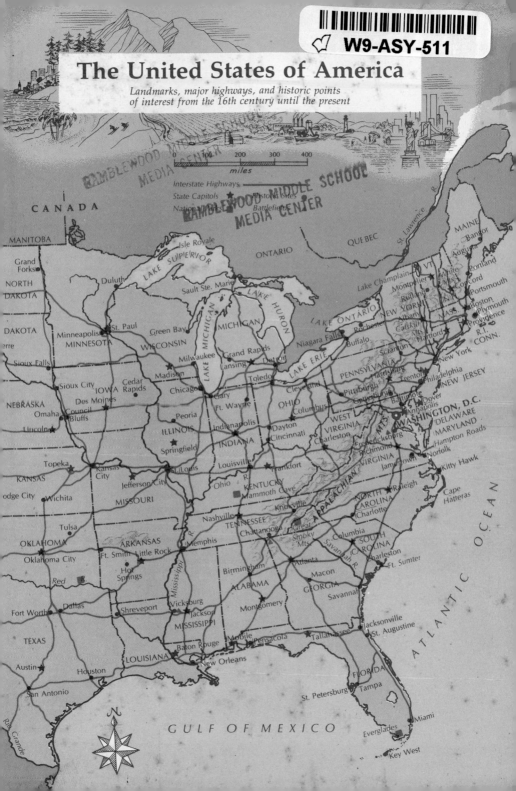

The United States of America

*Landmarks, major highways, and historic points
of interest from the 16th century until the present*

KNOW YOUR AMERICA

KNOW YOUR AMERICA

A Guide to Every State in the Union

VOLUME II

The Midwest · The Plains States
The Rocky Mountain States
The Southwest · The Far West

Edited by

MARION PATTON *and* MARY SHERWIN

Maps designed by John Morris

DOUBLEDAY & COMPANY, INC., Garden City, New York

CONTENTS

Contributing Writers to Know Your America   vii

Table of Maps   xi

THE MIDWEST   1

    Illinois   3

    Indiana   33

    Iowa   55

    Michigan   81

    Minnesota   107

    Missouri   135

    Ohio   165

    Wisconsin   191

THE PLAINS STATES   217

    Kansas   219

    Nebraska   245

    North Dakota   265

    South Dakota   285

THE ROCKY MOUNTAIN STATES   307

    Colorado   309

    Idaho   327

    Montana   345

    Nevada   365

    Utah   383

    Wyoming   401

THE SOUTHWEST 425

    Arizona 427
    New Mexico 449
    Oklahoma 467
    Texas 487

THE FAR WEST 509

    Alaska 511
    California 541
    Hawaii 571
    Oregon 605
    Washington 631

    Photographic Credits 657

    Index 659

Contributing Writers to
KNOW YOUR AMERICA

JANE ABRAMS, New York *News* travel writer, has covered the world on her assignments but retains a strong interest in New England, where she was born and went to school. A graduate of New York University, former faculty member of Pratt Institute, Ms. Abrams is a member of the Society of American Travel Writers, and New York Travel Writers' Association.

MARGO MASON BARRETT is a free-lance editor and writer who has at various times been an associate editor at Prentice-Hall and *Newsweek* magazine. She writes frequently for magazines, TV, and radio on a wide range of subjects. She has covered stories abroad as well as doing in-depth articles about the United States. She attended Columbia University and the Alliance Française in Paris.

HENRY and VERA BRADSHAW are a husband and wife team whose travel articles and photographs have appeared in such magazines as *Good Housekeeping, Reader's Digest, Outdoor Life,* etc. Wyoming is one of their real enthusiasms, and they have covered every inch of that beautiful state. The Bradshaws are members of the Outdoor Writers Association of America and the Society of American Travel Writers, of which Mr. Bradshaw is a former chairman of the board.

RICHARD M. BRAUN, a native New Yorker, graduated from C. W. Post College, studied journalism at the University of Missouri, and received his M.A. degree from New York University. He has been a reporter and editor for the New York *News* and has also written articles on travel abroad and in this country for the New York *Times*.

TED BREDT is a reporter for the Sunday section of the San Jose *Mercury & News*. He has lived in most of the Far Western states and has traveled extensively through all of them. His piece on Alaska reflects the diversity and color of one of our most unusual states.

JOHN J. CORRIS has worked as a public relations representative in the travel field for a number of years. As a free-lance writer he has written for the Science Program published by Nelson Doubleday, Inc., and is a contributing writer on the Third Revised Edition of the *Encyclopedia of World Travel*. A former newspaper reporter/feature writer and wire correspondent, Mr. Corris is active in the National Press Club, the Society of American Travel Writers, and the Aviation/Space Writers' Association. He lives in Falls Church, Virginia.

NED CRABB has had a varied career as a writer-reporter for the Miami *Herald*, Miami *News*, New York *News*, New York *Post*, and is presently on the staff of the *Wall Street Journal*. His articles on travel and nature have appeared in *Connecticut* magazine, *Fodor's Guide to the South*, the Miami *Herald's Tropic* magazine, *The Floridian* of the St. Petersburg *Times*, and the *National Enquirer*. He has also written for *The Florida Naturalist, The Miamian*, and *Frontiers*. He lives in New York.

PAULA DRANOV has been a reporter for the United Press International, covering national news and editing and supervising distribution of regional news stories in this country. She has also been based in London as a news editor for the Los Angeles *Times*-Washington *Post* News Service. Ms. Dranov has done extensive traveling in this country and is currently living in New York.

SETH GOLDSTEIN is a business journalist by occupation and has contributed articles to *Dun's Review, Barron's,* and *Commonweal* and is currently managing editor of Knowledge Industry Publications, Inc. A tireless traveler, Mr. Goldstein has explored the Far West and the Southwest on both Army leave and civilian vacation. With his wife, Marjorie, he is co-author of "Native Voices: A Calendar of American Writers." He lives in Larchmont, New York.

WILLIAM E. HAGUE was on the staff of Condé Nast for many years where he traveled to virtually every section of the country on stories for the *House & Garden Guides*. The author of *Your Vacation Home: How to Plan It, How to Live in It*, Mr. Hague was born in Duquesne, Pennsylvania, went to school in New Jersey (Princeton), and now lives in San Francisco. His piece on California captures the uniqueness and variety of that state with its climate, people, and history.

BRUCE HAMBY has been on the staff of the Denver *Post* for thirty years as executive sports editor, Sunday editor, and assistant managing editor. His current assignment as travel editor has taken him a million and a half miles to some 110 countries around the globe. He remains convinced there's no place to live better than Colorado and he writes of it with knowledge and enthusiasm.

KATIE KELLY is a native Nebraskan with a particular love for her home state. She attended the University of Nebraska, received her Bachelor of Arts degree in Journalism from the University of Missouri, and taught high school in rural Humphrey, Nebraska. The author of *The Wonderful World of Women's Wear Daily,* Ms. Kelly has also been a contributing editor to *Time* magazine. She is currently living in New York.

LEW LARKIN was born in Missouri and received his journalism degree from the University of Missouri. He was the Missouri history editor of the Kansas City *Star,* and many of his columns have been published in several volumes. He is author of the book *Missouri, Mother of the West.* He lives in Kansas City, Missouri.

MARILYN WAGNER LITHGOW grew up in the farming community of Chenoa, population 1826, in the heart of the Illinois prairies. She has a master's degree in social work from Wayne State University in Detroit, has worked with emotionally disturbed children, and has done family counseling. An avid enthusiasm for patchwork quiltmaking resulted in the book *Quiltmaking and Quiltmakers.* Ms. Lithgow's articles have appeared in many magazines. She is currently at work on a book about her Mennonite heritage and she commutes between New York and Illinois.

MILTON and JOAN MANN are a husband and wife team who specialize in photography related to the fields of travel and education. During the past ten years their free-lance assignments have taken them all over many regions of this country and the world. Their work has appeared in many magazines and they are the authors of *Washington, D.C.,* and *New Guinea,* both of which are part of the series "This Beautiful World," published by Kodansha International. Their film strips on customs and living in this country and foreign countries are used in high schools and appear in current editions of major encyclopedias and textbooks. They are members of the Society of American Travel Writers and are based in the Chicago area.

EDMUND G. ROSE, born in Bedford, Massachusetts, is an editor, writer, and research specialist. A graduate of Carnegie Tech's famed drama school, he won a nationwide contest with his television play, *Smile Me a Word,* and became Playwright-in-Residence at the Erie (Pennsylvania) Playhouse. Mr. Rose has a degree in history from New York University and is at work on a study of Portuguese and Spanish whaling ventures in the New World. Co-author with Mr. Rose for the article on Virginia is LENORE D. WARD who has written and researched extensively in the fields of business, health, social welfare, and travel.

TABLE OF MAPS

Alaska	510
Arizona	426
California	540
Colorado	308
Hawaii	573
Idaho	329
Illinois	2
Indiana	35
Iowa	57
Kansas	218
Michigan	83
Minnesota	109
Missouri	137
Montana	347
Nebraska	244
Nevada	367
New Mexico	448
North Dakota	267
Ohio	164
Oklahoma	469
Oregon	607
South Dakota	287
Texas	486
Utah	385
Washington	630
Wisconsin	193
Wyoming	400

KNOW YOUR AMERICA

THE MIDWEST

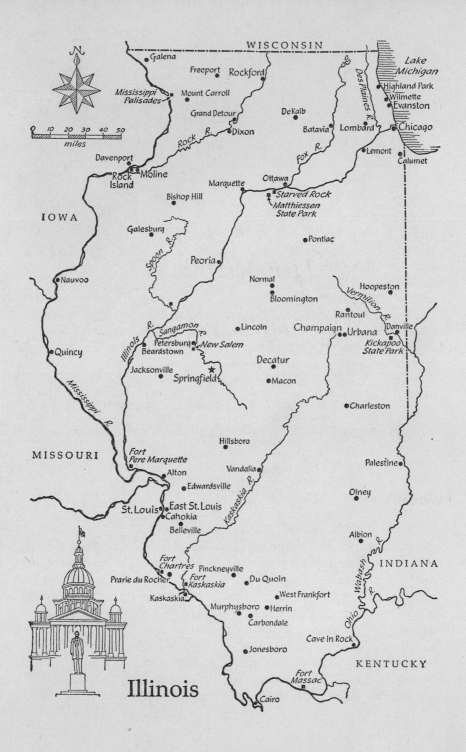

ILLINOIS

MENTION Illinois, and most Americans think of Chicago, the second-largest city and third-largest metropolitan area in the United States. But Chicago is only part of the dynamic state of Illinois. More than half of Illinois's residents (11,131,000 in 1974) live downstate, as the natives call it, where the corn grows tall and vast reserves of coal and oil lie hidden beneath the fertile soil. The industrial might of Chicago and the agricultural riches and mineral resources of downstate combine to make Illinois one of the nation's leaders in both industry and agriculture, and give the people of Illinois the sixth-highest per capita personal income in the nation.

What makes Illinois dynamic is the contrast between the hustle and bustle of rush-hour traffic in Chicago's Loop and the silent beauty of the covered bridge across Spoon River in Knox County, birthplace of Carl Sandburg, Chicago's unofficial poet laureate. Illinois is the eerie glow of the huge Calumet blast furnaces against the night sky, and the rocky hills of the Illinois Ozarks where the white-tailed deer browse; a blizzard howling across the wide-open spaces of the prairies that gave Illinois its nickname, "the Prairie State," and the cotton fields and magnolias in Little Egypt in the southernmost tip of the state. Illinois is the clash between the Chicago Democratic political machine and the conservative Republicans downstate; Lincoln's tomb in Springfield and a monument to the 1,354 Confederate prisoners of war who died of smallpox at Alton. Illinois is the Chicago Symphony Orchestra playing Beethoven and the Bluegrass Music Festival at the Crazy Horse Campground in Jacksonville. Most important of all, Illinois is a hodgepodge of people—southern blacks and third-generation descendants of Polish and Czech immigrants working side by side in the Chicago factory; men and women with German and Irish, Scandinavian and Italian names farming the land and working in the mines downstate. "I am the people—the mob—the crowd—the mass," wrote Carl Sandburg. "Do you know that all the great work of the world is done through me?"

THE LAND

The first explorers and settlers who ventured westward through the dense forests and along the great waterways of North America could scarcely believe their eyes when they reached the fringes of the Illinois prairies—stretching ahead as far as they could see lies an empty ocean of grass with perhaps a solitary clump of trees on the horizon. One Englishman who visited the prairies in springtime when a profusion of gaily colored flowers blossomed among the tall grasses exclaimed that the view rivaled any park in England, but a homesick young bride from Massachusetts who pioneered at Hillsboro in southern Illinois in 1822 thought she had never seen anything more dismal than the prairies, for she had the misfortune to arrive when the tall grasses had been burned over by autumn fires, leaving a black and empty landscape.

Whether they saw the prairies as beautiful or dismal, the early pioneers were reluctant to settle there and with good reason. No trees grew to provide fuel or shelter, and the tall grasses concealed marshy ground that provided treacherous footing for men on horseback or heavily loaded wagons. In summer, insufferable heat, stinging gnats, and lack of good drinking water during the droughts made even traveling across the prairies, much less living there, a miserable experience, and in winter, when fierce blizzards howled across the level land, only the foolhardy or the desperate would venture into the wide-open spaces.

For nearly 150 years after the first white men came to Illinois, the prairies in the northern and central parts of the state remained uncultivated, while the hilly, forested southern third of the state became the center of population growth. The first homesteaders, the French, chose to settle in the river bottoms along the east bank of the Mississippi, where centuries before, the prehistoric Indian Mound Builders had lived and planted their crops. The alluvial soil of the river bottoms, deposited by the periodic flooding of the Mississippi, is exceptionally fertile, but despite the gigantic levees which have been constructed, today's farmers still run the risk of being flooded out when the Mississippi leaves its banks.

As pioneers from the eastern American seaboard began drifting into Illinois, they also settled along the two major rivers that form the state's natural boundaries—the Mississippi to the west and the Ohio to the southeast. Gradually the pioneer settlements spread out along the Illinois River, which flows diagonally southwest across the state to empty into the Mississippi; the Rock River, which cuts across the northwestern corner of the state; and the other more than five hundred streams and smaller rivers that cover the state. The timber, a term peculiar to Illinois meaning woods, that grew along the rivers not only provided the new settlers with fuel and material for building cabins and fences, but also food to supplement their diet of wild game and corn meal—hickory and hazel nuts, wild grapes and plums and luscious wild strawberries, and maple sugar for sweetening. Clearing the timber to plant a few acres of corn was hard work, but the fertile soil—deposited in depths of two to one hundred feet by a glacier that once covered all but the southernmost tip of Illinois and overlaid in many areas with a dark, rich loam—produced abundant crop yields.

Originally 40 per cent of Illinois was covered by hardwood forests, but as the pioneers cleared the land for farms, the forested areas dwindled to about 10 per cent, posing a threat to the balance of nature. In recent years, however, the state has established four forests containing about 11,000 acres of woodland, in addition to the Shawnee National Forest, which covers more than 240,000 acres of the Illinois Ozarks, the plateau region in the southernmost tip of the state that was not leveled off during the Ice Age. Efforts also are being made by both private concerns and the state to reforest land that has been laid bare by strip mining for coal, and two state parks which boast numerous small lakes well stocked with fish have been developed out of reclaimed strip-mining land.

Today, the prairies that awed the early Illinois pioneers are neatly divided into a checkerboard of field dotted by farmhouses and buildings surrounded by windbreaks of trees. Although he never saw the Illinois territory, Thomas Jefferson is responsible for that checkerboard design, for the Land Ordinance of 1785, drafted by Jefferson, provided that the prairies be surveyed in rectangular blocks. Each six-mile-square block, called a township, was subdivided into thirty-six sections containing 640 acres each, and the sections were to be sold for a dollar an acre. Farm land in the heart of the prairies has increased as much as a thousandfold in value per acre since it was originally surveyed, but the blacktop country roads still follow the old rectangular section lines and visitors are puzzled by the right-angle jogs that occur regularly along the north-south roads, the compensations that the surveyors had to make to keep the section lines running due north.

CLIMATE

The weathermen may agree that Illinois has a temperate climate, but anyone who has experienced a typical August day when the combination of heat and high humidity rivals a steam bath would question that. The highest temperature ever recorded in Illinois was 117 degrees at East St. Louis during the unforgettable summer of 1954 when the thermometer hovered above 100 degrees for a stretch of almost two weeks. But complain to an Illinois farmer about the hot, sticky weather and he's bound to reply cheerfully, "Well, that's what makes the corn grow," and what is good for the corn is good for the economy of Illinois. The people of Illinois take refuge in air conditioning, which they consider to be a necessity rather than a luxury, and these days even the enclosed cabs of the huge tractors which cultivate the cornfields are air-conditioned.

Illinois is blessed with ideal weather conditions for agriculture—a growing season long enough for a variety of crops in addition to corn to mature; adequate precipitation averaging 35 to 45 inches annually; and the temperate climate according to the weathermen's standards. There is a catch, however, for the weather in the Prairie State is noted for its unpredictable and violent changes. The temperature has been known to drop as much as 65 degrees within a few hours. Spectacular but frightening lightning storms are commonplace events in summertime, and the hail and high winds that sometimes accompany these storms can destroy a farmer's entire crop in a matter of minutes. Most frightening of all are the tornadoes, incredible in their fury and destructiveness. Southern Illinois probably has more severe tornadoes per number of people than any other area in the United States, and in 1925 the most disastrous tornado on record killed more than seven hundred people in the southern part of the state.

Since Illinois is 382 miles long, the climate varies noticeably between the extreme northern and southern areas. Temperatures of 20 degrees below zero are not uncommon in the northern part of the state during winter, and the lowest temperature recorded was 35 degrees below zero at Mount Carroll in 1930. Chicago gets its nickname of the "Windy City" because of the icy winds that blow off Lake Michigan creating a wind-chill factor well below the recorded winter temperatures. But at Cairo at the southern tip of the state where the Ohio River flows into the Mississippi, the climate is mild enough to grow cotton and the area around Cairo is nicknamed "Little Egypt." In early spring when ice and snow still blanket northern Illinois, thousands of magnolia trees are blooming in Cairo, and the cypress trees lend an aura of the old South.

THE PEOPLE OF ILLINOIS

Although the French were the first white men to explore and settle in the Illinois territory, which they claimed for nearly one hundred years, their presence hardly made a dent in that wilderness of prairies and river forests. Domesticating the wilderness was the task of the hardy woodsmen from Virginia and the Carolinas who drifted westward over the mountain trails to the Cumberland Gap and down the Ohio River, first to Kentucky and then on to Illinois, where game was plentiful and land was to be had for the taking.

With their missus and the young'uns in tow, these intrepid southern woodsmen carried all they needed for survival in the wilderness on a packhorse or their own backs—a rifle and an ax, a bag of corn meal to make hoecakes, a big iron kettle and a skillet, salt for preserving game and seeds for planting, carding combs and a spinning wheel, and one luxury, the family Bible with all the births and deaths recorded. They were called "squatters," a restless vanguard who made a clearing in the forest where no white man had ever set foot before, built a cabin, and planted a few acres of corn. They lived in one spot for a year or two, then sold out the "improvements" they had made in the wilderness and moved on again, ahead of the tide of permanent homesteaders who came with their livestock and wagons filled with household goods and settled down to stay.

When the territory became a state in 1818, four out of every six of Illinois's scant 40,000 residents were southern-born, but in the following decade, the population of Illinois increased almost threefold and the Yankees and the European immigrants far outnumbered the Southerners. Most of these early pioneers, having arrived in Illinois via the Ohio or Mississippi rivers, settled in the forested southern third of the state. They were leery of the prairies that covered central and northern Illinois where few trees grew to provide fuel and shelter and a team of heavy oxen was needed to cut through the tough sod, and few ventured to settle there.

Chicago in 1830 was only a little settlement situated in a swamp, and one traveler from St. Louis complained that he couldn't even find it, but three years later, the U. S. Congress voted to construct a harbor at Chicago and almost overnight the settlement of some 350 people became a city. Hundreds of thousands of European immigrants poured through the port of Chicago in the mid-1800s; some of them kept on traveling West but many settled down in Illinois—Germans, English, and Scandinavians who staked out farms on the prairies, and Irish who dug the canals and built the railroads that soon crisscrossed the state. Within forty years after Illinois entered the Union, its population had jumped past the 1.5 million mark and the wide-open prairies avoided by the early pioneers had become the center of the state's economic life.

Among the settlers who came to Illinois in the first half of the 1800s were social and religious groups who established their own close-knit communities like the English colony at Albion in southeastern Illinois which Charles Dickens came to visit on his American grand tour. A group of Quakers settled on the Fox River in the northeastern corner of the state in 1835, and around the same time, Swiss-German Mennonites fleeing religious persecution in Europe began settling in central Illinois near Peoria. Today the fifth- and sixth-generation descendants of these Mennonites still live in the small farming communities established by their ancestors, although many of the other groups who came to Illinois seeking the freedom to practice their own beliefs have disappeared. A group of Swedish settlers established a community at Bishop Hill in northern Illinois in 1846 on the basis that all property was owned in common, but like many other noble experiments in communal living, the Bishop Hill settlement was eventually split by internal strife and disintegrated. The Mormons, who had been hounded out of Missouri, settled in Nauvoo on the Mississippi River in 1839, making it the largest town in Illinois at that time, with a population of 20,000. However, the resentment of the prosperous and polygamous Mormons by their Illinois neighbors grew increasingly bitter until in 1844, their leader, Joseph Smith, and his brother, Hyrum, were lynched by a mob, and the Mormons under the new leadership of Brigham Young packed up and moved on West to Utah. Later, a French communal society called the Icarians also settled at Nauvoo, but like the Bishop Hill community their lofty principles could not withstand the pressure of human disagreements and the Icarian community faded away.

In the second half of the 1800s, thousands of the European immigrants arriving at the port of Chicago stayed on to work in the city's rapidly growing industries, and by the beginning of the twentieth century Chicago was a booming metropolis populated by immigrants from every country in Europe. The Polish community was the largest group; next came the Germans and the Italians; and then all the central and southern European peoples—the Czechs, Russians, Hungarians, Greeks, and Yugoslavians—each group living in their separate communities with the boundaries strictly maintained. Many of the old European neighborhoods have all but disappeared in recent years as the latest wave of immigrants, the southern blacks, arrived to work in the defense plants during the hectic years of World War II, and today these newcomers comprise one third of Chicago's 3.1 million residents.

A list of all the famous men and women who came from the state of Illinois would be a long and impressive one, but first place on the list could only be given to one man, Abraham Lincoln, the Great Emancipator. To set the record straight, though, Lincoln was born in Kentucky and didn't settle in Illinois until he was a grown man, as was true of his opponent in the famous slavery debates, Stephen A. Douglas, who was a transplanted Vermonter. The famous Indian chief Black Hawk, who made a hopeless stand against the encroachment of the white man on the land of his ancestors, was a native of Illinois, as were James Butler "Wild Bill" Hickok and Wyatt Earp, heroes of the Wild West. William Jennings Bryan, orator and statesman; Jane Addams, social reformer; and Adlai Stevenson, statesman and delegate to the United Nations, were also born in Illinois, and the state has produced a number of notable poets and writers including Carl Sandburg, Vachel Lindsay, Ernest Hemingway, Archibald MacLeish, John Dos Passos, James T. Farrell, John Gunther, and Gwendolyn Brooks, who is now the official Illinois state poet. Louis Sullivan and Frank Lloyd Wright, working in Chicago, revolutionized architectural design, and the unique contributions of the Chicago school of jazz, which included Louis Armstrong and Benny Goodman, were just as revolutionary in the

earning for himself a place in Illinois history as the Father of Chicago.

Illinois was admitted to the Union as the twenty-first state on December 3, 1818, with its first capital established at the old French town of Kaskaskia. New settlers began pouring into Illinois in the first decade after it became a state, and as the center of population shifted farther north, the capital was moved, first to Vandalia in 1820, and then to its present location at Springfield in central Illinois in 1837. The choice of Springfield as the permanent state capital was in part due to the efforts of an up-and-coming young lawyer and politician who made his home there: Abraham Lincoln was his name, and he was destined to change the course of American history.

Like many young men of his era who later became prominent in Illinois politics, Lincoln had served in the state militia during the Black Hawk War of 1832 when the last of the Indians were expelled from Illinois. Ironically, one of the regular army officers who also saw action in the Black Hawk War was Jefferson Davis, who later became the President of the Confederacy.

With the danger of Indian attacks finally removed and the opening of the Erie Canal which made travel to the western states easier for the New England farmers tired of trying to scratch out a living from the rocky soil and the European immigrants landing in New York City, thousands of new settlers arrived to carve farms out of the Illinois wilderness before the government had even put the land up for sale. New agricultural techniques which made it possible to adequately drain and cultivate the rich prairie soil and the construction of a system of canals and railroads crisscrossing the state also contributed to the rapid development of Illinois in the mid-1800s.

On the eve of the Civil War, Illinois was a state divided between the northern antislavery groups and the proslavery faction from the southern part of the state. Slavery had been introduced in the Illinois territory by the early French settlers, and although the Northwest Ordinance of 1787 prohibited slavery, many of the settlers in southern Illinois were from slaveholding states. An attempt to amend the state constitution to permit slavery was defeated in 1824, but in 1837, Elijah P. Lovejoy, a firebrand Presbyterian minister, was murdered by a proslavery mob at Alton in southern Illinois for attempting to publish an abolitionist newspaper. During the Illinois senatorial race of 1858, the famous debates on the slavery issue between Abraham Lincoln, grandson of a Virginian, and Stephen A. Douglas, an immigrant from New England, brought national recognition for the lawyer from Springfield. Although Douglas won the senatorial campaign, Lincoln was elected President two years later, and the state of Illinois elected to remain in the Union during the Civil War.

Industry was already well established in Chicago and northern Illinois by the time of the Civil War, and with the wartime need for food and supplies, there was a tremendous spurt of industrial growth. The first steel rails in the nation were fabricated at Chicago in 1865, and the same year marked the opening of the Union Stock Yards that were to make Chicago a world-famous meat-packing center. By the 1870s manufacturing had outstripped the state's agricultural products in value, and despite the wealth produced by the Illinois farmers, manufacturing still leads agriculture in the state's economy today.

The growth of Chicago as an industrial center was temporarily halted by the Great Fire of 1871, which began, if popular legend is to be believed, when Mrs. O'Leary's cow kicked over a lantern which set the dry hay in the barn on fire. By the time the fire could be put out, almost every building in the heart of the city, most of them flimsy wooden structures, had been destroyed and more than 250 people had died. However, the stockyards and most of the grain stores and factories were undamaged, and within three years the people of Chicago had built a new and more soundly constructed city.

The industrial expansion in Illinois during the second half of the nineteenth century was not without problems. The Illinois farmers suffered because agricultural prices failed to keep pace with the prices of manufactured goods, and freight rates were very high. In 1867 farmers organized the Order of Patrons of Husbandry for co-operative buying, and later many Illinois farmers were active participants in the Grange movement. At the same time, laborers in the factories, railroads, and mines were organizing to secure higher wages and better working conditions. The laborers' discontent culminated in two violent incidents that shook the nation—the Haymarket Square Riot in Chicago in 1886 and the Pullman Strike in 1894. Seven strikers were sentenced to death for the murder of one policeman in the Haymarket Square Riot; four of the seven were hanged but the rest were later pardoned when it was revealed that the jury at their trial and the presiding judge were prejudiced against them. The Pullman Strike, during which traffic was halted on all twenty-four railroad lines leading out of Chicago, resulted in the death of four men and injury to many others after federal troops were sent in to combat the strikers. Out of the strong trade union movement which developed in Chicago emerged the Socialist party headed by Eugene Debs and the Industrial Workers of the World, known as the Wobblies.

In the early twentieth century, Illinois became a leader in progressive social legislation with the enactment of a child labor law in 1903, a law limiting the working hours of women in 1909, and a workmen's compensation law in 1911. But violence—economic, racial, and political—continues to rear its ugly head in Illinois history to the present day. Chicago was the scene of a race riot in 1919 which left twenty-three blacks and fifteen whites dead, and an eviction riot in 1931 during which three people were killed and many more wounded by police. Striking coal miners at Herrin in 1922 murdered nineteen strike breakers, while at Chicago on Memorial Day, 1937, ten men were killed, of whom six were shot in the back by police, during a meeting of steelworkers organized by the CIO. Chicago was again the scene of violence during the Democratic National Convention of 1968 when confrontations between the police and convention participants and observers led Senator Abraham Ribicoff to denounce the "Gestapo tactics in the streets of Chicago" from the floor of the convention itself.

On the other hand, one of the most significant events in the history of our civilization took place in Chicago on December 2, 1942, when physicist Enrico Fermi and other scientists at the University of Chicago produced the first controlled nuclear chain reaction, and the atomic age began. The Atomic Energy Commission maintains a major research and development laboratory, the Argonne National Laboratory at Lemont, which is under the direction of the University of Chicago, as is the Argonne Cancer Research Hospital. In 1971 the AEC completed construction of the nation's largest atom smasher at Batavia, near Chicago, and three other nuclear power reactor centers have been built by private electrical companies operating in Illinois.

Education has always been a vital concern to the people of Illinois, and as early as 1825, when much of the state was still wilderness, the legislature passed an act establishing a system of free public schools. In the mid-1800s Illinois pioneered in supporting higher education for women and some of the earliest coeducation facilities in the country. Today, the state of Illinois is noted for its distinguished private colleges and universities as well as its outstanding system of public institutions of higher education: the main campus of the University of Illinois at Champaign-Urbana with a rapidly growing commuter branch at the Circle Campus in Chicago, and five state universities located at Carbondale, Normal, De Kalb, Macomb, and Charleston. Although the Illinois Indians long ago vanished from the Prairie State, every fall when the corn is almost ready for harvesting, the "Fighting Illini," nickname of the University of Illinois football team, take the field to defend the honor of Illinois.

INDUSTRY

Illinois is one of the industrial leaders of the nation, producing almost every kind of manufactured goods imaginable from steel rails and diesel engines to soft drinks and candy bars. In terms of value added by manufacturing, Illinois ranked fourth highest among the states in 1976 with a total of close to 30 billion dollars.

Seventy per cent of Illinois's industry is concentrated in the Chicago metropolitan area, which alone accounts for 5 per cent of the gross national product. Industry got an early start in Chicago because a few visionary men recognized that the village in a swamp at the southern end of Lake Michigan could become the link between the breadbasket of the Midwest and the hungry cities of the eastern seaboard and Europe. Even before Chicago was incorporated as a city in 1837, it had a packing house capable of handling 5,000 hogs, and with the opening of the famous Union Stock Yards in 1865, Chicago became, in the words of poet Carl Sandburg, the "Hog Butcher for the World." The Union Stock Yards had to be closed in 1971 after many of the major packing houses had moved out West, but Chicago's Board of Trade is still the largest grain market in the world, and the processing of food, especially grain, beverages, and bakery goods, is a major industry in Chicago and the state of Illinois.

The Chicago industrial complex, which includes the blast furnaces, rolling mills, and oil refineries in the Calumet area to the southeast, is also the nation's second-biggest steel-producing center, and the iron and steel that come out of the Chicago mills are manufactured into hundreds of different metal products. The production of agricultural machinery has been an important industry in Illinois since 1847 when Cyrus McCormick opened a factory in Chicago to mass-produce his mechanical grain reaper, an invention that revolutionized farming. About the same time, another inventive genius named John Deere settled in a village named Grand Detour near Moline where he built the first steel plow, which could cut through the thick prairie sod and turn it over, an almost impossible task for more primitive plows. With the steel plow, cultivation of the fertile prairies became a practical reality, and John Deere's one-man business grew into a multimillion-dollar farm machinery concern. Today, Illinois leads all other states in the manufacture of farm machinery, as well as machinery for construction and industrial use and transportation equipment.

Electronics is another major Illinois industry, and the state is a leading producer of telephone equipment, radios, and television sets. Rubber and plastic products, chemicals, and scientific instruments also rank high on the long list of manufactured goods produced in Illinois. A major printing and publishing industry flourishes in Chicago, and many of the nation's magazines and catalogues are printed there. Furniture, safety glass, footwear, athletic goods, soap—you name it, Illinois manufactures it.

The nineteenth-century visionaries who foresaw the possibilities inherent in Chicago's geographical location in the heartland of America with access to both the Great Lakes and the Mississippi River would be delighted to know that their predictions of the city's importance came true—today Chicago is the transportation hub of the nation. O'Hare Airport outside of Chicago is the largest and busiest commercial airport in the world. Chicago also is the biggest rail center in the country—a "Player with Railroads and the Nation's Freight Handler," said Carl Sandburg back in 1916, and that's still true today. Interstate trucking operations center in Chicago too, and with the opening of the St. Lawrence Seaway in 1959, the city has become a major port for overseas shipping, handling more than two million tons of overseas cargo in 1974. The new Calumet Harbor, completed in 1962, provides docking facilities for the ocean vessels that have crossed the Great Lakes, and the sixteen-mile-long Calumet-Sag Channel links into the Illinois Waterway, an ingenious combination of canals and rivers that leads to the Mississippi, making it possible for goods to be transported by water from the St. Lawrence Seaway all the way to the Gulf of Mexico. In addition to Chicago, two other major transportation centers have developed in the state—Peoria, on the Illinois River, and East St. Louis, on the Mississippi.

East St. Louis also is one of the largest of the downstate industrial areas, producing a variety of manufactured goods including iron and steel products, chemicals, glass, and meat products. Some of the downstate industries moved there from Chicago because of lower taxes, but many developed to process the agricultural produce raised in the neighboring areas. Decatur, in central Illinois, for instance, is called the Soybean Capital because its industries specialize in manufacturing soybean-based products, while in Peoria the factories convert grain into breakfast food, livestock feed, or whiskey. Downstate industry is also being developed in areas where the natural resources have been depleted, leaving local residents jobless, as in Danville, which was a major coal-producing area for nearly a century until the mines gave out. Once in danger of becoming a ghost town, Danville now has nearly 150 plants employing more than 16,000 people, and the city is enjoying a new prosperity.

AGRICULTURE

Towering above the level farm land near Pontiac in central Illinois stands a newly constructed grain elevator with a capacity of holding 4.5 million bushels of corn. It is one of the largest grain storage facilities in rural Illinois, and its two enormous grain bins, each capable of holding 2 million bushels, are among the largest individual bins ever constructed in the world. Nevertheless, the bountiful 1975 harvest of corn in central Illinois was more than this and other storage facilities in the area could handle, and a veritable mountain of corn, 680,000 bushels, had to be piled up on the ground until it could be shipped out to market.

Illinois ranks second only to Iowa in the production of corn, and is the leading state in the production of soybeans, an increasingly valuable crop in recent years as a wide variety of new products utilizing soybeans have been developed. Fields planted in corn one year are often planted in soybeans the next year as part of a crop rotation plan, since the nodules on the roots of the growing soybeans replenish the vital nitrogen in the soil leached out by the corn. In addition, Illinois farmers utilize vast quantities of liquid nitrogen and other fertilizers and insecticides to maintain high levels of crop yields.

Instead of selling the corn they raise, many Illinois farmers prefer to use their crop to fatten hogs or beef cattle for market. Again, Illinois ranks second only to Iowa in the production of hogs and is one of the leading producers of beef cattle. Large quantities of oats, wheat, and hay are also raised in Illinois. The northern portion of the state near the Wisconsin border is a major dairy production area; the extreme southern part of the state is noted for its peach and apple orchards; and small truck farms producing a variety of vegetables and fruits are located near the metropolitan areas, particularly outside Chicago. Together, the production of crops and livestock earned 6.3 billion dollars for the Illinois farmers in 1974, making Illinois the third-ranking state in total cash farm receipts.

Approximately four fifths of the total land area of Illinois, 56,400 square miles, is farm land, but since World War II, the amount of land given over to farming has gradually diminished as the metropolitan areas have spread out and new industry has been developed in downstate Illinois. While there has been a progressive decrease over the past thirty to forty years of the number of people living on farms, the size of the average farm has been steadily increasing. Back at the turn of the twentieth century when the grandparents of today's farmer were getting married and setting up for themselves, 180 acres was considered a good-sized farm. Today, more and more land is being bought up by corporations or leased by individual farmers who may farm as much as 9,000 acres of land.

The modern farmer tends to think of his occupation as a business enterprise, and big business at that, because of the financial investment needed to purchase land at today's high prices and the expensive equipment required by modern agricultural methods. He tends to specialize in raising one or two major crops rather than a variety, and if he feeds beef cattle or hogs for market, he will stock hundreds of them. Unless he is in the dairy business, the modern farmer no longer keeps a dairy herd and his wife buys milk at the local supermarket like the town folks do. Gone too is the flock of hens scratching in the barnyard, for poultry and egg production also are big businesses run on the system of an assembly line with conveyor belts to carry feed to the hens and carry away their eggs. It is sad to think that the old-fashioned American farm with its work horses and milk cows and pigs and chickens may someday be preserved only as a curiosity, but with the world population explosion and the prospect of starvation facing future generations, every effort must be made to produce the largest amount of food in the most efficient way, and that means specialization and modern production methods.

NATURAL RESOURCES

Beneath the fertile Illinois soil is another gift of nature—large reserves of coal and oil. The deposits of soft (bituminous) coal, known as the Eastern Interior Basin, which underlie more than half of the state, are the largest deposits in the United States and among the richest in the world. The coal-mining operations center around West Frankfort in southeastern Illinois, and the oil reserves also are found primarily in the southern part of the state. Illinois ranks fourth in the nation in the production of coal and ninth in the production of crude petroleum, but with the current energy crisis, new ways to make the most of Illinois's vast coal and oil reserves are being explored in the race to meet America's energy needs.

Currently, more than half of the Illinois coal mines employ the strip method of mining, whereby power shovels operating on the surface of the earth dig trenches deep enough to reach the coal seams. While strip mining is an efficient and economical technique, it has the major disadvantage of creating a barren landscape where the soil is washed away with every rainfall. A congressional bill that would have forced private mine owners to restore land laid waste by strip mining to its former condition was defeated by presidential veto in 1974, but pressure from conservationists continues and some mine owners have taken the initiative in reforesting the sites of former strip-mining operations. The state of Illinois also is developing two parks on reclaimed strip-mined land—Kickapoo State Park near Danville, which was the top coal-producing area in Illinois for nearly a century until the mines finally gave out, and Pyramid State Park near Pinckneyville in southern Illinois.

In addition to its coal and oil reserves, Illinois is rich in other commercially important minerals. Lead was being mined at Galena in the northwestern corner of the state as early as 1700, only thirty years after the first white men set foot in the Illinois territory. In the 1830s when much of the state was still wilderness, the boomtown of Galena was famous for its wealth and elegance. More than half of the nation's current output of fluorspar, a mineral used in the ceramics, chemical, and steel industries, is mined in Illinois. The remarkably pure St. Peter sandstone, found near Ottawa, is used in glassmaking. Other commercially significant minerals mined in the state are limestone, sand and gravel, zinc, clay, peat, and tripoli—amorphous silica used for industrial polishing.

Twenty-four conservation areas and wildlife preserves are scattered across the state. The buffalo, elk, and bear that once roamed the Illinois territory disappeared well over a hundred years ago, and the white-tailed deer were almost extinct by the beginning of the twentieth century. However, in the 1930s the Department of Conservation released four deer on a state game refuge and since then their numbers have steadily increased in southern and northwestern Illinois. Major bird migratory routes cross the state, and thousands of Canadian geese winter every year at the Union County conservation area near Cairo, but by far the most rare species of nature's handiwork to be found in Illinois are the world-famous white squirrels which make their home in a small town named Olney, near the Wabash River. A virgin stand of white pine are preserved in the White Pines Forest near Dixon in the northwestern part of the state, while at nearby Mississippi Palisades State Park, springtime brings a profusion of the native wildflowers that once covered the prairies— violets, bluebells, bellworts, and wild geraniums. The Beall Woods Natural Preserve, 270 acres of primeval woodland bordering on the Wabash River, is listed in the United States Register of National Landmarks, and the largest Shumard red oak in the country can be seen there.

CITIES

The skyline of **Chicago,** the second-largest city in the United States, looms tall above the prairies, for the city's newest landmark, the Sears Tower, is the tallest building in the world. Chicago was the birthplace of the skyscraper—the first steel skeleton building was constructed there in 1885, and from its modest 10 stories have sprung the 110-story Sears Tower and its rival, "Big John," the 100-story John Hancock Center, which dominate the other glass and steel towers clustered in downtown Chicago. The people of Chicago pride themselves on building big, whether it be skyscrapers or the world's largest ornamental fountain, Buckingham Fountain in Grant Park, whose central jet shoots up 135 feet in the air, or the two-block-square Merchandise Mart, the world's largest wholesale shopping and buying center. Even the Chicago sewage system is credited as being one of the engineering feats of the world, for constructing it involved making the Chicago River flow backward instead of emptying into Lake Michigan.

The problem for a visitor to Chicago is deciding where to begin— there's so much to see and do. A five-story-high Picasso sculpture, a gift from the artist to the people of Chicago, graces the plaza of the new Civic Center in downtown Chicago. One block over is State Street, "that great street," said to be the most highly concentrated shopping area in the world and the location of the huge Marshall Field's department store whose fantasy-world Christmas window displays have delighted generations of Midwest children. The rumble and squeal of the elevated trains passing by overhead is another Chicago tradition, and the downtown area is called the Loop because the elevated rail tracks make a loop around it.

Along the eastern edge of the Loop runs elegant Michigan Avenue, a thoroughfare of culture and fashion. Two beloved bronze lions guard the entrance to the Chicago Art Institute on Michigan Avenue, and inside is the world's outstanding collection of French impressionist and postimpressionist paintings, as well as an internationally renowned school of art and the Goodman Theater. A few blocks north is the main branch of the Chicago Public Library, considered to be one of the best in the country; the nucleus of the library's collection is the 8,000 volumes sent by Queen Victoria after the Great Fire of 1871 destroyed downtown Chicago. Traffic on Michigan Avenue crosses the Chicago River via one of the more than fifty drawbridges, connecting the different parts of the city, that can be raised to let ships travel up and down the river. Some of the city's most elegant and expensive boutiques and restaurants are located on North Michigan Avenue, along with two of Chicago's other landmarks, the Gothic Tribune Tower and the tower of the Wrigley Building, whose four-dial clock is illuminated at night. There are many art galleries and the Museum of Contemporary Art in the vicinity of North Michigan Avenue, and nearby Rush Street is the night-club center of the city.

Chicago has one of the biggest park systems in the world, 568 parks covering more than 6,000 acres, and one of the loveliest aspects of the city is the parks and parkways which extend for miles along Lake Michigan. The best way to see Chicago is to drive along Lake Shore Drive from Jackson Park near the University of Chicago on the south side of the city to the "Gold Coast," the towering stretch of apartment buildings on the north side, especially after dark when the flood-lit skyscrapers in the Loop are silhouetted against the sky. Jackson Park was the site of the World's Columbian Exposition in 1893, and the building that was the exposition's Palace of Fine Arts is now the Museum of Science and Industry, the most visited attraction in Chicago, which contains working models of all the inventions of modern man from a cyclotron to a realistic coal mine. Farther north on Lake Shore Drive is mammoth Soldier Field and McCormick Place, the city's huge exposition center where more than two million people attended trade shows and conventions in 1974. Not far from the Loop on Lake Shore Drive are the Field Museum of Natural History; the Shedd Aquarium, the largest in the world; and the Adler Planetarium, the first of its kind to be built in the nation. Lincoln Park, site of the famous Saint-Gaudens statue of old Abe, covers more than a thousand acres along Lake Shore Drive on the near north side of the city; there is a well-known zoo in Lincoln Park, as well as a golf course, playing fields, public beaches, yacht harbors, and acres of greenery to be enjoyed.

Chicago has been noted for its innovative architecture since the days of Louis H. Sullivan, the father of the "Chicago style." One of Sullivan's famous buildings, the Auditorium built in 1889, was recently restored and now houses Roosevelt University. The Robie House, located near the University of Chicago, is one of the finest examples of Frank Lloyd Wright's "prairie architecture" developed during his working days in Chicago around the turn of the twentieth century. The internationally known modern architect Mies Van Der Rohe designed the clean-cut glass and steel buildings of the Illinois Institute of Technology on Chicago's west side, and his latter-day contemporary Eero Saarinen created the over-all plans for the integration of new buildings into the traditionally designed campus of the University of Chicago. In contrast to the modern styles of Van Der Rohe and Saarinen stands the nine-sided Baha'i Temple whose high dome is covered with glittering quartz; the temple is the American center of the oriental cult of Bahaism and is located in Wilmette, just north of the Chicago city limits.

Chicago also is an education center, boasting ninety-five institutions of higher learning—the best known among them being the University of Chicago, Loyola University, the Circle Campus of the University of Illinois, and Northwestern University located at Evanston, just north of Chicago proper. There are six medical schools located in the city as well as three dental schools, one college of pharmacy and one of osteopathy. Other educational resources include the John Crerar Library, the largest public library in the world devoted to science and technology; the Chicago Historical Society, which has an outstanding collection of Lincoln memorabilia; the Newberry Library, noted for its collection of rare books and a haven for scholars; and the Oriental Institute on the University of Chicago campus.

Highlighting the cultural scene in the city are the performances of the renowned Chicago Symphony Orchestra and the Lyric Opera. During the summer months, the symphony hosts the Ravinia Festival of classical, jazz, rock, and folk music held in the suburb of Highland Park, northwest of Chicago. Ballet and dramatic productions, not to mention picnicking on the lawn, are added attractions at this nationally known festival of music. Another outstanding cultural event is the annual invitational show of contemporary American artists sponsored by the Chicago Art Institute which is considered to be one of the most prestigious shows in the nation's art world.

Not everything is big and beautiful in Chicago, however. Like all major American cities today, Chicago is confronted with the problems of unemployment, rising crime, inadequate housing, and racial strife, and on the days when the industrial pollution hangs over the city, the Indian word for the swamp where the city sprang up—Checagou, meaning a powerful smell (possibly of wild onions)—seems a very appropriate name for modern Chicago. But despite its problems, Chicago is a dynamic, exuberant city, "a tall bold slugger set vivid against the little soft cities," in the words of poet Carl Sandburg, and an exciting place to visit.

North of Chicago, along Lake Michigan, is the city of **Evanston,** one of the showcase suburbs in the metropolitan area with its stately homes and wide tree-lined streets. Northwestern University is located in Evanston, as is the headquarters of the Woman's Christian Temperance Union, and generations of Northwestern undergraduates have amused themselves in their more whimsical moments by depositing empty beer cans and whiskey bottles on the front lawn of the WCTU. Rotary International also has its headquarters in Evanston, and two schools of theology, the Garrett Biblical Institute (Baptist) and the Seabury Western Theological Seminary (Episcopal), along with Northwestern, contribute to the city's reputation as a lively educational and cultural center.

Other major cities in northern Illinois are **Rockford,** an industrial center noted for the production of machine tools, and the Tri-Cities of **Moline** and **Rock Island,** Illinois, and Davenport, Iowa, which together comprise the leading center in the world for the manufacture of agricultural machinery. **Peoria,** in central Illinois, is the home of the internationally known Caterpillar Tractor Company, which provides daily tours of its plant facilities for the public, and of Bradley University, noted for its basketball teams and the Corn Stock summer theater-in-the-round. Several national insurance companies have their home offices in **Bloomington,** which also is the county seat of McLean County, Illinois's richest agricultural area; Illinois Wesleyan University in Bloomington and Illinois State University in its twin city, **Normal,** serve as the focus of educational and cultural activities for the surrounding mid-state area.

The main campus of the University of Illinois, located at **Champaign-Urbana,** in central Illinois, boasts one of the largest university libraries in the nation, as well as the Krannert Art Museum and Center for the Performing Arts. At nearby **Rantoul,** the Chanute Technical Training Display Center—named for Octave Chanute, a Chicago inventor who developed airplane construction principles—graduates 25,000 air force technicians each year. **Springfield,** in addition to being the capital of the state, is a rapidly growing educational center, home of Sangamon State University and the new Southern Illinois School of Medicine. In southern Illinois, the bustling campuses of Southern Illinois University at **Carbondale** and **Edwardsville** are a vitalizing force in the economic and social life of what was, until a few years ago, a relatively backwater area of the state, and the six-week-long Mississippi River Festival held annually on the campus at Edwardsville is known as one of the most popular music festivals in the country.

SPORTS AND RECREATION

Although there is no prettier sight to a corn belt farmer than field after field of tall corn, its broad leaves rustling in the breeze on a sunny day, for scenic beauty most Illinoisans prefer the more than 280,000 acres of state parks, forests, and conservation areas. Two of the most popular recreation areas in northern Illinois are the Mississippi Palisades State Park and the Matthiessen State Park on the Vermilion River. Rugged cliffs rising above the Mississippi dominate the

1,300 acres of the heavily wooded area named the Mississippi Palisades. Deep canyons cut through the Palisades and there are many unusual rock formations, some resembling human figures, and a famous cave where a boy named Bob Upton hid for days from Indians on the warpath. Matthiessen State Park, on the eastern side of the state, was once a favorite spot of the Illiniwek, the Confederation of Illinois Indians, who probably were as impressed as today's visitors by the spectacular Dells, a gorge two hundred feet deep through which the Vermilion River flows. Visitors who hike through the Dells can explore the caves which have been given fanciful names like the Devil's Paint Box and the Giant's Bath Tub. This state park also is a favorite haunt of nature lovers because of its four hundred varieties of plant life.

In the Illinois Ozarks, which cut across the southern tip of the state, there are more than a dozen recreational areas which offer hiking and camping facilities for outdoor enthusiasts, not to mention breath-taking scenery. Giant City State Park, one of the state's largest park areas, got its name because of the gigantic bluffs and natural stone structures which resemble the streets of a metropolitan city, and the Garden of the Gods near the Pound Hollow recreation area is famous for its rock formations with colorful names like Needle's Eye, Camel Rock, and the Devil's Smokestack. The nearby Mermet Lake conservation area offers some of the finest bass and bluegill fishing in the southern part of the state, and other lakes scattered throughout the Illinois Ozarks provide facilities for swimming and boating.

Sailing and boating on Lake Michigan have been popular pastimes for many years, and with the development of man-made lakes to provide water supplies for downstate communities, more and more Illinoisans are becoming water sports enthusiasts. Some of the man-made lakes also provide good bass fishing, and the catfish still lurks in the Illinois rivers and streams, although Illinoisans allow that you have to be a native to appreciate the catfish's distinctive flavor. For the hunter, the Mississippi and Illinois river valleys provide excellent duck shooting, pheasant thrive in the central Illinois cornfields, and deer hunting is allowed in some of the state conservation areas.

The people of Illinois are avid sports fans too and there is always a big turnout for sports events, whether it be the professional baseball, football, or hockey games in Chicago, or the home-town high school athletic contests. Amateur softball is a favorite summer pastime in the small farming communities, and golf courses and tennis courts proliferate along the edges of the cornfields.

POINTS OF INTEREST

Illinois is justly proud of its most famous son, Abraham Lincoln, and the area around Springfield where he made his home and now lies buried is known as Lincoln Land. There is a town named Lincoln too, which old Abe himself christened with watermelon juice in 1853, and a Lincoln College for which ground was broken on Lincoln's last birthday before his assassination while he was President of the United States.

Visitors young and old enjoy the living museum of New Salem Village, located in a state park twenty miles northwest of Springfield, where log cabins, the general store, and the tavern have been authentically reconstructed, so the village appears much as it did when Lincoln lived there from 1831 to 1837. Lincoln was a twenty-two-year-old uneducated backwoodsman when he arrived in New Salem; he worked there as a storekeeper and postmaster, acquired some book learning and became a country lawyer, and was elected to represent Sangamon County in the legislature in 1834. Visiting New Salem Village is a fascinating trip into the past, for the visitor comes away with a real sense of what daily life must have been like for those hardy pioneers of nearly 150 years ago.

Nearby New Salem is the town of Petersburg, where Lincoln's first sweetheart, Ann Rutledge, is buried. Ann died in 1835, and the inscription on her tombstone reads "Beloved of Abraham Lincoln, wedded to him, not through union, but through separation. . . ." Poet Edgar Lee Masters, author of *Spoon River Anthology,* also is buried in Petersburg, and his boyhood home there is open to the public.

In Springfield, Lincoln delivered his famous "house divided" speech at the Old State Capitol Building, which was painstakingly dismantled a few years back, and modern housing for the State Historical Society was constructed below ground before the Greek Revival-style building was carefully put back together again, stone by stone. Other sites associated with Lincoln in Springfield are the white frame house where the Lincoln family lived for nearly a quarter century, which has been refurnished in period pieces, and the Lincoln Tomb in Oak Ridge Cemetery where the Great Emancipator is buried beside his wife, Mary Todd, and three of their four sons. Visitors also will enjoy seeing the archaeological displays in the Illinois State Museum and the miniature three-dimensional scenes of important events in Illinois history, of which the favorite by far is a frightening version of the Great Chicago Fire of 1871.

The Lincoln Trail Homestead State Park on the banks of the Sangamon River marks the site of Lincoln's first home in Illinois, and the Lincoln Log Cabin State Park near Charleston commemorates his father and stepmother, who are buried nearby. Scattered throughout central and southern Illinois are a number of towns which Lincoln regularly visited during his career as a circuit-riding lawyer. In Beardstown on the Illinois River, Lincoln successfully defended his client in a famous murder trial, which is usually re-enacted every year by the townspeople in the original courtroom that looks much as it did during Lincoln's day. At Vandalia, Illinois's second capital, visitors can see the Madonna of the Trail Monument, one of twelve erected by the DAR along the "National Old Trails Road," as well as the old State House where Lincoln held a seat in the General Assembly in the company of Stephen A. Douglas. History buffs will want to visit the seven towns where the famous Lincoln-Douglas debates on the slavery issue took place—Ottawa, Freeport, Jonesboro, Charleston, Galesburg, Quincy, and Alton—and pay their respects to the now-forgotten "Little Giant," Stephen A. Douglas, at his tomb in Chicago.

Many of Illinois's sixty-six state parks are memorials to the Indians who once roamed the Illinois territory and the French who were the first white men to settle there. Cahokia Mounds State Park near East St. Louis preserves more than eighty temple and burial mounds built by prehistoric Indians, including the hundred-foot-high Monk's Mound, the biggest man-made earthwork of prehistoric origin in the United States. At the nearby village of Cahokia are the Church of the Holy Family built by French missionaries and the old French Courthouse, which are reputed to be the oldest permanent structures west of the Alleghenies. Fort Kaskaskia and its neighbor, Fort Chartres, built by the French on the Mississippi below East St. Louis, are now state parks, as is Fort Père Marquette at the junction of the Illinois and Mississippi rivers, and traces of French culture are still visible in the village of Prairie du Rocher, one of the earliest French settlements.

Fort Massac State Park on the Ohio River preserves another site of an old French fort which is being restored. George Rogers Clark and his frontiersmen camped here on their way to capture Fort Kaskaskia from the British during the Revolutionary War, and a statue of Clark overlooks the river. A tour of the historical sites in southern Illinois would not be complete without seeing famous Cave-in-Rock on the Ohio River where outlaws, counterfeiters, and murderers hid out during the early frontier days.

One of the better known state parks in northern Illinois is Starved Rock, built around the enormous outcropping of sandstone which towers above the Illinois River. According to legend, Starved Rock got its name because a band of Illinois Indians who had taken refuge there starved to death rather than surrender to an enemy Indian tribe. A monument at the top of Starved Rock marks the site of Fort St. Louis, built by Cavelier, Sieur de La Salle, to claim the Illinois territory for the French, but today nothing remains of the old fort. The rest of the park is rich in Indian relics, including Skeleton Cave, where a pre-Columbian burial ground has been recently discovered.

At Dickson Mounds, near the Mississippi in northwestern Illinois, a new state museum houses over two hundred prehistoric Indian skeletons and a fine collection of Indian tools and artifacts. Farther north, on the Rock River in Lowden State Park, stands a statue of the famous Indian chief Black Hawk, leader of the Sac and Fox tribes, who fought the white men to preserve the Rock River country for his people and finally had to give up in defeat. Today, visitors can drive through the beautiful Rock River country along the Black Hawk Trail from the northern boundary of Illinois to the Tri-Cities of Davenport, Rock Island, and Moline on the Mississippi, with a detour to Grand Detour, the village where John Deere built the first steel plow and where his blacksmith shop and home have been preserved.

Not far from the Tri-Cities is the restored village of Bishop Hill, Illinois's first commune. A group of Swedish immigrants led by Eric Janson set up the Bishop Hill community in 1846 on the basis that all property was owned in common, but before long the settlers were quarreling among themselves and the community dissolved. Now, folk crafts such as weaving, candle-dipping, and blacksmithing are taught at Bishop Hill during the summer months.

At Galena, tucked away in the extreme northwestern corner of the state, time seems to have stood still, for this charming town has changed relatively little since the 1830s when the nearby lead mines were booming and the cultural life of Galena was a bright spot in the wilderness. Visitors will enjoy seeing the lovely old homes and churches built in Galena's heyday, as well as the restored Ulysses S. Grant home, a two-story brick house presented to the general by the grateful citizens of Galena after his return from the Civil War. Galena, New Salem Village, Cahokia Mounds—these are only a sampling of the many historical sites and places of interest waiting to be visited in downstate Illinois.

SPECIAL EVENTS

July and August are red-letter months on the Illinois calendar, for it's fair time in the Prairie State. Local fairs are held in every county, and the blue-ribbon prize-winning livestock and home-economic entries go on to compete in the Illinois State Fair, the largest agricultural fair in the nation, which is held the second week of August in Springfield. More than 700,000 Illinoisans, farming people and city folks, attend the State Fair every year, for there is something for everyone to enjoy —livestock shows; displays of prize-winning cakes and needlework; home-economic and farm-equipment demonstrations; carnival rides and auto races; top-name entertainment and harness racing; and that sticky sweet cotton candy to top off a special fair lunch of Illinois pork tenderloin sandwiches and corn on the cob dripping with butter. Fair time is fun, but it is serious business too, for the competition especially in the livestock judging is keen, and the greatest achievement for an Illinois 4-H Club member is to have his entry chosen to compete in the State Fair.

Visitors from across the nation come to the Du Quoin State Fair held the end of August to see the Hambletonian, "the Kentucky Derby of Harness Racing," considered to be the most prestigious trotting race in the world. Another world-famous event is the International Livestock Exhibition and Horse Show held annually in December at Chicago.

The Lilac Festival in Lombard, the Indian Pow Wow at Black Hawk State Park near Rock Island, the National Sweet Corn Festival at Hoopeston, and the Railsplitting Contest at Lincoln are only a few of the special events that take place each year in Illinois. Palestine, on the eastern side of the state near the Wabash River, plays host to the largest rodeo east of the Mississippi held every Labor Day weekend, while across the state at Nauvoo, visitors can sample homemade wine and blue cheese during the Wedding of the Wine and Cheese, an annual ceremony introduced by French immigrants who settled there over a century ago. The annual Fort de Chartres Rendezvous commemorates the early French days in Illinois with activities such as greased-pole contests and canoe races, and the Steam Boat Days at Peoria celebrates the era of the great paddle-wheelers with a race between the *Julia Belle Swain* of Peoria and the *Delta Queen* out of Cincinnati. There is an International Carillon Festival at Springfield, a Deutschfest at Belleville, and an Apple Festival at Murphysboro in the heart of the southern Illinois orchard country. A re-enactment of a Civil War battle takes place every year at Galena during the U. S. Grant Civil War Cantonment, which also features tomahawk- and knife-throwing contests as well as a military ball. A listing of the dates of these and the many other special events, including art shows and craft demonstrations, held annually throughout the state can be obtained from the Illinois Office of Tourism in Springfield.

M.L.

CHRONOLOGY

1673 Father Jacques Marquette of France and Louis Jolliet of Canada were the first known white men to travel through Illinois.

1699 French priests founded a mission at Cahokia, the oldest permanent town in Illinois.

1717 Illinois became part of the French colony of Louisiana.

1763 Illinois was included in the territory ceded by France to Great Britain after the French and Indian War.

1778 George Rogers Clark's forces captured Cahokia and Kaskaskia from the British during the Revolutionary War.

1787 Congress made Illinois part of the old Northwest Territory.

1800 Illinois became part of the Indiana Territory.

1809 Congress made Illinois a separate territory.

1812 Indians massacred white settlers fleeing from Fort Dearborn on the site of present-day Chicago.

1818 Illinois became the twenty-first state on December 3.

1832 Illinois settlers defeated the Sac and Fox Indians in the Black Hawk War.

1844 Mormon leader Joseph Smith and his brother, Hyrum, were lynched by mob at Nauvoo. Mormons were forced to flee the state.

1848 The Illinois and Michigan Canal, the shipping link between the Chicago and Illinois rivers, was completed.

1858 Abraham Lincoln and Stephen A. Douglas debated the slavery issue in their senatorial campaigns throughout Illinois.

1871 The Chicago Fire destroyed much of the city.

1886 Discontent among industrial laborers led to the Haymarket Square Riot in Chicago.

1893 The World's Columbian Exposition was held in Chicago.

1900 The Chicago Sanitary and Ship Canal was completed, making the Chicago River flow backward.

1933 The Illinois Waterway linking Lake Michigan with the Mississippi River was completed.

1933–34   The Century of Progress Exposition was held in Chicago.

1942   Scientists at the University of Chicago controlled an atomic chain reaction for the first time.

1965   Illinois Senate and House of Representatives were reapportioned.

1968   Participants and observers of the Democratic National Convention held in Chicago claimed police harassment.

1969   Illinois adopted individual and corporate income taxes.

1970   Illinois voters approved a new constitution, which went into effect July 1, 1971.

1971   The Atomic Energy Commission completed the nation's largest atom smasher at Batavia, west of Chicago.

1975   Richard J. Daley won a sixth term as Chicago mayor. He died during his term of office in December 1976.

1976   James R. Thompson, a Republican, was elected governor of Illinois.

1979   Sweeping all of the city's forty-four wards and capturing 82 per cent of the vote, Jane Byrne became the first woman mayor of Chicago.

INDIANA

THE VERY MENTION of Indiana is usually enough to start people humming. It could be because a lot of Americans still subscribe to the notion that life is better out there on the front porches of rambling houses in well-kept small towns. More likely, it's because Indiana has produced more than its share of the nation's song writers, many of whom have paid loving musical tribute to their home state. The one who did it best was writer Theodore Dreiser's brother Paul Dresser. He composed Indiana's state song, "On the Banks of the Wabash Far Away."

But Dresser was not the only Indiana boy with musical talent. A fellow from Indianapolis named Harry Gumbinsky changed his name to Harry von Tilzer and wrote three thousand songs, among them "I'll Be with You in Apple Blossom Time" and "Wait 'Til the Sun Shines, Nellie." One of his most popular compositions, "In the Evening by the Moonlight," evokes the simple pleasures of his home state.

Cole Porter and Hoagy Carmichael were from Indiana too, as was Thomas Westendorf who wrote "I'll Take You Home Again, Kathleen." Poet James Whitcomb Riley conveyed in verse what Paul Dresser did in music—his vivid descriptions of his home state have gained in popularity over the years.

Much of the state's image, of course, is just wishful thinking. Today, it is an industrial powerhouse, producing more steel and manufactured goods than farm products. Politically and socially it's changing, too. It's no longer as solidly conservative as it once was. During the first half of the 1970s, Indiana sent two liberal Democrats to the United States Senate.

THE LAND

There's pretty strong evidence that nature intended Indiana to be a state of prosperous farms and quiet towns. The plan was laid back in the Ice Age thousands of years ago when glaciers covered most of the state. After all the ice had melted, Indiana was left with enough rich soil to convince even the most reluctant farmer to put down roots.

The most appealing farm land of all is in the center of the state which is crossed by the great Midwestern corn belt. Geologists call this part of the country the "till plain" to indicate that it is composed of "till" or earth materials that once were part of the glacial mass. Here, the land is low and level, the plain rising only occasionally to form low hills and then dropping modestly to mold shallow valleys. At only one point is this gentle landscape interrupted by a hill of significant height—for Indiana, that is. There's a point in Wayne County on the Ohio border where the hills mount 1,257 feet above sea level.

In northern Indiana the glaciers left somewhat more dramatic evidence of their presence. A visitor from the east coast brought here blindfolded might imagine he was back on the Atlantic beaches when he gets his first look at the great sand dunes that border Lake Michigan in Indiana. So spectacular are these dunes—and so unexpected in the Midwest—that what remains of them has been set aside by the Federal Government as the Indiana Dunes National Lakeshore.

Elsewhere in the Great Lakes Plains area, swampland has been drained, leaving rich black soil for farming. The glacial residue in this northernmost part of Indiana also includes marshes and moraines or low ridges or mounds made up of materials deposited by the melting glaciers. Here, too, are most of Indiana's thirty-six lakes of significant size. The largest, Lake Wawasee, covers 4.6 miles in Kosciusko County in the northeast.

Geologists will tell you that through the Great Lakes Plains area runs the east-west divide which separates the rivers and streams that drain into the Mississippi from those that empty into the St. Lawrence.

The only area of Indiana untouched by those glaciers of the distant past is to the south where the lowlands surrounding the Wabash River are flat and fertile. Farther east, however, the territory is more

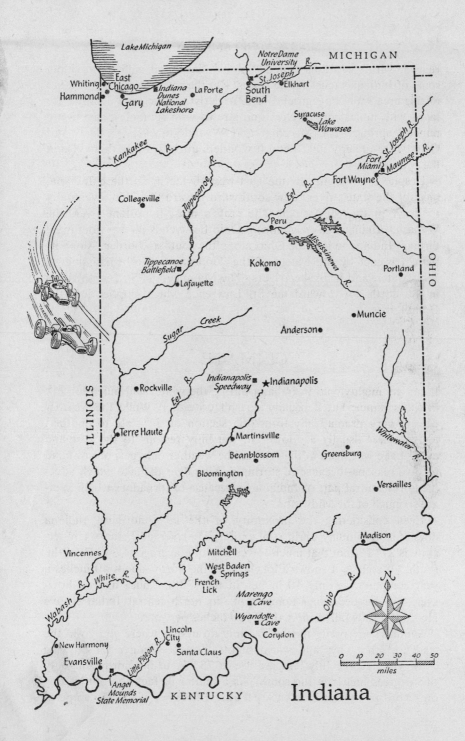

Lake Michigan

MICHIGAN

Notre Dame
University
St. Joseph R.

Whiting
East
Chicago
St. Joseph
Hammond
Indiana
Dunes
National
Lakeshore
La Porte
South
Bend
Elkhart

Gary

Syracuse
Lake
Wawasee

Kankakee R.

St. Joseph R.

Fort
Miami
Maumee R.

Collegeville

Eel R.

Fort Wayne

OHIO

Tippecanoe R.

Peru

Mississinewa

Tippecanoe
Battlefield

Kokomo

Portland

Lafayette

R.

Sugar Creek

Anderson

Muncie

ILLINOIS

Rockville

Eel R.

Indianapolis
Speedway

★ Indianapolis

Terre Haute

Martinsville

Whitewater R.

Beanblossom

Greensburg

Bloomington

Versailles

Madison

Vincennes

Mitchell

White R.

West Baden
Springs
French
Lick

Marengo
Cave

Ohio R.

N

Wyandotte
Cave

Corydon

Wabash R.

Lincoln
City

Little Pigeon R.

New Harmony

Santa Claus

0 10 20 30 40 50
miles

Evansville

Angel
Mounds
State Memorial

KENTUCKY

Indiana

rugged, with steep hills called "knobs" and deep valleys providing some of Indiana's most scenic vistas. But the most spectacular feature of this area isn't aboveground. The underlying limestone deposits are laced with underground rivers and strewn with sinkholes, caves, and mineral springs. The Marengo and Wyandotte caves in Crawford County are underground natural wonders unrivaled anywhere else in the country.

Despite the presence of the east-west divide in northern Indiana, most of the state's rivers flow southward toward the Ohio, eventually to drain in the Mississippi. The state's most important river, the Wabash, originates in neighboring Ohio but wends its way southwest through Indiana to join the Ohio along the southern border. Along its path it is met by the waters of the Tippecanoe, Eel, Mississinewa, Whitewater, and Kankakee rivers. The Maumee and St. Joseph rivers in the north flow toward the St. Lawrence which empties into the Great Lakes.

CLIMATE

It can get mighty cold in Indiana during the winter and much too hot in the summer, but it usually doesn't do either. While the weather doesn't vary dramatically from one section of the state to another, temperatures usually are lower in the hilly regions to the east and along Lake Michigan in the north. The weather only gets out of hand for two reasons—because of storms moving over the lake which affect the north-central part of Indiana or because of tornadoes which menace so much of the Midwest.

Even considering the proximity of the lake, northern Indiana doesn't suffer unduly during the winter. The average January temperature is 27° F.—not that much lower than the average of 34° F. in the south. Of course, it snows a lot more in the north—about 40 inches a year compared to only 10 inches in the south. Those figures, however, can be deceiving. Some spots in north-central Indiana have recorded a snowfall of more than 100 inches per year.

Summers are pretty much the same no matter where you go in the state . . . hot days and warm nights, perfect weather for growing corn. The average July temperature is 75° F. in the north and only two degrees higher in the south. As a matter of fact, the hottest day on record in Indiana was back on July 14, 1936, when the temperature in Collegeville in the northwest soared to 116° F. And just to prove that you can't make any generalizations about Indiana's weather, the coldest day on record was in Greensburg in the southeast when the mercury fell to a very chilly −35° F. on February 2, 1951.

As far as rain is concerned, the difference is minimal, with the north getting about 36 inches per year compared to the south's 43 inches. The tornado season begins in the spring and lasts through early summer, adding an element of uncertainty to the state's climatic conditions. All things considered, the best time to be in Indiana is the fall, when the days are clear and crisp and the nights are illuminated by a glowing harvest moon.

THE HOOSIERS

One of the easiest ways to stir up controversy in Indiana is to ask why people there are called "Hoosiers." No one has been able to pin down the origin of the term, and explanations of how it came into being differ widely. There are some who subscribe to the theory that it comes from an English dialect in which "hoo" means hill and someone who lives on the hill is a "hoozer." Still others are certain it's a corruption of "who's here?"—the question pioneers called out as they heard or saw someone approach. Then, there's the story about Sam Hoosier, a canal contractor who preferred to hire men from Indiana because they were such good workers. His crews were known as "Hoosier's men."

Whatever the origin, the name stuck and anyone who lives in Indiana today is a Hoosier. They're a pretty homogeneous lot, most of them white, native-born Americans whose parents also are native-born Americans. There are also a few foreign-born Hoosiers—mostly the Poles, Hungarians, Belgians, Italians, and Mexicans who live and work in the industrialized Calumet area in the north of the state. That's where Indiana's black population is concentrated—50 per cent of the residents of Gary and 25 per cent of the people in East Chicago are black. Those figures are derived from the 1970 United States Census which also determined that 70 per cent of the people of Indiana are Protestants, 15 per cent are Catholics, and 1 per cent is Jewish.

Indiana wasn't always so homogeneous, but it never did have the ethnic mix to be found in so many other states. The earliest white men in the area were the French, who were mostly interested in fur trapping and trading and viewed the area that is now Indiana as a link in their route from Canada to New Orleans via the Ohio and Mississippi rivers. The French built Fort Miami in 1704, Fort Ouiatenon in 1719, and Fort Vincennes in 1732 to protect their access to the route. They established the first permanent white settlement at Fort Vincennes.

Ultimately the English began challenging the French for control of the territory. At the same time, they were intent upon ousting the Indians to make room for white settlers. The Delaware, Mohican, Munsee, Shawnee, Kickapoo, Piankashaw, Potawatomi, and Wea Indians had populated the area long before the arrival of either the English or the French. Some of the tribes had been pushed into Indiana from as far east as Pennsylvania and as far north as the Great Lakes by the white man.

Once the French had been disposed of and the Indian question resolved, more and more white settlers from the new United States to the east arrived in Indiana. Most of them came from the south—from the Carolinas, Virginia, Kentucky, Tennessee, and Maryland. A few came from the east and northeast. But all had the same idea—to take advantage of the cheap land available in Indiana, then part of the Northwest Territory, and to farm on the rich, fertile soil.

When they first took a census in Indiana in 1810, 24,520 people were living there, mostly on farms. Fifty years later, the population had grown to 1.3 million, but Indiana was still an agricultural state with 90 per cent of the people living in rural areas and the largest city, Indianapolis, inhabited by fewer than 19,000 residents. About this time Indiana acquired a bit of a German flavor as the result of an influx of immigrants who introduced rathskellers, singing societies and, more seriously, the Lutheran Church. Indeed, the German music lovers helped change the tastes of the Indianapolis population—one of the singing societies began importing concert artists and continued to sponsor concerts for years. At the time, most of Indiana's people lived in the southern half of the state, a situation that wasn't to change until the early 1900s when heavy industry came to the Calumet area along Lake Michigan to the north.

Even today, Indiana remains a state of small towns. Indianapolis' population has grown to 1.1 million but most of the people live in 42 other cities with populations ranging from 10,000 to 100,000. More than half a million people live in the Gary-Hammond metropolitan area, the second largest urban complex in the state. But when you figure that all those city dwellers—those in both Indianapolis and Gary-Hammond—constitute just under 35 per cent of all the people in the state, you can see why Indiana still has a reputation as a state of small towns. The other 65 per cent of the population is divided between the rural areas and cities like Fort Wayne, Evansville, South Bend, Anderson, Terre Haute, and Muncie. Of those six, Fort Wayne is the largest with 374,550 people in the metropolitan area.

HISTORY

Thousands of years before the Indians settled in what was to become Indiana, it was inhabited by the prehistoric Mound Builders or Hopewell Man. Archaeologists know very little about these early Midwesterners. The only clue to their existence is the gigantic earthen mounds they built to bury their dead in style. Like the ancient Egyptians, the Mound Builders apparently had the idea that the dead would have to be properly equipped for the next world. They buried them with carved tobacco pipes, ornaments of shell, bone, and copper, hoes and other implements to till the soil, and even musical instruments, again of bone and copper. But in spite of all that archaeologists have been able to deduce from the Mound Builders' artistic and engineering ingenuity, they have not been able to trace where they came from or where they went.

By the time the first Europeans arrived to scout out the area that is now Indiana, tribes from other parts of the country had begun converging on the densely wooded land. From the east came the Delaware, Mohican, Munsee, and Shawnee—all displaced by white settlers. From the Great Lakes region came the Huron, Kickapoo, Piankashaw, Potawatomi, and Wea. They hoped that here, perhaps, they would be undisturbed by the westward push of white colonization.

For a while, the Indians co-existed peacefully with the French, who were the first to explore and settle in what is now Indiana. The French explorer Robert Cavelier, Sieur de La Salle was there as early as 1679 seeking a water route to the Pacific. Once he learned that the

St. Joseph and Kankakee rivers didn't take him in that direction, he turned his attention to northern Indiana. La Salle soon was followed by French fur traders, who swapped beads, blankets, knives, paint, and whiskey with the Indians and then built trading posts at Miami and Ouiatenon. They established the first permanent European settlement at Vincennes in 1731 and two years later built a fort there.

It wasn't long, however, until the French were challenged by the English, who had designs on both the fur trade and the land. The English had the notion that they were entitled to all the territory that stretched west from their colonies along the Atlantic coast. Needless to say, the French took the opposite point of view. The resulting disagreement, known as the French and Indian War, lasted from 1754 until 1763, when the defeated French ceded to Great Britain all of Canada and the eastern half of the Mississippi Valley. The Indians who had fought with the French failed in their attempt to hold back white settlement, but to appease them, the British, by the Proclamation of 1763, reserved all the lands west of the Appalachians for the Indians. That decision didn't set too well with the American colonists who already were beginning to complain about British rule. They were even more upset eleven years later when the British invoked the Quebec Act guaranteeing religious freedom for the French settlers in the area wrested from France and attaching Indiana and the surrounding territory to the Canadian province of Quebec.

During the American Revolution, the English lost Fort Vincennes in 1778 to colonial troops led by George Rogers Clark. They won it back only to lose it again a year later to Clark and a band of frontiersmen who regained control after a grueling winter march from Kaskaskia, Illinois.

Once the revolution was won, the new United States Government had to decide what to do with the vast Northwest Territory of which Indiana was a part. The first move was to enact the Ordinance of 1785 which specified how the land was to be surveyed and then sold to companies or individuals. Fifteen years later, Congress separated Indiana from other areas of the Northwest Territory and William Henry Harrison was named the first governor.

Meanwhile, the settlers were still having trouble with the Indians who were giving vent to their hostility by burning villages and killing pioneers. General "Mad Anthony" Wayne finally put a stop to some of the resistance when he defeated the Miami Indians at the Battle of Fallen Timbers in Ohio. But it wasn't until 1811 when William

Henry Harrison defeated Indians led by the Shawnee chief Tecumseh at the Battle of Tippecanoe near Lafayette, Indiana, that the territory really was considered safe for white settlement.

There were about 64,000 people living in Indiana when it became the nineteenth state in the Union on December 11, 1816. At the time, southern Indiana was the most populous area, and it was to this region that George Rapp, a German religious ascetic, came in 1815 to establish Harmonie, a communal settlement. Harmonie flourished until 1825 when Rapp and his followers moved to Pennsylvania and sold their town to Scottish economist Robert Owen. He changed the name of the community to New Harmony and continued the experiment. It attracted international attention among scholars as Owen introduced such innovations as a trade school, the first kindergarten in the United States, a free public school system, free library, and civic drama club. In 1827, however, the experiment failed, primarily because members of the community lacked the dedication and idealism to make it work.

Meanwhile, the state itself was in trouble. Reckless spending for road and canal construction plunged the government into debt by 1840. The following decade and the advent of the railroads brought better times. It was during this period that Clement and Henry Studebaker opened their blacksmith and wagon shop in South Bend—a thriving little business that was to become the nation's largest wagon manufacturer and eventually a major automobile company.

For all its economic progress, Indiana maintained the social attitudes of the Southern states from which many of its earliest residents had emigrated. Although slavery was prohibited by federal law, it continued to exist well into the nineteenth century. Moreover, in 1831 a law was enacted requiring all Negroes entering the state to deposit a $500 surety bond as a means of demonstrating that they would not become public burdens. And the new state constitution adopted in 1851 totally excluded blacks from Indiana. That law stood until the U. S. Supreme Court declared it unconstitutional in 1866. Blacks did not feel welcome in Indiana through the first half of the twentieth century. The Ku Klux Klan flourished there in the years after the Civil War, and it wasn't until after World War II that all forms of segregation were declared illegal.

Despite its Southern heritage, Indiana fought with the North during the Civil War. It didn't see much action, though. Apart from a raid on Corydon, Indiana, by Confederate General John Hunt Morgan and his Raiders, the state was unscathed during the conflict.

After the war, Indiana's industrialization accelerated. One reason was the discovery of natural gas near Portland in 1886 and another was the decision of the Standard Oil Company in 1889 to build one of the world's largest refineries at Whiting, a little village on Lake Michigan. In 1894, a Kokomo man, Elwood Hayes, designed one of the first gasoline-powered cars that worked, and by 1902 the Studebaker brothers were turning out the first electric-powered automobiles.

But perhaps the most important industrial development of all was the U. S. Steel Company's decision to build a giant steel mill in northern Indiana and to establish there the city of Gary. Since then, Indiana's industry has never looked back. Today it far surpasses agriculture as the source of the state's income. As a result, the population has shifted away from the rural areas to the state's small towns and cities and to its two large urban areas, Indianapolis and Gary-Hammond.

Politically, despite some Democratic inroads, Indiana has been a Republican state since the Civil War. However, the political tide may be turning. The state sent two liberal Democratic Senators to Congress in the early 1970s and in 1967 Gary elected a black mayor, becoming one of the first major American cities to do so.

INDUSTRY

A good many Hoosiers are employed in Indiana's factories smelting steel or in the oil refineries tending to the petroleum that flows into the state from the southwest via a thousand-mile pipeline.

Somehow, all that industry just doesn't fit Indiana's bucolic image. But the fact is that Indiana is one of the nation's ten leading manufacturing states. Steel mills in Gary, Hammond, Whiting, and East Chicago produce some 18 million tons a year, placing Indiana among the foremost steelmaking states. All four cities are located in the Calumet region on the shores of Lake Michigan and adjacent to Illinois on the west. Here too are Indiana's giant oil refineries. The one at Whiting is among the nation's largest.

Farther west in Elkhart there's music as well as smoke in the air.

This is where they make 70 per cent of all the band instruments sold in the United States.

While steel is Indiana's most important product, there's a surprising diversity of other manufactures. They make aircraft engines, automobile parts, drugs, electronic equipment, paper products, and telephones in Indianapolis; aluminum, auto parts, and tools in Anderson, Evansville, Muncie, and South Bend; farm machinery in Fort Wayne and La Porte; and parts for military aircraft in Lafayette. Add all that to the bedding, electrical machinery, furniture, hardware, pottery, pumps, railroad equipment, glass, foundry, leather, and rubber products produced elsewhere in the state, and you've got a pretty complete picture of Indiana's industrial output. It totals nearly $12 billion a year, far more than the state takes in from farming.

The state's aforementioned industrial diversity is partly due to the ready availability of labor and the excellent interstate highway system and partly to the state's location within 800 miles of forty of the fifty largest consumer and industrial markets in the United States.

AGRICULTURE

Although Indiana has far fewer farms than it used to—just over 100,000 of them averaging about 170 acres each—it still ranks among the nation's leading agricultural states, with corn the chief crop. It grows all over, but primarily in the corn belt, which passes through the center of Indiana. Farther south there are wheatfields and to the north are soybeans, an increasingly important crop.

But Indiana is just about as diversified agriculturally as it is industrially. Tomatoes, cabbage, onions, peas, potatoes, and snap beans grow in most areas of the state, as do such fruits as apples, grapes, melons, peaches, and strawberries. And, Indiana is one of the leading producers of mint for flavoring. Both peppermint and spearmint grow there.

These days, however, crops are secondary to livestock as the source of Indiana's farm income. Hogs bring in most of the money, followed by cattle and calves. Of lesser importance are the sheep raised in central Indiana and the chickens hatched on farms scattered throughout the state.

NATURAL RESOURCES

In the days when Indiana was settled, the state was covered with thick forests of black walnut, hickory, maple, oak, ash, beech, willow, elm, sycamore, tamarak, and the yellow poplar or tulip tree. Most of the woods are gone now, cleared for farming. Only one-sixth of the state is still forest.

Indiana used up its supplies of natural gas which were found in the state late in the nineteenth century. The first well went into operation near Portland in 1886 and hundreds soon were drilled in the Indianapolis area. Within twenty years the supply ran out.

Today the most valuable minerals found in Indiana are bituminous or soft coal mined in the southwest and building limestone which is quarried in Allen, Clark, Lawrence, and Putnam counties. Indiana supplies a full two-thirds of all the limestone the United States uses in buildings, road construction, and cement making. As for the coal, it's used mostly for heating and for generating electric power. Some 18 million tons are mined each year, placing Indiana among the nation's leading coal-mining states.

Indiana also has some producing oil wells in the southwest and north-central sections. Of lesser importance are the sand and gravel, peat, and clays found throughout the state.

CITIES

Indianapolis is a bustling industrial city that affords most of the advantages of small-town living that Hoosiers prefer.

Back in the 1820s the area that is now Indianapolis was just a nameless part of the woods populated by a few settlers who certainly had no intention of building a city. The state legislature, however, had other ideas. It was wrestling with the problem of where to locate the capital of the new state of Indiana. The logical solution was to place it right in the center of the state, despite the fact that at the time there was not so much as a primitive village in the neighborhood.

By 1825 the first state offices had moved from the original capital at Corydon to the new one at Indianapolis. It took another eleven years before the population reached the point where Indianapolis could be incorporated as a town and eleven years after that until it was big enough to be considered a city. That was in 1847, the same year that the Madison railroad reached Indianapolis. It was one of the first major transportation routes that were to converge there. So many routes meet in Indianapolis today that the city calls itself the Crossroads of America.

Over the years Indianapolis has attracted more and more industry, which in turn drew more and more people. It's now the largest metropolitan area in the state and the only one with more than one million inhabitants. Despite the fact that it is not located on navigable water, Indianapolis has emerged as an important industrial center producing truck motors and bodies, airplane motors, road machinery, saws, refrigerators, electrical equipment, furniture, and pharmaceuticals. It's become an educational center, too, with three colleges, including Butler University and the prestigious Indiana University Medical Center.

Indianapolis fans out from Monument Circle, which occupies the very center of the original mile that was selected as the capital of the state. From the top of the 285-foot Soldiers and Sailors Monument, there's a panoramic view of the city which now encompasses 54 square miles. But even from the top of the monument you have to look up to see the elegant gold dome atop the State Capitol, a massive structure of Indiana limestone completed in the 1880s.

The national headquarters of the American Legion are in Indianapolis, situated on World War Memorial Plaza, a five-block area set aside to honor Indiana's dead in World Wars I and II. The complex of buildings along the plaza includes the memorial building housing an auditorium and meeting rooms and a military museum displaying combat maps, pictures, and such military memorabilia as a World War I French 75 cannon and a Navy Terrier missile.

There's another impressive collection at the Art Museum—ranging from oriental treasures dating back four thousand years to seventeenth-century Flemish and Dutch paintings, eighteenth-century French, English and Italian decorative arts, and nineteenth-century British and American paintings.

Benjamin Harrison lived in Indianapolis except for the years he lived in the White House as the twenty-third President of the United States and when he was serving in Congress. His home is now a national shrine and is furnished as it was before Harrison's death in 1901. Another local boy who made good was poet James Whitcomb Riley. His house on Lockerbie Street has been preserved too.

Most visitors to Indianapolis have a one-track mind. And that track is the Indianapolis Speedway where the Indianapolis 500 has been run every Memorial Day since 1911. The Speedway has its own museum and a bus that you can take around the track for a fee.

The Calumet district along Lake Michigan is the twenty-mile stretch where most of Indiana's heavy industry is located. Here is **Gary**, the town built by U. S. Steel in 1906, now the second-largest city in Indiana and still home of one of the nation's largest steel mills. It's pretty hard to determine where Gary leaves off and **Hammond** begins or to fix the exact boundaries of **Whiting** where Standard Oil built a huge refinery years ago. There actually is a city in those parts called **East Chicago.** It's a big town, but like the others, indistinguishable from the rest of Calumet. Along with blacks, there's an interesting ethnic mix of people who work in the area—Poles, Italians, Hungarians—and who also make their homes here.

South Bend is industrial too, and its population is the same kind of ethnic mix found in the Calumet. But it's famous for something other than factories. It's the home of the University of Notre Dame and its legendary football teams. The golden dome of the university's administration building is the most famous landmark. Topped by a statue of the Virgin Mary, it can be glimpsed from just about anywhere in the city. The 1,500-acre campus is open to visitors during the summer. Its most famous sights are the Grotto of Lourdes, a reproduction of the one in France, and a replica of a log cabin built in 1830 by Father Stephen Badin, the first Roman Catholic priest ordained in the United States. Scholars are interested in Memorial Library, one of the largest college libraries in the world. It has the capacity to store two million books and can seat thousands. Sacred Heart Church, another campus landmark, is regarded as one of the finest Gothic structures in the United States. Like the administration building, it contains several murals by artist Luigi Gregori.

Fort Wayne was built on the fort established by General "Mad Anthony" Wayne after he defeated the Miami Indians at the Battle of Fallen Timbers in 1794. Before that, there was a settlement—just a tiny British trading post in the wilds that somehow survived the constant wars between pioneers and Indians, French and English, and Indians and English. The city has tried to re-create the old days by having an area designed to look the way the fort did in Wayne's day.

Today Fort Wayne sponsors a Fine Arts Foundation, which in turn supports the Philharmonic Orchestra, Festival Music Theater, Civic Theater, and a ballet company. Two of the biggest attractions in town are the Lincoln Library and Museum and Concordia Senior College. The museum, sponsored by the Lincoln National Life Insurance Company, contains a collection of oil paintings and original photographs of the Lincolns as well as books, letters, and curios belonging to several members of the family. Concordia College, a Lutheran institution, is an architectural prize-winner. The late Finnish architect Eero Saarinen designed the buildings in the style of a North European village. To date, they've won thirty-one international awards.

The industrial town of **Evansville** has a Southern flavor that stems in part from its location just across the Ohio River from Kentucky. It is home to more than a hundred factories, continuing an industrial tradition that dates back to the early years of the nineteenth century. The big attraction in the area is the Angel Mounds State Memorial where a prehistoric Indian village once stood. Replicas of the ancient dwellings have been constructed on the site using some of the artifacts unearthed by archaeologists.

Paul Dresser and Eugene V. Debs both were born in **Terre Haute.** Dresser was Theodore Dreiser's brother, and he won a place in the hearts of Hoosiers by composing the state song, "On the Banks of the Wabash Far Away," which we mentioned earlier. Debs, labor organizer and political reformer, served in the Indiana legislature and ran for president four times on the Socialist ticket, from 1900 to 1912. His birthplace is located on North 8th Street.

SPORTS AND RECREATION

There are two things guaranteed to generate excitement in Indiana: the Indianapolis 500 on Memorial Day and high school basketball, a passion of such proportions that it's been dubbed "Hoosier hysteria." The races have been going on since 1911, when Indianapolis was an automobile manufacturing center. Over the years it has escalated in both importance and excitement, drawing some 200,000 spectators from all over the world. The excitement starts building up long before the race is run—the whole month of May has become a festival of anticipation, and lately events have been spilling over into June, most notably the festival golf tournament for professionals.

High school basketball is to the small towns of Indiana what the Indy 500 is to Indianapolis. From the late fall when the season begins to March when the finals of the annual high school basketball tournament are played in Indianapolis, the whole state is preoccupied with the game. College football and basketball also have an enormous drawing power, particularly when Notre Dame, Purdue, or Indiana University are concerned. In recent years, Indiana University, located in Bloomington on a beautifully wooded campus, has given Hoosiers something new to brag about—its championship swimming and diving teams.

For all its devotion to spectator sports, Indiana hasn't neglected the outdoorsman. It has thirty-three state parks and forests with recreation facilities ranging from picnic grounds to hiking trails, horseback riding, swimming, boating, and camping. The most popular resort area is along Lake Michigan among the dunes, but the inland lakes, particularly Wawasee near Syracuse, draw thousands of vacationers each year. Elsewhere, the lakes and streams are well stocked with pike, perch, and bass and, in season, hunters stalk quail, pheasant, and deer in the Cumberland foothills and Hoosier National Forest.

POINTS OF INTEREST

Abraham Lincoln was born in Kentucky and is buried in Illinois, but he grew up in Indiana, a historical fact you're not likely to forget after a few days in the state. The Lincolns moved to southern Indiana from Kentucky when Abe was seven and for fourteen years farmed in Spencer County near Little Pigeon Creek. The tales of Abe Lincoln trudging miles to school, reading and writing by firelight and learning to split rails, are derived from his years in Indiana.

The Lincoln Boyhood National Memorial near Lincoln City evokes many of those early experiences. Built on the site of the Lincolns' farm, it contains the grave of Abe's mother, Nancy Hanks Lincoln, who died when he was nine. A walk through the Exhibit Shelter on the southwest corner of the farm brings to mind those days in the

1820s when Lincoln was growing up there. The log buildings have been reconstructed and the fields and gardens are kept as they would have been when the Lincolns were in residence. The memorial is only one stop along the Lincoln Heritage Trail, which begins in Kentucky and follows the Lincoln family to Indiana and then to Illinois where Honest Abe became a lawyer, then a politician, and eventually a presidential candidate.

Back in Lincoln's day when visitors came to Indiana they usually wanted to observe the social experiment, mentioned earlier, at New Harmony—an experiment that had begun in 1814 when a German religious ascetic named George Rapp arrived with his followers. Their aim was to create a communal society by sharing both the work and the fruits of their labor. They cleared more than 30,000 acres for farm land and within ten years had evolved into a prosperous and peaceful community. In 1825, however, Rapp sold out, moving with his followers to Pennsylvania and turning over the town to Robert Owen, a Scottish industrialist who had his own ideas about Utopia. He changed the name from Harmonie to New Harmony, recruited educators, scientists, social reformers, and artists, and set about creating his own communal society. Despite the expense and the high-level theorizing that went into the experiment, this one was a failure. It seemed that artists and educators were idealistic about communal living, except when it came to performing the menial tasks necessary to keep things running.

Today, New Harmony is a state memorial and a major tourist attraction. Many of the buildings used by the original Harmonists have been restored. Among them are a dormitory which Rapp's followers built for bachelors and which was used later by the Owen group as a cultural center and school, the fort-granary, the poet's house, and a few other homes. There's also a tricky maze of garden hedges called the Labyrinth that dates back to Rapp's day. With a little time and patience, you can work your way to the center.

New Harmony still attracts artists, scholars, and educators, who come to lecture or perform during the summer. As a matter of fact, descendants of Robert Owen are still around and thinking about putting New Harmony back in business as an artistic and cultural center. It obviously still has its appeal. Architect Philip Johnson was inspired to design one of the most unusual new buildings, a Roofless Church, and sculptor Jacques Lipchitz contributed a bronze called "Descent of the Holy Spirit."

Some of the early visitors to Indiana were more concerned with the body than with the human spirit. Quite a few of them were convinced that the medicinal waters at French Lick were just what they needed for health, if not for happiness. At first, enthusiasts simply arrived at the hot springs in their wagons, filled up bottles, and drove home. But in time, the place became a fashionable resort, attracting guests from all over the country. It was especially popular early in the twentieth century. They even called the West Baden Springs Hotel there the Carlsbad of America. It was—and still is—a rather spectacular watering hole. The main building is eight-sided, six stories high, and contains 708 rooms. Small wonder that it cost $7 million to build in 1906. The elegant marble lobby is topped by the largest glass-enclosed dome in the world. It weighs more than eight tons and at its highest point is 150 feet above the floor. When guests weren't restoring themselves with the waters, they could stroll through the grounds, which covered 700 acres, golf on the nine-hole course, attend the little theater, or gamble in the casino. A lot of them were gambling on the stock market, too. The hotel fell upon hard times after the 1929 crash and was closed. Later, it was used as a Jesuit seminary and now houses a college, the Northwood Institute.

Ever since the West Baden Springs Hotel closed, Indiana visitors have had to settle for less luxurious but not less spectacular resorts. Today, most people come to see the dunes that form the sandy beach along Lake Michigan. The dunes used to line the lakefront for twenty-five miles between Gary and Michigan City. But as the area became increasingly industrial, the dunes were cleared away, leaving just seven miles untouched today. What remains is a breath-taking sight—small dunes, shifting daily with the wind, and large ones (the tallest is 190 feet high and has a name, Mount Tom) anchored by plants and vines and an amazing variety of wildflowers. Botanists have identified twenty-six varieties of orchids growing here. In order to make sure that industry doesn't encroach on the area any more, Congress in 1972 set aside 8,329 acres as the Indiana Dunes National Lakeshore.

The dunes aren't Indiana's only natural wonder. The caves in the southern part of the state are just as awe-inspiring, particularly Wyandotte with its twenty-three miles of tunnel winding down five levels beneath the ground. One of the huge chambers even contains a mountain—an honest-to-goodness underground mountain 185 feet high. Two smaller caverns are nearby, Marengo Cave with its eerie stalactites and stalagmites and Squire Boone Caverns, named for Daniel's brother who discovered them almost two hundred years ago.

People also come to Indiana to see some picturesque examples of human ingenuity—the covered bridges of Parke County. There are thirty-six of them, spanning creeks and streams on winding back roads that once were major arteries but now are frequented mostly by tourists and Hoosiers out for leisurely drives in the country. The longest of the bridges, over Sugar Creek, measures 207 feet.

Santa Claus is in Indiana, too. Not jolly Old St. Nick, but a tiny village named Santa Claus where it's Christmas all year round. That's where all the mail addressed to Santa goes. When it gets there, it's postmarked and returned to the sender. And should some of the senders happen to drop by in person, there's plenty to remind them that Christmas is always on the way. Starting June 15, Santa himself arrives. He's on the job until Christmas Eve when the whole town closes for a short winter's nap.

SPECIAL EVENTS

At one time, the circus came to Peru, Indiana, every year. And not just one circus—so many of them maintained winter headquarters there that Peru looked upon itself as the Circus Capital of the World. But times have changed, and the big top is no more. The people of Peru, however, still love circuses, so much so that they decided they should have one of their own, and some professional circus people stayed around to train local school children. Now, Peru has its own circus and holds a festival every July to celebrate that fact.

The fall is festival time throughout Indiana—Versailles has one focusing on the pumpkin crop, Mitchell goes all out for persimmons, and the fall foliage is cause for celebration in Martinsville. But one of the biggest events is in Rockville, which whips up two weeks of excitement every year at the Covered Bridge Festival. There are thirty-six of these covered bridges throughout Parke County, all of which you can see on a bus tour and then browse in the Farmer's Market where you can even pick up some papaws.

Unquestionably, the biggest event of the year in Indiana is the Indianapolis 500 on Memorial Day. But gaining in importance are the U. S. National Drag Races held at the Indianapolis Speedway each Labor Day. There's another big race in June—this one on water. It's the Madison Regatta on the Ohio River when hydroplanes vie for the Governor's Cup.

Music lovers throughout the world have long been aware that the Romantic Music Festival in Indianapolis in May is well worth the trip. That same month, Fort Wayne holds its annual Fine Arts Festival, and, lately, the town of Beanblossom in Brown County has been attracting national attention with its Blue Grass Music Festival in June.

P.D.

CHRONOLOGY

1679 French Explorer Robert Cavelier, Sieur de La Salle explored the area that is now Indiana.

1731 The first permanent settlement was established by the French at Fort Vincennes.

1763 As a result of the French and Indian War, Indiana became English territory.

1778 George Rogers Clark ousted the English from Fort Vincennes. The British recaptured the Fort, and Clark routed them again in 1779.

1787 Indiana became part of the Northwest Territory.

1800 The territory of Indiana was separated from the Northwest Territory.

1811 William Henry Harrison defeated the Indians led by Tecumseh at the Battle of Tippecanoe.

1815 George Rapp founded a communal settlement called Harmonie.

1816 Indiana was admitted to the Union as the nineteenth state.

1825 George Rapp sold Harmonie to Robert Owen who began his own experiment and renamed the town New Harmony.

1851 The Indiana state constitution excluded blacks from the state.

1889 One of the world's largest oil refineries was built by the Standard Oil Company, at Whiting on Lake Michigan.

1894 Elwood Haynes of Kokomo designed one of the first gasoline-powered automobiles that worked.

1906 The U. S. Steel Company began building Gary and the huge steel mill there.

1911 The first 500-mile automobile race was held at Indianapolis.

1933 The governor was given greater powers under a reorganization of the state government.

1949 Racial segregation in the public schools was outlawed by the Indiana legislature.

1966 The Indiana Dunes National Lakeshore was established by Congress.

1967 Gary elected a black mayor, Richard D. Hatcher, thus becoming one of the first major U.S. cities to do so.

1971 Indianapolis' sesquicentennial was observed.

1975 Indiana Senator Birch Bayh entered the race for the Democratic presidential nomination in 1976.

1976 Republican incumbent Otis R. Bowen was re-elected governor.

1979 As a significant part of a pilot program of the National Park Service to improve mass transportation to urban parks, it was estimated that $62,000 would be needed by Indiana Dunes National Lakeshore to create several new bus routes and educate the public to the availability of rail service to the region.

IOWA

LOOKING AT Iowa today, it is hard to imagine that 150 years ago the land was Indian territory, off limits to the settlers pushing westward to farm. In the early days of the nineteenth century the Mississippi River was still the dividing line between civilization and the wilderness. The white men who crossed the barrier were the adventurous few, the explorers and scouts who preceded the rush to tame the continent.

Without a doubt, what drew the white man to Iowa was its farm land, endless stretches of prairie, and a rich soil that still serves Iowa well. Farming is the very essence of the state: hogs and corn and soybeans, towering grain elevators, enough slaughterhouses to process 6.5 billion pounds of meat every year. And Iowa's people continue to cling to the land. Only two of its cities have populations of more than 100,000, not enough to qualify either of them as an urban giant. Indeed, Iowa is one of the few states where the number of people still living on farms matches the number of city dwellers.

But it would be a mistake to imagine that Iowa is just an endless vista of cornfields. There are the quiet country lanes, the log cabins the pioneers built just over a century ago, the Mississippi River towns rich in the lore of the steamboat era, and more than 275,000 acres of lakes, rivers, and streams. Herbert Hoover was born in Iowa, Wyatt Earp grew up there, and for a time Mark Twain worked there. Each came from a different tradition, each from a strain of American life that Iowa reflects. Hoover, the first President born west of the Mississippi, came from a Quaker background and imbibed the spirit of these unpretentious people who settled and prospered on the Iowa frontier. Earp grew up in Pella, a town built by immigrants from Holland who nurtured their Old World heritage while they adapted to the New World. Mark Twain lived in Keokuk during its heyday as a river town and a port of call on the route south to New Orleans.

Iowa assimilated those traditions and more—the Germans and Irish and Scandinavians who crossed the ocean to farm on the raw frontier. There, a new tradition took root and eventually flourished, the tradition of a hard-working and self-sufficient people willing to brave the howling snowstorms of winter, the terrible tornadoes, and the blistering heat of the sun-drenched summers to cultivate the land. Today's Iowa is a living tribute to their perseverance: a land of agricultural abundance and a bastion of solid, simple values passed on from generation to generation of people who live on the land.

THE LAND

Iowa is flat, a vast plain leveled off thousands of years ago by the glaciers of the Pleistocene epoch which slid over the state depositing fertile black soils to fill the ancient valleys. The first of these glaciers was the Nebraskan ice sheet that covered Iowa more than two million years ago. Next came the Kansan drift, a glacier that blanketed everything but what is now the extreme northeast corner of Iowa. Two other glaciers followed, and by the time all that ice melted some 10,000 years ago, Iowa was flat.

Geologists say that some parts of the state are flatter than others. The northern and central sections are flattest of all. Here, in the so-called Young Drift Plains the glacial deposits, or "drift," have become the richest and most fertile soil in the state. To the west and south, however, the lay of the land is more diverse: although it's still flat, this area, called the Dissected Till Plains, has some hills and ridges formed over many thousands of years by the streams that cut through or "dissected" the plains. The wind whipping across the plains piled soil along the Missouri River to form bluffs that in some spots reach as high as three hundred feet. Geologists call northeastern Iowa the "driftless area" because only one of the four glaciers touched it. The land here is comparatively hilly, and the soil is too poor for farming.

Two mighty rivers flank Iowa to the east and west. The Mississippi curls its way southward on the east while the wide Missouri flows along the western border en route to its rendezvous with the Mississippi farther south. All the rivers in Iowa empty into one or the other of these two major waterways. The Des Moines River makes its way

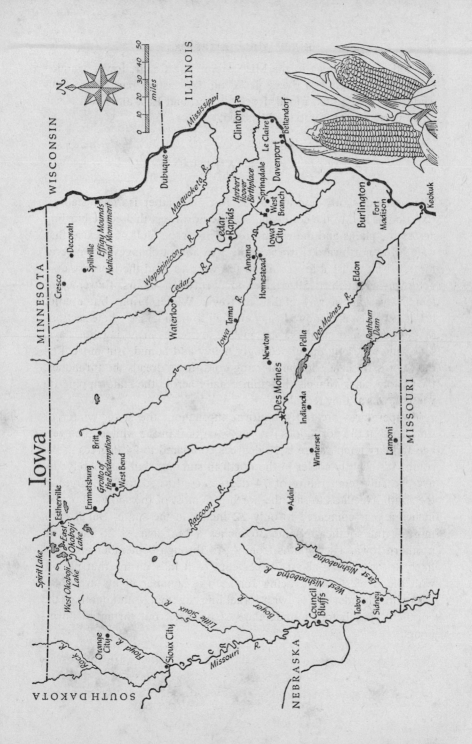

485 miles across Iowa to the Mississippi. The Cedar, Iowa, Maquoketa, and Wapsipinicon rivers also drain the eastern part of the state
while the Little Sioux, Floyd, Rock, Boyer, and East and West Nishnabotna rivers empty into the Missouri.

CLIMATE

The best one-word description for Iowa's weather is "changeable."
Exposed as it is to the cold winds of the northwest that come hurtling
across the plains and the warm breezes from the Gulf of Mexico that
waft softly northward, Iowa is subject to abrupt changes in temperature: It isn't unusual for a shift in the wind to send the mercury up—
or down—as much as 50 degrees in twenty-four hours. Extremes of
temperature are a way of life in Iowa: Winter brings bitter cold,
howling winds, and snows heavy enough to immobilize whole sections
of the state, and summers are just as extreme—blistering hot days,
scorching sun, and air suffocatingly heavy and humid. But more than
the oppressive heat and the piercing cold, Iowa dreads the tornadoes,
the deadly black funnels that spin crazily across the state ripping up
whole towns as they reel along.

Temperatures are fairly uniform throughout the state, winter or
summer, but the north does get the worst of it in the winter; the average January temperature is 18 degrees compared to 24 degrees in the
south. It's slightly cooler in the north in summer—but just barely: an
average July temperature of 74 degrees contrasted to 77 degrees in
the south. Needless to say, the north gets most of the snow—about 50
inches a year compared to only 22 inches in the south. But it rains
most in the southeast, some 36 inches a year against 26 inches in
northern Iowa. The months from April through September are most
likely to bring rain; about 70 per cent of it falls during that period,
with the rainiest month being June. Iowa summer nights are noted
for wild thunderstorms with crackling lightning illuminating the
cornfields just before thunderclaps signal brief but torrential down-
pours.

PLATE 1 Lincoln's tomb in Springfield, Illinois.

PLATE 2 Marina City twin towers (left) flank the Chicago River.

PLATE 3 The Museum of Science and Industry is one of Chicago's most popular tourist attractions.

PLATE 4 The Roofless Church, in New Harmony, Indiana, the site of two religious communal colonies in the early 1800s.

PLATE 5 Statue of General Lafayette at Tippecanoe Battlefield, Indiana.

PLATE 6 George Rogers Clark National Memorial in Vincennes commemorates the winning of the Northwest Territory.

PLATE 7 The world-famous Indianapolis "500."

PLATE 8 Des Moines's imposing State Capitol.

PLATE 9 Inside Henry Ford Museum, Dearborn, Michigan.

PLATE 10 The Soo Locks at Sault Ste. Marie, Michigan.

PLATE 11 Michigan's Mackinac Bridge, one of the world's longest suspension bridges, overlooks Fort Michilimackinac.

PLATE 12 Children don native costumes for Holland, Michigan's annual Tulip Festival.

PLATE 13 Detroit's skyline.

PLATE 14 Carl Milles's rotating
Indian God of Peace in
St. Paul's City Hall and
Courthouse is thirty-nine
feet high and made of
sixty tons of onyx.

PLATE 15 Minnesota's Split Rock Lighthouse on Lake Superior's
North Shore Drive.

THE IOWANS

For more than thirty years after it became part of the United States with the Louisiana Purchase in 1803 Iowa was largely ignored. At the time there was still plenty of good farm land back East and the territory west of the Mississippi was still full of Indians, many of them tribes that had been displaced from their homelands elsewhere. There were some seventeen tribes in Iowa when French explorers came in 1673. The Illinois, Iowa, Miami, Ottawa, and Sioux lived along the Mississippi while the Omaha, Oto, and Missouri were farther west pursuing the great herds of buffalo. Later, the Sac and the Fox came down from Wisconsin and the Winnebago and the Potawatomi arrived from the East.

As long as they had only the French explorers and fur traders to contend with, the Indians were pretty peaceful. Although there were occasional outbreaks of violence among them, hostility against the white man didn't erupt until 1735 when the Sac and Fox battled and beat a small French force near what is today Des Moines.

During the early years of the nineteenth century, the Indians of Iowa began to lose their lands by treaty. Chief Black Hawk of the Fox fought back in an effort to regain some of the million and a quarter acres his tribe once controlled, but his battle proved futile and by 1845 the defeated Indians agreed to move west. The Sioux clung to their Iowa lands until 1851, but then they, too, were uprooted.

White settlers began drifting into Iowa in the 1830s—about 50 of them lived there in 1832, but by 1840 the population had soared to 43,000, mostly farmers who moved in from neighboring states. Homesteaders from Kentucky settled in southern Iowa while farmers from Ohio, Indiana, Illinois, and the East Coast congregated in the north.

The 1850s brought a rush of immigrants from Europe, particularly from Germany and the Scandinavian countries. Parts of Iowa still retain some of the ethnic flavor introduced by those nineteenth-century settlers. A Nordic fest is held every year at Decorah in northeastern Iowa as a tribute to the Norwegian heritage of the people of the area. Dutch settlers left their mark on two Iowa towns, Pella in Marion

County and Orange City in northwestern Sioux County. Pella was founded in 1847 by eight hundred Dutch immigrants. Today, the town is famous for its annual spring tulip festival and as the boyhood home of the legendary Wyatt Earp. Orange City gets equally enthusiastic about its Dutch heritage at tulip time.

Iowa's most famous German community dates back to 1855 when members of the Amana Society arrived from Buffalo, New York, where they originally had settled. The Amana Colonies were founded by a group of Inspirationists led by Christian Metz. Members lived communally in seven villages and owned and operated their own industries, including the famous refrigerator equipment company. Another German sect, the Old Order Amish, settled in Iowa's Washington County in 1846. The descendants of these nineteenth-century settlers still live as their great-grandfathers did. They farm without the aid of modern equipment, travel in horse-drawn carriages, and get along without electricity, telephones, and other necessities of twentieth-century life.

The Mormons came to Iowa in the nineteenth century, too, but most of them stayed only long enough to build the hand carts they needed for the long journey west to Utah. One group did remain behind and their descendants live today in Lamoni in southern Decatur County.

Quakers settled in eastern Iowa near Springdale and West Branch. This area was a major station on the underground railroad which smuggled slaves out of the South prior to the Civil War. Among the Quakers of West Branch were the parents of President Herbert Hoover, the first United States President born west of the Mississippi. The Hoover Memorial Library is there today, adjacent to the two-room cottage where the thirty-first President was born.

Although it has been more than one hundred years since the Indians left Iowa, remnants of the Sac and Fox tribes came back during the nineteenth century and bought 3,600 acres of timberland along the Iowa River. The two tribes, today known as the Mesquakies, have been there ever since. For the most part the Indians of the Tama Settlement farm or work in nearby towns. Some are craftsmen who make beads, baskets, and Indian jewelry for sale to tourists.

Despite the visibility of some of Iowa's ethnic groups—the Indians, the Dutch of Pella and Orange City, the Amish, and the Czechs who live in Cedar Rapids—most of the state's immigrants were easily assimilated. More than 80 per cent of Iowa's 2.8 million people were born there, and most of them are Protestants of one denomination or another. The most recent arrivals have been blacks from the South who have come to Iowa to work in the factories of Des Moines and Waterloo. Although the black population is small, Iowa, like most other states, has experienced some racial tensions.

Iowa is one of the few states where the rural and urban populations are about evenly matched. Some 200,000 persons live in Des Moines, the state's largest city, and another 111,000 live in Cedar Rapids. No other Iowa city has more than 100,000 people. While the farm population has been declining over the years, Iowa, along with North Carolina and Texas, has one of the three largest farm populations in the United States.

HISTORY

Historians would love to know more about Iowa's first residents, the mysterious Mound Builders, prehistoric Indians who inhabited the Mississippi Valley a thousand years before the first white men arrived. Remnants of their civilization are scattered all over Iowa—some 10,000 burial mounds from 3 to 10 feet high and 30 to 90 feet in diameter. One of the biggest is the "Woman Mound" in Clayton County—it is shaped like a huge female and measures 135 feet long and 70 feet across the figure's arm spread. From the tools and pottery buried with the dead, archaeologists have learned that the Mound Builders were farmers and craftsmen who made ornaments out of shell and bone and painted their bodies with red ocher.

Although the Mound Builders were long gone when the first Europeans arrived in Iowa in 1673, some seventeen Indian tribes, including the Illinois, Iowa, Miami, Ottawa, Sioux, Omaha, Oto, Missouri, Sac (Sauk), and Fox, lived throughout the state. The Sac and the Fox, branches of the Algonquin nation, made their homes in southern Iowa, while the Omaha, Oto, and Missouri Indians inhabited the west and southwest. The other tribes lived along the Mississippi and befriended the French explorers and fur trappers who were the first foreign visitors to push that far down the Mississippi.

Louis Jolliet and Father Jacques Marquette canoed down the Mississippi and came ashore at what is now Iowa on June 25, 1673. They followed a path through the prairie until they came to an Illinois Indian village where they were warmly welcomed, according to Marquette's account of the visit.

In 1680 Robert Cavelier, Sieur de La Salle, began his historic voyage to the mouth of the Mississippi, and, at its conclusion, claimed all the land drained by the mighty river for France. He called the whole territory Louisiana. But no one seemed very interested in the vast new land. Only a few French missionaries, fur trappers, and soldiers came to see what was there. One of the visitors, Nicholas Perrot, found lead near what is now Dubuque and taught the Miami Indians how to mine it, but none of the Frenchmen founded settlements.

Meanwhile, Louisiana changed hands. In 1742 France transferred her lands west of the Mississippi to Spain, but the Spanish showed no more inclination to colonize than did the French. Finally, in 1788 a white man came to stay. He was Julien Dubuque, a French Canadian who made a deal with the Fox Indians to mine lead on a strip of land that stretched twenty-one miles along the Mississippi. He remained until his death in 1810 when the Indians took over the mines. A few other Frenchmen settled during the final decade of the eighteenth century, but by and large Iowa remained an Indian wilderness.

The Louisiana Territory was returned to French control in 1800 and three years later was acquired by the United States. The Americans showed much more curiosity about their Louisiana Purchase than either the French or the Spanish. President Thomas Jefferson dispatched Meriwether Lewis and William Clark to see what was there in 1804. It took them two years to travel west across the vast territory to the Pacific, a journey that took them north through Iowa. A member of their team, Sergeant Charles Floyd, died along the way and was buried near what is now Sioux City.

There was a major obstacle to the settlement of Iowa once it became American—it was Indian country and the red men showed little inclination for moving farther west so that the whites could take over. For the quarter of a century after the Louisiana Purchase, only fur traders ventured across the Mississippi. The Army did build Fort Madison in 1805, and for jurisdictional purposes Congress designated the area as part of the Territory of Missouri in 1812 following the admission of Louisiana to the Union. Finally, after the Army put down an uprising of Indians led by Fox Chief Black Hawk, a fifty-mile-wide strip along the Mississippi was opened for settlement and attached to the Territory of Michigan. That area and the adjacent lands to the west were to become part of the Territory of Wisconsin in 1836. Two years later Congress created the Territory of Iowa, which included all of what is now Iowa and sections of Minnesota and North and South Dakota.

Becoming a state required some compromises. In the first place, Iowa settlers were not too enthusiastic about the idea when it was first proposed by territorial governor Robert Lucas in 1839. Their objections were understandable: Most of them were poor farmers who couldn't afford the higher taxes they would have to pay to support a state government. As long as Iowa remained a territory, the federal government paid the salaries of the officials. Another problem was a disagreement with Congress as to where the boundaries should be set. The people of Iowa insisted that the Missouri River form the western boundary and twice rejected congressional attempts to draw the state line farther east. Finally, Iowa was admitted to the Union on December 28, 1846.

The 1840s also brought a rush of foreign immigrants to Iowa. Irish, Scots, Swedes, Germans, and Dutch came by the thousands to join the farmers from adjacent states who had moved in earlier. The arrival of these newcomers pushed the state's population to 192,000 by 1850, quite a jump considering that only 50 people had been there in 1832. But the 1850s were just the beginning of Iowa's boom. During the next decade Czechs came to Johnson and Linn counties, a group of Frenchmen established a communal settlement in Adams County, the Amana Colonies were formed in 1855 by Germans who moved to Iowa from Buffalo, New York, where they originally had settled, Danes came to Benton County in great numbers. In all, there were enough new arrivals during the 1850s to more than triple Iowa's population.

Those were the years that also brought the railroad to Iowa. The first locomotive arrived in Davenport in 1853, and the next twenty years saw a frenzy of railroad construction and keen competition among Iowa towns to lure the railroads their way. Although Iowa urgently needed the railroads, there soon was discontent about unregulated freight rates. The state's farmers resented the rates enough to organize politically. Members of the Grange, a national union of farmers, were able to gain enough power in the state legislature to enact a series of laws designed to regulate the rates. Although the laws were repealed in 1878, four years after their enactment, the state assumed an active role in railroad regulation.

The outbreak of the Civil War found Iowa firmly in the Union camp. There was no question about the slavery issue here. Iowa had been admitted to the Union as a free state at the same time that Florida had come in as a slave state to maintain the ratio of slave to free states. Furthermore, the Quakers of southern Iowa had long been active in the operation of the underground railroad which ferried runaway slaves out of the South.

The years after the Civil War brought controversy on two fronts: the attempts to regulate railroad freight rates and the issue of temperance. The first move to prohibit the sale of alcohol in the state was made in 1838, and in 1855 voters adopted a law prohibiting the sale of liquor. That statute was modified two years later by a licensing system and again in 1870 when liquor sales were permitted on a local option basis. In 1882, however, Iowa adopted a constitutional amendment barring the sale of alcoholic beverages. It was declared unconstitutional, but two years later a law was adopted again prohibiting liquor sales. Another change in 1894 allowed counties to decide the issue for themselves, but that liberalized statute was repealed in 1915, four years before nationwide prohibition became a fact. Today, Iowa permits the sale of beer in retail stores and allows the sale of other alcoholic beverages in state stores. Liquor is now sold in taverns.

Iowa started to develop industrially in the 1880s, and early in the twentieth century the state began building its modern road system. However, farming continued to generate most of Iowa's income. Bumper crops in the early years of the twentieth century and the ease in marketing farm products via Iowa's new roads stimulated the state's economy. The advent of the Farm Bureau Federation and its program to bolster Iowa's agriculture by introducing new farming methods and teaching farmers how to employ them was soon followed by the organization of the Farmers' Union to promote co-operative buying and selling.

The demand for Iowa's farm products during World War I meant continued prosperity, but afterward many farmers who had mortgaged their land to buy more property found themselves deep in debt. More than half of them lost their land during the Great Depression of the 1930s. Droughts in 1934 and 1936 brought more hard times, but by then the federal government was offering subsidies to aid the hard-hit farmers and later the farmers themselves organized to buy and sell their crops co-operatively.

The state's economy picked up again during World War II, and

following the war industrial activity in Iowa accelerated. Manufacturing provided jobs as mechanization lessened the need for farm
workers. Although more and more people moved to the cities to work
in the factories, Iowa's population today remains about evenly divided between urban and rural areas.

Since before the Civil War Iowa has traditionally been a Republican state. But it has shown some leanings to the Democratic party in
recent years. Former Governor Harold Hughes and the popular
young Dick Clark, both Democrats, represented Iowa in the U. S.
Senate in the early 1970s. One explanation for their success is the
reapportioning of the state legislature to give more power to Iowa's
city dwellers. The reapportionment plan was modified several times
before winning approval from the voters in 1968.

INDUSTRY

Iowa's industry is closely tied to its agriculture. And, surprisingly, the
state's income from manufacturing falls just short of its agricultural
earnings. The manufacture of farm machinery and food processing
are Iowa's biggest industries. John Deere has been an important name
in the state since the 1850s when he introduced his sodbuster iron
plows. Today, there are two huge John Deere Company plants in
Iowa—one in Waterloo where tractors are made and another one in
Des Moines, the state's largest city. Farm machinery is also manufactured in Bettendorf, which is also the home of an aluminum processing plant that produces everything from aluminum foil to the wing
panels for the Boeing 747.

In terms of food processing, meat packing is the major activity.
Hogs are slaughtered at stockyards all over Iowa and meat-packing
plants are scattered throughout the state. Corn has to be processed,
too, and plants in Cedar Rapids, Clinton, and Keokuk make corn oil,
cornstarch, corn sugar, and glucose. Breakfast cereal is made at the
Quaker Oats Company plant in Cedar Rapids.

A man by the name of F. L. Maytag invented the motor-driven
washing machine in Newton, Iowa, in 1911, and the city still has a
big Maytag plant. Amana is famous for refrigeration equipment produced by a joint stock company owned by members of a German
commune that settled in Iowa back in the 1850s.

In addition to the John Deere plant, Des Moines has two large tire factories, Firestone and the Armstrong Company. The city also is a big midwestern insurance center—about fifty firms have their headquarters here.

AGRICULTURE

Iowa has always been farm country, and it looks like it always will be. It raises 7 per cent of the nation's total food supply, enough to rank it second only to California in the value of its agricultural output. A full 95 per cent of Iowa's land is under cultivation—almost 34 million acres divided into more than 150,000 farms.

Many of the farmers are the descendants of the settlers who rushed to Iowa in the 1800s to homestead. They raised corn just as the Indians had before them, and today corn is still Iowa's most important crop. The state produces more than 850 million bushels a year, about as much as farmers in neighboring Illinois grow. Some years Iowa ranks first in corn production, and sometimes Illinois does. Most of the Iowa-grown corn is used for livestock feed to fatten the hogs and cattle raised on other Iowa farms. Hogs are by far the most important livestock. Iowa raises more of them than any other state, providing almost one fourth of the nation's total supply. There are six hogs for every Iowa resident! Beef cattle are important here too, especially in the eastern, southern, and western sections. But while hogs and beef cattle predominate, Iowa ranks among the leading states which supply both dairy products and chickens and eggs. It produces about 6 per cent of the eggs consumed in the United States.

Although corn is king in Iowa, farmers there raise a wide variety of other crops. Soybeans are grown on almost every farm, and oats and hay are important, too. Most of the alfalfa and red clover raised in Iowa goes for cattle feed. Fruit and vegetable crops are less important, but cabbages, cucumbers, melons, onions, potatoes, and tomatoes are grown. Apples are the most important fruit crop, followed by peaches from the orchards in the southern part of the state and grapes from the vineyards near Council Bluffs.

NATURAL RESOURCES

Iowa's rich black soil is the state's most valuable natural resource. The state's farm land is the best in the country—rich, black, and fertile enough to produce abundant crops year in and year out.

But nature has not been so generous with minerals in Iowa. Although the state has deposits of limestone, shale, sand, and gravel, as well as some clay and reserves of bituminous coal, minerals bring the state only 1 per cent of its annual income. Much of that comes from the production of gypsum, the mineral used in cement making and building materials.

Figuring that 95 per cent of Iowa is farm land, it isn't surprising that most of the state's forests have long since been plowed under. But wildflowers add color and charm to the flat landscape—blue pasqueflowers, bloodroots, marsh marigolds, and violets in spring; prairie lilies, purple phlox, and wild roses in summer; and gentians, goldenrod, and sunflowers in the fall.

Iowa's wide-open spaces discourage most animal life, but there are plenty of rabbits, opossums, and some white-tailed deer. The birds love it there, though. Iowa is a stopping-off place for migratory birds as they wing south for winter and north in the spring. Thousands of ducks and Canada geese make rest stops in Iowa to feed off the grain fields where quail and pheasants nest.

CITIES

If the Army hadn't thought it in such bad taste, **Des Moines** might be known today as Raccoon, Iowa. The name was suggested by the first military contingent to establish itself at the spot where the Des Moines River forks off to a smaller stream, the Raccoon River. The War Department was shocked at the notion of calling a military outpost anything as undignified as "Fort Raccoon," and insisted on "Fort Des Moines" instead.

No one is quite sure how the name Des Moines came about in the first place. It could stem from the Indian name for the river itself—they called it Moingona, or River of the Mounds, because of the prehistoric Indian mounds in the area. Or it could be a corruption of *moyen,* the French word for middle. At any rate, the place got its name in 1843 when a company of Dragoons arrived to establish the fort. That was two years before the area was officially opened for white settlement. After it was, the town developed slowly, but in 1857 the legislature decided to move the state capital there from Iowa City.

Today, Des Moines is a city of over 200,000 people, the largest town in Iowa, home base for forty insurance companies, and a busy midwestern convention center. Hardly a week goes by that some farm group or another isn't holding a convention in Des Moines's 14,000-seat Veterans Auditorium.

It took Iowa sixteen years to construct the ornate state capital building that now crowns a hill in the center of an eighty-acre park. Work began in 1870 but had to be interrupted every time the state ran out of money for the project. The legislature first used the gold-domed Renaissance capitol in 1886. The dome itself is the largest gold one in the country, and the inside of the building is just as splendid as its wedding-cake exterior: Twenty-nine different kinds of marble were used to decorate it, the wood and stone trim is hand-carved, and the sweeping grand staircase would do credit to a Renaissance palace.

Just a stone's throw from the capitol is the Iowa State Department of History and Archives, with exhibits dating back billions of years. Among the displays are ancient rocks and fossils found in the state, prehistoric Indian artifacts, the handiwork of Iowa's more modern Indians, as well as such relics of pioneer times as a prairie schooner, a stagecoach, and tools with which the early settlers confronted the wilderness.

Another state building well worth a look is Terrace Hill, an imposing Victorian structure that is to become the governor's mansion. Built in 1869, the three-story brick building is trimmed with carved woodwork and topped by a tower that soars two stories over the roof.

The architecture is sleek and modern at the Des Moines Art Center, hub of the city's cultural life. Designed by architect Eliel Saarinen, the center was expanded by an addition that is the work of another world-famous architect, I. M. Pei. Exhibits range from displays of folk art to paintings by such European masters as Goya, Daumier, Pissaro, Courbet, and Rodin.

Des Moines is also a city of parks and lakes. The deer and buffalo still roam at nearby Lewis A. Jester Park, and there are camping facilities at Walnut Woods Park on the banks of the Raccoon River within the city limits.

Cedar Rapids, the second-largest city in Iowa, is an industrial town that dates back to 1838 when a lone log cabin stood alongside the Cedar River. The electronics industry is important here today, but most Americans are more familiar with the Quaker Oats Company, which makes cereal in Cedar Rapids. Artist Grant Wood once lived here and the Gallery of the Cedar Rapids Art Association has a valuable collection of his paintings.

Waterloo is an industrial town, too. There's a big John Deere tractor plant that employs many of Waterloo's 75,000 residents. Originally known as Prairie Rapids when it was settled in 1845, Waterloo got its present name when it was petitioning for a post office in 1851. There was no particular reason for the change—folks just liked the way "Waterloo" sounded. The arrival of the Illinois Central Railroad put the place on the map in the 1870s, and it became a shipping point for the surrounding farm country. Novelist Sinclair Lewis worked for the Waterloo *Courier* in 1908 and 1909 before he became famous as the author of *Main Street*.

Iowa's oldest city is **Dubuque** on the banks of the Mississippi. It is named for Julien Dubuque, a French Canadian who mined lead in the area during the eighteenth century. The Fox Indians were awed by Dubuque and the supernatural powers they thought he possessed— legend has it that he once threatened to set the Mississippi afire if they didn't co-operate with him. The Indians withstood all Dubuque's threats until he threw a torch into the river and flames shot up immediately. Dubuque had arranged for a companion to pour oil on the water, but the Indians never knew that, and he got what he wanted.

Dubuque died in 1810, and the Indians remained in control of the area for another twenty years. White settlement was not permitted until 1833 after Chief Black Hawk signed a treaty with Washington. The first village built by the settlers wasn't far from where Dubuque had once mined. It was a pretty rough frontier town, full of saloons and brawling lead miners. But eventually it attained respectability and some importance as seat of Dubuque County. By the 1850s the town had three colleges: the University of Dubuque, Wartburg Seminary, and Clark College. The 1860s brought prosperity: The railroad arrived, lumbering became an all-important industry, and sawmills were built all over. By then, mining was already a thing of the past and all that now survives as a reminder of Dubuque's heyday as a mining town is Old Shot Tower, where ammunition was made by dropping molten lead from the top to the bottom through several levels of screens into a vat of water. Other reminders of Dubuque's early days are to be found at Ham House, a restored 1857 mansion that serves as the local museum.

Historically speaking, **Davenport** is distinguished by the fact that it was the first of Iowa's cities to get railroad service. This Mississippi River town dates back to 1836, four years after the Sac and Fox Indians signed a treaty with General Winfield Scott. Even before that an officer named George Davenport had established his own fur-trading post with the aid of Antoine LeClaire, a French half-breed.

Davenport was still a relatively small settlement when the first locomotive was ferried across the Mississippi. But between 1850 and 1860 the population mushroomed, mostly due to the arrival of Germans seeking new homes on the frontier. Although the railroad had a lot to do with Davenport's development, the place was a romantic river town, too. It was a major stop on the steamboat route between St. Paul and New Orleans. In fact, one of the boats, the *Effie Afton,* kicked off a cause célèbre when it rammed a pier on the first bridge built across the Mississippi and burned. The bridge became the focal point of a lawsuit brought by rivermen who protested the construction of bridges in general on the grounds that the river was a "navigable waterway consecrated by nature" for their use. Stephen Douglas represented the rivermen and Abraham Lincoln represented the railroad which had built the bridge. Lincoln won.

Today, Davenport is one of the four "Quad Cities," the others being Bettendorf, Iowa, and Rock Island and Moline, Illinois. It is still an important shipping center.

Iowa City, the first capital of Iowa, is the home of the University of Iowa. Now a town of 46,000, it was founded in 1839 and was nothing but a few log cabins and frame houses when the cornerstone for the original capitol building was laid in 1840. The capital was moved to Des Moines in 1857, two years after the university opened. The school took over the graceful, columned capitol when the legislature left for Des Moines, and today it serves as the university's administration building. The campus itself occupies 706 acres and includes a hospital, the Virgil M. Hancher Auditorium for stage shows and concerts, and a museum of art.

Iowa's most important cities on the Missouri River are **Council**

Bluffs and **Sioux City.** Council Bluffs was named for the bluffs that tower over the river below. It first was called Hart's Bluffs, but when a group of Mormons arrived in 1846 they changed it to Miller's Hollow and later to Kanesville. The name became Council Bluffs after the Mormons went off to Utah to join Brigham Young in 1852. The place was a terminus for the Union Pacific Railroad before the Civil War, and afterward, five rail systems connected with the Union Pacific there. Today, it is an industrial town and a transportation center for the surrounding corn and wheat country. The chief local attraction is the restored Victorian home of nineteenth-century railroad magnate Grenville M. Dodge.

Sioux City, a town of 85,000, is famous for its stockyards and meat-packing industry. It traces its history back to the days of the Lewis and Clark exploration of the Northwest Territory. One of their party, Sergeant Charles Floyd, died en route and was buried along the Missouri. There's a monument today marking his grave. The hill where Floyd is buried is a good spot for a look at the surrounding territory. You can see three states—Iowa, Nebraska, and South Dakota—from there. The grave of the Sioux Chief War Eagle also overlooks the Missouri from a bluff where the old Indian once sat to watch the comings and goings along the river.

SPORTS AND RECREATION

Feeding the chickens may be all in a day's work for Iowa's farmers, but lately people from the cities have been paying for the privilege. The idea of a farm vacation is catching on there. About fifteen farms accept paying guests who want to sample such rural pleasures as feeding chickens, baling hay, or simply watching the grass grow.

The farmers themselves don't have to go very far from home for a change of pace. Interspersed with Iowa's corn and wheat fields are 275,000 acres of lakes, ninety-eight state parks and preserves, and three federal reservoirs offering all kinds of water sports plus camping, picnicking, and lazing in the sun. One of the state's newest resort areas surrounds Rathbun Dam, ninety-nine miles southeast of Des Moines. The two-mile long dam has formed an 11,200-acre lake bordered by one state park and several federal parks.

Northern Iowa has a big resort complex, too, the so-called "Great Lakes," Okoboji, Spirit Lake, and West Lake Okoboji. There's a little something for everyone here, from amusement parks to sandy beaches, a herd of buffalo, a summer theater, campgrounds, water-skiing, golf courses, and yachting lessons. Iowans will remind you that West Lake Okoboji has been compared to Lake Geneva in Switzerland and Lake Louise in Canada for sheer size and beauty. It's pretty deep, too—134 feet in some spots. The lakes attract thousands of visitors in winter and summer. Fishermen who don't mind the cold can drop a line through the ice, but the big winter attraction is the snowmobile racing sponsored by the Okoboji Racing Association.

Iowa prides itself on its fishing and with all that water there's bound to be something for just about everyone but deep-sea fishermen. The "Great Lakes" are known for walleye and northern pike, while the man-made lakes in southern Iowa are well stocked with bluegill, crappie, largemouth bass, catfish, and bullheads. The streams of northeast Iowa attract both fishermen and canoeists. There's plenty of rainbow and brown trout in French Creek, Bloody Run, North and South Bear Creeks, Little Paint Creek, and the Upper Iowa River. And there's always the Mississippi for walleye and sauger, northern pike, largemouth bass, white bass, and crappie.

Hunters come to Iowa for ring-necked pheasants and take about 1.5 million of them every year. But there also are bobwhite quail, Hungarian partridge, ruffed grouse in season, as well as good duck and goose shooting around the inland lakes and marshes. Deer and turkey hunting are permitted but restricted to Iowa residents.

As far as spectator sports are concerned, Iowa offers a little bit of everything. Des Moines has a professional baseball team, the Iowa Oaks of the American Association (Catfish Hunter and Vida Blue started with the Oaks) as well as a hockey team, the Capitols of the International Hockey League. Football fans watch the University of Iowa in the Big 10 Conference.

POINTS OF INTEREST

In addition to being farm country, Iowa is a colorful blend of folk cultures, a vivid reminder of pioneer times, and a place where the word "old" can have many meanings. Iowa's effigy mounds, the graves left by prehistoric Indians who lived there a thousand years ago, are old by anybody's standards. Not so old, relatively speaking, are the log cabins dating back to the 1850s when the state was settled, the imposing Victorian mansions of the first men to get rich on the Iowa frontier, the covered bridges of Madison County, and the picturesque churches built by settlers less than two hundred years ago.

Among the early immigrants to Iowa were a group of Germans who arrived in the 1850s via Buffalo, New York. The newcomers called themselves the Amana Society and lived a communal life sharing their resources, pooling their incomes, and even eating all their meals together. They established seven communities called the Amana Colonies southwest of what is now Cedar Rapids. The villages—East Amana, West Amana, High Amana, Middle Amana, South Amana, Amana, and Homestead—are situated one hour's drive by oxen from each other. You can travel between them a lot faster these days, but much of what Amana was then it is now. The Society still operates factories manufacturing woolens and furniture, baking bread, and even making wine. The Amana Refrigerator Company is headquartered there, too, although it is no longer owned and operated directly by the members of the Society.

The factories offer tours as does Amana Heim in Homestead, a clay and timber house furnished as it was more than one hundred years ago. Among Amana's biggest attractions, however, are its restaurants, justly famous for hearty German cooking, an art that most definitely has survived the transition to modern times.

Not far from Amana is West Branch, where Herbert Hoover, thirty-first President of the United States, was born and raised. No doubt about it, Hoover put the little town on the map. It is still the same Quaker village it was when he lived there, but now it's also a National Historic Site, home of the Hoover Presidential Library, the repository of Hoover's papers, books, and correspondence. The library, operated by the National Archives, contains an 8,000-volume collection pertaining to the American political, economic, and social scene of the twentieth century.

The tiny white frame cottage where Hoover was born is still there. It has been restored to look as it did when his father, the local blacksmith, built it in 1870. The blacksmith shop has been restored, too, complete with all the tools of the trade, circa 1870.

Like most of their neighbors, the Hoovers were Quakers and part of the congregation at the Quaker Meetinghouse, which also has been carefully preserved and is still where it stood when Hoover was a boy. Nearby are the graves of Hoover and his wife.

Without a doubt, the most intriguing of Iowa's tourist attractions are the effigy mounds built by prehistoric Indians who inhabited the area more than one thousand years ago. Although mounds can be found throughout the state, the most imposing group are along the bluffs of the Mississippi in northeast Iowa, where nearly 1,400 acres have been set aside as the Effigy Mounds National Monument.

The mounds, shaped like huge birds and serpents, have told archaeologists a lot about the culture of the ancient Indians who built them. The tools, primitive jewelry, and utensils buried with the dead, presumably to help make life easier in the next world, suggest that the Mound Builders, as they are called, were peaceful people—farmers and craftsmen who tilled the soil with hoes fashioned from stone or shells, smoked tobacco in carved stone pipes, and played music on pipes of bone and copper. Curiously, the dead were buried without weapons, leading some historians to believe that the Mound Builders were a peaceful people and may have been wiped out by warrior tribes.

Just west of the Effigy Mounds Monument is the little town of Spillville, where Czech composer Anton Dvořák spent the summer of 1893. Spillville is enormously proud of that visit and of the work Dvořák did while vacationing there. Folks are sure his *American Quartette* was composed and first played in Spillville, that he did some work on the *New World Symphony* that summer, and that he found inspiration for *Humoresque* during his stay.

But memories of Dvořák aren't all Spillville has to offer. There are also the Bily Clocks, a collection of intricately carved clocks fashioned by hand by two home-town boys, Frank and Joseph Bily. One features a parade of the Twelve Apostles as the clock chimes the hour. Another, the American Pioneer Clock, depicts scenes from American history. There's also the Lindbergh Clock, another called the Parade of Nations, a clock model of the world's smallest church (located in nearby Festina), and a Dvořák memorial clock in the shape of a violin and featuring a likeness of the Czech composer. The clocks are displayed in the Spillville house Dvořák rented for his 1893 vacation.

Even without the clocks and the memory of Dvořák, Spillville would be an interesting stop. It dates back to 1854 when a Czech immigrant built a sawmill there. Later, more immigrants came from Bohemia and Switzerland. The elm-lined streets, the public square with its brick and tile bandstand, and St. Wenceslaus Church, one of the most beautiful in Iowa, give the place a touch of European charm in a uniquely American setting.

A Catholic priest is responsible for north-central Iowa's most famous tourist attraction. Father Paul Dobberstein worked for forty-two years to build the Grotto of the Redemption at West Bend. Today, it's the largest grotto in the world, a collection of more than one hundred carloads of rocks and minerals valued at $2.5 million. Father Dobberstein set the rocks into cement to construct nine separate representations drawn from the life of Christ. Among the most valuable minerals is a 300-pound Brazilian amethyst in the Christmas Chapel of the adjacent Church of St. Peter and Paul. Dobberstein died in 1954, and since then, another priest, Father Louis Greving, has continued his work.

The rich farm country of southeastern Iowa has a bit of an Old World flavor. The town of Pella, for instance, was settled by Dutch immigrants in 1847 and has preserved its cultural heritage through the intervening years. They still make wooden shoes there, as well as Dutch sausages and pastries. Lawman Wyatt Earp lived there as a boy and Pella has restored the house where he grew up as well as some other nineteenth-century buildings, including a country store, a log cabin, a gristmill, and a blacksmith shop.

There's a familiar sight in Eldon, Iowa—the house artist Grant Wood used as a backdrop in his famous painting "American Gothic." Nearby Washington County is Amish country and has been ever since four groups of Amish settlers arrived in 1846. Members of the sect are farmers who still travel by horse and buggy in keeping with the plain and simple ways their beliefs prescribe.

Iowa usually isn't associated with Mark Twain or Buffalo Bill, but if you drive along the Mississippi on the Great River Road, you're sure to learn that Twain once worked in Keokuk and that Buffalo Bill was born in Le Claire. Keokuk's library has a display of some of Twain's possessions as well as a large collection of his works. Le Claire has a riverboat museum devoted to the life and times of Buffalo Bill. There's a riverboat museum in Keokuk, too—the town has restored the old paddle-wheel towboat, the *George M. Verity*, to display memorabilia from the riverboat days. Clinton, a river town north of Le Claire, uses its relatively modern steamboat as a theater, but visitors can inspect its engines, its paddle-wheel shafts, and the Captain's Lounge furnished Victorian style.

Steamboats also plied the Missouri River, Iowa's western boundary, and one of them, the *Bertrand,* sank in 1865 with a cargo of $250,000 in mercury. Two Nebraska men found the wreck in 1967 and much of what they recovered is now on display at the DeSoto National Wildlife Refuge north of Council Bluffs.

Southwestern Iowa has a lively and colorful history. There's a restored house in Tabor that once was a station of the underground railroad. John Brown used to stay there and actually hid the rifles there that he later used for his raid at Harpers Ferry.

Jesse James robbed a moving train in Adair County, Iowa, and escaped with between $1,700 and $4,000. James robbed many trains, but this was the first *moving* train to be held up. There's a train wheel marking the spot near the town of Adair.

Madison County is famous for its covered bridges. Seven of the sixteen scattered throughout the county have been restored, and they're working on the rest. Winterset, the county seat, has another claim to fame: Movie actor John Wayne was born there in 1907. His father was a local druggist.

SPECIAL EVENTS

Iowa may be as American as apple pie, but folks out there haven't forgotten that their ancestors came from Europe. In fact, they take advantage of every opportunity to salute their varied ethnic heritage. Bettendorf celebrates with its annual International Folk Festival in June. More than twenty nationalities are represented by their music, dress, dance, crafts, and foods.

Things are a bit more partisan in Emmetsburg on St. Patrick's Day. The town was named after Robert Emmet, an Irish patriot executed by the English in 1803 during Ireland's fight for independence. Emmetsburg considers Dublin its sister city and usually has a guest from Ireland on hand on St. Patrick's Day when it honors its Irish founders.

They scrub the streets in Pella and Orange City when the two towns separately celebrate the blooming of the tulips every May. The street scrubbing is a Dutch ritual that's been preserved by the descendants of the immigrants who settled both towns in the nineteenth century. Dutch costumes and wooden shoes are the order of the day at the two tulip festivals.

Decorah was settled by Norwegians, as evidenced in their annual Nordic Fest in July. Street dancing, Nordic field events, a parade, a show of Scandinavian folk arts, and opulent smörgåsbords take place during the three-day Nordic Fest, which attracts thousands every year.

The Amana Colonies were settled by German immigrants and, naturally, the Oktoberfest is a tradition there.

The Mesquakie Indians hold their annual powwow in August. The Mesquakies are descendants of the Sac and Fox tribes of Iowa and returned to the state in the nineteenth century to buy land at Tama, where they maintain a tribal community.

Iowans are as sentimental about the good old days as they are proud of their ethnic heritage. Burlington likes to reminisce about the romance of the Mississippi when the paddle-wheel steamboats chugged their way south to New Orleans. It stages a week-long celebration, Steamboat Days, every June and imports jazz, rock, and country and western musicians to liven things up. Another river town, Clinton, focuses on theatrical attractions on its steamboat, the *Rhododendron,* during Riverboat Days in July.

And lest you forget that Iowa is a farm state, there's plenty going on during the summer to remind you. The Midwest Old Settlers and Threshers Reunion at Mount Pleasant during the Labor Day weekend features an exhibit of steam engines and steam-powered machines and puts them to work in demonstrations of what farming used to be like.

Biggest and best of all the farm-related events is the Iowa State Fair, one of the largest state fairs in the nation. It's held in Des Moines every August and draws crowds from all over the Midwest for its exhibits of the latest in agricultural equipment and technology, plus the big-name entertainers who are always on hand.

And there's lots more—the Annual Hobo Convention in Britt every August, complete with gallons of mulligan stew and a contest to select the king and queen of the road; the Sidney Rodeo, with some of the nation's top cowboys, which comes to Sidney in August and moves on to Fort Madison after Labor Day. A relatively new event is the National Hot Air Balloon Contest at Indianola in August. It's a colorful festival with more than two hundred balloons drifting through the skies.

Things don't quiet down much in wintertime despite Iowa's frigid temperatures and heavy snows. Cresco holds a snow festival in January highlighted by championship snowmobile races. Esterville and Holiday Mountain stage a winter sports festival in February with skiing and snowmobile racing, an ice skating competition, and an ice sculpture contest.

P.D.

CHRONOLOGY

1673   Father Jacques Marquette and Louis Jolliet, French explorers, visited what is now Iowa.

1682   Robert Cavelier, Sieur de La Salle, claimed for France all the land drained by the Mississippi River.

1762   France transferred its lands west of the Mississippi to Spain under the terms of the Treaty of Fontainebleau.

1788   A French Canadian, Julien Dubuque, settled along the Mississippi to operate lead mines controlled by the Miami Indians.

1800   Spain returned to France the lands west of the Mississippi.

1803   Iowa came under control of the United States through the Louisiana Purchase.

1804   Meriwether Lewis and William Clark passed through Iowa on their expedition through the Northwest Territory.

1808   Fort Madison, the first American fort in Iowa, was built.

1832   A treaty with the Fox and the Sac Indians opened for settlement a fifty-mile-wide strip along the Mississippi known as the Black Hawk Purchase.

1834   Iowa became part of the Territory of Michigan.

1836   Iowa was attached to the Territory of Wisconsin for jurisdictional purposes.

1838   Congress created the Territory of Iowa, including parts of Minnesota and North and South Dakota.

1846   Iowa was admitted to the Union, becoming the thirty-first state.

1853   Construction begins on Iowa's first railroad.

1857   Iowa's first constitution was adopted.

1873   Members of the Grange seeking to regulate railroad freight rates gained control of the Iowa legislature.

1913   The Keokuk Dam was completed.

1917   Construction of Iowa's modern highway system was begun.

1934–36   Severe droughts worsened the predicament of Iowa's farmers, many of whom lost their heavily mortgaged land during the Depression of the 1930s.

1953   Iowa's public schools came under the direction of a board of public instruction.

1955   Laws against Sunday dancing, hunting, and horse racing were repealed.

1962   The Iowa court system underwent reorganization.

1968   Iowa voters approved a plan to reapportion the state's legislative districts.

1972   Democrat Dick Clark, a political unknown, was elected to the U. S. Senate replacing Republican Jack Miller.

Construction of Living History Farms was announced—a multimillion dollar, 500-acre panorama of agriculture, northwest of Des Moines.

1975 $9.3 million raised in private funds to build Des Moines's civic center, performing arts theater, and plaza.

1977   Saylorville Lake, created by the U. S. Corps of Engineers, opened north of Des Moines.

Ground-breaking for $2 million Botanical Center in Des Moines.

1979   Itinerary of American visit of Pope John Paul II called for a four-hour visit on October 4 in Des Moines. He presided at a Mass at the Living History Farms Foundation. Located on the outskirts of the city, the facility is a 600-acre working model of a farm.

MICHIGAN

MICHIGAN is a state of startling contrasts: huge industrial cities on the edge of a wooded wilderness, miles of modern highways that slash through the state, and narrow dirt roads that wind deep into its peaceful forests. It takes about six hours to drive from Detroit in the southeast to Michigan's Upper Peninsula—from the boom and bustle of the state's industrial hub to the cool stillness of its dense forests and rustic villages. And Michigan has yet another side: farms as well as factories, dairy cattle grazing on rolling green pastureland, cherry orchards, even vineyards.

Most of Michigan's nearly nine million residents are clustered in and around its big cities. More than half of them live in the Detroit metropolitan area including the independent city of Hamtramck, the populous suburbs of Dearborn, Royal Oak, Pontiac, and Bloomfield Hills. Automobile manufacturing is the all-important industry here— the "Big Three," the Ford Motor Company, General Motors, and the Chrysler Corporation are the area's biggest employers.

Although Michigan was one of the first regions of the United States to be explored by Europeans, the state wasn't settled until the second quarter of the nineteenth century after the Erie Canal opened up a convenient water route east. But as far back as the early seventeenth century French explorers, missionaries, and fur traders came down from Canada to map the virgin territory. They found thousands of lakes—more than eleven thousand of all sizes—and miles and miles of rivers and streams, to say nothing of the four Great Lakes—Michigan, Superior, Huron, and Erie—which surround Michigan on three sides. The French put their stamp on Michigan; names like Detroit, Cadillac, and Sault Ste. Marie pay tribute to their early claim on the territory. Then came the British, temporarily, before Michigan became American and immigrants of all nationalities bypassed the big cities of the East for the western frontier which by the early 1800s had extended as far as Michigan.

It didn't take Michigan's raw young cities long to catch up with the rest of the country. By the turn of the century, Detroit was the fifteenth largest town in the United States. Mining of iron ore and copper in the Upper Peninsula and the lumbering industry which developed during the mid-1800s gave the state's economy a tremendous boost. But the big boom came after the invention of the automobile when Henry Ford offered his factory workers the unheard of wage of five dollars a day plus a share of the profits. Thousands more rushed to Detroit to work the assembly lines.

The auto industry has dominated the state's economy ever since. But in recent years tourism has played an increasingly important role in the scheme of things in Michigan. The remote Upper Peninsula has attracted millions of visitors from all over the country, city dwellers in search of a respite from the daily grind, the young and the old who want to savor the pleasures of the forests and the lakes, and the nature lovers who want to make sure that it's all still there.

THE LAND

The Great Lakes dominate Michigan. Four of them—Erie, Huron, Michigan, and Superior—surround the state on the east, west, and north. In addition, there are eleven thousand inland lakes in Michigan ranging in size from tiny bodies of water to the thirty-square-mile Houghton Lake in the north-central region of the Lower Peninsula.

In describing Michigan, "peninsula" is the key word—the state is made up of two of them. The land area which borders on Indiana and Ohio to the south is the Lower Peninsula, the more populated and industrial area of the state. The big cities of Detroit, Grand Rapids, Flint, and the state capital of Lansing are here. Lake Michigan forms the western border dividing the state from Wisconsin and Illinois while Lake Huron separates Michigan from Canada to the north and northeast. Lake Erie laps at the southeastern border.

The Upper Peninsula—a land of forests and mineral resources—is divided from the Lower Peninsula by the four-and-a-half-mile-wide Straits of Mackinac. This part of the state stretches from west to east,

Michigan

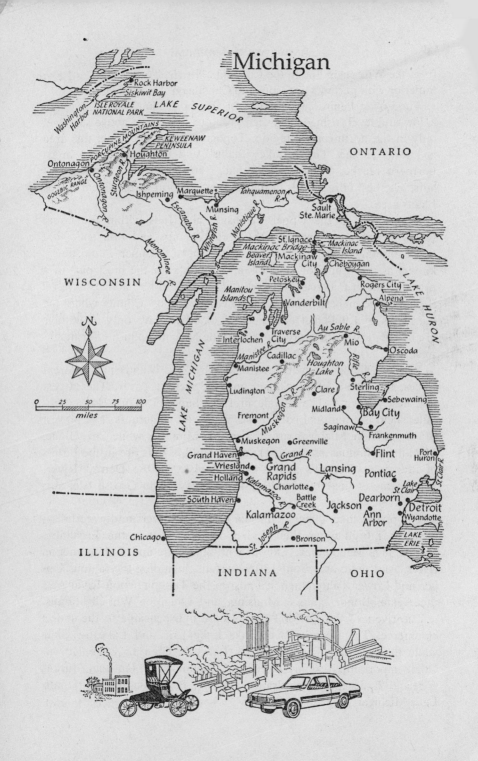

from the Wisconsin line to the Canadian border. To the north is Lake Superior with part of Minnesota and Canada on the other side.

The Lower Peninsula is the largest area of the state. Here, the land is low and level, rising to between 1,200 to 1,400 feet above sea level only in the north-central region. Topographically speaking, this area is known as the "Great Lakes Plains" and is characterized in its northern reaches by sandy soils and, here and there, some rolling hills. The best farm land is in the southern section of the Great Lakes Plains area.

About half of the Upper Peninsula also falls within the Great Lakes Plains area, but here there are swamps and thin soils that make farming difficult. The other half of the Upper Peninsula is known as the "Superior Upland" and consists for the most part of a rugged plateau that rises to nearly two thousand feet above sea level in spots. The highest point in the state is in Baraga County where the land rises to 1,980 feet above sea level. Michigan's only mountains are in this region—they are the Porcupine Mountains in the far northwest.

Part of Michigan's land area consists of the islands in the Great Lakes, the Straits of Mackinac, and the Detroit River. The largest and best known is Isle Royale in Lake Superior. This 210-square-mile island is a national park that is nearly all wilderness. The biggest islands in Lake Michigan are Beaver and Manitou, while Bois Blanc, Mackinac (famous as a resort), and Round islands are in the Straits of Mackinac. Detroit's zoo is on Belle Isle, in the Detroit River, while some of the city's wealthiest residents live on Grosse Isle, also in the river.

The picturesque Upper Peninsula has lots of rivers and waterfalls—some as intriguing as their Indian names. There's the Escanaba, Manistique, Menominee, Ontonagan, Sturgeon, and Tahquamenon rivers. And there are about 150 waterfalls, including the famous Upper and Lower Tahquamenon Falls on the Tahquamenon River plus the Agate, Bond, Miners, Munsing, and Laughing Whitefish Falls.

The rivers of the Lower Peninsula are indispensable to the state's commerce. The Detroit River links Lake Erie and Lake St. Clair while the St. Clair River connects Lake St. Clair to Lake Huron. Other important rivers are the Grand, Kalamazoo, Manistee, Muskegon, and St. Joseph which drain the Lower Peninsula and empty into Lake Michigan.

CLIMATE

Michigan isn't as cold as you might expect considering that it borders on Canada and is mostly surrounded by water. In fact, it owes its relatively mild climate to the Great Lakes, which warm the air in the winter and cool it in summer.

The average Michigan temperature in January ranges from 15 degrees in the western Upper Peninsula to 26 degrees in Detroit and elsewhere in the southern Lower Peninsula. Summer temperatures are pleasant—an average of 65 degrees in July in the Upper Peninsula and about 73 degrees in the Lower Peninsula. In terms of record temperatures, in July 1936 the mercury hit 112 degrees in Mio, Michigan. The coldest day recorded was February 9, 1934, when the temperature in Vanderbilt fell to 51 degrees below zero.

The southern part of Michigan gets the most rainfall, an average of thirty-three inches a year, while the central part of the state and the Upper Peninsula get about twenty-five inches. The heaviest snowfalls occur in the Upper Peninsula and along the shores of Lake Michigan in the southern part of the state. The southwestern part of the state gets the least amount of snow—about thirty inches a year. They get quite a bit more in the Upper Peninsula, an average of 160 inches. It isn't unusual for the snowfall there to measure fifty feet or more in a single winter.

THE PEOPLE OF MICHIGAN

The French staked the first European claim to what is now Michigan but, as Count Louis de Frontenac put it at the time, all they cared about was saving souls and trading furs. The souls in question belonged to the Indians, some fifteen thousand of them who lived in Michigan in the early seventeenth century when the French began their explorations. The Ottawa and Chippewa were particularly helpful to the early fur traders, while the Hurons in the southeast tended to their farming and the Miami and Potawatomi prowled the territory's deep forests.

Frenchmen like Étienne Brulé and Jean Nicolet, both explorers, and the Jesuit missionaries René Ménard and Jacques Marquette were the first European arrivals. Marquette founded the first white settlement in Michigan at Sault Ste. Marie in 1668. It was the forerunner of a series of French trading posts, forts, and missions that sprang up throughout the territory during the 1600s.

The Indians weren't any happier than the French when the British took control of the territory in 1763 at the conclusion of the French and Indian War. To the British, Michigan was of strategic importance during the American Revolution and had an added economic attraction: the British too were interested in the fur trade. At this time, settlement was sparse. It didn't begin in earnest until after Michigan was firmly in American control after the War of 1812 and wasn't really significant until the opening of the Erie Canal in 1825 made possible convenient transportation between Michigan and the East.

Among the first to arrive in Michigan were settlers from New York and New England looking for virgin territory to farm. But they soon were followed by European immigrants, particularly Germans and Irish who settled throughout the state. As early as the mid-1830s Detroit had a large German community and not long afterward the Irish constituted a sizable ethnic group. Dutch pioneers arrived in 1847 and settled in the western part of the Lower Peninsula. Their presence is still obvious in towns like Holland, Harlem, Vriesland, and Zeeland. Holland lives up to its name with a two-hundred-year-old windmill brought over from the Netherlands and the only wooden-shoe factory in the United States.

The Germans still have their own communities, too. One of the best known is the little village of Frankenmuth, south of Saginaw, where the residents cling to their German language and traditions.

Poles came to the Bay City area in the mid-1800s to homestead, and the Irish arrived in large numbers as the timber industry began to flourish. Their descendants are still around, as is a group that traces its ancestry to the French Canadians who came to fish long before Bay City became the largest port in northeast Michigan.

There's considerable ethnic diversity in the Upper Peninsula too. Cornishmen, Finns, Swedes, Italians, and Frenchmen were attracted seventy-five years ago by the area's mining and lumbering industry. You still can get a genuine Finnish sauna in these parts, complete with wet birch whisks to rev up the circulation and a dip in Lake Superior to close up your pores.

There's an Irish enclave on Beaver Island, thirty-five miles out in Lake Michigan from the port city of Charlevoix. The Irish supplanted a Mormon colony which was ensconced on the island in the mid-1800s. Today's residents are fishermen who also run the island's resort hotels. You're aware of their Irish heritage the minute you arrive—the "welcome" sign at the ferry slip is in Gaelic.

As Michigan's industry expanded, immigrants from all over the world moved in. Poles, Ukrainians, Germans, Bulgarians, Italians, Russians, and Hungarians came to work in Detroit's huge automobile assembly plants. And a later wave of immigration brought American blacks from the South. In 1900 there were less than sixteen thousand blacks in all of Michigan, but the 1970 census found that their number had increased to more than one million. About two thirds of the blacks live in Detroit, which constitutes 45 per cent of the city's population.

Most of Michigan's people are city dwellers today—75 per cent of them clustered in the metropolitan areas of Ann Arbor, Bay City, Detroit, Flint, Grand Rapids, Jackson, Kalamazoo, Lansing, Muskegon-Muskegon Heights, and Saginaw. Only 4 per cent of the total population, some three hundred thousand people, live in the Upper Peninsula.

The population of the Detroit metropolitan area stands at 4.1 million, making it the fifth largest city in the United States. But Michigan has other sizable cities. Dearborn, Flint, Grand Rapids, Kalamazoo, Lansing, Pontiac, Royal Oak, Saginaw, and Warren, all in the Lower Peninsula, have populations exceeding eighty thousand. Marquette with about 22,000 people is located in Michigan's Upper Peninsula.

Demographers expect Michigan to keep on growing. Some have predicted that by the year 2010 the population of Detroit's six-county area will reach 7,500,000. Since 1950, however, the population of the city proper has been dropping: it had reached 1,845,000 in 1950 but by 1970 was down to 1,575,000. During that period the suburbs expanded rapidly.

HISTORY

While the English were carving out their colonies along the East Coast during the seventeenth century, the French were exploring America's interior, gliding over the Great Lakes in canoes they learned to make from the Indians, mapping the lakes and rivers of what is now Michigan and developing their lucrative fur trade. The French explorers came to Michigan via Canada from the outpost at Quebec. The first known expedition was undertaken by Étienne Brulé, an explorer dispatched by Samuel de Champlain, governor of New France, in 1622. Twelve years later, De Champlain directed another explorer, Jean Nicolet, to find a water route to the Pacific. Nicolet's search led him to Michigan's Upper Peninsula and then through the Straits of Mackinac before he concluded that he was on the wrong track.

The explorers were soon followed by the missionaries, Jesuits who came to the wilderness to save the souls of the Indians. Father René Ménard founded the first mission at Keweenaw Bay in 1660 and eight years later Father Jacques Marquette established the first permanent white settlement at Sault Ste. Marie. Marquette was as much explorer as he was missionary. He and other Frenchmen, including Robert Cavelier, Sieur de La Salle and Louis Jolliet, traveled throughout Michigan mapping its lakes and rivers and visiting the trading posts, missions, and forts built along the routes of the fur trappers. But the French, who were preoccupied with fur trading and converting the Indians to Christianity, did little to encourage settlement.

By the late 1600s the British had begun to challenge the French for the American interior. The struggle finally culminated in the French and Indian War, which ended in 1763 with the British the victors. The change didn't suit the Indians, who had maintained a close alliance with the French. They attacked British outposts at Fort Michilimackinac and at Detroit, which had been founded in 1701 by the Frenchman Antoine de la Mothe Cadillac as Fort Pontchartrain. Even after the hostilities ceased, the British didn't try to stimulate settlement of the region. Instead, they concentrated on fur trading and governed Michigan as part of the Province of Quebec. Detroit became a British stronghold during the Revolutionary War and even after the war the British refused to surrender their Michigan outposts to the Americans. The United States didn't gain control until 1796, thirteen years after the war had ended.

Detroit and Fort Mackinac were to change hands again when they were captured by the British during the War of 1812. All of the fighting in the area kept settlers away until after 1814. But then the state began to develop rapidly, thanks to the territorial governor Lewis Cass, who fostered the growth of a system of roads linking Detroit with Chicago, Saginaw, and Port Huron. Transportation was further improved by the initiation of steamboat service between Detroit and Buffalo, New York, in 1818 and by the opening of the Erie Canal in 1825.

By 1835 there were enough people on hand to draw up a constitution and to petition Congress for admission to the Union. But action was delayed pending settlement of a boundary dispute between Michigan and Ohio. Both laid claim to a strip of land near what is now Toledo, Ohio, and tempers grew so hot over the issue that the two almost went to war. President Andrew Jackson finally settled matters by giving the strip to Ohio and compensating Michigan with the entire Upper Peninsula instead of just the eastern half of it. The next year Michigan was admitted to the Union.

Soon Michigan's agricultural economy was bolstered by the discovery of iron and copper in the Upper Peninsula. Miners flocked to the area, and it soon became apparent that the mineral wealth was so extensive that some way had to be found to transport the ore to the industrial centers developing along the Great Lakes. The solution was the Soo Canal, constructed at Sault Ste. Marie in 1855.

The Civil War slowed Michigan's development somewhat. The state sent ninety thousand men to fight for the Union and took tremendous losses—fourteen thousand men were killed. At the time, Michigan was a Republican state—the state claims the party was founded there in 1854 at a state convention in Jackson.

After the war, lumbering emerged as a major industry and more and more settlers arrived to farm. By the end of the nineteenth century all of the state's eighty-three counties had been settled. But the most momentous growth began after the turn of the century with the emergence of the automobile industry. Ransom E. Olds was actually manufacturing cars in Detroit as early as 1899 and was mass-producing Oldsmobiles in 1901. Two years later Henry Ford went into business in Dearborn armed with his belief that the automobile should be a necessity, not just an expensive toy for the rich. Ford had some other new ideas; he established a profit-sharing plan for his workers in 1914 and paid five dollars a day minimum wage at a time when most unskilled workers made a mere dollar a day. Detroit's factories switched to the manufacture of war materials during World War I and afterward the state, not surprisingly, devised a highway system to complement the growth of the automobile industry.

Business was booming in the 1920s but the Great Depression of the 1930s was devastating for the state. Thousands lost their jobs and things got so bad that copper mining in the Upper Peninsula was virtually abandoned because it cost so much to get to the deposits buried deep in the earth. The Depression was followed by a period of labor strife as unions struggled to gain a foothold in the automobile plants. The United Automobile Workers finally won collective bargaining rights from the manufacturers in 1937 and by 1941 had won recognition and pay increases from all the major auto companies.

During World War II, Detroit's auto makers again switched to war production, turning out planes, ships, and tanks for the American armies.

Since the war, Michigan's economy has been dominated by the fortunes of the automobile manufacturers, which in turn are dramatically affected by any swing in the nation's economy. The recessions of the late 1950s and early 1970s brought about slumps in auto sales and consequent large-scale unemployment in the industry. During the same period, Michigan's cities were experiencing racial tensions brought about after large numbers of blacks from the South arrived to work in the automobile plants. The tensions had first erupted in a major race riot in 1943 and then exploded again in 1967 when Negroes in Detroit rioted for eight days during which $45 million worth of property was damaged and destroyed and forty-three people were killed.

For all of these problems, Michigan has not been lax in the area of public welfare and education. Spending for school aid, mental health facilities, welfare for the aged, disabled, and impoverished has been generous. And despite the racial tensions, blacks have made gains both politically and socially. Several have been nominated for state offices by both the Democrats and Republicans.

INDUSTRY

Detroit is synonymous with the automobile industry even though it is not the only city in Michigan where cars are made. There are big plants in Dearborn, Flint, Kalamazoo, Lansing, and Pontiac, but since the early years of the twentieth century, Detroit has been the headquarters of the automobile industry and remains so today.

Actually, they don't put cars together in Detroit anymore. The big assembly plants of the nation's three big auto manufacturers—Ford, General Motors, and Chrysler—have moved out of the city proper to the surrounding suburbs. But there are many plants in Detroit where auto parts are made—just about everything that goes into a car is manufactured in the city and its environs. As a matter of fact, transportation equipment was being made there even before the automobile was invented. Carriages, wagons, bicycles, and marine engines were manufactured in Detroit during the nineteenth century, but that early preoccupation with transportation equipment doesn't explain why Detroit developed as the nation's automobile manufacturing center. It did have the advantages of inexpensive water transport for coal, iron, and steel, good rail connections with the rest of the United States and Canada, and it was convenient to the greatest markets in the country. But it really was sheer coincidence that Detroit developed as an auto manufacturing center. It just happened that innovators like Henry Ford and Charles B. King lived there, that Ransom Olds was from Lansing, and W. C. Durant was from Flint. These were the men who helped make the automobile industry what it is today, and they all were in Michigan when the horseless carriage became a reality.

Today, it goes without saying that Michigan is the leading manufacturer of automobiles in the United States—the industry employs more than a quarter of all the industrial workers in the state, uses two thirds of the total U.S. rubber supply, two fifths of the plate glass, and more than three fifths of the nation's upholstery leather. All told, the automobile industry brings in 40 per cent of Michigan's manufacturing income.

Pre-eminent though it is, the automobile industry isn't the only important manufacturing activity in Michigan. The state also produces machinery for agriculture and manufacturing, as well as office machines, pumps, stoves, and furnaces. In fact, the manufacturing of machinery is the second-largest industry in the state, earning more than $1.6 billion a year.

Michigan is a big steel producer, too—and has been since the middle of the nineteenth century. Detroit, with some of the largest steel mills, foundries, and refineries in the United States, is the center of this industry. Related to the steel production is the manufacture of nails, bolts, and other basic metal products such as castings. And factories in Detroit, Flint, and Grand Rapids produce such fabricated metals products as cutlery, hand tools, and hardware.

In addition to all that heavy industry, Michigan is one of the nation's leading food-processing states. They call Battle Creek the "Cereal Center of the World" because it produces more breakfast cereal than any other city. Both Detroit and Grand Rapids are important food-processing centers, and Fremont is the home of the largest baby foods plant in the United States. All that food processing brings the state nearly $800 million a year.

Industrially diverse Michigan also produces lots of chemicals and allied products at plants in Ludington, Marquette, Midland, Muskegon, and Wyandotte. There are important drug manufacturers in Ann Arbor and Kalamazoo, and Detroit is the home of the nation's oldest and largest pharmaceutical products manufacturer, the Parke-Davis Company.

Grand Rapids, the home town of President Gerald R. Ford, has another claim to fame: it calls itself the "furniture capital of America" for the obvious reason that it is a big furniture-manufacturing town. Kalamazoo is the center of the state's paper-manufacturing industry, Muskegon makes billiard and bowling alley equipment, Alpena has the largest cement plant in the United States, and elsewhere in the state they make clothing, scientific instruments, lumber and wood products, petroleum and coal products, rubber and plastics, as well as stone, clay, and glass products.

AGRICULTURE

Considering that Michigan manufactures so much breakfast cereal, it is appropriate, if not coincidental, that its leading agricultural product is milk. Dairy farms throughout the Lower Peninsula make Michigan one of the most important milk-producing states in the nation.

Although Michigan's agriculture doesn't come close to producing the amount of income its manufacturing industries do—$922 million compared to $13 billion annually—farming is important. There are more than 93,000 farms covering about 40 per cent of the state's land area. Cattle and calves rank second to dairy products but the state's farmers also grow a wide variety of crops. Wheat is the most important cash crop, followed by dry beans grown in the "thumb" of Michigan's mitten-shaped Lower Peninsula.

The state ranks first nationally in the production of cherries. Most of them are grown in the Traverse City area along Lake Michigan.

There are more than 1.6 million cherry trees on farms throughout a five-county area. Michigan also grows a lot of blueberries—enough to rank first among the states in this crop too. Most of them are produced on farms surrounding South Haven on the southwest coast of Lake Michigan.

Apples, cantaloupes, grapes, honeydew melons, peaches, pears, plums, and strawberries also grow in profusion in the fertile fruit-producing area along Lake Michigan. And farmers there also make money selling the honey produced by the bees attracted by all the fruit trees.

In addition to dry beans, Michigan grows a wide variety of vegetables, among them asparagus, cabbages, carrots, cucumbers, lettuce, onions, potatoes, snap beans, sugar beets, and tomatoes. More than a thousand vegetable farms are concentrated around Grand Rapids, Muskegon, and other industrial cities. However, the western counties produce a big celery crop and farmers elsewhere raise alfalfa, corn, hay, and oats—most of which is used as livestock feed.

NATURAL RESOURCES

In addition to its enormous industrial wealth, Michigan is rich in natural resources. It shares with its neighbors Wisconsin and Minnesota the greatest iron-ore region in the world. In Michigan, the deposits are concentrated in the Marquette, Menominee, and Gogebic ranges in the Upper Peninsula. Millions of tons have been mined since the iron was discovered near Ishpeming and Negaunee in 1844. So great are Michigan's reserves that during the last half of the nineteenth century it was the nation's leading producer of iron ore. Minnesota occupies that position today, but Michigan still contributes about one fifth of the United States' supply. The ore is shipped east via the Great Lakes to the steel-producing centers of the Midwest and East.

The Indians were the first to find Michigan's "treasure chest"—the copper deposits in the Keweenaw Peninsula in the northern part of the state. During the 1800s more than two thirds of the nation's copper came from the mines of Houghton, Keweenaw, and Ontonagon counties in the western Upper Peninsula. Michigan remains one of the leading copper-producing states today.

There's salt in Michigan, too, enough to supply the whole world for the next million years. And most of it is under Detroit. That's right, miles of salt mines some thousand feet deep underlie the city. Most of what they yield is used for industrial purposes. And the state also produces salt from natural brines found in Gratiot County and from artificial brines in Manistee, Midland, Muskegon, St. Clair, and Wayne counties.

Michigan also has oil, coal, natural gas, gypsum, peat, clay, marl, sand, and gravel, as well as limestone—one of the world's largest limestone quarries is at Rogers City. The oil is in the southern and central sections of the Lower Peninsula.

An inventory of Michigan's natural resources wouldn't be complete without including the fertile glacial soils in the southern half of the Lower Peninsula, the lush forests that still cover more than half of the state, and the deer, badgers, black bears, bobcats, minks, muskrats, and other animals that populate the woods. The lakes, rivers, and streams are full of fish—more than enough bass, crappie, perch, pike, and trout to attract even the most indifferent fisherman.

The forests are made up of hardwoods like aspens, beeches, birches, elms, maples, and oaks and such softwood trees as cedars, firs, hemlocks, pines, and spruces. They are interspersed with blackberry, currant, elder, gooseberry, raspberry, and rosebushes, as well as bittersweet, clematis, grapes, moonseed, and similar plants, all growing wild in the woods.

CITIES

For obvious reasons **Detroit** is known as "Motown," "Motor City," and "the Automobile Capital of the United States." It is the nation's fifth-largest city and a town to be reckoned with even without the automobile industry. Detroit was fifteenth in size before the days of the automobile, a booming industrial town with a long and colorful history and a rich ethnic heritage. It dates back to 1701 when French explorer Antoine de la Mothe Cadillac came along and shrewdly recognized that the west bank of the Detroit River was an ideal place for a settlement. He established Fort Pontchartrain there, and under the French it quickly became an important trading center. The Indians brought in furs to exchange for gunpowder, bullets, cloth, brandy, and nails. The British continued the fur trade after they expelled the French in 1763, but they were forced to surrender it to the Americans in 1796. By then, the place was known as Detroit, from the French word *détroit* meaning "strait." The "strait" they had in mind is now called the Detroit River.

Detroit really didn't begin to thrive until steamship service connected it with Buffalo, New York, in 1818 and the Erie Canal opened in 1825. After that, it grew quickly as English, Irish, and German immigrants arrived to join the descendants of the original French settlers. Then came the discovery of iron in Michigan's Upper Peninsula and the transformation of Detroit into a flourishing industrial town. By the turn of the century, the population had reached 286,000.

The city got bigger and bigger after Henry Ford and Ransom E. Olds opened their automobile factories in the early years of the twentieth century. Thousands more arrived to work the assembly lines— Irish, Hungarians, Middle Easterners, Ukrainians, Russians, Poles, Germans, Swedes, Greeks, even Chinese—enough of an ethnic mix to give Detroit a cosmopolitan flavor. The immigrants clustered together in neighborhoods that reflected their national backgrounds. Some twenty-five thousand Greeks still live in the area referred to as Greektown, Detroit has its own Chinatown, and the independent city of Hamtramck completely surrounded by Detroit proper still has an almost exclusively Polish population.

Needless to say, no visit to Detroit would be complete without a tour of an automobile plant to see how cars are put together. All of the large manufacturers offer guided tours. In addition, the headquarters of the auto makers are local landmarks. The General Motors Technical Center, a futuristic complex designed by Finnish architect Eero Saarinen, is considered a "must" for tourists.

Although much of what there is to see and do in Detroit is related to the automobile industry, the city is justifiably proud of its Civic Center, its park system, museums, art galleries, and theaters. The Civic Center is a gleaming, modern complex along the waterfront, a $100 million project undertaken in 1951 to revitalize the area. Tenements, small industries, and old warehouses were mowed down to make way for a complex which is dominated by Cobo Hall, one of the largest convention centers in the world. It seats up to fourteen thousand persons, accommodates seventeen thousand cars, and offers display space equivalent in size to twelve football fields.

The twenty-story white marble City-County Building is part of the Civic Center, as is the Henry and Edsel Ford Auditorium, home of the Detroit Symphony Orchestra. Nestled among all the new buildings is Mariner's Church, a place of worship and shelter since 1848 for the men who work the lake freighters.

Detroit's cultural attractions are grouped together along Woodward Avenue, one of the city's main thoroughfares. The Public Library, the Art Institute, the Historical Museum, and the Children's Museum are known collectively as the "Art Center." The Institute of Art has a valuable collection of Dutch and Flemish masters, including Pieter Brueghel's "Wedding Dance." Mexican artist Diego Rivera stirred up a local controversy with his interpretation of Detroit's industrial life in a series of frescoes in the Institute's Garden Court. When they were unveiled, they were severely criticized by those who didn't find Rivera's view of Detroit particularly flattering. The Institute's collection also includes a display of African art and artifacts contributed by former Michigan Governor G. Mennen Williams and an exhibition of medieval armor that once belonged to publisher William Randolph Hearst.

The Historical Museum traces local history back to Cadillac's arrival in 1701. Some of the city's early streets have been reconstructed and there's an exhibit showing how the standard of living for Americans has changed over the years. The nearby Children's Museum was designed to give youngsters an appreciation of history—the displays here are scaled down to a child's-eye view. A doll and toy collection and a bird room are especially popular with the kids.

The Detroit Zoo is another attraction that delights both children and adults. A miniature railroad winds through its 122 acres past animals living in their natural habitats—an African swamp, an Australian plain, and a polar region among them. The Zoo, with its thirty-three hundred animals, is one of the largest and most modern in the country. There's a second zoo especially for children on Belle Isle, the thousand-acre island park in the Detroit River. Here, animals are displayed in a Mother Goose setting and children are encouraged to pet them.

Detroit's most spectacular tourist attraction is in **Dearborn,** the city that grew up around the headquarters of the Ford Motor Company. Henry Ford chose Dearborn, still considered a Detroit suburb, as the site for Greenfield Village and the Henry Ford Museum, both designed to show how Americans lived and worked from colonial times to the present. In constructing the village, Ford sought out the homes of famous Americans and had them moved to Dearborn. Among them are the Menlo Park, N.J., laboratory of Thomas A. Edison, the homestead and workshop of aviation pioneers Orville and Wilbur Wright, the homes of William Holmes McGuffy, Noah Webster, Luther Burbank, Robert Frost, and Stephen Foster. Greenfield Village is made up of nearly a hundred buildings laid out along shaded lanes that crisscross 240 acres. Visitors can stroll from one authentic old shop to another, dine at the Clinton Inn (once a stagecoach stop), visit the Susquehanna House (once the Maryland home of a king's tax collector), watch craftsmen at work, ride a 1913 merry-go-round, take a trip on a century-old steam train, tour the village by carriage, by Model T Ford, or—on snowy winter days—by sleigh.

The Henry Ford Museum also is devoted to American history. An enormous collection ranging from colonial furniture and tools to automobiles and aircraft has been assembled in an eleven-acre hall. The main attraction is the Great Hall of Transportation—exhibits here include a Russian cart, an early American automobile, a 1930s sports car, and a 600-ton, 125-foot-long steam engine.

Detroit's motor magnates built huge homes for themselves on the outskirts of the city. Henry Ford's "Fair Lane" is in Dearborn on the campus of the local branch of the University of Michigan. But other automobile millionaires chose Grosse Pointe, a wooded area along Lake St. Clair. It is still one of the most desirable residential areas, although the newer homes are considerably more modest than the palatial mansions built by the city's early industrialists.

Detroit was the capital of Michigan until the state legislature in 1847 decided to move the seat of government farther inland—in those days they still worried about the possibility of foreign invasion. The story goes that after months of debate someone jokingly suggested that the capital be moved to **Lansing,** then just a sawmill and a single log house in the wilderness. The place had been named by settlers after the town they came from in New York.

Although a frame capitol was erected once the move became official, Lansing remained a backwoods town until 1870, when the railroad connected it with other Michigan cities. The legislature celebrated by appropriating $1.2 million for the construction of a permanent capitol, which was completed in 1878. The town already had a college—an agricultural school established in East Lansing in 1857. There were a few carriage and wagon factories, too, but industrially speaking the town wasn't particularly notable until a local fellow named Ransom E. Olds built the world's first practical automobile. That changed everything—by 1904 Lansing was the world leader in the manufacture of automobiles and gasoline engines. It remains an important automobile and parts-making center today, home of the Reo Division of the White Motor Company, Oldsmobile, and the Fisher Body Division of General Motors.

The agricultural school eventually became Michigan State University. It expanded to cover nine hundred acres divided by the Red Cedar River. Some three hundred buildings surrounded by tall trees, shrubs, and covered with vines now make up the main campus. Another three thousand acres farther away constitutes the University's agricultural experiment centers and farm installations.

Michigan's other big university town is **Ann Arbor,** just a village of less than two thousand people when it bid for the University of Michigan in 1837. Today, Ann Arbor has a population of 100,000 and has become a cultural center that offers theater, dance, music, art, and six museums. The sports-minded are likely to be impressed by Michigan Stadium, the largest college stadium in the country—it can seat 105,000. The university library contains more than four million volumes and the Kelsey Museum of Archeology houses an impressive array of classical exhibits. The Gothic Law Quadrangle is one of the most picturesque sections of the campus, the Museum of Art boasts a collection that spans fourteen centuries, and the Baird Carillon in the Burton Memorial Tower provides weekly spring and summer concerts. There are fifty-three bells ranging in size from twelve pounds to twelve tons.

Flint, Michigan's third-largest city, is an automobile town. Most of its factory workers are employed by General Motors, which has a huge Buick factory and a Chevrolet assembly plant there. Before the advent of the automobile, Flint was just another small town established back in the early 1800s when the fur trade still flourished in Michigan. Later, lumbering became the main industry—sawmills proliferated and in the mid-1800s Flint began making road carts and, later, carriages.

The Buick Motor Company started manufacturing cars in Flint as early as 1904 and the place has never been the same since. It had its share of labor strife during the 1930s and 1940s—violence erupted in 1937 when the United Auto Workers staged a strike that successfully transformed Flint into a solidly union town. Needless to say, the sights to see in Flint include the Buick and Chevrolet plants, but the town also is the home of the Michigan School for the Deaf and the

Robert T. Longway Planetarium, the main attraction of the Flint Community Junior College.

Grand Rapids was on the map long before Gerald R. Ford became President. Its main claim to fame before Ford went to the White House was as the "furniture capital of the United States." Indeed, the city's furniture factories employ more than eight thousand skilled craftsmen. The local museums will give you a pretty good idea of what Grand Rapids has contributed to American homes: both the Public Museum and the museum at the Baker Furniture Company display the work of Grand Rapids' furniture makers and the styles of furniture popular in the United States since its early days. In addition, the Public Museum, gift of logging millionaire T. Steward White, has a section devoted to Michigan wildlife and the new Roger B. Chaffee Planetarium. The art museum is known for its collection of German Impressionist paintings.

Kalamazoo got its name from the Potawatomi Indians—it means "place where the water boils." Today, it's a place where automobiles, drugs, and paper are made. It was the first city in the country to create a pedestrian-only shopping mall to relieve downtown traffic congestion. The top local attraction is the Kalamazoo Nature Center, with five hundred acres of nature trails and animal displays. The Center is considered the best of its kind in the Midwest.

SPORTS AND RECREATION

Most people who come to Michigan in the summer as vacationers usually bring a fishing pole, water skis, or at least a bathing suit. The one thing you can't get away from in the state is water—nowhere are you more than six miles from one of the Great Lakes, one of the state's 36,350 miles of rivers and streams, or one of its 11,037 lakes. Michigan's Great Lakes' shoreline is longer than the Atlantic coast from Maine to Florida, and that means more than three thousand miles of beaches of one kind or another. Visitors can take their pick of a vacation spot: a sandy beach, a cool stream or river for boating, swimming, or fishing, or one of the inland lakes. Four national forests and seventy-three state parks offer just about every water-related sport, plus camping, hiking, and picnicking.

You can even tour parts of the state by water. The adventurous can canoe down the Rifle River from Sterling and the very brave can shoot the rapids. For the more sedate, there's a two-hour scenic cruise down the Au Sable River aboard the *River Queen,* an old paddlewheel that makes a nineteen-mile trip from Five Channels Dam near Oscoda. And they say the best way to see the famed Pictured Rocks along the Lake Superior shore is from one of the boats that sail out of Munising. The sandstone rocks, truly one of Michigan's most spectacular natural wonders, have been pounded by Lake Superior's waves for centuries into intriguing shapes and arresting colors.

Fishermen don't have to be coaxed into trying their luck in Michigan no matter what time of year. Spring is probably the best time to angle for steelhead and lake trout in the Great Lakes. There are other varieties of trout—brook, brown, and rainbow—in the inland lakes. Fishing continues right through the winter with sportsmen dropping their lines through holes in the ice and erecting ice shelters to protect themselves from the wind and cold while they wait for a bite.

Winter also brings skiing, sledding, and snowmobiling. There are seventy winter resorts throughout the state and ski slopes for every level of skill. Tobogganing is popular, but the big local enthusiasm in recent years has been snowmobiling. Hundreds of trails have been marked throughout the state and competition is keen at countless snowmobile races. The I-500 Snowmobile Race at Sault Ste. Marie is the one that gets the most attention, but Traverse City's TC-250 and the Thunder Bay 250 at Alpena are gaining in importance.

Michigan has its share of spectators, too—the folks who'd rather crowd into one of the university stadiums to watch the state's college teams in action or cheer on Detroit's professional football, baseball, basketball, and hockey teams.

And just in case you're under the impression that culture takes a back seat to sports in Michigan, consider this: theater attendance in Detroit is second only to New York's. There's a professional repertory company at the city's Fisher Theatre, plus the productions at Wayne State University and the University of Detroit. Summer theaters scattered throughout the rest of the state attract enthusiastic audiences.

POINTS OF INTEREST

Tourism is one of Michigan's leading industries. More than ten million people come to the state every year to get away from it all. And there are plenty of places to do just that. The entire Upper Peninsula qualifies by anybody's standards. It's got 16,000 square miles of woods, 4,300 lakes, 153 waterfalls, 12,000 miles of streams, and 1,700 miles of Great Lakes shoreline. There's nothing much to do there except unwind, breathe clean air, daydream in the deep, cool forests, fish the clear streams, and bask on the sandy beaches. During Michigan's mining and lumbering heyday in the nineteenth century, the UP, as they call it, was a pretty busy place. That's all changed now. Today, the biggest city in the Upper Peninsula, Marquette, has only about 22,000 people and most of the other towns are small and rustic, quiet places inhabited by the descendants of the Finns, Swedes, Italians, and Frenchmen who once came to work the mines and fell the trees.

Sault (pronounced "Soo") Ste. Marie is a historic city, the oldest town in Michigan, and the third oldest settlement in the United States. And it is situated on a vital link between Lake Huron ports and Lake Superior and the water route east to the Atlantic Ocean. The locks on the St. Marys River connecting Lakes Huron and Superior make possible an enormous amount of shipping. Without them the river would be impassable to the thousands of ships that stream through each year bearing more cargo than the amount handled annually by the Suez, Panama, and Kiel canals combined!

If you had to pick a single place to go in the Upper Peninsula, the obvious choice would be the Isle Royale National Park on Isle Royale, the largest island in Lake Superior. To get there you take a fifty-mile boat trip from Houghton, Michigan, or a twenty-mile trip from Grand Portage, Minnesota. Automobiles aren't permitted on the islands so, if you go, expect to hike to the campsites or to the Inn at Rock Harbor or the other one at Washington Harbor.

Isle Royale is just what you would expect an inaccessible wooded island to be. It's a wilderness tamed by man only to the extent of marking hiking trails through the National Park, setting aside campsites, and providing boats and guides for the adventurous who want to explore the smaller nearby islands. Moose, wolves, mink, and beaver live in the woods, the streams are full of trout, and wildflowers brighten the dark green woods.

Prehistoric Indians once lived on the island and mined copper there, according to archaeologists who have found ancient pits on the island. In the late nineteenth and twentieth centuries, miners crossed over from the mainland to dig for copper at McCargo Cove, Rock Harbor, Siskiwit Bay, and Washington Harbor. Those mines have long since been abandoned but are still among the island's only man-made sightseeing attractions.

The water of Lake Superior is much too cold for swimming, even in summer, and the beaches are rocky. But there are more than a hundred miles of hiking trails, lots of opportunities for boating, and an ample supply of peace and quiet.

Mackinac Island is a short ferry ride from St. Ignace. No automobiles are permitted here either, except for a utility truck, a fire engine, and an ambulance. Everybody else has to get around on foot, on horseback, by bicycle, or in carriages. The Indians had a long name for the island. They called it "Michilimackinac" which means "Great Turtle," an apt description for the three-mile-long, two-mile-wide island covered by picturesque rock formations. The history of the island dates back to 1780 when the British built Fort Mackinac to guard the straits. The fort is there today, just as it was in colonial times—the ramparts, guardhouse, cannon, and blockhouse still intact. John Jacob Astor was another early arrival. He located the headquarters of his American Fur Company on the island in 1817. The offices and warehouses have been preserved and are open to the public.

Several hundred people live on Mackinac Island year-round keeping the place in shape for the tourist season in summer. Supplies have to be flown in once the straits freeze over in winter, although you can drive a team of horses over the ice to the mainland. Summer brings a rush of visitors to savor the serenity of the island and to golf, hike, and swim.

Another Michigan island with a "past" is Beaver Island, thirty-five miles off Charlevoix in Lake Michigan. The place was ruled more than a hundred years ago by a fellow named James Jesse Strang, who proclaimed himself king of a colony of Mormons in 1847 and tyrannized them for nine years before he was shot during the inevitable revolt. After Strang's death, Irish fishermen took over. Their descendants are still there making a living fishing for bass and catering to visitors. Predictably, Beaver Island is popular with fishermen.

One of the most famous spots in Michigan is Interlochen, a village of some eight hundred people that triples in population when the National Music Camp opens in the summer. Students from all over the country enroll for the eight-week summer session to practice up on their musical instruments, singing, dancing, and acting. The daily concerts, plays, and recitals are open to the public.

Michigan happens to have the biggest sand dune in the world. It's at Glen Haven on Lake Michigan and is called "Sleeping Bear"—a name derived from an Indian legend about a mother bear who swam the lake and lay down to wait for her two cubs to join her. She fell asleep and, so the Indians said, still sleeps, waiting for her young. The dune rises 480 feet above the surrounding beach and moves inland about two feet each year. There is a spectacular view of the lake from the top of the dune. Scooters are available for those who want to take in the view but would rather forego the uphill hike.

For all its natural wonders, Michigan offers some attractions that are strictly man-made. A favorite tourist stop is at Holland, a town settled by Dutch immigrants in 1847. The newcomers did everything they could to insure that they'd feel at home in the wilderness. Importing a two-hundred-year-old windmill from the Netherlands gave the place a distinctly European touch. It had to be disassembled into seven thousand pieces for the trip across the Atlantic and a Dutch millwright came along to put them all together again. Come spring, the town is full of tulips, so many that it's called the Tulip Center of America. There's a wooden-shoe factory and two museums, one with an exhibit of furniture and another with a display of Dutch kitchens.

One of Michigan's principal cultural centers is in Bloomfield Hills near Detroit. It's the Cranbrook Foundation, established by the Booth family, publishers of a chain of Michigan newspapers. The Foundation includes five private schools as well as an Art Academy and an Institute of Science. The Gothic Christ Church at Cranbrook is one of the center's most distinctive landmarks. Finnish architect Eliel Saarinen, father of Eero Saarinen, designed the buildings which are set on three hundred landscaped acres enhanced by fountains, archways, and the work of artists who teach and study at Cranbrook. Carl Milles, the Swedish sculptor, taught there for many years.

SPECIAL EVENTS

There is a toll to drive across the Straits of Mackinac Bridge, but you can get to the other side for free if you walk it on Labor Day along with the governor and thousands of others who make the annual trek on foot. The Labor Day Bridge Walk has been a tradition in the state ever since the $100 million bridge was completed. It's a four-and-a-half-mile stretch from Mackinaw City to St. Ignace on the Upper Peninsula.

Hardly a day goes by in Michigan during the spring, summer, or early fall without a celebration of some kind. Every September some three hundred vintage automobiles are oiled and polished for the annual Old Car Festival at Greenfield Village in Dearborn. The newest car participating was made in 1925—the others date from the nineteenth century. September is also a big month for rodeos—the towns of Clare, Charlotte, and Sparta each hold one annually. But Iron River plans ahead for July when it stages the Upper Peninsula Championship Rodeo.

One of the state's more colorful festivals occurs each May in Holland, a little town in western Michigan just south of Muskegon. Folks there hold a four-day Tulip Time Festival each May when the flowers are scheduled to bloom. The townspeople first scrub the streets just like they do in the Netherlands and then put on their wooden shoes for the traditional dancing, parades, and pageants.

In June Mackinac Island holds its annual Lilac Festival. And July is the big month for fruit festivals—Traverse City's Cherry Festival, Manistee's National Strawberry Festival, South Haven's National Blueberry Festival. There's also Sebewaing's Sugar Festival and Munger's Potato Festival, both in July.

The most famous of Michigan's ethnic festivals is Frankenmuth's Bavarian Festival in June. The village was settled by German immigrants, and residents still observe their ethnic traditions and speak German. The town of Wyandotte holds a Greek Festival in May and German and Hungarian festivals in June. Bronson stages Polish Festival Days in July and Sault Ste. Marie salutes its Italian community with a two-day fete, Soo Italian Days, in July. Greenville has its Danish Festival in August; Ann Arbor holds its Ethnic Fair in September. And Petoskey honors the state's Indians with its All State Indian Pageant in July, featuring Indian dancing and a powwow.

Special events during the winter include snowmobile races, ski races, and winter carnivals of every description.

P.D.

CHRONOLOGY

1622   French explorer Étienne Brulé visited Michigan under the auspices of the governor of New France in Canada.

1634   Jean Nicolet, another Frenchman, explored Michigan in search of a route to the Pacific.

1668   Father Jacques Marquette, a Jesuit, established the first permanent white settlement at Sault Ste. Marie.

1701   Antoine de la Mothe Cadillac founded Fort Pontchartrain, later to become Detroit.

1763   The British took control of Michigan following the French and Indian War.

1783   The United States acquired control of Michigan following the Revolution.

1805   Congress created the Territory of Michigan.

1825   The Erie Canal linked Michigan with the East.

1837   Michigan became the twenty-sixth state.

1845   Iron ore was discovered at Negaunee in the Upper Peninsula.

1854   The Republican Party was founded at Jackson, Michigan.

1899   Ransom Olds began manufacturing automobiles in Detroit.

1903   Henry Ford founded the Ford Motor Company in Dearborn.

1937   The United Automobile Workers won collective bargaining rights at Fisher and Chevrolet plants in Flint, Michigan.

1954   Work was begun on the Mackinac Bridge connecting the Upper and Lower Michigan peninsulas.

1963   Michigan voters approved a new state constitution.

1967   Forty-three people were killed during an eight-day race riot in Detroit.

1976   Pontiac Stadium, with one of the world's largest air-supported sports domes, was completed.

1979   In an attempt to reduce litter, Michigan became the first heavily populated state to ban throwaway beer and soft-drink containers.

MINNESOTA

IF Minnesota had to be summed up in a single word, the only one that would do is "clean." The air is clean, the state's lakes and rivers are clean, and to the constant astonishment of outsiders, even the state's politics always have been free of patronage and corruption. Although Minneapolis–St. Paul is the fifteenth largest metropolitan area in the nation and heavily industrial, the eleven lakes within the Minneapolis city limits are clean enough for swimming.

More than half of Minnesota's three million residents live in one of the Twin Cities or in the surrounding urban area. That leaves a lot of space in the nation's twelfth largest state for farming and recreation. Most of the farms are in the south on the prairies that border Iowa or along the Red River Valley separating Minnesota from North and South Dakota to the west. But the state's appeal, especially for visitors, is its vast northern wilderness, the forest and lake country populated by the deer and elk and the beaver, mink, and otter that the French Canadian fur traders sought so eagerly two hundred years ago. Six huge Indian reservations occupy much of northern Minnesota. Here live the descendants of the Sioux and Chippewa who once waged a bitter struggle for the hunting lands, the fields of wild rice, and the deep blue lakes of the territory.

This Minnesota is a land of mystery—the secrets of nature and the secrets of history lay hidden for centuries among the tall trees and cool blue waters. Historians are still arguing about whether or not the Vikings were here 130 years before Columbus discovered America. They've spent years evaluating some highly controversial evidence: the Kensington runestone found in Alexandria, Minnesota, in 1898 and tools of Scandinavian design unearthed later. The stone is engraved with the names of members of a Viking party that is said to have followed the inland waterways as far as northwestern Minnesota in the fourteenth century.

Hundreds of years later more modern explorers came to northern Minnesota in search of the source of the great river that led them south through the continent. The Mississippi trickles forth from Lake Itasca, not the largest or even the most picturesque of Minnesota's twenty-two thousand lakes. Here, in one of the nation's few remaining wilderness areas, it is easy to understand why Minnesota calls itself the "land of the sky-blue waters." The lakes and rivers sparkle in the sun as they have for centuries, pure and clear and clean. The air is perfumed by woodsy smells of leaf and bark and flower. And the deep greens and browns of the forest offer a soothing contrast to the chrome and steel of the modern world a few hours away.

Although parts of the state have been scarred by the men and machines who came to take away the timber and iron ore Minnesota once had in such abundance, much of it remains the silent wilderness it was when only the Indians knew the paths through the forests and the canoe routes through the rivers and streams. All things considered, it's not really an exaggeration to suggest that Mother Nature is alive and well and living in Minnesota.

THE LAND

Part prairie and part woods, Minnesota shares some of the features of Wisconsin, its lake-studded neighbor to the east, and some of Iowa, North and South Dakota, the corn and wheat belt states to the south and west. Sculpted by the glaciers of the Pleistocene Epoch, Minnesota is a land of wide, deep lakes (more than twenty-two of them), lush green forests, and rolling plains. Only the southeastern slice was untouched by the glaciers that slid over the state thousands of years ago. This southeastern sliver is low and level and crisscrossed by streams that over the centuries have carved valleys along their path toward the Mississippi on the state's eastern border.

The glaciers left their mark everywhere else, smoothing the surface of the plains that swing southeast across Minnesota from the Canadian border to the north and depositing rich soil composed of sand, gravel, and clay in the southwest corner. Almost half of Minnesota—the vast northeastern area with its famous deposits of iron ore—lies over the southern tip of the Canadian shield, the hard rock that underlies most of Canada. Even the power of the glaciers didn't smooth

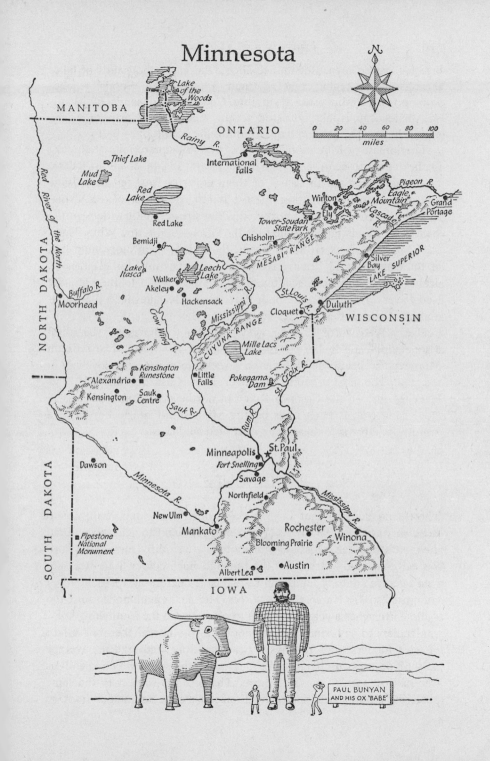

Minnesota

N

MANITOBA

ONTARIO

Lake of the Woods

Rainy R.

0   20   40   60   80   100
miles

Thief Lake

Mud Lake

Red Lake

Red Lake

International Falls

Pigeon R.

Winton

Eagle Mountain

Ely

Grand Portage

Tower-Soudan State Park

Cascade R.

Bemidji

Chisholm

MESABI RANGE

RED RIVER OF THE NORTH

NORTH DAKOTA

Lake Itasca

Leech Lake

Walker

Akeley

Hackensack

Silver Bay

LAKE SUPERIOR

Buffalo R.

Moorhead

Crow Wing R.

Mississippi

CUYUNA RANGE

St. Louis R.

Cloquet

Duluth

WISCONSIN

Mille Lacs Lake

Kensington Runestone

Alexandria

Little Falls

Pokegama Dam

St. Croix R.

Kensington

Sauk Centre

Sauk R.

Rum R.

Dawson

Minneapolis

St. Paul

Fort Snelling

Minnesota R.

Savage

SOUTH DAKOTA

Northfield

Mississippi R.

New Ulm

Rochester

Mankato

Winona

Pipestone National Monument

Blooming Prairie

Albert Lea

Austin

IOWA

PAUL BUNYAN AND HIS OX 'BABE'

out this rugged area. But the ice sheets did carve thousands of lakes throughout the region. One of them, Lake of the Woods, reaches from northern Minnesota deep into Canada. Thousands of islands dot this enormous lake bordered on the west by the Northern Angle, a tiny chunk of Minnesota that lies alongside Manitoba.

The largest of Minnesota's lakes is the 430-square-mile Red Lake in the far north-central section of the state. Big lakes aren't unique here: more than ten thousand of them cover at least ten acres. One that attracts lots of attention is Lake Itasca, the source of the Mississippi which emerges as a narrow, shallow stream. As it widens to the south, the Mississippi is joined by the Minnesota, Crow Wing, Rum, St. Croix, and Sauk rivers. Between them they drain more than half of the state. The St. Louis River, which empties into Lake Superior, drains the northeastern section of Minnesota, while to the west the Red River flows north on a path that eventually takes it to the Canadian river system that empties into Hudson Bay.

Henry Wadsworth Longfellow wrote about Minnesota's beautiful Minnehaha Falls in his poem *The Song of Hiawatha*. The falls on Minneapolis' beautiful Minnehaha Creek are among the loveliest in the state. The most dramatic, however, is the Cascade Falls that tumbles 124 feet on the Cascade River in northeastern Lake County. A close runner-up is High Falls on the Minnesota-Ontario border in a remote area that is to this day an unsettled wilderness.

CLIMATE

There's no denying that Minnesota's winters are long, snowy, and very, very cold, but severe as they are, it's difficult to generalize about the state's weather. Most of Minnesota is covered by snow from mid-December to mid-March. But the north is much colder than the south —an average January temperature of just 2 degrees above Fahrenheit compared to 15 degrees in the south. The north gets more snow, too —about 70 inches a year compared to 40 inches in the southwest.

Needless to say, summers are cooler in the north—the area is free of frost for less than 90 days a year and July temperatures average only 68 degrees compared to 74 degrees in the south which usually is free of frost for 160 days or more. The south is subject to the same blistering summer heat spells as Minnesota's corn belt neighbors. One day in July 1936 the temperature at Moorhead shot up to 114 degrees. The record low was set twice—once at Leech Lake Dam in 1899 and again at Pokegama Dam in 1903 when the mercury tumbled to 59 degrees below zero.

Southeastern Minnesota gets the most rain, some 32 inches a year compared to 20 inches in the far northwest.

THE MINNESOTANS

By the time the first white men arrived in Minnesota, the Chippewa, a branch of the Algonquin Indians, had pushed the Sioux out of their forest villages and west toward the Great Plains. Indeed, when French explorers and fur traders arrived from Canada late in the seventeenth century, the Chippewa were on hand to assure them that they held most of Minnesota north and east of the Mississippi. Until the Chippewa hounded them out of their forest preserves, the Sioux had been peaceful Indians cultivating wild rice and hunting in the lush woods. But the conquering Chippewa were just the beginning of their troubles. Their lucrative fur trade suffered during the Revolutionary War, and early in the nineteenth century they traded away most of the land surrounding what is now Minneapolis–St. Paul for practically nothing.

The Chippewa, too, were victimized by the white man's treaties. Little by little they ceded most of their Minnesota lands, sometimes for prices so low that one chief bitterly told the white negotiators: "You forget that the land will be yours as long as the world lasts."

It was more than a hundred years after the first French explorers arrived that Minnesota was opened for settlement. No one is sure just which explorer arrived first, but it is generally agreed that the fur traders Pierre Esprit Radisson and Médart Chouart probably visited Minnesota as early as 1660. Nearly twenty years later Daniel Greysolon, Sieur Duluth penetrated the Minnesota woods during an expedition he hoped would end at the Pacific Ocean. At about that time, Father Louis Hennepin, a Belgian missionary, was captured by the Sioux who held him for months as they wandered through the forests. Hennepin was the first white man to visit the site of what one day would be Minneapolis. When he saw the falls of the Mississippi there, he named them after St. Anthony.

During the eighteenth century Minnesota remained a wilderness frequented only by the Indians and the French fur traders and missionaries. The French who ruled a vast region of Canada from Quebec showed no interest in colonizing the wilderness to the south. They just wanted all the furs they could get their hands on. France abandoned its holdings in the New World to the British in 1762, but that meant nothing to Minnesota. The Indians adapted easily by trading furs with the British. Even after the American Revolution, Minnesota remained a wilderness, although the advent of the nineteenth century saw the first efforts to relieve the Indians of their lands so that the white man eventually might move in.

Once the Indians relinquished much of their holdings in 1838 the first settlers arrived, eyeing the fortunes to be made from Minnesota's vast timberlands. Most of the newcomers were shrewd Yankees from New England. Within twenty years they had done so well that Minnesota became a mecca for Northern Europeans lured across the ocean by an avalanche of advertising. Those ads would do credit to the best Madison Avenue has to offer today: they boasted of the rich soil, the unlimited opportunities for wealth through manufacturing, railroading, or farming. They even claimed that the climate could cure tuberculosis.

The first to respond to all the publicity were Germans, followed by the Irish, Canadians, and eventually the Swedes, Norwegians, Danes, and Finns. There were just over five thousand people in all of Minnesota in 1850 but by 1880 the population had soared to 780,773. More than 70 per cent were first or second generation European immigrants.

The Swedes came by the thousands in response to the "American Letters" of Peter Cassel who went to Iowa in 1846 and was so enthusiastic about what he found there that he sent impassioned descriptions back home. The democratic life he wrote about had enormous appeal in class-conscious Sweden, and the rich farm land that was to be had practically for the asking was a powerful incentive to emigrate. East-central Minnesota still bears the imprint of these nineteenth-century immigrants, although it is estimated that, all told, the Swedes cultivated more than two million acres throughout the state.

The Norwegians came at the height of the lumber boom. But when they had earned enough felling trees to buy land, they showed no affinity for the company of their fellow Scandinavians, the Swedes. Instead, they headed west to the fertile Red River Valley.

Germans came in great numbers in the 1880s and 1890s. They settled in St. Paul, in New Ulm on the Minnesota River, and in Stearns and Brown counties in central Minnesota. For years, whole communities clung to their German language and customs. New Ulm was virtually destroyed during a Sioux massacre in 1862, but the survivors rebuilt the town and it still reflects its German heritage. The Finns also have carefully preserved their traditions. Most of them arrived late in the nineteenth century to work the mines of the Mesabi and Cuyuna ranges. And today communities like Chisholm are made up of the descendants of those early immigrants. The Finns brought the sauna to Minnesota, and many Finnish families still have bathhouses in their back yards.

The last major wave of immigration to Minnesota came early in the twentieth century when workers were needed for the meat-packing plants of St. Paul. Poles and Lithuanians responded to the advertisements this time, and their descendants still constitute a sizable ethnic group in South St. Paul.

Minnesota today reflects the patterns of settlement of its nineteenth-century immigrants. The counties north of Minneapolis–St. Paul are still predominantly Swedish while the Norwegians remain concentrated in the Red River Valley. The Germans constitute a recognizable ethnic group in the center of the state and along the south-central border, while the Finns are still to be found in the northeast.

There has been a population shift away from the farms as Minnesota has become increasingly industrial. Almost half of the state's population is now concentrated around the Twin Cities, now the fifteenth largest metropolitan area in the United States. And although Minnesota has six Indian reservations, about half of its twenty-three thousand Indians now live in Minneapolis–St. Paul. Almost all of Minnesota's blacks are there, too, although Negroes constitute only 1 per cent of the state's total population.

HISTORY

If the Vikings discovered America, as some say, they very well may have gotten as far west as Minnesota. The idea that they did is based on the Kensington runestone, a rock inscribed with the names of twenty-one Viking explorers. A Minnesota farmer found it in 1898, and it immediately stirred a still-unresolved controversy. No one has been able to authenticate the stone, and most historians now say it's a hoax, but to some it serves as tangible proof of the "Vikings-were-first" theory.

Another Minnesota discovery proves conclusively that the place was inhabited more than ten thousand years ago. The skeleton of a young girl found in 1931 generated a lot of anthropological excitement. The girl, who became known as "Minnesota Man," was at first thought to be older than any of the prehistoric Indians known to have lived on the North American continent. However, after careful studies, scientists reached the conclusion that this was just another Indian skeleton dating back eleven thousand years.

Minnesota's recorded history begins with the arrival of French explorers and fur traders about 1660. Pierre Esprit Radisson and Médart Chouart, Sieur de Groseilliers are believed to have arrived from Canada at a spot north of Lake Superior. Next came Daniel Greysolon, Sieur Duluth en route, he hoped, to the Pacific Ocean. Greysolon soon discovered that he was mistaken but still claimed the whole area for France. The next year Father Louis Hennepin and two companions launched an exploration of Minnesota and got as far as Mille Lacs before they were kidnapped by the Sioux. News of the capture spread and Duluth eventually heard about the "three white spirits" the Sioux were holding and managed to engineer their release.

Starting in 1762 the land was alternately controlled by the French, the Spanish, and the English. First the French gave all their land west of the Mississippi to Spain in 1762. The next year the British won the French and Indian War and as a result acquired from France all of its territory east of the Mississippi. Ultimately, Spain gave its holdings back to France—this happened in 1800—and three years later the United States gained control via the Louisiana Purchase.

Two famous explorers arrived in Minnesota around the turn of the eighteenth century. The first was Jonathan Carver, who visited what is now St. Paul and ventured inside a cavern that has been known as Carver's Cave ever since. Carver is said to have negotiated a treaty with the Sioux for a huge slice of Minnesota and Wisconsin, but if he did, it was repudiated by Congress after the matter was debated, on and off, for twenty years. Zebulon Pike, a U. S. Army lieutenant, was the second explorer. He was charged in 1805 with extending American authority over Minnesota. Pike succeeded in making a deal with the Indians for military posts at the mouths of the St. Croix and Minnesota rivers, but the Indians were more loyal to the British than

Pike had bargained for. They took the whiskey and $200 worth of trinkets he paid for the sites, but as soon as he left, they co-operated with the British fur companies in resuming what by then was considered illegal trade.

It took the War of 1812 to oust the British and their fur interests from the area once and for all. As soon as they were gone, John Jacob Astor moved in and took over where the British concerns had left off. But even so, Minnesota's settlement proceeded slowly. Colonel Henry Leavenworth arrived in 1816 and plied the Indians with whiskey and money until they allowed him to build a military post on lands they controlled. Five years after that, several Swiss families arrived to farm, but although a steamboat chugged up the Mississippi to Fort St. Anthony (later Fort Snelling) in 1823, settlement didn't begin in earnest until the "Indian problem" was resolved.

It took a whole series of treaties to edge the Sioux and the Chippewa out of Minnesota, but the two treaties signed in 1838 were the signal for Easterners to swoop into the territory to farm and to exploit its vast timber reserves. Many of the newcomers were lumbermen from Maine who had an idea of Minnesota's potential wealth. Others were farmers and tradesmen from elsewhere in the East. By the time Congress created the Territory of Minnesota in 1849, more than 4,000 persons lived there. Even more came after 1851 when the Indians gave up millions of acres west of the Mississippi. The territorial population had reached 150,000 when Minnesota was admitted to the Union as the thirty-second state in 1858. Many of the new arrivals were European immigrants who came in response to a flood of advertisements abroad about the richness of Minnesota's soil, the ready availability of jobs in the lumbering industry, and even the miraculously "curative" powers of the air itself.

When the Civil War began in 1861, Minnesota was the first state to offer troops to support the Union. But the following year the Army had to dispatch forces to Minnesota to suppress an Indian rampage. The Sioux, desperate to drive the white man out of their hunting lands, went on the warpath, devastating frontier towns and killing hundreds of settlers. By the time the federal troops arrived, whole towns like New Ulm settled by German immigrants had been virtually destroyed.

The war interrupted Minnesota's boom only temporarily. As soon as it was over, the state renewed its call for immigrants. Germans, Swedes, Danes, Norwegians, Irish, and Finns came by the thousands, some to farm, some to work in the lumber camps until they could save enough money to buy land, and, after iron was discovered in the Vermilion Range in 1884, some to work the mines.

Meanwhile, wheat farms sprouted where the Sioux once hunted and flour mills were built to process the grain. Most of them were concentrated in Minneapolis, so many that the place was nicknamed "Mill City." The railroads snaked across the state bringing still more people through the 1880s—the population reached one million in 1885.

But for all its prosperity, Minnesota had its share of troubles. There was the blizzard of 1873 which took seventy lives on the prairies, a national financial panic the same year that practically bankrupted the whole city of Duluth, an invasion of grasshoppers that wiped out crops in twenty-nine counties in 1876, and a flour mill explosion in Minneapolis that claimed eighteen lives in 1878. But by far the worst disasters were two forest fires that swept huge sections of the state in 1894 and in 1918. The first killed more than four hundred persons and destroyed more than $1 million in property, while the second killed four hundred persons in Carlton and St. Louis counties and wiped out $25 million in property.

On the plus side were the discoveries of vast iron reserves in the Vermilion Range in 1884, in the Mesabi Range in 1890, and in the Cuyuna Range in 1911. A major event in 1889 was the decision by the Sisters of St. Francis to place Dr. William Mayo and his sons in charge of St. Mary's Hospital in Rochester, Minnesota. The Mayo Clinic put Rochester on the map, and its worldwide fame now attracts more than 150,000 patients every year.

The early years of the twentieth century bolstered Minnesota's economy. The first of the state's huge steel mills began operating in Duluth in 1916 and with the advent of World War I the state was called upon to accelerate production of iron, lumber, and wheat.

Even before the war many of Minnesota's farmers had been voicing discontent with railroad freight rates and the cost of doing business with the banks and grain companies. They began forming cooperatives, and the movement eventually generated its own political party, the Farmer Labor Party. But no political influence could soften the effect of the Great Depression of the 1930s. The state's economy virtually ground to a halt, with rampant unemployment and a drastic decline in farm income.

World War II pulled the state out of the doldrums. Again, the mines, lumber companies, and farms were called upon to produce everything they could to feed and supply the armies. The mines outdid themselves producing 84 million tons of iron in 1943 alone.

The decade following the war saw the depletion of Minnesota's richest iron ore. The economy of the northeastern part of the state went into a decline as mines closed, throwing hundreds out of work. The opening of a plant at Silver Bay in 1955 to process taconite, a lower-grade iron ore, helped a little, but the mining region still had a long way to go to recover its former prosperity. One device was the formation of industrial development corporations to lure new business into the region, a move that was strongly supported by the state government.

At the same time, mechanization on the farm was lessening the need for agricultural workers and Minnesotans began leaving the land and flocking to the cities. The population shift had political repercussions resulting in a statewide reapportionment bolstering the legislative representation of the urban areas. The 1960s also saw stepped-up efforts to aid Minnesota's industry. A special loan fund was created in 1961 to pump money into the northeastern mining region, a group of private citizens organized in 1964 to help attract new industry to the state, and in 1967 a special council was created to promote development of the Twin Cities area. In 1971 the state legislature passed a bill stipulating that 40 per cent of the property taxes collected from new industries within the Twin Cities metropolitan area be returned to the area for redistribution to municipalities and school districts.

Whatever its economic troubles, Minnesota always has been a leader in providing health and social services to its citizens. Its state politics have remained notoriously honest over the years. Evidence of corruption is so hard to come by that *Time* magazine once wrote that "Minnesota politics is unnaturally clean—no patronage (at least for the most part) and virtually no corruption."

INDUSTRY

Once primarily agricultural, Minnesota, like the rest of the nation, has become more and more industrial since the end of World War II. Even mining and lumbering, for many years important sources of income, have taken a back seat to manufacturing, which now brings the state more than 60 per cent of its annual income. Most of Minnesota's heavy industry is concentrated in the Twin Cities of Minneapolis–St. Paul. Here is the center of the state's most important industry: the manufacture of farm machinery as well as heavy nonelectrical equipment for construction, mining, printing, and papermaking. But most Americans are more familiar with the products of Minnesota's second-ranking industry: food processing. Supermarket shelves across the nation are lined with the canned vegetables Minnesota produces. And meat-packing plants in towns like Albert Lea, Austin, Duluth, South St. Paul, and Winona process the beef cattle, hogs, and lambs raised on Minnesota's farms.

Earlier in the twentieth century, flour milling was Minnesota's most important industry. Indeed, during the 1920s the state was the world's leading producer of flour. The economic importance of this industry has declined dramatically, but Minnesota still is a leading producer of wheat flour. In fact, about one tenth of the nation's total supply still comes from the state, which also turns out a hefty supply of breakfast cereals and cake mixes.

Much of Minnesota's huge soybean crop is processed into oil at plants throughout the state. There are big ones at Blooming Prairie, Columbia Heights, Dawson, Mankato, Minneapolis, and Savage. And the sugar beets which grow so profusely in the Red River Valley are refined at plants throughout the area.

The increasing diversity of Minnesota's industry is evident in the St. Paul–Minneapolis area. Here, there are plants for the manufacture of electrical equipment for industrial use as well as several large printers and publishers, among them the nation's largest publisher of law books. The manufacture of paper and paperboard products has been a thriving industry in Minnesota since the lumbering days of the 1800s, and today huge paper mills still operate in Cloquet and St. Paul. Other Twin Cities plants make chemicals, sandpaper, abrasives, all sorts of adhesive tapes, and industrial adhesives. There's an automobile assembly plant in St. Paul, and elsewhere in the state they make railroad equipment, linseed oil and meal, carpets, cement, cosmetics, fur, knitted goods, furniture, glass, leather, and stone products.

AGRICULTURE

Farming in Minnesota isn't what it used to be: descendants of the hardy pioneers who battled the elements in the northern part of the state a century ago have all but deserted the land. But while the state's manufacturing far surpasses agriculture in its earning power, one in fifteen Minnesotans still works on the land raising beef and dairy cattle, tending sheep, or cultivating the vegetables Minnesota cans and ships to the rest of the nation.

Although Minnesota is edged on the west by both the corn and the wheat belts, the state's agriculture is dominated by livestock: beef and dairy cattle, sheep, hogs, chickens, and turkeys. Cattle raising is an important industry, but more than 1.75 million dairy cattle supply enough milk to make Minnesota one of the nation's leaders in milk, butter, and cheese production. The dairy cattle graze on pastureland that sweeps southeastward through the state, while beef cattle and hogs are raised throughout the state. Most of Minnesota's sheep farms are in the northwest corner where poor soils and a short growing season make the land unsuitable for crops.

The Red River Valley on Minnesota's western border is one of the most heavily agricultural areas of the state. Here, wheat, oats, and barley grow along with potatoes, sugar beets, flaxseed, and enough hay to rank the state among the nation's biggest hay suppliers.

Farther south, Minnesota shares part of the corn belt with South Dakota and Iowa. Oats and soybeans also grow in this fertile region as well as corn, which is used mainly for cattle feed.

Minnesota, as most Americans know, is the home of the Jolly Green Giant. Most of the green peas, sweet corn, and potatoes that find their way to the nation's dinner tables via cans plucked from supermarket shelves are grown and processed in Minnesota.

NATURAL RESOURCES

Minnesota has run out of the high-grade iron ore that made its Mesabi, Cuyuna, and Vermilion ranges famous. But the state still supplies more than half of the iron ore used in the United States today.

Once the high-grade iron ore ran out—the Mesabi Range alone yielded 1.5 billion tons since they started mining it in the 1880s—the state's vast reserves of taconite were tapped. This ore, a lower-grade mineral, needs processing to concentrate it into high-grade iron. There seems to be limitless supplies of it in Minnesota, more than enough to maintain the state's supremacy as the nation's most important source of iron.

Before they found iron in the Mesabi Range in 1884, another of Minnesota's valuable resources had generated its own boom. The forests that covered the northern and central part of the state lured lumbermen from the east who came to Minnesota with no thought of conservation: they virtually stripped parts of the state of vast stands of pine, balsam, and spruce. Those were the days of Paul Bunyan, the giant logger who swooped through the woods exuberantly felling trees right and left. By the 1920s, however, Minnesota's forests were sparse, its seemingly endless supply of lumber nearly exhausted. What remains of Minnesota's lumber industry depends on trees that have been planted to replace the natural forests. Luckily, some segments of the thick pine woods have been preserved by both the federal and state governments.

Of all Minnesota's resources, the most valuable today is the rich soil deposited millions of years ago by the glaciers. The most fertile areas are in the north of the state where the soil is formed by grayish drift from the glaciers. The reddish soil of the northeast is the least fertile while in the southern part of the state the topsoil is composed of loess, a silt-like material carried by the wind and smoothed over the glacial drift.

Although iron is by far Minnesota's most valuable mineral, the state also has important deposits of manganese used in steel-making as well as extensive reserves of granite along the upper Minnesota River. Limestone and sandstone are quarried in southern Minnesota and are that region's most important mineral resource.

Despite the ravages of the lumber boom, 40 per cent of Minnesota is still forest—lush woods of jack, Norway, and white pine in the north and groves of ash, black oak, black walnut, elm, and maple in the south. The northern woods are enlivened by wild roses and geraniums, rue anemones, blackberries, raspberries, blueberries, honeysuckle, lilies of the valley, and wintergreen. The prairies of the south have their share of wildflowers too: violets, goldenrod, prairie phlox, and asters.

There's still some big game in the north woods: black bears and moose prowl the forests and white-tailed deer are prevalent. But wildlife is abundant throughout the rest of the state: lots of beavers, foxes, gophers, bobcats, minks, muskrats, in addition to the quails and pheasants that frequent the grain fields, the ducks along the lakes, and the bass, muskellunge, pike, and trout of the rivers and lakes.

CITIES

People who live there will go to considerable time and trouble to tell you how different **Minneapolis** and **St. Paul** are. The idea that the rest of the country regards the two cities as twins—or worse, as one indistinguishable metropolis—perturbs the natives who don't see things that way at all. Minneapolis, they will tell you, is big and beautiful, the commercial and industrial hub of the state, a town that is building for the future with verve and imagination. St. Paul, on the other hand, is small and serene, the seat of the state government, a city so proud of its history and heritage that it remains intent on preserving the New England traditions of the settlers who transformed it from a frontier hamlet called "Pig's Eye" to the "Boston of the West."

St. Paul was settled, first, by a stubborn group of squatters who parked themselves on land the government had reserved for construction of a fort at the confluence of the Minnesota and Mississippi rivers. It came by its original name when the settlers, led by a French Canadian fur trapper who called himself "Pig's Eye" Parrant, came to the area in 1840. The following year a Catholic priest suggested that the little grouping of log cabins be named something more dignified and "Pig's Eye" became St. Paul, after the priest's patron saint. The place wasn't particularly attractive in those days—an 1843 visitor described it as a primitive outpost populated by mosquitoes, snakes, Indians, and about twelve white people. Nevertheless, it was there to stay—by 1849 there were 642 buildings and 800 people, a polyglot group of French Canadians, Swedes, Norwegians, and New Englanders who came to the frontier for a fresh start and because of the territory's vast reserves of timber.

Some of them settled on the other side of the Mississippi in an equally crude village that was to become Minneapolis. But in the mid-1800s St. Paul was the more important of the two. It became the territorial capital in 1849, and when Minnesota became a state in 1858, it retained the seat of government. The following decades brought the railroads and men like James J. Hill, a ruthless entrepreneur, who for all his questionable financial wheeling and dealing gave St. Paul much that it still treasures. His support of the Catholic Church was largely responsible for the size and splendor of the St. Paul Cathedral, and he gave the town its first reference library.

St. Paul's character was molded by the Yankee businessmen who arrived after the Civil War and set about making their fortunes in banking, lumbering, and railroading. They built their homes along Summit Avenue, still St. Paul's most handsome residential street. This graceful boulevard lined with Victorian mansions testifies to the taste and refinement of the families which set the tone for the town as it struggled to achieve the Eastern ambience it still prizes.

F. Scott Fitzgerald lived on Summit Avenue years later—he wrote *This Side of Paradise* at his parents' home there when he was twenty-three years old. St. Paul is as proud of that as it is of its imposing state capitol, an ornate, white-domed structure of sandstone and marble set on two hundred acres of parkland in the heart of the city. St. Paul's gleaming new city hall is an attention-getter too. Its eighteen floors are paneled in woods representing every country in the world.

Como Park Zoo always has been one of the city's main attractions. Many of the animals are housed in cages or out-of-doors in settings designed to reflect their natural habitats. But as far as museums and other cultural attractions are concerned, St. Paul must yield to her neighbor across the river. Minneapolis, an industrial city, has managed both to preserve its natural beauty and to offer its citizens an ample smörgåsbord of art and theater.

It's come a long, long way since its rough and tumble beginnings during the lumber boom of the late 1800s. A steady stream of newcomers, many of them Scandinavian immigrants, felled trees with lusty exuberance so that they could make money to buy farm land. Flour-milling was another early industry—St. Anthony's Falls in the Mississippi provided the water power for the mills that were to become the city's economic foundation. Today, giant corporations still operate mills there—namely the huge Nabisco, General Mills, and Pillsbury plants.

But industrial though it is, Minneapolis has avoided the kind of urban problems that characterize so many modern American cities.

The eleven lakes within the city limits remain unpolluted—you can still swim in them when it's warm enough. There are 153 parks, green oases encircling the lakes and threading their way through the town. Minnehaha Park overlooking the Mississippi was named for the sparkling falls Henry Wadsworth Longfellow never saw but described so vividly in *The Song of Hiawatha*.

As evidence of its determination to enhance the quality of life for its 434,000 residents, Minneapolis has replaced a decaying seventeen-block section of its downtown area with the elegantly modern Nicolet Mall, a meticulously landscaped cluster of shops and cafes linked by pedestrian walks—no cars are permitted here. On the mall is the city's shining new pride and joy, the fifty-seven-story IDS Tower, tallest building between Chicago and San Francisco.

Culturally speaking, Minneapolis has much to boast about. Its Tyrone Guthrie Theater has earned a nationwide reputation for the excellence of its repertory productions; its Walker Art Center has a first-class collection of contemporary American paintings as well as valuable Oriental stone and pottery exhibits. The Minnesota Institute of Arts is equally impressive: its treasures include works by Rembrandt and Van Gogh. The University of Minnesota has an art gallery, too, housed in the Northrop Memorial Auditorium, home of the Minnesota Orchestra. In addition to the University, which has campuses in Minneapolis and St. Paul, Minneapolis has two other colleges, the Augsburg College and Seminary and the Minneapolis School of Art and Design. There are seven colleges in St. Paul, including Macalester College and Hamline University.

Duluth, Minnesota's third-largest city, has a unique appeal during the hay fever season. The pollen count is so low that the place is a mecca for hay fever sufferers seeking relief. In fact, that's why the Hay Fever Club of America maintains its headquarters there.

Duluth is a long, narrow town stretching for more than fifteen miles along the shore of Lake Superior. You can see just how narrow it is from the Skyline Parkway in the hills above the city.

For a while in the nineteenth century it looked as though Duluth was going to become nothing more than a Minnesota ghost town. It didn't even have a name in 1856 when rumors of copper to be found along the lake shore brought a rush of speculators. At the time, Duluth was just a few cabins surrounding the home of George Stuntz who came to survey the area for the government and decided to stay. The boom brought on by the discovery of copper didn't survive the national financial panic of 1857. And most of the people who stayed through that disaster left in 1859 when a scarlet fever epidemic broke out. In fact, Duluth lost so many residents that by 1865 only two houses were occupied. Things improved after financier Jay Cooke decided to make Duluth the northern terminus of the Lake Superior and Mississippi Railroad, but when Cooke went broke in 1877, most of Duluth's five thousand residents left. Eventually the town improved its harbor, which was a very important undertaking. Today, it is one of the nation's foremost inland ports and the third largest grain center.

The best way to see Duluth is from Skyline Parkway or via a sightseeing cruise along the harbor which offers an excellent view of the massive grain elevators and the forbidding ore docks. The city also is the starting point for one of the nation's most scenic roads, the North Shore Drive, which winds along the lake from the north of the city.

Without a doubt, the Mayo Clinic is more famous than the town that surrounds it. **Rochester,** Minnesota, traces its history back to 1854 when settlers first began arriving in Olmsted County. By 1858, when the town was incorporated, there were fifteen hundred people there, most of them farmers. Dr. William Mayo arrived much later, but he was on hand to treat the victims of a vicious tornado in 1883. At the time, the Sisters of St. Francis, an order of Roman Catholic nuns, was so appalled by the lack of medical facilities that they decided to build a hospital and asked Dr. Mayo and his sons to run it. St. Mary's Hospital opened in 1889, but by the early 1900s it had evolved into a private group practice run by the Mayos and the doctors they invited to join them. Today, the Mayo Clinic draws patients from all over the world and is housed in a huge complex of buildings connected by a maze of underground passages. Since 1972 it has had its own medical school and for many years has operated one of the world's largest programs for medical residents, doctors who are learning their specialties.

Although the Mayos and medicine dominate Rochester, the town also serves as headquarters for one of IBM's big manufacturing plants. For visitors, though, the main attractions are: the clinic; the medical museum with its demonstrations of how the human body works and how such devices as the heart-lung machine and the artificial kidney operate; and Mayowood, the sprawling forty-room mansion built by Charles H. Mayo and donated by his son, the late Dr. Charles W. Mayo, to the Olmsted County Historical Society.

SPORTS AND RECREATION

For sportsmen and nature lovers Minnesota is a dream come true— more lakes, streams, and rivers than even the most dedicated fisherman could try in a lifetime; forests still teeming with deer and moose, even bear and coyotes; and mile upon mile of canoeing waters and hiking trails. Even in the eight-county area surrounding Minneapolis–St. Paul the opportunities are limitless. Fishing is good in three lakes within the Minneapolis city limits and the hunting lands in its outskirts abound with ducks, squirrels, rabbits, muskrats, foxes, and woodcocks. Only the bear and moose hunters have to make the trek north to find what they're looking for.

In Arrowhead Country, the triangle of northeastern counties that border Lake Superior and Canada, hunting and fishing are a way of life. Year after year hunters armed with rifles or bow and arrow come to stalk white-tailed deer, elk, moose, bear, bobcat, and coyotes. Most of the fur-bearing animals—the raccoon, otter, beaver, mink, and muskrat—are now protected species, but even they may be taken within prescribed periods.

The twelve-county Minnesota "Heartland" area farther west is popular with grouse and duck hunters. Tens of thousands of Canadian geese, snow geese, and blue geese are to be found here, especially along the borders of the Thief Lake and Agassiz refuges.

Fishing is legendary in these parts. Muskellunge, walleye, sauger, northern pike, large and smallmouth bass, brook and rainbow trout are all available for the modest price of a license that is good for a year.

Minnesotans have taken to canoeing lately, an enthusiasm that has swept the state and which had a lot to do with the opening of the Boundary Waters Canoe area, more than fourteen thousand square miles of lakes and rivers that crisscross over the Canadian border. Here, the adventurous can find the challenge of rushing white water while others can slip silently along the streams the voyageurs of the past followed in their search for furs and fortunes. The canoe area is part of the National Wilderness section of the vast Superior National

Forest. The wilderness area is just that—a true wilderness with no public roads, no big recreation areas, and no lumbering.

While the wildest country is in the northern part of the state, the south provides a multitude of similar, if tamer, pleasures. Lakes throughout the southwest abound with bullhead, while Albert Lea Lake and smaller fishing areas are known for bluegills, crappies, bass, walleyes, and northern pike.

Hunting is good in the fall when ducks and geese sweep down from the north on their annual migration. And while they are protected species today, the woods are full of the kind of animals the fur trappers once coveted—beaver, otter, mink, muskrat, and fox. You can't shoot them here, but you can watch them scamper through their natural habitat, and, if you're lucky, catch a beaver building his dam or an otter slipping through the mud along a river bank.

With all its sky-blue waters Minnesota offers innumerable opportunities for water sports of every variety—swimming, sailing, water-skiing, skin-diving, powerboating, houseboating. You name it, and it's there.

The state's long cold winters haven't daunted its outdoorsmen. They just trade their canoes for snowmobiles, their sailboats for ice yachts, their hiking boots for cross-country skis. All the fishermen have to do is don heavier clothes and drop a line through a hole in the ice. Snowmobiling has become a virtual winter passion—there are more than 250,000 of these zippy machines in the state, and snowmobile races have captured the attention of just about everybody.

While the state has thirty-five ski areas, the downhill racers are almost outnumbered by the cross-country skiers, who are content to forego the thrills of the slopes for the less challenging pleasures of gliding gently across the countryside.

There's even something in this land of nature lovers for those who would rather watch others exert themselves. The Minnesota Twins brought professional baseball to Minneapolis–St. Paul and the Minnesota Vikings have collected an enthusiastic following of pro football fans. And then there are the Minnesota Knicks competing against the nation's top professional soccer teams and the Minnesota North Stars, the pro hockey team. The Twin Cities also boast a rugby club with an active schedule.

POINTS OF INTEREST

The first men to visit Minnesota more than two centuries ago came to hunt, to follow Indian paths through the wilderness, and to learn what nature had to offer in this rich land of deep green woods and clear, crystal lakes. It has been a long time since those early French explorers first intruded on territory known only to the Indian, the deer and the elk, the mink and otter and muskrat, but people still come to Minnesota for much the same reason. Although they know they aren't the first to mark the paths and stand awed and silent in the vast, lush forests, they come because Minnesota still offers the mystery of a dark, green wilderness and the unforgettable sights of cascading white water pouring over rocks arranged by nature with an artistry man can never hope to duplicate.

Since more than half of Minnesota's three million residents are clustered around Minneapolis—St. Paul, most of its 84,000 square miles are undisturbed oases—mile upon mile of woods and lakes interspersed with small towns and smaller villages, some of them rustic and some of them quaint throwbacks to an earlier and quieter time. There's Sauk Centre, the village Sinclair Lewis wrote about in *Main Street*. His boyhood home is there, a trim frame house like many you'll see in this part of the state.

Minnesotans call their state's northwest corner "Viking-land" because of legends generated by some controversial historical evidence that Viking explorers were here 130 years before Columbus discovered America. The discovery of the Kensington Runestone in Alexandria, Minnesota, in 1898 set off the speculation that has preoccupied the populace in these parts ever since. The theory is that thirty Vikings had been sent in 1355 to track down settlers who had abandoned a Norse colony in Greenland. They are said to have followed a route north along the coastline to Hudson Bay and then southwest down the Nelson River to Lake Winnipeg and from there to the Red River of the North to the Buffalo River and a string of lakes in Minnesota that have since been drained. The runestone upon which the names of the Viking party were carved was found in this lake country. Later, more artifacts purportedly of fourteenth-century Scandinavian design were unearthed. Most historians dismiss them all as lacking in authenticity, but the legend of those early Viking visitors persists. Alexandria has built a museum to display the runestone and the other disputed evidence of the Viking presence.

Whether or not the Vikings really were there, northwestern Minnesota holds the key to a mystery that was much easier to solve. Here at Lake Itasca a tiny stream bubbles along a rocky course for a while and then deepens and widens and gathers power eventually to slash through the continent on its inexorable path to the sea. At its source, the Mississippi is a trickle so shallow and so narrow that you can step across it without wetting your feet. Every year thousands of tourists make the trek to wonder at the modest beginnings of the waterway that divides east from west and that once formed the natural barrier that our forefathers never dreamed their fledgling republic would cross.

The first white men to venture into Minnesota came ashore in an area that remains almost as remote and wild as it was in the eighteenth century. The fur traders who first settled at Grand Portage at the tip of what is now Cooke County wanted only a way station en route to their markets in Canada. They built a crude outpost—a wooden stockade and some blockhouses—that recently has been restored and designated a national historic site. Grand Portage is still Indian country. As a matter of fact, the approval of the local Chippewa was needed before the restored buildings of the old North West Company could be opened to the public. The Grand Portage Indian Reservation is now part of Superior National Forest, 3,400 square miles of pine stands and lakes and streams edged on the north by the Pigeon River which forms the Canadian border. The towns of Ely and Winton are takeoff points for canoeists bent on exploring the wilderness by water. Nearby is the Tower-Soudan State Park, home of the oldest and deepest iron mine in Minnesota. The Soudan Underground Mine is no longer in operation but it has been revamped for safety so that visitors can descend twenty-three hundred feet below the earth's surface to see how the iron ore was once extracted and hauled away.

All of this part of Minnesota is mining country and near Chisholm in the heart of the Mesabi Range five mines still operate. The area has been carved by man into massive gaping canyons to gain access to the rich minerals the earth once shielded. Chisholm has a museum of mining built as a government works project in the 1930s that traces the history of the industry in the state.

Farther north, at the Canadian border, sportsmen from both nations rendezvous for fishing and hunting trips through an area designated as the Voyageur National Forest. A bit farther south, toward the center of the state, the emphasis is on Indian lore and the exploits of that legendary logger Paul Bunyan. There's a larger-than-life replica of Bunyan at Pioneer Village in Brainerd who introduces himself and talks about the old logging days. But if you want to see where the real man was born, go to nearby Akeley and see his cradle and then pass through Hackensack where there's a monument to his sweetheart, Lucette Diana Kensack.

The south and west shores of Mille Lacs, technically a part of the Mille Lacs Indian Reservation, are popular with youngsters because of a live animal park and the Mille Lacs Historical Society Indian Museum.

Another American hero, aviator Charles Lindbergh, Jr., was born in Little Falls, Minnesota, where his boyhood home has been maintained as a memorial to him and to his father, once a respected Minnesota congressman.

Life seems more placid, more civilized in southern Minnesota, but despite the fact that the prairies are now cultivated, there are still spots of stunning natural beauty and historic towns which offer vivid insights into the drama of pioneer life. Northfield, for instance, fought off Jesse James and his gang and Waseca County still maintains its Anti-Horse Thief Detective Society, a holdover from the days when stealing a horse was regarded as almost as bad as murder, if not worse.

The Minnesota River winds through this part of the state along a green valley toward its rendezvous in the east with the Mississippi River. Germans settled along its path in the mid-1800s and built the town of New Ulm, which retains to this day a distinctly European flavor.

New Ulm's existence testifies to the courage and spirit of those early German settlers. The town was just taking shape in 1862 when the Sioux, bitter about the treaties that had allowed the white man to infringe upon their lands, made one last brutal attempt to regain what they had lost. Bands of Sioux swept through Renville County, driving the settlers out, raiding town after town, slaughtering everyone except the few lucky women and children who managed to hide and eventually to escape. Many who did never went back, but after the Sioux were subdued and thirty-nine of their leaders had been executed, New Ulm rebuilt and didn't neglect to erect a monument to the settlers who perished on those terrible nights in 1862.

The area is still rich in Indian lore due largely to the Pipestone National Monument, the quarry from which the Sioux took the red stones they used to carve their ceremonial pipes. The surrounding park includes Lake Hiawatha, Winnewissa Falls, and Leaping Rock, a twenty-three-foot natural column.

For all the drama of frontier life, there was never any trouble at Fort Snelling, the first military outpost in Minnesota built in 1820 to ward off Indian attacks. It is now a historic site near Mendota, an early settlement built at the spot where the Mississippi and Minnesota rivers meet. Mendota's chief attractions today are two old homes, one of which served as the first capitol of the territory. The oldest of the two was built in 1835 by Henry Hastings Sibley, who was to become Minnesota's first governor. It has been restored and some of his original furnishings are on display there. The house next door was the home of Sibley's fellow fur trader, Jean Baptiste Faribault. It is colonial in style, and today contains some of the original furnishings as well as Indian artifacts, including some outstanding examples of artistic beadwork.

SPECIAL EVENTS

St. Paul has a positive attitude toward winter which is about the only kind to have, considering how cold and snowy it gets in those parts. In fact, the city goes overboard to show just how much fun you can have when the temperature is near zero and the snow is piled high. It stages a winter carnival to end all winter carnivals—two whole weeks of sled dog races, ski jump competitions, ice fishing contests, parades, tobogganing, the crowning of a carnival queen, and the finish of the famous Winnipeg "400" Snowmobile Race. All that activity doesn't change the fact that it's mighty cold up there during the last week in January and the first week in February, but it sure takes your mind off it.

The St. Paul carnival may be the biggest and best of Minnesota's winter celebrations, but it is far from the only one. There are too

PLATE 16 Paul Bunyan and Babe the Blue Ox greet visitors entering Bemidji, Minnesota.

PLATE 17 The world's largest open-pit iron mine, in Hibbing, Minnesota.

PLATE 18 The Mayo Clinic in Rochester, Minnesota, operates one of the world's largest programs for medical residents.

PLATE 19 Memorial to a by-gone era. St. Joseph, Missouri.

PLATE 20 A paddleboat on the Mississippi River recalls
the stories of Mark Twain.

PLATE 21 Mark Twain's boyhood home in Hannibal, Missouri.

PLATE 22 The nightlights of St. Louis, with its graceful Gateway Arch.

PLATE 23 Giant stalactite in the Ohio Caverns in West Liberty.

PLATE 24 Professional Football Hall of Fame in Canton, Ohio.

PLATE 25 Cleveland's mall and convention center.

PLATE 26 Perry's Victory and International Peace Memorial on South Bass Island in Lake Erie.

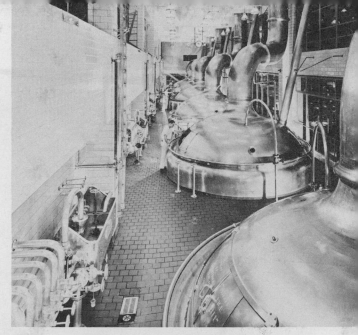

PLATE 27 Inside one of Milwaukee's breweries.

PLATE 28 An aerial view of Riverfront Stadium and the Cincinnati skyline.

PLATE 29 The wooded hills of Little Norway, Wisconsin.

PLATE 30 The imposing State Capitol in Madison, Wisconsin, is set on a hill in a wooded park.

many snowmobile races to count and any number of ice-fishing and ski-jumping contests. The town of Winona added an ice-sculpture contest to its winter carnival to challenge the artistic types who don't ski.

Not to be outdone by St. Paul's boast that it is the home of the nation's biggest winter carnival, Minneapolis makes a big splash every summer with its Aquatennial, which it claims is the biggest *summer* festival in the United States. For ten busy days in July the town revolves around the festivities—240 different events on land and water. And just to make sure everybody hears about it, they choose a queen each year and send her on a world-wide tour to promote the city.

Minnesotans celebrate or commemorate all sorts of. things that have nothing to do with the weather. Every year the little town of Northfield re-enacts its most famous crime—Jesse James's robbery of its bank in 1876. The James gang shot up the town after robbing the bank and killing one of the clerks. A posse gave chase and didn't come back until it had killed three of the outlaws and captured three others. They didn't get either Jesse or his brother Frank, who were forced to lie low and to give up robbing banks in the area. Northfield is still proud of its role in this episode and every September stages "Defeat of Jesse James Days" to make sure that nobody forgets what happened.

New Ulm, the town settled by German immigrants and devastated by the Sioux in their rampage of 1862, is a happier place now. It pays a boisterous tribute to its Teutonic heritage with a Polka Festival every July. It's one big party with everyone dancing in the streets to the music of two dozen polka bands and taking time out to sip beer from the local brewery and sample German sausages.

Rivaling New Ulm's Polka Festival is the annual Svenskarnas Dag in June at Mendota's Minnehaha Park. Thousands of Minnesotans of Swedish ancestry gather here for folk dancing and folk songs.

Even Minnesota's Indians get in on the summer festivities. At Pipestone Monument the Sioux stage the "Song of Hiawatha Pageant" on consecutive weekends in July and August. July 4 brings the annual powwow at Red Lake and all summer long the Indians hold powwows at Walker up north.

Add to that the rodeos, fishing contests, ethnic festivals of all descriptions, arts and crafts shows, Bemidji's Paul Bunyan Festival in June, Duluth's annual International Folk Festival in August, the Minnesota State Fair just before Labor Day, and it's hard to find an uneventful day on the Minnesota summer calendar.

P.D.

CHRONOLOGY

1660   Two French fur traders, Pierre Esprit Radisson and Médart Chouart, Sieur de Groseilliers, are believed to have visited what is now Minnesota.

1679   Daniel Greysolon, Sieur Duluth, explored Minnesota's Lake Superior shores.

1680   Father Louis Hennepin, a Belgian missionary, became the first white man to see what he named St. Anthony Falls.

1762   France granted its lands west of the Mississippi, including part of today's Minnesota, to Spain.

1763   The French, defeated by the British in the French and Indian War, relinquished their lands east of the Mississippi.

1800   Spain gave its lands west of the Mississippi back to France.

1803   With the Louisiana Purchase the United States acquired all the land west of the Mississippi, including parts of Minnesota.

1805   Lieutenant Zebulon Pike was sent to Minnesota to establish American authority.

1821   The first settlers arrived to farm in Minnesota.

1823   The steamboat *Virginia* reached Minnesota via the Mississippi.

1838   The Sioux and the Chippewa signed treaties with the United States, opening much of Minnesota for white settlement.

1849   The Minnesota Territory was created.

1858   Minnesota became the thirty-second state.

1862   The Sioux destroyed Minnesota frontier towns in their last attempt to recover their hunting lands.

1884   Iron was discovered in the Vermilion Range.

1889   Dr. William Mayo and his sons established their clinic at Rochester, Minnesota.

1894   Iron was discovered in the Mesabi Range.

         A forest fire swept across eastern Minnesota killing four hundred persons and destroying $1 million in property.

1911   Another rich source of iron was discovered in the Cuyuna Range.

1918   A forest fire took four hundred lives and destroyed $25 million in property in Carlton and St. Louis counties.

1930s   Minnesota's economy was devastated by the Great Depression.

1943   Minnesota's iron mines produced 84 million tons of ore, an all-time record.

1955   The first taconite processing plant opened in Silver Bay.

1961   A special loan fund was created to aid the economically depressed northeast mining areas.

1967   A metropolitan council was created to promote industrial development in the seven-county Twin Cities area.

1968   Minnesota's Democratic Senator Hubert H. Humphrey lost his race for President of the United States.

1971   The state legislature passed a revenue-sharing bill to return tax money to municipalities and school districts.

1972   Hubert Humphrey won more than four million primary votes but failed to win the Democratic presidential nomination.

1974   The nation mourned the death of Charles A. Lindbergh, a native of Little Falls, Minnesota.

1975   The worst blizzard of the century occurred in January.

1976   Walter F. Mondale, a Democratic senator from Minnesota, was elected U. S. Vice President.

1978   The nation mourned the death of the renowned statesman Hubert H. Humphrey.

1979   In a year which saw state department budgets scrutinized with unusual care, the legislative appropriation for the Tourism Bureau's fiscal year was $1,271,500. Tourism-industry support came from key legislators as well as tourism-field leaders.

MISSOURI

MANY Missourians are often asked by non-Missourians two major questions:

"Do you pronounce it 'Muhzooree' or 'Muhzooruh'?"

Missourians pronounce it either way!

The other, "How did Missouri become known as the Show Me State?"

Missouri Congressman Willard Duncan Vandiver in 1899 became irked at a colleague boastfully extolling the virtues of his state, and Vandiver acidly commented, "I come from a country that raises corn, cotton, cockleburs, and Democrats. I'm from Missouri and you've got to show me."

The precivilization beginnings of Missouri were buried hundreds of feet beneath the present surface millions of years ago when the entire continent, now known as North America, lay under a vast ocean.

Thousands of miles of rainbow-hued lilies covered the ocean floor. The waters began to recede and with air and enormous pressure combined to form coal, marble, limestone, iron ore, and various other minerals that would be discovered millenniums later.

The eons passed and the northern half of Missouri was covered with ice during the glacial periods. The ice age, which began about one million years ago, was characterized by periodic melting retreats. Melting was slow, however, and the final retreat occurred some 25,000 years ago. These huge glaciers gouged out the Great Lakes and thousands of smaller lakes and canyons.

Today lush forests and rich meadows cover a large part of the state and swift streams tumble through the woody and hilly regions.

And today the citizens of the Show Me State contend that it has shown the world through such distinguished men as Harry S Truman, John J. Pershing, Omar Bradley, U. S. Grant, Mark Twain, George Washington Carver, Thomas Hart Benton, and the rugged and colorful Kit Carson, Jim Bridger, Daniel Boone, and, of course, Jesse James!

THE LAND

Missouri has four main natural topographical regions. One includes almost the entire area north of the Missouri River where the ice sheet left a fertile deposit of soil.

The second region, the Osage Plains, consists of low-rolling prairies in western Missouri that were never covered by ice.

The Ozark Plateau is the third region, the largest land area in the state, which consists of forested hills and Taum Sauk Mountain, 1,772 feet high; about 10,000 springs, the largest gushing 800 million gallons daily; numerous rivers and man-made lakes, including the Lake of the Ozarks, which is one of the largest artificial lakes in the nation.

The fourth region, the Alluvial Plain, in deep southeast Missouri, is known as the "Bootheel," because a portion projects itself south of the normal east-to-west southern boundary. It is a thick layer of mud, sand, and decayed stump roots and very productive of cotton, soybeans, and rice.

Over 50 per cent of Missouri's borders are formed by riverbanks. Most of the larger cities including St. Louis and Kansas City and more than half of the state's population are located on either the Missouri or the Mississippi River. Missouri is located in the center of the huge Missouri-Mississippi-Ohio watershed that drains about 40 per cent of the nation's total area.

The Missouri River, second-longest river in the nation, bisects the state from west to east. Including the headwaters, the Missouri River is 2,714 miles long. Its nickname is the "Big Muddy," because it transports a large load of sediment and drops it wherever and whenever the current wills. This creates the rich bottom land.

Because the Missouri flows erratically across almost 3,000 miles, both humorous and serious comments have been made. One river historian wrote, "Of all the variable things in creation, the most uncertain of all are the action of a jury, the state of a woman's mind and the course of the Missouri River!"

Marquette said upon viewing the river for the first time, "I have never seen anything more frightful."

Missouri

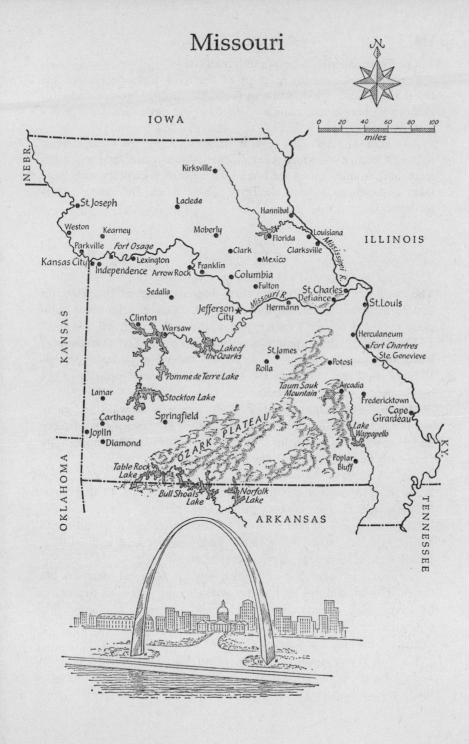

The Sioux called it "a furious and mad river."

Concerning the muddy make-up of the river, farmers contend it is too thick to drink and too thin to plow! But it does provide water for millions of people and millions of acres, plus navigation for a heavy towboat traffic.

Although Missouri lies several hundred miles from the nearest ocean or lake, it has more miles of navigable streams than any other state, and, in addition to the Lake of the Ozarks, includes such large lakes as Stockton, Pomme de Terre, Table Rock, Bull Shoals, Norfork, and Wappapello.

CLIMATE

The Missouri climate is almost as unpredictable as the Missouri River and it has generated the comment, "One should never complain about Missouri's weather; just wait awhile and it will change!"

The diversity of the climate is emphasized by the fact that one may travel in a straight line 450 miles from the warm and almost subtropical southeast corner to the chilling, wind-swept prairies of the northwest corner near Nebraska.

Within the state there occur periodic extremes of wind and calm, heat and cold, drought and flood. Because it is between the northern and southern weather belts of the country, Missouri's temperature frequently fluctuates between the two.

An indication of the wide variance is shown by the record temperatures of 118 degrees at Clinton in 1936 and minus 40 degrees at Warsaw in 1905. They are only thirty miles apart.

The state's general climate may be summarized as a humid continental type, consisting of a fairly long summer and a five-to-six-month winter, marked by capricious temperatures.

Normality is somewhat of a misnomer in Missouri weather, but "normal" temperatures in January will average about 33 degrees at St. Louis and 30 degrees at Columbia and Kansas City. Normal July temperatures will average about 80 degrees at St. Louis and 78 to 79 degrees at Columbia and Kansas City.

Rainfall averages are uncertain, about 50 inches in the southeast and 32 inches in the northwest. About one third of the annual rainfall occurs in the spring months.

The snowfall average is from 18 to 20 inches, sometimes higher north of the Missouri River where the snow remains on the ground longer than in southern Missouri.

Records reveal that about every ten years there will be one severe drought and one disastrous flood, the former state-wide, the latter regional.

Missouri is subject to tornadoes, usually in the hot summer months, but the state, through the United States Meteorological Service, has an excellent warning system.

THE MISSOURIANS

For many generations the United States of America has been referred to as a "melting pot" because of the tremendous ethnic diversity of the population. The same appellation might be applied with the same reasoning to the state of Missouri.

The first settlers were Indians. It is believed they came to the continent, and eventually Missouri, between 10,000 and 25,000 years ago. Indian artifacts and bones have been dated beyond the 10,000-year figure.

The first white men to enter the territory were Spanish conquistadors from the Southwest in the 1500s, but they did not remain long. More than 150 years later Catholic missionaries came from Canada. About 1700 the first white settlers, French miners who lived at Kaskaskia, Illinois, crossed the Mississippi River daily to mine lead in Missouri.

This commuting continued until 1723 when large groups came with some degree of permanency to join the camp of Philippe Renault who came from Paris to mine lead on a grand scale. He brought two hundred miners and laborers, stopping en route at Santo Domingo to buy five hundred Guinea Negroes.

The Renault camp at Fort de Chartres was near a settlement of a few houses that became Ste. Genevieve. Within a short time Renault's crew was mining 1,500 pounds of lead daily. He made a fortune and in 1742 sold his holdings and returned to France.

The founding of St. Louis in 1764 and other Mississippi River towns brought settlers to the territory but not in any large numbers. The Louisiana Purchase in 1803, the Lewis and Clark Expedition, and the explorations of Captain Zebulon Pike, Lieutenant Stephen H.

Long, and John C. Frémont focused anew attention on the area and brought more settlers from the East and Southeast.

Captain William Becknell and his men of Franklin, Missouri, opened the Santa Fe Trail in 1821, which also provided added impetus to immigration.

In 1845 and 1846 the potato famine struck Ireland, and approximately 50,000 people immigrated to this country. Missouri received its share of the brawny Irishmen who helped to build the rail lines westward and add a volatile fillip to the ethnic diversity.

In 1848 and 1849 revolutionary movements for a German Union, and liberty, erupted and differences between Germany and Prussia caused the old Bund to be restored. General dissatisfaction grew and many thousands of Germans immigrated to America. Again, Missouri proved to be a magnet. Many Germans already in Missouri wrote glowing letters to friends and relatives in the fatherland which somewhat accelerated the movement overseas.

In the decades after 1850 thousands of Italians immigrated to this country and many of them settled in St. Louis, Kansas City, and smaller Missouri cities and towns. The general immigration movement in the last half of the nineteenth century also included British, French, Chinese, and people from middle European countries.

Missouri's ethnic heritage is remarkably diversified. In the major cities and smaller towns there are descendants of immigrants from a score of nations, both European and Asian.

As you can see, Missouri is indeed a melting pot. Just as there is no typical American, so there is no typical Missourian.

HISTORY

Although the conquistadors may have entered the territory now known as Missouri, the actual record of history for this state began in 1673 when Fathers Jacques Marquette and Louis Jolliet sailed down the Mississippi River and discovered the mouth of the Missouri River.

And, in 1682, Robert Cavelier, Sieur de La Salle, paddled down the Mississippi and claimed the Mississippi Valley for France, which included present-day Missouri. There followed a trickle of fur trappers, Catholic missionaries, and explorers.

In 1702 Jesuit priests established a mission at what is now St.

Louis and about that same time French miners from Illinois began working Missouri lead mines.

In February of 1764 St. Louis was founded by Pierre Laclède, a New Orleans merchant and fur trader, and his fourteen-year-old stepson, Auguste Chouteau. The two had visited the site earlier and became convinced that a trading post should be established there. On the second trip they brought twenty-eight workers from New Orleans and landed at what is now the foot of Market Street in St. Louis. Laclède's vision went beyond a trading post and he decided to establish a town there, which he named for King Louis IX of France. The first settlers were French and Spaniards, plus a few Indians and Negroes. By 1800 the population was 949 and the town was formally incorporated in 1808.

The event that was to have a tremendous impact on St. Louis, as well as the rest of the immediate area, was the Louisiana Purchase. President Jefferson decided to buy New Orleans and as much of the Floridas as possible to give American manufacturers and producers a peaceful door to the Gulf and then to European markets.

James Monroe and Robert Livingston were dispatched to France to try to buy the land. Their negotiating coincided with Napoleon's need of a healthy sum for a possible war with England.

The Americans were stunned when France's Foreign Minister asked if the United States would be interested in buying all of Louisiana, as the vast territory was referred to then.

The Americans asked how much. Fifteen million dollars!

There were no transatlantic telephones or wireless then and the Americans felt Napoleon might renege if they depended on ships for communication with Washington. Time was of the essence. More negotiation followed. Finally a treaty was signed.

On March 10, 1804, at St. Louis, Captain Amos Stoddard, forty-two years old, of Connecticut, a veteran of the Revolutionary War and the Army's official representative at New Orleans, formally took over the vast territory in the name of the United States. He was the President's personal selection to perform this important mission.

The westward gates of empire, with unestimated billions in natural resources, now swung open. And Missouri, or Upper Louisiana, would be vitally affected.

There were about 10,000 citizens in the territory, mainly French with a goodly number of Spaniards and some Anglo-Saxons. The melting pot was bubbling and settlers began trickling in from Ken-

major competition, the railroads, that would eventually win. In 1859 the Hannibal and St. Joseph Lines became the first to be completed across the state.

But not everything could be rosy for Missouri, nor the nation. The Missouri Compromise became one fuse and the Dred Scott decision another. Scott, a slave, sued for his freedom in Missouri and the case went to the United States Supreme Court, which held that because he was a slave he could not file a federal court suit.

The Civil War, that fratricidal conflict, cut down the nation's young manhood. Although Missouri was admitted as a slave state, it resisted all efforts to secede or to become part of the Confederacy. It furnished 109,000 men to the Union armies, more than several "Northern" states larger than Missouri, and 30,000 Missourians to the Confederacy. More battles were fought on Missouri soil than all other states except Virginia and Tennessee.

The Industrial Revolution burgeoned and affected the economy of the nation following the Civil War. Inventions that changed the lives of Missourians, and of the entire world, included the telegraph, wireless, telephone, incandescent lamp, horseless carriage, and diesel engine.

After the Civil War the use of farm machinery increased. During the last three decades of the century the machines included the cultivator, gang plow, tractor, combines, huge drills, reaping and harvesting machines, harrows, and others. Electricity came to the farms around the turn of the century.

This mechanical revolution drove large segments of farm labor to the cities, and the first movement toward formation of labor unions in Missouri occurred in St. Louis. The Workingmen's Union was organized there in 1864 and two years later published its first newspaper, *The Industrial Advocate*. One year later the General Assembly passed a law setting eight hours as the daily maximum for workers. It soon became virtually unenforceable. The union movement languished in Missouri for several years. The American Federation of Labor was formed in 1881 and the union cause began to revive in Missouri during the late 1880s.

Thus, there developed a rather unseen competition for economic progress between industry and agriculture in Missouri, but today the state may be fairly evenly divided between the two. And in recent years there has been some sort of "marriage" that is termed "agribusiness."

The Spanish-American War of 1898 placed the United States in the position of a colonial power for the first time. It vitally affected Missouri. At El Caney the courageous conduct of a young army lieutenant caught the attention of his superiors. He was a Missourian, John J. Pershing.

Missouri furnished 8,083 volunteers and 3,000 regular troops, topped by only four other states. The University of Missouri set a national record by sending one fourth of its total enrollment into the armed forces.

One of Admiral Dewey's crack gunners was A. L. Smith, of Sedalia, Missouri. Edward P. Stanton, of St. Louis, raised the first American flag over Manila, Arthur L. Willard, of Kirksville, raised the first flag on Cuban soil, and Frank Fulton, of St. Louis, did it atop San Juan Hill.

Missourians again distinguished themselves in World War I. At the tomb of Lafayette in Paris, General Pershing saluted and commented, "Lafayette, we are here."

In the 1920s, Missourians along with millions of other Americans enjoyed their affluence but in the next decade many sold pencils and apples on street corners.

Missouri passed its $60-million highway program in 1921, and during the 1930s its legislature enacted important laws and established the Highway Patrol, one of the first in the nation, despite dire threats it would make Missouri a police state. It has become one of the finest among the states.

Missouri was one of the first states to enact a broad social security program which included old age pensions, aid to dependent children and the blind, and relief for the unemployed and unemployables.

Missouri voters also adopted a constitutional amendment that established a Conservation Commission which restored and preserved the state's wildlife and forest resources.

In 1940 the voters adopted another constitutional amendment that set up the Missouri Non-Partisan Court Plan. This removed the judges of the Missouri Supreme Court and Circuit Courts of St. Louis and Kansas City from politics.

Missourians again displayed their wartime courage when World War II occurred. Omar Bradley, of Moberly, Missouri, commanded the largest army ever to serve under an American, which invaded France on D-Day, June 6, 1944. That army contained 221,000 Missourians. Lieutenant Commander Mildred H. McAfee, of Parkville, became the first commander of the WAVES.

In 1965 Missouri voters approved the amendment allowing a governor to serve two consecutive four-year terms. (Governor Phil Donnelly served two terms but they were not consecutive.)

INDUSTRY

Missouri is among the top twelve states in terms of the number of industry-manufacturing plants and their employees.

According to industrial economists, this is due to the state's abundant electrical power and water, a favorable climate and topography, a central location with tremendous rail, river, highway, and air facilities, enough coal to last one hundred years, the largest lead deposits in the nation, and unestimable iron-ore deposits.

Before the Industrial Revolution most of Missouri's so-called manufacturing was done in the home—spinning, weaving, and the making of shoes, clothing, and furniture.

The first manufacturing done outside the home was the grinding of grain. Water power was plentiful and by 1839 there were 64 steam flour mills and 640 gristmills in Missouri.

The first move toward both industry and manufacturing, as such, occurred in 1827 when Joseph Murphy, an Irish immigrant blacksmith, built his first wagon for the Santa Fe trade. He sold it for $27. Murphy then began turning out wagons on a mass-production basis. During the westward trek he built 100,000 wagons. Pioneers heading for Santa Fe, California, or Oregon liked his sturdy wagons. The United States Army was one of his best customers.

The manufacturing of lead products began sometime in the late 1700s. Shot for the War of 1812 was produced at Herculaneum. Moses Austin mined lead and turned out lead products at Potosi. Associated with him was his son, Stephen Austin, who would later become the "Father of Texas."

Today some of the nation's largest industrial plants are located in St. Louis and Kansas City. These two cities contain two thirds of the 7,000 factories in Missouri, with approximately 400,000 employees. In St. Louis the McDonnell-Douglas Aircraft Corporation has 36,000 employees. In addition to producing airplanes, it has made fourteen space capsules for the astronauts.

One of the three largest beer-producing companies in the nation, Anheuser-Busch Brewery, is located in St. Louis.

In Kansas City the largest employer is the Trans World Airlines employing 12,000 workers at its home base for world-wide overhaul and maintenance. The second-largest employer is Hallmark Cards, the world's largest greeting card maker, with 9,500 employees, including 500 artists. Kansas City also has three automobile assembly plants which, with those in St. Louis, sets Missouri up as the second-largest car producer among the states. Michigan, of course, is first.

Kansas City is also the nation's largest manufacturer of envelopes and a leader in farm equipment distribution and the development of underground storage space.

Something unique in the Middle West is the Midwest Research Institute, a multimillion-dollar organization in Kansas City that conducts scientific, technological, and nuclear laboratory tests and experiments for corporations and organizations in twelve states.

Missouri, in addition to turning out space capsules, also produces liquid propellant engines, solar batteries, material for launching pads, and special optical instruments for space flights. Two Kansas City engineering firms, with contracts in more than a score of foreign countries, did highly classified construction work at Cape Kennedy.

Throughout the state are cement plants, glassmaking companies, shoe factories, food-processing plants, clothing manufacturers, and factories for clay and metal products, furniture, leather goods, electrical machinery, chemicals, meat packing and transportation equipment, flour milling, and stoneware.

The state's principal wood products are furniture, railroad ties, barrels and barrel staves, business buildings and residential homes, and gunstocks. There are over 200 furniture making plants in Missouri and 650 lumber mills and wood-products plants.

The transportation equipment production—planes, automobiles, trucks, golf carts, etc.—ranks second in the number of employees, close to 60,000 and a payroll around $300 million.

Another major industry in Missouri is the manufacture of various electrical machinery, including control devices, meters, motors, generators, switches of all types, and wiring equipment. Several of the 150 factories in this category are among the largest in the nation.

Missouri has the largest firebrick and refractory plants in the world at Mexico. Also in the state are 190 factories turning out leather goods and shoes. Chemicals, fertilizers, and allied products are turned out at 395 plants by their 20,000 employees.

Printing and publication is also a major business. There are 1,200 plants in Missouri that include newspapers and commercial printing, lithography, periodicals, textbooks, catalogues, pamphlets, and handbills. The two major cities account for the bulk of this production.

AGRICULTURE

Agriculture in Missouri today is second in the economic yardstick, but a close one to industry and manufacturing.

The Indians were the first farmers in Missouri. They were followed by the French, whose principal crops were corn, wheat, beans, pumpkins, barley, oats, apples, and melons. They also raised a large variety of livestock.

The soil was so rich that the French only scratched the surface and dropped in the seed, just as the Indians had done. Little or no attention was given the crop from planting to harvesting.

The American farmers from Virginia, Kentucky, and other southeastern states brought new standards of cultivation. They moved into the wilderness and squatted on public lands. They built their own houses, barns, corrals, and furniture from timber, and then planted and harvested their crops while fighting off Indians.

Agriculture was the dominant occupation in almost all of the frontier settlements and the developing nation until new inventions and industrial technocracy burst upon the economic scene.

Corn is the most valuable cash crop in Missouri. The 1976 calendar year production was 170 million bushels, slightly more than the previous year, despite low rainfall in some areas. For many years Missouri farmers have planted about one third of their acreage in corn.

The 1976 soybean crop produced 86 million bushels and the cotton production was 200,000 bales. Wheat production was 54,450,000 bushels. Kansas City is the hard winter wheat capital of the nation, and the third-largest general grain market.

Other Missouri crops of note include oats, barley, sorghum, alfalfa, clover, timothy, and lespedeza. Tobacco, growing along the western Missouri border north of Kansas City, is a multimillion-dollar crop.

Some of the largest strawberry fields in the nation are in southern

Missouri. Grapes thrive profusely. Wine making is both a home and commercial enterprise in Missouri. The 1976 crop produced approximately 100,000 gallons. The crop is sometimes difficult to estimate because the home makers of wine have no reporting agency.

There are apple, peach, and pear orchards throughout the state. Cherries, raspberries, blackberries, dewberries, and loganberries are widely cultivated, and watermelons are a major crop.

Thousands of acres are planted annually in potatoes, sweet potatoes, sweet corn, beans, peas, onions, squash, cabbage, carrots, and other vegetables.

The raising of beef cattle and hogs is a very profitable enterprise in Missouri. The abundance of water, grazing grass, hay, corn, and small grain for feeding purposes shrinks production costs.

The West Plains area in south-central Missouri is the nation's feeder pig capital. Missouri produced 3 million hogs in 1975, for a value of $100 million, and slightly topped that for 1976.

Missouri is one of the top ten states in dairy cows. The largest dairy complex in the world is in the Springfield area in southwest Missouri which processes over one million pounds of milk daily, in addition to turning out ice cream, butter, cheese, and powdered, condensed, and evaporated milk.

Poultry production is another major economy in Missouri. In 1976 sales totaled almost $100 million from over 100,000 flocks and 200 hatcheries. Almost 2 billion eggs were laid and 40 million broilers produced. Turkey production was around 5 million.

A College of Agriculture was established at the University of Missouri at Columbia in 1870, one of the first in the nation. Norman J. Colman, a Missourian, was the first U. S. Secretary of Agriculture.

NATURAL RESOURCES

The major categories of Missouri's diversified natural resources are arable land, minerals, forests, and wildlife.

More than twenty-one different kinds of minerals are found in 107 of the state's 114 counties.

Lead mining is second to agriculture in Missouri. It began around 1700 near Ste. Genevieve. In 1975 Missouri mined 400,000 tons of lead, which was 79 per cent of the national total. The known lead deposits will last more than half a century.

The University of Missouri School of Mines at Rolla was opened in 1871. It is located in a mining area, operates an experimental mine, has a nuclear reactor, and ranks among the ten top engineering colleges in the nation.

Iron ore ranks next to lead in volume production. Hematite, an iron ore, was discovered in 1815 at Arcadia, and in 1826 the first furnace was built at St. James.

There are large deposits of iron ore in Washington County, Missouri—many of the deposits are 1,800 feet thick. The reserves have been estimated at between 10 and 25 billion tons.

Coal is another leader in Missouri. It has been discovered in fifty counties. Reserves have been estimated at 85 billion tons.

Missouri's major zinc-producing region is in the southwest area near Joplin and Carthage. It is found in smaller deposits in central Missouri.

Copper is mined in the state but in small amounts. The main deposits are in Shannon and Ste. Genevieve counties. Germanium, a rare metal used mainly in transistors, is found in rather small pockets near zinc-ore areas.

Cobalt is mined near Fredericktown and has a variety of uses, especially in jet engines, in magnets, and the medical profession. If a cobalt isotope is added to a nuclear device, it creates a deadly radioactive agent. Or, the bomb! It is believed that Missouri has produced more cobalt than any other state but production figures are a highly classified security secret.

Missouri mines small amounts of pyrite, manganese, and tungsten. It is one of the largest producers of limestone used in highway construction, buildings, smelting, cement, and rock wool.

Missouri ranks second in the mining of barite, or "tiff," which is used in the drilling for oil. Barium, a derivative, is used in rubber, paper, and glass manufacturing.

From limestone comes cement and Missouri is a major producer of cement. In recent years the average produced has been between 4 and 6 million tons annually, valued at approximately $100 million. The world's largest rotary kiln is at Clarksville, Missouri.

Missouri also mines large quantities of marble, mainly Carthage marble, known for its gleaming white attractiveness. It is mined near Carthage and used throughout the nation. The Missouri capitol at Jefferson City is constructed of Carthage marble.

Missouri also has a very unusual natural resource that is always alive and kicking—the Missouri mule! For well over a century Missouri has been the mule capital of the world. In the early 1820s Captain Becknell and his men brought back jackasses from Santa Fe for breeding purposes. Today, Missouri is famed for its breeding of sturdy mules.

About one third of Missouri is forest land, or approximately 15 million acres. The state has twice as much forest cover as the combined total in Kansas, Iowa, Nebraska, and Illinois.

Missouri's forests played an important role in the early history of the state, providing log cabins, corrals, barns, outbuildings, and furniture for the settlers.

There is forest growth, large and small, in every Missouri county. Shannon County has the largest acreage. Other large forest growth is found in the Ozark region and along the Missouri and Mississippi rivers.

The shortleaf pine is the main softwood. The hardwoods include elm, walnut, maple, cottonwood, the various oaks, hickory, and ash. Missouri leads in the growing of walnut trees and in the production of walnut wood items. Tree thieves concentrate on walnut because of its higher value.

In 1937 Missouri citizens approved creation of a Conservation Commission long before the ecologists launched their crusade. The commission is charged with the responsibility of restoring and preserving the state's wildlife and forest resources. Commission agents distribute several million tree seedlings annually and launch a broad program to assist farmers and others to promote forest growth.

The commission has also played a major role in protecting wildlife and in propagating the species that were doomed to extinction. Annual quotas were established for the killing of deer, wild turkeys, geese, ducks, quail, and various other game. Hunting seasons were set in designated areas. These protective measures resulted in increased reproduction.

The commission also attacked the fish problem in a similar manner. Size limits were set and the number that could be caught also established. Fish hatcheries were launched.

As a result of this slow but successful program Missouri has become a national mecca for hunters and fishermen. In 1975 the state issued 500,000 hunting permits and 900,000 fishing permits.

Swan Lake in Chariton County, Missouri, is regarded as the Canada goose capital of the nation by virtue of the flight stopovers. The peak goose population in 1975 was 196,000.

CITIES

Ste. Genevieve, named after the patron saint of Paris, is the oldest city in Missouri, the oldest permanent settlement west of the Mississippi River. It has many old homes including those of Commandant Jean Baptiste Valle and that of Mons. Ribault, both more than two centuries old. The French culture is evident, predating the antebellum period by a century.

The date of the founding of Ste. Genevieve has generated some historic disagreement. Some historians place it at 1723 when Philippe Renault from Paris began working the lead mines with his French laborers and Guinea Negroes. Even before that there existed a small settlement. The year 1732 has been mentioned, also 1735. The latter date apparently has some official precedence because the city observed its bicentennial in 1935.

St. Louis, the largest city in Missouri, was founded in February 1764 by Pierre Laclède Liguest and Auguste Chouteau, merchants and traders from New Orleans. Their original plan was to establish a fur-trading post but Laclède entertained more ambitious plans to build a town here. He did this and the town was incorporated in 1808.

The French influence initially predominated but as the city grew the citizenry included Germans, English, Italians, Scots, and Spaniards.

The 1970 United States Census listed the population of St. Louis at 622,236.

Today St. Louis is a city of vast manufacturing enterprises, the largest raw fur market in the world, a leading grain market, and one of the nation's chief hog-shipping centers. It is also a major center of culture, including the arts and architecture, education, music, literature, and painting.

The Great Cathedral in St. Louis contains mosaics among the most beautiful in the world. Only in Italy are there cathedrals with mosaics more exquisitely breath-taking.

St. Louis may well be considered a City of Flowers. The Missouri Botanical Garden (Shaw's Garden) has 12,000 different plants and trees, one of the largest collections in this hemisphere. It also contains the world's first geodesic dome greenhouse.

The St. Louis Art Museum has a collection of Chinese bronzes, ceramics, paintings, several period rooms, and a Gothic court. The Jewel Box in Forest Park contains a cathedral of waterfalls and flowers.

Astronomers will be attracted to the McDonnell Planetarium in St. Louis, which can show star positions at any point in time and from any place on earth.

The city is rich in books. The St. Louis Mercantile Library, established in 1846, has a large collection of rare and current books, including parts of Auguste Chouteau's original journals. For many years the library possessed, among its many art treasures, 112 sketches by George Caleb Bingham, the famous Missouri artist of the last century. In the spring of 1976, after considerable negotiations, Missouri citizens contributed $1.8 million to buy the sketches. They will be placed on exhibition in various cities of the state.

The large Concordia Theological Seminary in St. Louis has many rare books on the Protestant Reformation.

At St. Louis University, founded in 1818 and the oldest Catholic University west of the Mississippi River, there is one of the most unusual libraries in the nation. Some 10 million pages of rare manuscripts were microfilmed at the Vatican Library in Rome and brought to St. Louis many years ago.

Both young and old devotees of aviation will enjoy the 10,000 items of memorabilia on Charles A. Lindbergh, who made the first solo flight across the Atlantic in 1927 in the *Spirit of St. Louis*. These objects are in the Missouri Historical Society at St. Louis.

Both the French and the Germans made major contributions in music at St. Louis. Several Germans launched the Philharmonic Society in 1859 and later founded the St. Louis Choral Society. This was followed by the present Symphony Orchestra.

There have been hundreds of beer garden songfests and the city once vied with New Orleans for the nebulous crown as the jazz capital of the nation. One of the most memorable and best known blues song is "St. Louis Blues," composed in 1914 by W. C. Handy. He followed this with "Beale Street Blues."

Nationally known by lovers of music and light opera is the Muny Opera of St. Louis, established in 1919, which seats 12,000 in an open-air amphitheater. It features Broadway shows, musical comedies, light operas, and varied performances by New York, Hollywood, and television personalities.

In the field of higher education in St. Louis, Washington University and St. Louis University are academically prominent. There are seven other institutions of higher learning in St. Louis.

The first public kindergarten in the nation was established in St. Louis in 1873, and the Manual Training School, launched in 1880, became a model for other American cities.

Kansas City's founders, unlike those of St. Louis, were mostly from the British Isles. Daniel Morgan Boone and others had trapped in that area around 1800 and by 1830 there were a few log cabins along the Missouri River.

The early settlers began calling the cluster of cabins, "Town of Kansas," after the Kansas River that flowed into the Missouri River. There are many who still believe that Kansas City, Missouri, was named after the state of Kansas, but the "Town of Kansas" blossomed in 1839, or twenty-two years before the Kansas Territory became a state.

Several years later, fourteen town incorporators paid $4,200 for 250 acres. Names such as Wilson, Caldwell, Collins, Chick, Tate, and Owens were among the Anglo-Saxon cofounders.

In 1853 the name was changed to "City of Kansas," and that soon became "Kansas City." It prospered early and fast as a trading community, a center for fur trappers, and a springboard to the West for pioneers heading for California, Oregon, Santa Fe, and other areas.

The 1970 United States Census listed the population of Kansas City at 507,087.

Today Kansas City is a city of trade, commerce, manufacturing, and a gateway to vast agricultural enterprises such as wheat, corn, and livestock.

Although the appellation "Cowtown" has carried a derogatory tone, the city has made vast strides in the arts in the past half century.

In the art and culture area in Kansas City, the William Rockhill Nelson Gallery of Art and the Mary Atkins Museum of Fine Arts are national attractions. The gallery structure, which also houses the museum, has an outstanding collection of oriental art including works from India, China, Japan, and Indochina; several period rooms; sculpture; and hundreds of paintings and prints.

In Kansas City a singing society was formed in 1853, a band in

1858, and a symphony orchestra in 1896. The present Philharmonic Orchestra began in 1933.

The Starlight Theater, located in Swope Park, was founded in 1951 and seats 7,500. Its performances are similar to those of the St. Louis Muny Opera.

In architecture the Kansas City Country Club Plaza has received national attention since it was built in 1920, becoming the first shopping center. A Spanish architectural motif prevails with fountains, statues, and tree-lined walks.

Kansas City is also a strong center of education. The University of Missouri campus there enrolls around 10,000 students. The University of Missouri was founded in 1839 at Columbia, Missouri, and is the oldest state university west of the Mississippi River. In addition to the main campus at Columbia and the one at Kansas City, there are others at Rolla and St. Louis. Total enrollment for the four is 50,000 students.

There are eight other institutions of higher learning in Kansas City including Rockhurst College, Avila College, several junior colleges, and the Kansas City Art Institute, which attracts students from other countries.

The Kansas City Public Library has 1,157,000 volumes, and the Linda Hall Library at the University of Missouri Kansas City has the largest collection of scientific-technological books and papers in the nation next to Harvard University. There are 500,000 volumes and 13,000 scientific journals in thirty-five languages at Linda Hall. Special security personnel guarded the library before and during World War II because it contained valuable information on the atom bomb. It brings students, scholars, and scientists from scores of foreign countries.

Independence, which abuts Kansas City, counts 111,662 people and is best known as the home of President Truman, and the Truman Library. More than a century ago it vied with Kansas City as the springboard for pioneers westward.

The Harry S Truman Library at Independence contains his official papers and many hundreds of books. It has brought between 300,000 and 400,000 visitors annually. Mr. Truman is buried in the courtyard of the library.

St. Joseph, fifty-five miles north of Kansas City, with a population of 72,891, competed with Kansas City and Independence for those going to California and Oregon. It was founded in 1826 by Antoine

Robidoux, soldier, trapper, trader, and one of several Robidouxes who achieved impressive records in settling the West.

Springfield, in southwest Missouri, with a population of 120,096, is the capital of the biggest dairy complex in the world and, historically, the site of one of the bloodiest battles of the Civil War.

Jefferson City is Missouri's capital, almost midway between St. Louis and Kansas City, whose population is some 32,500. It became the capital in 1826. The capitol of white Carthage marble is modeled after the Pennsylvania capitol at Harrisburg.

Columbia, with 58,804 population (not counting almost 30,000 university students), thirty miles north of Jefferson City, is another historic city.

The State Historical Society of Missouri at Columbia publishes and preserves information on Missouri history and has an extensive collection of rare books, maps, manuscripts, journals of exploration, newspapers, and paintings by George Caleb Bingham, Thomas Hart Benton, and other artists. The society was established in 1898 and now has 14,000 members, the largest of any state historical organization in the nation.

SPORTS AND RECREATION

It is doubtful if any state has two professional football teams and two professional baseball teams contending year after year for the top spot and sometimes winning it.

The St. Louis Cardinals baseball teams have won many pennants and World Series over the decades. The Cardinals football team has always been in contention in its league. Both play in Busch Stadium, which seats 49,000 fans.

The Kansas City Royals baseball team also has its share of loyal fans.

The Kansas City Chiefs football team has won two league championships the past ten years; in 1967 they lost 35–10 in the Super Bowl against the Green Bay Packers and in 1970 they defeated the Minnesota Vikings 23–7 in the Super Bowl.

The Harry S Truman Sports Complex in Kansas City is a $64-million project with separate sports fields. The football stadium seats 78,000 and the baseball stadium holds 42,000.

Football has been popular in almost all of Missouri's colleges and universities. The University of Missouri, always drawing about 60,000 fans when playing at home (Columbia), has been in the top ten teams nationally for most of the past twelve years and has won many conference titles the past thirty years. The annual and highly emotional battle between Missouri and Kansas universities is almost a replay of the Civil War!

Kansas City's basketball team, the Kings, has been in contention the past several years. The city's hockey team was discontinued in 1975 for a lack of support. St. Louis has a hockey team that is frequently in contention.

St. Louis and Kansas City, as well as the smaller cities and towns, sponsor baseball leagues for younger players which produce the stars for the big leagues.

Golf and tennis are other sports that are popular throughout the state. Missourians are avid about fishing and hunting. Under the long and constructive program by the Conservation Commission there is plenty of wild game, and in the numerous streams, rivers, and lakes there are over a hundred species of fish.

Mark Twain National Forest and Clark National Forest are located in Missouri. The state also has six state forests totaling 30,000 acres and state parks totaling 80,000 acres. These recreation, camping, and general tourist attractions drew 14 million visitors in 1975.

Boating, water-skiing, and other aquatic sports are popular on the state's several lakes.

Both major cities have many parks and playgrounds. Forest Park in downtown St. Louis contains 1,380 acres. Swope Park, just south of the city limits of Kansas City, has 1,386 acres. The two are among the largest metropolitan parks in the nation.

Thomas H. Swope, a Yale graduate, came to Kansas City around the turn of the century and became wealthy in real estate. When William Rockhill Nelson, founder of the Kansas City *Star,* began pushing mightily for parks and boulevards in Kansas City, Mr. Swope bought the large parcel of undeveloped land and gave it to the city. It has six hundred picnic tables, two golf courses, two lakes, many tennis courts, and a zoo with 250 mammals, 335 birds, and other species of animal life.

POINTS OF INTEREST

Missouri has a wealth of diversified attractions for persons of all ages plus the advantage of what might be termed "geographical accessibility," or easy to reach from anywhere!

Perhaps the most awesome attraction in St. Louis is the spectacular stainless-steel Gateway Arch, designed by Eero Saarinen, 630 feet high, on the Mississippi River front. It is the tallest man-made national monument in the nation and commemorates the opening of the West after the Louisiana Purchase. The supporting legs contain a train elevator to lift visitors to the top, which offers a fantastic view.

Other St. Louis tourist attractions include the birthplace of Eugene Field, the children's poet, and a three-story building as a museum and shrine to the writer.

On the Mississippi River front the Old Courthouse harks back to 1839, and the Manuel Lisa warehouse, no longer filled with furs, recalls the first decade of the 1800s. The National Museum of Transport reflects travel and transportation from the horse and oxen, the prairie schooner, canoe, flatboat and keelboat, and steamboat, train, automobile, and airplane to the space age.

Hallowed is the spot near the Old Courthouse where U. S. Grant freed his one and only slave and where Phoebe Couzins became the first woman United States marshal in the nation.

Jefferson Barracks Park rambles along the west bank of the Mississippi River. The barracks cloak memories of hundreds of thousands of American soldiers and the tribal ghosts of Chief Black Hawk who was imprisoned there in 1832 after the war bearing his name.

In Kansas City the Liberty Memorial to World War I war dead contains hundreds of wartime exhibits and the largest war mural in the world done by Kansas City artist Daniel MacMorris. The monument has a 216-foot-high shaft with an eternal flame on top. An elevator within the shaft takes visitors to the pinnacle.

Thomas Hart Benton, a Missouri native and one of the nation's great painters, died in January 1975 at his home in Kansas City. The home and adjoining studio are now national shrines. He painted the murals in the Missouri capitol at Jefferson City, many portraits of his close and long-time friend and crony, Mr. Truman, and the mural in the Harry S Truman Library at Independence.

Fort Osage stands on a Missouri River bluff a few miles east of Kansas City. It was the westernmost fortified trading post, built in 1808. All buildings have been restored as originally constructed. William Clark selected the site on his expedition. Nathan Boone directed construction.

Not all of the interesting tourist attractions in Missouri are in St. Louis and Kansas City.

There are many beautiful and graceful ante-bellum homes in Weston, Lexington, Mexico, and Louisiana. In Lexington one may visit the Civil War battlefield and stand in the trenches, or prowl through the Anderson house, now a museum, which was used as a hospital by both armies during and after the battle.

Watkins Mill, not far from Kansas City, also a national shrine, is a plantation dating back to pre-Civil War days. It contains old wooden gristmills and original weaving looms, blacksmith shops, and the restored home of the original owner.

At Arrow Rock State Park, eighty-five miles east of Kansas City, the tavern built in 1834 has been restored. It was the main lodging and watering place for travelers between St. Louis and Kansas City. The park contains the home built by pioneer artist George Caleb Bingham, a jail, seminary, courthouse, and old homes.

The Mark Twain State Park has the small home in which the writer was born. It was moved from nearby Florida and now serves as a museum. Samuel Clemens, otherwise known as Mark Twain, grew up in Hannibal and his home there is part of another museum. The whitewashed fence gleams brightly and near the Mississippi River one may wander in the cave where Tom Sawyer and Becky Thatcher got lost.

In an area of virgin prairie grass and a giant cottonwood tree at Laclede is the birthplace of General John Joseph Pershing. At Lamar, more than 100 miles south of Kansas City, stands the birthplace of President Harry S Truman. And at Clark, southeast of Moberly, one may see the birthplace of General Omar Nelson Bradley.

The George Washington Carver National Monument was established at Diamond, Missouri, in 1951 on 210 acres of the farm where he was born. It contains many exhibits.

Nathan Boone's home at Defiance, not far from St. Louis, is still in excellent condition and contains the room where Daniel Boone died plus the seven wooden mantels he carved. In the yard the Judgment Tree still stands where Daniel, as a local magistrate, dispensed justice.

Jesse James's home is preserved at Kearney, north of Kansas City, where he is buried. Dozens of tombstones have been chipped away over the decades by souvenir hunters.

SPECIAL EVENTS

Celebrating the New Year, one of the most colorful customs in Missouri is La Guignolée, which is observed by the French in Ste. Genevieve and, to a limited extent, in other Mississippi River towns where French culture predominates.

One of the year's big events in Kansas City is the American Royal Livestock and Horse Show, the largest saddle horse and livestock show in the United States. It is held in early October for ten days and attracts between 250,000 and 300,000 persons.

The show began in a tent in 1899 as a Hereford Fat Stock Show with 540 of the breed exhibited. The show gradually expanded to include prize-winning contests for various bovine breeds and horses, mules, sheep, and swine.

In the Royal show there are a dozen equestrian contests featuring the finest horses and most expert riders from all parts of the nation; there is also equestrian precision riding by military units, and harness racing.

A parade of forty bands and forty floats sprinkled with guest celebrities from Hollywood and television provides a nonfarm touch. A "Secret Six" committee selects the Belles of the American Royal and the queen who will reign over the Royal and the Coronation Ball.

The Future Farmers Association and the 4-H Clubs from throughout the nation hold their annual conventions during the Royal, bringing an estimated 15,000 young people to Kansas City.

The Missouri State Fair at Sedalia is held the latter part of August and is second to the American Royal in general agricultural importance in Missouri. It brings approximately 100,000 visitors. The Sedalia fairground is one of the largest in the nation and has a mile track for harness racing, stunts, and equestrian showmanship.

There are two large district fairs held annually, one at Cape Girardeau, covering several counties in southeast Missouri, and the other at Springfield in southwest Missouri, also a multiple-county event. There are annual fairs in many counties.

One of the most convivial events held annually in Missouri is the Hermann Maifest (May Festival). Hermann is on the Missouri River between St. Louis and Jefferson City and was founded in 1836 by the German Settlement Society of Philadelphia. The Maifest is usually held May 1–15 and the entire German town, plus thousands of visitors, revel in gaiety and fun, quaffing the brew, sipping the wine, and gourmandizing on ambrosial German food.

Following are other annual events in Missouri which attract both natives and visitors:

The Missouri Botanical Garden in St. Louis stages an orchid show in January.

The National Intercollegiate Basketball Tournament is held in Kansas City early every year. There are also college and university tournaments held in St. Louis.

The Missouri Valley Fox Hunters Association holds its annual hunt at Kearney September 12–15. There are field trials held in the Ozarks, not on any definite dates.

Turkey shoots are held in many communities, usually just before Thanksgiving.

Journalism Week is held the first week in May at the University of Missouri at Columbia. It was begun sixty years ago by the late Dr. Walter Williams, founder of the first School of Journalism at Missouri in 1908. Outstanding editors, writers, and political leaders address the graduating seniors and prizes for excellence in writing are awarded.

The annual Apple Blossom Festival is held the first week in May at St. Joseph; the Ozark Jubilee is at Poplar Bluff May 26–27; the Silver Skates Tournament takes place in St. Louis in December; and the Pony Express Commemoration is at St. Joseph the third week in April.

L.L.

CHRONOLOGY

1673   Jolliet and Marquette discovered the mouth of the Missouri River.

1700   Jesuits opened a mission at the present site of St. Louis.

1702   French miners crossed the Mississippi River to work mines near Ste. Genevieve.

1723   Renault and his miners and slaves arrived to work lead mines.

1735   First permanent settlement was established at Ste. Genevieve.

1764   Pierre Laclède and Auguste Chouteau founded St. Louis.

1780   George Rogers Clark defeated British-led tribes near St. Louis.

1798   Daniel Boone walked to Missouri from Kentucky.

1804–6   Captain Amos Stoddard took over Louisiana Purchase Territory. Lewis and Clark left St. Louis on their expedition to the Northwest.

1808   *Missouri Gazette,* state's first newspaper, began publication in St. Louis.

1811–12   Disastrous earthquake occurred in southeast Missouri.

1812   Territorial status was granted to Missouri.

Victories were scored near St. Louis in United States war with England.

1814   Battle of New Orleans; many Missourians involved.

1820   Missouri Compromise was enacted; a constitution was drawn up.

1821   Missouri was admitted to the Union.
Captain William Becknell opened the Santa Fe Trail.
Stephen Austin left to colonize area that became Texas.

1826   State capital moved from St. Charles to Jefferson City.

1835   Mark Twain born at Florida, Missouri.

1837   Six hundred Missourians went to Florida for Seminole War.

1839   University of Missouri was founded at Columbia.

1846–47   Missourians won important victories in United States war with Mexico.

1857   Dred Scott decision was upheld by the Supreme Court.

1861   Missouri refused to secede from the Union.

1873   First public kindergarten was opened in St. Louis.

1882   Jesse James was killed at St. Joseph.

1908   First School of Journalism in the world was opened at Columbia.

1917   General John J. Pershing led allied armies in World War I.

1921   Missouri launched its first big road-building program.

1927   Charles A. Lindbergh made first overseas solo flight to France.

1928   Republican National Convention was held at Kansas City.

1937   Voters approved Missouri Conservation Commission and Department.

1940   Voters established the nation's first Non-Partisan Court Plan that removed State Supreme and Circuit courts from politics.

1944   Brigadier General Omar Bradley assumed command of 1.3 million Army combat troops during World War II.

1945   Harry S Truman became President. Omar Bradley became a full general.

1946   Winston Churchill delivered famous "Iron Curtain" speech at Fulton.

1965   Legislature approved two consecutive four-year terms for governor.

       Gateway Arch in St. Louis was completed.

1972   St. Louis and Kansas City launched multibillion-dollar building projects in their respective downtown areas.

1976   Republican National Convention was held at Kansas City.

1979   The state celebrated its first Volksmarch (Walkfest) in Hermann. The non-competitive event—its goal was exercise and enjoyment—was enjoyed by people of all ages and was routed past historic and scenic areas. The Missouri Volksmarch was sanctioned by the International Federation of Popular Sports, formed in 1968, which now has fourteen member nations and sponsors events in which more than 8 million participate annually.

Ohio

MICHIGAN

LAKE ERIE

Ashtabula

Toledo
Maumee

CAN.
U.S.
Bass
Islands

Kelleys Island
Cedar Point

Chardon

Cleveland

Lorain
Elyria
Sandusky
South
Amherst
Bellevue

Twinsburg
Hudson
Kent

Warren
Youngstown

New Bavaria

Findlay

Barberton
Akron

Alliance

Van Wert

Bucyrus

Ashland

Massillon

Canton

Lisbon

Zoar
Village

Mansfield

Schoenbrunn
Village

Lima

Marion

Millersburg

Steubenville

New Bremen

Scioto R.

Greenville

Springfield

Columbus

Zanesville

London

Grove
City

Crooksville

Dayton
Miamisburg

Lancaster

Monroe

Wilmington

Circleville

Marietta

Lebanon

MOUND CITY
GROUP
NATIONAL
MONUMENT

Chillicothe

Hocking R.

Ohio R.

Cincinnati

WEST
VIRGINIA

Jackson

Thurman

Ohio R.

Portsmouth

Gallipolis

KENTUCKY

INDIANA

PENNSYLVANIA

Maumee R.

Portage R.

Sandusky R.

Huron R.

Vermilion

Cuyahoga R.

Little Miami R.

Miami R.

Muskingum R.

N

0   25   50   75
miles

OHIO

OHIO started out as farm country, then discovered its potential for industrial wealth. And like the nation as a whole, the state now has some regrets about having rushed into industrial development. The state is now restoring some of the sparkling waters muddied and oiled by industrial waste and rehabilitating a landscape ravaged by strip mines.

Over the years, people have moved off the land in Ohio, abandoning farms for factory work. Today, the overwhelming majority of the population live in great urban centers—cities like Cleveland, Cincinnati, Columbus, Akron, Toledo, and Dayton. But like the rest of the country, Ohio still has its share of quiet towns with elm-shaded streets where the pace of life has quickened very little in the jet age and where the old America and traditional values are very much alive.

Out in Monroe County, for instance, the Amish and Mennonites pursue the same quiet lives they've been leading for generations, shunning automobiles, farm machinery, and other labor-saving devices. They're one of the many ethnic groups still visible in Ohio. For the most part, the immigrants to this midwestern melting pot have assimilated so well that today distinctions barely exist.

That word "midwestern" is likely to raise a few hackles in Ohio. The state simply doesn't consider itself part of the Midwest. Of course, it doesn't look upon itself as eastern either, so it's probably best to concede that this state can't be characterized all that easily.

THE LAND

Ohio might be described as a bridge between the industrial East and the agricultural Midwest. Bordered on the north by Lake Erie and on the south by the Ohio River, the state shares some of the physical features of western Pennsylvania to the east and of the plains states to the west. Kentucky's famous blue grass country pokes into south-central Ohio, while to the north the state is edged by the plains that surround Lake Erie and once formed part of the lake bed itself.

Ohio's terrain was etched thousands of years ago by the movement of glaciers that once covered all but the southeastern corner of the state. Thanks to this Ice Age activity, most of the state is blessed with fertile soil and gently rolling hills. Only the southeastern reaches of the Allegheny Plateau, which spills into Ohio from Pennsylvania and West Virginia, were untouched by the glacial shifts. As a result, the rugged terrain in this part of the state lacks the fertile soil found in the north, but it does contain valuable deposits of clay, coal, natural gas, oil, and salt.

The lay of the land changes west of the plateau. Although hilly in spots (Ohio's highest point, Campbell Hill, which rises 1,550 feet above sea level, is in this area), the level, rich farm land beyond the plateau marks the eastern reaches of the vast central plains, the famed corn belt which sweeps west beyond the Mississippi. To the north, this plains area is joined by the fertile lowland that once formed part of the bed of Lake Erie. At its narrowest point in Ohio, the Great Lakes Plains area is only ten miles wide, but to the west, it broadens to encompass much of the Maumee Valley surrounding Toledo.

The Blue Grass Region which spills over into south-central Ohio from Kentucky is barely distinguishable from the central plains. In its level stretches farmers are able to grow tobacco, but the hills are less fertile and not suitable for farming.

Threading their way through the state toward Lake Erie in the north or the Ohio River in the south are 44,000 miles of rivers and streams. Roughly one third of the state is drained by the Cuyahoga, Grand Huron, Maumee, Portage, Sandusky, and Vermilion rivers, which empty into Lake Erie. The largest section, however, is drained by tributaries to the Ohio, which meanders westward from Pennsylvania toward the Mississippi. The 237-mile-long Scioto River is the largest tributary to the Ohio, followed by the Miami, Little Miami, Mahoning, Hocking, and Muskingum. Separating the two drainage areas is a series of low hills—a topographical divide that follows an irregular path from the northeastern section to the Indiana border on the west.

Ohio's waters also include more than 2,500 lakes, most of them carved by those Ice Age glacial movements. Although most of the lakes are tiny, a few cover more than forty acres. And as if nature hadn't been all that generous, more than 180 of the lakes are man-made, many of them built during the nineteenth century to feed the Ohio and Erie Canal connecting Cleveland with Portsmouth in the south or the Miami and Erie Canal linking Toledo and Cincinnati.

The 3,457 square miles of Lake Erie that fall within Ohio's boundaries are edged in the state by a 312-mile shore line that's mostly rocky apart from a few stretches of sandy beach and some good natural harbors. Ohio's principal lake ports are at Cleveland, at Toledo where the Maumee Bay flows into the lake, and at Sandusky where there's another bay. The lake itself has been heavily polluted by industrial waste, and, to date, the clean-up efforts haven't been successful enough to permit safe swimming and water sports in many areas.

CLIMATE

When it comes to weather, things are pretty routine in the Buckeye State. The winters are cold, but not impossibly so. January temperatures average 31 degrees. And it does tend to snow a lot but not nearly as much as it does in parts of neighboring Pennsylvania and Indiana. As for the summers, they're hot, though the average July temperature is 74 degrees.

The state's weather is determined largely by its unobstructed position. It's open to cold, dry fronts from Canada as well as to warm, moist fronts from the Gulf of Mexico. If both fronts arrive over Ohio at the same time, the result is usually rain or snow—an average of 32 inches of rain and 29 inches of snow every year. The driest area is along Lake Erie in the north, while the southwest, particularly around Wilmington, gets the most precipitation, some 44 inches per year.

Of course, even typical Ohio has its extremes. In Thurman, on July 4, 1897, the mercury hit an uncomfortable 113 degrees. It happened again at Gallipolis on July 21, 1934. And it got very cold at Milligan on February 10, 1899—39 frigid degrees below zero.

THE OHIOANS

There is great curiosity about Ohio's first residents. They were there quite some time ago—between 5,000 and 7,000 years before the territory was settled. These prehistoric Indians known as the Mound Builders, or Hopewell man, left plenty of intriguing evidence of their presence, such as burial and effigy mounds and beautifully crafted ornaments. But to date no archaeologist has been able to trace where they came from or where they went.

When the white man arrived in Ohio back in the seventeenth century, the place was populated by Shawnee, Miami, Wyandot, and Delaware Indians who were glad to trade furs with the new arrivals from France via Canada but didn't like the prospect of having them for neighbors. The Delaware Indians had already been displaced by the English and Swedes who had taken up residence in Pennsylvania. The Indians tolerated the white man until it became obvious that the newcomers had designs on their territory as well as their furs. Their hostility toward the English erupted in the French and Indian War, which began in 1754. That conflict was to settle which white men were to dominate the vast Northwest Territory of which Ohio was a part—the French who were there first, mostly trading, or the English who were anxious to annex territory.

The war resolved the political question, and the defeat of the Indians seemed to quiet things, at least temporarily. But the red men weren't going to concede defeat until the end of the eighteenth century after two more bloody wars with the newcomers.

Once everything had simmered down, white settlers from the East began arriving in ever greater numbers. The first group from New England came down the Ohio River in 1788, found land that appealed to them, and called it Marietta. Then, a party from New Jersey arrived and settled on the site of what is now Cincinnati.

For the next forty years, Ohio was a magnet attracting both Southerners, mostly from Virginia, and New Englanders. They came because they had heard that all you had to do was "tickle Ohio's rich soil with a hoe to laugh with the harvest." The word was that there was plenty for everyone in Ohio and just about everyone came. In a fit of "Ohio fever" whole villages in New England pulled up stakes to move west. Immigrants from Germany and Switzerland got off the boat and headed straight for Ohio. Irishmen who had worked on the Erie Canal came to help construct the Ohio canals and later the railroads. Scotch-Irish and Germans from Pennsylvania dominated most of the south, and by 1850 the Germans seemed to be everywhere in the state. Some drained the swamps to the northwest for farm land and established towns like New Bremen and New Bavaria.

Elsewhere, Lancaster, Columbus, Massillon, Alliance, Canton, and Steubenville were founded by German immigrants from either Pennsylvania or Germany. As a matter of fact, among the first white men to come to Ohio were German-speaking Moravian missionaries who hoped to Christianize the Indians. They arrived in 1760. Later, so many Amish and Mennonites from Germany, Switzerland, and Pennsylvania settled in Ohio that today there are more of these "plain people" in the state than in the Pennsylvania Dutch country itself. Most of them live in Holmes, Wayne, and Tuscarawas counties where roadside signs warn drivers to slow down their speed or they're likely to run into one of the horse-drawn carriages of the Amish farmers who still won't have anything to do with cars, electricity, violence, and other temptations of the modern world.

So many Swiss came to Ohio that parts of Tuscarawas and Monroe counties where they settled are still referred to as "little Switzerland." The Welsh who arrived in the early 1800s to work the mines in Jackson County clung to their language and traditions for generations. It wasn't so long ago that Welsh was the only language spoken in those parts.

As Ohio became more and more industrial, its population became more and more varied. The factories of Cleveland, Toledo, Youngstown, Akron, and Dayton were manned by Italians, Poles, Hungarians, Russians, Austrians, Greeks. Somebody once calculated that sixty-three different ethnic and nationality groups live in Cleveland alone, giving the city a cosmopolitan character not usually associated with the Midwest.

Ohio's population continued to grow and diversify until World War I when, of necessity, it halted for a while. After that, stricter immigration laws slowed the European influx. But Ohio's industries still needed workers, and there were plenty of Americans looking for jobs. Blacks from the South moved to Ohio in search of work during the 1930s and 1940s, boosting the state's black population from 62,000 in 1870 to 970,000 one hundred years later. In the recent past, newcomers have been Puerto Ricans and chicanos looking for factory or farm work.

Today, Ohioans are quick to point out that they've given the nation some of its most distinctive talents. The state calls itself the "Mother of Presidents," despite the contrary claims of Virginia, and boasts that eight of its sons have gone to the White House: William Henry Harrison, Ulysses S. Grant, Rutherford B. Hayes, James A. Garfield, Benjamin Harrison, William McKinley, William Howard Taft, and Warren G. Harding. To those who argue that William Henry Harrison was born in Virginia, Buckeyes patiently point out that he spent most of his life in Ohio.

If that roster isn't proof positive that Ohio produces some pretty remarkable people, there's more to come: Thomas Edison, the Wright brothers, Agnes Moorehead, Burgess Meredith, Clark Gable, James Thurber, Sherwood Anderson, Zane Grey, Hart Crane, Ambrose Bierce, and William Dean Howells, to name a few.

HISTORY

The Indians who lived in Ohio in the seventeenth century probably understood very well why the white man was drawn to the rivers and forests. After all, they, too, had been attracted by the thick woods populated by deer, mink, muskrats, opossums, rabbits, raccoons, foxes, and squirrels. The Erie Indians who lived along the south shore of Lake Erie were probably the first inhabitants of Ohio during recorded history. But at some point in the 1650s they'd been exterminated by the Iroquois. Later, other tribes began moving in—the Miami from Wisconsin, the Shawnee from the south, the Wyandot from Canada, and the Delaware from Pennsylvania.

If they objected when the French fur trader Louis Jolliet was exploring the south shore of Lake Erie in 1669, they didn't do anything about it. No Indians interfered with French explorer Robert Cavelier, Sieur de La Salle, when he found the Ohio River in 1669. La Salle may have explored the river rather thoroughly—some say he sailed as far as what is now Louisville, Kentucky—but historians have no proof. By the turn of the century, the Indians had probably become accustomed to seeing the fur traders, both French and English, along the river and near the lake.

For some reason, the Indians got along with the French a lot better than they did with the British. And when the French and English went to war in 1754 over the question of who should control the Northwest Territory, the Indians fought on the side of the French. By 1758 the French conceded defeat and left the territory to the British and Indians. The red men were still persistent, though. Pontiac, an Ottawa chief, led an uprising against the British in 1764—an uprising that was doomed and that put an end to Indian resistance to white settlement of the Ohio Valley. That didn't mean that the red men were ready to give up altogether. Indians supplied from Detroit continued to fight American frontiersmen. It wasn't until much later when General "Mad Anthony" Wayne won the Battle of Fallen Timbers near Toledo in 1794 that the Indians finally recognized that the white man was there to stay.

Meanwhile, back East, decisions were being made as to who was entitled to the land in the Northwest Territory. The British bowed out in 1783 with the signing of the Treaty of Paris, which gave the whole region to the Americans with the exception of a few English outposts, including one at Detroit and another at Fort Miami on the Maumee River in Ohio. That settled, it was a matter of which of the new United States could rightfully claim the land. Finally, New York, Massachusetts, Virginia, and Connecticut ceded to Congress the land they held north of the Ohio River. However, Virginia reserved an area between the Little Miami and Scioto rivers. This land, the Virginia Military District, was awarded to Virginia veterans of the Revolution. Connecticut engineered much the same deal, holding on to an area on Lake Erie called the Western Reserve. These lands were eventually granted to Connecticut residents whose property had been destroyed during the Revolution, though some were sold to speculators.

White settlers didn't arrive in any numbers in Ohio until 1786. It was then that the Ohio Company, a group of New England war veterans, purchased from Congress 1.5 million acres along the Ohio River. The New Englanders who settled Marietta in 1788 came to Ohio as a direct result of that purchase. After that, the territory was quickly populated, initially by New Englanders but later by immigrants from just about every corner of the new United States and from Europe. It wasn't long before Ohio became a state. On March 1, 1803, it was the seventeenth admitted to the Union. At the time, the state capital was at Chillicothe. In 1810 it was moved to Zanesville, where it remained until 1812, then back to Chillicothe until 1816, when Columbus became the permanent capital.

The War of 1812 brought some excitement to northern Ohio. General William Henry Harrison, who later became President of the United States, commanded troops battling the British in the north, and Commodore Oliver H. Perry gave him some invaluable assistance by defeating an English naval force in the Battle of Lake Erie in 1813.

After the war, construction of transportation routes to serve Ohio were begun. The opening of the Ohio and Erie Canal between Cleveland and Portsmouth in 1832 and the Miami and Erie Canal from Cincinnati to Dayton and Toledo in 1845 gave a big boost to the state's economy. The era also saw the inauguration of the first railroad in the state, the Erie and Kalamazoo, linking Toledo to Adrian, Michigan.

At the same time, Ohioans were becoming increasingly occupied with politics. The anti-Nebraska movement was organized to oppose the extension of slavery to the Nebraska territory. It became the Republican Party in 1855, and it wasn't long before the approaching Civil War heightened the political controversy. A man by the name of Clement L. Vallandigham organized the Peace Democrats, popularly known as the Copperheads, to support the southern cause. But Ohioans clearly didn't see things his way. He was soundly defeated when he ran for governor in 1863. Meanwhile, Ohio supplied 300,000 troops for the Union in the Civil War, but few of them saw action within the state's borders. In fact, the closest the war got to Ohio was when a raiding party led by Confederate General John Hunt Morgan crossed into the state in 1863. Morgan's Raiders were captured, but their incursion went down in history because it turned out to be the farthest north the South managed to get throughout the war.

In the years that followed, Ohio politics were to become more controversial, and to tell the truth, pretty corrupt. The city governments of Cincinnati, Cleveland, and Toledo were graft-ridden and tightly controlled by political bosses. Marcus A. Hanna, the Republican boss of Cleveland, and George B. Cox, of Cincinnati, proved to be masters of political maneuvering. It was Hanna who singled out William McKinley and propelled him from the House of Representatives to governor of Ohio in 1891 and finally into the White House in 1896.

By the turn of the century, however, people in Ohio had had their fill of political corruption. Two men, Tom L. Johnson and Samuel (Golden Rule) Jones managed to clean things up in Cleveland and Toledo, and a state-wide referendum in 1912 resulted in approval of amendments designed to modernize the state constitution. The next year, massive flooding devastated the Miami, Scioto, Muskingum, and Maumee valleys, killing about 500 people and causing $147 million in property damage, most of it in Dayton.

The next thirty years were difficult ones for Ohio. The state sent 225,000 men to World War I, then reveled in prosperity during the 1920s, only to be stunned later when the Great Depression cost thousands of workers their jobs and closed factories throughout the state. The farmers, too, were not immune to the economic crisis. Many of them lost their land when the bottom fell out of farm prices. Economic recovery came hand in hand with World War II and 840,000 Ohioans went off to fight.

After the war, the state entered the Atomic Age with the construction of the Portsmouth area project which produces uranium 235 for atomic uses, an Atomic Energy Commission research laboratory in Miamisburg, and a uranium refining center near Cincinnati. And the space age came to Ohio in 1956 when the National Aeronautics and Space Administration opened the Lewis Research Center in Cleveland. That's where NASA scientists research chemical, electric, and nuclear space propulsion systems. The fifties also saw the completion of the 241-mile Ohio Turnpike.

In more recent years, Ohio has been busy with programs designed to attract more industry, solve its problems with juvenile delinquency, expand and improve its public schools and universities.

And it has been the scene of some headline-making events. Rioting by blacks in Cleveland in 1966 cost four lives. Two years later, a Negro, Carl B. Stokes, was elected mayor of Cleveland. But that wasn't a first for Ohio. Springfield had elected a black mayor in 1967 and Dayton did the same in 1968.

Even more traumatic for the state and the nation than the riots was the tragedy that took place in 1970 on the campus of Kent State University, near Akron. Four students were killed when national guardsmen opened fire during a demonstration protesting the United States bombing of Cambodia. The deaths aroused intense bitterness in Ohio and throughout the nation.

INDUSTRY

Ohio's booming industrial area around Youngstown is most often likened to Germany's Ruhr Valley. Situated near the Pennsylvania border just north of the Ohio River, Youngstown, a metal-producing city, is right in the heart of Ohio's industrialized northeast. Nearby Canton produces roller bearings, bank vaults, and vacuum cleaners, and Akron, near Cleveland to the north, is the rubber capital of the world, manufacturing more than a third of the tires and tubes made in the United States.

Ohio produces more than $22 billion a year in manufactured goods and leads the nation in the production of bus and truck bodies, motorcycles, and truck trailers as well as rubber tubes and tires.

The state's proximity to Detroit is responsible to a large degree for Ohio's concentration on the production of transportation equipment. Factories in Cincinnati, Cleveland, Columbus, Hudson, Lorain, Toledo, and Twinsburg turn out auto bodies and parts, while Elyria has the largest plant in the United States for the manufacture of automobile air brakes. But the transportation industry isn't confined to automobiles. Airline parts are made in Dayton, and elsewhere in the state locomotives and railway cars are produced.

Not all the machinery made in Ohio is designed for keeping America moving. The state leads the nation in the manufacture of machine tools and is one of the most important producers of blast furnaces, rolling mills, heating and cooling equipment, office machinery, and refrigerating devices.

Ohio rivals—but so far hasn't topped—Pennsylvania in the production of iron and steel, turning out about 23 million tons a year at mills in Cleveland, Lorain, and Youngstown. And an Ohioan who really wants to impress you can boast that Cincinnati leads the world in the manufacture of machine tools, soaps, detergents, and playing cards. Dayton is the nation's largest producer of cash registers, magazines, putty, and plastics. Toledo has the largest factory in the United States for the manufacture of weighing scales. Elyria is the home of the nation's biggest factory for the production of golf balls, and the state itself is the national leader in the manufacture of clay and glass products.

If all that doesn't convince you of Ohio's industrial might, consider the slaughtering and meat-packing industry, shipbuilding, the production of aluminum, bicycles, butter, cement, matches, musical instruments, paints, varnishes, sporting goods, clothing, shoes, textiles, paper, coke for steel-making, chemicals, fertilizers, and tar.

AGRICULTURE

Long before the days of steel mills and rubber factories Ohio was the envy of the nation for an entirely different reason. The glaciers that had covered much of the state during the Ice Age had left fertile soil, perfect for farming. And that's why people originally came to Ohio. The place didn't disappoint them. By 1850, only sixty-two years after the first white settlers arrived, Ohio led the nation in agricultural production.

Although today farming brings Ohio only a fraction of its annual income, 60 per cent of the state is still farm land supporting more than half a million people. Ohio remains a leading state in the production of corn and wheat as well as oats, popcorn, and soybeans. Other important crops are barley, red clover, rye, and timothy seed. But today many of the state's farmers are concentrating on raising meat animals. As a result, Ohio is among the leading hog-producing states. It was here that Poland China hogs were first bred back in the 1800s. The development was so important that a monument to the Poland China hog was raised near Monroe.

Equally significant was the development of American Merino sheep, a breed with especially fine wool. Ohio still produces more wool than any other state east of the Mississippi.

The state's dairy farms have helped put Tuscarawas County on the map as "America's Little Switzerland"—needless to say, it produces great quantities of Swiss cheese. Van Wert on the other side of the state—in the west—makes all the Liederkranz cheese produced in the United States.

Throughout the state vegetables and fruits are grown in abundance, with the plains along Lake Erie yielding enough grapes to allow Ohio's fifty wineries to produce about 1 million gallons a year.

NATURAL RESOURCES

In addition to its industrial wealth and agricultural abundance, Ohio also has vast mineral reserves. The state produces more than 40 million tons of bituminous (soft) coal each year, much of it taken from fields in the south and southeast near the state's borders with Pennsylvania and West Virginia. Coal has been mined in Ohio since the early 1800s, and geologists estimate that some 42 billion tons remain to be extracted from the ground. Much of it lies so close to the surface that it has been taken up by strip mining, a procedure that has mutilated the landscape, polluted the waters, and finally provoked such an outcry from environmentalists that the state has enacted laws to curb abuses. So far, however, not much progress has been made in restoring the landscape.

But even if coal mining were banned entirely, Ohio would still have plenty of underground wealth. Oil was found in western Ohio in 1885, and since then the state's wells have been producing more than 5 million barrels a year. More than 21,000 wells are in operation today. There also are about 7,000 natural gas wells yielding approximately 37 billion cubic feet of gas each year.

There's even more in the way of minerals. Salt, for instance. The state's enormous reserves of rock salt and salt-water brine are so extensive that geologists say Ohio could supply the whole country with all the salt it can use for thousands of years. The deepest salt mine in the United States—it reaches some 2,000 feet below the ground—is at Barberton in Medina County near Akron. Ohio also leads the nation in the production of clays and building stone. It supplies approximately one quarter of the clay used in the manufacture of bricks, tile, cement, pottery, and stoneware. The largest sandstone quarry in the United States is in South Amherst, Ohio. It's one of the many that help the state supply one fourth of the nation's store of sandstone.

Still another mineral that Ohio produces in abundance is the limestone used for glassmaking and also for the production of lime, cement, chemicals, fertilizer, and steel. Most of it is quarried chiefly in north-central Ohio. The deepest limestone quarry in the country is at Barberton—the same town that boasts the deepest salt mine.

CITIES

The people of **Cleveland** have many good reasons to brag about their city. Its Museum of Art, for instance, is second only to the Metropolitan in New York in the value of its collection. Its 18,000-acre park system has long been recognized as one of the country's finest. The Cleveland Playhouse is the oldest professional resident theater company in the United States. And anyone who has never heard of the Cleveland Symphony Orchestra isn't much of a music lover.

Cleveland's cultural distinction is linked to its cosmopolitan character. It's been called the melting pot of the Midwest for good reason. Immigrants representing sixty-three different ethnic and nationality groups flocked to the city during the nineteenth century and the early years of the twentieth century to work in the factories that made Cleveland rich. Today, however, the descendants of many of those early immigrants have deserted the old neighborhoods for the burgeoning suburbs. The population of the city proper has been declining—down to less than 800,000 today. But Greater Cleveland—the city itself and the more than seventy suburbs that surround it—ranks as one of the nation's largest metropolitan areas.

Cleveland isn't writing off its downtown area as a victim of age and decay. It has poured $250 million into a massive urban face lift, specifically the Erieview project, consisting of forty modern buildings on a 200-acre site. Cleveland's Convention Center, one of the largest in the country, is located in the midst of a 17-acre mall. Clustered together nearby are the Cuyahoga County Court House, City Hall, Public Library, Federal Building, Municipal Stadium, and Horticultural Gardens. You can look down at it all from the Terminal Tower at Public Square, which is a fifty-two-story structure that's still one of the tallest buildings in the Midwest.

Clearly, the city has come a long way from that day in 1796 when Moses Cleaveland arrived to survey the 3 million acres the Connecticut Land Company had purchased at forty cents an acre. The opening of the Ohio Canal in 1832 gave the town its first taste of importance, but it wasn't until the Civil War that Cleveland came into its own. By then iron ore had been found in the upper Great Lakes and coal was being mined nearby—a combination that was to give Cleveland the beginnings of its steel industry. Almost a century later, the opening of the St. Lawrence Seaway gave the port of Cleveland access to the ocean. Today, it handles 20 million tons of cargo a year.

Industrially, Cleveland has never stopped growing. Just about everything is made in Cleveland—steel, auto parts, electronics, light bulbs, missile components. But all that industry has its disadvantages. The plants lining the banks of the Cuyahoga River that divides the city have so polluted the water that the river itself once caught fire. And the waters of Lake Erie are still too dirty for swimming in many areas.

But you don't have to leave Cleveland to return to nature. The city's park system has something for everyone. Connected by more than eighty miles of parkways, the "emerald necklace" of ten parks and a zoo surrounds the city with picnic grounds, beaches, riding stables, horse and hiking trails, golf courses, fishing streams, and man-made lakes. The Cleveland Zoo features lions and tigers roaming free on islands surrounded by deep moats and a unique display of hoofed animals in their natural habitat. The aquarium in Gordon Park has marine and fresh-water plants and animals, and the cultural gardens in Rockefeller Park (John D. Rockefeller was a local boy who made good) have been designed to represent the native countries of twenty of Cleveland's nationalities.

Cleveland is very proud of its Museum of Art with its $33-million collection of paintings and sculptures from all over the world. There's also the nearby Museum of Natural History with its exhibits of birds, mammals, gemstones, and fossil fish, and Western Reserve Historical Society's two museums: the Frederick C. Crawford collection of antique cars and airplanes and the Historical Museum. The Auto-Aviation Museum exhibits more than 130 cars and eight planes, including a 1911 model called the Bumblebee, which was one of the first planes used along the Cleveland lake front. The Historical Museum boasts the largest Napoleonic collection in the United States, as well as displays of early American costumes, Indian relics, and miniature rooms depicting American homes from 1620 to the present.

While you're museum hopping, don't forget the private collection of Salvador Dali's works at the Dali Museum. It contains, among other masterpieces, "The Discovery of America by Christopher Columbus," "The Ecumenical Council," and "The Hallucinogenic Toreador." There's also the Cleveland Health Museum and Education Center, with hundreds of exhibits demonstrating how the human body works. "Juno, the Talking, Transparent Lady" will give you a pretty vivid picture of how she functions.

Severance Hall near the campus of Case Western Reserve University is the home of the Cleveland Orchestra, which gives regular concerts there when it's in town from September through May. Then the orchestra moves out of town to its summer home, Blossom Music Center, near Akron. Theater buffs will always find good entertainment at the three theaters which make up the Cleveland Playhouse or at Karamu House, an interracial theater featuring the performing arts.

In the early days of the nineteenth century, **Cincinnati** was attracting immigrants by the thousands. In a poem that enhanced the city's appeal, Henry Wadsworth Longfellow paid tribute to Cincinnati as the "Queen of the West," and, to tell the truth, those words were not poetic overstatement. When they were written in 1854, Cincinnati was the largest city west of Philadelphia—a booming river town that was to continue to grow and prosper throughout the steamboat era.

Cincinnati's history goes back to 1788 when settlers built Fort Washington on the banks of the Ohio. It was here that the first legislature to govern the Northwest Territory assembled in 1799. Once land companies started peddling acreage back East, the people came in ever increasing numbers. Many of those early settlers were Germans who introduced beer halls and *Gemütlichkeit* to the frontier. But the city also took on a southern flavor. After all, it's just across the river from Kentucky and was linked by the river to points throughout the South. You can still board a steamboat in Cincinnati and cruise down the Ohio to the Mississippi en route to New Orleans.

The river continues to play a major role in Cincinnati's commercial life. It handles more shipping than any other inland waterway in the world. But the town has attracted industry of all types. It produces more machine tools than any other American city and is the home of Proctor and Gamble, one of the largest soap manufacturers in the world.

You can still glimpse the past, though. Tucked away in modern Cincinnati is the home of Harriet Beecher Stowe's father. Now a museum of Negro history, it was Miss Stowe's residence while she worked on *Uncle Tom's Cabin*. Even older is the Kemper Log House, built in 1804, which displays the furnishings that belonged to the family of the Reverend James Kemper. And you can get a sampling of another era by visiting the showboat *Majestic* docked at the public landing. The showboat is the winter home of the Cincinnati Symphony Orchestra and the Cincinnati Ballet Company.

Residents are justly proud of both and also are inclined to brag about the Conservatory of Music and the Art Academy at the University of Cincinnati. And when they really want to stress their town's cultural attractions, they'll tell you about the art collection donated to the city by Mr. and Mrs. Charles P. Taft. It includes works by Rembrandt, Turner, Goya, Gainsborough, and Corot, as well as some priceless French Renaissance enameled plaques and dishes. All are housed in the Taft Museum, a mansion built in 1820. There's another impressive collection at the Cincinnati Art Museum.

For all its lively history and industrial activity, Cincinnati has slipped from its place as the largest city in the state to third in size. Ranking second after Cleveland today is the state capital, **Columbus,** a bustling town with more than eight hundred factories, the state university, and a new museum complex.

Settled in 1797, Columbus became the state capital in 1816. It's the biggest city in the world named in honor of Christopher Columbus. The capital has taken on a whole new look in recent years. It has put $60 million into a massive urban renewal project constructing new office buildings, hotels, motels, and vast underground parking facilities. One of the newest buildings is the Ohio Historical Center with archaeological, historical, and natural history displays. Among them is "Ohio Village," a reconstruction of a nineteenth-century Ohio county seat.

A few prize buildings did escape the wreckers when downtown Columbus was renovated. One of them was the state capitol itself, a limestone structure dating from 1861. It's considered the purest example of Doric architecture in the United States. Also untouched was the nearby German Village constructed by settlers who came to Columbus between 1840 and 1860. Its solid brick homes have been restored, and historic St. Mary Church has been preserved.

You can get an idea of what Columbus used to look like at the Center of Science and Industry. One of its exhibits is "Durell Street of Yesteryear"—a reconstruction of the town's main street as it looked between 1830 and 1910. Most of the center's other exhibits are science- and health-related. There's the Battelle Planetarium and "Valida," a mechanical transparent lady who explains what's going on in her see-through body.

The Wyandot Indians used to camp in the winter in the Olentangy Indian Caverns, a series of limestone caves 55 to 105 feet underground, located in the outskirts of Columbus. When you emerge you can witness one of the gun fights staged every fifteen minutes at the replica of an old frontier town.

Dayton is a pretty modern city, too. But it didn't necessarily plan it that way. Much of original Dayton was destroyed by the floods that devastated the Miami Valley in 1913. Ever since then, the townspeople have been determined that it won't happen again. To make sure, they built a series of five flood-control dams designed to hold back the rising waters. All five were built by Dayton alone with no help from the state or the federal government.

Today, the city's main claim to fame is as the headquarters of National Cash Register Company, a firm founded by John Patterson in the late 1800s. One of Patterson's employees gave the town another major industry when he quit to develop the automobile self-starter. But for all that, the town's two most famous sons are Orville and Wilbur Wright, who went to Kitty Hawk, North Carolina, to test their flying machine successfully.

Dayton got one of their original planes and the city displays it at Carillon Park, a museum that traces the history of transportation. In addition to the plane, there's a Concord stagecoach, an early locomotive, a fire engine, a Conestoga wagon, and Dayton's oldest building, Newcom Tavern. More planes are exhibited at the Air Force Museum at Wright-Patterson Air Force Base, eleven miles east of the city. Among the displays are aircraft used during World Wars I and II by the Germans, the Russians, and the Japanese.

Dayton also has a fine art institute of which it is justly proud. The institute, an Italian Renaissance villa with a graceful curved entrance stairway, contains a first-rate collection of seventeenth-century paintings, a pre-Columbian collection, and two medieval cloisters. This is the place where Dayton's music lovers come for regular weekly concerts.

Toledo, Ohio's fourth-largest city, just missed being part of Michigan. Both states wanted the small town on the shores of Lake Erie when it was just a dot on the map. In fact, they nearly went to war over the issue in 1835. Guns were being loaded when President Andrew Jackson forestalled catastrophe by awarding Toledo to Ohio and giving Michigan its upper peninsula. Toledo has since turned into the eleventh-largest port in the United States and claims to be the glass capital of the world. There's plenty of truth in that boast: The town's four glass manufacturers have a combined annual net income of more than $1 billion.

The history of glass is the main attraction at Toledo's Museum of Art, which has the most extensive glass collection in the United States. It also displays an outstanding collection of paintings, including some by Rubens, Rembrandt, El Greco, and a variety of American artists. The museum is ranked among the ten finest in the nation.

Equally outstanding is the Toledo Zoo, one of the biggest in the country. It covers more than thirty acres and features one of the largest fresh-water aquariums in the United States.

What glass is to Toledo, rubber is to **Akron.** It's been that way ever since Benjamin Goodrich went into the rubber business there in 1870. His company, B. F. Goodrich, is still around, along with Firestone, Goodyear, General Tire and Rubber, and Mohawk. One of the rubber millionaires, Frank A. Seiberling, of Goodyear and Seiberling, is responsible for Akron's most spectacular showplace. His family gave the city its Stan Hywet Hall, a sixty-five-room Tudor revival manor house complete with its antiques and art treasures, fine furniture, tapestries, oriental rugs, glass, china, and silver. The house itself cost $3 million to build in 1915 and is worth many times that today. The exterior was modeled on several Elizabethan manor houses. The inside is paneled in hand-carved oak, walnut, and sandalwood. Surrounding the house are gardens of tulips, daffodils, roses, peonies, irises, and chrysanthemums. There's also a formal Japanese garden with a seven-foot antique granite lantern weighing more than a ton.

Magnificent though it is, Stan Hywet Hall is only one of several spectacular Akron tourist attractions. You can't go inside one of them—the Goodyear air dock, the world's largest building without interior supports. It's the equivalent of twenty-two stories tall and is big enough to house ten football fields—so enormous that it even creates its own weather. It's been known to rain inside the air dock when it's sunny and clear outside. Goodyear built the giant dirigibles *Akron* and *Macon* here.

The summer home of the Cleveland Symphony, Blossom Music Center, in **Cuyahoga Falls,** is considered a miracle of architectural ingenuity. It's a $9.6-million pavilion that seats 4,600 but has been so flawlessly designed that another 10,000 people can spread blankets on the lawns and still hear and see clearly. The acoustics are perfect and the view completely unobstructed.

SPORTS AND RECREATION

When you're in Ohio you're in football country, a state of passionate sports fans who divide their loyalties among a score of college teams but usually unite to back the professional Cleveland Browns. Some 80,000 enthusiasts jam Cleveland's Municipal Stadium to cheer on the Browns whenever they're in town. And you can be pretty sure that around the state millions more are following the action on television.

There are, of course, those who prefer college football. The Ohio State Buckeyes, one of the Big Ten teams, have plenty of ardent fans throughout the state, as have the squads of Miami University, Bowling Green, Ohio University, Dayton, Western Reserve, and Xavier.

When the baseball season arrives, Ohio residents have a choice to make. They can follow the Cincinnati Reds or the Cleveland Indians. The true baseball fan keeps an eye on both teams. The Reds are a special source of pride, not only because they won the World Series in 1975, but because their history dates back to 1916 when the Cincinnati Redstockings became the first professional baseball team in the world. In Toledo, they keep track of the action in the International League to see how the home team, the Toledo Mud Hens, are doing.

The winter season, once devoted solely to basketball and the Cleveland Cavaliers, now offers a new diversion—four professional ice hockey teams: the Cleveland Crusaders, the Cleveland Barons, the Columbus Seals, and the Toledo Blades. As if that isn't enough to keep even the most avid sports fans satisfied, Ohio has sixteen race tracks, including those at Cincinnati, Cleveland, Columbus, and Grove City. There's also the Mid-America Sports Car Course at Mansfield and, for the younger set, the annual Soapbox Derby in Akron.

All this is not to suggest that you can't get Ohioans away from the stadiums or their television sets. A state with so many inland lakes and with all those resorts along Lake Erie is bound to have its share of swimmers, sailors, water-skiers, and just plain sun worshipers. Once summer comes to Sandusky Bay the waters are dotted with sailboats and motorboats and the beaches crowded with bathers. The scene is the same all along the Lake Erie shore line—the unpolluted parts, that is.

Cedar Point, on Lake Erie, has attracted vacationers since 1882. Its mile-long beach is just as popular as ever, and its continually expanding amusement park has strengthened its appeal.

Cedar Point isn't all Ohio has to offer in the way of lakeside resorts. The shore line from Vermilion west is scattered with vacation cottages and docks. Put-in-Bay on South Bass Island, northwest of Sandusky, has long been a favorite vacation spot. In the old days it was a pretty exclusive spa. Millionaires congregated at the Victory Hotel which, before it burned down in 1919, was said to be the largest summer resort in the United States. It was a rather scandalous place at the time, too, after its swimming pool became the first in the United States where men and women were permitted to bathe at the same time.

Ohio's state parks and forests also provide all sorts of recreation, from swimming, boating, and water-skiing to camping, hiking, and picnicking. There are sixty-seven separate recreation areas scattered through the state parks, the Wayne National Forest, and the Muskingum Conservancy District. Some permit hunting in season and fishing all year round, and more and more are providing facilities for skiing, ice skating, snowmobiling, tobogganing, and other winter sports.

POINTS OF INTEREST

One of the most vivid impressions a visitor takes away from Ohio is of a quarter-mile-long snake with a ball in his mouth. The serpent has been there for more than 5,000 years ever since the prehistoric Mound Builders constructed it out of stone and clay. Undulating along the crest of a hill near Locust Grove in the southeastern part of the state, the serpent measures more than twenty feet across and, in places, five feet high. Experts say it is the best example to be found in the United States of the handiwork of the Mound Builders, or Hopewell man. But they still haven't managed to agree about what the ball represents—some say it's the sun, others think it's an egg.

The serpent is only one of the effigy mounds left in Ohio by its primitive inhabitants. Eleven of them are maintained by the Ohio Historical Society while the National Park Service has set aside one group, including Serpent Mound, as national monuments. Fort Ancient on a hilltop near Lebanon is said to be the largest such structure in the country. It's made up of earthen walls rising to a height of twenty feet and encircling an area of more than one hundred acres.

Once you've marveled at the sophisticated engineering achievements of those early Indians, the later stages of Ohio's history are likely to seem commonplace by comparison. But who can resist the romance of the frontier, the drama of Indian wars and the vivid reminders of the fortitude and courage of the pioneers. A visit to Schoenbrunn Village in northeast Ohio, for example, can be especially poignant. It was here that the first white men to settle in Ohio—Moravian missionaries who had hopes of Christianizing the Indians—battled the elements and withstood the hostility of the British and Indians. When they finally gave up in despair, they razed their own church to prevent it from being desecrated. The abandoned village was destroyed but not forgotten. It has been reconstructed, complete with sixty log cabins, the church and schoolhouse. You can see the original textbooks used by the missionaries at the village museum.

Just twenty years after Schoenbrunn Village was abandoned, General "Mad Anthony" Wayne subdued the Indians at the Battle of Fallen Timbers. The site, southwest of Maumee, is now a park, as is Fort Recovery, near the Indiana border, where General Arthur St. Clair was defeated by Indians in 1791. Two years later, the bones of his massacred troops were buried by General Wayne's men, who built a stockade. They named it Fort Recovery to point out the fact that they had recovered the area from the Indians.

When it comes to military monuments, Fort Recovery takes second billing in Ohio to the International Peace Memorial, erected between 1912 and 1915 to commemorate Commodore Oliver Hazard Perry's naval victory over the British in the Battle of Lake Erie during the War of 1812. The 352-foot-high fluted Doric column is one of the chief attractions of Put-in-Bay on South Bass Island in Lake Erie. The island, which can be reached by ferry from Port Clinton on the mainland or by airplane, draws thousands of tourists every year. They come not only to see the monument but to take advantage of excellent fishing year round and to swim, picnic, and explore the island's caves during the summer. Another attraction is the Heineman Winery, one of several that can be visited on the Lake Erie islands. Others are located on Middle Bass Island, a short hop away, and are open to the public for tours and wine tasting.

There's a state park on Kelleys Island, also in Lake Erie, that has facilities for camping, biking, and golf. But the chief attraction here is the glacial grooves carved in limestone by those prehistoric sheets of ice that etched so much of Ohio's terrain centuries ago.

Back on the mainland nearby are some other natural wonders that have fascinated men for centuries. One of the most picturesque is the Blue Hole near Castalia. It's a spring that gushes 7,519 gallons of water a minute from an underground river. Flashing through the crystal-clear waters are several varieties of trout. Since fishing is prohibited, the trout have gotten into the habit of coming to the surface for food and can be easily glimpsed by sight-seers who toss them tidbits. South of the Blue Hole near Bellevue is Seneca Caverns, formed when nature wrenched apart rocks millions of years ago. If the ceiling were lowered and the floor of the cavern raised, the rocks forming them would fit together perfectly, like parts of a jigsaw puzzle. Underlying the caverns is "Old Mist'ry River," so called because scientists have never been able to measure its depth or locate its source.

You can get a pretty accurate picture of how those early pioneers lived in Marietta, where one of the original buildings erected by the first permanent settlers still stands. Built in 1788, it's now the Campus Martius State Memorial Museum displaying the china and furniture of the period, along with some personal possessions of the Rufus Putnam family who lived there.

One of the most unique of Ohio's early settlements was Zoar Village in the northeast part of the state near Canton, founded in 1817 by a group of Germans who continued to live there communally until 1898. They say that the outside world finally proved too tempting for the young people of Zoar who began drifting away from communal life until the society finally disintegrated. The fine hotel that the Zoarites operated remains in business, and tourists can see what life was like there over a century ago by paying a visit to the museum that once was the home of the society's leader, Joseph Baumeler.

Entrancing as it is to wander through Ohio's little towns in search of the past, the present has its own allure. And in this industrial state, that means the pulsating factories that supply so much of the nation's manufactured goods. You can see how some of the products are made on tours of giant plants run by Goodyear Tire and Rubber, Proctor and Gamble, Eastman Kodak, Lotus Glass, National Cash Register, Armco Steel, and many more. For some, however, all that industrial might can't compete with the National Professional Football Hall of Fame in Canton. It pays tribute to football greats from all over the country and displays some of the equipment used in scoring a few of the more famous touchdowns in history.

After a few days in Ohio, visitors are not likely to ever forget that the state was the birthplace of some of the most distinguished men and women in American politics, arts, science, and technology. Aside from the fact that you can visit the birthplaces of or memorials to eight American presidents—William Henry Harrison, Ulysses S. Grant, Rutherford B. Hayes, James A. Garfield, Benjamin Harrison, William McKinley, William Howard Taft, and Warren G. Harding—you also can see the birthplace of Thomas Alva Edison in Milan, and, for good measure, the house of the doctor who delivered him. Edison spent only the first seven years of his life in the unpretentious brick house where he was born, and although the house is now filled with Edison family possessions, the doctor's house, now the Milan Historical Museum, contains more antiques.

Annie Oakley was born in Ohio—in tiny North Star near the Indiana border. She had a considerable reputation for sharpshooting by the time she was fourteen and made enough money killing game to pay off her mother's farm mortgage. You can see some of the medals and trophies she later collected at the Garst Museum in neighboring Greenville.

Just in case you're getting the idea that Ohio's famous sons and daughters all lived in the distant past, the tourist guides are sure to remind you that John Glenn, the first American in space, was born in Cambridge and grew up in nearby New Concord, and that Neil Armstrong, the first man to walk on the moon, was from Wapakoneta. That city's big tourist attraction these days is the Neil Armstrong Air and Space Museum, which displays, along with other exhibits depicting the history of flight, the *Gemini 8* capsule in which Armstrong completed the first spacecraft docking in orbit.

SPECIAL EVENTS

The return of the buzzards to their roosts near Hinckley is one of the biggest events of the year in Ohio. The whole town plus the curious from other parts of the state turn out the first Sunday after March 15 to welcome the birds home.

During the rest of the year the people of Ohio seem preoccupied with food. They've got festivals for just about everything edible the state produces. In Chardon there's a Maple Festival in April; in Burton, a Butter Churn Festival in June. The people in Bucyrus wait until August for their annual Bratwurst Festival, and since the corn is at its peak that month, Millersport holds a Sweet Corn Festival.

But the fall is when Ohioans get down to serious eating. It starts off with melons in Milan in September and then honey in Lebanon. Lisbon's Johnny Appleseed Festival features all the apples you can eat and all the cider you can drink. There's another Apple Festival in Jackson, and at the Ohio Swiss Festival at Sugarcreek, everyone dresses up in Swiss costumes, yodels, and eats lots of—you guessed it —Swiss cheese. Burton holds its annual Apple Butter Festival in October, and a 300-pound pumpkin pie is the main attraction at Circleville's Pumpkin Festival in late October.

Youngsters come from all over the world to compete in the All-American Soapbox Derby in Akron every August, the same month that yachtsmen converge on Put-in-Bay on Lake Erie for the Inter-Lake Yachting Association Regatta, and on the Ohio River for the Portsmouth Regatta. For music lovers the big month is May, when Cincinnati holds its Music Festival and Baldwin-Wallace College in Berea pays its annual tribute to Johann Sebastian Bach.

Holmes County, where many of Ohio's Amish live, stages an Antique Festival in Millersburg each October, but collectors who don't want to wait that long can pick up antique pottery in June at the pottery festival in Crooksville-Roseville.

The "good old days on the farm" is the theme of the Steam Thresher's Festival in London in July, the same month that Quaker City holds the Ohio Hills Folk Festival.

P.D.

CHRONOLOGY

1669   Robert Cavelier, Sieur de La Salle, purportedly explored the Ohio River as far south as Louisville, Kentucky.

1747   The Ohio Company of Virginia was established with the purpose of colonizing the Ohio River Valley.

1764   The French and Indian War, which began in 1753, ended with the defeat of Indians led by the Ottawa chief Pontiac.

1783   The British signed the Treaty of Paris giving the Northwest Territory to the United States.

1788   White settlers from New England established the first permanent settlement in Ohio at Marietta.

1794   Mad Anthony Wayne defeated the Indians at the Battle of Fallen Timbers near Toledo, thus finally crushing the red men's resistance to white settlement.

1803   Ohio became the seventeenth state on March 1.

1813   The British were defeated on Lake Erie by a naval force commanded by Commodore Oliver H. Perry.

1832   The Ohio and Erie Canal connecting Cleveland and Portsmouth was opened.

1845   The Miami and Erie Canal linking Cincinnati, Dayton, and Toledo was completed.

1863   The Civil War came to Ohio when a Confederate raiding party led by General John Hunt Morgan was captured in Columbiana County.

1870   Benjamin F. Goodrich opened his rubber manufacturing business in Akron.

1913   Floods took 500 lives in the Miami, Scioto, Muskingum, and Maumee valleys.

1922   The Miami River Valley flood-control project was completed.

1938   The Muskingum River Valley flood-control project was completed.

1955   The Ohio Turnpike was opened to traffic.

1966   Rioting by blacks in Cleveland took four lives.

1970 Four students were shot and killed by Ohio national guardsmen on the campus of Kent State University.

1975 Guardsmen charged in the Kent State shootings were acquitted.

1977 Thirty-one-year-old Dennis Kucinich became mayor of Cleveland.

1979 Cleveland's feuding Democrats paralyzed the city's efforts to correct its financial problems in a year when the mayor (Kucinich) and all City Council members were up for re-election. Kucinich was defeated.

WISCONSIN

JUST OVER one hundred years ago, Wisconsin was a vast territory of trees and lakes populated mainly by Indians who had been driven out of their homelands to the north and east. Although French fur traders and explorers had charted its interior back in the seventeenth century, there wasn't a real interest in Wisconsin until lead was discovered there back in the 1820s. That announcement touched off a "get rich quick" rush to places like Hazel Green on the Illinois border not far from the Mississippi River. Indeed, in the nineteenth century Wisconsin was primarily noted for its lead and lumber. The dense forests to the north were leveled by rapacious lumber barons during a boom that spawned the legend of Paul Bunyan, boosted Wisconsin's economy, and devastated its landscape.

It is small wonder that a state that experienced so much manipulation at the hands of the lumber barons and the railroad interests took a progressive political turn in the late years of the nineteenth century. In a way, Wisconsin came by its politics naturally: many of the German immigrants who flocked to the state during the 1850s were artisans and intellectuals who left their homeland mainly for political reasons. As it happened, though, the man who led Wisconsin's progressives wasn't German. Robert M. La Follette was a Madison lawyer who challenged the hold of the lumbermen and railroad interests and, after he was elected governor in 1900, led the fight for reforms that made Wisconsin an early leader in the enactment of such social welfare programs as workmen's compensation, minimum wages for women and children, and civil and property rights for women.

Wisconsin has other claims to fame, too: it produces much of the milk and cheese that Americans eat. Dairy farming is still a way of life: More than 3 million cows produce upward of 2 billion gallons of milk a year. And Milwaukee is famous for yet another beverage: beer, a drink introduced by the city's German immigrants.

Wisconsin industry has come a long way since the days of lead mining and lumbering. It is a leading producer of heavy machinery, electrical appliances, and even automobiles: The American Motors plant in Kenosha is the largest auto factory in the United States.

Much of the damage inflicted during the lumber boom has been overcome by a massive reforestation program, and today, Wisconsin's great north woods have been restored to their original lush, green beauty. Four of Wisconsin's five vast Indian reservations are scattered through the north woods. Here, the Chippewa still hunt and fish in the lakes their ancestors knew so well. But the year-round population up north is sparse—most of Wisconsin's 4.4 million residents are concentrated in the industrial southeast near Milwaukee, Racine, and Kenosha.

THE LAND

At a glance, Wisconsin's landscape seems rather undramatic: some hills and valleys, rich level farm land, and lots of lakes. But a closer look reveals a startling diversity—scenic gorges, limestone and sandstone bluffs lining the Mississippi River, steep hills and ridges, and the remnants of ancient mountain ranges with evocative names—the Baraboo Range, Rib Mountain, and the Gogebic Range.

The glaciers of prehistoric times were responsible for Wisconsin's natural beauty. A million years ago these giant sheets of ice slid over the state, carving valleys and depositing rich soils ideal for farming. When they retreated, they left behind blocks of ice that melted, forming the eight thousand lakes that dot the state. The glaciers once covered all but the southwestern part of the state, a section now known as the Western Upland, characterized by steep slopes and winding ridges. It is here that the sandstone and limestone bluffs rise spectacularly along the Mississippi.

Wisconsin has four other topographical regions. Adjacent to the Western Upland is the Great Lakes Plains, which extends from the center of the state south to the Illinois border. Here is Wisconsin's best farm land, rolling plains composed of fertile soil overlaying limestone ridges that run from north to south.

The Central Plain that sweeps across the mid-section of the state,

Wisconsin

N

| 0 | 25 | 50 | 75 | 100 |

miles

LAKE SUPERIOR

Apostle Islands
National
Lakeside

Bayfield
Peninsula

Bayfield
La Pointe · Madeline
Island

Superior

Ashland

GOGEBIC RANGE

Presque Isle

Land O'Lakes   MICHIGAN

Danbury
Grindstone Lake

Hayward

Boulder
Junction

Menominee R.

St. Croix R.

Spooner

Eagle
River

Three Lakes

Rhinelander

Timms Hill

Tomahawk

Peshtigo R.

Rib Mountain

Peshtigo

Ephraim

Oconto R.

Egg
Harbor

Chippewa R.

Eau Claire

Sturgeon
Bay

Black R.

Fort Howard

Green
Bay

MINNESOTA

Mississippi R.

Fox R.

Manitowoc

La Crosse

Oshkosh

La Crosse

Ripon

Sheboygan

Westby

Wisconsin
Dells

BARABOO RANGE

Spring
Green

LAKE MICHIGAN

Cave of the
Mounds

Lake Mendota
Lake Monona
Lake Waubesa

Milwaukee

Wisconsin R.

Madison

IOWA

Belmont

New
Glarus

Fox R.

Racine

Hazel Green

Beloit

Kenosha

ILLINOIS

from the Mississippi on the west to the Lake Michigan shore, once was covered by glaciers except in its southernmost portion. There, the Wisconsin River flowing southwest to the Mississippi has etched the Wisconsin Dells, a gorge that the local folk modestly describe as "scenic." Between the Central Plain and the lowland along the shore of Lake Superior to the north lies the Superior Upland, an area of woods and hills and hundreds of lakes. Timms Hill, the highest point in the state, is in this section. It towers 1,953 feet above sea level in Price County.

The Superior Lowland along the lake is Wisconsin's smallest topographic region. Its sandy beaches edge the lake but the whole section extends inland only a few miles before it ends abruptly at a cliff that marks the beginning of the Superior Upland.

The rivers that drain Wisconsin flow north to Lake Superior, east to Lake Michigan, or west to the Mississippi. An east-west divide cuts across the northern part of the state separating the rivers flowing toward Lake Superior from those heading south to either the Mississippi or Lake Michigan. The principal rivers emptying into Superior are the Bad, Montreal, and Nemadji. A north-south divide separates the rivers flowing toward the Mississippi from those emptying into Lake Michigan. The Black, Chippewa, La Crosse, St. Croix, and Wisconsin empty into the Mississippi while the Fox, Menominee, Milwaukee, Octonto, and Peshtigo drain into Lake Michigan.

CLIMATE

Although you can get a good tan on Wisconsin's beaches during the summer, the state is no place for those who would rather live in bathing suits than overcoats. Pleasant though they are, Wisconsin's summers are short. The winters are very long and very cold.

Predictably, winter is most severe in the northwestern part of the state, where the January temperature averages 12 degrees. It's not quite as cold in the southeast—there, the temperature in January averages 22 degrees. Surprisingly, the areas with the mildest winters are along the shores of Lakes Michigan and Superior—the very places you'd expect to be coldest in winter. However, the winds off the lakes moderate the temperatures, keeping the air warmer in winter than that of the inland regions and cooler in summer than that of other areas of the state.

It can get pretty hot during a Wisconsin summer, but generally, it doesn't. July temperatures in the southeast average 73 degrees, while it's only a little bit cooler in the northwest—69 degrees is the average July temperature. The hottest day on record was July 13, 1936, when the mercury hit 114 degrees in Wisconsin Dells. The temperature fell to a record low in Danbury on January 24, 1922—the thermometer dropped to 54 degrees below zero.

The northwest gets the brunt of Wisconsin's snowfall—an average of more than 100 inches isn't unusual for Iron County, while the southern part of the state generally gets about 30 inches each winter. Wisconsin gets most of its rain between May and October. The state averages about 30 inches of rainfall each year.

THE PEOPLE OF WISCONSIN

Until lead was discovered in Wisconsin in the 1820s nobody paid much attention to the place except the Indians and a few French fur traders. Most of the Indians who lived there before the white man arrived in the seventeenth century were Winnebagos, Dakotas, and Menominees, all peaceable tribes of skillful craftsmen who also fished, hunted, and farmed. But as white settlement pushed west, the region that is now Wisconsin became a refuge for many tribes uprooted from their eastern and northern homes. The Chippewa came from Canada to the southern shore of Lake Superior, the Sacs moved in from Michigan to the Green Bay area, while the Foxes settled along the Fox River and the Ottawas encamped along the southern shore of Lake Superior. The Kickapoos, Hurons, Miami, Illinois, and Potawatomi eventually arrived, too.

None of the red men expressed any vehement objections when the first white explorer arrived. He was a Frenchman, Jean Nicolet, and it was more than twenty years before any other Frenchman ventured that far again. And when they did begin to arrive from their outpost in Quebec they were interested only in fur trading and converting the Indians to Christianity, not in settling down.

Even after the United States acquired control of the territory in 1783, few white men came to stay. It took the discovery of lead in the next century to bring about the area's first population boom—and boom it did. Miners and prospectors came from the East, and from Europe came the Irish, fleeing famines at home, along with Germans,

Poles, Scandinavians, Swiss, and English. To clear the way for them, the U. S. Army ruthlessly dispensed with the Indians and their claims during the Black Hawk War in 1832.

Many of the Germans and Poles settled in Milwaukee, a city that to this day proudly bears their imprint. Other Germans went to farm in the area between Racine and Sheboygan, while the Swiss clustered in the south-central region around New Glarus and some Poles headed toward the center of the state.

The Finns and Swedes found work in the woods felling trees during Wisconsin's nineteenth-century lumber boom, and other ethnic centers sprang up elsewhere. There's an island in Green Bay that once was believed to have the largest Icelandic colony in the United States, until a 1961 survey determined that only 18 per cent of Washington Island's Scandinavian population traced their ancestry to Iceland.

Despite the rout of the Indians in the 1832 Black Hawk War, there are enough Indians in Wisconsin today to warrant five reservations. All of Menominee County 35 miles northwest of Green Bay once was a reservation, but since 1961 it has been a county governed entirely by the Indians who live there. Indians also live on the Red Cliff Reservation on the tip of Bayfield Peninsula in the northwest, the Bad River Reservation along Lake Superior, and the Lac Court Oreilles Reservation near Couderay in the northwest. Here, the Chippewa still hunt and fish in the Grindstone Lake and Lac Court Oreilles. The fifth reservation, Lac du Flambeau, is popular with tourists, particularly when the powwows are held during July and August. Nearby is Strawberry Island, which the Chippewa have controlled since 1745. The Chippewa are believed to be the only survivors of the Ojibway nation, once the largest of the Algonquin tribes. All told, 19,000 Indians live on Wisconsin reservations.

Until the 1960s Wisconsin had only a small black population. But during that decade it increased 72 per cent and the 1970 census found that 130,000 blacks were living in the state, most of them in Milwaukee.

Although Wisconsin's population began to decline during the Great Depression of the 1930s it recently has begun to increase again. But today most of the people live in the southeastern industrialized area of the state around Milwaukee. The 1970 census found that 70 per cent of the population is there, concentrated in 20 per cent of the state's land area. Over the last forty years people have been migrating to the urban areas from the northern regions although the trend now appears to be slowing. However, like the rest of the country, Wisconsin in the past twenty years has seen a tremendous growth of suburban areas at the expense of the cities. Milwaukee, the twelfth-largest city in the United States, registered a population decline in the 1960s while the surrounding suburbs experienced a population boom.

HISTORY

Wisconsin's recorded history goes back to 1634 when a French explorer named Jean Nicolet beached his canoe near what is now Green Bay and stepped ashore convinced he had arrived in China. He was dressed for the occasion—a robe of Chinese damask, just the thing for an Oriental reception, but not what the awe-struck Winnebagos were accustomed to. Nicolet had been dispatched by the governor of New France to find a route from Quebec to China. He set out in a canoe laden with gifts and with seven Huron Indians to act as guides. After a three-month trip to Wisconsin, all he had found was that the New World was bigger than anyone had imagined.

That fiasco put an end to French exploration for a while. It was twenty years before a second contingent arrived. It was composed of Pierre Esprit Radisson and Médart Chouart, Sieur de Groseilliers, who were seeking to expand the French fur trade. The missionaries soon followed. A Jesuit, Father René Ménard, established a Catholic mission in 1660 and five years later Father Claude Jean Allouez founded five more.

For the most part, relations between the French and Indians in Wisconsin were peaceful. But trouble did break out in 1712 over whether the French or the Fox Indians should control the Fox and Wisconsin rivers. It took the French more than twenty-five years to establish supremacy. By then, the British were casting covetous eyes at the American interior and at Canada, which then was held by the French. In 1754 the two nations clashed in the French and Indian War, which didn't end until 1763. The victorious British took over the fur-trading posts and annexed the area that is now Wisconsin to the Province of Quebec, but they didn't get a chance to do much more before the Revolutionary War began in 1775. The United States gained control of Wisconsin at the end of the war and added it to the vast Indiana Territory in 1800. Eventually, it became part of the Illinois Territory and then part of the Michigan Territory.

Wisconsin remained a virtual wilderness until lead was discovered in 1824. When word got around that 17,000 pounds had been unearthed at a mine in Hazel Green in one day, there was no stopping the rush of prospectors. Some were in such a hurry to get to the ore that they didn't bother to build houses. Instead, they burrowed shelters into the hills and earned the nickname "badgers." But all the hurrying paid off—by the 1840s Wisconsin was supplying half the nation's lead. And Wisconsin still calls itself the Badger State in tribute to those early miners.

All of this was none too pleasing to the Indians, many of whom had retreated to Wisconsin after being uprooted from their homes farther east or in Canada. The Sacs were most aggressive in trying to regain their territories and their efforts brought on the Black Hawk War in 1832. Abraham Lincoln, Jefferson Davis, and Zachary Taylor all took part in the army rout of the Indians. Afterward, the surviving red men were forced into Iowa.

In April 1836 the Wisconsin Territory was created and the first legislature met in Belmont. At the time, the territory included part of Minnesota, Iowa, and North and South Dakota. Wisconsin's present-day boundaries weren't set until just before it became the thirtieth state in 1848. The decade between 1840 and 1850 saw a mushrooming of Wisconsin's population from 31,000 to 305,000.

The years leading up to the Civil War were turbulent politically in Wisconsin. Sentiment there was vehemently against the extension of slavery into the new territories of the west and political protest coalesced in 1854 at a meeting in Ripon when the state's Republican party was founded. Needless to say, Wisconsin was firmly in the Yankee camp during the Civil War. Thousands of men went off to fight for the Union, many of them in the Iron Brigade, one of the North's most respected fighting units.

After the war, timbering in Wisconsin took on the excitement that once had been generated by lead mining. These were the days of the lumber barons who masterminded the felling of millions of trees heedless of the fact that they were devastating the landscape. Nobody thought much about the damage they were doing in those days. Instead, the lumber boom gave rise to exuberant legends . . . the story of Paul Bunyan swinging his ax through the wilderness was one of the most popular.

The 1870s also saw one of the worst tragedies in Wisconsin's history—a forest fire broke out the night of October 8, 1871 and swept through part of northern Wisconsin, wiping out the village of Peshtigo and several other hamlets. Some eight hundred lives were lost. Ironically, the Great Chicago Fire occurred the same night, killing three hundred people. The Peshtigo fire did $5 million worth of damage in Wisconsin.

Although the state remained staunchly Republican, by the 1880s the party was firmly in the hands of the big businessmen who represented lumber and railroad interests. Their control in the last years of the nineteenth century was challenged by a Madison lawyer, Robert M. La Follette, Sr., who gained enough support to win the governorship in 1900. La Follette described himself as a Progressive and his political, social, and economic reforms did much to upgrade the quality of life in Wisconsin. Under his influence, the state imposed an inheritance tax, a railroad property tax, began to regulate railroad rates and service, and passed a law establishing direct primary elections. La Follette was elected to the U. S. Senate in 1906 and continued to serve until 1925. But he had set the wheels in motion for other reforms in Wisconsin: a commission to settle labor disputes and enforce labor laws, a workmen's compensation law, minimum wage laws for women and minors, pensions for mothers, full civil and property rights for women, pensions for teachers, and model laws for the incorporation of co-operatives.

La Follette himself achieved national political prominence as a Progressive leader in the Senate and as the Progressive candidate for President in 1924. At his death in 1925 his son Robert was elected to his Senate seat. The younger La Follette continued to hold it for twenty-one years. Ironically, Senator La Follette's career in Congress was terminated when he lost the 1946 Republican primary to Joseph R. McCarthy, who gained notoriety with his Communist "witchhunts" of the early 1950s.

Another La Follette served Wisconsin during the 1930s—Robert Sr.'s younger son Philip, who was elected governor three times. During his first administration in 1932, Wisconsin passed the first state unemployment compensation act.

Wisconsin's progressive approach to education, public welfare, and other programs has imposed some financial hardship. Because economic growth has sometimes faltered, the state has had to hike taxes dramatically since 1950. Coupled with the increases has been the imposition of a state sales tax. Politically, Wisconsin has moved away in recent years from its Republican and Progressive tradition. Democrats have shown increasing strength, and the state's Democratic presidential primary has taken on national significance.

INDUSTRY

Despite Wisconsin's pastoral image, it's a highly industrial state, a producer of such heavy machinery as engines, turbines, power cranes, and other construction equipment, as well as automobiles, ships, aircraft, motorcycles, household appliances, radios, and television sets. Manufacturing accounts for four fifths of Wisconsin's income. It brings the state more than $5 billion a year compared with slightly more than $1 billion generated by agriculture.

The most important industry in the state is the manufacture of non-electrical machinery—engines, farm machinery, machine tools, and metalworking machinery to name a few. The factories that turn out these products are located in Milwaukee and elsewhere in the southeastern corner of the state. In this area, too, are the state's big automotive plants, while shipbuilding takes place farther north along the lake shores—at Manitowoc and Sturgeon Bay on Lake Michigan and at Superior on Lake Superior.

The industrial area surrounding Milwaukee includes factories that produce railroad equipment, house trailers, motorcycles, and such electrical equipment as appliances, motors, and radio and television sets. And there's a big papermaking industry, sizable enough to place Wisconsin first among the states in the value of paper production. Its mills turn out tissue paper, wrapping paper, and paper boxes. This industry is an offshoot of the state's lumbering activity, once so extensive that its forests were virtually destroyed in the last years of the nineteenth century. Today, Wisconsin produces about 400 million board feet of timber a year.

Food processing is of enormous importance in Wisconsin. The state's dairy farms provide huge supplies of milk used in the production of butter, ice cream, evaporated and dried milk, and other dairy items. Wisconsin is the source of the nation's entire supply of malted milk products and produces more milk and cheese than any other state. It is the source of 45 per cent of the nation's cheese supply and 15 per cent of the milk.

Wisconsin brews a lot of beer, too, more than any other state, and more than enough to justify Milwaukee's nickname of "Beer Capital" of the United States. The state also cans a lot of fruits and vegetables —the sweet corn, peas, snap and lima beans, cranberries, and sour cherries grown on the state's farms.

AGRICULTURE

Wisconsin calls itself America's dairyland and with good reason: It produces 15 per cent of the milk and 45 per cent of the cheese Americans consume. The state has been famous for its dairying for more than a century and since 1912 has led the nation in the production of milk, cheese, and butter. More than 3 million dairy cows produce more than 2 billion gallons of milk a year.

Dairying has been big business in the state since 1870. Only two years after that, the Wisconsin's Dairymen's Association was established to promote and improve the state's dairy products. Eventually, it urged farmers to market their products co-operatively and some still do. As late as 1967, dairy interests were powerful enough in the state legislature to prohibit the sale of margarine with yellow food coloring in Wisconsin. That law has since been changed.

Not all of Wisconsin's 119,000 farms are devoted to dairying. Some farmers raise beef cattle and hogs, and others raise hay to feed the livestock—enough hay to make Wisconsin first in the nation in hay production.

Most of the green peas and sweet corn Americans buy in cans is raised in Wisconsin. And farmers there grow lots of beets, cabbages, lima and snap beans, as well as carrots, cucumbers, onions, and potatoes. Fruit crops include raspberries, strawberries, apples, and cranberries.

Wisconsin farmers also raise bees and minks—bees for their honey and the beeswax used in lipstick and candle manufacturing, and minks for coats and collars.

NATURAL RESOURCES

Ask a vacationer about Wisconsin's natural resources and he's likely to sing the praises of the lakes, the woods, the foliage, and the animal life. A businessman, on the other hand, might think in terms of the sand and gravel deposits, the granite, the iron ore, and the lead and zinc. And a farmer would probably speak of the fertile soils in the southern and western parts of the state.

Originally, Wisconsin's forests were its richest natural resource. Unfortunately, those days are gone. Lumbering in the latter years of the nineteenth century destroyed much of the state's north woods and the area is only just beginning to recover as a result of massive reforestation programs. But to a visitor's eye, Wisconsin's woods leave little to be desired: Forests cover half the state with ash, aspen, basswood, elm, maple, oak, yellow birch, balsam, fir, hemlock, pine, spruce, tamarack, and white cedar. Bears, coyotes, deer, and foxes still populate the forests and the lakes abound with bass, muskellunge, pickerel, pike, sturgeon, and trout.

Mining in Wisconsin isn't what it once was. During the 1800s the state produced about half the country's lead. Today, the most valuable minerals are sand and gravel found throughout the state, limestone and sandstone in the south, granite in the center and north, and iron ore in Iron County. Valuable clays are mined in Brown, Dunn, Fond du Lac, Manitowoc, Racine, Sauk, and Waupaca counties, and there's still some lead and zinc in Grant, Iowa, and Lafayette counties.

CITIES

What Pittsburgh is to steel and Detroit is to cars, **Milwaukee** is to beer. The city's famous breweries date from the arrival of thousands of German immigrants who bypassed the big cities of the East for the northwestern frontier when it hadn't extended much farther than the western shores of Lake Michigan. In the mid-1800s, Milwaukee was just a dot on the map, a rude outpost where the Milwaukee, Menominee, and Kinnickinnic rivers emptied into the lake. When the

PLATE 31 Tourists, riding an authentic wagon train, stop in front of Castle Rock, Kansas.

PLATE 32 Wheat harvest in Kansas.

PLATE 33 The only unaltered Pony Express Station in the country still stands near Hanover, Kansas.

PLATE 34 President Dwight D. Eisenhower's boyhood home in Abilene.

PLATE 35 Chimney Rock, the guidepost in Nebraska for
pioneers on their route west.

PLATE 36 The discovery of oil in western North Dakota has boosted the state's economy.

PLATE 37 The rugged terrain of the Badlands, northwest of Crawford, Nebraska.

PLATE 38 Scotts Bluff National Monument in western Nebraska evokes memories of the famed Oregon Trail and Pony Express.

PLATE 39 The Snake River winding its way through northwestern Nebraska.

PLATE 40 A herd of buffalo roams North Dakota's Theodore Roosevelt National Park.

PLATE 41 This cairn, or mound of stones, indicates the geographical center of North America at Rugby, North Dakota.

PLATE 42 The annual trip of the Fort Seward Wagon Train in North Dakota, en route to one of the state's many historic sites.

PLATE 43 Aerial view of Garrison Dam and Reservoir on the Missouri River in central North Dakota.

PLATE 44 This unusual "Byzantine" structure is Mitchell, South Dakota's Corn Palace.

PLATE 45 Korczak Ziolkowski stands next to the Crazy Horse Monument he sculpted, near Custer, South Dakota.

Germans began to arrive, the population of the area was insignificant—an 1840 map indicates between two and eighteen persons per square mile. But there was rich farm land for the asking, and no obstacles to the burgeoning German community, which clung to its language, its traditions, and, of course, its beer.

Almost two hundred years before the arrival of the German immigrants, French explorers, missionaries, and fur traders had roamed the shores of Lake Michigan. The Jesuit Jacques Marquette visited the area as early as 1674, but although others came after him, it wasn't until 1795 that another Frenchman, Jacques Vieau, settled and built a trading post. The location he picked was midway between the old French settlement at Green Bay and a new one farther south along the lake that was to become Chicago.

During the first half of the nineteenth century, southeast Wisconsin was rural, the German settlers apparently content to tend their farms and sip their beer. All that changed during the 1880s after iron ore was discovered on the shores of Lake Superior to the northwest. Factories sprang up at Milwaukee to process the ore and convert the raw metal into manufactured goods. Now the twelfth largest industrial city in the United States, Milwaukee's most important products are heavy machinery and electrical equipment.

By the late nineteenth and early twentieth century Milwaukee was no longer an exclusively German city. Poles, Italians, and other ethnic groups came to work in its factories. But in some ways the city still retains some of its early German character. Its famous restaurants are German, its civic festivals are usually described as "fests," and its breweries are a constant reminder of the city's German heritage. A visit to one of them is a must for any tourist who comes to town. Anyone old enough to drink gets a free sample after taking a tour.

For many visitors, Milwaukee is a pleasant surprise. It's cleaner and more orderly than many of today's large industrial cities. The graceful residential areas along the lake front blend into the park that extends northward along the shore. A stop at the public museum provides a reminder that it wasn't so very long ago that the whole area was virgin territory known only to the Indians and a few fur traders. The museum is famous for displays which trace the evolution of plant and animal life from their earliest stages to their present recognizable forms. Another unique exhibit is the museum's collection of rare rocks. But for those who care more for human than for natural history, there's a section where the streets of old Milwaukee have been re-created.

One of the city's biggest attractions is the County Zoo, a carefully designed and landscaped park where animals appear to be wandering about in the open, unprotected from each other. What you can't see are moats which separate natural enemies of the animal world from one another. Among the zoo's prizes are three white rhinoceroses, several camels, polar bears, and Siberian tigers. The antics of a gorilla usually draw a crowd of youngsters once they realize that he can't break the glass that surrounds his cage.

Among Milwaukee's landmarks are two churches which are architecturally unique for different reasons. The St. Joan of Arc Chapel on the campus of Marquette University was brought from France stone by stone and reassembled on Long Island in New York. Then it was taken apart again and moved to Milwaukee. Dating from the fifteenth century, the Gothic-style chapel is a local treasure, authentic in every detail. The other church is the dramatically modern Annunciation Greek Orthodox Church designed by Frank Lloyd Wright. The city's art center and war memorial is the work of another great architect, Eero Saarinen. The center, considered a work of art in itself, overlooks the lake.

The story of how **Madison** got to be the capital of Wisconsin will give you a notion of the shrewdness of the land speculators who forged into the wilderness ahead of anyone else. A onetime judge named James Duane Doty was exploring the backwoods of Wisconsin in 1829, nearly twenty years before the territory became a state. He managed to acquire quite a bit of property for himself, land that was to come in handy in 1836 when the territorial legislature was trying to decide where to put the capital. He persuaded the lawmakers to choose an uninhabited spot he owned and had named Madison. At the time it was just some trees and underbrush picturesquely situated between Lake Mendota, Lake Monona, and Lakes Waubesa and Kegonsa. The place had been bypassed by the pioneers, who dismissed it as "beautiful but uninhabitable." Once the decision was made to locate the capital there an enterprising family of settlers went out to Madison in 1837 to set up a boardinghouse to accommodate the workmen who were to build a capitol. By the time the legislators arrived in 1838 Madison consisted of the boardinghouse, a general store, a cabin used as a school, and the uncompleted capitol. Things were so bad that when the lawmakers assembled, one of the first proposals they considered was to move the capital somewhere else.

Conditions improved once the railroad arrived in 1854, but the University of Wisconsin, established in 1849, was barely managing to survive. The Civil War gave Madison's economy a boost—by the time it was over, the town's businesses were solidly established, its factories were busily producing farm tools, tinware, flour, beer, clothing, and shoes. Even the non-denominational university, lambasted at one time for its "godlessness," recovered from the setback it suffered during the war when most of the students went off to fight. Today, Madison is a city of nearly 175,000 persons and the university is one of the most respected institutions in the country. The capitol building the early legislators grumbled about is long gone. The current one, considered one of the most graceful in the United States, was built in 1848. It's an Italian Renaissance structure with an exterior of gleaming white Vermont granite and a 282-foot dome second only in height to the dome of the U. S. Capitol in Washington.

The University of Wisconsin now occupies 1,000 landscaped acres on Lake Mendota and serves as the center of Madison's cultural life. The library contains 2.5 million books, including the prized Thordardson Collection on the history and development of English science, ornithology, and botany, and the Duveen Collection of alchemy and chemical history. There's always something going on on campus —a concert, a play, a lecture, a forum.

Once you've seen the university, checked out the State Historical Society Museum downtown, and taken a look at all the things that can be made out of wood at the U. S. Forest Products Laboratory, you ought to take a camel ride. The Vilas Park Zoo on Lake Wingra provides the camel (it's got a whole herd of them) and if you've ever wanted to take a trip on the "ship of the desert," drop by any Sunday during the summer for a free ride.

Green Bay, the oldest town in Wisconsin, is famous for its professional football team, something that no doubt would astound the French explorers who thought the beaver was the most important local attraction. The French came in the seventeenth century to trade with the Indians. There aren't many Indians around Green Bay today, and the dollar has long since replaced beaver skins as the accepted currency. Even the water isn't the same as it used to be—it was so green when the British arrived in 1761 that they changed the name of the French settlement from La Baye to Green Bay. The British also built Fort Howard, which they eventually surrendered to the Americans. The fur trade continued to dominate the economy of the Green Bay area until after completion of the Erie Canal in 1825. Then the town became a shipping center and a market for the farms established on its outskirts. Later, the town turned to lumbering. Today, shipping is still important although Green Bay has become a city of paper mills and cheese processing plants.

Without question, the most important local landmark in Green Bay is Lambeau Stadium, home of the Green Bay Packers, and the adjacent Green Bay Packer Hall of Fame with its display of the trophies the team has collected over the years. And for those people with an interest in local history, the Fort Howard Hospital Museum is an intriguing stop. Built as a hospital in 1816, it is all that remains today of the old fort. It's a simple white frame structure containing nineteenth-century furniture brought from the East by the officers assigned to the fort after the British turned it over to the Americans.

Another local point of interest is the Tank Cottage, the oldest house standing in Wisconsin. A French trader, Francis Roi, built the original section in 1776. The second owner expanded it, and the third owner, a Norwegian named Nils Otto Tank, improved it by covering the outside of the log cottage with clapboard and plastering the inside walls. The furniture displayed there today was brought from Holland by Tank's wife.

One of Green Bay's distinguished nineteenth-century citizens built his house, Hazelwood, on the other side of the Fox River. Morgan L. Martin, a New York lawyer, came to Green Bay in 1827. He became a member of the legislative council of the Michigan Territory and later served as president of the convention that drew up Wisconsin's state constitution. Hazelwood, a white frame house set back from the road, has a colonnaded porch overlooking the river and another facing the road.

Racine and **Kenosha** have two things in common: Both are industrial cities and both are on Lake Michigan south of Milwaukee. They are so close together that you can see Racine from Kenosha and vice versa—only 12 miles separate the two cities. Racine is older. It goes back to a settlement established by Jacques Vieau, a French fur trader, in the eighteenth century. The place was unnoticed until the middle of the nineteenth century, when the railroad connected it to Beloit and Milwaukee. Enough Czechs, English, Irish, Germans, and Danes arrived then to give it a unique cosmopolitan flavor. The manufacture of farm machinery was the town's first important industry, but today Racine has numerous industries, including the production of metal products.

Kenosha was settled by native Americans in 1835. Irish, English, and German immigrants came after the city managed to improve its harbor and built up its shipping activities. Kenosha is still an important lake port, but it's better known as the home of American Motors Corporation. And, just for the record, the largest automobile plant in the United States is in Kenosha, not Detroit.

La Crosse is the largest Wisconsin city along the Mississippi. It got its name when it was just a Winnebago campsite: Visiting fur traders noticed the Indians playing a game that reminded them of the French sport *la crosse*. The first settlers arrived in 1842, and six years later the Winnebagos were removed to Minnesota, a development that put a big dent in the local fur trade. The economy improved when the railroad came through and lumbering began to develop. German immigrants arrived via the railroad, bringing their culture, their love of singing, and their taste for beer. They established breweries in short order, but until the turn of the century, the local economy was dominated by sawmills and lumber markets. Today, La Crosse manufactures a variety of products, among them farm tools and beer.

A local landmark you can't miss—even if you try—is Granddad Bluff, a 1,172-foot crag that towers over the center of the city and affords a spectacular view of the Mississippi and, on a clear day, of two neighboring states, Iowa and Minnesota.

SPORTS AND RECREATION

Bordered on three sides by water and laced with 1,700 rivers and streams and more than 8,000 lakes, Wisconsin has something for everyone who loves the out of doors. Needless to say, the fishing is terrific: muskie, walleye, northern pike, and bass in the inland lakes and rivers, and fighting fish like coho and Chinook salmon, brown trout, and sturgeon in the waters of Lake Michigan and Lake Erie. There's swimming, sailing, canoeing, and even skin-diving for the asking. The state has mapped miles of canoe trails for both experienced adventurers who want the thrills of shooting the rapids and for novices who just want to paddle down a quiet stream and admire the scenery.

Bicycling has become increasingly popular in recent years and got a big boost when the state established a bikeway that spans the 300 miles from Kenosha to La Crosse. Elsewhere, bike trails have been set aside in more than thirty counties—Milwaukee, Waukesha, and Racine counties alone offer more than 200 miles of trails and streets reserved exclusively for cyclists. And the state has adopted a policy of putting in a bikeway along any highway it improves, safety permitting.

Winter in Wisconsin has come to mean skiing and snowmobiling. The state has more than 250 slopes of every description, from gentle hills for beginners to long, steep courses for the experts. Cross-country skiing has been gaining adherents—they call it "ski touring" in Wisconsin. Hundreds of areas have been set aside for the sport, which requires less skill than downhill skiing and generally means just gliding across the snow.

The snowmobile has become a virtual lifeline in parts of northern Wisconsin, where residents can be housebound for weeks on end in winter if they don't have a means of traveling across the snow. Elsewhere, however, snowmobiling means zipping along marked trails or across fields that farmers often open to snowmobilers for a fee.

Fall is hunting season, a time for sportsmen to take to the north woods in search of black bear and white-tailed deer. And there's plenty of small game, too: geese, duck, grouse, pheasant, woodcock, rabbit, and squirrels. Wisconsin sets aside a special period for those who prefer to hunt with bow and arrow.

Milwaukee is a sports-minded town of baseball, football, basketball, and polo fans. Milwaukee has not one but two polo teams. The season begins in June and, throughout the summer, crowds of five thousand or more watch the matches at the city's Uihlein Stadium, built by the president of the Jos. Schlitz Brewing Company, a polo player himself. The sport has caught on to such an extent that Milwaukee's polo club bills itself as the "Summertime Polo Capital of America."

The city's baseball team, the Milwaukee Brewers, has plenty of fans, too, as do the Milwaukee Bucks, the pro basketball team. Come football season and the eyes of Wisconsin are on the Green Bay Packers.

POINTS OF INTEREST

Even in the last century people enjoyed a vacation in Door County, the peninsula that juts out into Lake Michigan. Green Bay separates it from the mainland. Door County's appeal has remained the same over the years—cool breezes off the lake, picturesque villages, white frame resort hotels, and leisurely summer days. There are wide green lawns, shade trees, and little towns that haven't changed much in the past hundred years. And the area's got a Scandinavian flavor—Norwegians and Swedes settled here in towns like Ephraim, Egg Harbor, Sister Bay, Ellison Bay, and Gills Rock.

Ephraim, with just over two hundred people, is considered the summer capital of the county. Moravians from Central Europe settled here back in 1853 after life in Green Bay got too hectic for them. They built a church and went about the business of leading quiet, unworldly lives. Even today, the town reflects their principles: You can't get an alcoholic drink there, not even Milwaukee's beer. Ephraim is particularly popular with golfers—its Peninsula State Park is considered one of the two best courses in the state. The other one is Bay Ridge in nearby Sister Bay.

Just off the tip of the peninsula is Washington Island, a Scandinavian settlement of some three hundred people. Every summer, thousands make the trip from the mainland to fish or just to wander through the woods. The boat ride across the infamous "Death's Door"—the strait that separates the island from the mainland—is a good deal safer on today's sturdy ferries than it was in the days when the flimsy ships of French explorers fell victim to the treacherous currents.

Lake Superior has its islands, too—a group of twenty-two of them that constitute the Apostle Islands National Lakeshore. The Chippewa were the first to take refuge on these islands—they fled the marauding Foxes and Sioux and encamped on the largest of the Apostles, Madeline Island. The French fur traders came along later in the seventeenth century and in 1693 one of them built La Pointe, a fort that eventually became an important trading post. Today it's a museum that will give you some idea of what island life was like when only the Indians and fur traders were around and how things have changed over the years. Now the Apostles are a wilderness preserve and recreation area administered by the U. S. Department of the Interior. To get there, you take a ferry from Bayfield.

If you'd like a look at the islands but don't want to make the trip, you can get a pretty good view from the Red Cliff Indian Reservation on the tip of Bayfield Peninsula. The reservation is one of four in the northern part of the state. Visitors are welcome at all of them. Red Cliff is somewhat remote, so tourists usually stop off at Lac Court Oreilles (pronounced, and sometimes spelled, "Corderay"), where the Chippewa still hunt and fish. An enterprising businessman at Hayward, just north of the reservation, has restored the tiriy village as it was when logging was the main industry in these parts, and Chippewa demonstrate their age-old crafts at his Historyland Indian Village. For the price of admission you can see how the Indians made their canoes out of birch, tanned leather, and processed wild rice.

The Chippewa at the Lac du Flambeau reservation farther east stage powwows all summer and visitors can explore their reservation any time of the year. Lac du Flambeau once was controlled by the Sioux, who yielded the territory to the Chippewa after a battle in 1645. The Chippewa have been there ever since. The place got its name from some French fur traders who happened along one night in the seventeenth century while the Indians were fishing by torchlight. *Flambeau* means "torch" or "flame" in French.

What draws most visitors to Wisconsin's north woods is fishing. The lakes of the area are well stocked with muskies, fish that can grow to tremendous size: Someone once caught a 60-pounder, and the little towns throughout the area are engaged in continuous competitions to see if anyone can land a bigger one. The muskies are bred at the State Fish Hatchery at Spooner, one of the two main attractions of this little town west of the Lac Court Oreilles Reservation. The other one is the Museum of Woodcarving, famous for artist Joseph Barta's life-size representation of *The Last Supper*.

Wisconsinites call the whole northwestern part of their state "Indian Head Country" because on the map it looks like the profile of an Indian chief facing west. Eau Claire, an industrial town of some 45,000 people, is poised on the edge of the wilderness to the north and likes to call itself the "Gateway to Indian Head Country." Sixteen state parks and forests are scattered through the eighteen-county region.

Tomahawk to the northeast is generally conceded to be the jumping-off spot to the Great North Woods—what the local folks call the wilderness of northeast and north-central Wisconsin. Serious fishermen know and love these parts—little towns like Manitowish Waters and Manitowish have a big reputation among anglers. The population thins out the farther north you go. In fact, it's not too much of an exaggeration to say that there are more lakes than there are permanent residents of these parts. Rhinelander has just over 1,300 people today, but it once was the logging capital of the north woods. There's a logging museum in the town now that'll give you an idea of how the nineteenth-century lumberjacks lived and worked. Along with all the relics of the old days—the tables set with tin plates and cups, the bunkhouse, and the fully equipped kitchen—there's a replica of a somewhat unusual beast that once terrified pioneers in the area. It's a monster 7 feet long and 30 inches high with tusks and a backbone of a dozen horns. When it first appeared, the pioneers called it a "hodag," and nobody knew what to make of it. It turned out that the creature was a hoax—a man-made monster of oxhides and wood. You'll see lots of references to it around Rhinelander—now that no one's afraid of it, the hodag has become something of a local mascot.

The north woods still have a healthy bear population, and the creatures have learned that the town dumps near Land O'Lakes, Presque Isle, and Three Lakes offer a free lunch. You can spot them there at dusk sifting through the trash in search of tasty tidbits. Dusk is also a good time to see the deer that live deep in the woods. They're timid, but they do venture out to the roadside at twilight to nibble at the grass.

In southern Wisconsin, the most famous of Wisconsin's tourist attractions is just a short drive from Madison. The Wisconsin Dells are an awe-inspiring sight—a scenic wonder that has fascinated generations of visitors to the area. The Dells were carved by the currents of the Wisconsin River, which over the centuries shaped the surrounding soft sandstone into intricate shapes—here, a rock that looks like a chimney; there, one that reminded the early rivermen of "Black Hawk's Head." The most fantastic is Stand Rock, a pillar that rises 45 feet into the air to form a sandstone slab. A cruise down the river has always been the best way to see the Dells. The state has maintained the beauty of the area, prohibiting commercial enterprises that would mar the natural setting.

There's another breath-taking sight not far away, but this one's underground. The Cave of the Mounds, between Mount Horeb and

Blue Mounds, was discovered in 1939 by a road construction crew quarrying limestone on a farm belonging to a family named Brigham. It was quite a find. The cave contains fourteen rooms connected by narrow underground passages, an eerie wonderland with stalactites hanging from the ceiling and stalagmites rising from the floor. Embedded in the walls are the fossils of shellfish that lived 400 million years ago! Indeed, geologists say it took millions of years for seeping water to carve the cave out of sedimentary rock.

Many people who come to this part of Wisconsin are interested in Taliesin, the home architect Frank Lloyd Wright built, in the village of Spring Green on the Wisconsin River. Wright also established a school of architecture on the grounds, and since his death, the house has become part of the school. Ironically, another house in the neighborhood arouses even more interest and awe. The House on the Rock built by Madison sculptor Alex Jordan perches precariously on a chimney rock that towers over the Wyoming Valley below. It took more than 15,000 feet of steel wire to anchor the house firmly to its moorings.

There's a definite European flavor to south-central Wisconsin. Norwegians settled around Mount Horeb in the 1800s, and if you want to see how they lived, stop by at the "Valley of the Elves," also called "Little Norway." A local promoter restored the sod-roofed house and farm buildings of the first Norwegian family to settle here as the core of his Scandinavian village.

But far more famous than the Norwegians are the Swiss of Green County to the south. So many of them settled in these parts that the county is referred to simply as "Switzerland." The town of New Glarus is thoroughly Swiss—they even celebrate Switzerland's Independence Day here on the first Sunday in August with a *Volkfest* that features lots of yodeling. Many of the buildings lining the main street look like Swiss chalets, and two local museums, the Chalet of the Golden Fleece and the Swiss Historical Village, are devoted to Swiss traditions and culture. There's even a lace factory on the outskirts of town which still produces fine Swiss embroidery.

Anyone who doesn't know that the five Ringling brothers got their start in Wisconsin will doubtless be surprised to hear that the state calls itself the "Mother of Circuses." The Ringlings were from Baraboo and put on their first show in the back yard of the local jailhouse in 1884. For the next thirty-four years, Baraboo was the winter home of the circus. Now it's the home of the Circus World Museum, a dazzling collection of paraphernalia from the days of the big top.

It took Baraboo more than forty years to decide to pay tribute to the Ringlings, but when it opened the museum in 1959, it did it in style: In addition to the original wagons, posters, and a 25,000-piece miniature of the Ringling Brothers Circus as it once was, the museum puts on a daily display of how the traveling circus worked in its heyday. Teams of horses unload the wagons from railroad flatcars, a calliope plays in almost continuous concert, world-famous performers are on hand periodically, and, just for good measure, when the weather is good, the elephants go out to bathe in the Baraboo River.

Once a year, the wagons, horses, and other animals get a real workout. They travel to Milwaukee for the Fourth of July Circus Parade, an event that's gotten more and more popular since its inception in 1963. Some five hundred horses draw the wagons through the streets and two dozen elephants tromp alongside.

SPECIAL EVENTS

During late June and early July the circus comes to Milwaukee from Baraboo, home of the Circus World Museum, Wisconsin's tribute to five of its most famous sons—the Ringling brothers. The circus is a big attraction during Old Milwaukee Days, lasting for nearly a week, when the city salutes its history and heritage. A visit to the circus during Old Milwaukee Days is free, courtesy of the city. There are fireworks, too, and free concerts, part of a grand celebration that winds up on the Fourth of July when thousands of spectators line the downtown streets for the annual circus parade. It's all done with a flourish that even the Ringlings could envy.

Old Milwaukee Days is just the beginning of a series of summer events in Wisconsin's biggest city. In July, there's the Summerfest, the Greater Milwaukee (golf) Open, and the 4-H Club Junior Fair to keep things exciting. Elsewhere in the state, the emphasis is on ethnic festivals: New Glarus, the little Swiss town in Green County, holds a Heidi Festival in June, celebrates Switzerland's Independence Day in August, and winds up the summer season with the Wilhelm Tell Pageant on Labor Day. Racine honors its Danish heritage with Kringle Day in May; Ephraim pays tribute to its Norwegian settlers with the Fry-Bal Fest and Regatta in June; Sheboygan serves up the beer and bratwurst on Brat Day, the first Saturday in August, and La Crosse stages a week-long Oktoberfest with lots of dancing, beer, and bratwurst.

Up north, the towns of Hayward and Boulder Junction both claim to be the "muskie capital of the world" and spend the summer trying to outdo one another to prove it. Hayward gets things started with its Muskie Festival in June, a celebration featuring parades and Indian dancing. Boulder Junction counters with its Muskie Jamboree, famous for the free meal of baked muskie and wild rice served to the thousands of visitors who come. In July, Hayward hosts its Lumberjack World Championships, a series of logrolling, chopping, sawing, and tree climbing contests.

During the winter, the action in northern Wisconsin switches to the towns of Eagle River, Rhinelander, and Three Lakes, which pool their resources for the annual Snowmobile Marathon and Derby in January. It's considered the biggest and best of the state's innumerable winter snowmobile races. The other big January event is Beloit's Silver Skates Racing Derby. On the agenda in February are Iola's Winter Carnival, the Presque Isle Fishing Jamboree, and Westby's ski jumping tournament.

P.D.

CHRONOLOGY

1634 Jean Nicolet, a French explorer from Quebec, landed on the shores of Green Bay believing he had arrived in China.

1660 Father René Ménard, a Jesuit, established a mission near what is now Ashland, Wisconsin.

1712 The French and the Fox Indians began a twenty-eight-year struggle for control of the Fox and Wisconsin rivers.

1763 Wisconsin was annexed to the Province of Quebec by the British after the French were defeated in the French and Indian War.

1783 Wisconsin came under U.S. control at the end of the Revolution.

1824 Lead was discovered at Hazel Green.

1832 U.S. troops defeated the Sac Indians in the Black Hawk War.

1836 The Wisconsin Territory was created by Congress.

1848 Wisconsin was admitted to the Union as the thirtieth state.

1854 The Republican party was founded at Ripon.

1870 The lumber boom began, attracting thousands to the state.

1871 Some eight hundred persons were killed in the Peshtigo forest fire.

1872 The Wisconsin Dairymen's Association was founded.

1900 Robert M. La Follette, Sr., was elected governor.

1911 Wisconsin approved creation of pensions for teachers and establishment of a commission to settle labor disputes.

1924 Robert M. La Follette, Sr., was defeated in his bid for the U.S. presidency as a Progressive party candidate.

1930 Philip F. La Follette was elected governor.

1932 The first state unemployment compensation act was passed in Wisconsin.

1946 Joseph R. McCarthy defeated Robert M. La Follette, Jr., in the Republican primary and went on to election to the U. S. Senate.

1958 Gaylord Nelson became the first Democrat elected governor of Wisconsin since 1932.

1964 The U. S. Supreme Court reapportioned Wisconsin's legislative districts.

1969 Reopening of renovated Pabst Theatre in Milwaukee for performing arts concerts; originally built in 1895.

1976 For nation's Bicentennial, Old World Wisconsin Museum opened in Eagle.

1978 The 1977–79 state budget reflected about $400 million in surplus funds in the state treasury. Proposals on what to do with the money spurred political debate.

1979 A $942 million tax-cut bill was signed into law by Governor Lee Dreyfus, in office less than eight weeks. After an eight-week tax moratorium starting in May, a new, lower tax rate went into effect.

THE PLAINS STATES

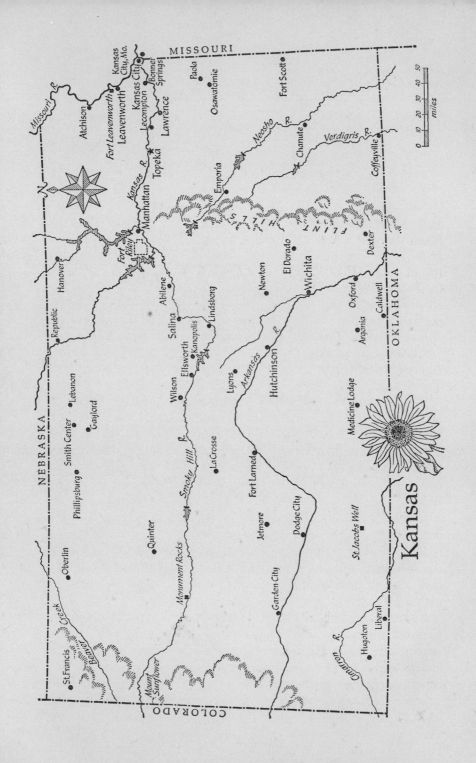

Kansas

KANSAS

MOST PEOPLE believe Kansas deserves to be called the plainest of the Plains states. It is an unfair evaluation that is based upon experiences of those who speedily traverse the seemingly flat landscape on their way to "spectacular" scenery. People who dig below the surface of the endless ocean of grains and grasses discover a land fertile in rip-roaring history. Furrowed deep are famous trails like Santa Fe, Oregon, and Chisholm, over which came pioneers of exceptional stamina. It was a quality necessary to overcome a host of climatic disasters and locusts, gunslingers, rustlers, and law officers of dubious quality. Abilene, Wichita, and Dodge City became synonymous with law and disorder.

Kansas statehood was the final major issue over which the North and South split. Kansas was where abolitionist John Brown tested his handful of men before heading for Harpers Ferry. It was the land upon which antislavery and proslavery groups battled with ferocity sufficient to earn the territory the nickname "Bleeding Kansas." A less horrific appellative for modern times is "Breadbasket of the World." Kansas is America's number one wheat producer. Agriculture and agribusiness are major industries along with manufacturing and mining.

Every pilot knows the state as the "Aircraft Capital of the World." Airplane buffs will find the main manufacturing facilities for Beech-craft, Cessna, and Lear in Wichita. Together they produce over 60 per cent of all the airplanes made in the United States.

Kansas is the Sunflower State. The yellow-rayed blossoms bloom as prolifically across the grasslands as once did American buffalo, the state animal. Bison are found today only in parks and zoos, and the largest herd is located at Maxwell State Game Preserve along with a collection of other prairie wildlife.

There are two state birds. The western meadow lark officially won the title on Kansas Day in 1925 when school children overwhelmingly voted in its favor. Unofficially, the jayhawker is the Kansans' favorite. It is a legendary bird whose origins date back to a pioneer of minimal resources who said he would make the rugged journey across Kansas by "jayhawking" his way. A cross between the quarrelsome blue jay and fighting sparrowhawk, the jayhawker embodies qualities Kansans believe inherent in themselves. It takes a stubborn, tough, resilient individual to survive in a gentle rolling land whose history is frequently punctuated with violence, hardship, and disaster. Therefore, it is not surprising that the State Legislature in 1861 voted to adopt the motto "Ad Astra per Aspera," "to the stars through difficulty." It is a saying befitting the land and the character of its people.

THE LAND

Kansas would be a perfect rectangle if the Missouri River didn't clip off the northeast corner. East to west the state stretches 411 miles. It is 208 miles wide and encompasses a total of 82,264 square miles.

Contrary to belief, this fourteenth-largest state is not entirely without vertical scenery. True, much of the central and western portions are tableland with few trees. However, the eastern half has hills which are particularly well timbered near the Missouri River border. Mount Sunflower in Wallace County, next to the Colorado border, reaches the highest point of 4,026 feet. Gradually, the land slopes toward the east. Near Coffeyville on the Oklahoma border it dips to the low of 686 feet.

A series of chalk pinnacles along the Smoky Hill River near Quinter are outcroppings of sedimented remains of ancient marine life. Millions of years ago much of Kansas was covered by an inland sea and important prehistoric fossils have been found.

Two main rivers drain the state. In the south, the Arkansas predominates. It shares the landscape with the Cimarron to the west and Verdigris and Neosho rivers to the east. Eleven principal rivers and numerous smaller streams make up the Kansas River basin in the north. Initial inquiry as to the location of the river may bring puzzlement to the newcomer. Locals refer to it only as the "Kaw." Actually, none of these waterways is truly navigable. Kansas also has few natural lakes. However, several man-made bodies of water have been created as part of the system providing irrigation and flood control.

CLIMATE

With little to impede them, the winds that cut through central Kansas make it one of the windiest inland areas in the nation. Icy Arctic blasts from the north and hot moist breezes from the Gulf of Mexico create short periods of extremes in weather conditions which can bring sudden blizzards or heat waves of over 100° F. January, the coldest month, has a mean temperature of 30° F. while in July, the warmest, it hovers around 79° F. The annual temperature averages 55° F.

Kansas averages fifty tornadoes a year, which is low compared to other states in the Great Basin Region. One of the most damaging single tornadoes in the nation did occur June 8, 1966, when it ripped through the heart of Topeka, destroying an area eight miles long and four blocks wide. Sixteen people were killed, 406 injured, and over $100 million in property was damaged.

Sunshine abounds. There are anywhere from 275 clear or partly clear days in the east to 300 such days in the west. Rain, and at times lack of it, is the nemesis. Average rainfall ranges from a high of 40 inches a year in the southeast to a low of 26 inches in the west. Fifteen inches along the Colorado border is not uncommon. Devastating floods covered much of the eastern and southern portions of the state in 1951. The first severe recorded drought occurred in 1860. Although others followed, none reached comparable magnitude except those of the 1930s and 1950s.

THE KANSANS

The original territorial Kansans were principally Anglo-Saxons from New England. After the Civil War, the building of railroads attracted Central Europeans. A few dollars and the offer of free land when the track-laying job was finished brought many Russians, Germans, Bohemians, and Scandinavians. It is from these ancestors that the majority of the 93 per cent native white population are derived. German ancestry predominates. Mexicans and Canadians also found Kansas to their liking.

Migration patterns eventually mixed the population. However, small communities persist where the majority of people are of one ethnic background. Annual events such as the After Harvest Czech Festival in Wilson or Mexican Fiestas in Topeka and Garden City remember these heritages. Lindsborg, known as "Little Sweden, U.S.A.," was honored by a visit from King Carl Gustaf of Sweden in 1976. Today, foreigners continue to immigrate to Kansas but represent a small 1.2 per cent of the total 2,246,578 population.

The history of blacks in Kansas is more impressive than the small 4.5 per cent minority they represent. Slavery was the major issue in the battle for statehood. Proslavers used Lecompton as their capital. Abolitionists headquartered in Lawrence and made the town an important station in the Underground Railway which helped slaves escape Southern servitude. However, no matter how fervent abolitionists were to set slaves free, they did not want blacks living in Kansas.

This attitude subsided somewhat after the Civil War. During the late nineteenth century, Kansas became one of the recipients of the Negro Exodus movement. The black population increased but personal freedom was as poor as anywhere else in the country.

In 1951 a Topeka clergyman took his nine-year-old daughter to the door of an all-white school. When she was denied enrollment, he found a lawyer. March 17, 1954, the Supreme Court decided that segregated education, "separate but equal," was inherently unequal and must be eliminated. Since then, *Brown* vs. *Board of Education of Topeka* has become the basis for most Civil Rights decisions concerning school segregation.

Kansas women were given complete suffrage in 1912. However, fifty-one years prior to that, they were voting in school elections and in 1887 gained the right to vote in municipal and bond elections. In 1887, antiprohibitionists in the town of Argonia decided to nominate a member of the Women's Christian Temperance Union for mayor as a joke. Mrs. Susanna Madora Salter was elected to the office, making her the first female mayor in the United States. Another female political first occurred when Mrs. Georgia Neese Clark was appointed Treasurer of the United States. A banker and businesswoman from Topeka, Mrs. Clark served as Treasurer from 1949 until January 1953.

Amelia Earhart is another famous Kansan. Born in Atchison in 1898, she was the first woman to fly the Atlantic as a passenger. Four years later, in 1932, she made a solo flight. Unfortunately, this recipient of the Distinguished Flying Cross disappeared five years later somewhere between New Guinea and Howland Island while attempting an around-the-world flight.

Perhaps the most forceful and annoying woman to emerge from Kansas, at least from the viewpoint of partakers of the brew, was Carry Nation. Mrs. Nation initiated vendettas against tobacco, foreign foods, corsets, skirts of improper length, and barroom paintings. But it was alcohol that gained her national prominence. She began her campaign in the 1890s in her hometown of Medicine Lodge where she attacked one of the town's saloons, which were ignoring state prohibition laws. A female chorus urged her on by chanting, "Those who tarry at the wine cup—they have sorrow, they have woe." Her weapon that day was an umbrella. Not until 1900 did she take up the hatchet, which became her prohibition symbol.

Among the male Kansans who attained prominence are two who created the state song, "Home on the Range." In 1873, Dr. Brewster Higley wrote the words and Daniel Kelly, a carpenter and musician from Gaylord, the music. Higley was a pioneer homesteader living in a cabin on Beaver Creek, seventeen miles from Smith Center. When it became a hit song in 1934, no one knew its origin. Not until a couple named Goodwin staked their claim to the royalties did a persevering lawyer for the opposition track its beginnings to Higley and Kelly. Higley's one-room cabin is now a museum.

The thirty-fourth President of the United States, Dwight D. Eisenhower, although not a Kansan by birth, always considered Kansas his home. Born in Denison, Texas, in 1890, he moved with his family to Abilene the following year. He and his five brothers were raised in a religion that was antiwar. Nonetheless, he attended West Point and served brilliantly as Commander in Chief of Allied Armies in Europe during World War II.

The Eisenhower Center in Abilene is a favorite visitor's stop. It consists of his family home, a $400,000 museum which stands on three acres of land he once tilled as a boy, the Presidential Library, and the chapel where he is buried.

Other Kansans in the race for the country's top political offices included Governor Alfred Mossman Landon. Landon made a bid for the presidency against Franklin Roosevelt in 1936. History remembers him for his resounding electoral vote defeat of 8 to 523. The vice-presidency was once held by Kansas Senator Charles Curtis, who was elected in 1928 with Herbert Hoover. His mother was part Kaw and part Osage, which made him the first man of Indian blood to be elected Vice-President. Another Senator, Robert Dole, was nominated in 1976 at the Republican Convention in Kansas City, Missouri, to run on the ticket with incumbent President Gerald Ford.

Throughout its history, Kansas has consistently had more newspapers per capita than any other state. Therefore, it is not surprising to find a number of excellent journalists and editors. The most outstanding among them was William Allen White. In 1895, at the age of twenty-seven, he became owner and editor of the Emporia *Gazette*. A year later he published an editorial entitled "What's the Matter with Kansas?" which made him an overnight success. The *Gazette* became the sounding board for his grass roots Republican liberal views and eventually he earned the title "Sage of Emporia."

Although he backed many of Democratic President Franklin Roosevelt's bills, he always campaigned against FDR during election years. Roosevelt once spotted White in a crowd during the 1936 campaign. To the crowd's delight, FDR expressed his appreciation for "Bill White's support for three and a half years out of every four."

Before White died in 1944, he had written numerous short stories, novels, two biographies, and many political-historical pieces. He won the Pulitzer Prize twice, the last awarded posthumously.

Other Kansan authors include William Inge, who won the Pulitzer Prize for his play *Picnic*. His best writings revolved around realistic psychological portrayals of ordinary people in small Midwest towns. Although his principal subject matter centered around New York City, Damon Runyon, prophetically, came from the town of Manhattan near Topeka. Black poet Langston (James) Hughes spent part of his childhood in the "mud town" district of Topeka and later moved to Lawrence. All his music, drama, and fiction reflected Negro problems.

Photography was a field that interested Gordon Parks of Fort Scott. *Life* magazine was his principal employer for many years. Winner of numerous awards for his sensitive and provocative still photography, he eventually entered the motion picture industry, starting as director of the movie *Shaft*.

Although not a Kansan by birth, photographer Brian Lanker did win many prizes while employed by the Topeka *Capital-Journal* from 1969 to 1974. Among the honors were a Pulitzer Prize for feature photography and National Newspaper Photographer of the Year award in 1970.

Not all achievers sprang from artistic sources. Track star Jim Ryun of Wichita and the University of Kansas became the world's fastest one-mile runner in 1966, and the following year set a new world's record of three minutes, fifty-one point one seconds. And, someone who took the state's motto to heart and reached for the stars was astronaut Ron Evans. Born in St. Francis and graduated from the University of Kansas, Evans was commander of the pilot ship during the Apollo 17 flight to the moon.

HISTORY

The recorded history that shaped Kansas began in 1541 with the arrival of the Spanish explorer, Francisco Vásquez de Coronado. He had left Mexico the year before and headed north in search of the fabled Seven Golden Cities of Cibola. Failing to find Cibola, he turned his attention toward another tale of golden streets and bejeweled houses, this time in the Land of Quivira. With a party of forty-two men he turned his expedition northeast into Kansas. Historians know Coronado crossed the Arkansas River at a point near Dodge City and reached the top of the great bend of the river. His explorations beyond that are unknown. In a message to his King, he expressed disappointment at not having found gold but described the province of Quivira as ". . . the best I have seen for producing all the products of Spain."

The following year a Franciscan monk, Juan de Padilla, who had traveled with Coronado, returned to Quivira to Christianize the Indians. He was murdered, however, and became the United States' first Christian martyr.

Coronado's legacy to the Plains Indians was the horse. Those left behind from his expedition multiplied during the next 150 years and made horsemen of the once foot-weary Kansas Indians, such as the Wichita, Pawnee, and Kansa tribes. Until the French explorer Claude du Tisne crossed into Kansas in 1719 while following the Missouri River, only a few French and Canadian trappers and hunters knew the area. Five years later Kansa villages were visited by Étienne

Venyard, Sieur de Bourgmenot, as he crossed Kansas to reach the Rockies.

Spain, France, and England laid claim to the area but the latter did nothing about it. In 1762 France conceded it was Spain's, but in 1800 France gained possession. Three years later Napoleon came to an agreement with James Monroe and sold the Louisiana Territory, an 828,000-square-mile lot which included Kansas, to the United States for a paltry three cents an acre. A year later, President Thomas Jefferson dispatched his shy but moody secretary, Captain Meriwether Lewis, and Lieutenant William Clark on an expedition to explore the Louisiana Purchase. During late June and early July they camped at several points on the Kansas side of the Missouri River. The word "Kansas" first appeared in the journals of this expedition. Contact was made with the Kaw Indians but the tribal name was recorded with fifty-four different spellings, many variations on the word "Kansa."

Captain Zebulon Pike of the United States Army arrived with an expedition in 1806. Besides further exploration, he acted as negotiator between the Indians and the new "White Father." It was he who convinced the Pawnee Indians to trade their Spanish flag for a United States one, thereby making it the first American banner raised over Kansas. Captain Pike's unfavorable impression of the region coincided with the opinions of many other explorers and prominent politicians of the day. They felt the land was wild and useless desert, best left to the savages. Stephen Long, an Army explorer who trekked across Kansas in 1820, reported the area ". . . almost wholly unfit for cultivation and, of course, uninhabitable by a people depending upon agriculture." On his survey maps he labeled the region "Great American Desert," a name that was to stick for many years.

As hunters, trappers, and traders continued to trickle through the region, trails were established. In November 1821 a Missouri trader, William Becknell, loaded three wagons of trade goods and set out for Santa Fe on a sporadically used trail. Becknell averaged fifteen miles a day on the 775-mile route, two thirds of which cut through Kansas. Within four years of his successful journey, the route had become important enough to have Congress authorize its survey. For the next fifty-nine years, the Santa Fe Trail was considered North America's most important commerce route until 1880 when the Atchison, Topeka and the Santa Fe Railroad began providing a more efficient means of traversing the distance.

During those years of the Santa Fe Trail's existence, Kansas experienced the bloodiest and most rip-roaring period of its history. It began in 1820 with the Missouri Compromise. Slavery was a burning issue in Missouri's bid for statehood. Congress finally decided it should enter the Union as a slave state while the rest of the "useless" Louisiana Purchase territory should be free. As financial prospects brightened, it became apparent that the territory was not as useless as originally believed. Both North and South envisioned future states but wanted them added to the Union with their personal moral convictions concerning slavery. The same year that Kansas was organized as an official territory, 1854, Congress tried to placate both sides by passing the Kansas and Nebraska Act. In principle, the Act stated that the citizens of each territory would be free to decide for themselves through popular sovereignty if they wanted to enter the Union as a free or slave state.

The democratic solution did not end the bickering. Instead, bloody warfare erupted as abolitionists and proslavers battled to make Kansas their own. To aid abolitionists, New Englanders began immigrating under the auspices of the fanatical antislave organization, the New England Emigrant Company. To curb the tide of Free Staters, so-called "Border Ruffians" from Missouri began making forays into towns known as abolitionist strongholds—barn-burning, stealing, and occasionally murdering.

For the first Territorial Legislature election in 1855, over six thousand votes were cast, although there were fewer than two thousand legal voters within the territory. Town populations mysteriously increased overnight as people slipped across the border to cast illegal votes. Others simply cast their ballots twice or more. One man voted 144 times! Slavery was chosen by a margin of seven to one.

For the next several years, partisan fighting raged. Farmlands were destroyed, homes, barns, and towns were sacked and burned, leaving many homeless or dead. Lawrence, the headquarters of antislavery partisans called "Jayhawkers," was attacked and burned by border ruffians in 1856. Two days later, John Brown and seven followers retaliated for the Lawrence raid by hacking to death five proslavers during the Pottawatomie Massacre. Brown, born in Connecticut in 1800, had followed his five sons to Kansas in 1855 and settled in Osawatomie. He was a strong advocate of abolition and constantly fanned the flames of antagonism between the two forces.

Retaliatory raids kept news of the Kansas Territory as headlines in

Union papers for years, earning the territory the nickname "Bleeding Kansas." With all the violence, it is surprising that only fifty-five men were killed during those years.

After three abortive attempts at drafting a constitution, Kansans convened again in 1859 at Wyandotte, which is now part of Kansas City. This time Free Staters were in full control. They wrote the final constitution which barred slavery and fixed the present boundaries of the state. Kansans accepted the constitution and the following year passed it on to Congress. The House of Representatives approved the Wyandotte Constitution but proslavers controlling the Senate vetoed it.

Kansas statehood became a national issue and eventually part of the Republican Party's presidential platform headed by Abraham Lincoln. With Lincoln's victory, the abolitionists became strong enough to outvote slavery and the South seceded from the Union and left the Republicans in control of Congress. On the eve of Lincoln's inauguration, January 29, 1861, Kansas became the thirty-fourth state of a disintegrating Union.

In terms of fighting men, Kansas contributed admirably to the Civil War. Some twenty thousand of the thirty thousand eligible Kansans of military age had joined the Union Army. They suffered the highest mortality rate of any state in the Union. Only one major engagement was fought on Kansas soil, the battle of Mine Creek on October 25, 1864, in Linn County. Around twenty-five thousand men were involved in this battle which the Confederates lost.

Kansas Civil War fighting was done on a guerrilla basis and William Quantrill was the most notorious of their leaders. He led a band of cutthroats that included such apprentices of violence as Jesse James and Cole Younger. On August 21, 1863, he directed the worst raid of the war against the town of Lawrence. One eyewitness wrote, "The whole business part of the town, except two stores, was in ashes. The bodies . . . were laying in all directions." The raid cost Lawrence a million and a half dollars' worth of property looted and burned and 150 residents slaughtered.

Despite the violence and the Civil War, settlers never stopped coming. Wagon trains first traversed the northeast portion of Kansas over the Oregon Trail in 1842. Under the Homestead Act of 1862, land was given free of charge to Union soldiers and for a nominal fee to anyone else who worked the land for five years. Railroads pushing westward across the state often searched Europe for immigrants to whom they promoted land development.

As settlers poured onto lands that had been designated Indian territory since 1830, Indians, fearful of further encroachment, fought back. During the height of Indian attacks in 1867, 130 settlers lost their lives. Later that year, the Indians agreed to migrate to Oklahoma in exchange for food, homes, money, and clothing from the United States Government. When these promises were broken, sporadic fighting continued. The last Indian raid occurred in Decatur County near Oberlin in 1878.

Indians were only part of the pioneers' problems. Lacking trees, they had to live in homes built from clumps of sod. Throughout much of the northwest, fence posts were constructed of stone upon which barbed wire could be strung. Lawmen, lacking proper wooden jails, resorted to chaining criminals to fence posts and, later, telephone poles or dropping them into cisterns for safekeeping. Crops able to survive the climate and the insects often brought little income due to high freight costs for shipping goods to market. Bank interest rates on loans were sky-high. During winter the animals grazed far from the homesteads, leaving settlers little more than grain upon which to subsist.

Railroads contributed toward easing some of the farmer's hardships by providing more efficient methods of transporting crops to market. The Kansas Pacific reached the Colorado border in 1869 while the Santa Fe did the same farther south in 1872. It was during the construction of the Kansas Pacific that William Cody earned his title "Buffalo Bill." During an eighteen-month period beginning in 1868, he killed an estimated 4,280 bison to provide meat for the railroad builders.

The most exciting times for the railroads began in 1867 when an Illinois livestock shipper, J. G. McCoy, convinced the Union Pacific, Eastern Division (later the Kansas Pacific), to establish low rates for beef shipped from McCoy's stockyards in Abilene to Chicago. Word spread in Texas that steers could be driven to Kansas on lush grass and flat plains without interference from farmers or bushwhackers.

Kansas cowtowns were born. Named for a trader, the Chisholm Trail, stretching a thousand miles from Texas to Abilene, became the prominent route of cattle drivers. For one dollar a day and beans and bacon, cowboys drove over a million cattle into Abilene's stockyards during the first three years. In the record year 1871, seven hundred thousand cattle were penned in the town by five thousand cowboys.

The work on the trail was boring, dust choking, and long on hours with not nearly as many dangers from rustlers and Indians as Hollywood portrays. It was the cowtown infested with gamblers, conmen, and prostitutes who preyed on cowhands and railroad crews alike that did in many a fine man. T. A. McNeal, a Kansan, remarked, "In competitive examination for wickedness, they would have given Hell a neck and neck race." Weary cowboys often lost their meager wages and sometimes their lives the first night in town.

Considering the prevalent lawlessness, it is not surprising that Kansas produced the best-known frontier marshals. Unfortunately, Wild Bill Hickok, Bat Masterson, and Wyatt Earp, much romanticized in modern-day fiction and films, were little better than the criminals they fought. Less colorful lawmen who contributed more to the taming of the West were best described by the Western fiction writer William MacLeod Raine as ". . . usually quiet men. They served fearlessly and with inadequate reward. Their resort to the six shooter was always in reluctant self defense." Ham Bell and Bill Tilghman of Dodge City were two of these men.

However, the most courageous but short-lived career was that of Thomas James Smith, marshal of Abilene. The fighting Irishman was hired near the beginning of a cattle season, replacing yet another marshal who lasted but a few weeks. He subdued his antagonists mainly with fists and within a few months had Abilene peaceful enough that his job was discontinued. Later, as the newly appointed Deputy United States Marshal for Abilene, he was killed while trying to arrest a defiant homesteader. He was given Abilene's biggest funeral. In 1904 a monument was erected in the city proclaiming him "fearless hero of frontier days who, in cowboy chaos, established the supremacy of law."

As settlers in the east began fencing property, cattle capitals moved west. Abilene was replaced by Newton, Ellsworth, Caldwell, Wichita, and finally Dodge City. "Cowboy Capital of the World," Dodge City began in 1872 as a town on the Santa Fe Railroad. At first it was headquarters for buffalo hunters, who in 1873 shipped four million hides east. When the buffalo herds dwindled, cattle became king and cowboys made the town the wildest and wooliest in the West. Lawlessness was on the decline in 1885 when the last big cattle drive occurred, a million steers driven by five hundred cow-

boys. Because of cow fever the state passed a law that same year forbidding cattle to enter from Texas.

By 1890, settlers occupied most of the prime land and mass immigration ceased. Although a variety of mineral deposits were discovered
and developed between 1890 and 1930, agriculture remained the
state's principal source of income. Farm production reached a new
peak during World War I as warring Europeans increased their demand for food and mechanized equipment began replacing farm-
hands needed to manufacture war materials. As additional farmers
lost their livelihoods during the drought-ridden 1930s, Kansas began
attracting industry as a means of providing employment.

Today, Kansans are profitably engaged in manufacturing, farming,
and mining—the state ranks first in the production of helium.

INDUSTRY

Long before World War II began, the aircraft industry was firmly
entrenched in Wichita. The contribution of the Wichita Division of
the Boeing Company to the war was the production of 44 per cent of
all the Army and Navy trainer planes, while it took thirteen other
manufacturers to produce the remainder. Simultaneously, the Kansas
plant was constructing more than four B-29s a day. As the state's
second-largest employer, Boeing continues to produce military and
commercial aircraft parts and assemblies and does overhauls and
modifications of existing planes.

The state's largest employer is Cessna Aircraft, which is headquartered in Wichita. Sixty per cent of the nation's aircraft are made
in Kansas by Cessna, Beechcraft, and Lear. These range from small
two-seaters to corporate jets. Naturally, with all those planes, Kansans are aircraft-oriented and use them extensively for farming and
business. It is not uncommon to see a runway instead of a back yard
in new housing developments.

With Kansas ranking sixth in the nation in total railroad mileage
and Kansas City the third-largest rail center, it follows that railroads
should also be a leading industry. Santa Fe is the largest and maintains one of its three general offices in Topeka. It is the most self-
sufficient railroad in terms of building its own equipment. Shops
located in Atchison, Topeka, and Wichita manufacture and repair
railroad cars and locomotives.

In addition to trains and planes, the production of cars, trailers, campers, ships, and boats combined make transportation the state's leading manufacturing industry.

A measure of the increase in industrialization can be found in the statistic that 66 per cent of the population now resides in urban areas. Over forty-five hundred manufacturing plants are scattered throughout the state but the heaviest concentration lies around the three largest cities: Wichita, Kansas City, and Topeka. Among the variety of goods manufactured are processed food, chemicals, printed matter, soap, and electronics.

AGRICULTURE

Although manufacturing replaced agriculture as the leading source of income in the early 1950s, in truth both go hand in hand. Food and kindred products processing is the number two manufacturing industry, bringing in over two billion dollars annually. Kansas has long been a leader in meat packing and the foremost flour milling state. This is understandable since it ranks fourth in the country in beef production and first in wheat, growing one sixth of the nation's crop.

Wheat wasn't always the leader. The early settlers mainly planted corn. But in 1874, the year of the worst plague of locusts that came "like storms of rain to almost deluge the land," a group of Russian Mennonites seeking religious freedom arrived. They brought with them seeds of a hardy breed of winter wheat called Turkey Red which proved better suited to the climatic conditions of Kansas. In twenty years, it became the leading crop.

During the droughts of the 1930s, many envisioned the demise of agriculture in Kansas. Each year during that decade had below-normal precipitation and the "Great Dust Bowl" originating in Kansas eventually covered half the state and portions of five others. This disaster followed several years of prosperity during which the demand and price for wheat and beef rose rapidly. Encouraged by premium prices and a spell of higher precipitation than normal from 1901 to 1915, farmers overgrazed and ploughed under a larger percentage of the sod so necessary for retention of moisture in dry times. Eventually, through conservation programs and flood control projects, Kansas was saved from turning into a desert. By the time the droughty 1950s came, farmers had learned to control existing water supplies and what and how to plant, thereby avoiding a total economic disaster.

During the past few years, grains have edged out beef cattle as the leading income in agribusiness. The decline in cattle production has been done by the ranchers in an effort to raise beef prices to profitable levels. Kansas now ranks first not only in wheat but in sorghum silage produced. Other crops grown include sorghum grains, lespedeza seeds, alfalfa, popcorn, and corn.

Whether it's livestock or grain, one seasoned traveler described his attraction to Kansas as a place where he can see the mere 11.3 per cent of farming Kansans at work with a fascinating collection of mechanical monsters. "Successful Kansas farmers are skilled not only in food production, but in management, economics, and mechanics and often know more about foreign policy than politicians in Washington." Despite their declining numbers, now at seventy-nine thousand, Kansas farms have been increasing in size to the present average of 632 acres. With 49.9 million acres in production, Kansas ranks third in the nation in total farm acreage.

NATURAL RESOURCES

Minerals represent 10 per cent of the value of all goods produced in Kansas. Petroleum, first discovered near Paola in 1855, is the leading product. Not until the discovery of crude oil near El Dorado in 1915 did the industry boom. Some forty thousand wells are now in operation, mainly in the south-central portion of the state. Natural gas is the second and natural gas liquids the third most important minerals. Hugoton Field (named for the French novelist Victor Hugo) in the southwest covers nine counties and is one of the largest gas deposits in the world. Despite reserves of 395 million barrels of oil, 11.7 trillion cubic feet of natural gas, and 394 million barrels of natural gas liquids, the mining of these minerals is considered to be in the mature stage and Kansas has slowly declined from its position among the top ten mineral producing states to the top fifteen.

The nation's first helium was discovered near Dexter in 1903. Liberal is the site of the world's largest helium-processing plant, built in the 1960s. Zinc, bituminous coal, lead, and building materials including cement, stone, clay, and gravel are other important natural re-

sources, in addition to vast quantities of salt. Six companies produce
salt from mines or brine water wells near Hutchinson, Kanopolis, and
Lyons. Kansas' known reserves alone are said to be sufficient to keep
the nation in salt for the next 375,000 years!

CITIES

"Come to **Wichita** and bring a six-shooter," is an axiom no longer
true. "Cow Town," situated on the banks of the Arkansas River, is a
re-creation of the infamous town as it was in the 1870s. Five of the
original buildings, including the jail used by Wyatt Earp, along with
thirty-two others faithfully reconstructed from old photos, contain
fixtures, furnishings, and memorabilia from structures of the era.

"Cow Town" bears little resemblance to the Wichita of today.
Home to over a quarter million people, it ranks amazingly low in the
areas of crime, unemployment, and cost of living. It is the largest city
in Kansas and its center of industry. Within ten years of 1917, when
the first airplane was built in Wichita, the city's inhabitants were constructing more private aircraft than any other place in the world.
Flour milling, meat packing, oil refining, chemical production, and
printing are foremost industries. It is also known as the home of the
world's largest camping equipment manufacturer, Coleman, and
western apparel store, Sheplers.

Wichita, named for the Indian word meaning "painted faces," likes
to boast it traded its six-guns for music, theater, and art. Roland P.
Murdock's famous American Painting and Sculpture Collection is a
permanent part of the Wichita Art Museum. The Wichita Art Association has traveling exhibitions and a superb Children's Theater. Three
drama groups, a music theater, and a symphony orchestra round out
the cultural offerings. Many performances are presented in the blue-
domed Century II cultural and convention center downtown. Completed in 1969, it covers 10.8 acres and includes an auditorium, concert hall, theater, and convention and exhibition halls.

The 1950s saw the construction of Mid-Continent Airport, the
major international port of call in Kansas. More recently, the new
five-million-dollar Sedgwick County Zoo was added, a natural habitat zoological garden featuring domestic animals of North American
and Asian farms. More than 16,500 students are drawn to attending
one of the city's three universities—Friends University, Kansas New-

man College, and the first municipal college built west of the Mississippi, Wichita State University.

Six miles southeast lies McConnell Air Force Base and at the confluence of the Big and Little Arkansas rivers stands Blackbear Bosin's forty-four-foot metal sculpture, *Keeper of the Plains*. It marks the site of the Mid-America All-Indian Center.

Topeka, the state capital, is located on the Kansas River. The rich bottom soil of the river, which was a "good place to dig potatoes," gave Topeka its Indian name. With over 140,000 people, it is the third-largest city in Kansas.

It became the permanent capital in 1861. The Capitol, patterned after the one in Washington, D.C., took thirty-seven years to complete. In 1957, to house the ever-expanding government agencies, a modern state office building was added adjacent to the Capitol. Construction of a new Supreme Court building began in 1975. Both the Kansas State Library and the State Historical Society, located in Topeka, contain excellent collections of newspapers. The Historical Society's Library features an almost complete assemblage of Kansas newspapers dating from 1875.

One of the city's founding fathers, Cyrus K. Holliday, also founded the Santa Fe Railroad. Santa Fe Industries' general offices and shops in Topeka employ over forty-five hundred people and represent a major industry. Also located in the city is Goodyear Tire Company's second-largest factory, producing, among other items, giant earthmover tires.

Culturally, Topekans listen to their own Civic Orchestra, have several theater companies to see, and enjoy a variety of programs at Washburn University's Mulvane Art Center, which also contains a valuable collection of paintings. Municipal Auditorium provides facilities for large conventions or traveling entertainment. Gage Park, with its AAU standard swimming pool, Reinisch Rose Garden, and Zoo, is well attended. Incidentally, the Zoo's tropical rain forest houses the man-made but, nonetheless, largest waterfall in the state.

Topeka's international fame centers around the Menninger Foundation, which was founded as a clinic in 1919 by a father and his two famous psychiatrist sons. It works closely with the Veterans Administration Hospital and the Topeka State Hospital, thus making the city a center for the treatment and prevention of mental illness.

Kansas City began as a Wyandot Indian settlement in 1841 when the tribe migrated from Ohio. Wyandotte, as the town they established was called, didn't become Kansas City until 1869. Now with a population of 182,213, it is the second-largest in Kansas. The Missouri River divides it from its twin city, Kansas City, Missouri.

"Gateway to Kansas" was a title that evolved as settlers and goods migrated into the state mainly through the city. Railroads established a main terminus in Kansas City by 1870, filling the newly established meat-packing houses with cattle. Meat packing remains a prime industry. Over three hundred companies located in the city also produce flour, food products, autos, detergents, refined oil, and milled steel. Kansas City, Kansas, pioneered in the development of industrial parks and in 1973 was granted a Foreign Trade Zone designation by the Commerce Department. Interestingly, the second-largest employer is not in industry but is, rather, the prestigious University of Kansas Medical Center.

Kansas City Kansans rely on their sister city in Missouri for cultural amenities. However, there are several major shopping areas on the Kansas side, with Indian Springs Shopping Center the largest such complex in the Midwest.

Urban renewal projects during the last decade have revitalized the downtown area. Center City Plaza is a two-block mall of fountains and waterfalls which depicts typical Kansas landscape. Nearby Civic Plaza contains the eleven-story Municipal Office Building, completed in 1973.

Of historical interest is the old Huron Cemetery in the heart of the business district. The Wyandots were members of the Huron tribe. When they sold their Kansas holdings to the government, the treaty contained a clause which protected in perpetuity the resting place of the Indians and white people who founded the city. On the outskirts of the city at Bonner Springs is the Agriculture Hall of Fame, a visual aid in the study of the evolution of farming.

Other noted Kansas cities include **Leavenworth,** located on the Missouri River. It is the oldest city in Kansas, having been established as Fort Leavenworth in 1827. The Fort remains and headquarters the senior tactical school of the Army. Leavenworth is best known for its institutions: the Federal Prison, State Penitentiary, and Veterans Hospital.

The old abolitionist city of **Lawrence** is located on Interstate 70, west of Kansas City. Although city planners have been trying to diversify income with the introduction of industry, the University of Kansas remains the major employer. Dyche Museum on the campus has one of the largest collections of prehistoric fossils found in Kansas. Once the largest Indian school in the country, Haskell Institute in Lawrence prepares students for careers in modern business and industry.

Another university town is **Manhattan.** Kansas State University, founded in 1863, is the oldest in the state. In addition to the 315-acre campus, the university owns four thousand acres used for experimental farm work.

SPORTS AND RECREATION

There are no professional football teams in Kansas and only one professional baseball team, the Wichita Aeros. Many Kansans feel a close affinity to the Chiefs (football) and Royals (baseball) of Kansas City, Missouri, but for the most part enjoy the outstanding basketball and track teams of their own universities. Jim Ryun brought the state international fame when he set two world's records in distance running. Of all sports events, rodeos are the best attended.

Greyhound racing fans meet twice a year in April and October at the National Coursing Meets near Abilene, "The Greyhound Capital of the World." Abilene recently erected the Greyhound Hall of Fame as a tribute to the outstanding racers.

Most Kansans prefer participating in outdoor sports like hunting, golfing, and horseback riding. They make extensive use of their growing system of recreational parks and lakes. Swimming, boating, fishing, and water-skiing are popular not only in the state lakes but also in the twenty-one Federal Reservoir areas.

POINTS OF INTEREST

With its numerous airports, extensive railroad network, and as third leading state in total highway mileage, getting to the tourist attractions of Kansas is relatively easy. Dodge City is the current center of tourism. Thanks to the TV series *Gunsmoke,* thousands visit its replica of Front Street and Boot Hill Cemetery every year. The present county marshal boasts he's never drawn his gun in the twenty years he's been in office. The stockyards continue to exist but cattle are rounded up via cowboys on motorcycles or jeeps. Both Wichita and Abilene also have replicas of the bygone age of cowtowns, although many people visit Abilene for the newer attraction, the Eisenhower Center.

Unusual museums are scattered throughout the state, including the Osa and Martin Johnson Safari in Chanute, the Barbed Wire and Rock Post museums in LaCrosse, and the MicroZoo of Abilene, where one can study microscopic life. History is remembered at the Hollenberg Station, two miles northeast of Hanover near the Nebraska border. It is the only Pony Express station on the entire route which stands intact. Honoring the first inhabitants of Kansas are the Pawnee Indian Village Museum near Republic and the Indian burial pits of Salina, where 140 skeletons, some more than six feet tall, have been found.

Scientific interests will be satisfied by standing in the Geographical Center of the country (if not counting Hawaii and Alaska) near Lebanon in north-central Kansas. Nearby Meades Ranch in Osborne County is the Geodetic Center of North America. It serves as the reference point, or point of origin, for all government maps of the continent.

If only one point of interest must be chosen to exemplify Kansas, then the half-mile-long grain elevator in Hutchinson is it. Most Kansas towns boast grain elevators, but no others can store seventeen million bushels of wheat in one thousand bins.

Forts, once protectors of travelers, now attract them as tourist destinations. Fort Riley began as an army post in 1853. So many cavalry regiments were organized there, including General Custer's 7th, that it became known as the "cradle of the Cavalry." Custer's home and the first Capitol of Kansas are on the military reservation. Fort Larned, built to protect Santa Fe Trail travelers, is a National Historical Site.

A National Park does not exist in Kansas, although the Department of the Interior is considering the Flint Hills region for that status. This area of bluestem grass prairie is considered to be the finest pastureland in the world. Ranchers are protesting against the proposed park. They feel government control would mean cessation of grazing rights.

Although there are no really spectacular land features in Kansas, there are several points of interest. South in Comanche County lie ten acres of vividly colored and unusual formations called Hell's Half

Acre. Near Jetmore is Horse Thief Canyon, a mini-version of the Grand Canyon. In the Smoky Hill River region is Castle Rock, a prominent landmark rising seventy feet above the level plain. Farther west are the Monument Rocks, which resemble Egyptian sphinxes. These rocks were designated the first National Natural Landmark in Kansas. St. Jacob's Well is said never to run dry, no matter how severe the drought. Located in the Little Basin area of Clark County northwest of Ashland, it was used as a waterhole by early pioneers. Thought to be bottomless, the well is in a region famous for sinkholes formed when underground caverns had their supporting rock strata undermined by water.

SPECIAL EVENTS

Rodeos and county fairs make up the bulk of special events attended by thousands of Kansans annually. The two most popular attractions are the Kansas State Fair in Hutchinson and Topeka's Mid-America Fair, both held in mid-September. Every July, Phillipsburg is the site of the state's biggest rodeo.

Among the prominent events is Handel's *Messiah,* an annual program in Lindsborg since 1882. A chorus of four hundred area people perform Handel's music at Bethany College on Palm and Easter Sundays.

On Shrove Tuesday, the International Pancake Race in Liberal is run simultaneously with a race in Olney, England. First mentioned in English history in 1445, the quarter-mile course is run by women tossing pancakes in skillets. According to the *Guinness Book of World Records,* the current record time holder is America's Kathleen West, who ran the course at Liberal on February 10, 1970, in 59.1 seconds.

Perhaps the most intriguing event listed on the Kansas calendar is Oxford's "Anti-Horse Thief Day." The celebration was first sponsored in 1890 by the Anti-Horse Thief Association Number Three. The highlight of the fair was the capture and hanging of a horse thief by a posse after a wild chase through town. For a number of years the event was not held, until three decades ago when the Lions Club revived it. A new innovation was introduced for the state's Centennial celebration in 1961. This time the thief stole a motor scooter and the posse tracked him down on lawn mowers and garden tractors.

Modern innovations on historical themes are a part of the Kansan character. They have a fondness for history, learning from past errors how to adapt themselves to the adversities of their land. The historian Carl Becker wrote: "With Kansas history back of him, the true Kansan feels that nothing is too much for him. How shall he be afraid of any danger, or hesitate at any obstacle, having succeeded where failure was not only human, but almost honorable? Having conquered Kansas, he knows there are no worse worlds to conquer."

J.M.
M.M.

CHRONOLOGY

1541   Francisco Vásquez de Coronado, exploring the Land of Quivira, crossed the Arkansas River near what is now Dodge City.

1542   Father Juan de Padilla became the first Christian martyr in the United States.

1719   Charles Claude du Tisne explored the northeastern corner of Kansas.

1724   Kansas villages were visited by Étienne Venyard, Sieur de Bourgmenot, as he crossed Kansas to the Rockies.

1803   James Monroe negotiated with Napoleon for the purchase of the Louisiana Territory.

1804   Lewis and Clark expedition camped at several points on the Kansas side of the Missouri River.

1806   Captain Zebulon Pike explored Kansas and persuaded the Pawnee Indians to replace their Spanish flag with a United States one.

1820   Missouri Compromise admitted Missouri as a slave state but provided that all future states west of the Mississippi and north of 36°30′ should be free.

1821   William Becknell established the Santa Fe Trail as a trade route.

1835   First Kansas periodical, the *Shawnee Sun,* published by a missionary, the Reverend Jotham Meeker.

1854   Kansas-Nebraska Bill gave the two territories the right to self-determination in settling the question of slavery.

1856   Lawrence sacked by border ruffians. John Brown retaliated by executing five proslavers at Pottawatomie Creek. Missourians avenged the massacre at the Battle of Black Jack.

1859   The ratified Wyandotte Constitution abolished slavery and set the present boundaries of the state. A provisional state government was elected.

1861   On January 29, Kansas became the thirty-fourth state in the Union. On November 5, Topeka was chosen as the state capital.

1862   Homestead Act brought additional settlers.

1863   Quantrill's guerrillas attacked Lawrence, murdering 150.

1864   Confederates defeated at Mine Creek, the only Civil War battle fought on Kansas soil.

1867   Height of Indian attacks—130 settlers killed.

Joseph McCoy turned Abilene into the first cowtown with the arrival of its first Texas longhorn cattle.

1874   Great Grasshopper Plague.

Russian Mennonites introduced Turkey Red wheat.

1878   Last Indian raid, in Decatur County.

1878–80   Negro Exodus brought forty thousand from former slave states.

1880   Prohibition laws passed.

1885   Texas cattle drives terminated.

1887   Women's suffrage extended to cover municipal and bond elections.

Town of Argonia elected Mrs. Susanna Medora Salter its mayor, the first woman in the United States to hold the office.

1900   Carry Nation began her national campaign for prohibition.

1903   State Capitol at Topeka completed after thirty-seven years of construction.

1912   Kansas became the seventh state in the Union to give women full suffrage.

1928   Senator Charles Curtis was elected Vice-President of United States on Hoover ticket, the first man of Indian ancestry to hold the office.

1933–35   "Dust Bowl" Era had its origins in Kansas.

1936   Governor "Alf" Landon lost his bid for the presidency by a landslide electoral vote.

1948   State's prohibition amendment was repealed.

1951   Worst floods in state's history hit the eastern and southern portions of the state.

1952   Population of Kansas passed two million.

1954   Manufacturing surpassed agriculture as the state's major source of income.

Brown vs. Board of Education of Topeka set a precedent in Civil Rights cases involving segregated education.

1966   Worst tornado in state ripped through the heart of Topeka.

1967   Jim Ryun became the world's fastest one-miler for the second time, at 3:51.1, breaking his world's record of the previous year.

1972   Astronaut Ron Evans, pilot ship commander during flight of Apollo 17, became first Kansan to circle the moon.

1973   Kansas City, Kansas, was given Foreign Trade Zone designation, a tax-free status for certain areas of business.

1974   Terms for governor and other top state officers were increased from two to four years.

1976   Senator Robert Dole was nominated to run for the vice-presidency on the Ford ticket at the Republican Convention in Kansas City, Missouri.

1979   A photographic portrait of the late President Dwight David Eisenhower, made from a color transparency owned by the Eisenhower Center in Abilene, went on permanent display in the State Capitol building in Topeka. The portrait was presented to Kansas by David Eisenhower, grandson of the former U. S. President.

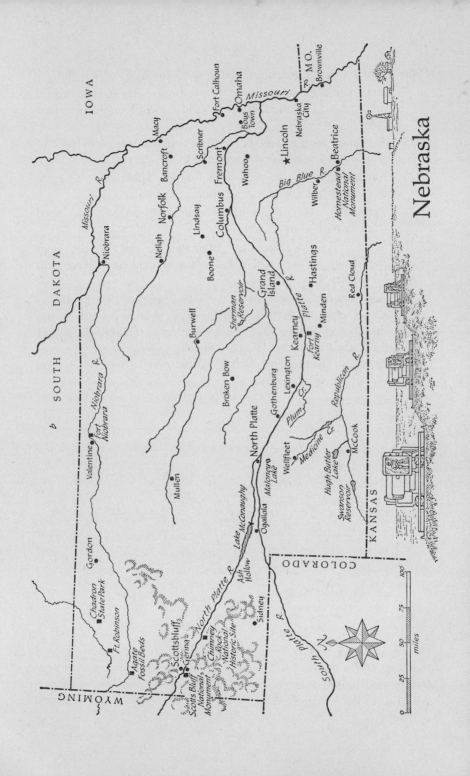

Nebraska

NEBRASKA

NEBRASKA, the Cornhusker State, has always been defined in terms of land. Where other areas of this country drew settlers for everything from intangible reasons like freedom and the pursuit of happiness to those very tangible reasons like gold and silver, Nebraska's lure has always been the land. The Oto Indians named it Nibrathka, meaning "land of the flat water," in reference to the wide, lush valley that gently cradles the Platte River. And if others were less than charitable (notably Major Stephen Long who wasted no time in scrawling "The Great American Desert" across his map in 1819), no matter. The land was always there, ready and waiting. "We come and go, but the land is always here," Nebraska author Willa Cather wrote in *O Pioneers!* her masterpiece about the settling of Nebraska. "And the people who love it and understand it are the people who own it—for a little while."

Those who have loved it and owned it—for a little while—form a line of land lovers stretching far back into the mists of prehistory. The prehistoric pioneers were hunters and farmers, tied to the land. At the beginning of Nebraska's recorded history in 1750, many of the Indian tribes were farming tribes: the Oto, Omaha, Ponca, and Pawnee. The settlers who followed were looking for land, for they knew that land was also freedom and the pursuit of happiness. And that land was, in its own way, golden.

THE LAND

Generally, when people think of Nebraska, they think of something low, flat, and wide. And to the quickly passing glance her major attribute would indeed seem to be a sameness; a fertile flatness, if you will. But to the loving eye of the native beholder, Nebraska is a land of gradual gradations. A gentle lifting from the low-slung bluffs hugging the banks of the Missouri in the east, on through to the gently rolling Sand Hills of central Nebraska, and finally the eerie moonlike landscape of the far west.

The entire eastern portion of Nebraska is defined by the Missouri River and it is true river territory. There are stands of piney woods folded into a gently rounded landscape while stalwart bluffs stand guard over the rolling Missouri. The Sand Hills, an egg-shaped portion of mid-Nebraska roughly 200 miles long and 150 miles wide, are certainly one of Nebraska's most unusual and most distinctive features. Formed during the Ice Age when the glaciers scraped across the land and laid down a layer of sand and powdered rock, this area is a series of high sandy ridges covered over with still-virgin grass, untouched and unturned by man for centuries. Today it is prime cattle-grazing land, dotted with hundreds and hundreds of fresh-water lakes.

West of the Sand Hills is the panhandle, that portion of the state that juts out and seems to head west from the rest of the state. Here are the Wildcat Hills, the foothills of the Rockies. And it is here that Nebraska reaches her highest point: 5,426 feet in Kimball County, that county occupying the far southwest corner of the panhandle. Due north of this, in the opposite corner, is Sioux County, which contains Toadstool Park, an area so eerie it seems to have been snatched out of a moonscape. Great, flat, swirling sandstone formations clot the landscape like gritty finger paintings.

CLIMATE

The weather of Nebraska can only be considered in terms of extremes: bitter-cold winters, searing-hot summers, breath-takingly soft springs, and crisp refreshing autumns. Winter temperatures average 12–14 degrees with most natives barely batting an eye at temperatures of 20 or even 30 degrees below. Summer is just as extreme: The average temperature is in the upper 80s with the 100-degree temperature often experienced in August being accepted as familiar summertime fare.

Winters are generally thought of in terms of heavy snowfalls, with the snow being layered upon the by-then sleeping landscape like frosty icing on a cake. "Night was a howling chaos of snow, and dawn a blind white ghost of day without a sun," wrote John Neihardt, Nebraska's Poet Laureate. As for those still, hot summer days, no one described them better than Neihardt: "When the white-hot sun glared in upon the tortured world, it was as though a sky-wide furnace door were opened."

These temperature extremes cause all sorts of climatic aberrations which drove the early pioneers both out of the state and out of their minds. Hailstones as big as golf balls will rain down, cutting crops to ribbons and making mush out of rooftops in a matter of minutes. An average of twenty hailstorms a year pummel the state. Tornadoes are all-too-common occurrences. They are signaled by an unearthly stillness, then the far-off vision of the tornado's funnel moving silently and effortlessly across the landscape, sucking and whirling. Then, suddenly, the ear-shattering roar as it hits, tearing everything in its path asunder. A tornado is quick, touching down here and there for a matter of seconds, but devastating.

THE NEBRASKANS

The myth of the West has it settled by John Wayne and Randolph Scott. Needless to say, the reality is somewhat different. It was not settled by handsome square-jawed men who rode out of the Hollywood Hills nor was it settled by women in neat gingham aprons strewing petunia seeds in their wake. It was settled by very real human beings with very real reasons for being there—and some of those reasons weren't very romantic. Just practical.

For every dreamer that hit the Oregon Trail or the Overland Trail in Nebraska, there was a drifter. For every troubador a tramp, for every wanderer a wastrel. They came leaving something behind—everything from crime and punishment to poverty; they came going to something—freedom or a selfish dream of betterment. And if these reasons are less than noble, they are at least real.

And the painful process of opening up the West—that vast stretch of unrelenting frontier west of the Mississippi—was not glamorous or romantic. It was very hard work. For when they arrived at their destination they found an inhospitable area that would freeze them to death in the winter, burn them up in the summer, then dash their frail hopes before reluctantly yielding up the richness of her land to these intruders.

The migration that began as a trickle with the great westward movement of the 1830s and 1840s became a roaring flood with the end of the Civil War and the coming of the railroad in the 1860s. And Nebraskans came from all over, dropping out of the westward rush like place names from a globe. The tough Irish laying track westward for the Union Pacific dropped out or came back to settle along the railroads they had built, particularly in Greeley and Colfax counties. The English went to nearby Hall County while Scandinavians set up settlements in Boone and Nance and Madison counties. The Czechs and Bohemians settled south of the Platte in and around Webster County. And the French and Swiss, led and often misled by the enthusiastic letters of old Jules Sandoz, Mari's tough but determined father, found themselves in the bitter barrenness of Keith and Perkins counties in the far southwest. The railroads, anxious to settle the routes and protect their investment, advertised in foreign newspapers to entice immigrants, even paying their passage all the way from Europe to Nebraska.

Granted the people who settled Nebraska were tough; they had to be. But despite that toughness of character—or, perhaps, because of it —Nebraska has turned out a passel of creative types in the past century. Nebraska author Mari Sandoz may have been right when she figured, "Perhaps it was to be expected that many would be stirred to tangible make-believe by the vast horizons, the deep nights and the summer whirlwinds, heat dances and mirages of the high country." And out of these summer whirlwinds and mirages have come the likes of dancer Fred Astaire, puppeteer Bil Baird, actors Marlon Brando and Henry Fonda, television personalities Johnny Carson and Dick Cavett, and movie mogul Darryl F. Zanuck, who came from the Victorian houses of Wahoo, Nebraska.

Nebraska's literary heritage includes Pulitzer prize-winner Willa Cather, renowned mystery writer Mignon Eberhart, political New Frontiersman Ted Sorenson, novelists Mari Sandoz and Bess Streeter Aldrich, and John G. Neihardt, Nebraska's Poet Laureate. Politicians like William Jennings Bryan, "The Silver-tongued Orator," and George Norris, "The Fighting Liberal," both sprang from the heart land of Nebraska. Bryan was a three-time presidential candidate and served as U. S. Secretary of State from 1913 to 1915. Fred Seaton, a newspaper publisher, served as President Eisenhower's Secretary of the Interior from 1956 to 1961. Former Nebraska Governor Val Peterson was U. S. Ambassador to Denmark from 1957 to 1960.

And, of course, there is the local color: Calamity Jane staked out the Platte River as if it were Times Square, wandering from barracks to barracks. Jesse James is said to have taken refuge with the Santee Sioux near the mouth of the Niobrara. James Butler Hickok was able to change his nickname from Duck Bill to Wild Bill because he murdered a man in Nebraska. And the range wars that pitted the cattlemen against the farmers were as bitter in Nebraska as in any other state.

HISTORY

Nebraska is essentially thought of as a pioneer state, conjuring up visions of covered wagons and calico dresses. And for the most part, that is true, for in the great push to explore and exploit the New World, the area that was to become Nebraska was, for centuries, ignored. When the Spaniards, first in 1541 and later in 1601, climbed that watery ladder of rivers and streams that stretches northward from the Rio Grande, they were in search of the legendary City of Quivira, a glittering city where warriors were said to ride in golden canoes and drink from jeweled cups. Instead, they found Nebraska. They took one look and left.

Indeed, until the great pioneer migrations of the mid-1800s, this was to be the historic destiny of Nebraska in general; of the Great Plains in particular. People always came looking for one thing, and when they could not find it, they passed through, unable to see the incredible riches Nebraska held: millions of acres of fertile land.

After the Spanish came the French. In 1682, under an expedition led by Robert Cavelier, Sieur de La Salle, the entire Mississippi River Basin was claimed for his patron, King Louis XIV. The French were looking for furs to trap, and unfortunately Nebraska was hardly the place to do that. Instead, it was the rich fur-trapping prospects along the Mississippi that excited the French. When Napoleon, who knew little of his American holdings and cared less, sold the entire territory —to be known as the Louisiana Purchase—to Thomas Jefferson in 1803 for $15 million, few on either side of the ocean cared.

When Meriwether Lewis and George Rogers Clark made their famous expedition in 1804 to map the Louisiana Purchase, the area that would one day become the state of Nebraska was duly noted, a few forts were established, and then Nebraska was, once again, promptly forgotten. Then came the opening of the Oregon Territory in the 1840s, and settlers came streaming through Nebraska, particularly along the south bank of the Platte River, that wide, flat ribbon that ripples across the broad face of Nebraska. The Platte became the Interstate of the 1830s and 1840s as a mixed bag of dreamers, adventurers, wanderers, and wastrels streamed westward. The Platte gave them direction, water, shade, and food, and the settlers gave it a name: the Oregon Trail.

Then came the California gold rush in 1849 and still more people streamed across Nebraska. When the Mormons set out from Nauvoo, Illinois, in 1846 for their self-promised land in Utah, they, too, used Nebraska as their route, choosing the north bank of the Platte and calling it the Mormon Trail. Between 1840 and 1866 more than 2.5 million people crossed Nebraska in covered wagons. The deep-cut ruts of those wagons are still visible today, worn forever into both the landscape and the memories of Nebraskans.

Obviously, though, some of those settlers broke away from the wagon trains and stayed behind. Soon they were joined by settlers whose goals were not Oregon or California or Utah, but Nebraska itself. They founded settlements which turned into villages which turned into towns which became cities. They defied blizzards and droughts and grasshoppers and locusts. They fought loneliness, insanity, boredom, and disease. One of the first public institutions to open in Nebraska was the Norfolk Insane Asylum to handle all the broken spirits and crushed hopes. It is still there today.

Nebraska's political fortunes changed drastically in 1854 when Congress passed the Kansas-Nebraska Act, formally creating the Territory of Nebraska (which included most of North Dakota, South Dakota, Colorado, Wyoming, Montana, as well as Nebraska) and opening it to sanctioned settling. In 1862, in the midst of the Civil War, President Abraham Lincoln signed the Homestead Act, giving 160 acres of government land to anyone willing to pay fourteen dollars and able to live on the land for five years. The first person to take advantage of this offer was a Union soldier, Daniel Freeman, who put down his money and picked up his claim: 160 acres near Beatrice, Nebraska, on the banks of the Big Blue River.

The pioneer business boomed, and in 1867 Nebraska became the thirty-seventh state in the Union with a population of 50,000 people. By 1870 that figure had soared to 123,000.

But it was not an easy business, settling Nebraska. In addition to the many physical hazards—blizzards, hot winds, droughts, grasshopper attacks, sickness and death—there were frequent and bloody encounters with the Plains Indians. It was an obvious and inevitable conflict between the Indians who claimed the land by right of heritage and the settlers who claimed the land by the right of recently written law. As more and more settlers pushed into the Indian lands, followed by the Army to enforce their right to be there, the conflict broke open into bitter battles. It was, obviously, an unequal struggle. Outnumbered, outmaneuvered, and outgunned, the Indians finally surrendered to army troops.

This chapter of the conflict closed with the murder of Crazy Horse in 1877 and the subsequent end of Sioux resistance. The Cheyenne held out until 1879 when they were arrested and held in Fort Robinson stockades. Most were killed—including women and children—by army troops during an escape attempt.

Despite physical hardships and emotional upheavals, Nebraska was settled. And the first two decades of the twentieth century seemed to repay those early pioneers for all their troubles. Prosperity was the name of the game and the future looked not rosy, but golden. Then came the Great Depression and Nebraska was not left out of the crash that had sent the eastern financial empires crumbling. In the farm states, the Depression was compounded by the droughts of the 1930s. Farms were lost as land burned out and hope dried up.

By 1940, the Depression and the droughts were over and Nebraska had to face what the rest of the world was facing: a world war. If Pollyanna saw goodness in the face of evil, this was surely the case for America in the 1940s. The national war effort saw Nebraska, along with the rest of the country, gearing up for the national war effort. Farms increased production, new industries came in to diversify the economy and provide more job opportunities.

By the time the 1950s rolled around, the twentieth century had roared into Nebraska. And today, missile silos at the Strategic Air Command base in Omaha are as much a part of the Nebraska landscape as the grain silos that dot the rich face of the rest of the state.

INDUSTRY

Although Nebraska is primarily an agricultural state, industrial development has become an integral part of Nebraska's economic life, particularly with the industrialization that came during World War II and with the intense mechanization of farming itself. Because it is now more practical to farm larger and larger spreads, more and more small farmers have left the land. Hence: industrial development to diversify both the economy and the job market. Omaha, for example, has over six hundred manufacturing concerns turning out everything from TV components to TV dinners. Today, some 62 per cent of Nebraska's 1.5 million people live in urban areas, and only 18 per cent are engaged in farming, while some 11.7 per cent are employed in manufacturing.

Not surprisingly, much of Nebraska's industrialization is in farm-related enterprises such as farm equipment, truck trailers, motors, and engines. As more and more farmers expand their operations, for example, irrigating becomes important. Thus, the manufacture of sophisticated irrigation equipment—some so futuristic in appearance it seems to have been dropped from a far-off space odyssey—becomes vital. The Lindsay Manufacturing Company, specializing in irrigation equipment, has its home in the town of the same name. Population: 291. Behlen Manufacturing, which started out making corrugated aluminum grain storage bins, now includes everything from silos to home garages.

Food processing is another obvious industrial spin-off for an agricultural state. Everything from frozen TV dinners to popcorn processing plants are located in Nebraska. More than half of the industrial activity is devoted to the processing of food and food products, a $1-billion industry in Omaha alone. Currently, research is under way to develop new markets for Nebraska's abundant and nutritious soybean crops.

One of the largest industries in Nebraska is meat packing, and Omaha has twelve plants, including those of the major names in meat packing and processing—Swift's and Swanson's. Where Chicago once held the title of meat packer to the world, that title now goes to Omaha.

AGRICULTURE

Nebraska is first and foremost an agricultural state, blessed with some of the richest soil in the world and people whose love affair with this land has withstood the toughest of tests for over a century now.

Corn and wheat are her major crops, with mixed grain production —rye, sorghum, alfalfa, barley, and soybeans—following close behind. With 48 million acres in production, Nebraska ranks fourth in corn production with 434 million bushels, while also producing 86 million bushels of wheat, 850,000 bushels of barley, and 115 million bushels of sorghum. Nebraska ranks first in alfalfa meal production and great northern bean production. In 1975, cash receipts from farm marketing hit nearly $4 billion.

These staggering production totals are a tribute and a testimony to modern science and technology and a lot of hard work on the part of Nebraska's farmers. Nearly all of Nebraska's corn, for example, is hybrid and has undergone carefully controlled breeding specifically for Nebraska's soil and climate. Additionally, thousands of dollars' worth of fertilizer—as much as thirty dollars per acre—is used to keep the soil from becoming depleted during a century of nearly continuous single-cropping. And, finally, that expensive machinery: tractors, grain combines, corn pickers, hay balers, forage harvesters, field choppers, trucks, and wagons. Where the first farmer started off with his homestead of 160 acres and a strong back or two—usually his wife's—with all the modern scientific and technological aids available today, three people can plant and cultivate 640 acres of land, raise 500 to 600 hogs, and feed 300 beef cattle.

As a result, farms are getting larger and larger. Some are so-called commercial farms, like those being run by large concerns like Purina. But most farms in Nebraska, so far, are still privately owned and operated. And the typical farm is big—600 acres—because only a large spread like this makes it economically feasible for an adequate return on that huge mechanical investment.

Because of those temperature variations—so necessary yet so frustrating and, often, so destructive—irrigation has come to play a more and more important role to the modern Nebraska farmer. Fortunately, Nebraska has one of the greatest underground water reserves in the nation, estimated at nearly 1.9 billion acre-feet, or enough to cover the state to a depth of 34 feet. This water has accumulated over the centuries and makes irrigation very feasible.

In the fertile soil of eastern Nebraska, corn is the leading crop. The western and panhandle portions of the state yield wheat, the second most important crop in the state. The rich soil of the Platte River Basin, which cuts east to west through the mid-section of the state, produces a cornucopia of agricultural products: sugar beets, potatoes, beans, alfalfa, and corn.

The native grasses of the sand hills along with the feed lots dotted across the state feed the herds of Herefords and Angus cattle so famous in Nebraska. The state ranks first in carcass beef production, second in cattle marketed.

NATURAL RESOURCES

Heading west across Nebraska, one is caught up in a symphony of nature. Cornfields and wheat fields ripple off into the distance. Stacks of hay sit like plump loaves of bread browning on the landscape. Herds of cows gaze impassively at the passing parade of people, automobiles, trucks, campers, and even horseback riders. Mother Nature has laid a peaceful patchwork quilt of organic beauty over Nebraska.

Oil was discovered in the panhandle of western Nebraska in 1939 and there has been a steady output ever since. Oil is now produced in sixteen of Nebraska's ninety-three counties. Petroleum accounts for 45 per cent of the value of all minerals in Nebraska. Natural gas was discovered in 1949. Although petroleum production has declined recently—down from over 24 million barrels in 1962 to 11 million in 1970—production is currently holding steady. And the cattle of the panhandle have learned to stoically share their traditional turf, standing shaggy cheek by metallic jowl with these mechanical monsters.

Sand and gravel along with cement, chalkrock, and limestone are also produced in Nebraska, plus gypsum, salt, pumice, and potash. Deposits of shale and clay are found and used in brick manufacturing. According to the U. S. Bureau of Mines, mineral production in Nebraska in 1975 brought in $103 million.

CITIES

As this nation's Bicentennial approached, a rather visionary artistic plan evolved in Nebraska: the commissioning of monumental outdoor sculptures to be placed at ten of the twenty-five rest stops along the Nebraska portion of Interstate 80 which, for a great distance, follows the old Oregon, Mormon, and Overland trails. These works of art would thus form, in the words of one of the plan's most ardent backers, "a 455-mile sculpture garden."

Not surprisingly, this remarkable plan was developed in **Lincoln,** the state's capital, at the equally remarkable Sheldon Memorial Art Gallery on the University of Nebraska campus. The Sheldon is one of the finest small galleries in the country, housing one of the best collections of international art in the country. Designed by Philip Johnson, the Sheldon contains a masterful collection of art including works by Picasso, Edward Hopper, and Georgia O'Keeffe and sculpture by Brancuşi, Nadelman, and Noguchi.

Lincoln, along with Omaha, has the distinction of being the cultural heart of Nebraska. The Nebraska Art Association, founded in Lincoln in 1888, is one of the oldest art organizations in the country devoted to the exclusive acquisition of contemporary art. No public funds are used and their magnificent collection is now valued at more than $5 million. Each year, national and international artists are presented in programs by the Lincoln Symphony, the Broadway Theatre League, the Community Playhouse, and the university music and drama departments. For film buffs there is the Foreign Film Society plus periodic film series presented in the Sheldon Gallery. Additionally, the gallery is used for concerts by the Lincoln Friends of Chamber Music and the Sheldon Trio.

The University of Nebraska, founded in 1869 (just two years after Nebraska became a state), is based in Lincoln along with Nebraska Wesleyan University. And, attesting to Nebraska's great outdoor heritage, there are forty-eight parks and three zoos in Lincoln plus thirteen public and private golf courses, nine swimming pools, thirty-one tennis courts, and twelve ice skating ponds. And practically within shouting distance of the State Capitol there are twelve recreation areas for boating, fishing, hunting, swimming, camping, horseback riding, and nature walks. A 238-acre industrial park, along with other manufacturing concerns, turns out everything from boats, bricks, and brooms to furniture, farm fencing, and footwear.

Omaha, forty miles to the northeast of Lincoln, is commonly called "The Gateway City," a term that goes far back into its history, but is just as true today. Omaha was founded as a riverbank village in 1853 and developed first as a river town. When the railroad started west from Omaha in 1865, Omaha became the crosspoint for rail traffic, and the Union Pacific still maintains its head office in Omaha. It is the hub of a nine-state trucking industry and a junction point for air travel in all directions. In 1953, with the resumption of regularly scheduled barge service on the Missouri, Omaha came full circle to become once again a river town.

Culturally, Omaha contains the fine Joslyn Memorial Art Museum and its $15-million collection of painting and sculpture. The Joslyn also provides a series of concerts, lectures, and special exhibits throughout the year. The Omaha Symphony, an eighty-piece orchestra, plays there each winter, and the museum also sponsors summer pops concerts. For twenty-eight years the Joslyn has been sponsoring a series of Sunday afternoon chamber music concerts. The Omaha Playhouse is noted for its fine productions and full seasons: six each year, including two musicals and four plays. Henry Fonda got his start here, taking his first acting lesson from Marlon Brando's mother.

Omaha's Great Artists Concerts—which go back to 1892—feature the likes of the Dubrovnik Festival Orchestra and the noted violinist Eugene Fodor. The Omaha Opera's 1975–76 Bicentennial season had productions of *La Traviata* and *Manon,* which starred the celebrated Roberta Peters.

Father Flanagan's Boys Town, that famous refuge for homeless boys, sits on a hilltop ten miles from town. Founded in 1917 with ninety dollars in borrowed money by the Roman Catholic priest Father Edward J. Flanagan, Boys Town has grown from a population of five lads in one building to a population of some one thousand boys in a modern complex that now sprawls over 1,500 acres.

Omaha also boasts of three universities, three colleges, two schools of medicine, two pharmacy schools, one law school, eight nurses' training programs, thirty business and technical schools, and five Montessori preschools.

Appropriately enough, in 1967—as if to celebrate Nebraska's statehood centennial—Omaha saw the resurgence of her Old Market into an artistic and cultural center. Once an old fruit and vegetable market, it had fallen into disuse and disrepair only to be rescued by a combination of artists and businessmen. The Old Market now has artists' lofts, restaurants, shops, pubs, and boutiques. A dinner theater performs in an old fire barn while a crafts guild operates out of a banana warehouse. A once seedy hotel has become work and living space for artists, and paintings are for sale in an old potato storage room.

SPORTS AND RECREATION

For water enthusiasts (yes, water enthusiasts) landlocked Nebraska—with literally thousands of rivers, streams, and lakes—is a paradise. Boating and water-related sports are among the leading recreational activities in Nebraska. People use everything from peaceful paddle-it-yourself canoes to speedboats on Nebraska's waterways.

For fishing enthusiasts, Nebraska boasts excellent casting and catching. Lake McConaughy—"Big Mac" as it is called—is chock full of walleye, bass, trout, and pike. Other prime spots are Whitney Lake, the Sherman Reservoir, and Lake Maloney for walleye fishing; Hugh Butler Lake for bass; the Swanson Reservoir, Medicine Creek, and the Missouri for catfish.

Chadron State Park, set high on the crest of the Pine Ridge in the northwest panhandle, offers swimming, trail riding, camping, hiking in the timbered buttes, and excellent trout fishing. The Fort Niobrara Wildlife Refuge near Valentine, in north-central Nebraska, provides a safe sanctuary for elk, buffalo, antelope, and Texas longhorns, all of which make excellent scenery for the good hiking that is available there. For canoe enthusiasts, there is the challenging white water of the Niobrara River.

Hikers have the entire state to wander through with predesignated nature trails or trails of their own making through timber, Indian territory, pioneer pathways, or the great outdoors in general. More specifically, there is Toadstool Park and those eerie geologic formations, the Wildcat Hills, the timbered hills of Chadron State Park, the buttes of Chimney Rock, the nature trails at Fort Calhoun. Most of these areas also have excellent camping plus trail riding for the outdoor lover.

Scattered throughout the state are 5 state parks, 8 state historic parks, 55 state recreation areas, 23 state wayside areas for roadside picnics and resting, and 134 state special-use areas for activities ranging from fishing to hiking to just lazing around.

Hunting is another sport avidly followed by Nebraskans. Carefully licensed and monitored by the State Game Commission, their rules are rigidly followed by Nebraska hunters. Pheasant, turkey, grouse, quail, duck, geese, deer, and an occasional wild boar are there during the tightly defined seasons.

But by far the biggest sport in Nebraska is a stand-up-and-shout sport: fanatic backing of the University of Nebraska football team, the Cornhuskers, or, in deference to the university's colors of red and white, The Big Red. Big Red fans buy their tickets months, years in advance. They arrive at Memorial Stadium in Lincoln wearing red cowboy hats, red ties, red coats, jackets, T-shirts, sweat shirts—anything red. They drink red beer, a quietly lethal combination of tomato juice and beer. Flying over the stadium on a Saturday afternoon is like flying over a can of red paint that has been spilled over the prairie. And the wall-busting shouts of the fans can be heard for miles across the midlands.

POINTS OF INTEREST

If the first of those early westward wanderers thought of Nebraska merely as a place to go through, many of today's wanderers (translation: tourists) see Nebraska somewhat differently. And well they might, for Nebraska holds a treasure of attractions that spring directly from her link with natural history and our nation's pioneer history.

Nebraska has an abundance of scenic treats and none is more intriguing than Toadstool Park, in the northwest corner of the panhandle, a do-it-yourself haven for hikers, nature lovers, and amateur archaeologists. The wildly swirling and mildly grotesque sandstone formations here are 40 million years old and look just like what they are: leftovers from a fantastic voyage through time. Nearby are the Agate Fossil Beds, a national monument with a remarkable cache of prehistoric fossil remains and, again, more hiking and nature trail opportunities.

Out west, in the Wildcat Hills Recreation Area and the nearby game preserve, you can still see buffalo and elk roaming through the timber breaks. Near here are some of Nebraska's biggest tourist attractions, the massive soaring rock formations of Chimney Rock, Courthouse and Jail Rocks, and Scotts Bluff. All were guideposts along the Oregon Trail for the early pioneers. Today the Scotts Bluff National Monument has a fine museum dedicated to telling the story of the great migration of the 1800s.

The route of the prairie schooners traveling westward included a precipitous trek down Windlass Hill, twenty-five miles northwest of Ogallala. Once maneuvered, travelers found themselves in Ash Hollow, where they rested up for the long trip ahead. The graves in Ash Hollow are grim reminders of the terrible toll taken by the settling of the West.

For history buffs, there are restored army posts around the state— Forts Robinson, Hartsuff, Niobrara, Kearney, and Sidney—complete with parade grounds, general stores, and historic memorabilia. The entire town of Brownville (pop. 174), on the banks of the Missouri, has turned itself backward to become the eighteenth-century river front town it once was, including restorations of historic homes. In Gothenberg, one of the nation's few remaining Pony Express stations has been preserved, paying tribute to a mail service that guaranteed eight-day delivery of a letter from St. Joseph, Missouri, to Sacramento, California.

Buffalo Bill Cody, who introduced the rodeo to the world in 1882, lived in North Platte, and his home, Scouts Rest Ranch, is now a national monument. For those who want to experience the Wild West firsthand, there is Front Street in Ogallala out in the western part of the state. Once the trail's end for cowboys and cattle drivers, Ogallala re-creates those flashy days with a series of saloons, dance halls, and shoot-outs along with a museum, Boot Hill, and a refurbished Victorian mansion. And for more down-to-earth western activity, try Wellfleet: Every Sunday afternoon in the summertime there is calf roping on Main Street.

Historic preservation has been going on vigorously for the past few years in Nebraska. The Kennard House in Lincoln, built two years after statehood in 1869, was the home of Thomas P. Kennard, Nebraska's first secretary of state. It is a charming yellow frame Plains Victorian house with cupolas, porches, and a picket fence. Inside is an authentic period house complete with horsehair furniture, marble-top dressers, and patchwork quilts. Fairview, the magnificent turn-of-the-century Victorian mansion built for William Jennings Bryan, is also in Lincoln. Bryan, "The Silver-tongued Orator," was the fiery advocate of the silver standard and one of the best trial lawyers in the country.

The Norris Home in McCook was the home of Senator George Norris, "The Fighting Liberal," who was the father of the Tennessee Valley Authority, the Rural Electrification Administration, and Nebraska's own unique one-house unicameral legislature. In 1931 Norris had the house, a solid no-nonsense frame house, remodeled as his own "private relief act" to help his home town during the Great Depression.

Other historic restorations include the Wildwood House in Nebraska City, a ten-room brick house built in 1869. Set in its own park, this mid-Victorian house has imported French wallpaper, period lighting, and a rosewood sofa that came up the Missouri by steamboat in 1865. The Carson House in Brownville was begun in 1860, and traces of the original floor stenciling can still be seen.

Three modest but charming historic spots to visit are the Homestead National Monument in southeast Nebraska, complete with a museum and a log cabin. Visitors can walk the grounds of that first homestead claim, put down in 1863. The Neligh Mill is a restored, red-shingled flour mill built in 1874 and set in the middle of Nebraska's lush wheat farming area. In Phelps County in south-central Nebraska, the County Historical Society has a lived-in sod house now open to the public.

All over the state, towns and counties and cities are involved in preserving the past through historic restorations and the establishing of historic societies. Some are elaborate affairs set up in restored mansions. Others, such as the charming museum in Scribner, occupy modest store fronts on Main Street. The Nebraska State Historic Society also has three mobile museums for visitors. Each summer the three trailers appear along Nebraska highways telling the history of the area in which each is located.

Two of the best historic museums in the country are in Nebraska, within forty miles of one another. The Stuhr Museum of the Prairie Pioneer in Grand Island and Harold Warp Pioneer Village in Minden (both directly off Interstate 80) have assembled thousands and thousands of artifacts from this nation's pioneer past. Additionally, both have re-created entire villages and areas inside their grounds. There are houses, railroad stations, churches, country schools, and general stores.

The home of Pulitzer prize-winning author Willa Cather (*My Ántonia, O Pioneers!*) in Red Cloud has been restored and filled with Cather memorabilia. In tiny Bancroft (pop. 545) the one-room study once used by Poet Laureate John G. Neihardt (*Black Elk Speaks, Cycle of the West*) has been restored along with an Indian prayer garden and a new museum. Author Mari Sandoz (*Cheyenne Autumn, Old Jules*) lived in the Sand Hills and is buried out in the wild, virgin prairie grasses of that area. Many of her papers and manuscripts are on display in Gordon, Nebraska.

Arbor Lodge, a fifty-two-room mansion located in Nebraska City, was once the home of ardent conservationist J. Sterling Morton, who gave America Arbor Day in 1872. It is a magnificent piece of architecture set on sixty-five acres of lush landscape which contains thousands of varieties of trees, flowers, shrubs, and bushes.

Art lovers have the Sheldon Art Gallery in Lincoln and the Joslyn Memorial Art Museum in Omaha to visit. Additionally, there is the Nebraska State Capitol building, one of the most distinctive state capitols in the country. Designed and built in the 1920s and 1930s—after a nationwide competition to choose the designer—it is a bold Art Deco design, a far cry from the more familiar Greco-Roman imitations that dot the country. It is a magnificent building that artistically and organically incorporates many of those things symbolic of Nebraska and the Great Plains—buffalo, sheaves of wheat, stalks of corn—into its decorative motifs.

For those interested in Nebraska's far distant past, the State Museum in Lincoln contains the restructured skeletons of many of the prehistoric animals that once roamed Nebraska—including the world's largest elephant.

SPECIAL EVENTS

Nebraska seems in constant celebration of her pioneer past, exuberantly involved in a look backward to the days of sodbusters, cowboys, Indians, trail drivers, and her own prairie pioneers. The result: everything from Wild West rodeos to quiet poetry readings.

Rodeos and county fairs are held almost weekly throughout the summer months, and harvest festivals hold sway into the autumn.

Rodeos range from small affairs in small towns, to the granddaddy of them all, the Burwell Rodeo held every August up in that Sand Hills town. But Mullen might be Rodeo City: The High School Rodeo is held in Mullen every May, followed by the Mullen Rodeo on the Fourth of July and topped off by the 4-H Rodeo in August. Another big Sand Hills bronco bust-out is held every July in Broken Bow.

County fairs, a good way to sample small-town life in rural Nebraska, come fast and furious during August and early September. Complete with parades, the high school marching band, baking contests, calf roping, tractor pulls, bingo games, cattle judging, and mountains of homemade food for sale, county fairs are true Americana.

Nebraska's early settlers are remembered in such annual celebrations as Plum Creek Days (named for the creek around which the settlers built their dugouts and sod houses), which are held in Lexington, and Oregon Trail Days, held in Gering. And the biggest of them all: the Czech Festival held every August in Wilber (pop. 1,483) to celebrate the rush of Czechoslovakian immigrants who came to the area during the pioneer period of the late 1800s. People parade in colorful native costumes, there is dancing in the streets, and stacks of kolaches and other native dishes are eaten, making an enticing collage of sights, sounds, and smells.

Nebraska's own Mardi Gras celebration is the gaudy, baroque, and splendiferous Ak-Sar-Ben celebration (that is "Nebraska" spelled backward) sponsored by the civic group of the same name. There are parades, marching bands, a rodeo, and a huge formal dance where a king and queen—resplendent in fur-trimmed robes and jewel-bedecked crowns—are named to rule over the mythic Court of Quivira. This is an annual event, held in October.

Nebraska's Indian heritage is celebrated on the Omaha and Winnebago Indian reservations. During the annual Winnebago Powwow, held for two days in August, two important tribal ceremonies, the Medicine Dance and the Winter Feast, are still celebrated. The Omaha tribe holds its annual Powwow Council in August in a grove of oak trees just outside the village of Macy. Ceremonial dances and the speaking and chanting of myths and songs are a part of the occasion. Cody Park near North Platte has Indian dances daily during the summer.

For sailing fans, there is the McCook Regatta held each July, and Brownville, Nebraska's spiffed-up old river town, has an old-fashioned steamboat plying the Missouri plus good old summertime band concerts. The National Old Fiddlers' Contest in August draws contestants and spectators alike from all around the country to the soft, grassy banks of the Missouri to hear the old-time music.

One of Nebraska's best-loved residents, the late John G. Neihardt, was made her Poet Laureate in a special session of the state legislature in 1921. Every August, special tribute is paid to "the little gent" (as one farmer from rural Wilber once called him) during Neihardt Days. Much of Neihardt's moving poetry was concerned with the settling of the West, the terrible conflicts between the settlers and the Indians, the hardship that was endured by all.

K.K.

CHRONOLOGY

1541   Coronado reached Nebraska.

1601   Oñate reached Nebraska.

1682   Mississippi Basin was claimed by the French.

1823   Bellevue, first settlement, was established.

1841   Oregon Trail extended through Nebraska.

1846   Mormon Trail extended through Nebraska.

1849   California gold rush. People left and some people passing through en route stayed.

1854   Kansas-Nebraska Act created the Nebraska Territory.

1861   Pony Express route extended through Nebraska.

1863   First homestead in the United States was claimed in Beatrice, Nebraska.

1867   Nebraska became the thirty-seventh state in the Union.
Union Pacific Railroad was completed across Nebraska.

1869   University of Nebraska was founded.

1872   Arbor Day was proclaimed.

1877   Crazy Horse was murdered at Fort Robinson.

1904   Kincaid Act gave 640-acre sections of free land to farmers.

1917   Boys Town was founded by Father Edward Flanagan.

1921   John G. Neihardt was named Poet Laureate of Nebraska.

1932   Nebraska State Capitol building was finished.

1934   Unicameral form of government was adopted.

1946   Offut Air Force Base, south of Omaha, was made headquarters of the U. S. Strategic Air Command (SAC).

1953   Resumption of barge service on Missouri River from Omaha.

1967   Resurgence of Omaha's Old Market area.

1975   *Harper's* magazine cited Omaha as tenth of top fifty cities in quality of life.

1979   Nebraska cattle ranchers battled one of the most bitter winters in the history of the state. Governor Charles Thorne declared several counties in the Sandhills disaster areas. A prime difficulty was getting feed in to stranded ranchers who had exhausted their supplies.

NORTH DAKOTA

ANYBODY who has ever been to North Dakota can tell you that the population explosion hasn't caused any problems there yet, especially in the western part of the state where there is only an average of four people per square mile. The state has thus far escaped some of the problems that plague other parts of the United States, such as air pollution, crime, and racial tensions.

The air in North Dakota is clear and crisp. And with no huge urban centers, North Dakota has been able to avoid the conflicts that so often characterize city life.

Not that everything is perfect in the state. It would like to bolster its industry and create more jobs as farming becomes more automated and people leave the land. Agriculture is by far the biggest industry, and wheat is the major crop. In fact, settlers first came to North Dakota because they heard they could get rich growing wheat. That was back in the 1880s just after the Indian Wars when North Dakota was considered remote even by frontier standards. The railroad made it easier to get there, and immigrants from northern Europe—Scandinavians, Russians, and Germans—came by the thousands to farm in the wilderness.

Teddy Roosevelt went to North Dakota in the 1880s, too, to shoot buffalo. He liked it so much that he bought two ranches and might have stayed on if politics hadn't called. The Indians also liked the land, but they didn't stand a chance to hold on to it once the white man began arriving en masse. Tribes like the Mandan, the Hidatsa, the Chippewa, and the Sioux were settled on reservations once they stopped resisting the intruders from the East.

Today, less than a hundred years after it became a state, North Dakota still resembles the pioneer land it once was. True, super highways and the jet age have arrived, but those wide open spaces are still wide open. The famed Badlands in the southwestern part of the state are still a breath-taking natural wonder. And despite the amenities of the twentieth century, life in general seems simpler, quieter, more in keeping with the land, the seasons, and the elements than it is in places less remote. North Dakota hasn't yet lost touch with its heritage. It is a living reminder that the country is still young and that the old times weren't really so long ago.

THE LAND

Even on a topographical map, North Dakota looks flat. Its rectangular shape lends to its image: a vast expanse of prairie stretching westward . . . a remote, vaguely alien land, sparsely populated by a tough breed of farmers who tend their cattle and grow their wheat far from the hustle and bustle of America around it.

While it is true that North Dakota *is* pretty flat, there are shades of difference—contrasts that belie the starkness of its image to the outsider's eye. The eastern part of the state, for instance, was once a glacial lake, Lake Agassiz. Today, it is rich and fertile farm land that surrounds the Red River which flows northward into Canada to empty into the Hudson Bay.

Topographically speaking, the entire Red River Valley and the area to the west of it—the Young Drift Plains—are part of the Central Lowland that covers much of the North American continent from the Appalachians until it meets the Great Plains which extend west to the Rockies. The Young Drift Plains are separated from the Red River Valley by a steep slope or escarpment which reaches its highest point in the Pembina Mountains in the north of the state. Elsewhere, the Young Drift Plains range from 300 to 2,000 feet above the Red River Valley. Here, too, the soil is rich and fertile, another remnant of those great glaciers which once slid over the entire surface of the state. They carved lakes throughout the area, including Devils Lake, a body of salty water that has no outlet and is steadily shrinking. And, the glaciers etched shallow valleys and rolling hills into the countryside—hills that rise into genuine mountains in the north of the state. The Turtle Mountains rise only about 550 feet above the plain.

To the southwest of the Young Drift Plains lie the Great Plains, and here, again, the two areas are separated by an escarpment, this one rising 300 to 400 feet on the east bank of the Missouri River. The lowlands on either side of the river are known locally as "the

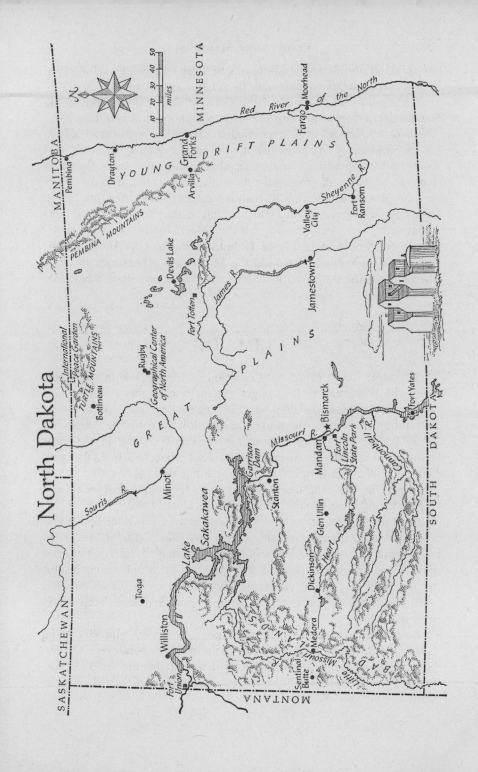

North Dakota

MANITOBA

SASKATCHEWAN

MINNESOTA

SOUTH DAKOTA

MONTANA

miles
0 10 20 30 40 50

Red River of the North

Moorhead

Fargo

YOUNG DRIFT PLAINS

Pembina

Drayton

Grand Forks

Arvilla

PEMBINA MOUNTAINS

Sheyenne R.

Valley City

Fort Ransom

Devils Lake

James R.

Jamestown

Fort Totten

G R E A T   P L A I N S

International Peace Garden

TURTLE MOUNTAINS

Rugby

Geographical Center of North America

Bottineau

Souris R.

Minot

Lake Sakakawea

Garrison Dam

Stanton

Missouri R.

Bismarck

Mandan

Fort Lincoln State Park

Cannonball R.

Fort Yates

Tioga

Williston

Fort Union

Glen Ullin

Dickinson

Heart R.

Medora

Sentinel Butte

Little Missouri R.

B A D L A N D S

slope." Dotting this region are buttes or steep hills which stand alone and are separated from each other by small, rugged valleys.

The most interesting part of the Great Plains is the section in the southwestern corner of the state—North Dakota's famous Badlands. Here, nature has allowed her imagination free rein to carve a long and narrow valley and embellish it with buttes, domes, pyramids, and cones, all composed of sandstone, shale, and clay and colored in tones of brown, red, gray, and yellow. Adding to the array of colors are the pink and red clays—the above ground indication that lignite coal beds below ground are still burning as they have been for centuries.

The western part of North Dakota is drained by the Missouri River, which flows south toward the Mississippi. The James River in the center of the state eventually joins the drainage pattern formed by the Missouri.

CLIMATE

Most people shiver at the very mention of North Dakota's weather. And with good reason. It does get extremely cold there. Winters are harsh with temperatures dipping as low as 60 degrees below zero and with biting cold winds that make the situation even worse. But what a lot of people don't realize about North Dakota is that its summers can be just as extreme as its winters. As a matter of fact, the state holds the Western Hemisphere record for temperature range in any one year: in 1936 the mercury dipped to 60 degrees below zero in February and in July soared to 121 degrees above zero.

If those statistics come as a surprise, consider this one: North Dakota has more hours of sunshine than any other state in the Union . . . some 15 hours a day from mid-May through July. For the most part, those summer days are pretty pleasant with July temperatures averaging 69 degrees in the north and 72 degrees in the south. And even when it does get very hot, the low humidity helps keep things comfortable.

Even under the best of circumstances, however, winters can be downright awful if you're not used to subzero temperatures. The average January temperature in the northeast of the state is 3 degrees while it is 14 degrees in the southwest corner. And then there's the snow—about 32 inches a year.

In general, the weather is better in the western part of the state where the humidity is lower, the rains and snows are less, and the winters are milder than in the east. For instance, annual precipitation in the west averages about 15 inches, compared to 18 inches in the southeast.

THE NORTH DAKOTANS

In the 1800s, while the West was being won, North Dakota wasn't exactly what you'd call a magnet for settlers. In fact, a railroad had to be built to attract people to the area. But once the Northern Pacific Railroad reached North Dakota things changed dramatically, largely because the railroad waged a massive advertising campaign. It concentrated on spreading the word in northern Europe about North Dakota's "choice prairie . . . hardwood timbered lands . . . natural meadows . . , healthful climate." And it got results: settlers by the thousands began to arrive from Norway, Germany, Poland, Iceland, and Russia.

Before the advent of the railroad and the "Dakota Boom" it fostered, North Dakota was pretty much Indian territory. The Arikara, Cheyenne, Hidatsa, and Mandan tribes farmed the land of the Missouri Valley while such hunter and warrior tribes as the Assiniboin, Chippewa, and Sioux wandered throughout the northeast. The first white man to arrive was a French Canadian, Pierre Gaultier de Varennes, Sieur de La Verendrye. He visited the Mandan Indians at their village near the present-day site of Bismarck in 1738, but after that the only visitors of any importance until the early years of the nineteenth century were the fur traders and trappers who came down from Canada.

The Dakotas became U.S. territory with the Louisiana Purchase in 1803 and the following year President Thomas Jefferson dispatched Meriwether Lewis and William Clark to take a look at the vast area the nation had acquired. Lewis and Clark made it as far as what is now Stanton, N.D., by October 1804 and camped there through the winter before pushing west to the Pacific. But even their celebrated exploration did little to spur settlement. Two major factors discouraged it: hostile Indians and the inaccessibility of the place. Some permanent settlers did arrive from Canada in 1812 and put down roots at Pembina, but they didn't stay long. Once the border between the

Dakotas and Canada was officially set at the 49th parallel, most of them moved back across the line.

Congress tried to encourage settlement in 1863 by opening the area for homesteading—that is, it made land available free to anyone who lived on it and improved it. But still, fear of the Indians and the remoteness deterred even the boldest pioneers. Trouble with the Indians was chronic at the time. The Sioux had massacred hundreds in neighboring Minnesota in 1862 and that same year government troops were dispatched after them. The bloody reprisals took place in North Dakota. Despite a series of treaties between the government and the Indians, the battles continued—mostly because the treaties were so often ignored. The Indian Wars finally ended in 1881 when Sitting Bull, the great Sioux chief, surrendered to U.S. troops.

By then some enterprising eastern corporations had decided to brave the hazards of North Dakota to establish huge wheat farms. For a while those tremendous spreads—ranging in size between 3,000 and 65,000 acres—were so successful that individuals began drifting into the area with hopes of reaping the same enormous profits or "bonanzas" that the companies had realized.

The biggest population boom took place after North Dakota became a state in 1889. The next year the U.S. Census reported that there were about 191,000 people in the state but twenty years later, in 1910, about 577,000 were counted. Many of the newcomers were Europeans; as a matter of fact, the 1890 census found that 43 per cent of the new state's population was foreign born. And many of those Europeans were Norwegians. Even today, there's a strong Norwegian accent to North Dakota. Norwegian language and literature are taught at the University of North Dakota and in some of the public schools.

Many Indians still live in the state, too—four reservations, with a total population of 11,000. The largest is Turtle Mountain Reservation, just south of the Canadian border. This is the home of the Turtle Mountain band of the Chippewa tribe. The Sioux live on two reservations, Fort Totten at Devils Lake and Standing Rock in Sioux County. The Three Affiliated Tribes—the Mandan, Hidatsa, and Arikara—are on the Fort Berthold Reservation at Lake Sakajawea.

According to the 1970 census, there were about 618,000 people in North Dakota, making the state one of the least populated in the nation. It ranks forty-fifth. Through the years, the population has been steadily dwindling due to the lack of job opportunities. Although

farming remains the most important industry, there has been a continuous movement of people away from the land to the cities. Today,
most of North Dakota's population is concentrated in the Red River
Valley around Fargo and Grand Forks. The number of people per
square mile declines as you go west—there are 23.9 persons per
square mile in the Red River Valley, only 8.9 in the center of the
state, and only 4 in the west.

The state has been trying to create new jobs through programs to
lure industries, and to an extent it has been successful. North Dakota
now has a high rate of industrial growth. So far, however, even that
encouraging development has neither stopped the natives from leaving nor attracted newcomers in significant numbers.

HISTORY

At one time or another, four countries have laid claim to North
Dakota—or at least to parts of it. But until the United States gained
control of the territory with the Louisiana Purchase in 1803, the area
was largely ignored. Then in 1682 Robert Cavelier, Sieur de La Salle,
claimed all the land drained by the Mississippi River for France.
Since part of North Dakota was drained by the Missouri, which eventually flowed into the Mississippi, the region technically became
French territory. Another part of the state also became nominally
French when that country laid claim to all the land south of the Hudson Bay.

All of this meant nothing to the Indians who were living in North
Dakota at the time. In those days, the Arikara, Cheyenne, Hidatsa,
and Mandan tribes were peacefully farming, unaware of the foreign
claims and concerned only with the periodic attacks by the Assiniboin, Chippewa, and Sioux. The first hint the Indians had that
anyone else was interested in their land was the arrival of French Canadian explorer Pierre Gaultier de Varennes, Sieur de La Verendrye,
who visited the Mandans at their village near what is now Bismarck
in 1738. By then, France had given her Hudson Bay territory to
Great Britain. But from the Indians' point of view, Varennes' visit
was a novelty that wasn't repeated. They didn't have much contact
with the Spanish either after 1762, when France gave its land west of
the Mississippi to Spain. So uninterested were the Spaniards in this

vast area that they gave it back to France in 1800. The United States acquired it all in 1803 with the Louisiana Purchase.

By then, the Indians had some indication that they wouldn't be alone much longer. Trappers and traders came and went, uninterested in anything but furs, but by the early years of the nineteenth century, trading posts and transportation routes had begun to appear. It is said that the oldest trading post in North Dakota was built at Pembina in 1797. Along with the new routes and trading posts came the U. S. Army. Forts sprang up in the wilderness manned by federal troops whose responsibility was to insure the safety of the trappers and traders and keep the Indians in line.

At this stage, there still were no signs of permanent settlement. But by 1812 a few Scots-Irish from Canada had moved into the Pembina area. They wanted to farm but did not intend to become U.S. citizens. Once an official survey determined that Pembina was in the United States, not Canada, the settlers moved back across the border.

One of the most important early outposts was Fort Union, established by the American Fur Company in 1829. Three years later a steamboat named *The Yellowstone* traveled up the Missouri River to the fort. But even that new mode of transportation didn't do much to spur settlement of the Dakotas. The area officially became the "Dakota Territory" in 1861 and two years later was opened to homesteading. Still, hostile Indians and the remoteness of the area discouraged settlement. At the time, U.S. troops were kept busy battling the Sioux who had killed settlers in neighboring Minnesota.

Two events finally convinced people to come and farm in North Dakota: the arrival of the Northern Pacific Railroad in 1872, followed by the Great Northern Railroad in 1880, and the "bonanzas" or huge profits made by eastern corporations which bought up enormous sections of North Dakota to grow wheat. Corporate farming didn't last long, but while it did, it was so successful that families came by the thousands to get rich quick by growing wheat in North Dakota.

During this period, the town of Yankton, now in South Dakota, served as the territorial capital, but the centers of population were widely separated. Eventually the capital was moved to Bismarck, a change that wasn't acceptable to those in the southern part of the territory. Finally, in 1889 Congress divided the area, creating North and South Dakota. That same year, both were admitted to the Union.

Since then, North Dakota has gone through several phases. Its farmers, fearful of exploitation by Eastern business interests, formed the Nonpartisan League in 1915, a group that managed to elect its candidate as governor the following year. He was a Republican by the name of Lynn J. Frazier who was able to realize some of the League's proposals. During his term of office, the Bank of North Dakota was established and plans were made for the opening of a state-owned flour mill and elevator in Grand Forks. Both were responses to the League's demand for state ownership of grain elevators, flour mills, packing houses, and cold storage plants.

The 1930s brought two disasters: the Great Depression, which affected the rest of the world and devastated North Dakota's agricultural economy, and a severe drought and accompanying dust storms that struck another blow at the farmers. As farm production declined during the Depression, thousands began leaving the land and the state. During World War II, agricultural production zoomed ahead, and after the war, the threat of droughts was somewhat alleviated by the construction of the huge Garrison Dam in 1946. A further spur to the economy came in 1951 when oil was discovered at Tioga.

Today, North Dakota's biggest challenge is the diversification of its economy and the creation of new jobs. Farming remains all important, but while 97 per cent of the land area is occupied by farms, fewer and fewer people are needed to run them. Over the years, the population has been shifting to the cities of Fargo and Grand Forks, but many North Dakotans have left in search of jobs that simply don't exist in the state. For all its problems, though, North Dakota has much to boast about: lots of clean air, plenty of wide open spaces, and a natural beauty that remains pretty much as it was when only the Indians were around to appreciate it.

INDUSTRY

North Dakota is the least industrial state in the nation. Nonetheless, food processing ranks as one of its most important industries, and North Dakota is one of the leading states in the production of butter.

It was inevitable that a state as heavily agricultural as North Dakota would make an effort to process or refine the products of its farms. The state established a flour mill in Grand Forks in 1922 which today produces about 1.5 million barrels of flour a year. And it also processes flax and soybeans. Wheat flour and cereals are processed elsewhere, at Devils Lake and Glen Ullin, for instance. And there's a sugar refinery at Drayton—it opened in 1965 to process sugar beets grown in both North Dakota and Minnesota.

Some oil refineries have sprung up since the discovery of oil in Tioga in 1951. Today, there are refineries in Dickinson, Mandan, and Willston as well as a plant in Tioga where gasoline, propane, butane, natural gas, and sulfur are extracted from petroleum.

Taken as a whole, North Dakota's industries account for only 10 per cent of its income—the lion's share comes from agriculture, while the rest comes from the mining of the state's natural resources.

AGRICULTURE

Farming is of primary importance in North Dakota. The rich soil in the Red River Valley and the fertile Young Drift and Great Plains encouraged the early pioneers to put down roots and stay awhile. Today, North Dakota is virtually border-to-border farm land. In 1970 it had about 45,000 farms, many of them with more than 1,000 acres. The most important crop in the state is wheat, both spring and durum. North Dakota ranks as the second most important wheat-producing state in the nation, harvesting about 180 million bushels annually and devoting 6.5 million acres to the crop.

In addition, North Dakota farmers raise more than half the nation's supply of flaxseed—between 13 and 20 million bushels a year. And the state also leads the nation in the production of both barley and rye. Barley is grown chiefly in the eastern part of the state while most of the rye comes from both the southeast and north-central regions. There are other important crops, too—farmers in the Red River Valley grow sugar beets, potatoes, and corn. Elsewhere they raise oats, soybeans, alfalfa, hay, safflower, sunflowers, and sweet clover.

Then there's the livestock industry. Plenty of good grazing land for cattle exists in the center of the state, but all told, some 12 million acres or one-fourth of the state's total farm land is used for pasturing. In the west where the land is more rugged and less suited to crops, sheep raising has become an important industry.

As a whole, farming brings in about four fifths of the value of goods produced in North Dakota. But only about one fifth of the state's workers are employed on the farms. In many cases, farms ac-

PLATE 46 Mount Rushmore National Memorial towers majestically over the pine-covered Black Hills.

PLATE 47 South Dakota's Badlands, with its awesome ridges and ravines.

PLATE 48 Red Rocks Theater, west of Denver,
is a natural amphitheater of red sandstone.

PLATE 49 The Homestake Gold Mine in Lead, South Dakota, has been
in operation since 1872.

PLATE 50 Cliff dwellings occupied by Pueblo Indians about 800 years ago in southwestern Colorado's Mesa Verde National Park.

PLATE 51 A panoramic view of Denver, with the snow-capped Rockies in the distance.

PLATE 52 Hagerman Peak towers over Snowmass Lake, near Aspen.

PLATE 53 Sparkling white sand of Great Sand Dunes National Monument, near Alamosa, Colorado.

PLATE 54 The grandeur of Pike's Peak, rising over the plains of Colorado.

PLATE 55 The multi-spired
United States Air Force
Academy Chapel is set
at the foot of the
Colorado Rockies.

PLATE 56 Craters of the Moon National Monument near Arco, Idaho,
is an area of lava beds and volcanic rock formations.

PLATE 57 Panoramic view of the popular year-round resort area of Sun Valley-Ketchum.

PLATE 58 The Snake River winds through the rugged gorge of Hells Canyon, Idaho.

PLATE 59 Elkhorn, a ghost town in Montana, fascinates tourists.

tually are owned by people who live elsewhere—the so-called "suit-case" farmers who are on hand only twice a year, for planting and then again for harvesting.

NATURAL RESOURCES

North Dakota has enormous reserves of both coal and oil. Oil was struck at Tioga in 1951 and subsequently the state has ranked ninth in the nation in terms of oil reserves. The oil fields lie in the Williston Basin and are so large that they stretch across the state's borders into South Dakota, Montana, and Canada. There are wells in thirteen of North Dakota's western counties.

As for the coal, there are about 350 billion tons of lignite in Mercer County. About four million tons are mined a year using strip-mining techniques. No other state has such enormous reserves of this fuel. Despite that fact, mining dropped off during the 1950s when other forms of fuel were plentiful. But the energy crisis of the 1970s has spurred production. As a matter of fact, plans are afoot to estab-lish a series of lignite gasification plants to generate energy by burn-ing an estimated 10 million tons of lignite apiece.

And there's more in terms of minerals—natural gas wells in Bow-man County and the oil-producing counties in the northwest, and de-posits of sand and gravel throughout the state. There's also lots of clay of just about every variety to be found throughout the southwest.

But for all that mineral wealth, North Dakota's chief natural re-source is its rich fertile soil—the soil that made the state's agriculture what it is today. The state has abundant wildlife, too. It isn't unusual to see white-tailed deer grazing or to spot mule deer or proghorn antelope in the western plains. Visitors to the Badlands usually are intrigued by the "dogtowns" built by the prairie dogs. And the state's lakes and marshes always have been breeding grounds for ducks and waterfowl—naturalists will tell you that more waterfowl hatch here than in any other state.

The state's forests are sparse, however—only about 1 per cent of the land area is covered by woods. But the countryside is enlivened in spring and summer by the colorful blooms of black-eyed Susans, gaillardias, pasqueflowers, prairie mallows, red lilies, and wild prairie roses, the state flower.

CITIES

Fargo, with a population of about 53,000, is the biggest city in North Dakota. Figuring that the population of the state hovers around the 600,000 mark, Fargo can be considered a fair-sized urban area—especially since about 123,000 people live in the Fargo-Moorhead City, Minnesota, metropolitan area.

The railroad is responsible for the growth of Fargo. When the Northern Pacific extended its line across the Red River in 1872, the place was just a tiny settlement called Centralia until they renamed it in honor of William George Fargo of the famed Wells, Fargo & Company. Today, it's a major shipping point for the three thousand farms that surround it in the fertile Red River Valley. The area's major crops are grains, potatoes, and sugar beets, and although Fargo likes to think of itself as an increasingly sophisticated city in the arts and industry, agriculture is still the backbone of its economy. North Dakota State University conducts agricultural experiments at its campus in northwest Fargo and the Institute for Regional Studies also maintains a research center there.

Residents are likely to point out that Fargo was designated an "All American City" after its urban renewal efforts and erection of a $10 million Civic Center. In terms of the arts, there's a bit of everything: the Fargo-Moorhead Civic Opera, the Prairie Stage at North Dakota State University, the Fargo-Moorhead Community Theater, the Northwest Stage Company, the Fargo-Moorhead Symphony, and the Bison and Fargo galleries.

For the sports-minded, there are four swimming pools and a golf course in the city parks, and for history buffs, the Forsberg House with its unique collection of memorabilia dating back to pioneer days.

Grand Forks, about 75 miles north of Fargo on the Red River, is a shipping center, too. The big industry here is potato processing—about two million pounds per day. The Western Potato Service makes french fries for shipment throughout the nation. Wheat is another big local crop and quite a bit is milled at the State Mill and Elevator in Grand Forks, one of the largest and most modern of its kind in the country. The local economy has gotten a boost from the nearby Grand Forks Air Force Base, home of the 321st Strategic

Missile Wing and the 319th Bomb Wing. The base controls 150 Minutemen ICBM's and an assortment of alert aircraft.

Grand Forks can be considered the educational center of the state. It was here in 1883 that the University of North Dakota was founded, a school that today is the state's largest educational institution. The University Gallery on campus displays the arts and crafts of both students and professionals and the Hughes Fine Arts Center is the place to go for concerts and theater. But the University isn't the only local tourist attraction. There's the Scandinavian Cultural Center with its exhibits relating to the heritage of the predominantly Norwegian and Swedish populace of the area and the Grand Forks County Historical Society Museum. Its collection includes the town's first post office restored to its original condition.

Bismarck, the state capital, is the fastest growing city in North Dakota. Located in the western part of the state on the Missouri River, it dates back to 1872 when it was called simply "Crossing on the Missouri." The Northern Pacific Railroad brought new life to the area in 1873 and the gold rush in the Black Hills added to the excitement of the times. About 40,000 people live in Bismarck today, and while the city is proud of its colorful past, it tends to emphasize what an up-to-date place it is now. For instance, residents are especially proud of the city's Civic Center, which can seat up to 7,850 people. The center is used for meetings, stage shows, concerts, basketball games, ice shows, hockey, and rodeos.

But the town's most important tourist attraction is the state capitol, a nineteen-story edifice known as the "skyscraper capitol of the plains." You can get a pretty good look at those plains and Bismarck itself from the observation deck on the eighteenth floor, but what usually intrigues visitors are the bronze statues on the grounds. There's one of Sakajawea, the Indian girl who guided Lewis and Clark on their explorations of the Northwest; one of North Dakota statesman John Burke; and another representing a pioneer family that helped settle the state. Inside is the "Roughrider Gallery" with its portraits of famous North Dakotans, including television commentator Eric Sevareid, bandleader Lawrence Welk, singer Peggy Lee, and baseball star Roger Maris. The 1935 building replaces the previous capitol that was destroyed by fire that same year.

There's a state historical museum on the grounds that gives visitors an insight into North Dakota's past. Among the exhibits are Indian relics, early weapons, and mounted specimens of the state's wildlife.

The Indian collection is said to be one of the finest in the world. But for a look at exhibits relating to the early pioneers, the place to go is the Camp Hancock Museum on the site of the original Camp Hancock built in 1872. Among the displays of furniture and tools, there is a cannon used by the U. S. Cavalry during the gold rush days.

The Dakota Zoo is another must for sightseers. It is on the banks of the Missouri River and has some unusual attractions, such as a friendly 1,600-pound Kodiak bear named Clyde, a Prairie Dog Town, buffalo, and about a hundred other kinds of animals.

Bismarck's park system is pretty extensive—a total of 1,250 acres divided into twenty parks with baseball diamonds, tennis courts, archery ranges, three golf courses, and several swimming pools. The city has two colleges: Mary College on the city's outskirts, noted for its impressive ultramodern architecture, and Bismarck Junior College.

Minot is the fourth-largest town in the state. At first it was just a city of tents erected when the Great Northern Railroad was building its line. Its importance today stems from its location in the middle of a rich farming area that got richer after they started mining lignite and later when oil was discovered nearby. The U. S. Air Force has established a base in the town's northern outskirts.

Once considered a "wide open town," Minot has settled down to a more sedate routine, a pace that's leisurely enough to have fostered a theater company, the Mouse River Players; the Allegra Dance Ensemble; and the Linha Art Gallery.

SPORTS AND RECREATION

Curling is very popular in North Dakota. It is a winter spectator sport imported from Canada which can best be described as a cross between shuffleboard and bowling played on an ice lane. It is most popular in the eastern and northern parts of the state, and every year the National Curling Finals are held at Grand Forks.

Needless to say, North Dakota is a land of winter sports. Since the land is pretty flat, cross-country skiing has generally been more popular than downhill skiing, even though the state now has six downhill ski areas at Fort Ransom, Rolla View, Devils Lake, Arvilla, Minot, and Bottineau Winter Park. Snowmobiles have caught on in popularity—whole families go on snowmobile "safaris" following marked trails in the state parks, and snowmobile races draw large crowds.

Fishermen in the state have learned not to be deterred by the long, cold winters. They simply drop a line through a hole in the ice and, with any luck, can hook a trout, northern pike, walleye, sauger, crappie, or bluegill. It is always fishing season in North Dakota, except in April when game fish are off limits. And there are some pretty big fish in the state's waters. Somebody once caught a thirty-seven-pound northern pike. Anybody who lands one of the big ones is encouraged to report it to the State Game and Fish Department. If it meets their standards, they'll reward the fisherman with membership in the Whopper Club.

Hunters have their choice of more than a hundred areas. Duck and goose hunting is especially good, and the western part of the state abounds with big game—whitetail deer, mule deer, and antelope.

Lake Sakajawea is North Dakota's largest summer playground and also the largest man-made fresh-water lake in the nation, some fourteen miles wide in spots. The lake was created by the Garrison Dam across the Missouri River and named for the Shoshone Indian woman Sakajawea who guided Lewis and Clark on their exploration of the Northwest. There are five recreation areas surrounding the lake offering facilities for boating, swimming, fishing, camping, and picnicking. Throughout the state there are more than 150 camp grounds with a wide range of facilities.

Hiking and trail riding—guided or unguided—are two popular ways to get away from it all, particularly in the Badlands. But for the visitor who would prefer a less active means of soaking up the local color, there are rodeos all over the state at all times of the year.

POINTS OF INTEREST

It isn't hard to understand why Theodore Roosevelt fell in love with North Dakota's Badlands. He went there in 1883 to hunt buffalo and was immediately entranced by the "fantastic beauty" of the place, an eerie, almost barren jumble of knolls, cones, and hills colored in shades of gray and burnt clay. One visitor wrote that "viewed from a distance at sunset it looked exactly like the ruins of an ancient city."

Outdoorsman that Roosevelt was, he bought a share in the Maltese Cross ranch near Medora and invested in four hundred head of cattle. A year later he bought another ranch, Elkhorn, about forty miles away and threw himself into the Western way of life with his customary vigor. Before he went back east Roosevelt had won the respect of the tough men of the frontier and had organized a local cattlemen's association.

Roosevelt hasn't been forgotten in the Badlands. Today most of the area is within the confines of the vast Theodore Roosevelt Memorial Park sprawling over some 70,000 acres near Medora.

The town itself is a tourist attraction. Medora dates back to 1883 when a French nobleman, the Marquis de Mores, arrived and was so captivated by the area that he decided to stay and tried in vain to operate a packing plant so that the cattlemen wouldn't have to ship their stock east. De Mores named the town after his wife, and to make sure they were comfortable there, he built a twenty-six-room château and imported the furnishings from France. The château is now a historic site, an oddity of European elegance amid the western simplicity of what is now known as "rough rider country."

Medora has been restored to look pretty much like the rugged town it was in Roosevelt's day. In addition, there is the "Medora Doll House," a unique museum with an enchanting display of dolls dating back three centuries and an exhibit of toys from all over the world. There's a Western-style museum, too, with a collection of relics from pioneer days and an array of Indian arts and crafts.

Throughout North Dakota there are vivid reminders that a hundred years ago this was still Indian and buffalo country. For the Indians, the buffalo was more than just a source of food. They used the hides to make teepees, the neck skin as a shield to protect them from arrows, the sinews as sewing thread, the bones as tools. When the white man began to arrive back in the 1830s there were about forty million bison roaming the Great Plains. By 1900 only three hundred remained in all of North America. Today, they are a protected species and about twenty-two thousand live in the United States and Canada, with the largest North Dakota herds in Roosevelt Memorial Park.

The Sioux were the great buffalo hunters and Sioux from the Standing Rock Reservation made possible the last great buffalo hunt in North Dakota in 1882. Some six hundred braves killed five thousand buffalo in three days. The biggest buffalo in the area today is a sixty-ton concrete and steel replica of the American bison that overlooks the city of Jamestown.

The Mandan Indians hunted buffalo, but they were primarily an agricultural tribe living near what is now Bismarck. The state has restored one of their early encampments—Slant Village, so called because it is located on a slope in Fort Lincoln State Park. The Mandan lived there between 1650 and 1750, when they moved farther north. The reconstructed lodges at Slant Village give you a pretty good idea of how the Mandan lived. Each dwelling is about ten feet high and thirty to forty feet in diameter. The Mandan placed their beds along the wall at the left of the entrance and stabled their horses on the right. A fireplace was dug into the ground at the center of each lodge and directly overhead was a vent to allow the smoke to escape. The lodges all faced the center of the village where religious ceremonies were held.

Not far from Slant Village is another Indian community—Fort Yates on the Standing Rock Reservation, occupied by the Sioux. It was at Fort Yates that Sitting Bull, the most famous Sioux of them all, was buried. There's an ongoing controversy about whether or not Sitting Bull's bones are still there. Indians from South Dakota who had always resented the fact that the chief was buried at Fort Yates, opened his grave one night in 1953 and removed the bones, which they took back to South Dakota for reburial at Mobridge. This escapade doesn't seem to worry the North Dakota Sioux, who claim that the chief was buried in lime and that no bones could remain. They seem satisfied that Fort Yates is still Sitting Bull's last resting place.

Fort Lincoln State Park has its own ties with Sitting Bull's era. It was from Fort Abraham Lincoln that Lieutenant Colonel George Custer set out to battle the Sioux at Little Big Horn in Montana in 1876. Before Custer's disastrous defeat, Fort Lincoln had been one of the most important military outposts in the West. Life there was either very dangerous or very dull. The danger came from the continual Indian raids, the dullness from the isolation and lack of diversion in the wilderness. Today the blockhouses from which the soldiers surveyed the river valley have been restored and the surrounding park provides amenities that those soldiers couldn't have imagined—picnic grounds, campsites, hiking trails, and even showers.

Another reconstructed fort dating from the Indian Wars is Fort Totten near Devils Lake. It is considered the best preserved military post of the period west of the Mississippi. It was constructed of brick and mortar in 1868 and at one time four companies—about 150 men —were stationed there. Life was a little more interesting at Fort Totten than at Fort Lincoln. There were dances, baseball games, foot-races, and even variety shows put on by an enlisted men's entertainment troupe. Today, the big attraction there is the Fort Totten Little Theatre on the restored Cavalry Square. Other original buildings have been reconstructed and along with the theater there is an art gallery, a museum, and a general store.

The oldest community in North Dakota is tucked up in the northeast corner of the state. The town of Pembina dates back to 1797 when it was a fur-trading outpost. You can take a look at some of the relics of that early settlement at the local museum, but the biggest tourist attractions in the northern part of the state are farther west. The most famous is the International Peace Garden in the Turtle Mountains. Half of the garden is in North Dakota and the other half is in Manitoba, Canada. It was dedicated in 1932 to commemorate 150 years of peace between the United States and Canada. All told, there are 2,339 acres encompassing a colorful formal garden, music and athletic camps, an All Faiths Chapel, and an eighteen-foot electrically operated clock with a face composed entirely of flowers.

Not far from the Peace Garden is the geographical center of North America at the town of Rugby. The flags of the United States and Canada flank a stone marker at the exact spot determined by the U. S. Geological Survey in 1931. There's a museum nearby that occupies several blocks in Rugby. Its diverse collection includes an old train engine, five hundred dolls, an ancient "water closet," and an array of pioneer furniture and farm implements.

One of the newest and most faithful representations of pioneer life in North Dakota is Bonanzaville near Fargo. It was founded in 1967 by an enterprising North Dakotan who managed to relocate some old log cabins, country houses, a rural church, a school, a general store, and other early buildings to form a town.

SPECIAL EVENTS

Twice a year in June and July a wagon train sets out from Jamestown in southern North Dakota across the prairie en route to Fort Lincoln near Bismarck. It's a week-long trip that re-creates pioneer days for some 350 local people and tourists who ride along on horseback or in covered wagons. Most participants dress as the settlers of a hundred years ago did—boots and Stetsons for the men, and long dresses and bonnets for the women.

The Indians re-create the old days too. Each September the Sioux of the Standing Rock Reservation play host to Indians from all over the United States at the All American Indian Activities Association Powwow and Rodeo Finals. It is just one of the many powwows that take place in North Dakota annually, but it's the biggest one and draws huge crowds to the reservation.

As might be expected, rodeos are a feature of just about every kind of get-together in North Dakota. Some are pretty special, though, like the one they always hold during the Roughriders Festival at Dickinson in July; the Champions Ride Rodeo at Sentinal Butte in August; and the three-day rodeo that's an annual event at the North Dakota Winter Show, the largest agricultural exposition in the Northwest held at Valley City every March.

On the cultural scene, the big events are the International Festival of the Arts, an eight-week affair that begins in June at the International Peace Garden, and the Imagination Art Festival that spotlights the arts in Fargo every September.

February is a big month in Minot. People come from all over the state for the Winterfest, a week-long series of activities including the North Dakota Ski Race Championship, the Minot International Cross-Country Citizens race, and the Regina-Minot 250 Snowmobile Race.

P.D.

CHRONOLOGY

1682   Southwestern North Dakota became French territory when Robert Cavelier, Sieur de La Salle, claimed for France all the land drained by the Mississippi.

1738   Pierre Gaultier de Varennes, Sieur de La Verendrye, came from Canada to explore North Dakota.

1803   The United States gained control of North Dakota through the Louisiana Purchase.

1804   Meriwether Lewis and William Clark wintered at Mandan during their exploration of the Northwest Territory.

1812   Scottish and Irish farmers from Canada settled at Pembina in the northeast corner of what was to be North Dakota.

1861   Congress created the Dakota Territory.

1863   The territory was opened to homesteading.

1875   Eastern corporations began wheat farming operations and reaped financial "bonanzas."

1889   Congress divided the Dakota territory in two and North and South Dakota were admitted to the Union.

1915   The Nonpartisan League was founded.

1922   The state-owned North Dakota Mill and Elevator in Grand Forks began operating.

1946   Work began on Garrison Dam on the Missouri River.

1951   Oil was discovered at Tioga.

1965   Work was completed on the first plant, at Stanton, of a lignite-burning power project.

1967   Work on Garrison Dam completed.

1972   Bismarck's centennial.

1977   State legislature continued its appropriation of funds, begun in 1973, for a New Heritage Center on the capitol grounds.

1979   With President Carter's energy program calling for the increased use of the country's coal reserves, a consortium of five pipeline companies readied itself to begin work on the A.N.G. Coal Gasification plant, the nation's first synthetic fuel facility, at rural Beulah.

SOUTH DAKOTA

MOST Americans probably know more about South Dakota than they realize. Everybody recognizes the Indian names Sitting Bull and Crazy Horse, the famous chiefs who led the Sioux in their battles to remain supreme on the plains. The name George Armstrong Custer is a familiar one too—his last stand at Little Big Horn wasn't in South Dakota, but he did something important there. It was Custer who verified reports back in 1876 that there was gold "in them thar hills" —the famous Black Hills of South Dakota.

A good deal of our Western lore stems from the gold rush in the Black Hills. In fact, the cowboy towns we learned to recognize from western movies look just like the "one street" South Dakota town of Deadwood on the edge of the Black Hills gold fields. Wild Bill Hickok was shot and killed in Deadwood and the graves of such famous Western figures as Calamity Jane, Preacher Smith, and Deadwood Dick are here.

Mount Rushmore is in the Black Hills, too, and is famous for the towering carved faces of Presidents Washington, Jefferson, Lincoln, and Theodore Roosevelt.

The western part of the state was—and is—cattle country. The east is more sedate, more like the Midwest than the Wild West. It was settled by farmers, many of them from northern Europe who came out west by railroad to put down roots in South Dakota's rich soil. Farming is still all important here, but industry is beginning to make some inroads encouraged by the state's efforts to diversify its economy and provide jobs as automation lessens the need for farm workers.

Most of South Dakota's cities are concentrated in the southeast corner of the state, including the biggest one, Sioux Falls, with a population of 77,000, and two of the oldest cities, Yankton and Vermillion. Although more and more Dakotans are moving to the cities, there's still plenty of space for whoever wants to get away from it all.

The state figures that it has just over eight people per square mile. About forty thousand of them are Indians living on seven reservations, including Pine Ridge, home of the Ogala Sioux.

Nobody in South Dakota has forgotten that less than a hundred years ago the area was still Indian territory. Tales of the pioneer days abound, and there are still plenty of people who can tell them firsthand. Much about South Dakota is still new and raw. It's hard to forget there how fast times have changed.

THE LAND

There are two South Dakotas—the part to the east of the Missouri River and the part to the west of it. The difference is very important to the natives and even a newcomer can easily spot the distinctions. The eastern part of the state, for instance, is an area of low, rolling hills shaped by ancient glaciers that slid across the state. This area contains two topographical regions, the Young Drift Plains and the Dissected Till Plains, both part of the central lowland that occupies much of the midwestern United States from the Appalachian Mountains to the Great Plains in the west. The largest of the two areas, the Young Drift Plains, is mostly gently rolling countryside, except in the extreme northeast of the state where the Prairie Hills rise steeply from the plain. The James River flows south through the entire Young Drift region forming a wide basin.

The southeast corner of South Dakota is part of the Dissected Till Plains, so called because the glaciers left deposits of assorted materials known to geologists as "till." The word "dissected" also has a specific meaning here—the area is literally dissected or cut up by streams.

The Great Plains cover the western part of South Dakota. Here, the land is flat for miles and miles except for the *buttes,* flat-topped hills that poke upward from the prairie, some of them reaching 400 to 600 feet above the surrounding plain. But the most interesting parts of this western region are the Badlands and the Black Hills, both dazzling displays of nature's handiwork. The Badlands are steep hills and gullies carved by wind and water into the soft rock of the area. In South Dakota they stretch for about 100 miles along the White and Cheyenne rivers.

The Black Hills along the state's western border are an intriguing

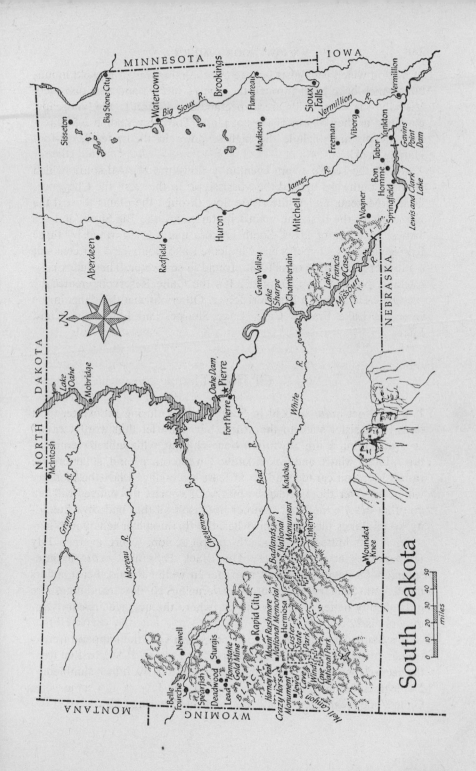

MINNESOTA

IOWA

MONTANA

WYOMING

NORTH DAKOTA

NEBRASKA

Sisseton

Big Stone City

Watertown

Big Sioux R.

Brookings

Flandreau

Madison

Sioux Falls

Vermillion

Vermillion R.

Viborg

Freeman

Yankton

Gavins Point Dam

Tabor

Bon Homme

Springfield

Lewis and Clark Lake

Aberdeen

Redfield

Huron

James R.

Mitchell

Wagner

Gann Valley

Lake Sharpe

Chamberlain

Lake Francis Case

Missouri River

Mobridge

Lake Oahe

McIntosh

Grand R.

Moreau R.

Oahe Dam

Pierre

Fort Pierre

Bad R.

Cheyenne R.

White R.

Kadoka

Belle Fourche R.

Newell

Sturgis

Deadwood

Spearfish

Lead

Homestake Gold Mine

Rapid City

Mount Rushmore National Memorial

Hermosa

Custer

Harney Peak

Crazy Horse Monument

Jewel Caves

Custer State Park

Wind Cave National Park

Hell Canyon

B L A C K

Badlands National Monument

Interior

Wounded Knee

South Dakota

0 10 20 30 40 50
miles

formation which geologists believe are the remnants of age-old mountains which once burst through the earth's surface and then subsided. Visually, the Black Hills are a spectacular addition to the landscape, emerging as they do out of the flat plain. They tower some 3,500 feet into the air and include the highest point in the state—7,242-foot Harney Peak.

All of the state's rivers eventually flow into the Missouri, which courses southward toward the Mississippi. In the west, the Cheyenne, Grand, Moreau, and White rivers flow through the plains toward the Missouri. In the east, the main tributaries are the Big Sioux and the James. In terms of lakes, South Dakota has a few formed by those Ice Age glaciers. One of them, Medicine Lake, contains 4 per cent salt —a higher proportion of salt than found in sea water. The state's largest lake, however, is man-made. It's the Oahe Reservoir created by the Oahe Dam on the Missouri River. Others formed by dams in the river are Lake Francis Case, Lake Sharpe, and Lewis and Clark Lake.

CLIMATE

It doesn't get *quite* so cold in South Dakota during the winter as it does in its sister state to the north, but don't let that word "south" fool you. Winters are downright bone-chilling, with subzero temperatures, biting winds, and lots of snow. On the other hand, summers are rather hot: you can depend on at least a few days when the mercury will zoom over the 100-degree mark. Of course, the natives will tell you that despite the heat, summer here isn't all that bad: low humidity keeps things pleasant even when the thermometer tells you otherwise. It gets hottest in the south-central region, where average July temperatures are 78 degrees. The Black Hills are cooler in midsummer—68 degrees is about average. In winter the northeast suffers most, with January temperatures averaging 10 degrees. Things are only slightly better in the southwest, where the average January temperature is 22 degrees.

If a South Dakotan wants to impress you with the temperature extremes recorded in the state, he'll tell you about 1936. In that year the record low was set when the temperature in McIntosh tumbled to 58 degrees below zero on February 17. In July of the same year, Gann Valley registered the all-time high: a blistering 120 degrees.

The whole state gets a good deal of snow in the winter—anywhere from 22 to 60 inches. The Black Hills, of course, get the most. It rains more in the southeast—here they get about 24 inches a year compared to only 14 inches or less in the northwest corner and between 18 and 20 inches in the center of the state.

THE SOUTH DAKOTANS

South Dakota belonged exclusively to the Indians until French Canadian fur traders began infiltrating the territory in the early 1800s. The Arikara farmed along the Cheyenne and Missouri rivers while the Cheyenne hunted in the Black Hills and other western areas. The Sioux or Dakota roamed the plains chasing buffalo and periodically attacked their traditional enemies, the Arikara. No question about it, the Sioux were a warrior tribe who sometimes didn't live up to their name Dakota, which means "friend" in their own language. Once the white man began moving into the territory in earnest in the 1850s, the Sioux were to cause them considerable trouble—and vice versa.

The fur traders didn't seem to disturb the Indians much at first. In fact, those early white visitors remained on friendly terms with the Indians, who seemed content to let them come and go, since, inevitably, they did go. A French trader, Joseph la Framboise, established a permanent settlement—Fort Pierre—in 1817 on the Bad River, but even that didn't touch off any major Indian hostilities. By 1823, however, the Arikara felt threatened enough to attack a fur-trading party from Missouri. Retaliation came swiftly from federal troops in league with the Sioux. In the years that followed, more and more trading posts were built along the Missouri River, but the rich farm land didn't attract many settlers until big eastern land companies began carving up the territory and establishing towns they called Sioux Falls, Medary, Flandreau, Yankton, Vermillion, and Bon Homme.

By the time the Dakota Territory was created by Congress in 1861 the Indians were on the warpath. The Sioux Chief Red Cloud led his braves against U.S. troops surveying the western part of the state near the Powder River for a road. Red Cloud persisted in his raids for two years until the government gave up the project. Hostile Indians were a major deterrent to settlement of the western part of the state, but even their uprisings couldn't hold back the white man after gold was discovered in the Black Hills in 1874. The gold rush brought prospectors, adventurers, and such legendary characters as Wild Bill Hickok and Calamity Jane to Deadwood, the lawless mining town that has been immortalized in tale after tale of the wild, wide-open West.

Only a few years after the gold rush began, South Dakota experienced a "land rush" touched off by the advent of the railroad. Settlers poured in from neighboring states in the Upper Mississippi Valley and thousands more came from northern Europe—Danes, Norwegians, Swedes, Germans, Russians, Czechs, Dutch, Welsh, and Finns. By 1890, one year after South Dakota became a state, one third of the white residents were foreign-born. There are still Danish and Swedish communities in the southeastern part of the state and the Norwegians still constitute a major ethnic group.

The immigrants brought their religions. Most were Lutherans or Catholics, but by 1890 there also were Methodist, Presbyterian, Episcopal, and Baptist churches. Mennonites and Hutterites made up a small but highly visible segment of the immigrant farmers. The Hutterites lived in colonies that held all property and goods in common— a sort of religious communism.

Ultimately the Indians were subdued and assigned to seven reservations. There are some forty thousand Sioux in South Dakota today, but life for them is a far cry from the time when they were led by the great chiefs Red Cloud, Sitting Bull, and Crazy Horse. For the most part, the reservation Sioux farm or tend their herds of sheep. Poverty is the rule rather than the exception. Many young Indians leave, hoping to find jobs in the cities. What they often find instead is social and economic discrimination—a holdover from pioneer days when whites viewed the Indians as savage enemies who constituted an impediment to the taming of the frontier.

By the time South Dakota was admitted to the Union in 1889, its population stood at 350,000. But an eight-year drought discouraged immigration and it wasn't until after 1900 that thousands more arrived to take advantage of the land the government had opened for settlement in the west. The population kept growing until the Depression and dust storms of the 1930s played havoc with the state's agricultural economy. According to the 1930 census, there were about 693,000 people in the state. So many left during that difficult decade that today the population stands at just over 685,000—still below the 1930 peak.

People are still leaving the state, but for different reasons. Although South Dakota remains one of the most predominantly agricultural states in the nation, fewer and fewer people are needed to run the farms. As a result, more and more farm workers are moving to the cities—cities which offer only limited job opportunities because of the state's lack of economic diversity. Just over 77,000 people live in Sioux Falls, the state's largest city, but statewide there's a ratio of slightly more than eight residents per square mile!

HISTORY

South Dakota's history is a colorful mélange of romance and tragedy . . . of exuberance and excess once gold was discovered in the Black Hills, of bloody battles as the once mighty Sioux fiercely defended their hunting lands, of the senseless slaughter of two hundred Indians at Wounded Knee Creek now recognized as one of the most shameful episodes in the winning of the West.

The land that is now South Dakota changed hands three times before it became American territory in 1803. Originally it was claimed for France by Robert Cavelier, Sieur de La Salle, as part and parcel of a vast area drained by the Mississippi River. That was in 1682. Eighty years later France turned over the territory to Spain, which held it until 1800, when it was returned to France. The United States acquired it as part of the Louisiana Purchase. By then, the only white men to venture into the vast prairie area bisected by the Missouri River were French fur trappers. Indeed, the first explorers didn't arrive until 1743. They were François and Louis-Joseph La Vérendrye, French-Canadian brothers who left a lead plate as a token of their visit near what is now Fort Pierre. The first white man to settle in South Dakota was the French fur trader Pierre Dorion who married a Sioux and decided to live near what is now Yankton.

The year after the Louisiana Purchase explorers Meriwether Lewis and William Clark were sent by President Thomas Jefferson to see what promise the new land held. They passed through South Dakota twice—en route to the Pacific and on their way back in 1806. At that point, there still was no permanent white settlement—that was to come eleven years later when the French fur trader Joseph La Framboise established a trading post at the mouth of the Bad River.

In those early days, troubles with the Indians were minimal. The Arikara were farming peacefully along the Missouri and Cheyenne rivers, the Cheyenne were out in the west of the state hunting, and the Sioux were chasing buffalo and making war, when the occasion demanded, on the Arikara.

The peaceful Arikara were responsible for the first major outbreak of Indian hostility against the white man in South Dakota. They attacked a fur-trading party from Missouri in 1823, only to be attacked in return by a combined force of federal troops and Sioux warriors. In those days, South Dakota was considered rather remote, accessible only by a long overland journey. But things began to change in 1831 when the steamboat *Yellowstone* sailed up the Missouri River from St. Louis. Its arrival at Fort Tecumseh (today's Fort Pierre) was a boon to the fur-trading business but didn't convince farmers to take advantage of the rich South Dakota soil. They began to drift in about twenty years later after some shrewd eastern land companies decided to organize things for their own benefit—laying out townsites and parceling out farm land. All of the development in those days was on the east bank of the Missouri River. The west bank was Indian territory, and the Sioux were in control.

The Sioux were relentless in defending their hunting lands from the white man. Chief Red Cloud blocked construction of a road to Wyoming by repeatedly attacking the Army surveying party until it simply gave up the effort. Those raids led to a treaty giving the Sioux all the land west of the Missouri—a treaty that was blatantly ignored once gold was discovered in the Black Hills.

An Army expedition led by Colonel George A. Custer confirmed reports of the gold discovery in 1874 and two years later the richest vein in the Western Hemisphere was tapped near Lead, South Dakota—the Homestake Mine, still going strong. Predictably, the Sioux were enraged by the treaty violation. Crazy Horse and Sitting Bull led a series of futile uprisings which ended with their surrender of their claims to the Black Hills.

After that, Sitting Bull remained quiet for several years until 1890 when a Nevada Paiute named Wovoka had a "vision": the buffalo were replenished, the white men were driven from the earth, and the Indians were restored to their early position of happiness and supremacy. That vision had an obvious appeal to the Indians, and they elevated it to a religion. Soon, all the Sioux in South Dakota were fervent believers and were expressing their faith through the "Ghost Dance," a ritual for which the dancers wore a shirt that was supposed to protect them from the white man's bullets.

It might have been just harmless fantasizing had not the military taken it seriously. The authorities thought the only way to put an end to the "Ghost Dance" and the "vision" was to take into custody the Indian leaders Kicking Bar, Short Bull, Big Foot, and Sitting Bull. When Sitting Bull resisted, he was killed. His followers fled to Big Foot's camp and managed to elude the army until soldiers caught up with them at Wounded Knee Creek. There, one shot fired by a resisting Indian touched off a massacre during which two hundred Indian men, women, and children were slaughtered and sixty soldiers died.

With the Indians subdued and confined to reservations, South Dakota's settlement proceeded more rapidly. Thousands of farmers arrived once the railroads extended their lines into the territory at the end of the 1870s. Many were from northern Europe, particularly the Scandinavian countries, Germany, and Russia. But the centers of population were so far apart that in 1889 Congress divided the Dakota territory and admitted to the Union the newly created states of North and South Dakota.

Dust storms in the last decade of the nineteenth century discouraged settlement, but by 1900 Indian lands in the west were made available for farming and ranching and immigration picked up. The early years of the twentieth century were prosperous ones for South Dakota—a state bank was established in 1915 and lent millions of dollars to farmers. However, many of the programs initiated in those days failed due to mismanagement. The 1930s brought more hard times in the form of the Great Depression during which farm prices toppled and severe droughts and dust storms made matters even worse for the farmers. During those years, thousands left the land and moved away from the state in search of jobs. Although the agricultural economy recovered during World War II and was further revitalized after the war by the massive Missouri River Basin Project designed to provide flood control, electric power, and irrigation, the population by 1970 hadn't recovered from that exodus of the 1930s.

Today, South Dakota is determined to diversify its economy. Development corporations have been established in 128 areas and localities and in 1964 the state legislature authorized municipalities to issue revenue bonds to finance projects designed to stimulate the economy. Farming is still the leading industry, but many people who live on farms commute to jobs in the new factories. In recent years, South Dakota has been encouraging tourism so aggressively that it now ranks as the second most important source of the state's income.

South Dakota made the headlines in the early 1970s for two reasons—first, when its Democratic Senator George McGovern ran for the Presidency and lost, and again in 1973 when two hundred Sioux led by militants from the American Indian Movement took over the little village of Wounded Knee in order to protest the failure of the federal government to initiate an intensified program of Indian education. Two persons were killed during the seventy-one-day siege before the dissidents surrendered to authorities.

INDUSTRY

Industry in South Dakota runs third to agriculture and tourism in terms of generating income for the state. As a matter of fact, about the only manufacturing there has sprung up as a direct result of the state's agricultural abundance. Food processing is the leading manufacturing activity. There's a big meat packing and processing plant in Sioux Falls and others in Huron, Madison, Mitchell, and Watertown. Poultry processing plants and creameries are located in Rapid City, Sioux Falls, and a few other towns, and there are flour and feed mills in Rapid City and some more feed mills in Sioux Falls.

A state-owned cement manufacturing plant operates near Rapid City and some factories in Belle Fourche process a type of clay called bentonite. All told, there are less than six hundred manufacturing or processing plants in the state, most of which employ less than fifty persons. Even gold mining, while important, hardly makes a dent in the state's overall preoccupation with farming. It accounts for just 2 per cent of the state's income, while mining of other minerals found in the Black Hills and elsewhere in the state accounts for another 2 per cent.

AGRICULTURE

South Dakota is a state of farms—thousands of them averaging about 800 acres in size—and agriculture is the main source of the state's income. Cattle raising is particularly profitable—in fact, three fourths of the income from agriculture is generated by the cattle raising operations of ranchers who maintain big spreads in the western part of the state. South Dakota's statistics reveal that more than half of its 77,000 square miles is used for the grazing of beef cattle. And if those figures impress you, how about this one: farms of all types occupy nine tenths of South Dakota's total land area.

In addition to cattle, the state raises enough sheep and lambs to make it a leader in wool production. Farmers in the southeast raise hogs and elsewhere in the east dairy farming is a big industry.

As far as crops are concerned, South Dakota is one of the leading producers. It is part of the gigantic corn belt that stretches across the midwestern United States and, naturally, corn is one of its most important agricultural products. In addition, the state is a leader in the production of alfalfa seed, flaxseed, and rye. Most of the crop farming goes on in the eastern part of the state where the soil is especially rich—the result of those enormous glaciers that slid over the area back in the Ice Age.

As well suited as South Dakota is to agriculture, farmers there have had their troubles in the past. Droughts and dust storms were periodic and devastating hazards before 1944, when Congress established the Missouri River Basin Project to provide for flood control, irrigation, and power production. A few of the major dams built in the state since then have allowed for the irrigation of more than 250,000 acres—land that today is producing crops that once wouldn't grow there: alfalfa, alfalfa seed, vegetables, and fruits. The biggest of the dams on the Missouri River are the Oahe, Gavins Point, and Big Bend.

NATURAL RESOURCES

"There's still gold in them thar hills"—the Black Hills, that is, in South Dakota. Gold was found at French Creek in 1874, and by 1876 eager prospectors had zeroed in on the immensely valuable Homestake Lode near Lead, South Dakota. That one mine has since yielded millions of tons of gold ore and is today the largest gold-producing mine in the Western Hemisphere. About 500,000 ounces of pure gold are extracted from the Homestake Lode each year—more than one third of all the gold mined in the United States and enough to make South Dakota the leading gold producer in the nation. Another fourteen million tons remain to be mined.

While gold is certainly the most important metal in the Black Hills, it is not the only one. There are more than sixty others, including antimony, arsenic, bismuth, iron, lead, manganese, tellurium, tungsten, and zinc. However, even when you add the molybdenum, uranium, and vanadium found in the state, you find that mining doesn't generate much income for South Dakota. Even taking into consideration the oil wells in the west of the state and the gravel, granite, and sand to be found elsewhere, mineral resources bring in only 2 per cent of South Dakota's total income.

The most valuable natural resource when it comes to generating income is the state's rich soil, which has made agriculture the leading industry. The eastern half of the state is covered with rich, dark soil suited to the raising of corn and wheat, two of the state's most important crops. The western half of the state has a shale-based soil that's ideal for grazing lands.

All that grass and growing land takes up so much space that forests occupy only a tiny percentage of South Dakota. The wooded area of the state is in the Black Hills, where trees like juniper, ponderosa pine, and spruce are common. Elsewhere there are hardwoods like ash, cottonwood, and oak trees.

You still can see buffalo in South Dakota. The nation's largest herd, about two thousand strong, is at Custer State Park in the Black Hills. And then there are the white-tailed deer, the antelope, the mule deer, the bighorn sheep, elks, and Rocky Mountain goats scattered throughout the state. The plant life is just as varied—the prairies are enlivened in spring with black-eyed Susans, goldenrod, Mariposa lilies, poppies, sunflowers, and wild orange geraniums, while the Black Hills are abloom with bluebells, forget-me-nots, lady's slippers, and larkspurs.

CITIES

Try out your French accent in **Pierre,** South Dakota's capital, and you're likely to get some puzzled stares from the natives, who call the place "Peer." It is smack in the geographic center of the state, a town of just over thirteen thousand persons that traces its history back to the 1743 visit of François and Louis-Joseph La Vérendrye. The two French-Canadian explorers buried a lead plate to signal to posterity that they had been there. Almost two centuries later, in 1913, some schoolchildren at play found it. The plate now occupies a place of honor in the Robinson Museum in Pierre's Soldier's and Sailor's Memorial building along with relics of the pioneer days and an Indian collection. Pierre is only six miles from the Oahe Dam and Reservoir on the Missouri River, the largest dam of its type in the world. It was designed to meet the needs for flood control, irrigation, navigation, municipal water supply, power development, and recreation.

The State Capitol is the pride of Pierre. It was completed in 1910 and features a collection of murals depicting the settlement of South Dakota. Just across the Bad River is old Fort Pierre, the site of the first permanent white settlement.

South Dakota's largest city is **Sioux Falls,** which thinks of itself as the "gateway to the West." This city of 77,000 in the southeast corner of the state was settled before the Sioux uprising of 1862 but abandoned when the Indians went on the warpath. The settlers returned in 1865 after a fort was built for their protection. Today, Sioux Falls is a stockyard and meat-packing center—the Morrell plant there processes 100 beef cattle, 200 sheep, and 750 hogs *every hour*. Needless to say, you can get a good steak dinner in Sioux Falls.

The town has other attractions, too, among them, three museums and a zoo with ninety species of animals. The most unusual of the museums is the Sioux Empire Medical Museum with its exhibits relating to medical history and concentrating on frontier medicine. There's an Indian collection, exhibits of rocks, minerals, and mounted animals at the Pettigrew Museum of Natural Arts and History. Just west of town is a memorial to the battleship U.S.S. *South Dakota* and the men who served on her during World War II. The ship itself isn't there, of course, but the memorial building is about the same size and is full of war mementos.

Yankton, not far from Sioux Falls, is a college town—the home of the first college established in the Dakota Territory. The city was the original capital of the territory—in those days the legislature met in the home of William Tripp, now the Yankton County Territorial Museum. The office of the first governor has been restored there and the other rooms are furnished as they would have been during the 1860s.

Today, however, it looks like the peaceful college town it is. In addition to Yankton College there's Mt. Marty College with its beautiful Gothic-style architecture. Among the other local attractions is a marker on the spot where Jack McCall was hanged for the murder of Wild Bill Hickok—a shooting that took place in Deadwood during the gold rush. McCall was the last person hanged in South Dakota and that happened in 1877. In addition to the Territorial Museum there are four others in Yankton, but what visitors usually want to see most is the Gavin's Point National Aquarium three miles west of town. It's a federal establishment with tanks featuring rainbow trout, catfish, bass, and northern pike. The show stealer, though, is the paddlefish, a curiosity because of the long, flat paddle that grows where its nose ought to be. These fish, a remnant of prehistoric times, have been found only in the Missouri River and in the Yangtze River in China.

When South Dakota was just getting organized as a state, Sioux Falls decided that it ought to be the site of the state penitentiary and Vermillion chose to have the state university. As a result, **Vermillion** today is regarded as the cultural center of the state. The University of South Dakota is the focus of life here. It has two important museums: the W. H. Over Dakota Museum and the Arne B. Larson collection of musical instruments. The W. H. Over Museum is on the University campus and is noted for its displays of stones, fossils, pioneer memorabilia, and the paintings of Oscar Howe, a Sioux who is artist in residence at the University. The musical collection, sometimes called the "Shrine to Music," is part of the W. H. Over Museum and contains an impressive display of antique instruments.

The second biggest city in South Dakota is **Rapid City** in the western part of the state. Tourism is important in this city of 43,000 nestled against the eastern slope of the Black Hills—thousands of visitors come annually to admire the surrounding scenery. The city has a lot to pay tribute to: the mineral wealth of the Black Hills, the Indians, the pioneers, and the dinosaurs. The dinosaurs? Yes, some skeletons were found in the area and life-size models of the ferocious Mesozoic beasts have been reproduced at Dinosaur Park just off Skyline Drive southwest of the city.

There's a full skeleton of a real marine dinosaur at the Museum of Geology at the South Dakota School of Mines and Technology Rapid City campus. But to get a look at some live reptiles, the place to go is Reptile Gardens south of the city where youngsters can ride on a giant tortoise. Other local attractions are the Minnilusa Pioneer Museum, the Marine Life Museum with its trained seals and porpoises, and the Timber of the Ages Petrified Forest which has a big collection of cut and polished petrified wood, minerals, and Indian artifacts. About five miles west of town is a replica of an 800-year-old Norwegian church, Borgund Stavkirke (which translates as "Stave

Church"). It is called the Chapel in the Hills and is a unique fir and pine building, intricately carved, with rooflines at six different heights and a "must" for thousands of tourists each year.

SPORTS AND RECREATION

When the natives talk about the "great lakes" in South Dakota, they don't mean Erie, Michigan, or Superior. The state has its own great lakes—Lewis and Clark, Francis Case, Sharpe, and Oahe—all created by the series of dams on the Missouri River. The lakes have given South Dakota something nature didn't provide—miles of beaches and acres of surrounding recreation land for camping, picnicking, golf, and riding. Needless to say, water sports are popular here, not only on the "great lakes" but throughout the state. All told—counting the state's 530 lakes and reservoirs and 98 rivers and streams—there are 3,866 miles of water in South Dakota, enough, say authorities, to provide each resident with more than one acre!

With all that water, it's little wonder that so many Dakotans are enthusiastic fishermen—one out of five has a fishing license. The great lakes are jumping with walleye, northern pike, paddlefish (somebody once caught one weighing 114 pounds), white bass, crappies, and catfish. And fishermen in those parts don't put away their rods during the winter. They just knock a hole in the ice or move inside the ice houses built right there on the frozen lakes and keep on fishing.

Hunting is popular here, too. The state has been described as the "pheasant capital of the world." But there's lots of game of all types: grouse, prairie chicken, partridge, wild turkey, bobwhite quail, ducks, and geese. November is deer hunting season in the Black Hills and there are seasons on antelope, elk, bighorn sheep, and mountain goat.

Snowmobiling and skiing keep Dakotans out of doors in the winter. Indeed, snowmobiling has become more popular every year. There are miles of trails to follow in the Black Hills and some hotly contested competitions—particularly the Governor's Cup Snowmobile Race, the Lead Hill Climb, and the Black Hills Winter Wonderland Races. More than eight thousand snowmobiles are registered in the state.

Skiers have five areas to choose from, including Terry Peak, the highest ski area east of the Rockies. It has a 1,200-foot vertical drop from the crest of a 7,076-foot mountain. The other areas are Deer

Mountain not far from Terry Peak in the Black Hills near Lead, Great Bear near Sioux Falls, La Couteau in the northeast of the state near Sisseton, and Inkpa-du-ta at Big Stone City, also in the northeast.

POINTS OF INTEREST

The Black Hills of South Dakota aren't really black—they just look that way. The Indians were the first to notice that from afar the ponderosa pine-covered hills look black, not green. They called them "Paha Sapa" which translates to Black Hills. Technically, however, the Black Hills aren't hills at all but mountains that millions of years ago pushed through a fault in the earth's crust and rose upward to a height of 14,000 feet. Over the centuries, the mountains eroded to their present appearance, one of nature's scenic triumphs 120 miles long, 50 miles wide, and still thousands of feet high.

For thousands of tourists, a visit to the Black Hills begins at Custer State Park, 72,000 acres of forests and game preserves including the nation's largest herd of free-roaming buffalo. There also are white-tailed deer, mule deer, pronghorn antelope, and wide-antlered elk. But perhaps the most appealing animals are the wild burros, descendants of the burros that used to take visitors to the top of Harney Peak, the highest point west of the Rockies. If you climb it today, you may meet a Rocky Mountain goat surveying the view—mile after spectacular mile of wooded wilderness. There is no shortage of awe-inspiring sights in the Black Hills. From Needles Highway, for instance, you can gaze out at a grouping of rugged granite spires that some people liken to needles and others to the spires of a Gothic cathedral.

Ironically, the most famous sight in the Black Hills isn't a natural wonder but a man-made one—Mount Rushmore, just southwest of Keystone where the sculpted heads of Presidents Washington, Jefferson, Lincoln, and Theodore Roosevelt loom over the landscape. Sculptor Gutzon Borglum carved the huge heads—each one is between 60 and 70 feet high—as a memorial to the birth, growth, unity, and vigor of the United States. They stage a lighting ceremony there on summer evenings, and the climax—the floodlighting of the four famous faces—is well worth the wait until after dark.

After Mount Rushmore was completed, the Sioux decided that

there ought to be a Black Hills monument to one of their leaders. Accordingly, sculptor Korczak Ziolkowski was commissiond to carve a statue of Chief Crazy Horse astride his pony. When it is done, it will be 563 feet high and 641 feet long.

A visit to the Black Hills wouldn't be complete without a stop at one of the area's most famous caves. Jewel Cave in Hell Canyon was named for the calcite crystals that sparkle in a cool subterranean chamber discovered in 1900 by prospectors looking for minerals. They came across the cave after they noticed that wind was rushing out of a hole in the cliffs. They didn't find any minerals but were so entranced by the beauty of the cavern that they tried to attract tourists. In those days, the cave was too far out of the way to draw many sightseers. But spelunkers came to explore it and have mapped fifty-two miles of passageways on four different levels. Eventually, transportation improved and the cave became a national monument administered by the National Park Service. Underground tours are now available, and thousands of visitors have marveled at the calcite "jewels" formed by centuries of water seepage through limestone cracks and crevices.

Wind Cave, another limestone cavern, was discovered back in 1881 when a pioneer heard wind whistling through a hole in some rocks. No one knows yet just how big Wind Cave is—only twenty-three miles of passages have been explored. But there's a national park named after it, just south of Custer State Park in the Black Hills.

Although Rapid City is the Black Hills' largest town, the most colorful is Deadwood, the rough and tumble western outpost that earned its notoriety in the 1870s during the gold rush. Then, as now, Deadwood was a one street town—the "street" in question being the floor of Deadwood Gulch. This is the town where Wild Bill Hickok was gunned down. The trial of his killer, Jack McCall, is re-enacted nightly during the summer months. Visitors also can take a look at Hickok's grave, and the place where Calamity Jane is buried in Mount Moriah Cemetery, otherwise known as Boot Hill. Today, the whole town is a museum of sorts—it's been designated a National Historic Site.

You can get a look at early mining techniques at the Broken Boot Gold Mine just outside of Deadwood, but for the real thing, the place to go is Lead (they pronounce it "Leed") to tour the Homestake

Mine, the largest producing gold mine in the Western Hemisphere.

The town of Spearfish to the north of Lead is famous for the Black Hills Passion Play staged every summer for more than forty years. The dramatization which originated in Germany tells the story of the last seven days of the life of Christ.

In sharp contrast to the lush beauty of the Black Hills is an equally famous natural wonder—the barren Badlands in the southwestern corner of South Dakota. Geologists say that once the Badlands were a marshy plain. That was 25 to 35 million years ago during the Oligocene Epoch when saber-toothed tigers, dog-sized camels, and the titanothere—a prehistoric beast that must have looked something like a giant rhinoceros—roamed the area. Over the centuries wind and water eroded the land and carved canyons and cliffs, spires and ridges and crevasses. There's not much plant life here—a few yuccas, some junipers, and an occasional patch of cottonwood trees. The prairie dogs seem to like the place, but for the most part, the only other animals around are jackrabbits, cottontails, and snakes.

When the French fur trappers first saw this rocky, arid landscape they described it as "bad land to travel across"—hence the name Badlands. The whole area—170 square miles of it—has been a National Monument since 1939.

While South Dakota's most dramatic scenery is in the western part of the state, there are things to see elsewhere. In Mitchell, for instance, there's the Corn Palace, an ornate structure with turrets that make it look rather Russian and out of place in the Midwest. Up close, you can see that it is decorated—both inside and out—with corn and grasses woven into intricate patterns.

The state's Indian reservations welcome visitors. Pine Ridge, the largest, is the home of the Ogala Sioux. It also is the site of the massacre of 200 Sioux at Wounded Knee Creek. The tragic story is retold on an interpretive sign and not far away is a monument marking the mass grave of 120 of the Indians killed. The most famous Sioux of them all, Chief Sitting Bull, is said to be buried at Mobridge—a claim disputed by North Dakota. Sitting Bull was buried at Fort Yates in North Dakota, but one night in 1953 some South Dakota Sioux opened the grave and took his bones to Mobridge for reburial. North Dakota contends that Sitting Bull was buried in lime and no bones could have remained. There is no way to prove that one state is right and the other one wrong.

SPECIAL EVENTS

Spring and summer are the rodeo seasons in South Dakota and everybody participates—high school students, the 4-H Club, the Indians, and anyone else who gets a thrill out of bucking broncos. One of the first of the season is the Jackrabbit Stampede on the campus of South Dakota State University at Brookings. During the summer, however, just about every celebration means a rodeo. Chamberlain, Mobridge, Belle Force, Interior, Springfield, and Redfield all hold rodeos on the Fourth of July. Should you miss them, you can make up for it on Labor Day at Kadoka, Wagner, Hermosa, or Newell.

Deadwood salutes the Gold Rush of 1876 every August with a parade and—what else?—a rodeo. They pay tribute to those days at Custer, too, and that celebration each July includes a pageant and a re-enactment of Colonel Custer's war with the Sioux along with the rodeo.

The Indians have added rodeos to their annual powwows. The biggest is the one the Ogala Sioux stage on the Pine Ridge reservation in August.

When South Dakota isn't celebrating its western heritage, it is honoring its ethnic diversity. There's a Nordland Fest in Sioux Falls in June, the Schmeckfest at Freeman in March, Czech Days at Tabor, and Danish Days at Viborg, both in June.

A race of any kind is guaranteed to draw a crowd in the state. In addition to the snowmobile races during the winter (see Sports and Recreation), there is the Black Hills Motorcycle Classic at Sturgis in August and the Black Hills Speedway National Championship at Rapid City in September.

And, lest anyone forget what the pioneers used for fuel, there's the North American Buffalo Chip Flip Finals at Pierre every August.

P.D.

CHRONOLOGY

1682   The land that is now South Dakota was claimed for France by Robert Cavelier, Sieur de La Salle, along with all the other territory drained by the Mississippi River system.

1743   The first white explorers visited South Dakota. They were François and Louis-Joseph La Vérendrye, French-Canadian brothers.

1803   South Dakota became U.S. territory through the Louisiana Purchase.

1804   Lewis and Clark passed through South Dakota en route to the Pacific.

1817   The first permanent white settlement was established by Joseph La Framboise, a fur trader.

1831   The steamboat *Yellowstone* sailed up the Missouri to Fort Tecumseh, now Fort Pierre.

1861   The Dakota Territory was created by Congress.

1862   A Sioux uprising drove settlers from the southeastern part of the state.

1868   The Sioux, led by Chief Red Cloud, ceased hostilities against federal troops in the Powder River area and signed the Laramie Treaty.

1874   Colonel George A. Custer verified that gold had been discovered in the Black Hills.

1876   The Homestake Lode was discovered, the richest gold mine in the Western Hemisphere.

1889   South Dakota was admitted to the Union as the fortieth state.

1915   The Bank of South Dakota was established.

1927   Work began on Mount Rushmore. The artist was Gutzon Borglum.

1930s   Thousands left South Dakota due to falling farm prices caused by the Great Depression, droughts, and dust storms.

1944   The Missouri River Project was authorized by Congress.

1962   Titan missile bases were installed in South Dakota.

1964 The state legislature authorized municipalities to finance industrial development via revenue bonds.

1972 George McGovern, South Dakota's Democratic senator, lost his race for the presidency.

A disastrous flood in Rapid City resulted in 236 deaths.

1973 Sioux Indians staged a seventy-one-day protest at Wounded Knee in an effort to force the federal government to upgrade Indian education.

1974 Richard F. Kneip became the first three-term governor of the state.

1976 During the nation's Bicentennial year, about 2,170,000 people visited Mount Rushmore.

1979 A plague of grasshoppers grazed fields and croplands in an onslaught comparable to a great plague which hit the state in 1874.

THE ROCKY MOUNTAIN STATES

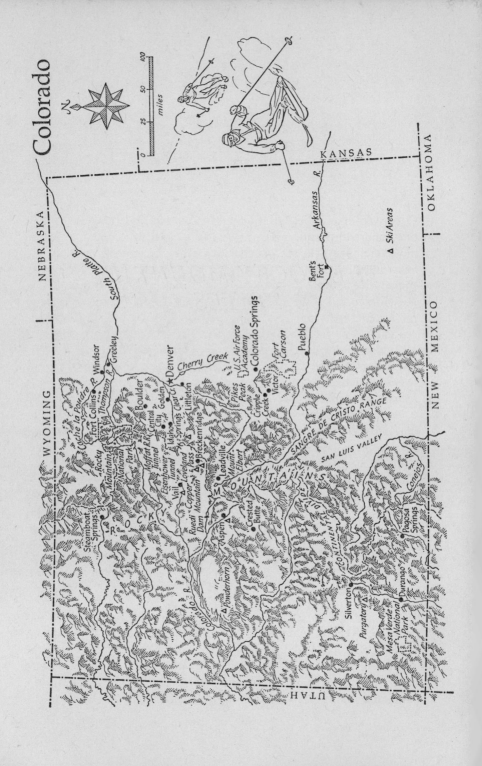

COLORADO

COLORADO entered its second century of statehood (it celebrated its one-hundredth birthday August 1, 1976) shed of its old frontier atmosphere. The gold and silver which attracted the first settlers have been mined out and the mountain men and the prospectors are gone. Indians live on reservations and cowboys now drive pickup trucks.

Colorado today is the new frontier, rich in energy-producing natural resources the nation sorely needs and with a stable, diversified economy.

But even with its lusty past and colorful pioneer figures faded into the history books, Colorado still exudes a magic attraction, luring twentieth-century settlers at a pace that makes it one of the nation's faster growing states.

Today's newcomers are drawn by a low-key atmosphere for pleasant, informal living, a sunny climate conducive to outdoor living, and, despite the population growth, great reaches of open space with unbounded recreational facilities.

Many of the once rich mining communities today are ghost towns that thrive on tourist curiosity, and the mountain peaks and valleys that yielded fortunes in gold and silver are irresistible attractions for skiers, fishermen, hunters, hikers, and campers.

THE LAND

While only a youngster in comparison with older eastern seaboard states, Colorado rightfully considers itself the nation's backbone. Highest of the fifty states, Colorado's 107,247 square miles average 8,600 feet in altitude, rising from a low of 3,350 feet on the eastern plains to the 14,431-foot summit of Mount Elbert, tallest of the state's fifty-four peaks that exceed 14,000 feet.

Actually Colorado boasts three distinct topographical areas: the arid eastern plains; the rugged Rocky Mountains, with the Continental Divide zigzagging from north to south; and high plateau country on the western slopes.

In the remote past, a shallow, narrow sea extended over the region, running from the Arctic south to the Gulf of Mexico. Marine life abounded in the waters that covered the area where present mile-high cities as Denver and Colorado Springs now exist. About 60 million years ago the earth's crust began to rise. Great folds and faults buckled the sedimentary rocks to as much as 15,000 feet above sea level.

Molten rock, finding outlets among giant cracks in the crust, forced its way into weak zones below the surface or spewed out as volcanoes and lava flows. Mineral-bearing solutions were squeezed out of the cooling magma to form the veins of gold, silver, copper, and other metals that played a major role in luring the first settlers.

Streams, eroding inexorably over millions of years, almost completely destroyed these ancient peaks. A great apron of rock debris, hundreds of feet thick, filled the valleys and plains, covered the foothills, and spread far out on adjoining plains.

Only gentle slopes remained, over which great rivers established meandering courses. In recurring periods of uplift, the peaks were rejuvenated to sculpture the complex rock structure into lofty peaks, ranges and ridges, and high mountain valleys.

Less than a million years ago, during the Ice Age, vast glaciers formed, flowing down the mountain valleys. When the climate again warmed, the glaciers began to slowly melt—but the ice-scouring they caused is still evident in the serrated peaks, the U-shaped valleys, and immense mountain lakes.

This sculpturing, by wind and water, continues to this day with rock waste carried from the mountains by streams and rivers deposited on plains and basins at lower elevations.

CLIMATE

Colorado's climate, thanks to its international reputation as a winter skiing mecca, is generally advertised on the frigid side. Actually it is mild and enticing, due to lack of humidity and an average of 300 days of sunshine each year.

The key to the state's climate is variation. It varies greatly not only from the eastern plains to the high mountains but almost from hour to hour; the daily temperature often drops 30 to 40 degrees from daytime to night, and there is an average variation of 35 degrees in mean temperature between the plains and the mountains.

In January, the coolest month, Denver's temperature chart shows an average high of 43.5 degrees and low of 16.2; in July, the warmest month, it ranges from 87.4 to 58.6. Temperatures in the mountains average about 35 degrees less.

Snowfall is often heavy at the high elevations but relatively light on the eastern plains. Cold spells seldom last long. Precipitation, averaging only 16.6 inches a year, is heaviest in the central mountains and on the more temperate western slope of the Rockies.

THE COLORADANS

Only 100 years old as a state and with a recorded history dating back only to the early 1700s, Colorado's first inhabitants go back 20,000 years. These ancient, unknown people of the Stone Age remain a mystery. No skeletal remains have been unearthed but numerous stone artifacts have been found in the northeast corner of the state.

The next culture is of far more recent date, the Indians. Somewhere around A.D. 100, Indians who grew corn and squash and built pit houses arrived in the high mesa land of southwestern Colorado. Their culture reached a peak in the Modified Basket Maker period when they built permanent habitations of poles, earth, and brush. Remains have been found throughout the San Juan Basin.

They were followed, some 800 years later, by Pueblo Indians who improved the crude pit dwellings with complete pueblos of mud and stone. They were constructed high on canyon walls as protection from enemies. Well-preserved ruins of these complexes are to be seen today in Mesa Verde National Park.

When the first white men explored what is now Colorado, they found two major American Indian groups: the mountain-dwelling Ute; and nomadic plains Indians, the Cheyenne, Arapaho, Comanche, and Kiowa. Almost alone among present western states, Colorado's Indian population was neither large nor permanent, other than the Ute, who numbered less than 10,000 in all.

They were never conquered but rather turned to the ways of peace and the white man. For their efforts they were treated shabbily and today reside on a small reservation in the unhospitable southwestern corner of the state.

The first white men to set foot in what is now Colorado were Spaniards, coming north from bases in Mexico and, later, what is now New Mexico.

The first recorded forays into the state came in the early 1700s. Some were exploratory treks led by Spanish missionaries; others were by trappers and early-day gold seekers.

There was a brief period of French influence, and an expedition in 1739 left behind such present-day reminders as the rivers named Riviere la Platte (now just the Platte) and the Cache la Poudre.

But both Spanish and the brief French interests came to an end in 1803 when Napoleon, hard pressed by his enemies in Europe, sold the vast Louisiana territory to the United States for $15 million. It included part of what is now Colorado.

This opened the gates to American exploration with the first major expedition in 1806, led by Lieutenant Zebulon M. Pike. Pike reached the area that is now Colorado Springs and gave his name to the towering peak which he unsuccessfully tried to scale. His journal notes his belief that such a peak could never be climbed; today a modern highway reaches its summit.

This and subsequent U.S. expeditions encouraged trappers who sought skins in the lower reaches of the Rockies and established trading posts. Trappers were followed by prospectors, the first wave stopping off in 1848 on their way to newly discovered California gold fields. The first settled along the banks of Cherry Creek, the site of present-day Denver. The hardier and more persistent ventured into the nearby Rockies, hoping to find richer sources.

As mining settlements grew, so did the ranks of merchants who set up shops to sell needed supplies. Then came farmers, who settled along the bottom lands of streams running down from the peaks.

Cattlemen came in the years following the Civil War, driving herds up from the southwest to forage on the grass of the eastern plains.

Descendants of these early residents—miners, merchants, cattlemen, and farmers—remain today. But Colorado residents now are basically city dwellers, with more than half of the state's 2.5 million population located in Denver and other cities along the eastern slope of the Rockies. They are employed in a wide spectrum of activities but all share in the common conviction that, best as possible, they want to conserve the land and its underground riches with the least possible damage to the once virgin terrain.

It is interesting to note that despite the strong pioneer influence of Spain, the state's largest foreign-born and second-generation group is German, followed by Russians, British, and Mexicans.

HISTORY

Colorado became the thirty-eighth state on August 1, 1876, only a few weeks after the nation observed its centennial and 270 years after the first Spanish explorers probed into the area.

Those two and a half centuries were a period of turbulence, early foreign influence, and, in the years before statehood, political wrangling that delayed admission into the Union for nearly twenty years.

There were Spanish expeditions pushing north to seek new routes to their missions established in California; trappers who came in the early 1800s and in 1832 established Colorado's first community, Bent's Fort, home to many of the great figures of the early-day West —Jim Bridger and Kit Carson among them.

But the major factor in the settlement was gold, and its discovery was largely by chance. Gold-hungry Easterners, headed for the California gold fields, stopped off in 1848 at the confluence of Cherry Creek and the Platte River and made meager "finds" in the sandy river beds.

While the initial strikes were small, accounts reaching the East prompted a small stampede of fortune hunters. They gathered in a ramshackle community, Auraria, with few making more than enough for subsistence.

A few hardier and more persistent ventured into the nearby Rockies hoping to find richer sources. Finally, in 1859, George Jackson found gold along Chicago Creek, near the present community of Idaho Springs. Then John Gregory made one of the richest strikes of all, on North Clear Creek near Central City. Later, even richer strikes were made at Cripple Creek and Victor, on the western slopes of Pikes Peak, and silver was discovered high in the Rockies at Leadville.

The rush was on with thousands heading west to search instant fortunes. Prospectors were followed by merchants, who set up shops to sell needed supplies. Then came cattlemen who in the years following the Civil War drove herds north to forage on the grass of the eastern plains. Finally, farmers came whose produce was eagerly sought by the settlers.

The many settlements along the eastern slope grew into full-fledged communities, notably Denver (originally Auraria), Colorado Springs, and Pueblo. As they emerged from gold camp status, schools were established, merchants enlarged their quarters—and city governments came into existence.

The first overtures to establishing the area as a political body came in the 1850s with attempts to give Colorado territorial status. There were many acrimonious years of internal debate before anything happened.

The first attempt was in 1859, when, without knowledge or consent of the U. S. Congress, a small group drew up a state constitution. An election to determine whether residents wanted statehood or territorial status resulted in a decision for the latter, named Jefferson Territory.

This proved an inept choice as a name, since leaders of the move for statehood were largely Republican and Thomas Jefferson was a Democrat. Search for a new name brought forth some curious suggestions: Yampa, Idahoe, Nemara, San Juan, Luca, Weapollao, Arapahoe, Tahosa, Lafayette, Columbia, Franklin, and Colorado.

Contrary to popular belief, say Colorado historians, the word "Colorado" does not come from the Spanish word for red. They say its source is coloreado, meaning "many colors together."

Official status as a territory, Colorado Territory, came in 1861, in the early days of the Civil War. Residents, almost solidly Republican, began to seek statehood. With the blessing of President Lincoln and the Republican Congress, an enabling act was passed in March 1864 to form state governments in both Colorado and Nevada.

But internal wrangling split the state and a constitution election resulted in a setback. Another move the following year brought approval, but by then Andrew Johnson was President and twice he vetoed bills favoring statehood, presumably because of his fear that the probable senators-elect would not support his administration. A third attempt at statehood was lost when it was found that the state's constitution included a provision against voting rights for blacks.

It wasn't until 1873, when U. S. Grant was President, that the Congress approved an enabling act signed by Grant in the final hours of the session. Colorado voters ratified still another constitution, which permitted blacks to vote. Grant's decision came on July 1, 1876, setting off Fourth of July celebrations that haven't been equaled since.

The state's first one hundred years were marked by a curious switch: from the original gold and other precious metals which drew the first settlers, through a largely agrarian era, back into the present period when natural resources, notably "black gold"—oil—again dominates the economic structure.

Through its first century Colorado's political overtones were mainly conservative, with major rifts developing between the "city folk" in Denver and other eastern slope cities and the largely agricultural areas on the western side of the Continental Divide.

In recent years this has been marked by a bitter division over the state's most critically needed resource: water. Colorado is far from short of water, with six major rivers flowing from the high valleys. But compacts with neighboring states restrict the amount available within the state boundaries. This problem has been compounded by a bitter rivalry between the eastern and western sectors. Attempts by Denver and neighboring cities to divert water from the less densely populated western portion have prompted power struggles reaching to the congressional halls in Washington.

An equable solution, still unreached, is considered vital to the future growth of Colorado's basic resources and over-all growth.

INDUSTRY

Few persons regard Colorado as an industrial state, but manufacturing is its number-one source of income, with an annual output of nearly $6 billion, with 144,000 persons engaged in it.

The state is the site of the nation's largest manufacturer of luggage (Samsonite) and the top producer of cement (Ideal Basic). The CF&I Steel Corporation at Pueblo is the nation's thirteenth-largest steel plant and Coors at Golden is the fourth-largest brewery. Major additions in recent years are Eastman Kodak film producing plant at Windsor, and IBM's facility near Boulder, where 4,500 employees turn out electric typewriters and computer machines.

Giant Titan rockets used in early space shots were produced near Denver by Martin-Marietta, which was also responsible for the $10 billion Viking Lander project which in 1976 tested the soil of Mars for life.

Several of the nation's blue-chip firms have selected Colorado as corporate headquarters. Johns-Manville, a diversified blue-chip producer of construction materials, for example, moved its headquarters from New York City in 1971 and five years later, on July 4, 1976, dedicated a $70 million world headquarters on a former ranch site southwest of Denver.

Denver, grown from its original ramshackle start on the banks of Cherry Creek, is the largest metropolis between Kansas City and California and the area's financial, transportation, and distribution center. In recent years it has become the hub of vital petroleum exploration.

Tourism is a major generator of income to Colorado's economy, with more than 8 million persons visiting the state each year to enjoy its year-round recreational possibilities. These tourists spend $630 million and are responsible for 45,000 jobs.

AGRICULTURE

Cattle, sheep, wheat, and sugar beets make the state's agriculture output a strong one, more than $2.5 billion annually.

It is a far cry from the pioneer days when a handful of farmers cultivated small plots along the streams at the foothills of the Rockies, their produce sustaining the area's mining camps.

They were followed in the 1880s by land-hungry Easterners who, unable to find suitable sites near water sources, began staking out homesteads on the dry plains. For a few years they prospered, thanks to accumulated moisture in the arid soil.

But with rains scarce and moisture exhausted, many pioneer "dry farmers" pulled up stakes and headed home. The few who remained, learning from bitter experience the need for soil and water conservation, made wheat a major crop, today valued at more than $1 million a year.

Their efforts were made easier by major developments which made water from rivers of the Rockies available for irrigation on the plains. Largest of these government-sponsored projects was the Colorado-Big Thompson, which carries some 300,000 acre-feet of water, through tunnels, pipelines, and canals, from the western side of the

Continental Divide to 720,000 acres in northwestern Colorado. Another, of more recent date, is the Fryingpan-Arkansas project, which brings water to the southeastern plains.

Sugar beets are a major crop, with annual production of more than 2 million tons a year, second only to California and Idaho. The high plateaus of western Colorado are dotted with peach and apple orchards, and the southern Arkansas Valley is noted both for its succulent melons and for the nation's most sought after malting barley, grown in the San Luis Valley.

The livestock industry has also changed greatly over the years. The onetime huge ranches and herds of semi-wild cattle have been replaced by smaller "spreads" specializing in purebred strains. With the decline in the cattle baronies came the era of the feed lots, where cattle are penned for fattening. The Monfort feed lots near Greeley, the nation's largest, handle up to 250,000 cattle on feed at one time, making that northern Colorado community the major livestock market between Omaha and the West Coast.

Today some 3 million cattle and 1 million sheep graze on the eastern and western slopes of the Rockies.

NATURAL RESOURCES

It was gold that started Colorado on the road to statehood.

Today it is gold, black gold, that is producing a twentieth-century "boom era." For the state, today, is a vast storehouse of energy-producing elements—crude oil, natural gas, and coal, which the nation so desperately needs to become self-sufficient.

Crude oil reserves in the state are estimated at 300 million barrels. In addition, 1.8 trillion cubic feet of natural gas is ready for recovery, and petroleum experts believe advanced technology will make it possible to tap another 300 trillion cubic feet in the Piceance Basin of western Colorado and the Denver-Julesburg Basin to the east.

Seven million tons of much-needed coal was mined in 1974 and reserves are estimated at 14 billion tons.

Colorado is also a major source of such steel-hardening minerals as molybdenum and tungsten. American Metal Climax annually extracts millions of tons of molybdenum from its high mountain mines on Mount Bartlett near Leadville.

Today's miners are bringing minerals from the earth which the early-day prospectors scorned or knew nothing about: uranium, which produced a boom era in the days of World War II, lead, vanadium, and zinc.

This vast, diversified search for minerals today contributes $700 million annually to the state's economy and provides employment for more than 16,000.

CITIES

Colorado is widely known as an outdoor state. Yet its residents are city dwellers, with three of every five of the state's 2.5 million based in the Denver area and four of five residing in municipalities stretching 150 miles along the eastern foothills of the Rockies, from Fort Collins south to Pueblo.

Known in earlier days as the "Queen City of the Plains," **Denver** today is better recognized as the "Mile-High City," with a marker on the state capitol steps noting the official altitude.

It ranks today as one of the nation's major trade, financial, transportation, and distribution centers, the marketing hub of a region extending five hundred miles in every direction.

The city spreads over nearly one hundred square miles. The downtown area, once a collection of rough shanties housing prospectors, boasts an impressive skyline with modern buildings soaring past forty stories. Yet it still retains many of the early-day stone structures built by pioneer mining tycoons.

Residential areas surround the downtown core, with tree-shaded parkways, spacious parks, and well-tended home gardens making it appear an oasis on the plains, the snow-capped Rockies providing a dramatic backdrop.

As with most major cities across the nation, Denver's population has sprawled past city boundaries into neighboring suburban areas. As of 1975, the city itself boasted around 520,000 residents, with the five adjoining counties home to nearly 1 million more.

Dominating the Denver skyline is the gold-domed state capitol building. The gold on the dome, residents are proud to note, isn't just gilt, but solid twenty-eight-carat gold leaf from the mines in the Rockies.

Across the landscaped Civic Center from the capitol is the Denver City and County Building, a four-story structure in classic lines. The southern edges of the Civic Center are the site of the new Denver Art Museum, a uniquely designed structure with glass-brick exterior, and modern Denver Public Library.

The steady growth of the Denver metropolitan area is based on many factors: the stable economic base, a relaxed, climate-blessed atmosphere for family living; a wide range of cultural pursuits; and plenty of open space. Despite the concentration of population in Denver and neighboring cities, the state's population density is 21.3 persons per square mile, one of the nation's lowest.

Employment is spread over a wide variety of enterprises, with the result that slowdowns in any one phase of the nation's economy have little over-all effect. One important stabilizing feature is Denver's major role as a federal center. More than two hundred federal bureaus, agencies, and regional offices in the area employ 31,500 persons, giving rise to Denver's claim of being the "western Washington, D.C." In addition, military facilities in and around Denver house more than 52,000, providing an annual federal payroll of nearly $700 million.

Also in Denver are the U. S. Mint, one of two remaining in the nation; the U. S. Air Force Accounting and Finance Center, which employs 2,500 civilian and military workers to supervise the $30 billion air force budget and supervise an annual payroll of $9.7 billion to 1.15 million active and retired personnel world-wide; the Federal Center, a vast complex of bureaus, with 6,800 employees; Lowry Air Force Base, now a technical training center; Fitzsimons Army Medical Center, includes one of the largest of the Army's eight hospitals; Rocky Mountain Arsenal, once the military's major producer of lethal nerve gas, now being deactivated; and Rocky Flats, producing components for nuclear weapons.

Denver is also the transportation hub of the Rocky Mountain states, with highway, air, and rail links to all major cities. But it hasn't always been so. In the early days the city at the foot of the formidable Rockies was bypassed in favor of the more geographically favorable plateau of southern Wyoming.

When the Union Pacific pushed its transcontinental route west in 1867, it went through Cheyenne, Wyoming, with only a spur line running south to Denver. Today the city is served by seven rail lines, including the home-based Denver & Rio Grande, which pioneered the first and only rail route across the Rockies. The route is one of the world's most scenic, highlighted by the six-mile-long Moffatt Tunnel carrying trains under the Continental Divide.

It was the same with highways. Congress did not include a route between Denver and Salt Lake City when it set up the interstate highway system in 1956. It took two years of intensive lobbying to persuade the legislators to include the transmountain route to Utah.

That prompted work on a long-desired tunnel under the Divide to facilitate year-round travel. The 1.7-mile-long Eisenhower Tunnel, world's highest auto facility, was bored under 11,992-foot peaks near Loveland Pass as a key part of east-west Interstate 70.

The first transcontinental airline routes also avoided Denver for years, but today the city-owned Stapleton International Airport, only fifteen minutes from downtown, is served by a dozen airlines, providing service to all major cities in the nation, as well as Canada and Mexico. It ranks as the tenth-busiest airport in the nation.

Denver's extensive park system offers residents a wide variety of recreational opportunities. There are more than one hundred, ranging from the large City Park, a few minutes from downtown, with an eighteen-hole golf course, the city's zoo, the Denver Museum of Natural History, tennis courts, and lots of room for picnicking and relaxing. The parks extend into the Rockies, one reserved for a city-owned herd of buffalo, and Winter Park, on the eastern side of the Continental Divide, one of the state's most popular ski centers.

Most famous is the Park of the Red Rocks, located fourteen miles west of downtown. This natural amphitheater, located in red rock formations at the base of the Rockies, provides 10,000 spectators with an acoustically perfect setting for concerts, ranging from rock 'n' roll to classic performances.

Seven universities and colleges are located in the city: University of Denver, Colorado Women's College, Regis College, and Loretto Heights College, all private institutions, and Metro State, Denver Community College, and the Denver campus of the University of Colorado.

Colorado's second-largest city is **Colorado Springs,** (pop. 135,000), scenically situated at the base of Pikes Peak. Founded by gold miners and developed by "bonanza kings" who struck it rich in Cripple Creek on the opposite site of Pikes Peak, Colorado Springs grew as a sedate retirement and resort center.

It still retains much of its pioneer aura, with palatial old homes and office structures built by early-day mining magnates. But its economy has been spurred by three major military installations. The U. S. Air Force Academy is only ten miles to the north, on an 18,000-acre site at the foot of Rampart Range. South is Fort Carson, Colorado's largest military base, headquarters of the 4th Infantry. The North American Air Defense Command (NORAD), the joint U.S.-Canadian force to defend the continent against air attack, is now headquartered at Peterson Air Force Base.

Alone among Colorado's cities, **Pueblo** (pop. 100,000) is industrially oriented. CF&I, the nation's thirteenth-largest producer of steel products, and its satellites employ more than 8,000. Pueblo is also the site of the Colorado State Hospital, the Colorado State Fairgrounds, and the Pueblo Army Depot, which handles a wide range of military matériel, including missiles.

Boulder, thirty miles northwest of Denver, is the seat of the University of Colorado, the region's largest institution of higher learning, with an enrollment of 20,000 in thirteen schools. In recent years Boulder's growth has been stimulated by major scientific laboratories and research agencies.

SPORTS AND RECREATION

Colorado is an outdoors-oriented state with year-round activities but best known for its winter skiing centers. Aspen and Vail are internationally famous and along with two dozen other developed areas annually attract more than 5 million skiers.

Coloradans are avid ski fans, as are the thousands who flock here in the winter, but they also enjoy many other recreational opportunities: some of the nation's finest fishing and big-game hunting, mountain hiking and climbing, camping, jeeping over high mountain passes.

There are fine facilities for competitive sports: some of the nation's better golf courses (Cherry Hills Country Club at Denver and the Broadmoor courses at Colorado Springs have been the scene of major tournaments) and a growing lineup of tennis facilities (including indoor courts for wintertime play).

Spectator sports enjoy tremendous popularity, with the Denver Broncos of the NFL and the Denver Nuggets of the NBA. Collegiate sports feature perennially strong teams from the University of Colorado, Colorado State University, and the U. S. Air Force Academy.

While Aspen and Vail are the favorite winter destinations of skiers from other parts of the United States and even overseas, Coloradans have a choice of twenty-six major winter sports areas, plus four others open only on weekends. Several—such as Breckenridge, Crested Butte, Keystone, Arapahoe Basin, Copper Mountain, Powderhorn, and Purgatory—are gaining major status with growing facilities for visitors.

Within the state borders are two national parks (Rocky Mountain and Mesa Verde), two national grasslands, six national monuments, and eleven national forests, with tourist and camping facilities. Grand Lake, at the eastern entrance of Rocky Mountain National Park, hosts the world's highest sailboat regatta each summer.

POINTS OF INTEREST

The wide scope of Colorado's tourist attractions is exemplified by the two most popular: Rocky Mountain National Park and the U. S. Air Force Academy. Rocky Mountain National Park, 410 square miles of ultrascenic alpine scenery, is the state's foremost attraction, drawing 2.8 million visitors in 1975. The academy, with an ultramodern campus on an 18,000-acre site ten miles north of Colorado Springs, lured 1.5 million the same year.

Rocky Mountain National Park, only sixty-five miles north of Denver, offers a broad spectrum of alpine scenery, from forested areas at its 8,000-foot eastern entry to the tundra above timberline. A major attraction is Trail Ridge Highway, a winding fifty-mile highway, well graded and paved, linking east and west entrances. For more than six miles it runs two miles and more above sea level, affording the unique opportunity of looking down on peaks soaring 10,000, even 11,000 feet.

The Air Force Academy is open to visitors daily, and although classrooms and dormitories are off limits, guests are welcome at the multispired chapel, with its sanctuaries for different faiths. It is considered the single most visited spot in the state. Prime time for an academy tour is at noon when the cadet corps, 4,400 in all, marches to the dining hall in formation to the strains of martial music.

Tucked away in the scenic southwestern corner of the state is Mesa Verde National Park, where well-preserved cliff dwellings of early-day Pueblo Indians offer a glimpse into pre-Columbian times.

Tourist facilities range from such plush resort complexes as the Broadmoor at Colorado Springs (with its own thirty-six-hole golf layout, skating rink, rodeo arena, and ski slopes) to dude ranches, many offering guests the chance to participate in ranch routines.

Railroad buffs are attracted by two pioneer narrow-gauge trains, both dating back to early mining days. The Denver & Rio Grande's "Silverton" runs daily from early May into September on spectacular trips up the Canyon of Las Animas Perdidas between Durango and Silverton. The Cumbres & Toltec, jointly owned by the states of Colorado and New Mexico, offers daily trips in summer months on a sixty-four-mile route that switches back and forth across the state line.

There's a revival of interest in the state's several communities boasting mineral springs. Best known today is Steamboat Springs, a major ski center with natural hot mineral pools and baths favored by overtired winter sports addicts. Pagosa Springs, in the southwest corner of the state, is the site of a new health spa built around hot springs.

Two of the state's most visited tourist attractions are in Denver: the U. S. Mint, which offers daily tours showing the operation that produces up to 900,000 coins an hour, and the Denver Museum of Natural History in City Park, one of the nation's finest show places with an annual attendance of 1.3 million, ranking it third behind Rocky Mountain Park and the Air Force Academy.

SPECIAL EVENTS

Aspen Music Festival (Aspen), last week of June through third week of August. Noted American and foreign musicians instruct and appear in recitals.

Central City Opera (Central City), Memorial Day through August. Nightly performances of operas at historic Central City Opera House.

Colorado State Fair (Pueblo), last ten days of August.

Little Britches Rodeo (Littleton), third week of August. Rodeo competition for teen-agers, bringing top young performers from across the nation to the Arapahoe County Fairgrounds.

National Western Stock Show (Denver), third week in January. One of the nation's major rodeos and stock judging events, opening the year-long competition among ropers and riders.

Pikes Peak or Bust Rodeo (Colorado Springs), last week in July. State's premier summer rodeo, held at Broadmoor Arena.

Pikes Peak Hill Climb (Colorado Springs), July 4. Grueling hill climb up Pikes Peak, drawing the nation's top race drivers for a stretch run over the twisting highway up the 14,000-foot peak.

B.H.

CHRONOLOGY

500 B.C. Basket Makers, earliest people known to have permanently lived on Mesa Verde; first Indian agriculturists of the Southwest.

1601 A.D. Juan de Oñate, hunting for gold, came from Mexico and penetrated as far north as the present site of Denver.

1776 Franciscan friars Silvestre Vélez de Escalante and Francisco Atanasio Domínguez explored southern Colorado while seeking a shorter route from the New Mexico to the California missions.

1803 United States acquired most of the eastern part of Colorado by virtue of the Louisiana Purchase.

1806–7 Lt. Zebulon M. Pike, sent to explore the southwestern boundaries of the Louisiana Purchase, reached the headwaters of the Arkansas River, and then crossed the Sangre de Cristo Range to the Conejos River in the San Luis Valley.

1848 By the Treaty of Guadalupe Hidalgo, Mexico ceded to the United States most of that part of Colorado not acquired by the Louisiana Purchase.

1859 Gold was found by George A. Jackson along the Chicago Creek on the present site of Idaho Springs; John Gregory made famous gold strike on North Clear Creek, stimulating rush of prospectors.

1861 Congress established Colorado Territory with the boundaries of the present state.

1867 Denver was chosen as territorial capital.

1870 Denver and Pacific Railroad was constructed to link Denver with the Union Pacific at Cheyenne, Wyoming; the Kansas Pacific entered Colorado from the Missouri River.

1874 Colorado College was founded at Colorado Springs; the legislature appropriated funds for the University of Colorado at Boulder.

1876 Colorado was admitted to the Union as the thirty-eighth state.

1878 Leadville was incorporated, and rich silver strikes on Iron,

Carbonate, and Fryer hills soon made it one of the world's greatest mining camps.

1915   Rocky Mountain National Park was created by Congress.

1958   U. S. Air Force Academy was established near Colorado Springs.

1959   Colorado-Big Thompson water project was completed.

1961   National Center for Atmospheric Research was created and located at Boulder.

1963   North American Air Defense Command (NORAD) was established at Colorado Springs.

1967   Start of construction of Fryingpan-Arkansas project to bring more water from the western slope of the Rocky Mountains to the Arkansas River Valley on the more densely populated eastern slope.

1969   Sugar Loaf and Ruedi dams, units of Fryingpan-Arkansas project, were completed.

1973   Eisenhower Tunnel, 1.7 miles long and the world's highest automobile tunnel (11,000 feet), opened to facilitate year-round travel over I-70 between Denver and Utah.

1976   Colorado celebrated its centennial birthday.

1979   The Federal Trade Commission negotiated its largest cash settlement ever, giving $14 million in canceled debts and refunds to 7,600 buyers of virtually useless homesites in the central part of the state.

IDAHO

ERNEST HEMINGWAY, who had lived a number of places in America and Europe, returned to the beautiful mountains and valleys of Idaho in his later years. He had a deep love for this state, which has a quality of wildness that appeals to men of action. In 1962 he died there, at his home in Ketchum, and his grave lies in a semiwilderness area where he had often hunted.

The widely diverse beauty and ruggedness which attracted Hemingway are now attracting many more people to Idaho, a state that was for so long generally passed over. As more and more Americans feel an urge to return to a more basic way of life as a reaction to overdevelopment, they are looking to places like Idaho. This is not to say that Idaho is experiencing a population boom, for it is still a decidedly underpopulated state, with only a little over 740,000 residents, although it ranks thirteenth in size in the nation with 83,557 square miles.

There is a great physical contrast in Idaho, which is nicknamed the Gem State, because of its mineral wealth. Northern Idaho, called the Panhandle, is mountainous and heavily forested, with many lakes, rivers, and streams. Central Idaho has mountain wildernesses as primitive as any in the United States, except possibly in Alaska. Southern Idaho is mostly desert, except in the Snake River Plain, where irrigation has created bountiful farm lands. And some vast areas of the southern region are sheets of hardened lava, volcanic craters, and cinder cones.

Idaho is also called the Spud State because it produces more potatoes than any other state in the nation. But the name "Idaho" is something of a mystery. Supposedly, it is an Indian word meaning "gem of the mountains," but there is evidence that the word was made up by white men. Lobbyists in Washington had been using the word extensively in referring to the territory, and the name had been used to designate certain mines and towns. When Congress had to choose a name for the new territory, it found "Idaho" to be the most convenient.

THE LAND

Idaho's widely diverse terrain usually is divided into four topographic regions: the Northern Rocky Mountains, the Middle Rocky Mountains, the Basin and Range Province, and the Snake River Plateau.

Almost all the northern half of the state lies within the Northern Rocky Mountains region, an area of high, rugged mountains. Some parts of this region are very primitive, with little or no development and no roads. It is marked by many swift mountain streams and rivers, deep canyons and gorges, and, in some sections, fertile valleys. Borah Peak, the highest altitude in the state, rises 12,662 feet in Central Idaho, about twenty miles northwest of the town of Mackay.

The Middle Rocky Mountains are in the western part of the state, along the border with Wyoming. There are eight north-south and northwest-southeast ranges in the area, with peaks rising to ten thousand feet.

The Basin and Range Province lies just west of the Middle Rocky Mountains. This small region has grassy plateaus and deep valleys in its mountains, and sand-and-gravel-floored basins in its desert areas.

The Snake River Plateau, which is also called the Columbia Plateau, contains the agricultural heart of Idaho. Following the path of the Snake River through southern Idaho, the Snake River Plateau is a crescent-shaped region, extending through much of the western and southern part of the state.

Idaho is truly a land of rivers and lakes. No one knows how many lakes there are in its hundreds of mountains and valleys, but the estimate is around two thousand. There are several large rivers and thousands of small ones. The greatest is the Snake River, which is 1,038 miles long, flowing from its source in Wyoming. It cuts one of the country's deepest and wildest canyons, a canyon almost one and a half miles deep at certain points. The Salmon River which flows across the state from east to west is frequently referred to as the "River of No Return"—the rapids make it virtually unnavigable to go upstream. Another important large river is the Clearwater, which

Idaho

BRITISH COLUMBIA

WASHINGTON

MONTANA

OREGON

WYOMING

NEVADA

UTAH

N

0   20   40   60   80   100
miles

Sandpoint
Pend Oreille Lake
Coeur d'Alene
Kellogg
Mullan
St. Maries

ROCKY MOUNTAINS

Lewiston
Lapwai
Clearwater R.
Grangeville
White Bird
Snake R.
Hells Canyon

Salmon R.
Salmon
Lemhi

BITTERROOT RANGE

Custer
Bonanza
Borah Peak

Weiser

Mackay
BOULDER MTS.
PIONEER MTS.
Idaho City
Caldwell
Boise
Boise R.
Nampa
Ketchum
Sun Valley
Craters of the Moon National Monument

De Lamar
Silver City

SNAKE RIVER PLAIN

Idaho Falls
Blackfoot
Fort Hall
Pocatello
Soda Springs

American Falls
Snake R.
Twin Falls

Lava Hot Springs

Oakley
Malad City

Teton R.

drains a large portion of north-central Idaho. It is a branch of the Snake River.

There are also hundreds of hot and cold springs in southern Idaho. Water from some of the hot springs is actually piped into some homes in Boise to provide heat.

CLIMATE

There is a wide diversity to the weather in Idaho which precludes making an overall statement about the climate. This is best exemplified by the precipitation pattern. In the southern and western parts of the state, most of which comprise the Snake River Plain, only an average of eight to twenty inches of precipitation falls each year, whereas an average of around fifty inches falls annually in the northern Rockies. Despite the fact that the southern regions get the lowest rainfall, they are the state's prime agricultural sections, because the low precipitation is balanced out by extensive irrigation of the rich soils.

Much of the precipitation is in the form of snow, which ranges from around an average sixteen inches annually in the Snake River Valley, to more than two hundred inches in some areas of the mountainous Panhandle. In Lewiston, the major city of that region, the snow cover lasts about twenty-five days a year, and in some of the highest elevations of the northern Rockies there is a snow cover year-round.

Idaho is not so cold, generally, as some of the other states of this western region, because the Rocky Mountains wall off the eastern part of the state and prevent cold air coming in from Montana and Wyoming to the east. That gives the westerly winds from the Pacific Ocean a chance to bring warm air over most of the state; the same situation makes Idaho a bit cooler than nearby states in the summer.

During July the temperatures are mild to cool over most of the state, with an average 60 to 70 degrees in the mountains, and 70 to 80 degrees in most other areas. January average readings are from 20 to 30 degrees, except in the mountains, where the averages are from 10 to 20 degrees.

THE PEOPLE OF IDAHO

Idaho, like some other western wilderness areas, was bypassed during the colonial era. Not until after 1800 did white men even enter the territory. In those early days a fur-trading post was established in the northern part of the state and a good many of the trappers were French. They gave French names to the land like Boise, Coeur d'Alene, Pend d'Oreilles, etc. Before that time only Indian tribes had inhabited the mountains and river valleys. In the mountainous northern part of the state were some smaller tribes like the Kutenais, Pend d'Oreilles, Coeur d'Alenes, and the more well-known Nez Percé. In the southern part, below the Salmon River, were Shoshone, Sheepeaters, Lemhi, and Bannocks.

In the decades following the Lewis and Clark expedition in 1805, pioneers of English, Irish, and Scottish ancestry migrated to Idaho, but there were few settlements in the rugged terrain. It was the discovery of gold in 1860 that brought the biggest surge of people to Idaho, so that by 1870, after a huge increase of population in the 1860s to over fifty thousand, there was a permanent population of around twenty thousand people. Also, just before the gold strikes, Mormons came over from Utah and set up the first farming communities in the southern part of the state. And sizable groups of Scandinavians came to settle in the forests and farm lands of the northern Panhandle region.

After 1900 Basque sheepherders came to the sheep country of the Boise valley in large numbers. Today there are about six thousand Basques living there, one of the largest colonies of these people outside the Pyrénées of Spain and France.

Modern Idaho reflects the pattern of late development. It is one of the most underpopulated of the states, with just over 740,000 residents, 70 per cent of whom live in the Snake River plain in southern Idaho.

The components of the population are as follows: about 98 per cent of the people in Idaho are native-born Americans, and 99 per cent are Caucasian. Of the remaining 1 per cent, there are around five thousand Indians, two thousand Japanese, and a little over two thousand blacks. Most of the Indians live on reservations, and their small numbers are a result of the brutal wars their ancestors fought

with the U. S. Army in the 1870s and the subsequent tribal reloca-
tions. The Japanese are the remnants of a population of about ten
thousand that was forceably removed from west coast areas to Idaho
during World War II. Most of the blacks moved to Idaho after 1940.

HISTORY

Idaho was uncharted wilderness until the early part of the nineteenth
century when Meriwether Lewis and William Clark entered the region on their famous trek to the Pacific Ocean. In 1805 the two
explorers and their expeditionary force crossed the Bitterroot Mountains into Idaho, then built canoes and traveled down the Clearwater
River and the great Snake River.

The trail blazed by Lewis and Clark provided the initial opening of
Idaho for other white men, for they were soon followed by fur trappers and traders, representing British trading companies, who for the
next several decades established trading posts in the northern part of
the state. One of the first permanent settlements in Idaho, however,
was established by an American from Massachusetts, Nathaniel
Wyeth, who built Fort Hall in eastern Idaho near the present-day city
of Pocatello.

As happened in other western states, missionaries came hard upon
the heels of the fur traders to convert the Indians. But in Idaho there
was a distinct difference—the Indians themselves asked the missionaries to come. In the early 1830s a delegation of Indians went as
far as St. Louis in search of religious teachers. The first to respond
were the Reverend and Mrs. Henry Spalding, who not only set up the
first mission near Lewiston in northern Idaho, but also established
the state's first sawmill, flour mill, church, school, and printing press.
Catholics came soon after, setting up a Jesuit mission among the
Coeur d'Alene Indians in 1842, and the Mormons started a short-
lived mission in eastern Idaho in 1855.

And so, Idaho's modern history began peacefully. But peace and
harmony were short-lived, shattered by a wild rush for gold. From
1860 to 1863 gold was discovered in the north, central, and southern
sections of western Idaho. The rich strikes caused gold seekers by the
thousands to stream into Idaho, and lusty boom-towns sprang up almost overnight. So many miners flocking to Idaho gave inducement
to the growth of farming and cattle ranching, for all those miners

needed to be fed. Within a relatively short time, however, the cattle and sheep herds, and the crop lands grew to such size that they were able to export their products, so that when the gold mines diminished and ghost towns began forming, the farmers were largely unaffected.

However, important discoveries of gold, silver, and lead continued to be made during the remainder of the century. One of the biggest finds was in 1884 in northern Idaho near the town of Kellogg, named after the prospector who uncovered one of the country's richest silver and lead producing regions.

The onrush of miners, cattlemen, and farmers caused the population to soar, so that by 1863 there were over fifty thousand people living in Idaho. The rapid population increase made possible the creation of Idaho Territory in 1863—a huge area including present-day Wyoming and Montana—with Lewiston as capital. (In 1864 Montana was made a separate territory, and in 1868 the same was done for Wyoming, giving Idaho its present shape.) After the creation of Montana had drastically reduced the size of northern Idaho, the capital was moved in 1864 from the northern city of Lewiston to Boise in the south. Boise's townsite had only been laid out the year before.

The huge population increase that made territorial organization possible caused trouble with the formerly peaceful Indian tribes, who were being pushed from their lands. When the U. S. Army tried to forcefully relocate the Nez Percé Indians, their leader, Chief Joseph, took them into battle. This relatively small tribe defeated the U.S. troops at White Bird Canyon in northwestern Idaho in June 1877, but as more soldiers were sent into the state, the Nez Percé were forced to retreat.

The Nez Percé War was one of the most dramatic in U.S. history. Chief Joseph's defeat of the U. S. Army and his success in eluding pursuing troops for many months despite the fact he was burdened with women, children, and old people, has earned him a lasting reputation as a military tactician. His strategies are still taught at West Point. He was also known as a man of great honor and oratorical skills. In 1976 a television documentary chronicled his life, its title taken from his most famous speech—"I will fight no more forever."

The Nez Percé War ended in 1877. In that same year and into 1878 there was also a war with the Bannock tribe. When their leader, Chief Buffalo Horn, was killed in a battle with federal troops, the spirit of the tribe was broken and they were defeated.

Shortly after Idaho's entry into the Union as the forty-third state on July 3, 1890, there was another bloody chapter in its history. Open warfare broke out in the northern Coeur d'Alene mining country between miners and mineowners, and among union and non-union mineworkers. Dynamitings, shootings, and general strife continued from 1892 to 1899, when Governor Frank Steunenberg called in federal troops to restore order.

Six years later, in 1905, Steunenberg, then no longer governor, was killed by a bomb attached to his front gate. Harry Orchard, a member of the Western Federation of Miners, confessed to the murder, and also implicated three union leaders. Orchard got a life sentence, but the others were freed. The trial, which attracted international attention, made a reputation for the state's attorney, William E. Borah, who went on to become a U.S. senator, a position he held until 1940.

During the two decades after 1900, Idaho enjoyed an economic upsurge, especially in lumbering and agriculture. World War I boomtimes were a particularly good period for the farmers, but their prosperity had a hard fall in the 1920s, a result of increased land and operating costs. However, during the 1930s, when the rest of the country was hit by severe economic depression, Idaho began to pick up, primarily because drought-ruined farmers from other regions moved into the state in large numbers to work in its extensively irrigated farm lands. Work done by the Civilian Conservation Corps in forestry, road construction, and other relief work also gave a big boost to Idaho.

The World War II era helped Idaho economically in a number of ways. Agricultural output increased to help feed the armed forces, and food processing industries began to grow into major segments of the economy. Employment increased as factories to produce aircraft, arms, and other military supplies moved into the state. Right after the war a housing boom gave a big boost to the lumber industry. Also in 1949 the Atomic Energy Commission built a nuclear reactor testing station near Idaho Falls.

In the 1950s and 1960s there was continued vigorous expansion of processing industries, manufacturing, and tourism, especially at Sun Valley, where facilities were enlarged. Also in those decades, hydroelectric power was greatly increased by a series of dams constructed on the Snake River. And in the 1960s there was political progress—the state legislature was reapportioned to conform to the U. S. Supreme Court's one-man, one-vote decision in 1966, and the following year many city governments were restructured.

On June 5, 1976, a controversial newly built dam on the Teton River, situated about thirty miles northeast of Idaho Falls, burst, and floodwaters rampaged over a wide area, inundating a number of towns. Ten people died in the floods, tens of thousands were left homeless, and more than fifty thousand acres were silted over or badly eroded. Total damage to this rich potato-farming and grazing region was estimated at over a billion dollars. Environmental organizations had opposed the dam on the grounds that it would interfere with wildlife and that it was located in an earthquake zone.

INDUSTRY

Idaho does not rank as an important manufacturing state, but it does have a sizable food processing industry that has developed around the large agricultural enterprises. This chief manufacturing activity includes about fifteen potato-processing plants. Over half the potatoes grown in the state are processed into quick-frozen and dehydrated specialty products. Also, most of the sugar beet crop is processed in the state. There are also meat-packing plants, canneries, creameries, and plants that process poultry and wheat.

Idaho's many forests have made it a leading timber-producing state, and now lumber and wood products are next to processed foods in importance. The products include plywood, veneers, pulp and paper, furniture, boxes, and railroad ties.

Although mining ranks fourth, behind tourism, as an income-producer, it is still vital to the state's economy. Silver mining is especially valuable, and Idaho is first in the United States in production of that ore. It also leads in the production of lead and zinc. Also significant in metals production are copper, tungsten, mercury, and vanadium. Gold used to have more importance in Idaho mining, but its production has dropped sharply because of increased mining costs and a static market price.

One of the fastest growing industries is tourism, which now brings in about $200 million annually. The number of tourists to Idaho more than doubled from 1950 to 1960, and by the early 1970s over six million people were visiting the state every year.

AGRICULTURE

The largest economic activity in Idaho is agriculture. On its more than three and a half million irrigated acres the state produces many crops, including the famous Idaho potatoes. Other main crops are beets, hay, barley, beans, and other vegetables, and fruit. The principal farming region is in southern Idaho along the fertile valley plains of the Snake River. Another large farming area is in the northern Panhandle, where wheat and peas are the principal crops. Idaho ranks as a top pea-producing state.

Although crop farming produces the majority of the farm income, livestock and livestock products are increasing in importance, so much so that Idaho is now considered among the leading cattle and sheep-growing states. Most of the cattle are grown in the Snake River region, with dairy farms concentrated in the western Snake River valley. A good many hogs are also raised in this area. Sheep graze in the mountains of the Columbia Plateau and the Great Basin during summer, and in the valleys and on the plains during winter. There is also a sizable poultry industry in southern Idaho, and in the north near the town of Washington.

All the agricultural enterprises together bring in about $750 million a year for Idaho, about half the value of all the goods produced in the state.

NATURAL RESOURCES

Other than its major mineral resources of silver, lead, zinc, and copper, Idaho's greatest natural resources are its bountiful forests, its deep, rich soils, and its abundant wildlife.

Forest lands cover about 40 per cent of the state. Most of these are evergreen forests, which include one of the country's largest stands of western white pine.

The state is particularly known for its many wild animals. For example, every year hunters harvest between 65,000 and 70,000 deer alone, along with nearly 14,000 elk. Other big game animals are mountain goats, moose, bighorn sheep, and antelope. There are many large predators roaming the state, such as grizzly and black bears, cougars, timber wolves, bobcats, coyotes, gray and red foxes, and wolverines. There are also great numbers of fur-bearing animals—beavers, otters, shrews, weasels, muskrats, and, in lesser amounts, martens and minks.

Idaho has an especially rich bird life. It has substantial populations of bald eagles, which are rare throughout the country, and large populations of egrets, gulls, buzzards, cormorants, kingfishers, herons, coots, pelicans, loons, swallows, terns, rails, sandpipers, and owls.

The thousands of streams, rivers, and lakes provide an abundance of fish. One of the most common and most popular of the game fish is the rainbow trout.

The area around the Snake River, the valley and the plain, have exceptionally rich soils. The Basin and Range region farther east also has excellent soils. The fertility of these gray and brown soils is derived from prehistoric lava flows and from alluvial and lake deposits.

CITIES

Three of Idaho's principal cities—Boise, Nampa, and Caldwell—are situated close together on the Snake River Plain in the southern part of the state near the western border with Oregon.

Boise, the capital, had its birth in the wild days of Idaho's gold rush shortly after 1860. In its first years it was overshadowed by nearby Idaho City. But in 1864 Boise became the territorial capital and began to outgrow its neighbor. Today, with a population of around 86,000, it is the state's largest city, and Idaho City is a tiny village of 165 people.

Boise's name is an outgrowth of its beautiful setting, for it is a corruption of the French "Les Bois," meaning "The Woods." French explorers and trappers were inspired to give this area that name when they came from desert country into Boise's heavily wooded hills. Extensive irrigation has made Boise Valley a flourishing agricultural region.

The Boise River bisects this city, which is now the economic heart of Idaho and its business, professional, and transportation center. Other than such manufacturing industries as steel fabrication and mobile homes, the leading economic activities include lumbering, livestock raising, dairy farming, fruit, and sugar beet farming.

One of the prime sights in Boise is the capitol, built in 1906. Patterned after the U.S. Capitol, it has a 195-foot dome, and is built of Idaho sandstone and Vermont marble. It houses a superb collection of mounted western birds.

Some of Boise's other attractions include Julia Davis Park, which has gardens, a zoo, a playground, and picnic areas; the Idaho Historical Museum, containing exhibits of pioneer and Indian life; the Boise Gallery of Art; and the Ann Morrison Memorial Park, 150 acres of formal gardens, sports and picnic areas. Boise State University, founded in 1932, is also located in the city.

Sixteen miles west of Boise is **Nampa,** population about twenty-one thousand. It is located in a lush agricultural area, and offers visitors some pleasant recreational opportunities. Lakeview Park is seventy acres of gardens, and sports facilities, with a natural hot water pool. Five miles southwest of the city is the Deer Flat National Wildlife Refuge, where there is fishing and hunting, in season, among the thousands of waterfowl and shore birds that migrate there.

Caldwell, about ten miles farther west from Nampa, is a peaceful city of around fifteen thousand, situated in the middle of irrigated crop farms and livestock ranches. Food processing plants are the main industry of Caldwell. The College of Idaho is located here, the oldest in the state, founded by the Presbyterian Church in 1891. It has a student body of around a thousand.

Approximately 125 miles southeast of Boise, on the Snake River, is **Twin Falls,** the major city of a prime, irrigated agricultural area that is considered one of the richest in the nation. It serves as a distributing center for farm products and contains food processing plants and sugar refineries. Other than being an agricultural and industrial center, Twin Falls is also a top resort area. There is good fishing in the Snake River, and hunting in the surrounding forests, and get-away-from-it-all resorts near alpine lakes in nearby mountains.

A little over a hundred miles northeast of Twin Falls is **Pocatello,** the largest industrial and railroad center of the state. This quickly growing city of over forty thousand is a shipping point for agricultural products, and includes phosphate plants among its industries.

Idaho State University, with eight thousand students enrolled in liberal arts, medical school, business, education, pharmacy, and vocational schools, is located in Pocatello.

Idaho Falls, an industrial city and agricultural center, with a population of around forty-two thousand, is about fifty miles north of Pocatello on the Snake River. Some of the main crops grown in the rich farm lands around Idaho Falls are potatoes, peas, and sugar beets. There is also considerable ranching and dairy farming, and the city has the largest stockyards in the state, plus the nation's largest chinchilla ranch.

Most of Idaho Falls' industry is an outgrowth of agricultural enterprises, especially food processing. Frozen french fries and dehydrated food products are among the most important.

Lewiston, situated in northern Idaho where the Snake River runs along the border with Washington, was founded in 1861 and was the state's first capital. Today, this city of around twenty-six thousand residents is Idaho's most important port, for a series of dams and locks has made it possible for barges to go from Lewiston down the Snake River to the Columbia River and to the Pacific Ocean. The city's most important economic activity is lumbering, but mining, livestock growing, grain crops, and fruit orchards are also important. And its mild climate and attractive setting have created a growing tourist business.

About a hundred miles north of Lewiston is the city of **Coeur d'Alene**, a lumbering and resort community of sixteen thousand people. It is ringed by mountains, lakes, and rivers, and is the center for large white pine logging operations. Lake Coeur d'Alene, surrounded by forested hills, is considered to be one of the loveliest lakes in the country. It is a popular resort spot, offering boating, swimming, fishing, a municipal beach, amusement park, and picnic grounds.

SPORTS AND RECREATION

Idaho's beautiful and often rugged landscape is a paradise for those who enjoy vigorous outdoor activities.

Sun Valley, located in south-central Idaho, a little town nestled in a great bowl-shaped valley, is one of the most famous resort areas in the United States. There are summer and winter activities there, but it is most favored for winter sports, especially skiing. People from all over the world go there to ski down its slopes. The lovely powder snow lasts from December into April, providing a much longer than usual skiing season. Other winter activities include ice skating, dog sledding, sleigh rides, and swimming in heated pools. Sun Valley's May through October summer season features golf, boating, kayaking, tennis, swimming, skeet and trapshooting, horseback riding, hiking, fishing, and in-season hunting.

The state's approximately two thousand lakes and fifteen thousand miles of rivers and streams make it one of the most superb fishing areas in the country. Nowhere in Idaho is an angler very far from a fresh-water fishing area. Trout are the favorite game fish, because they are the most widespread and are good fighters. Other popular catches are salmon, bass, perch, channel catfish, and sunfish.

Hunting takes place almost everywhere in the state. Mule deer are the most common game. Elk hunting is a big sport too, and the best country for that is in northern Idaho in the Salmon and St. Joe river regions. Other popular game are white-tailed deer, antelope, moose, bighorn sheep, mountain goat, and black bear.

Bird hunters go after ducks, particularly mallards, and Canada geese, doves, grouse, sage hens, ring-necked pheasants, and chukar.

Hells Canyon of the Snake River is the deepest chasm in North America. It runs for about a hundred miles along the Oregon border in western Idaho, and in some places has depths of about eight thousand feet. The Snake River is rapid and wild in this stretch, providing thrilling sport in fishing and boating.

Those seeking some genuine thrills can run the rapids of Hells Canyon in little jet-propelled boats. Cruises start at Lewiston and go ninety miles upstream. Such river running is popular in Idaho, and the Salmon River in the central part of the state is also considered one of the best rivers for the sport. Veteran river guides take parties on sixty-mile round trips.

Nearly three-quarters of Idaho is federally or state-protected land. There are fifteen national forests covering more than twenty million acres. (Seven of the national forests lie only partially in Idaho, such as Yellowstone National Park. Most of Yellowstone is within Wyoming, but a small portion of it extends into the northeastern corner of Idaho's eastern section.) There are also more than twenty parks and recreation areas run by the state.

POINTS OF INTEREST

Ghost towns, remnants of Idaho's frontier and gold rush days, dot the countryside, and have become favorite places for visitors seeking a glimpse of the past. Three ghost towns in the Boise area are Silver City, Dewey, and DeLamar. Silver City was the center for over two hundred mines during the 1860s, when it had a population of five thousand. The town is still much like it was back then, only now its winter population consists of one man. Dewey and DeLamar are within ten miles of Silver City, and each has only a few buildings left standing.

Other popular ghost towns are Bayhorse, in central Idaho, a boom town in the 1880s and 1890s; Lemhi, in east-central Idaho, a completely deserted town, where walls of an old fort built by the Mormons still stand; and the towns of Bonanza and Custer, in south-central Idaho, which were active in the 1880s.

Another way for visitors to experience the feel of nineteenth-century Idaho is to see Tressl's Frontier Town in Blackfoot, in the southern part of the state. This replica of a frontier town has shops, a school, church, trading post, and a collection of horse-drawn farm machinery.

Craters of the Moon National Monument is a fascinating 83-square-mile area of lava flows, cinder cones, and natural bridges. It was created by violent volcanic action millions of years ago and resembles a moonscape, cut by deep fissures and cones thrusting eight hundred feet into the air.

The little town of Ketchum, in south-central Idaho, has only about fifteen hundred residents, but it has become a year-round resort because of its location and the excellent hunting and fishing available nearby. It is situated amid the Boulder and Pioneer mountains of the Sawtooth National Forest, and has the look and feel of a rural mountain town. Ernest Hemingway loved the town, and the region, and spent the last years of his life there, as we've said earlier. A memorial bust of him has been placed a half mile north of nearby Sun Valley.

The state's more than two hundred mineral springs, hot and cold, are also popular with tourists, as well as residents. Not all of them have accommodations, however. Several of the best are: Indian

Springs, in American Falls, in southern Idaho, which has hot mineralized springs, pools, and baths; Lava Hot Springs, in the southeastern region, has thirty different springs feeding outdoor pools, ranging from hot to cold; Soda Springs, near Lava Hot Springs, the second oldest community in the state, contains dozens of mineral springs.

SPECIAL EVENTS

Idaho's rough-and-ready outdoor character is reflected in many of its seasonal entertainments. There are a good many rodeos, sporting events, Indian celebrations, and festivals commemorating the frontier days.

The capital city of Boise has one of the most fascinating events every midsummer, the Basque Festival, performed by the largest Basque colony in this country. The dancers in their colorful costumes are the main attraction. Boise also has a Music Week during May, which also features Basque dancing and music.

Every July the city of Nampa hosts one of the nation's top professional rodeos, the Snake River Stampede. Other big rodeos are the Night Rodeo in July in Malad City; the Pioneer Days Rodeo in Oakley, also in July; a five-day Night Rodeo in Caldwell in mid-August; the Hell's Canyon Rodeo at Weiser in late May or early June; the Pioneer Days Rodeo in Idaho Falls in late July; and the Border Days, a three-day rodeo in Grangeville on the July 4 weekend.

Lumberjack festivals also romanticize a part of Idaho's past. In late July or early August, on the Priest River in the Panhandle, there is the Priest River's Loggers' Celebration and International Rodeo, demonstrating lumberjack skills. And on Labor Day weekend the town of St. Maries hosts the Paul Bunyan Days, with logging events, a carnival, and a water show.

The town of Mullan, in northern Idaho, stages a Winter Carnival in February, which includes a state championship snowmobile race, fireworks, dancing, and a softball game in which the players wear snowshoes.

There are a number of Indian events in Idaho during the year. One of the best is in Fort Hall, every summer in late July or early August, featuring the traditional Sun Dances of the Shoshone-Bannock Indians. Another big celebration is the Nez Percé County Fair in mid-September, in Lewiston.

State fairs are also popular in the state. The Eastern Idaho State Fair in the town of Blackfoot in September features a parade, Indian dances, and horse racing; Boise hosts the Western Idaho State Fair in August; Sandpoint has the Bonner County Fair in late August or early September; and the Lemhi County Fair and Rodeo takes place in Salmon the weekend before Labor Day.

N.C.

CHRONOLOGY

1805 Lewis and Clark crossed Idaho.

1834 Fort Hall established in eastern Idaho.

1836 The Reverend and Mrs. Henry Spalding founded first mission at Lapwai near Lewiston.

1860 First of several gold discoveries made.

1863 Idaho Territory established.

1864 Boise became capital of territory.

1877 Nez Percé Indians, led by Chief Joseph, defeated U. S. Army in battle of White Bird Canyon. Later that year, Nez Percé tribe surrendered to the Army.

1878 Chief Buffalo Horn of the Bannock tribe killed, ending war with U. S. Army.

1890 Idaho became forty-third state on July 3.

1892–99 Warfare among miners, mineowners, and union and non-union mineworkers in northern Coeur d'Alene mining district.

1905 Former Governor Frank Steunenberg murdered.

1907 William E. Borah elected to U. S. Senate, beginning a thirty-three-year career.

1920s Farmers hit hard by agricultural depression.

1936 Sun Valley resort opened.

1949 Atomic Energy Commission built nuclear reactor testing station near Idaho Falls.

1959 Brownlee Dam, first of three hydroelectric dams on Snake River, completed.

1960s State legislature reapportioned and city governments restructured.

1976 On June 6, a newly built dam on the Teton River burst, killing ten people, leaving tens of thousands homeless, and causing about a billion dollars damage.

1979 Boise looked to its hot springs as a heat source in a major project (largest of twenty-two in the West) to gather scientific data on the potential of geothermal energy.

MONTANA

MONTANA'S two nicknames are truly indicative of its character—the Treasure State, and Big Sky Country. The treasure almost everyone had in mind when that first nickname was applied after Montana became a state in 1889 was gold and silver. Years before, the rich strikes of those precious ores had been responsible for giving the territory a sudden and large population spurt of white men, where for centuries there were only Indians.

Later, other minerals were added to the treasure—copper and oil, zinc, lead, manganese, and more gem sapphires than any other state. But Montana's treasure lay also in its vast herds of cattle and sheep that developed originally to supply the mining settlements of the gold and silver boom. Its treasure lay also in its great grain fields of the eastern plains that were homesteaded early in this century, and in the flow of its mighty rivers, which give it one of the greatest hydroelectric potentials in the world.

Then there is Montana's Big Sky—big because it covers such an immense land, 147,138 square miles. Only Alaska, Texas, and California are larger than Montana, and only Alaska, Wyoming, and Nevada have lower population densities. There is a lot of "living" room under the Big Sky.

The state takes its name from the Spanish *montaña,* meaning mountain, and early explorers called the region the Land of the Shining Mountains, although only the western third of Montana is mountainous. The rest of the country is a gently rolling terrain with wide horizons. Montanans are known for their fierce love of their big land and Big Sky, a love that visitors to its boundless beauty find fully justified.

THE LAND

Montana is divided topographically into the Great Plains, which cover the eastern three fifths of the state, and the Rocky Mountains, which cover the remaining western portion.

The Continental Divide winds through the Rockies of Montana to a point about two thirds the distance south from the Canadian boundary, where it turns abruptly west to the Idaho line, then again makes a sharp angle to the southeast.

The ranges of the Rockies trend mostly in north-south directions, with deep and very broad valleys and basins lying between the ranges. The valleys are flat and grassy and the mountains are heavily forested with evergreens. The mountains in the more than fifty ranges of this area were formed by glacier action about one million years ago, forming rugged, sharp peaks, deep U-shaped valleys, and thousands of small clear lakes. There are a few active glaciers remaining in the higher ranges, much smaller than the ones that formed the Rockies.

The terrain of the Great Plains, much less varied in contrast to the Rockies, is characterized by flat or gently rolling surfaces and occasionally interrupted by mountains and broad river valleys.

Montana has numerous and extensive rivers flowing from its mountains. The major rivers are the Missouri and its branch, the Yellowstone, which, with their tributaries, drain most of the state. This is the only state that has river systems draining into two oceans —the Missouri system flows into the Gulf of Mexico, and the Columbia system, whose tributaries drain the western part of the Rockies, flows into the Pacific.

Montana has numerous and extensive rivers flowing from its mountains. The major rivers are the Missouri and its branch the Yellowstone, which, with their tributaries, drain most of the state. This is the only state that has river systems draining into two oceans. The Continental Divide separates the waters running east and those running west: the Missouri system flows into the Gulf of Mexico, and the Columbia system, whose tributaries drain the western part of the Rockies, flows into the Pacific.

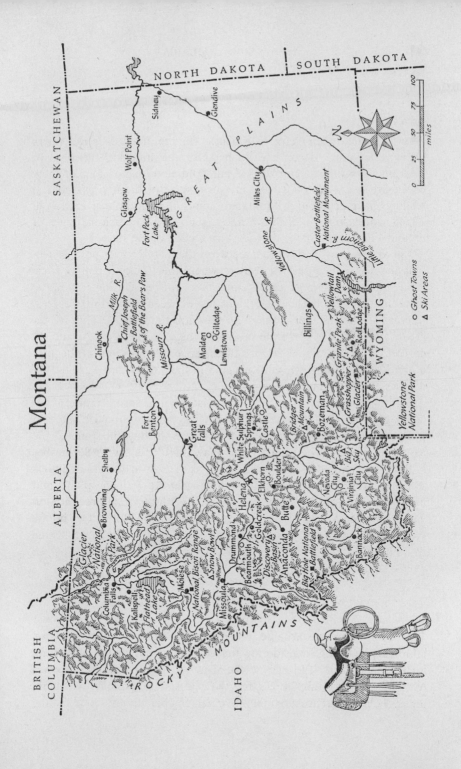

Montana

SASKATCHEWAN

ALBERTA

BRITISH COLUMBIA

NORTH DAKOTA

SOUTH DAKOTA

GREAT PLAINS

WYOMING

IDAHO

Sidney

Glendive

Wolf Point

Glasgow

Miles City

Fort Peck Lake

Milk R.

Chinook

Chief Joseph Battlefield

Battlefield of the Bear's Paw

Missouri R.

Shelby

Browning

Fort Benton

Maiden

Giltedge

Lewistown

Custer Battlefield National Monument

Yellowstone R.

Little Bighorn R.

Billings

Yellowtail Dam

Granite Peak

Red Lodge

Grasshopper Glacier

Great Falls

White Sulphur Springs

Castle

Bridger Mountain

Bozeman

Glacier National Park

Columbia Falls

Kalispell

Flathead Lake

Moiese

National Bison Range

Snow Bowl

Missoula

Drummond

Bearmouth

Goldcreek

Discovery

Anaconda

Big Hole National Battlefield

Bannack

Helena

Elkhorn

Butte

Boulder

Nevada City

Virginia City

Bridger Bowl

Big Sky

Yellowstone National Park

ROCKY MOUNTAINS

o Ghost Towns

△ Ski Areas

N

100

75

50

25

0

miles

CLIMATE

Montana cannot lay claim to a gentle climate. This does not mean the weather there is consistently bad, for the state has its share of pleasant days, but extremes of hot and cold, and long periods of snow cover, are not uncommon. For instance, some of the nation's coldest readings have occurred in Montana (minus 69 degrees near Helena in 1954), and also some of the warmest, such as the occasional highs of around 117 degrees in the northeastern section of the state.

The differences in elevations between the state's lower eastern section and the higher western section, where the Rocky Mountains are located, create a divergence of temperature ranges. During July in the mountainous west the average highs are between 50 and 60 degrees, whereas in the middle of the state they are between 60 and 70 degrees, and in the lower eastern section they are between 70 and 80 degrees. Average annual temperatures range from around 46 degrees in the Yellowstone River valley region in the southwest to around 35 degrees in the mountain valleys.

Killing frosts early in the fall and late in the spring make Montana's growing season rather short, ranging from around 120 days in the middle and eastern plains to fewer than 80 days in some of the mountain valleys. The killing frosts may come as early as September in the lower-lying sections and as early as August in the mountainous sections, with the last killing frost coming in April in the plains and in May or June in the mountain valleys. Average annual precipitation varies from less than 10 inches in the plains to 80 inches in the mountains, with a snow cover in most sections of the state lasting from 90 to 120 days.

THE MONTANANS

Two things are remarkable about Montana's people—their small numbers, especially considering the enormous size of the state, and their homogeneity. In 1970 the United States census reported 694,409 people living in this fourth-largest state of 147,138 square miles. Density averages less than five persons per square mile, making

Montana one of the nation's most thinly populated states. The Census Bureau estimated a population of only about 706,000 by 1975.

Most of the state's people are native-born whites of northern European heritage. Many of them, mainly Germans and Scandinavians, homesteaded farms in Montana's eastern prairie in the early years of the twentieth century. Earlier, in the nineteenth century, others from all across Europe had come to work in the gold, silver, and copper mines.

Before the white men began settling in Montana, the area was inhabited by a number of Indian tribes, including the Blackfoot, Assiniboin, Crow, Cheyenne, Shoshone, Atsina, Kutenai, Kalispel, and Flatheads. Over the years, as the white men began taking over their territory, the Indians were forced onto reservations. Today, populations of most of the above tribes, plus the Chippewa, Cree, and Sioux, live in seven reservations around the state.

The Indians, presently numbering around 27,000, are the state's only sizable racial minority. About three quarters of them live on the reservations which, for the most part, are poor in natural resources, except for grazing land, much of which is leased to non-Indian stock growers. Although unemployment is high on the reservations, most of the Indians are reluctant to leave their families and traditional ties and seek work among the white men, thus perpetuating their general condition of poverty.

Shortly after the Civil War, blacks began moving into Montana, but they never came in great numbers, and today their population is only around 2,000, about half of whom live in the Great Falls area.

HISTORY

Back in the days when Indians were the only inhabitants, access to what is now Montana was fairly difficult—there were the arid Great Plains to the east and mountains to the west. But despite the difficulties, explorers and trappers began penetrating the area in the eighteenth century.

The United States acquired Montana as part of the Louisiana Purchase in 1803, and in 1805 Meriwether Lewis and William Clark explored the area as part of their famous expedition to the Pacific Coast. Before that time, possibly as far back as the 1740s, explorers and fur traders, primarily Frenchmen, occasionally entered Montana, but there is no official record of exploration until the Lewis and Clark expedition.

After Lewis and Clark, waves of American and British fur traders began entering Montana. Their greatest contribution was exploration, for many of them took the trouble to record their findings and make maps. Canadian David Thompson, for instance, around 1810 mapped much of the northwestern Montana region, and John Colter, an American, discovered what is now Yellowstone Park in 1808. And it was a fur company that established the first permanent settlement—in 1847 the American Fur Company built Fort Benton on the Missouri River.

As in other western states, it was the discovery of gold that gave the greatest impetus to settlement in Montana. The first find was at Gold Creek in 1852, and strikes continued to be made until 1864. But it was the large strike at Grasshopper Creek in 1862 that really started a gold rush. In just a couple of years places like Virginia City, Bannack, and Helena became wild, populous boomtowns.

The gold rush created a period of lawlessness, and miners were preyed upon by bandits known as road agents. Because the mining towns had no effective means of law enforcement, the miners fought back by forming vigilante groups. Their most notorious enemy was the Plummer gang—the gang's leader, Henry Plummer, had actually been sheriff of Bannack and Virginia City before the vigilantes found him out. Plummer was hanged in 1864, as were a number of other outlaws, and the vigilantes soon became strong enough to drive most of the bandits from their territory.

The mining boom also was responsible for another violent chapter in Montana history—the Indian wars. Large numbers of white settlers began moving into Indian lands, slaughtering game and pushing the tribes into more and more confined and remote areas. The United States Government made treaties setting aside certain territory for the Indians, and most of the tribes, including the Flatheads, Blackfoot, and Crow, accepted the situation with a minimum of violence and retired to the reservations. But other tribes, particularly the Sioux and Cheyenne, began fighting back fiercely, beginning in the late 1860s.

The U. S. Army waged a major campaign against the Sioux and Cheyenne in Montana and other areas, involving a series of large battles, such as the Battle of the Washita, in November 1868, when a detachment under Lieutenant Colonel George Armstrong Custer massacred a Cheyenne village and killed the chief, Black Kettle; and the Battle of the Rosebud in the Black Hills region, in June 1876, when Sioux and Cheyenne warriors defeated a force commanded by General George Crook. The culmination of the war came on June 25, 1876, when a large army of Sioux and Cheyenne, led by Chiefs Crazy Horse and Sitting Bull, defeated and killed a force of U.S. cavalry, led by Custer, at the Little Bighorn River. That greatest victory was the last for the tribes, their last moment of full power and glory, for within a year their forces were broken and their leaders imprisoned or confined to reservations.

The last major Indian battle in Montana came in 1877, when, after several small engagements, Chief Joseph and the Nez Percé tribe fought a two-day battle with the United States Army at Big Hole, in southwestern Montana. Shortly after that conflict, the Nez Percé tribe was run to ground after months of successfully eluding the Army, and finally defeated, thus ending the Indian wars in that part of the country.

During the years of the mining boom and the Indian wars, the cattle industry was growing steadily in Montana. During the 1870s, as railroads entered the territory and Indians were pushed into reservations, ranchers expanded into central and eastern Montana, prospering with open-range operations. Farming and stock raising increased even more after completion of the Northern Pacific Railway in 1883. After that, cattlemen especially continued to expand and prosper until their major setback of 1886–87 when a severe winter killed thousands of cattle and wiped out a number of ranches.

However, by the time Montana became a state on November 8, 1889, the cattlemen had for the most part recovered, due mainly to their change in methods. They converted from open range to closed range and began growing winter feed.

During the four decades after becoming a state, Montana experienced a homesteading boom, the rise of corporate mining, and battles for political control among industrialists. Two men, William A. Clark and Marcus Daly, pioneered large-scale industrial mining, first of silver and then copper, and by the 1890s the companies these men had founded—especially Daly's Anaconda Copper Company—had become enormously powerful.

It was during the 1890s that Clark and Daly and a third copper baron, F. Augustus Heinze, became embroiled in what is known as the "War of the Copper Kings." For most of that time the feud was between Clark and Daly, with Heinze entering the fray in 1899.

What the copper kings wanted was political and economic control of the state. Some of their methods were less than admirable: the buying up of newspapers, attempts to influence the vote during selection of a permanent state capital, efforts to bribe state legislators, and the use of influence over judges in the courts of Butte, the center of the copper-mining industry.

Daly died in 1900, but not before he had sold his properties to a single corporation, which became the Anaconda Company. The others also eventually sold all their holdings to the company, and Anaconda became the single most dominant force in the state, and residents referred to it simply as "the Company." Its involvement in politics, symbolized by the chain of newspapers it owned until 1959, continued to be a controversial issue for many years.

The homesteading boom came in the early part of the twentieth century with the large-scale settlement of Montana's remote and semi-arid eastern plains region. Railroad advertising and promotion and the Enlarged Homestead Act of 1909 prompted homesteaders by the thousands to invade that area during the years 1910–17. A further stimulus was high wheat prices during World War I, but in 1918–19, falling crop prices, bank failures, and a series of droughts turned the agricultural boom into a bust that lasted until the mid-1920s. Then more droughts came in 1929 and did not let up until the late 1930s.

All aspects of Montana's economy suffered during the Great Depression of the 1930s, as demand for the state's metals dropped sharply. Not until World War II did the state's agriculture and industry recover, when the economy experienced a virtual boom. The state's meat and grain were in great demand, and its copper and other metals were used to make war materials.

Since 1950 the state's petroleum industry has expanded rapidly, as has its irrigation, water conservation, and hydroelectric power production programs. Tourism also has grown tremendously, becoming an important source of income.

Montana's major challenge today is to attract industries that will not destroy its famed natural beauty. This goal has been reflected in the many citizens groups that were formed in the late 1960s and early 1970s to help prevent pollution of natural resources and recreational areas.

Environmental concerns, plus the concerns for individual dignity and ethnic preservation, were reflected in the state's new constitution, drawn up in 1972. The document included guarantees of the right to a clean and healthful environment and the right to individual privacy. It also enjoined corporations as well as individuals and state agencies from discrimination, and stated that one of the state's goals was preservation of the cultural integrity of Montana's Indians.

INDUSTRY

A combination of circumstances has retarded the development of manufacturing in Montana—the state's remoteness from major markets, a small labor force, and an often severe climate. Consequently, most of the industrial activities are involved in processing raw materials from the state's forests, mines, and farms.

The most important of these is the manufacture of lumber and wood products, taking advantage of the forests, which cover about 22 million acres of Montana. The top commercial trees are several species of pine, fir, and cedar, which are made into softwood logs, finished lumber, fuel wood, fence posts, timbers for mine tunnels, pulpwood and paper, plywood, and Christmas trees. More than one third of the state's manufacturing labor force is employed in this industry, and about half of the products are used within the state.

Because Montana is rich in certain minerals, mining has been an important industry since the mid-nineteenth century. Gold and silver were the first ores mined extensively, and they are still significant, but today the most important minerals are coal, copper, petroleum, and natural gas. Coal and copper reserves are among the nation's largest, and petroleum reserves are more than 200 million barrels. Sand and gravel production ranks right behind oil and copper, and the state is also a leading producer of zinc, manganese, lead, phosphate, and chrome, of which it has 80 per cent of the known reserves. It also leads the nation in production of vermiculite, an important insulation material.

Industries that are an outgrowth of Montana's sizable agricultural activities include flour mills, sugar factories, canneries, meat-packing plants, and breweries.

Tourism has also become an important segment of Montana's economy, with its huge national parks, especially Glacier National Park, the major attractions. The development of reservoir and natural lakes recreation areas, dude ranches, and an open season on big game also have contributed significantly to the growth of tourism.

AGRICULTURE

Montana has extensive crop farming, and the most important crop is wheat, grown in the fertile soils of the central, eastern, and northeastern sections of the state. The farmers get premium prices for their wheat because it has a relatively high protein content. The state is the third-largest wheat producer in the country, ranked only behind Kansas and North Dakota.

Other important crops, also grown mainly in the eastern and central parts of the state, are barley, oats, rye, potatoes, sugar beets, great northern beans, and mustard, flax, alfalfa, and clover seeds. Corn is grown in the eastern half of the state and is used mostly for livestock feed, as is hay, which is produced in every county. In the mountain valleys of western Montana fruits and berries, particularly sweet cherries and apples, are grown.

Beef cattle and calves are second only to wheat in producing farm income for the state. The cattle and calves are raised mostly in the eastern part of the state, but livestock activities are important all across the southern part of Montana. Dairying and sheep raising are extensive in these areas. Livestock and livestock products brought Montana over $495 million in income in 1972.

NATURAL RESOURCES

Other than its abundance of minerals and forests, which are discussed in the section on industry, Montana's prime natural resources are its water systems, its soils and grasslands, and its wildlife.

The state's more than 1,500 lakes and 32,000 miles of rivers and streams are economically valuable in several ways—as areas for tourists and sportsmen and as sources for electric power and irrigation. Because so much of the state has a low rate of precipitation, irrigation is especially vital to agriculture, and today about one fifth of Montana's farm land is irrigated.

There are deep, rich soils in many sections of Montana. In the western mountain region many of the wide valleys have fertile soil built up by silt deposits from the rivers. This is also true of the river valleys in central and eastern Montana. And in some areas of the state fertile wind-blown dust accumulates in thick layers. In the plains areas of the eastern and central sections, the soils have limy subsoils, and, because of low rainfall, they are not leached, leaving many minerals in the earth which help produce rich crops. The soils of southwestern Montana have been enriched by ash from ancient volcanoes.

Big-game animals are especially plentiful in the state, including bears, deer, antelope, moose, mountain goats, mountain lions, and elk. There are also abundant game birds, such as ducks, pheasants, geese, partridges, prairie chickens, and grouse. And there are numerous smaller animals—wolves, porcupines, beaver, mink, muskrats, ground hogs, chipmunks, squirrels, coyotes, rabbits, and gophers. The many lakes and rivers and streams are fairly teeming with fish, primarily perch, bass, salmon, whitefish, trout, grayling, pike, and catfish.

CITIES

Billings, situated on the west bank of the Yellowstone River in south-central Montana, was built in 1877 by the Northern Pacific Railway. Today, with a population of around 64,000, it is the state's largest city, and the center of a huge, highly productive agricultural area. It also has a number of manufacturing industries, including glass, wood, and clay products, and refineries for processing oil and beet sugar.

In and around the city are some especially interesting historical sites. East of the city, Boothill Cemetery contains the graves of outlaws and lawmen who died in frontier gun battles, and southeast of the city is the Pictograph Cave State Monument, which preserves ancient Indian caves with pictographs inscribed on the walls. The Yellowstone County Museum and the Western Heritage Center both feature artifacts and art work of Indian and Old West history.

Southeast of Billings is the huge Crow Indian Reservation. In the northeast section of the reservation is the Custer Battlefield National Monument, which includes the ridge near the Little Bighorn River where on June 25, 1876, Lieutenant Colonel George Armstrong Custer and 225 men of the 7th Cavalry Regiment were killed in a battle against several thousand Sioux and Cheyenne.

Helena, in west-central Montana, the state's capital, was founded in 1864 in rather unusual circumstances. A band of prospectors who had had dismal luck in their search for gold wandered across a gulch that looked promising and decided to have one last dig. They named the huge ditch "Last Chance Gulch." What they thought was a last chance turned out to be a chance of a lifetime—the prospectors hit a gold deposit that eventually produced more than $20 million in gold.

After that, one of the state's biggest gold rushes began, and hundreds of cabins sprang up in the mining camp of "Last Chance." Eventually it was renamed Helena, and for many years it was a wild town of miners, outlaws, and gamblers.

Today, part of Helena's Main Street is that famous Last Chance Gulch, but the lawless old days are but a memory. This city of around 28,000 is a good place to raise a family, and it is also the center of the state's financial, political, civic, and social activities.

Visitors to Helena should not miss their chance to see the state capitol, a neoclassic building faced with Montana granite, completed in 1902. It is topped with a 100-foot-high copper dome that, in turn, is topped with a 65-foot-high statue depicting Liberty.

Part of the capitol complex is the Montana Historical Museum & C. M. Russell Art Gallery, containing dioramas of state history and a collection of the work of famous western artist Charles M. Russell.

Some other interesting sites are the Governor's Old Mansion, a restored twenty-room mansion dating from 1885, used by nine former governors; the gold collection at the Northwestern Bank & Union Trust Company on Last Chance Gulch Street; Reeder's Alley, an artists' colony that was home for miners and mule skinners in the old days.

Helena is surrounded by the Helena National Forest, 966,654 acres, offering camping and picnic areas, fishing, and hunting.

About fifty miles southwest of Helena is **Butte,** a city of around 22,000 residents whose major industry is copper mining. For over a century the thousand-acre mining areas around Butte have yielded copper, along with by-products of gold, silver, and other metals. The supply seems almost inexhaustible as the mines continue to produce high-grade ore.

Like other Montana cities, Butte has a wild, boomtown past, starting in 1864 with the discovery of silver. When the top-grade silver began running out, copper was encountered, and ever since copper has dominated the city's history. Today, the industry is consolidated and operated by the Anaconda Company.

As part of its mining heritage, Butte has developed one of the country's leading mining schools, the Montana College of Mineral Science and Technology (Montana Tech), founded in 1893. On campus is the Mineral Museum.

Visitors to Butte can see open-pit mining from observation towers and take free tours of mines arranged by the local Chamber of Commerce. Or they can visit the World Museum of Mining, one of the nation's finest. The Copper King Mansion, built in the 1880s, also is a popular attraction, a restored thirty-room house that was owned by W. A. Clark, a prominent political figure of the state's early history.

Sections of Deerlodge National Forest surround Butte, 159,000 acres of wilderness, lakes, fishing, hunting, camping, picnicking, riding trails, and winter sports.

The city of **Bozeman,** population around 20,000, lies about eighty miles southeast of Helena. It is the market place center for the grain, livestock, and dairying industries of Gallatin Valley. Bozeman was named for John M. Bozeman, who in 1864 led a group of immigrants from Wyoming to settle in this valley.

Montana State University, founded in 1893, is located in Bozeman. Its student body of over 8,000 is enrolled in colleges of agriculture, engineering, education, and science, professional, and graduate schools. On campus is the Museum of the Rockies, featuring pioneer and Indian exhibits, and art and science displays; and the Agricultural Field Complex, a working livestock area.

North and south of Bozeman is the Gallatin National Forest, covering 1,700,166 acres. Within it are mountains and large forests and facilities for camping, picnicking, backpacking trips, fishing, and hunting.

Great Falls, named for the falls in the Missouri River to the northeast, is Montana's second-largest city, with a population of around 60,000. Malstrom Air Force Base, with its Minuteman missiles, has contributed greatly to Great Falls' booming growth. Other growth factors have been expanding diversified industries, hydroelectric plants near the falls, Anaconda Company copper and aluminum plants, a fertile winter wheat production, and a thriving livestock industry.

The great western artist Charles M. Russell made Great Falls his home base, and today the city contains an outstanding display of his paintings, bronzes, and wax models in the Charles M. Russell Museum & Original Studio.

Near Great Falls is the Lewis and Clark National Forest, covering 1,862,018 acres of forests, mountains, and canyons. Visitors can enjoy scenic drives, fishing, hunting, camping, picnicking, and winter sports.

Missoula, located in the extreme western section of the state, is a center for agricultural activities and for the lumbering and paper manufacturing industries that are an outgrowth of the large reserves of timber that surround the city. It also serves as the regional headquarters of the United States Forest Service and the Montana State Forest Service.

The city was founded in 1860, and throughout its history has been a trading and transportation crossroads. Today, it has a population of over 29,000. Around 8,500 of that figure are students at the University of Montana, founded in 1893.

One of the most exciting features of Missoula is the Aerial Fire Depot, located about seven miles west of the city, where Forest Service members launch aerial attacks on forest fires. At the Smoke-jumper Loft, parachutists are trained and dispatched, and at the Northern Forest Fire Laboratory there is research into fire prevention and control and the beneficial uses of fire in forest management. There also is a visitor center, containing fire control exhibits and offering guided tours of the parachute loft.

Surrounding Missoula are the 2,076,641 acres of Lolo National Forest, which offers camping, picnicking, fishing, hunting, scenic drives, and winter sports.

SPORTS AND RECREATION

Western Montana has two things that make it prime skiing territory—the Rocky Mountains and plenty of snow. Anyone who can't find a good slope for a downhill run just isn't looking hard enough, for there are over twenty-five skiing areas from which to choose.

There are eight ski areas that are open daily from November to April. In northwestern Montana there is the Big Mountain, near Glacier National Park. And in the western and southern parts of the state there are Bridger Bowl, Big Sky of Montana, Red Lodge Mountain, Marshall Mountain, Montana Snow Bowl, Maverick Mountain, and Discovery Basin. All of these areas have lifts and tows, with slopes ranging from novice to expert. Some have cross-country and night-skiing areas. Accommodations in most are fairly elaborate, with lodges, ski shops, equipment rentals, restaurants, cafeterias, ski patrols, and ski schools. Some offer heated swimming pools.

There also are eighteen ski areas open on weekends and holidays, all offering lifts and tows, but with a variety of accommodations ranging from the remote and rustic to posh.

The most elaborate of the resort areas is Big Sky, forty-five miles southwest of Bozeman in southwestern Montana, developed by the late newscaster Chet Huntley. Besides the twenty-three miles of slopes for downhill skiing and thirty-five miles of cross-country skiing trails, Big Sky offers camping, golf, fishing, hunting, and horseback riding. One of its prime features is the new 204-room Huntley Lodge. There is also the Lone Mountain Guest Ranch, which has western cabins, a lounge, and skiing tours.

There are over twenty national parks and forests and state parks in Montana, offering a full range of summer and winter recreation and sports—fishing, hunting, boating, hiking, camping, picnicking, skiing, and scenic drives. The pride and joy of Montana is Glacier National Park, a 3-million-acre region of spectacular natural beauty which the state shares with Canada.

The park contains over fifty glaciers, feeding miles of rivers and streams and two hundred lakes. There are nearly 60 species of mammals, such as moose, bear, mountain goats, bighorn sheep, deer, and elk; around 235 species of birds; and more than 1,200 varieties of plants within the park.

Quite a bit of Glacier's grandeur can be seen from one's car, for there are about 240 miles of roads, but most of the park, including the glaciers, are accessible only by trails. There are 700 miles of trails, which can be traveled by foot or on horseback, leading to remote wilderness areas. There are also seven major and eight smaller campgrounds, with a limit of seven days of camping during the peak warm-weather season.

Although Yellowstone National Park lies mostly within the state of Wyoming, three of the five entrances to the park are through the small section within Montana's borders. The 3,472-square-mile park is America's first and largest national park, famous for its lakes, canyons, waterfalls, and two hundred geysers, including the world-renowned Old Faithful.

Another of the state's top recreation areas is Flathead Lake, in northwestern Montana, the largest fresh-water lake west of the Mississippi River. Its 190 square miles were formed by glacial action, and today it is a place of remarkable beauty, fringed by cherry orchards and dense conifer forests that rise abruptly from lake shore to mountaintop. On the east shore are resorts, marinas, and campgrounds. Besides the excellent fishing, favorite sports here are boating, swimming, water-skiing, hiking, and horseback riding.

Vacations on dude ranches and farms are a favorite form of recreation for Montana visitors, especially since there are hundreds of them available. There are two types: the working ranches where guests are another source of income, and the kind run primarily for guests. Both kinds usually feature horseback riding, pack trips, fishing, hunting, and side trips to points of interest. The best way to find these places is through the Montana Dude Ranchers Association in Billings, or through railroads and airlines operating in the state.

POINTS OF INTEREST

One of the best ways for a visitor to get a glimpse of Montana's wild gold-rush past is to visit the old mining towns of Virginia City and Nevada City in the southwestern corner of the state. Both towns are part of Alder Gulch, one of Montana's richest gold strikes, discovered in 1863. Around 35,000 people streamed into the region in search of the more than $100 million in gold that the area eventually produced. About a half-dozen towns sprang up along the gulch, but when the gold ran out, populations dwindled, and today only Virginia City and Nevada City remain.

Virginia City, with a permanent population of around 150, never became a ghost town, but Nevada City almost disappeared. However, most of Virginia City's historical buildings have been preserved, and a good part of Nevada City has been restored. Almost every building in Nevada City contains equipment and merchandise of the mining camp days. Even the houses are furnished in period style, and vintage buckboards line many of the streets.

There are other such vestiges of the past around the state. Castle Ghost Town, near White Sulphur Springs, in central Montana, was once a silver-mining boomtown. One of its famous citizens was Calamity Jane. Another is Bearmouth Ghost Town, near Drummond, in western Montana, where a million dollars in gold and silver was mined in 1866. Near Lewistown, in the central part of the state, are the gold-mining ghost towns of Maiden, Kendall, and Gilt Edge; and near Anaconda, in southwestern Montana, are the ghost towns of Cable and Southern Cross.

Another of the best-preserved ghost towns is Elkhorn, near Boulder, in southwestern Montana. Over thirty buildings still stand in this town that had a population of around 2,500 in its boomtown days of the 1870s and 1880s, when it was the center of a rich silver-mining district.

The Custer Battlefield National Monument is on the Crow Indian Reservation in southeastern Montana. On this site, on June 25, 1876, Lieutenant Colonel George Armstrong Custer and 225 men of the 7th Cavalry Regiment were killed in a battle against several thousand Sioux and Cheyenne. The battlefield remains much as it was on that day, and a national cemetery was established there in 1879, with headstones showing where the soldiers fell. A visitor center contains exhibits and dioramas.

There are two monuments to famous battles between the United States Army and the Nez Percé Indians, led by Chief Joseph. The Big Hole National Battlefield near Anaconda, in southwestern Montana, preserves more than 655 acres of the battlefield where the Indians were attacked by the Army on August 9, 1877. A self-guiding trail goes past trenches, a soldiers' memorial, and a memorial to Chief Joseph's band. The Nez Percé escaped after that battle but were pursued to the Bear's Paw Battlefield near the town of Chinook, in north-central Montana, where Chief Joseph surrendered after a six-day battle later in the year of 1877. That site has been preserved as the Chief Joseph Battleground Monument.

Fort Kalispell, in the northwestern corner of the state, is a replica of a frontier town, with saloon, stagecoach and trail rides, melodramas, and an art gallery. There is also an Indian village. In north-central Montana, near the town of Fort Benton, are the ruins of Old Fort Benton, on the river front of the Missouri. Parts of the old trading post and blockhouse remain, and there is a museum.

Visitors also can get a good view of bison in the wild at the National Bison Range, near the town of Moiese, in western Montana. Up to 500 bison roam over 18,541 acres, which include an exhibition pasture and picnic grounds near the headquarters.

At Red Lodge, in southern Montana, is the Big Sky Historical Museum, containing a large collection of western frontier guns, Indian artifacts, and antiques.

The Fort Peck Dam and Reservoir, in northeastern Montana, is the largest earth-fill dam in the nation, forming a huge reservoir with a 1,600-mile lake shore. A road follows the crest of the dam, which rises 250 feet above the Missouri River, leading to a mile-long spillway. South of the spillway are fossil beds. Guided tours of the power plant are offered, and there is a museum and information center.

Grasshopper Glacier, northeast of Cooke City, in southern Montana near the Wyoming border, is one of the largest icefields in the nation. It can be reached by hiking, horseback, or jeep.

SPECIAL EVENTS

People who like rodeos, horse shows, fairs, and river cruises find a great deal to do in Montana.

One of the state's best and oldest rodeos is the Wild Horse Stampede, at the town of Wolf Point in northeastern Montana, which takes place on the second weekend in July. Besides the activities in the corrals, there are Indian ceremonies and dances.

Another big one is the Northeast Montana Fair and Rodeo, during four days in mid-August at the town of Glasgow, also in the northeast. Other top cowboy events are the Montana State University Rodeo at Bozeman in mid-April; the Dawson County Fair and Jaycee Rodeo for three days in August at Glendive; the Last Chance Stampede and Fair at Helena in late July or early August; the Northwest Montana Fair and Rodeo at Kalispell; the Central Montana Horse Show, Fair, and Rodeo in late July at Lewistown; the Western Montana Quarter Horse Show in Missoula in mid-July; and the rodeos at Drummond in early July and in September. Billings has three outstanding western events: the Midland Empire Horse Show in mid-June; the Midland Empire Fair and Rodeo in mid-August; and the Northern International Livestock Exposition in late October or early November.

The town of Red Lodge, in southern Montana, has an exciting event lasting nine days in early or mid-August. It is the Festival of Nations, with craft exhibits and nightly entertainment that reflect several European cultures.

The line-up of fairs is impressive. One of the biggest is the State Fair at Billings from July 26 to August 3. Featured are a rodeo, livestock exhibits, horse racing, and nightly shows.

Some other fairs are the Eastern Montana Fair, for three days in mid-August at Miles City; the Western Montana Fair, in late August at Missoula; the Marias Fair, during the third week of July, at Shelby, featuring horse races with pari-mutuel betting, a rodeo, and agricultural displays; the Richland County Fair, four days of exhibits, livestock shows, and rodeos in early August at the town of Sidney; and the Montana Winter Fair at Bozeman.

An annual event which is particularly fascinating is the re-enactment of Custer's Last Stand. This outdoor drama is performed the first weekend in July about eighteen miles south of the town of Hardin, which is located near the Custer Battlefield National Monument in southern Montana.

Another celebration, and most attractive, is the North American Indian Days in mid-July at the town of Browning, in northwestern Montana, sponsored by the Blackfoot tribe and featuring native dances and ceremonies.

River cruises are popular in Montana. One of the biggest is the Yellowstone River Float Trip during the second weekend of July when a flotilla of anything from inner tubes to launches travels the river from Livingston east to Billings. Another top event is the Missouri River Cruise, a journey from Fort Peck to Fort Benton, with participants supplying their own boats.

N.C.

CHRONOLOGY

1803   United States acquired Montana through the Louisiana Purchase.

1805–6   Lewis and Clark explored Montana.

1852   First gold strike, at Gold Creek.

1864   Congress established Montana Territory.

1876   Sioux and Cheyenne defeated Custer and the 7th Cavalry on June 25 at the Battle of the Little Bighorn.

1877   Chief Joseph and the Nez Percé tribe surrendered to the United States Army after several battles.

1883   Northern Pacific Railway was completed across Montana.

1886–87   Major setback for burgeoning cattle industry when a severe winter killed thousands of livestock.

1889   Montana became the forty-first state on November 8.

1890s   "War of the Copper Kings" for political and economic control of the state.

1910   Congress established Glacier National Park.

1910–17   Homesteading boom in the eastern plains region of Montana.

1940   Fort Peck Dam and Reservoir was completed.

1951   First oil wells in the Montana section of the Williston Basin started production.

1955   The Anaconda Aluminum Company dedicated a $65-million plant at Columbia Falls.

1966   Yellowtail Dam was completed.

1972   New state constitution was drawn up.

1977   Redevelopment of Helena's downtown area, begun in 1974, included preservation of historic sites and creation of a pedestrian mall.

1979   With high world energy prices providing the incentive, the state experienced a sharp increase in the search for natural gas and oil.

NEVADA

UP UNTIL the 1850s Nevada was simply territory travelers passed through to get to California and the gold rush. Not until 1849 was there even a permanent settlement there. But then in 1859 some prospectors picked their way into some of the richest gold and silver veins this country has ever known. Boomtowns and mining camps began springing up overnight, and for about twenty years Nevada rivaled California.

But the strike-it-rich days faded as quickly as they began, and Nevada became depopulated about as fast as it had gained new citizens. Rapid boom-and-bust was to repeat itself several times in the state's history. It was the sort of thing that always assured a lot of wide-open spaces. And that's still true of Nevada—with 110,690 square miles, it is the seventh-largest state, yet it has the second-smallest population.

However, Nevada is one of the fastest-growing states in the nation. In the 1940s it entered another boom period and it hasn't looked back since. Laws that allowed almost every kind of gambling anywhere in the state were the cause of that boom. People still go to Nevada with the idea of striking it rich.

Its history of silver mining has earned Nevada the nickname of the Silver State. It is also called the Sagebrush State, because sagebrush grows all over its deserts. But dominating the deserts are the many rugged mountain ranges. The name "Nevada" comes from the mountains; it is Spanish for "snow-covered," referring to the towering Sierra Nevada (*sierra:* "mountain range") on the western edge of the state.

THE LAND

There is a large topographical region of the western United States called the Great Basin which includes parts of Oregon, Idaho, Wyoming, California, and Utah. The state of Nevada is situated almost entirely within the Great Basin, which is composed of about ninety isolated mountain ranges running generally north and south that are separated by broad, largely desert plains.

Nevada itself has three principal topographical regions:

The Columbia Plateau covers only a small part of the state's northeastern corner, and is one of the three small areas in Nevada that are not part of the Great Basin. The Columbia Plateau has deep canyons cut by rivers and streams.

West and south of Carson City, the rugged mountain range, the Sierra Nevada, cuts across a corner of the extreme western section of the state. This area, which includes the popular Lake Tahoe, is the second of the state's regions that are not part of the Great Basin.

The remainder of Nevada is covered by the Basin and Range Region, mostly upland areas divided by more than thirty mountain ranges running north and south. Boundary Peak, the state's highest point at 13,140 feet, is in this area, in the White Mountains on the California border. Buttes, mesas, and flat valleys with lakes or alkali flats (arid plains incrusted with alkaline salts) lie between the mountain ranges.

CLIMATE

Nevada has the dubious distinction of being America's driest state. That does not mean its citizens drink less—it means they get less rain than anybody else. During a typical year in the state, only about an average seven inches of rain falls. The driest areas are in the southeastern corner and the land near Carson Sink—only about four inches of rain, on the average, falls during the year in those areas.

The principal reason Nevada is so deficient in rainfall is that the high Sierras along the state's western boundary cause the clouds coming from the Pacific to drop their moisture before reaching the state.

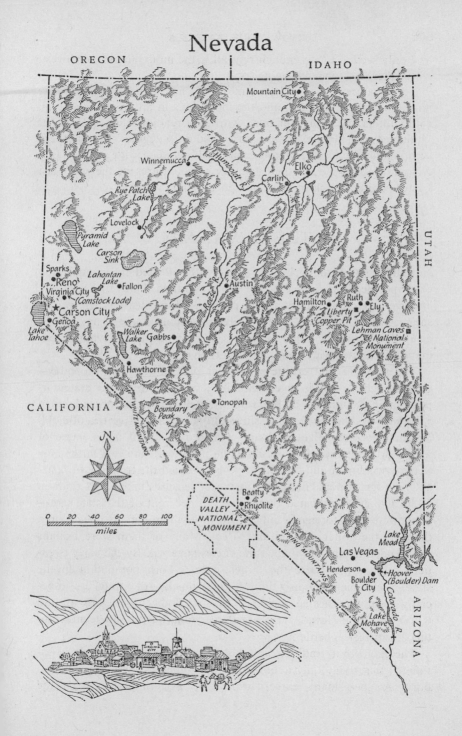

Nevada

OREGON   IDAHO

Mountain City

Winnemucca

Humboldt R.

Elko

Carlin

Rye Patch Lake

Lovelock

Pyramid Lake

Carson Sink

UTAH

Sparks

Lahontan Lake

Reno

Virginia City

(Comstock Lode)

Fallon

Austin

Hamilton   Ruth

Ely

Liberty Copper Pit

★ Carson City

Genoa

Lehman Caves National Monument

Lake Tahoe

Walker Lake   Gabbs

Reese R.

Hawthorne

CALIFORNIA

Boundary Peak

Tonopah

N

WHITE MOUNTAINS

0   20   40   60   80   100

miles

DEATH VALLEY NATIONAL MONUMENT

Beatty

Rhyolite

SPRING MOUNTAINS

Lake Mead

Las Vegas

Henderson

Boulder City

Hoover (Boulder) Dam

Lake Mohave

Colorado R.

ARIZONA

The only section to get enough rainfall is the mountainous northwest, where there is an annual average of twenty-four inches.

Temperatures vary widely, and there are some extremes. The northern part of the state, and the mountains in all areas, have long, cold winters and short summers, with July readings averaging about 70 degrees and January temperatures about 24 degrees. The southern sections have long, hot summers and mild winters, with average July temperatures in the 80s and January temperatures in the 40s. The western areas have short, hot summers and mild winters.

THE NEVADANS

Nevada's late-blooming history has greatly affected the composition of its people. It was the last area of the United States to be settled, and even then the primary motive people had for moving there was to seek riches in the newly opened silver and gold mines. They moved away just as quickly when the mines petered out, and Nevada's population fluctuated widely into the twentieth century.

The result of that erratic settlement pattern can be seen today— even though Nevada is seventh in size among the country's states, its population is only about 600,000. That leaves a lot of wide-open spaces in the state, especially since only 20 per cent of the 600,000 live in rural areas. The rest are clustered in urban areas, none of which—with the exception of Las Vegas and Reno—are very large.

Nevada's boom-and-bust history also created the tradition of a sizable immigrant population. For instance, censuses taken in Nevada in 1870 and 1880 indicated that about 40 per cent of the state's residents were from foreign countries, most of whom had also been lured there by the glitter of gold and silver. Many of them were Italians who tended to stay even when the riches gave out. By the early twentieth century they were the largest foreign-born population in the state. Sheep ranching also drew a good number of foreigners, especially from the Basque region of Spain. Today, there are around 6,000 people in Nevada who are descendants of the nineteenth-century Basque sheepherders.

The immigrant tradition still holds in modern Nevada. It is estimated that today only about a fourth of the residents are Nevada-born. A good many came from other western states, from the

Midwest, the South, and the East, but there are also close to 20,000 people from foreign countries.

Only about 8 per cent of Nevada's citizens belong to nonwhite groups, the largest being blacks, who account for about 6 per cent of the population. The Indian population is small, estimated at less than 2 per cent of the total. They are scattered in rural areas and reservations around the state, while the blacks live mostly in the Las Vegas area. There are also about 3,000 Mexican-Americans living in the southeastern section of the state.

Religious affiliations also reflect the patterns of settlement: More than a fifth of Nevadans are Catholic, and almost another fifth are Mormons, who were the first to make a permanent settlement in the state.

HISTORY

The theme of Nevada's early history is neglect—it was largely ignored by the Spanish who had extensively explored and settled so much of the western and southwestern United States, and later it was ignored by the many thousands of Americans who streamed westward to California. What those early explorers, and the pioneers, saw was a mostly dry desert region that did little to stimulate a colonizing urge. Consequently, Nevada was the last area of the coterminous United States to be explored and settled.

But the fact that Europeans and American pioneers did not find Nevada to their liking does not mean that certain Indian tribes found it totally disagreeable. However, the Indians encountered by the first white explorers—Paiute, Shoshone, Gosiute, Washo, and Mohave—did not live there in large numbers. There is archaeological evidence that Nevada was a more popular habitat in prehistoric times; sizable groups of primitive cultures apparently lived there as long as 12,000 years ago.

The initial organized expeditions into Nevada were led by English and American fur trappers and traders in the 1820s. One of the greatest was Jedediah Smith, who also explored other southwestern regions, including Utah. The adventurous Smith was the first white man known to have traveled all the way across Nevada, a feat he accomplished in 1826 and 1827. In the 1830s two other explorers—William Wolfskill and Joseph Walker—blazed trails across Nevada to

California. Wolfskill's route, which led from Santa Fe, New Mexico, to Los Angeles, became known as the Old Spanish Trail. Walker's route, which he established in 1833, became one of the most heavily traveled trails in the West some years later—thousands of wagons and people on horseback used the trail to get to California after gold was discovered there in 1848.

After the trail blazers came more intense, scientific expeditions, sponsored by the federal government. The first such expedition was led by John Frémont, who had explored other regions, such as Utah. His thorough investigations of the region between 1843 and 1845 provided the first accurate knowledge of Nevada's geography and natural history.

Strangely enough, while all these explorations were taking place, Nevada still officially belonged to Mexico. After the United States won its war with Mexico in 1848, it acquired what is now Nevada along with other southwestern regions. And also, despite the many explorations, there had been no permanent settlements founded. It took the Mormons from Utah to accomplish that. They had had good experience settling arid land in their own domain, and in 1849 they set up a trading post in west-central Nevada, which by 1851 was a settled community. It was called Mormon Station until 1855, when the name was changed to Genoa.

The federal government did not consider Nevada important enough to be a separate official territory, so it became a part of Utah Territory, established in 1850. But nine years later something happened that changed the government's attitude toward Nevada—the fabulous Comstock Lode of silver and gold was discovered in west-central Nevada, near the California border. That discovery changed nearly everyone's thinking about Nevada. The state became an overnight success as thousands of people rushed there to mine for the precious ores. Towns began forming rather suddenly as hundreds of people got rich fast. It was a heady boom-time era of newly made millionaires and reckless spending. The greatest of the new towns was Virginia City, which sprang up near the Comstock mines. Within a few years it was a wild, brawling city, the mining capital of the West.

Nevada's new-found wealth prompted a speedy reconsideration of its political position: It became Nevada Territory in 1861, and then, just three years later, on October 31, 1864, it became a state. During those early years of statehood, mining played the dominant role, although ranching and farming were getting a firm start in the general atmosphere of prosperity.

But the bawdy, bonanza days of America's new richling were to be short-lived. Within two decades the Comstock mines were exhausted, and the price of silver fell when it was demonetized. By 1880 the whole golden dream had collapsed. When the good times were gone, people packed up and "skedaddled," abandoning Nevada to the sagebrush and coyotes. By 1900 the state had lost one third of its population, and ghost towns were nearly as common as cactus.

However, after 1900 Nevada's luck changed again. New silver and gold deposits were found. Then copper ore was discovered at Ruth, Mountain City, and Ely. Miners by the thousands came rushing back to the state, prepared to give Nevada a second chance. When the new copper, silver, and gold mines proved to be large and stable, railroads began building lines to the mines. The new railways aided the cattlemen, who used them for shipping beef.

As World War I was beginning, Nevada's gold and silver mines were running out again. But the industrial demands of the war prevented another economic collapse, for the state's resources of copper, tungsten, zinc, and other metals were badly needed. Many new mines were opened and the miner got top dollar. But after the war, prices fell quickly, and, in the seesaw nature of Nevada's economic history, bad times hit its people once more.

Help was on the way, however. The federal government came to the rescue with aid for construction programs. The biggest project was Boulder (now Hoover) Dam, begun in 1930, which provides power and stores water for parts of Nevada, Arizona, and California. The government also completed the U. S. Naval Ammunition Depot at Hawthorne in 1930, which provided employment for large numbers of Nevada residents.

After that, Nevada began taking positive action in areas other than mining. In order to stimulate travel to the state, the legislature in 1931 reduced the residency requirement for divorce to six weeks. It also made gambling legal that same year, but the gambling casino boom did not come until after World War II. The war years helped Nevada's economy: Several air bases were built, and a huge magnesium-processing plant was built south of Las Vegas at Henderson.

In the 1940s the rest of the country discovered the joys of legalized gambling and began flocking to Nevada. The result was a fabulous tourist boom, and since then tourism, based on the lure of gambling, has become the state's leading industry. Las Vegas became the gambling capital and grew rapidly to become the state's largest city. Most all of the state's other towns and cities, such as Reno and Carson City, have also benefited tremendously from gambling revenues. Another economic stimulus was provided by the capitalistic enterprises of one man—Howard Hughes, one of the world's richest. He moved to Las Vegas in 1966, buying up hotels and casinos, land, TV stations, and airports.

Beginning in the 1950s, Nevada became the site of extensive nuclear research by the federal government. The U. S. Atomic Energy Commission began atomic testing in southern Nevada in 1951, at a site it had built the previous year about sixty miles northwest of Las Vegas. Tests are still going on there, but they are all underground, for since 1962 all above-ground testing has been banned. The nuclear projects greatly increased employment among Nevada residents, not only in the testing projects themselves, but also in the many technical industries that have grown up as adjuncts to the atomic industry.

INDUSTRY

Nevada is not a big manufacturing state. Although manufacturing has increased steadily since World War II, with significant expansion and diversification during the 1960s, it is the mining and processing of minerals that make up the largest industrial enterprise. In 1970 mineral production provided one third of the total value of goods produced in the state—and that was with only about one fourth of its land explored for resources.

The most important commercial mineral is copper, and copper smelting has become the primary industry, with the state ranking fifth nationally in annual output. Gold is Nevada's second most valuable mineral; the Carlin Mine in Eureka County became one of the top gold producers in the Western Hemisphere within two years after it began operating in 1965. Sand and gravel are ranked as the third most valuable of the state's minerals.

Factories in Henderson, the state's largest industrial center, produce titanium ore and industrial chemicals. Nevada also has the second-largest source of mercury and the second-largest mercury production in the country; its silver production ranks seventh.

Tourism is also recognized as an industry, and tourist-connected enterprises are the largest employers in Nevada. About 30 million people every year come to enjoy Nevada's night life, casinos, big-name entertainment, sports, and outdoor recreation facilities, providing the state with an annual income from tourism of around $950 million. That compares with the $165 million yearly income from mining.

AGRICULTURE

Nevada has a fairly strong livestock agriculture, but comparatively small crop farming. More than 75 per cent of the state's farm income is derived from livestock and livestock products. Most of the cattle and sheep ranches are large, averaging 5,070 acres, with the largest ones as much as 275,000 acres. Most of the largest ranches lie in the northern counties of Elko, Humboldt, Washoe, and White Pine.

The greater part of the state's crop farming is tied directly to the livestock industry, for the chief crops are alfalfa hay, barley, oats, and wheat—about 60 per cent of those crops are used to feed livestock. Cotton also is a big crop, and melons, grapes, and vegetables such as onions, potatoes, radishes, and tomatoes are also grown.

Because the state is so deficient in rainfall, crop farmers and livestock ranchers must depend on irrigation for most of their water. Even the farmers and ranchers located in river valleys are forced to pump in additional water.

NATURAL RESOURCES

Mother Nature was not stingy with minerals in Nevada—there are huge quantities of metal ore, particularly copper, gold, and silver, and large deposit of tungsten, mercury, manganese, lead, and zinc. Other minerals include antimony, barite, borax, clays, diatomite, fluorspar, iron ore, pumice, salt, gypsum, limestone, sand, and gravel. And there presumably is still a lot more to come in Nevada, for the majority of its land area is yet to be explored for resources.

The problem of lack of water has an effect on the types of animal life most abundant in Nevada, for those most adaptable to extremes of temperature and little moisture are most successful. There are many animals in the state, but they are mostly small ones. The few species of larger animals include mule deer, bighorn sheep, prong-horn antelope, and some mountain lions. The wolves that used to roam Nevada are extinct in that area now.

Among the abundant small animals are cottontail rabbits, jack rab-bits, and other rodents; predators such as coyotes, bobcats, badgers, and desert foxes are common, as are minks, marmots, muskrats, por-cupines, and raccoons. In the deserts is a large variety of reptiles such as geckos, horned toads, tortoises, and sidewinder rattlesnakes. The permanent bird population is not large, but a great variety of migra-tory birds come there at certain seasons. Among the chief game birds are sage grouse, pheasants, and quails.

CITIES

Las Vegas is the carnival that never stops. It glitters and whirls in perpetual motion twenty-four hours a day, every day of the year. Something like 15 million people go there annually, most of them re-sponding to the lure of quick money and adventure playing roulette, blackjack, baccarat, craps, or twenty-one at the casinos, or trying to hit the jackpot on the slot machines, called one-arm bandits. They also go there to see a spectacular line-up of big-name entertainers performing in the nightclubs of a Byzantine array of opulent hotels.

Most of Las Vegas' approximately 126,000 residents make their living directly or indirectly from the casinos, night clubs, and hotels. The center of all this money-making—and money winning and losing —is "the Strip," the stretch of Las Vegas Boulevard where the major resort hotels are strung out one after another. The Strip is where most of the top entertainment is concentrated.

Some of the leading hotels along the Strip are Caesar's Palace, the MGM Grand, the Dunes, the Riviera, the Desert Inn, the Flamingo, the Sands, the Sahara, the Stardust, the Thunderbird, the Frontier, the Las Vegas Hilton, and the Tropicana. In downtown Las Vegas, on Fremont Street, is "Casino Center," where there are such famous gambling halls as the Golden Nugget, the Mint, the Pioneer Club, the Golden Gate Club, and Binion's Horseshoe.

A recent phenomenon on the Strip is the Circus Circus, a "family casino." While parents are gambling on the ground level, their chil-dren can play on upper levels. The Mint Hotel and Casino lets visi-tors go behind the scenes to watch the money being counted, spy on gambling tables through one-way mirrors, and take a course in gambling.

Credit is tight in the casinos for first-time visitors, but with further visits, once credit has been established, those playing the tables can get loans for $1,000 easily. Anyone who is twenty-one years or older can go into the casinos.

Gambling and night life are only one facet of Las Vegas' character. It also has a university and a full range of outdoor activities. The University of Nevada, Las Vegas, established in 1951, covers three hundred acres. One of its most outstanding features, other than the ultramodern architecture of its buildings, is the Museum of Natural History, which contains a fine collection of historic and prehistoric Indian artifacts, items from the early mining and pioneer days, plus a display of live desert reptiles.

In and around Las Vegas are facilities for water sports, skiing, golf, fishing, and hunting. There are also many miles of hiking and riding trails in the surrounding countryside. The city has eleven golf courses and about seventy-five tennis courts.

While **Reno,** Nevada, has its share of hotels and gambling casinos and big-name entertainment, it is also a center of legal counsel for people seeking divorces. But the majority of the 73,000 Reno residents are more interested in the status of the crops in the fields around them. Reno is an important transshipment point for the agricultural produce of the Carson Valley.

Reno was first settled in 1858 (and was known as Lake's Crossing until 1868) and is just as much an established business and residential community as it is a gambling mecca. It has peaceful areas of homes and lawns, an industrial park, and convention facilities, particularly the 1,500-seat Pioneer Theater Auditorium, and the 8,000-seat Centennial Coliseum. On the outskirts of town are ranches, with low-slung ranch houses.

In back of the brightly lit gambling houses and night clubs that line the city's main streets is the staid and eminently respectable main campus of the University of Nevada. The university is particularly proud of its Atmospherium and Planetarium, at the northern edge of the campus, which is equipped with specially developed time-lapse cameras to study how and why storms and other atmospheric phenomena occur.

Carson City, with a population of around 16,000, was the smallest state capital city in the United States until recent years. (Juneau,

Alaska, is now the smallest.) Set into the forested eastern foothills of the Sierra Nevada, its Victorian gingerbread houses give it a fairyland appearance. The oldest public buildings can easily be identified by their rough-hewn sandstone walls, weathered and mellowed to a grayish-buff color.

The capital was named for Kit Carson when it was first plotted in 1858, and became a supply center for the area's mining activities. It was built on the site of a trading post which had been in operation since 1851. In 1861 real-estate speculators and politicians of the western mining region combined to have the site named the territorial capital, and in 1864 the town became the state capital. Orion Clemens, the first territorial secretary, had as an assistant, his brother Samuel—who later changed his name to Mark Twain. For a description of frontier Nevada, Twain's *Roughing It* is one of the best.

An outstanding feature of Carson City is the Nevada State Museum, which has superb exhibits of the mining industry, of natural history, and Indian life. A full-scale replica of a mine has been constructed in the museum, demonstrating completely the functioning of a typical mine. Between 1870 and 1893 the building that houses the museum served as a United States mint.

Also in Carson City is the Nevada State Prison, which was the first prison in this country to use lethal gas chambers for criminals. One unique thing about the prison is the geological quality of its grounds—bones of prehistoric animals, such as mastodons, have been unearthed within its walls.

SPORTS AND RECREATION

The chief recreation in Nevada is gambling, and the majority of those who make Nevada their destination have it in mind to try their luck at the casinos or with the slot machines. Those slot machines are seldom out of sight, at airports, train and bus stations, restaurants, grocery stores, and gas stations. However, the real centers of gambling in Nevada are Las Vegas, Reno, and Lake Tahoe. (For a discussion of Las Vegas and Reno see the section on "Cities.")

There are plenty of nongambling activities in Nevada. For outdoor lovers there is a choice of campgrounds in desert country, beside alpine or desert lakes, and high in forested mountains. For that matter, you are welcome to make camp in isolated areas, and Nevada has plenty of those. The state's two national forests, Toiyabe National Forest and Humboldt National Forest, have between them nearly 5 million acres of spectacular scenery. And there are nine state parks, all with facilities for camping and picnicking.

Hunting for rocks and old bottles has grown to be a popular sport in Nevada. The rock hounds search for a wide variety of minerals and gems throughout the state, particularly turquoise. Bottle hunters seek antique treasures in the dumps of ghost towns and mining camps.

Boating, swimming, and water-skiing can be enjoyed on several big lakes. The best, with the most developed recreation areas, are Lake Mead and Lake Mohave in southern Nevada, and Lake Tahoe on the western border. Other popular lakes with water sport facilities are Pyramid, Walker, Lahontan, and Rye Patch, all in the western part of the state. Pyramid Lake, which lies northeast of Reno, is named for a large pyramidlike island which rises above its surface. There are also many other smaller islands on the large lake.

Nevada has two winter sports centers—in the Sierras near Lake Tahoe, and in southern Nevada in the Spring Mountains northwest of Las Vegas. Besides skiing at these places there are snowmobile concessions, plus good snowmobiling and snow hiking throughout the state. Lake Tahoe has the most ski resorts, most of which are concentrated northeast of the lake.

The alpine Lake Tahoe is renowned for its beauty. It is one of the deepest in the world—1,645 feet at its deepest point. A variety of activities can be enjoyed at the lake—camping, hiking, horseback riding, picnicking, boating, fishing, and water skiing, or golf and tennis at various resorts, plus night club entertainment and casinos.

The state's rivers, streams, and lakes have abundant stocks of channel catfish, crappie, bass, and trout. Hunting is good too, mule deer being the most common game. Antelope and elk hunting is restricted to residents, however. But there is plenty of small game like cottontails and jack rabbits. Quail, sage grouse, chukar partridge, pheasant, geese, and ducks are also hunted. The area around Fallon, in west-central Nevada, is supposed to be one of the largest duck-hunting regions in the country.

POINTS OF INTEREST

Nevada's ghost towns hold a particular fascination for visitors to the state, and exploring them has become a popular pastime. They are towns that were built quickly near the sites where gold or silver was discovered, and often they died just as quickly when the mines gave out.

The most famous of the ghost towns is Virginia City, which was a thriving, wealthy city in the 1860s and 1870s. It has been restored for tourism, complete with museums, souvenir shops, and special tours. Virginia City grew suddenly as the result of the discovery of the Comstock Lode, one of the richest deposits of gold and silver ever discovered. The state has gone to a good deal of effort to make the ghost town resemble its appearance in the boom days, when it was a mining metropolis and the second-largest city in the West.

Virginia City was renowned for having more than a hundred saloons, but it also had dozens of stores, four banks, six churches, and several newspapers. One of those newspapers was Nevada's first, the *Territorial Enterprise,* and two of America's most famous authors— Mark Twain (Samuel Clemens in those days) and Bret Harte— worked on its staff as reporters. C Street has a lot of buildings that used to be stores, boardinghouses, and saloons, and now serve as souvenir shops, restaurants, craft shops, and museums. Some of the old saloons are still serving as bars. The Territorial Enterprise Building is still standing, and near it is the Mark Twain Museum.

Another famous ghost town is Hamilton, in the west-central part of the state, a boomtown in the 1860s and 1870s; another, in southern Nevada, is the town of Rhyolite, which has a number of elaborate ruins as reminders of a prosperous past. Other ghost towns are found in many areas of the state.

Along the southern border of Nevada near the towns of Beatty and Rhyolite, a corner of the 3,000-square-mile Death Valley National Monument juts into the state. The monument, which contains a wealth of geological phenomena, lies mostly in the state of California.

Fans of *Bonanza,* of television fame, can visit the Cartwright family's Ponderosa Ranch. The sets used for the series have been transplanted to a hillside setting at the north end of Lake Tahoe. Included are an amusement park complete with a street of false-front buildings and a full-scale reproduction of the Cartwright ranch house.

Hoover Dam, near the town of Boulder City in the southeastern corner of the state, at 726 feet, is one of the highest dams in the world. By backing up the waters of the Colorado River the dam created Lake Mead, one of the largest artificial lakes in the Western Hemisphere, 110 miles long with a 550-mile shore line. The Lake Mead National Recreation Area, which extends 240 miles along the Colorado, includes Lake Mead and Lake Mohave. There are six major recreational centers on Lake Mead and four on Lake Mohave.

Among other outstanding Nevada attractions are the Liberty Copper Pit, six miles west of Ely in the east, one of the world's largest open pit mines; the Berlin-Ichthyosaur Paleontologic State Monument, at the town of Gabbs in western Nevada, which has fossils of enormous prehistoric marine reptiles that are over 150 million years old; and a huge exhibit of classic antique cars in the town of Sparks.

The Lehman Caves National Monument, in west-central Nevada, contains caverns famous for their colorfully decorated limestone formations. The large vaulted rooms have stalactites, stalagmites, and many strange and beautiful formations, with dominant colors of red, orange, brown, and white.

SPECIAL EVENTS

The city of Reno knows how to put on a good show. One of the most exciting is in September when the Reno-Stead Airport is the scene of the annual Reno National Championship Air Races. Ex-fighter planes compete in pylon racing at speeds of nearly 450 miles an hour. There are also competitions in other categories, such as sport biplanes, plus aerobatics, sky-diving, formation flying, and hot-air balloon ascensions.

Also in September Reno hosts the Nevada State Fair, with agricultural, industrial, art, and other exhibits, plus a midway. In June the city has a rodeo, with top riders and cowboys from the United States and Canada competing for prize money, plus Indian ceremonial dancing and arts and crafts exhibits.

The biggest time of the year in Las Vegas is the celebration known as Helldorado, which takes place for several days in May. During this event, which has been held since 1935, citizens are encouraged to wear Western garb to enjoy the rodeos, the beauty contest, and the carnival attractions.

Also in the spring in Las Vegas is the Mint 400, a 400-mile off-road auto race in which drivers compete against rugged desert terrain as well as one another. And each fall, the Sahara Invitational Golf Tournament draws some of the top golfers to Las Vegas to compete for the $111,111.11 prize money.

Some other outstanding events in the state are the Nevada Rodeo and Fair at Winnemucca on Labor Day, one of the best rodeos in the West; the Nevada Day Celebration in Carson City on October 31, a pageant commemorating the state's admission to the Union; the National Basque Festival in Elko in July, which features sheep shearing, wood chopping, and other contests of skill and strength, plus a lot of colorful dancing; the World Championship Wild Burro Races in Beatty on Labor Day weekend; in August, Pony Express Days in Ely, and a Wagon Train Race from Placerville, California, to Lake Tahoe in Nevada; and, in September, a Lion's Stampede and 49er Show and a Kiwanis Chuck Wagon Breakfast in Fallon.

N.C.

CHRONOLOGY

1826   Explorer and fur trader Jedediah Smith led an expedition across southern Nevada.

1833–34   Humboldt River route across Nevada explored by Joseph Walker.

1843–45   John C. Frémont and Kit Carson explored Great Basin and Sierra Nevada.

1848   Treaty of Guadalupe Hidalgo gave Nevada and other southwestern land to United States.

1849   Mormon Station (called Genoa after 1855) became first non-Indian settlement in Nevada.

1859   Comstock Lode of silver discovered, bringing rush of prospectors to western Nevada; Virginia City settled.

1861   Territory of Nevada created.

Transcontinental telegraph completed, ending Pony Express which had begun in 1860.

1864   Nevada became the thirty-sixth state on October 31.

1877–81   Price of silver fell, causing many Nevada mines to close; also, many mines became exhausted of ore.

1880–90   Nevada's population dropped by about 15,000 as unemployed persons left.

1909   Nevada legislature passed laws making gambling illegal.

1931   State legalized gambling and reduced state residency requirement for divorce to six weeks.

1936   Boulder (now Hoover) Dam completed.

1951   U. S. Atomic Energy Commission began atomic testing in southern Nevada at Yucca Flat.

1963   Statewide Intertribal Council established by Nevada's Indians.

U. S. Supreme Court settled forty-year dispute by specifying how much water the states of Arizona, California, and Nevada could draw from the Colorado River.

1967   Nevada legislature changed state gambling laws to allow corporations that sell stock to the public to buy casinos and to hold gambling licenses.

1973 National Governors' Conference held at Lake Tahoe.

State Department of Human Resources and Nevada Indian Advisory Committee for Indian Education created.

1976 For the Bicentennial year, plans were underway in Las Vegas for an 800-seat Cultural Arts Center.

1978 Gamblers spent a record $1.3 billion at Nevada's casinos, gross revenues that were 21.5 per cent higher than in 1977.

1979 Claiming that the companies which sold it had overemphasized its merits, Nevada became the first state to repeal its no-fault auto insurance law, enacted five years earlier. Studies showed that the rates for the policies had gone up faster than the cost of living.

UTAH

ON JULY 24, 1847, in a mountain pass near the eastern edge of the Great Salt Lake Basin, Brigham Young, too ill to walk, was helped from his wagon to look at the land. Beyond the foothills below him he saw the beginning of one of the most desolate desert regions of the Southwest. He had led his Mormon followers across nearly half the American continent just to find this land.

"This is the place," Brigham Young said, a phrase that is now etched on a monument at that very mountain pass. It certainly did not look like "the place" to any of the other explorers who had passed that way, for that great barren valley with its dead inland sea did not seem a fit place for human habitation. But then that is just the reason Young and the Mormons sought it out, for they wanted to find a land thought to be so worthless that no one but other Mormons would come there, and they would thus be able to protect themselves from the violence they had known everywhere else.

Young was the spiritual leader of the Mormons—the Church of Jesus Christ of Latter-day Saints. The church's founder, Joseph Smith, had been murdered in the Mormons' former home of Nauvoo, Illinois. For a number of reasons, including their insularity and their polygamous marriages, the Mormons had been persecuted in Fayette, New York, where their church was founded in 1830, in Far West and Independence, Missouri, in Illinois, and in Omaha, Nebraska. Utah seemed just the place for them to get away from it all.

Despite predictions of disaster, the Mormons, in an incredible example of determination, industriousness, and ingenuity, made that barren land where they settled fertile and livable. They planned and built a beautiful city by Great Salt Lake, and began a prosperous agricultural enterprise through extensive irrigation. By using the same technique of irrigation they also established other successful colonies all over Utah.

For many decades the Mormons dominated the religious, economic, and social life of Utah. Non-Mormons also began to settle there, inevitably leading to the kind of conflicts—mostly religious persecution resulting from their practice of polygamy—the Mormons had sought to escape. But the Mormons continued for many years to dominate, politically and economically, until pressures from "Gentiles"—all who were not of the Mormon faith—and the United States Government lessened their power. In the twentieth century the Mormons have not "dominated" Utah, but they have been the single most influential force in shaping the character of the state.

There were Indians living in Utah before the Mormons came. The largest tribe was that of the Utes, and it is after them that the state is named. Utah is large, covering 82,096 square miles, ranking it eleventh in size in the nation. It is nicknamed the Beehive State, which is fitting: The Mormons called their land "Deseret," their word for honeybee, standing for hard work and industry, and "Industry" is the state's motto.

THE LAND

The three principal topographic regions of Utah provide an unusual variety of land forms.

The Rocky Mountains region has two ranges: the Wasatch Range, which runs north and south and splits the state in two; and the Uinta Mountains, a topographical oddity because it is the only major range of the Rockies that runs east and west. The Uinta Mountains form an angle in the northeast corner of the state with the Wasatch Range. Along the western side of the Wasatch Range is a series of valleys and plateaus called the Wasatch Front, which contains the bulk of the state's population and most of its major cities.

The western third of Utah is part of the Basin and Range Region, which covers areas of several states and is one of the driest regions in the country. This section in Utah is mostly desert land, interrupted by short mountain ranges. Great Salt Lake is in the northeastern part of this region. It is seventy-five miles long and twenty-five miles wide, but its deepest point is only twenty-eight feet. The lake's salt content averages around 25 per cent, making it six times as salty as any of the oceans. West and southwest of the lake is the Great Salt Lake Desert, covering around 4,000 square miles of flat salt beds as hard

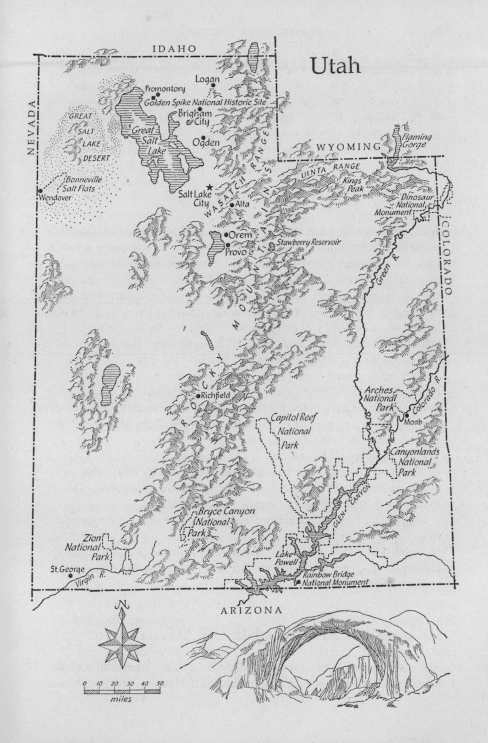

Utah

IDAHO

NEVADA

Logan

Promontory
Golden Spike National Historic Site

GREAT
SALT
LAKE
DESERT

Brigham
City

Great
Salt
Lake

Ogden

WYOMING

Flaming
Gorge

UINTA RANGE

Kings
Peak

Bonneville
Salt Flats
Wendover

Salt Lake
City

Alta

WASATCH

Strawberry Reservoir

Dinosaur
National
Monument

COLORADO

Orem
Provo

Green R.

ROCKY

Richfield

MOUNTAINS

Capitol Reef
National
Park

Arches
National
Park

Colorado R.

Moab

Canyonlands
National
Park

GLEN CANYON

Bryce Canyon
National
Park

Zion
National
Park

St. George

Virgin R.

Lake
Powell

Rainbow Bridge
National Monument

ARIZONA

N

0 10 20 30 40 50
miles

as concrete. It is here that the Bonneville Salt Flats, famous for land speed racing, is located.

South of the Uinta Mountains and covering the eastern half of Utah is the Colorado Plateau, an area of broad, rough uplands cut by deep, brilliantly colored canyons. The region is remarkable for its fiery, intricately carved natural bridges, arches, and other natural wonders that are the result of eons of erosion.

CLIMATE

Although Utah is generally an arid state, it does have considerable variations in its climate. In the desert regions, which cover about a third of the state, there is extremely dry heat, but in the northern mountainous areas there are severe cold winters and mild summers.

One thing the state has is plenty of sunshine, about 180 days' worth. But because of the low humidity, temperatures even on the hottest summer days will drop 20 to 30 degrees during the night. For instance, on any given July day in Salt Lake City, the thermometer may reach 90 degrees, and that night drop into the 60s.

Average seasonal temperatures illustrate the wide variations between the northeast part of the state and the southwest: for July the average is 60 degrees in the northeast and 84 degrees in the southwest; January is an average 20 degrees in the north, compared to 39 degrees in the southwest.

Utah's mostly arid condition is the result of the mountain systems of the West diverting much of the precipitation. Yearly averages of moisture vary from less than five inches in the Great Salt Lake Desert to up to fifty inches in the northeast, in the mountains.

Despite its aridness, there are sections of the state that get some rather spectacular snowfalls. For instance, the skiing region of Alta, near Salt Lake City, gets over four hundred inches of snow annually. However, the southwest part of the state gets very little snow each year, only a few inches.

THE PEOPLE OF UTAH

The single greatest influence on the character and composition of the people of Utah has been provided by the Mormons. They were the first to settle permanently this generally arid state that no one else seemed to want, made a great success of their first settlement, Salt Lake City, and then spread dozens more colonies all around the state. Today, Mormons still predominate numerically, composing about 70 per cent of Utah's approximately 1,146,000 residents.

In the centuries before the Mormons came in 1847, Utah was populated by small groups of Indians, primitive desert cultures like the Paiute, Gosiute, and Ute, who are classed as Shoshonean Indians. When white men first began entering Utah in the late eighteenth and early nineteenth centuries, they encountered tribes of the Shoshonean. Not much is known about the area in those earlier times, but it is presumed that the Shoshonean had lived there from about A.D. 400. Archaeological evidence indicates that from about 10,000 B.C. to A.D. 400 the area was inhabited by a Stone Age culture.

There are still a good many Indians in Utah—some are descended from the older, more primitive cultures, such as the Utes, who number about two thousand. Most of the others are from later tribes—the Navahos, who live in the Four Corners region of southeastern Utah, have the biggest tribe. Altogether, the Indians comprise the largest of Utah's minority groups, which include small numbers of blacks, Japanese, and Chinese. Most of the state's people, at least 97 per cent, are whites of predominantly northern European background.

Because there are so many wide-open arid regions in Utah, most of the state's residents—about 80 per cent—are clustered in urban areas. The majority of them live in the two chief metropolitan areas, Salt Lake City–Ogden and Provo–Orem.

Religious affiliation, as would be expected, is primarily Mormon, and about 70 per cent of Utah's citizens belong to that church. Most of the other church members are Roman Catholics or Protestants.

HISTORY

From the white man's point of view Utah's history is brief. From the Indian's point of view it is ancient, for there is evidence that certain tribes, such as the Paiute, Gosiute, and Ute, had inhabited the region that is now Utah since around the fifth century A.D. But those tribes were fairly primitive, being primarily desert wanderers who established no permanent settlements and left no written records.

Not until late in the eighteenth century did anyone from the outside world have a good enough look at Utah to write about it. The first were two Franciscan friars, Silvestre Vélez de Escalante and Francisco Atanasio Domínguez, whose accounts of their explorations were not encouraging, for they found the land mostly arid. Other Spaniards followed them, to trade with the Indians, but they did not stay.

It was the search for furs that finally prompted the first really extensive explorations of the Utah region. Between 1820 and 1840 fur trappers began going into Utah in ever increasing numbers, stalking the plentiful game that had been virtually untouched. Jim Bridger, a man who became famous for explorations in many areas of the Southwest, was one of those trappers. He is believed to have been the first white man to set eyes upon Great Salt Lake, which he reached in 1824.

Another of the famous "mountain men," as they were called, was Jedediah Smith, whose explorations were much more extensive than those of Bridger. Smith traversed the state from north to south and east to west. After Smith and Bridger, the United States Government sent forth official expeditions, the first led by Captain Benjamin Bonneville, in the mid-1830s. In the following decade John Frémont led official scientific expeditions to Utah to report on the landscape, the fauna and flora.

The opinion of Bridger and Smith and some of the other explorers was that Utah was good for game and trapping fur, but was barely livable as far as permanent settlements were concerned. The Mormons proved the mountain men wrong. The fact that Utah was land that no one else seemed to want was what attracted the Mormons. They had suffered religious persecution and violence in all of their homes since their founding in New York in 1830, and they were seeking a haven where no one would follow. From New York they had moved to Ohio, Missouri, and Illinois, experiencing the same persecution in each settlement. After their founding prophet, Joseph Smith, was murdered in Nauvoo, Illinois, in 1846, they began moving west.

The Mormons—the Church of Jesus Christ of Latter-day Saints—were led west by Brigham Young, who had assumed leadership of the church after Smith's death. Young and his followers arrived in the Great Salt Lake area in 1847, took one look at that nearly desolate land, and decided that "this is the place," a quote that has become legendary in their history.

The Mormons made the arid land livable and productive through irrigation, perseverance, and hard work. They were threatened with disaster in 1848 when great clouds of grasshoppers descended upon their fields. The settlers were helpless against the insects, but before their crops were destroyed great numbers of sea gulls swept in from Great Salt Lake and feasted on the grasshoppers. The sea gull is highly respected in Utah to this day, and a sea gull monument has been erected in Salt Lake City.

Between their first year in Utah and 1860 the Mormons founded 150 self-sustaining irrigated colonies all around the state. Their colonizing efforts were aided by the Perpetual Emigrating Fund, established in 1849, which provided money for Mormons who wanted to settle in Utah from other regions. Over a forty-year period the fund brought about 50,000 Mormons to the state from other parts of America and from such foreign countries as England, Scotland, Wales, Sweden, Norway, and Denmark.

Utah still belonged to Mexico when the Mormons came there in 1847, but in 1848, after the end of the war with Mexico, the United States acquired the region. That gave the Mormons the political freedom to found their own state, which they did in 1849, naming it Deseret. After Brigham Young was elected governor the State of Deseret requested admittance to the Union, but was turned down.

About the time the United States created Utah Territory in 1850, the Mormons began having serious trouble from two sources: the Indians and the "Gentiles" (the Mormon designation for anyone not of their faith) who had begun moving into Utah after they saw the success the Mormons were having with the formerly unsettled region. The Indian wars were mostly with the Utes, who resented the settlers, and the conflicts cost the Mormons lives and millions of dollars in property loss. Warring with the Indians did not end until 1867, when most of the Utes were persuaded to settle on a reservation in the Uinta Basin. The troubles with the "Gentiles" arose from what the non-Mormons claimed were the Mormons' political tyranny, their economic and social clannishness, and their practice of polygamy. The Gentiles felt frozen out by the Mormons' system and began to launch political attacks against their government and their church policies. Occasionally, the clashing of these two forces was violent, the very thing the Mormons had come there to escape.

Each time the Mormons applied for statehood they were refused on the basis of their sanction of polygamy, although a minority of

Mormon men had more than one wife. President James Buchanan wanted to take control of the territory away from the Mormons, and in 1857 he replaced Brigham Young as governor, sending federal troops to enforce the change. This period was known as the Mormon War, although little actual fighting occurred. The Mormons resented the U. S. Army's presence, but their resistance was minimal—however, the troops remained in Utah until they were forced to leave by the outbreak of the Civil War in 1861.

Congress passed a law against polygamy in 1862, but the Mormons refused to recognize it, and their refusal went unheeded for some years. But in the 1880s the federal courts began enforcing the law, and hundreds of Mormons were fined and sent to prison. Then the government came down hard on them—an 1887 law allowed the U. S. Government to seize church property of the Mormons for use by public schools. It was all too much for the Mormons, who realized further resistance was futile. In 1890 they officially prohibited polygamy among their own people.

Five years later the Mormons submitted a constitution to Congress that outlawed polygamy and prevented control of the state by any church. This time Utah was accepted, and became the forty-fifth state on January 4, 1896.

After the turn of the century Utah's prosperity increased, mostly as the result of railroad expansion that opened new markets for the state's farm and mining products. The first transcontinental railroad had been completed in 1869, when the Central Pacific Railroad and the Union Pacific lines met at Promontory, Utah.

Copper production increased greatly, as did the supplies of other nonferrous metals, and beef cattle and sheep became important state products. The state's prosperity increased steadily until the depression in the thirties, when Utah was hard hit, in mining and farming, ending up with one of the nation's highest unemployment rates. World War II brought renewed manufacturing and mining prosperity, and during the 1950s and 1960s the state changed from a basically agricultural to an industrial state.

For many years now, Mormons and Gentiles have lived peacefully side by side—the old days of misunderstanding and hostility are long gone. But Utah still faces some rather large economic problems. Some of the fiscal problems stem from Utahans' heavy spending on the school system, a result of the Mormons' emphasis on education as one of the most vital aspects of their lives. Today, the state is heavily dependent on federal aid, and the United States Government owns and administers about 70 per cent of the state's farm lands, forests, and mines.

INDUSTRY

Utah's industrial development has been dynamic in several areas, but probably the most dramatic development was the state's entry into production of parts and fuels for defense missiles. This defense-related industry did not get going on an important scale until 1957, and by the 1960s it had grown to the point that it was competing with Utah's two other important industries—production of primary metals and food processing. But the production of parts and fuels for missiles—and the related important industry of producing transportation equipment—were never to supersede metals and food processing, for in the late 1960s missile production began to decline. But this still remains an important part of the state's economy.

Primary metals production began with a steel plant built to supply World War II demands, and has expanded to a substantial steel-fabricating industry. Utah's metals plants smelt, refine, and roll metals, and also turn out basic products such as castings. Coke, pig iron, and steel are processed in the Provo area; uranium and potash are processed in the Moab area; and copper and lead are refined in Salt Lake City.

The manufacturing industries mentioned above, plus the manufacture of nonelectrical machinery, electrical equipment, fabricated metal products, the printing and publishing industries, and a long list of light industrial enterprises account for about half the value of goods produced in Utah.

Utah's industrial workers have been raised, for the most part, in the Mormon tradition of hard, well-disciplined work—consequently, the state's productivity per man hour is quite high.

The state's sunny climate, its many areas of natural beauty, and its attractive towns and cities have spurred the growth of two other industries—tourism and movie making. The state is now actively promoting tourism, and the number of visitors enjoying Utah's recreational facilities is increasing each year. There have been over sixty films shot in Utah, mostly in the eastern and southern sections of the state.

AGRICULTURE

There are 52.7 million acres in Utah but a sizable proportion of that acreage is taken up by mountains or by terrain with too high an elevation for farming. Poor types of soils and low annual precipitation eliminate a majority of the remaining acreage—consequently, only about 10 per cent of the state's land is considered arable.

One way of judging Utah's agricultural status is to look at the 1975 figures for the United States—Utah came in fortieth among the fifty states in total farm receipts. And the majority of that income—about 80 per cent—came from livestock and livestock products. The remaining income came from crops grown by irrigated farming and dry-land farming.

Cattle and calves are the foremost products of Utah's farms, but it is also a top sheep-raising and wool-producing state. Other important products are milk, hogs, turkeys, and eggs.

As for crop farming, about a million of the state's acres are irrigated by water from reservoirs, while another million and a half acres are made productive with the dry-farming method. The main crops are hay (which earns a hefty $10 million a year), wheat, and sugar beets, in the top three categories, followed in importance by such crops as apples, barley, cherries, greenhouse and nursery products, potatoes, and tomatoes.

NATURAL RESOURCES

Utah's mineral wealth makes up in large measure for its somewhat deficient agricultural resources. Around two hundred different minerals have been identified in the state and thirty-eight of those are mined commercially, giving Utah a ranking of fifteenth in the nation in 1970 in mineral production.

Copper is by far the principal mineral in Utah, accounting for more than half of the state's mineral production, and only Arizona produces more copper. One copper mine has even become a major tourist attraction because of its immensity—the Bingham Canyon Copper Mine, located twenty-seven miles southwest of Salt Lake

City. The largest open-pit copper mine in the country, it is two and a half miles wide and a half mile deep, and since 1904 it has produced about 9 million tons of copper.

The second most valuable mineral is petroleum, which, along with natural gas, began to be produced in significant amounts after World War II. The state is a major producer of coal west of the Mississippi, and Utah is the producer of uintaite, a form of solidified petroleum, which is a source of road oil, paving binder, and asphalt tile. Utah is also the country's top producer of beryllium ore and is among the top four states in production of gold, silver, lead, and molybdenum.

Utah also produces great quantities of magnesium, which is taken from Great Salt Lake; until recent years only salt was extracted from the lake, but beginning in the early 1970s plants were built to take magnesium and other minerals from the lake. The state also experienced a uranium boom after World War II with the discovery of extensive deposits in the southeastern part of the state. The mining of Utah's minerals amounts to about a third of the value of goods produced in the state.

CITIES

Salt Lake City, capital of Utah, is generally regarded as one of the most beautiful cities in the nation, the result of careful planning by its founders, the pioneer settlers of the Church of Jesus Christ of Latter-day Saints, commonly called Mormons, who came there in 1847.

Today, with a population of over 176,000 living in the city proper, or over 557,000 in the metropolitan district, Salt Lake City is by far the largest city in the state and one of the largest in the vast Intermountain Region of the western United States. It is the ecclesiastic center of the Mormons, a world-wide religious denomination; a nucleus of industrial and commercial activity, whose influence extends far beyond the local region; and an outstanding tourist center.

Modern skyscrapers are boosting the skyline of the city, but the copper-domed capitol still stands high above them all on a northern slope formed eons ago by the pounding waves of Lake Bonneville, a prehistoric lake that once covered the whole area. The city has a particularly dramatic setting: The Wasatch Range, snow-capped for eight months of the year, bends like a protective arm around the eastern borders of the city; the smaller Oquirrh Range rises to the southwest; and to the northwest, miniature ranges rise on the islands of Great Salt Lake.

Any visitor to Salt Lake City can have the experience of viewing almost unrivaled municipal beauty by taking the time for some casual strolling. The best place to start is Temple Square, the world center of Mormonism, which contains the Mormon Temple, the Tabernacle, the Bureau of Information, the Assembly Hall, the Visitor's Center, the Seagull Monument, the oldest house in the city, and bronze statues of Joseph and Hyrum Smith.

The Temple, which is built of solid gray granite blocks, was begun in 1853 and completed in 1893, costing $4 million. It has six spires rising to 212 feet. The Temple is not for worship or services, but for sacred ordinances such as baptism and marriage.

The Tabernacle, an enormous oval shell, has one of the largest domed roofs and unsupported arches in the world: The roof is seventy feet high in the center. The building is especially known for its remarkable acoustics—a favorite demonstration is the dropping of a pin, which can be heard about two hundred feet distant at the back of the Tabernacle. The building can seat eight thousand people to hear its famous organ and the recitals by the renowned Mormon Tabernacle Choir.

Two places that visitors should not miss are the Hansen Planetarium and the Salt Palace. The planetarium includes the one-hour "Star Chamber" shows, which take the audience on realistic trips into the solar system by means of the planetarium's space transit projector. The Salt Palace, which occupies a two-block area near Temple Square, is the city's convention and sports center and civic auditorium.

Salt Lake City is also the home of the University of Utah, the oldest state university west of the Missouri River, founded in 1850. It contains almost two hundred buildings on 1,168 acres. The campus has some outstanding museums and art center: the Museum of Natural History, which traces Utah history, among other exhibits; the Utah Museum of Fine Arts; and the Salt Lake City Art Center.

Ogden, settled by the Mormons in 1850, is now Utah's second-largest city, with a population of over 69,000. For many years it has been a vital railroad center, and it has been an industrial focal point ever since the first railroad line came to the town in March 1869. Nowadays it is an intermountain rail junction, a livestock and agricultural distribution center, and the home of the western Internal

Revenue Service center. It is also the home of Defense Depot Ogden and the Hill Air Force Base.

Ogden has a fine science museum, with a planetarium; it also has the John M. Browning Museum, which exhibits a large collection of Browning's original gun models. And it is also the home of Weber State College, which spreads across nearly 300 acres at the foot of the Wasatch Range; it was founded in 1889 as Weber Academy.

The city of **Provo,** south of Salt Lake City, is important for the production of steel, pig iron, and foundry products. This third largest of the state's cities, with a population of over 53,000, is situated in an area of outstanding natural beauty in the center of the Utah Valley at an elevation of 4,549 feet; it lies between a dramatic background of mountains and Utah Lake, the largest natural fresh-water lake in the state.

Brigham Young University, the world's largest private college, is located in Provo, and it is the city's center for music, art, theater, and many community activities. It was founded by Brigham Young in 1875 to train teachers for Utah schools and became a university in 1903. Mormons make up around 95 per cent of its student body.

Some exciting scenic attractions are near Provo, particularly American Fork and Provo canyons. There is a road that links these two canyons and circles Mount Timpanogos, which at 11,750 feet is the second-highest mountain in the Wasatch Range. The road is called the Alpine Scenic Loop and provides a traveler with some un-forgettable views.

Logan, which lies north of Ogden in the fertile Cache Valley be-tween the snow-capped peaks of the Wasatch Mountains, is Utah's fourth-largest city, with a population of over 23,000. One of the most beautiful temples of the Mormon Church is located here, overlooking town and valley. More than 9,000 students are enrolled in Utah State University in Logan; strong in engineering, agriculture, and forest sci-ences, the school offers both master's and doctor's degrees.

SPORTS AND RECREATION

Utah is famous for a good many things, and among them—as any re-ally serious fisherman can avow—is its fishing. And it is particularly known for the sport of casting for rainbow trout. The general season runs from the Saturday closest to June 1 through November, although about two hundred bodies of water are open all year round. Besides the mountain streams and swift-running rivers and a number of natural lakes, there are two large man-made lakes providing some spectacular sport for anglers—Flaming Gorge in northeastern Utah, and Lake Powell in the south-central part of the state.

Hunting is tops in Utah's many wilderness areas, where hunters go for deer, elk, antelope, jack rabbit, badger, woodchuck, gopher, quail, pheasant, chukar partridge, duck, and geese. Deer hunting is the most popular, and attracts sportsmen from all over the West. The season opens in mid-October.

One of the fastest-growing sports in Utah is "river running," which can be rough, but for pure thrill and adventure the sport can't be beat. The runs are made on large, unsinkable rubber rafts through the rough waters of the San Juan, Green, and Colorado rivers. Charter arrangements can be made at Moab, Green River, Bluff, and Mexican Hat.

There are plenty of mountains in Utah and plenty of snow; consequently, there is opportunity for a good deal of skiing, at fourteen different ski resorts.

Campers, picnickers, and hikers will have a fine time in Utah, for there are about three hundred developed areas for camping and picnicking, and hundreds of miles of trails for hikers through every sort of landscape, ranging from pleasant jaunts for the casual walker to the most rugged treks for the experienced adventurer. One of the best is the twenty-mile hike through Zion National Park's Virgin Narrows.

POINTS OF INTEREST

Zion National Park is considered to be the most beautiful section of Utah's Color Country. It covers 230 square miles, and its main feature is Zion Canyon, a spectacular multicolored gorge. The Zion Canyon Scenic Drive, a paved road, follows the North Fork of the Virgin River for seven and a half miles from the Visitor Center into Zion Canyon. Along this road visitors can see many of Zion's most majestic peaks. There are also more than 150 miles of trails which wind through the grassy canyon draws (a gully or ravine) and climb to high rocky rims within the park. The trails vary from casual strolls to rugged treks.

Arches National Park, in southeastern Utah, features natural rock spans formed by centuries of erosion. It covers 73,234 acres of rugged country. Bryce Canyon National Park, in the southwestern part of the state, is a 36,000-acre area of vast canyons of vividly colored spires and pinnacles, which have been eroded over the centuries into a myriad of shapes. There are twenty miles of roads among Bryce's brilliantly painted formations, and a series of fine trails.

A visitor can get a good geology lesson in Capitol Reef National Park, in south-central Utah. The 241,671-acre park was named after the white domes of Navaho sandstone—reminiscent of capitol domes —that jut from the top of the walls of the reef. The reef is a formation of sedimentary sandstone and shales that thrusts upward 1,500 feet. The various layers of these cliffs, which are beautifully multicolored, reveal the geologic evolution of the area. Navahos called these formations "sleeping rainbows."

Dinosaur National Monument covers about 325 square miles in Utah and Colorado—the Utah section is in the northeastern corner of the state. Within the monument are the most remarkable dinosaur fossils ever found. Dinosaur Quarry Visitor Center allows tourists to inspect fossils where they were discovered in the ground.

The Rainbow Bridge National Monument, in the southeastern part of the state, contains a natural arch of eroded sandstone that spans 278 feet and is 309 feet high. The name comes from its beautifully curved shape, like a rainbow, and from the red glow of its sandstone. For many years it was accessible only by a thirteen-mile journey on foot or horseback, but now there is a marina for mooring boats nearby. From the marina to the bridge is a hike of less than a mile.

SPECIAL EVENTS

Salt Lake City has three of the most popular events during July, August, and September: Days of '47, a time of parades and pageants commemorating the arrival of the Mormons in July 1847, is held July 15–24; the Utah State Fair in mid-September is ten days of livestock and agricultural shows, 4-H and Future Farmers of America competitions, entertainment by top performers, and an ice show that draws about 300,000 people; "Promised Valley," a dramatic re-enactment of the Mormon emigration, is presented every night except Sunday during July and August in an outdoor 2,000-seat theater.

Also in Salt Lake City are three outstanding Christmas performances: Handel's *Messiah* is presented free in the Tabernacle by the Salt Lake Oratorio Society on the Sunday before Christmas; *Amahl and the Night Visitors* by Menotti is performed at the Tabernacle by the University Opera Company the week before Christmas; and the *Nutcracker* is staged December 26–30 by Ballet West and the Utah Symphony Orchestra.

The ceremony of the "Driving of the Golden Spike" is re-enacted daily from Memorial Day to Labor Day at the Golden Spike Historical Site thirty-two miles west of Brigham City. The actual driving of the Golden Spike occurred on May 10, 1869, marking the joining of the Central and Union Pacific railroads, the nation's first transcontinental railway.

North of Salt Lake City, the town of Ogden has a Pioneer Days celebration in mid-July, with rodeos and a parade. Southeast of Salt Lake City, the town of Alta has some exciting skiing events every year, such as the national Gelande Contest, a ski-jumping competition, and the Snow Cup in March.

Memorial Day weekend marks the beginning of the Motorboat Marathon, a rugged 196-mile race down the Green River and up the Colorado River to the town of Moab.

In August, race car drivers from all over the world test their cars across the hard salt surface of the Bonneville race track, during the Bonneville National speed trials at the town of Wendover.

N.C.

CHRONOLOGY

1776   Two Spanish Franciscan friars made first far-reaching exploration of region that is now Utah.

1824–25   Jim Bridger visited Great Salt Lake, probably the first white man to do so.

1847   Mormon pioneer settlers, led by Brigham Young, arrived in Great Salt Lake region.

1848   United States won Utah area from Mexico.

1849   State of Deseret created by the Mormons.

1850   United States created Utah Territory.

1860–61   Pony Express crossed Utah.

1861   Telegraph lines met at Salt Lake City, providing first transcontinental telegraph service.

1869   First transcontinental railway completed at Promontory.

1890   Utah Mormons prohibited polygamy.

1896   Utah became forty-fifth state on January 4.

1913   State's first large reclamation project completed, called the Strawberry River Reservoir.

1952   Rich uranium deposits discovered near Moab.

1964   Flaming Gorge and Glen Canyon dams completed.

1967   Central Utah Project began, a program to provide water for state's principal growth areas.

1974   Oil companies invested millions of dollars to lease federally owned oil-shale land in Utah.

1976   For the nation's Bicentennial, Salt Lake City planned to plant one million trees for its one million population.

1979   Potential development of the coal-rich Kaiparowits Plateau in the southern part of the state became a source of controversy between environmentalists and energy companies. The coal lies beneath Indian reservations, archaeological sites, and national forests and parks.

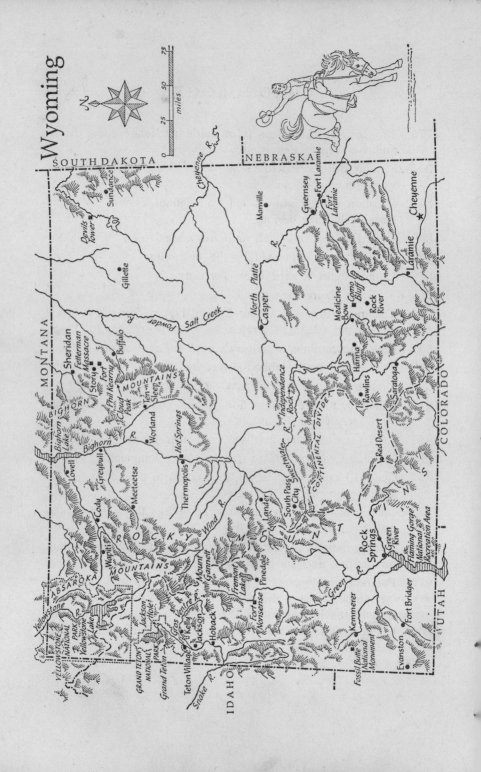

Wyoming

N

miles
0 25 50 75

SOUTH DAKOTA
NEBRASKA
MONTANA
COLORADO
UTAH
IDAHO

Sundance
Devils Tower
Gillette

Cheyenne R.

Manville
Guernsey
Fort Laramie
Fort Laramie
Cheyenne
Laramie

North Platte R.
Casper
Salt Creek
Powder R.

Sheridan
Fetterman
Massacre
Story
Fort Phil Kearny
Buffalo
BIGHORN MOUNTAINS
Cloud Peak
Ten Sleep
Bighorn Lake

Medicine Bow
Camp Bluff
Rock River
Hanna
Saratoga
Rawlins
Red Desert

Lovell
Greybull
Bighorn R.
Worland
Hot Springs
Thermopolis
Meeteetse
Cody
Wapiti
Wind R.
Bighorn R.

Independence Rock
South Pass City
Sweetwater R.
Lander
CONTINENTAL DIVIDE
S A N T A

ROCKY MOUNTAINS
ABSAROKA
Yellowstone R.
YELLOWSTONE NATIONAL PARK
Yellowstone Lake
GRAND TETON NATIONAL PARK
Grand Teton
Jackson Hole
Jackson Lake
Gros Ventre R.
Teton Village
Kelly
Jackson
Hoback
Snake R.
Mount Gannett
Fremont Lake
Pinedale
Fort Nonsense

Green R.
Rock Springs
Green River
Flaming Gorge National Recreation Area
Fort Bridger

Kemmerer
Fossil Butte National Monument
Evanston

WYOMING

WYOMING, though keeping pace in modern development, education, and culture, still remains the most truly "romantically" western of all our states.

Aromatic sage dots the hills. Tumbleweed rolls across lonesome roads. Mountains hump across almost two thirds of its land. In no other state are stores stocked as heavily with western gear. Saddles, leather belts, chaps, and lariats are still custom-made to suit the whims of cowboys and ranchers. Informality is the keynote. On Saturday nights, just as in years past, the cowboy comes to town to "whoop it up," although he'll come by car rather than horseback. Yet horses are much in evidence, since, summer long, a rodeo is going on some place. If one is to keep peace with the natives, it had better be pronounced "ro-dee-oh."

Ranches are so large that some are measured in sections rather than acres, and operations are much as they have always been. Cattle are still branded in the spring and driven by shouting cowboys to grazing lands. In summer, some ranchers make extra income from "paying dudes": city folks who want a genuine western experience. They get it. Even to joining the ranch family and hired help at meals of thick steaks and hot homemade bread and pastries.

Wyoming has long been known for its rugged mountains, thermal wonders, valleys, and wide-open spaces. Its population of 374,000 scattered over 97,914 square miles ranks it last among states in number of residents. Density is 3.7 people per square mile. The census reveals there are far more cattle and sheep in Wyoming than people! In size, it is ninth—smaller than Colorado, but three times the size of Ireland.

When Wyoming became a state in 1890, its population of 62,500 was not enough to qualify it for statehood, and it took some political maneuvering to get this accomplished. It is amazing that the state has only two cities with populations in the 30,000 and 40,000 range: Casper and Cheyenne, its capital. Perhaps it is this freedom of space, this lack of crowdedness, that has contributed most to making the people of Wyoming independent thinkers, unwilling to compromise when they believe they are in the right. It has also made them strong and self-sufficient, but with close ties with one another.

The state is often referred to as the Equality State. No state deserves this title more, for it was the people of Wyoming who had the foresight to enact the country's first woman suffrage act, and elect the first woman governor in the nation, Mrs. Nellie Tayloe Ross, who later became the first woman director of the U. S. Mint. Furthermore, they established the country's first successful county library system, and opened their own university at Laramie in 1887, so their young people need not leave the state in order to obtain higher learning. Since then, the state has added seven two-year colleges.

The name "Wyoming" was first given to a valley in Pennsylvania by the Delaware Indians. Translated, it means "large plains" or "end of plains," an apt description for one of Wyoming's outstanding topographic features. That is probably why James Ashley, early fur trader, suggested it for this rectangular state (then a territory), hemmed in by Montana on the north, Idaho and Utah on the west, Colorado and Utah on the south, and South Dakota and Nebraska on the east. Local Indians are responsible for the names of numerous Wyoming towns. For instance, Ten Sleep in the Big Horn Mountains was "ten sleeps" between camps. Other examples are Meeteetse, Medicine Bow, Greybull, and Sundance.

Wyoming has ten lovely state parks, two national parks (Grand Teton and Yellowstone, the latter the nation's first national park), two national monuments (Devils Tower being the country's first monument), two national recreation areas, and one Indian reservation, the Wind River. The largest Girl Scout encampment in the world is east of Ten Sleep.

Spring brings to this western state the promise of mountain meadows brilliant with wildflowers, especially Indian paintbrush, the official state flower. Winter brings glittering snowscapes, flocked trees, and frozen lakes.

John Gunther in his book *Inside U.S.A.* saw Wyoming as "America, high, naked and exposed . . . the friendliest state and the most unspoiled."

THE LAND

The natural setting of Wyoming is one of spectacular rugged beauty. Perpetually snow-capped peaks, roaring waterfalls, deep canyons, heavy evergreen forests, sparkling lakes, and rushing rivers add extraordinary magnificence to the topography of this mountain state. Among the phenomena are the bubbling hot cauldrons and the spouting geysers of Yellowstone National Park, and the world's largest mineral hot spring and its travertine formations at Thermopolis. Next to Colorado, it is the nation's highest state, with a mean elevation of 6,700 feet.

Creeping across Wyoming's eastern border to occupy approximately one third of the state is a portion of the Great Central Plain of North America. A mixture of flatlands and rolling hills, it gradually rises to approximately 6,000 feet before it terminates at the feet of the rocky wall of the Big Horn Mountain Range.

Over the western two thirds of the state spraddle various ranges of the Rocky Mountain chain. Besides the Big Horns, these include the Absaroka, Shoshone, Grand Tetons, Wind River, Gros Ventre, Sierra Madre, and other smaller ranges. The Big Horn Range, among the larger, has more than a dozen peaks that soar between 9,000 and 13,165 feet. On Cloud Peak, the highest, lies an amazing 137,000-acre wilderness area reached only by foot or horseback. Another prominent and beautiful peak is Grand Teton, 13,670 feet high, dominating the Alp-like Grand Teton Range in Grand Teton National Park. The craggy Wind River Mountains have the highest peak in the state: 13,725-foot Gannett, which crests the Continental Divide.

The Divide—that bony ridge of the Rocky Mountains dividing the water flow between the Atlantic and Pacific oceans—enters Wyoming mid-center of its southern border and extends northwesterly through Yellowstone National Park.

Between Wyoming's north and south ranges, the altitude gently tapers off and there exists a section of comparatively low, level land, a boon to early migrations. Through this welcome gap went the Oregon Trail; later, the Union Pacific Railroad.

Outstanding landmarks of Wyoming are its numerous deep-throated canyons, their colorful precipitous walls fencing in wild plunging streams. Some of the most sensational are the Yellowstone, Big Horn, and Shoshone.

Many streams, with headwaters within the state, feed three of the nation's important river systems: the Colorado, the Missouri, and the Columbia. The Yellowstone and its tributaries, the Big Horn and Powder, born in northeastern Wyoming, flow eastward to join the "Mighty Mo." So do the Cheyenne, North Platte, and Sweetwater. However, the Green River, in the southwestern corner, heads southerly for the Colorado, while the treacherous white-water Snake flows southwesterly out of Yellowstone Park to eventually hook up in the west with the Columbia.

Thousands of lakes, usually small and glacier-made, lie in hidden recesses high in the mountains. Others are more accessible. Yellowstone National Park has the state's largest: 140-square-mile Yellowstone Lake. Among the larger lakes, too, are Jackson in Jackson Hole and Fremont in the Wind River Mountains. Twenty-four Bureau of Reclamation Reservoirs provide recreation, flood control, electricity, and irrigation.

The Laramie and Cheyenne Plains in the south embrace some of Wyoming's most level land and are primarily grazing and ranching country. Near the heart of the state, north of Casper, on sandy rocky plains, lies one of the world's largest concentrations of light oil wells.

Out of place in this rugged mountainous land is the "Red Desert," a high treeless dry plateau west of Rawlins—an indentation in the Continental Divide that drains to neither ocean. Wyoming's last herd of bison roamed here; today, large herds of sheep graze on the desert floor.

Upstaging all topographical oddities is Devils Tower, the country's first national monument. Rising some six hundred feet above the Belle Fourche River in the northeastern part of the state, this queer monolith of igneous rock resembles a gargantuan tree trunk.

Eons ago, volcanic eruptions, movements of ancient seas and rivers, coupled with shifts in the earth's crust, were responsible for the uplift that is the Rocky Mountains, as well as the remainder of Wyoming's topography. Glacier-cutting and erosion did the rest. Left to verify the state's prehistoric story are its rocks, some of the oldest known to man, the huge dinosaur graveyard excavated at Como Bluffs, and the myriad of fossilized freshwater fish in the Green River formation at Fossil Butte National Monument, one of the few such repositories in the world. Actually, this is the only place in the world where the fossil of Mioplosus, a true perch, has been found. Palm fossils prove scientists' theory that this was once a subtropical land.

The landscape of Wyoming is ever changing. In June 1925 a rumbling in the earth caused the Gros Ventre slide, declared one of the largest earth movements in the world. Except for damming up the Gros Ventre River, it did little damage, until two years later when the natural earth dam broke, flooding and completely destroying the town of Kelly. The latest change came in August 1959, when a series of earthquakes violently shook the northwestern corner of Yellowstone National Park, causing much damage and loss of life, and forming new geysers and fissures.

CLIMATE

The sun shines bright on Wyoming. Take Lander: Daytime, there is always a 77 per cent probability of the sun being out. In Sheridan, 76 per cent, and in Casper, 75 per cent. Surprisingly, all three of these exceed that of Los Angeles and San Francisco. All residents enjoy sunshine 320 days of the year.

Air, filtered by pine forests and snow-capped mountains, is clean, crisp, and dry, with practically no humidity. Air in Cheyenne has been certified by the U. S. Department of Health as the purest of any city in the nation.

The state's average temperature is 57 degrees. Bringing the warmest temperatures are July and August, yet even during these months, rarely does it rise above 90 degrees, and nights are always cool. Coldest weather comes in December, January, and February.

Temperatures vary considerably between the mountainous west and the plains of the east. For instance, in Yellowstone and Grand Teton national parks, where elevations are high, winter weather sometimes closely resembles that of the subarctic, with temperatures dropping to 40 degrees below zero and unexpected high winds and blizzards shutting them in from the rest of the world. Blizzards are hazardous throughout the high country, and some mountain passes are closed. All of which goes to say that winter lingers longest west of the Continental Divide. In fact, the snowplow does not open Yellowstone National Park for traffic until May 15.

Rainfall is light. Average precipitation is 15.06 inches, most of which comes during the summer. A drought in 1930 and again in

1950 brought disaster to ranchers and farmers and instigated conservation practices and federal reservoirs to supply much-needed irrigation.

From the Rockies come the "chinook," a hot drying wind, a boon to stockmen in winter. Prevailing winds, too, come from the west, zooming in over the high peaks of the Rockies which alter their directions, and take much of the moisture out of the clouds. In southern Wyoming, winds often sweep across the countryside at forty to sixty miles per hour. The reverse is true in the Lander district, where winds have the lowest velocity in the nation (6.9), with Sheridan third (8.1).

THE PEOPLE OF WYOMING

"Spanish Diggings" near Manville have revealed the aboriginal stone quarries of a prehistoric age, but little is known about the people who worked them. Recent and very exciting are the archaeological diggings north of Ten Sleep on Medicine Lodge Creek, where a 10,000-year-old village is being excavated. In the Big Horn Mountains, another relic from the prehistoric past is "the Medicine Wheel," a strange huge circle of rocks with cairns at the base of its spokes. It is believed to have been built by sun worshipers.

When the white man came, twelve tribes of Indians roamed the plains: Crow, Blackfoot, Sioux, Ute, Bannock, Flathead, Cheyenne, Arapaho, Shoshone, Modoc, Nez Percé, and Kiowa. Besides hunting for buffalo, they were warring among themselves over the best hunting land. Later they united to battle the white man who was encroaching on their lands. Then, into the annals of history went names like those of Generals Custer, Crook, Sheridan, and Chiefs Dull Knife, Red Cloud, and Sitting Bull. In 1868, when the Shoshone tribe was reduced to 1,000, brave Chief Washakie reluctantly led his people to the Wind River Reservation, to which their hated enemy, the Arapaho, also came. In 1963, 1,861 Shoshones and 2,465 Arapaho lived on the reservation; a later census in 1970 indicated the total Indian count at 5,390, most of whom were on the reservation.

Although the notable Lewis and Clark Expedition (1804–6) missed Wyoming, one of its party did not: John Colter, trapper and guide. On its return, he left the expedition to become the first native-born American to enter what is now Wyoming. Following Colter was an influx of trappers and fur companies, rugged and daring mountain men who would pioneer settlement in western Wyoming.

It should not be overlooked that Sacagawea, the remarkable Shoshone woman guide, her work over, left the Lewis and Clark expedition about the same time as Colter to return to her people. Though disputed, it is claimed she died on the Wind River Reservation and is buried there.

Strange, but no important migrations west had Wyoming as their goal, or thought of it as a promised land in which to settle. Pioneers usually stayed because en route to the gold fields of California, or to homesteading in Oregon or Utah, it was here they ran into trouble. A wagon broke down. There was sickness. No money. Or some other catastrophe. But those that stayed never wanted to leave, and this fierce affection for the land exists in their descendants, many of whom live on land their pioneer forefathers homesteaded.

Pioneers were a hardy lot, adventuresome and brave. Foremost among them were Jim Bridger, known as the "Daniel Boone of the Rockies," Jim Baker, William Sublette, John Hoback. Colorful "Buffalo Bill" Cody, world-renowned for his Wild West show, guided buffalo hunts and fought Indians. Wild Bill Hickok was here, as were Calamity Jane and Kit Carson. Gamblers, outlaws, and cattle rustlers also hit the new territory and left their mark.

The greatest single event to bring settlers was the Union Pacific Railroad, which chugged into Cheyenne in 1867. Added to this lure was homesteading. This brought the first ranchers—big cattlemen from Texas, as well as cowboys who had driven up the huge herds of longhorns. Judges, lawyers, and congressmen also homesteaded. The discovery of gold and coal and the fact that there was now a railroad to transport these goods also had its bolstering effect on immigrants. Another thing: With the Civil War over, unemployed veterans came West to fight Indians or find employment.

South Pass City, scene of a big gold boom, was a flourishing community until the lode petered out. But not before fiery Mrs. Esther H. Morris was appointed the first woman justice of the peace in the world in 1870. Her statue is in the national Capitol, and a replica stands in front of the state capitol in Cheyenne.

While very few foreign-born emigrants singled out Wyoming (only 2 to 3 per cent of total population), among those who did were many nationalities. Greeks, Finns, Poles, and Italians headed for the coal mines at Rock Springs, Sheridan, and Hanna. Russian-Germans and

Mexicans harvested beets in the Big Horn Basin, the North Platte and Sheridan valleys. British, the largest number of foreign-born, settled mostly in big cattle country, especially between 1880 and 1890.

One of the largest concentrated settlements was that in the Star Valley, in southwestern Wyoming, when, in 1870, it became a part of Brigham Young's Mormon colonization. Over 90 per cent of the valley is still Mormon.

Among the esthetes who early discovered Wyoming was Thomas Moran, famous British painter. In 1871 he did some of his best work while with the U. S. Geological Survey expedition to Yellowstone Park. His pal, William H. Jackson, a photographer for the new Union Pacific Railroad, contracted with the state for a series of Wyoming scenery to be exhibited at the 1893 Columbia Exposition in Chicago. These photographs of Wyoming scenery have never been surpassed. Hans Kleiber, a forest ranger and self-taught artist, became famous for his paintings and etchings of Wyoming. And, for years, Archie "Teton" Teater has been capturing the beauty of the Teton Mountains on canvas.

Famous writers also flocked to Wyoming. Mary Roberts Rinehart, mystery writer, had a summer cabin in the mountains; Owen Wister lived on a ranch and wrote his popular novel *The Virginian,* with a setting in the nearby cow town of Medicine Bow; Bill Nye, famed humorist, lived and wrote in Laramie for almost seven years. Recently, name-writers, artists, and photographers, without fanfare, have been quietly locating in Wyoming.

Famed TV sports announcer Curt Gowdy, a native son, began his career in Cheyenne. In 1972 a state park was named for him.

For decades, Wyoming's sparse population did not grow. This was of no concern to the populace, who liked the wide-open spaces and the big country. A slight flurry occurred in 1912 with the spouting of a tremendous oil gusher in the Salt Creek oil country, when workers and people seeking fortunes descended on the area. But it was small, and soon dissipated.

Since 1940, there has been a sharp decline in ranchers and farmers. In fact, the trend for a long time was out-migration. Then in 1970 came a reversal. The nation needed coal to supply the energy needs, and a new look was taken at Wyoming's vast reserves. Between 1970 and 1974 came 14,000 new residents, mostly engineers and skilled workers. They are still coming. Hanna, once a ghost town, has experienced spectacular growth; so have Gillette and Rock

Springs. Green River's rise in population is attributed to soda ash mining and refining. It is predicted that within the next few years, Wyoming will have an unprecedented rise in population.

HISTORY

Wyoming's history reads like a fascinating Wild West novel. In fact, true historical happenings were the premise for hundreds of books, as well as TV and motion picture Westerns.

At the outset, five flags flew over portions of what was to become Wyoming: those of Spain, France, Great Britain, Mexico, and the Republic of Texas. A part of eight different territories, Wyoming is the only state born of four important annexations, one of which was the Louisiana Purchase. Most people avoided the newly acquired lands, believing them to be wild—unexplored—inhabited by Indians. All were true.

Territorial government did not come until 1868, and it would be yet another twenty-one years before Wyoming would gain statehood.

Plentiful beaver populations plus the demand for the pelts for beaver hats was the magnet that lured the first mountain men and the fur companies, especially to the Jackson Hole region. General William H. Ashley brought forty-three trappers as early as 1822 and started a rendezvous with trappers and Indians on the Green River. Beads, liquor, and merchandise were exchanged with the Indians for their furs. This colorful gathering is re-enacted annually by the townspeople of Pinedale and ranchers. Trapping reached its peak between 1825 and 1835, then dwindled because of the diminishing beaver and the loss of popularity of the beaver hat.

In 1832 Captain Benjamin Louis Bonneville arrived and on the site of the Green River Rendezvous built Fort Bonneville, or Fort Nonsense, as the fur traders dubbed it. Actually, Bonneville was not interested in trapping, but came to spy on the British camped on the other side of the mountains.

There were numerous expeditions. The daring young Lieutenant John Frémont came to find an acceptable route through the mountains and thus open the West to settlement. The first expedition to Yellowstone country was in 1870, headed by Henry Washburn and Gustavus Doane. Later that year, the second, a Department of Interior venture, was headed by Dr. F. V. Hayden. These two expeditions resulted in the establishment of this country's first national park, Yellowstone.

Crossing the Wyoming territory was the Oregon Trail with its numerous branches and cutoffs, such as the Overland Trail (used by the Pony Express and Overland stages) and the Bozeman Trail, which spurred northwesterly to the Montana gold fields. Hundreds of thousands of emigrants with their ox-drawn covered wagons plodded over these trails. Though they stayed to themselves, these included the Mormons en route to Utah. Many emigrants perished from the rigors of the journeys, some were killed by Indians.

The most significant historical record left is Independence Rock on the Oregon Trail. A mammoth boulder, it was nicknamed by Father Pierre Jean De Smet the "Register of the Desert" because nearly 50,000 emigrants scratched their names on its surface—500 are still visible. Independence Rock is near Guernsey, where ruts of the trail can be seen.

It was inevitable that the Indians, who had had this land to themselves, would become hostile.

To protect wagon trains, the government garrisoned forts along the trails. In 1849 Fort Laramie was acquired (now a national historic site), and it soon became the most popular with emigrants. Another important fort was Bridger (1842). And there was Fort Phil Kearny, the most hated by the Indians.

Numerous government treaties were made with the Indians and broken by the white man. Settlers could not be held back. The red man fought valiantly. And the year 1865 went down in history as the "Bloody Year on the Plains." Yet two of the most historic battles in Wyoming took place later along the Bozeman Trail: the Wagon Box fight near Story, in which the soldiers fought from behind circled wagon boxes (1867), and the Fetterman Massacre (1866), when soldiers on their way to gather wood were ambushed by Indians.

Finally, in 1868 a peace committee sent by the government signed new treaties with the Indians, and, after that, settlers lived in comparative safety.

With this, the face of Wyoming changed. The transcontinental Union Pacific Railroad was steaming across southern Wyoming bringing settlers and workers to the new coal and gold fields. However, stagecoaches still bounced across remote trails and were exposed to one daring holdup after another. They didn't stop rolling until 1887, when the Wyoming Central and Cheyenne Northern railways were built.

During the mid-sixties to mid-eighties, tens of thousands of cattle were being driven up the Texas Trail. A beef bonanza was on. It ended in the 1890s because of absenteeism of owners of ranches, a falling market, and a horrible blizzard that decimated the cattle.

Small farmers were now settling in Wyoming, fencing their lands with barbed wire. This aroused the animosity of the big ranchers, who had enjoyed the fenceless open range. There were killings and destruction. The farmers allied with "rustlers," the ranchers organized the Vigilantes. Confrontation took place in 1892, south of Buffalo, with the Vigilantes the aggressors. The Vigilantes killed two wanted-men on the KC Ranch, then headed for Buffalo, but surrendered before reaching the town. Things quieted down. But this so-called Johnson County Cattle War went down as an important turning point in Wyoming's history. For it marked the beginning of the end of the open range.

Yet there were more adjustments to come. Sheep were being introduced into the state in great numbers. Cattlemen resented the sheepmen, complaining that cattle would not graze where sheep had been. Many sheepherders were harassed by masked men; sheep were poisoned; and there were even some lynchings. During the late 1890s, sheepmen were granted use of public ranges, cattlemen compromised (some even placed sheep on their grazing lands), and peace came between the two factions.

In the years to follow, the oil sources of Wyoming were tapped vigorously with one of its fields the basis for an unforgettable oil scandal which sent the Secretary of Interior to prison. Gold and coal were mined, and boomtowns prospered. In fact, there were so many precious minerals it was once thought the state would be tax-free. Eventually, though, the gold mines were exhausted and coal lost its popularity. Settlements around them became faded ghost towns.

Only since the energy shortage of the 1970s has mining been reactivated in earnest. Today, it is believed that Wyoming, possibly more than any other state, will play a key role in helping solve the energy shortage. With this new stimulus, there will be exciting pages to add to the alluring Wild West history of this great and wonderful state.

INDUSTRY

Wyoming is not a heavily industrialized state. In 1973 there were 625 manufacturing firms and 405 mining companies. Most manufacturing is based on agriculture and mining products.

Number-one industry rests firmly on the refining of petroleum and mining of minerals: oil, gas, coal, betonite, uranium, soda ash, and the like.

Running neck and neck for second place are agriculture and tourism.

Farming, ranching, and the production of wool are high on the agriculture list. The Star Valley is noted for its dairy products, especially cheese. Beet sugar, lumber, and gypsum board factories are important.

An example of the impact of tourism, which is increasing by leaps and bounds, is the visitation to Yellowstone National Park. In July 1976, an incredible 764,486 visitors entered its gates. Dude ranches are popular, with ranchers making extra income by organizing pack and hunting trips.

Not to be overlooked is the late J. C. Penney, who opened his first store in Kemmerer in 1902, and went on to establish the nation's largest retail chain store. His first day's sales netted but $466.59, the year's gross $29,000.

AGRICULTURE

Being semiarid, only 5 per cent of Wyoming's soil has been plowed. The rest consists mainly of sagebrush and rugged mountains. Though thin, when irrigated, excellent crops of grain, sugar beets, barley, and wheat are produced.

Dry farming—farming without irrigation—exists mainly on the eastern plains, and is primarily livestock. Irrigated farming is found in river valleys and in scattered small areas, usually near reclamation reservoirs, which furnish the vital water for crops.

It is estimated that almost one half of Wyoming, or over thirty million acres, is grazing land. In these areas lie the big ranches. The state's exceptional prairie grasses provide outstanding forage for cattle and sheep.

In 1974, according to figures released by the State Department of Labor and Statistics, Wyoming had 8,200 farms and ranches, with 11.4 per cent of personal income derived from agriculture. The state's five leading commodities are cattle calves ($165 million), sheep and lambs ($22 million), sugar beet ($20 million), wheat ($18 million), and wool ($13 million). Among the states, Wyoming ranks second in wool production and fifth in sheep and lambs. Many ranchers breed fine horses.

Some historians credit the Mormons with being Wyoming's first farmers, even though they never stayed. Each year, the first group passing through plowed the wayside land; the group migrating in the spring sowed the seed; and the final group in the fall did the harvesting.

NATURAL RESOURCES

Wyoming is endowed with tremendous natural resources. Most important, it has the largest coal reserves in the nation: close to 20 million acres of workable seams. Because of the current energy shortage, these veins are being explored and mined at an accelerated pace, causing the state to experience a coal mining boom, a boom expected to continue through the 1970s and well into the 1980s. Controversy wages over whether or not permanent damage is done to the land by strip mining. However, Wyoming, always farsighted, has enacted laws governing strip mining, possibly tougher than any federal regulations, and the general feeling is that mining companies are showing a genuine concern for the land.

In other minerals, Wyoming ranks first in the production of bentonite, having the largest deposits in the nation, and first in sodium carbonate. Only New Mexico surpasses it in uranium deposits. In iron ore and petroleum it comes in fifth; seventh, in natural gas. Proof of its far-reaching gas and oil reserves is that they are found in twenty-one of its twenty-three counties.

Salt Creek, north of Casper, is the world's largest light oil field. This was the site of the Teapot Dome scandal. In 1927, oilman Harry Sinclair and Secretary of the Interior Albert Fall, along with others, were convicted of bribery.

Besides minerals, Wyoming is rich in magnificent stands of trees. Lodgepole pine, so named because the Indians used it to build their lodges, ponderosa pine, firs, spruces, and junipers are protected in five national forests, one of which, the Shoshone, is America's oldest national forest. Stands of aspens decorate lower reaches of the mountains, and graceful cottonwoods (the state tree) shade streams. These forests plus Thunder Basin National Grassland occupy 15 per cent of the state's area.

Although busy freeways cross the state, it is still possible to drive for miles seeing little or no habitation, only herds of antelope and deer roaming free on the vast plains. The state has the world's largest herds of pronghorn antelope and elk, as well as the largest number of Shiras moose in North America.

CITIES

Comparatively speaking, Wyoming has no truly big cities.

Cheyenne, its capital (40,914 pop.), is the largest. Founded in 1867, when the Union Pacific Railroad was built across the plains, it was so wild it was nicknamed "Hell on Wheels." It was here Wild Bill Hickok married a "circus gal." No longer an important grain and livestock shipping center, business focuses on legislative affairs around the three-story gold-domed capitol and the production of "Frontier Days," the world's largest and biggest rodeo, held annually in July.

There are memories. They lie in the State Museum with its exhibit of early-day cattle brands and in the quaint multicolored sandstone Union Pacific Depot, once the largest and grandest structure in the territory, and now a national historic site.

Cheyenne has always had a military base. Fort D. A. Russell, originally a frontier outpost, is now F. E. Warren Air Force Base. In July 1962 its 90th Strategic Missile Wing became the free world's largest intercontinental ballistic missile unit, with two hundred Minuteman missiles.

Although the number-two city in size, **Casper** (pop. 48,000) is number one in industry. Over four hundred oil companies and oil affiliates are located here. Also boosting the economy are agriculture, uranium, wholesale distribution, and small manufacturers. The current interest in gas and oil has added new impetus to its industry.

The city sprawls at the base of scenic Casper Mountain, on the site of the frontier fort once protecting the North Platte River crossing of the Oregon, Mormon, and California trails. The city's namesake, Lieutenant Casper Collins, was killed defending the fort.

Laramie, bearing a fur trapper's name, is Wyoming's third-largest city (23,143 pop.). It lies west of Cheyenne on the edge of the magnificent white-capped Snowy Range. Once a tent city and railroad center, it is now considered the state's cultural hub. This is because the University of Wyoming is here, the state's only four-year institution of higher learning, established four years before statehood. Among the two hundred buildings on the 719-acre campus is the outstanding Fine Arts Center, comprised of two art galleries and a concert hall, highlighted by an extraordinary Walcker pipe organ. The university's enrollment is 8,500.

In Laramie's proud history is Grandma Swain, who went to the polls in 1871 to become the first woman in the world to vote in a general election.

Sheridan, in mid-central Wyoming, just south of the Montana border, has a captivating western atmosphere. For years it has been a bustling center for big ranching operations, as well as dude ranching. Reflecting this are its western clothing shops and establishments where leather chaps and belts are hand-tooled, saddles repaired, lariats made to order. Yet talk on the streets these days is not only cowboy chatter, but serious discussions about the neighboring strip coal mines.

This town of nearly 11,000 people is surrounded by scenery. To its west rise the rugged spectacular Big Horn Mountains; to the east and south are rolling plains. It is headquarters for the Big Horn National Forest.

Upstaging the historical side is the huge brown-frame Sheridan Inn, built across from the depot in 1893 by the Burlington Railroad. The inn once had the reputation of having the most luxurious accommodations in the West. After all, where else could one have found bathtubs and electric lights? Or a telephone? Restored in the mid-1960s by Mrs. Neltje Kings, an area rancher, it has a fine restaurant, but no guest rooms. It is a national historic landmark.

On the outskirts sits stately Trails End, the mansion of the "Cowboy Senator," John B. Kendrick, who also served as governor from 1915 to 1917.

An interesting sidelight to Sheridan's past is that the telegram announcing the annihilation of Custer and his men was sent from here.

Possibly no other Wyoming town has retained as much genuine western color as has **Cody.** Shops handle all the paraphernalia dear to the heart of the cowboy. The Irma Hotel, built by "Buffalo Bill" Cody and named for his youngest daughter, is still open for business. Through the summer, every evening except Sunday, local children and cowboys stage a rousing rodeo. In the fall, big-game hunters come to be outfitted. Located near the eastern gateway to Yellowstone National Park, summer visitors often outnumber the 5,100 residents.

Founded by Buffalo Bill and a partner, the famous Wild West showman loved this town and his nearby T. E. Ranch so much he requested that he be buried here. But this was denied him. He died penniless in Denver.

Although most people are unaware of it, Buffalo Bill was recognized in the West for more than his showmanship, his fantastic buffalo hunts, and his scouting. For instance, it was he who pioneered the road into Yellowstone Park. And it was he who conceived the Buffalo Bill Dam, west of town on the Shoshone River, the first major reclamation project undertaken by the Bureau of Reclamation. When completed in 1910, this dam was the world's highest.

So it is only fitting that the magnificent Buffalo Bill Historical Center—the greatest repository of western art and artifacts in the world—should be located in Cody. Divided into three sections—Buffalo Bill Memorabilia, Plains Indian Museum, and Whitney Gallery of Western Art—the contents are valued at over ten million dollars. Among the western artists represented are Frederic Remington, Charles M. Russell, and Albert Bierstadt.

Adjacent to the forty-acre center grounds is the statue of Buffalo Bill on his favorite horse, Smoky, sculpted by Gertrude Vanderbilt Whitney. This is not only the largest bronze equestrian statue in the world, but one of the most photographed.

More noteworthy art is the Cody mural painted by Edward T. Grigware in the foyer of the Church of Jesus Christ of Latter-day Saints. It depicts the story of Mormonism and the Mormons' courageous westward migration.

Another small exciting western town is **Jackson,** southern gateway to Grand Teton National Park and a supply town for nearby dude ranches. It squats at the southern terminus of forty-eight-mile-long

Jackson Hole, the spectacular valley at the base of the Teton Mountains. Both valley and town were named for early mountain man Davey Jackson, who claimed this area as his private trapping grounds.

With a current population of over 2,000, in 1914 Jackson barely made the 500-resident requirement for incorporation and then only by counting visitors and unborn babes.

The beautiful setting of this popular tourist city—flowering meadows, the Teton Mountains, rushing rivers, heavy forests—has attracted the greatest concentration of artists in the state. As a result, excellent art galleries are side by side shops featuring exquisite Indian jewelry, fossilized fish, and souvenirs. These business houses fronted with boardwalks surround the city park, a landmark with its arches of elk antlers. Off the square is Crabtree Corners, a settlement of young folks engaged in glass blowing, pottery making, silversmithing, and numerous other handcrafts.

SPORTS AND RECREATION

The state abounds in outdoor recreation from thrilling float trips on wild or gentle rivers to backpacking to high mountain fastnesses. Innumerable easy trails lead to idyllic hideaways and roaring waterfalls. In the Tetons, mountain climbing challenges the daring. There's boating; canoeing, too. Water-skiing. Fishing (both stream and lake) and big-game hunting are superb.

Pack trips to base camps high above the timberline on towering mountains are one of the last purely western adventures left in the country. Following pack horses, laden with food and supplies, as they zigzag up a mountain, is unforgettable. These pack trips take photographers bent on capturing wildlife on film, fishermen going to remote lakes, hunters, and folks just seeking a refreshing wilderness experience.

Throughout the state, camping and picnicking are ideal, and there are literally thousands of opportunities in state parks, national parks, forests, and recreation areas.

Especially popular are early morning horseback rides with cowboys and wranglers, ending with a campfire-cooked breakfast of fried potatoes, eggs, pancakes, bacon, and sometimes steaks.

Rock hounds find that the rugged rocky area around Greybull conceals a treasure-trove of rare specimens, and the rock and fossil museum in town is one of the best.

When winter comes, outdoor activity does not decrease. Skiing is super, especially in the Jackson Hole region. North of Jackson, Teton Village, a counterpart of an Alpine settlement, huddling at the base of 10,446-foot Rendezvous Peak, has a rise of 4,139 feet, the largest vertical rise in America.

Yellowstone National Park with its winter wonders stays open, as does Grand Teton National Park. Ice fishing gets underway. So do snowmobiling, cross-country skiing, snowshoeing, commercial trips by snow-cats, and winter camping.

Both Jackson and Teton Village have dog-sled, old-fashioned cutter, and snowmobile races.

Year around, ranches ring with evening square dancing.

POINTS OF INTEREST

Topping all tourist attractions in the state and ranking high in the nation are Yellowstone and Grand Teton national parks.

Yellowstone National Park, the country's largest, with more than two million acres, is recognized as one of the finest wildlife sanctuaries in the world. Wild animals roam free in their natural habitat, and visitors are the trespassers. Among the large animals are bear, elk, deer, moose, and buffalo. Yellowstone Lake, the largest lake in America at such a high elevation (7,773 feet), provides exceptional fishing and boating. Yellowstone Canyon and Falls are predominant features. Weird geysers (Old Faithful is the most famous, though neither the largest nor the highest), gurgling hot pools—all in all over 10,000 thermal features—make Yellowstone Park the most extensive area of geyser activity in the world.

South of Yellowstone lies sublimely beautiful Grand Teton National Park. Its gray granite mountains rise abruptly from the valley floor and remind world travelers of the Swiss Alps. On the shores of Jackson Lake, the park's largest, are a splendid marina and campground. More than sixty species of mammals and over one hundred species of birds are found in this park. It is not at all unusual to watch moose feeding in swampy creeks at eventide, nor to observe the graceful trumpeter swans swimming on potholes.

Near Jackson is the National Elk Refuge, where some 9,000 elk

PLATE 60 Custer Battlefield National Monument in Montana marks the site of the Battle of the Little Bighorn.

PLATE 61 Makoshika State Park in eastern Montana is an area of colorful badlands created by wind and water erosion.

PLATE 62 Grinnell Lake, in the alpine grandeur of Glacier National Park in northwestern Montana.

PLATE 63 Massive limestone formations in Lehman Caves National Monument in eastern Nevada.

PLATE 64 Reno's downtown casino district.

PLATE 65 Natural stone arch in Arches National Monument, Utah.

PLATE 66 Hoover Dam and Lake Mead, one of the country's largest man-made lakes, are near Boulder City, Nevada.

PLATE 67 The Mormon Tabernacle in Salt Lake City.

PLATE 68 "This Is the Place" Monument Site, where Brigham Young
entered Salt Lake City Valley in 1847.

PLATE 69 Utah's Bingham Canyon Copper Mine, the largest open-pit copper mine in North America.

PLATE 70 The huge volcanic neck of Devils Tower National Monument in northeast Wyoming.

PLATE 71 Breath-taking scenery in Bryce Canyon National Park.

PLATE 72 Playful black bear cub in Yellowstone National Park.

PLATE 73 Grotto geyser in Yellowstone National Park.

winter. Visitors delight in accompanying the rangers on feeding sleighs of hay.

Appealing to tourists, too, are the exciting mountain drives that produce extravagant scenery: the Big Horns, Tetons, Absarokas, Wind River, and Snowy Range. And there are the stirring canyon drives with high colorful walls towering above the highway and river on the canyon floor. To name a few: Wind River between Thermopolis and Shoshone, Wapiti, Big Horn, and Hoback.

Scenery lovers and the outdoor-minded are attracted to the Flaming Gorge Recreation Area in the southern part of the state, which spills over into Utah, and is best known for its red-walled canyon, and fantastic fishing and boating on its dammed-up waters. Another is Big Horn Canyon National Recreation Area, stretching from Montana to near Lovell, so new that some recreation facilities, though open, are not completed. Called the "Land That Time Forgot," scenery is spectacular, and fishing and boating are considered the finest on the forty-seven-mile-long Big Horn Lake, born of Yellowtail Dam.

Historically, look to Fort Laramie National Historic Site, its early-day atmosphere heightened by period-costumed guides. Much of the fort has been restored. In addition, numerous towns have excellent pioneer museums, landmarks are still visible on the Oregon Trail, and battlefield sites, such as the Wagon Box and Fetterman Massacre, are marked.

Hot Springs State Park in Thermopolis embraces the world's largest single mineral hot spring. It flows an amazing 18.6 million gallons every twenty-four hours. Unique are the tepeelike travertine formations it has produced, and the marblelike terrace on the banks of the Big Horn River.

The Pryor Mountain Wild Horse Range in northern Wyoming is the first wild horse range ever established by the Bureau of Land Management. Here over two hundred wild horses roam free, and while BLM has recommended a loop drive, they are best seen by four-wheel-drive vehicles.

Reminiscent of cattle days is the Wyoming Hereford Ranch, six miles east of Cheyenne, one of the oldest and largest purebred cattle breeding ranches in the United States. Its original owner, Alexander Swan, in 1873 brought the first Hereford cattle into the West from England. Tours are conducted daily.

SPECIAL EVENTS

True to its logo of a cowboy on a bucking horse and its sobriquet of the Cowboy State, almost every town has a rip-roaring rodeo. Beginning in July, ringing over the plains and mountains, is the old-time cry of the cowboy, "Powder River, let 'er buck!"

In Frontier Days, Cheyenne claims the oldest (started in 1897) and biggest rodeo in the nation. Held annually in late July, the town relives with gusto its frontier days. Chuck wagon feeds, wild horse races, and the best of famous buckin' horse riders are on the program.

In mid-July cowboys gather for rodeos at Sheridan and Saratoga; July 3 and 4 at Cody. Kids under eighteen head for the Little Britches Rodeo at Rawlins and the Little Levi Rodeo at Gillette, both in mid-July. Rodeo season ends Labor Day weekend with Cowboy Days at Evanston.

County fairs get under way with the Central Wyoming Fair and Rodeo at Casper, July 31. The Western Plains Fair in Cheyenne is scheduled for August.

Early August brings a touching Indian pageant, "Gift of the Waters," at Thermopolis. Re-enacted is the ceremony in which the revered Chief Washakie of the Shoshone and Arapaho nations gives the hot springs to the white man with the reservation that a portion should be reserved forever for free public use.

Historically accurate is the Green River Rendezvous, commemorating the gathering of early trappers and Indians, staged on the original site near Big Piney and Pinedale, the second Sunday of July.

A unique happening is All-American Indian Days at Sheridan. The last weekend of July, Indians come from all sections of the country to choose a beautiful Indian girl as queen, and to remember ancient tribal customs.

In mid-June there's fun to be had at the wood-chopper jamboree at Saratoga, when lumberjacks get together to show their prowess.

Lively country music splits the air as square dancers swing their partners at the square dance festival held every August in Laramie.

Outstanding is the Grand Teton Music Festival in Festival Hall, Teton Village. For six weeks (late July through August), there are symphonic and chamber music concerts. Unique are "watermelon concerts," when watermelon is served after the concerts to audience and performers.

Through July and August, the famed Laubin Indian Dancers perform at Jackson Lake Lodge.

New and highly successful are the Governor's Canoe Races on the Snake River in Jackson Hole, Labor Day weekend. Thirty-two miles long and timed, they test the endurance of canoeists.

In mid-August, there is a regatta on beautiful mountain-ringed Fremont Lake. And the town of Worland remembers its German heritage with an Oktoberfest.

For persons wishing to realistically experience covered wagon days and camping along the trail, the answer is the trips with either the Teton Country Prairie Schooner or Wagons West. Wagon wheels roll on both trips from June to September.

V.B.
H.B.

CHRONOLOGY

1803 Wyoming became part of the United States as a result of the Louisiana Purchase.

1807 John Colter was the first white man to enter present Wyoming.

1825 Fur Rendezvous began.

1840 Father De Smet celebrated the state's first Catholic mass.

1842 John C. Frémont led an expedition to select sites for military posts with a view to territorial acquisition in the Far West.

Fremont Peak was named.

1847 Brigham Young led first group of Mormons across Wyoming.

1861 Transcontinental telegraph lines were completed and Pony Express was discontinued.

1867 Union Pacific Railroad reached Wyoming.

1868 Peace commission signed treaties with Sioux, Crow, Arapaho, Bannock, and Eastern Shoshone.

Wyoming territory was created.

1869 Cheyenne was designated territorial capital.

An act granting suffrage to women was approved, the first in the United States.

1870 Esther Hobart Morris was appointed first woman justice of the peace in the United States.

At Laramie City, the first mixed jury of men and women was impaneled.

1872 Yellowstone National Park, the nation's first national park, was created.

1886–87 Disastrous winter brought failure and bankruptcy to many stockmen.

1887 University of Wyoming opened its doors.

Capitol was completed.

1890 Wyoming became the forty-fourth state.

1892 Johnson County Cattle War.

1897 First Frontier Days celebration in Cheyenne.

1902   J. C. Penney opened his first store at Kemmerer.

1906   Devils Tower became first national monument.

1924   Mrs. Nellie Tayloe Ross was elected governor, first woman governor in the United States, and later became first woman director of U. S. Mint.

1925   Teapot Dome oil case was tried at Cheyenne.

1929   Grand Teton National Park was established.

1955   Uranium mining and prospecting on large scale.

1958   First ICBM base in the nation was established at Fort Warren Air Force Base, Cheyenne.

1959   A severe earthquake in Yellowstone National Park resulted in gigantic new geysers and scores of boiling springs and steaming fissures, previously inactive.

1972   Coal strip mining and oil production underwent acceleration as a result of the energy crisis.

1977   Development of natural resources and energy has resulted in a rapid population influx, sharply affecting the economy.

1979   Wyoming's challenge to the federally mandated 55 mph speed limit was defeated by compromise legislation in its House of Representatives.

       Governor Ed Herschler blocked plans by the Texas Eastern Transmission Corporation, which had planned for a $1.8 billion coal pipeline from Wyoming to the Texas Gulf Coast. His rationale was that the project posed too many questions as to its effect on Wyoming.

THE SOUTHWEST

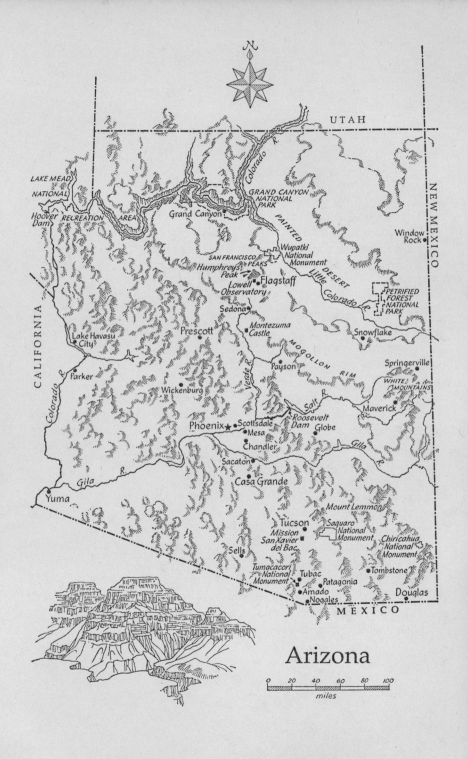

UTAH

NEW MEXICO

CALIFORNIA

MEXICO

LAKE MEAD
NATIONAL

Hoover
Dam

RECREATION   AREA

Grand Canyon

Colorado R.

GRAND CANYON
NATIONAL
PARK

PAINTED

Window
Rock

Wupatki
National
Monument

SAN FRANCISCO PEAKS

Humphreys
Peak

Lowell
Observatory

Flagstaff

DESERT

Little

Colorado

R.

PETRIFIED
FOREST
NATIONAL
PARK

Sedona

Lake Havasu
City

Prescott

Montezuma
Castle

Snowflake

MOGOLLON

Parker

Colorado

R.

Wickenburg

Verde R.

Payson

RIM

Springerville

WHITE
MOUNTAINS

Salt

R.

Maverick

Phoenix

Scottsdale

Mesa

Chandler

Roosevelt
Dam

Globe

Gila

R.

Sacaton

Casa Grande

Yuma

Gila

R.

Mount Lemmon

Tucson

Mission
San Xavier
del Bac

Saguaro
National
Monument

Chiricahua
National
Monument

Sells

Tumacacori
National
Monument

Tubac

Patagonia

Amado

Nogales

Tombstone

Douglas

Arizona

0   20   40   60   80   100
miles

ARIZONA

THERE WAS a time, some years ago, when Arizona was thought of as little more than a stretch of land that had to be crossed in order to get somewhere else. Considering that its 113,956 square miles make Arizona the country's sixth-largest state, that involved a lot of traveling.

That was in the days before people stopped long enough to find out what a pleasant place Arizona could be, or took time to experience its imposing beauty and grandeur, or to realize its wealthy potential. Well, times have changed. Nowadays, tens of thousands of people every year can't wait to get to Arizona—to visit and to take up residence.

Things started to change with the miracle of irrigation, which changed vast desert areas from brown to green and eventually made Arizona into a prosperous agricultural state. And the discovery of vast mineral wealth, especially copper, beneath some of those rocky deserts began making them look a lot more attractive.

Arizona is not all desert. It is true that most of the state's 1.8 million residents live in desertlike areas, where the climate is perennially warm and dry and allegedly health-giving, but it is also true that half the state is mountain and plateau country.

So Arizona has metamorphosed from wasteland to playground in the minds of the American people, but there are drawbacks to popularity. Because the state is one of the fastest-growing in the nation—in population and in industry—its once pristine skies, formerly touted as pollution-free, are beginning to be clouded with the residue of the phenomena of modern living.

THE LAND

Arizona is divided into only two principal physiographic regions. These are the Colorado Plateau and the Basin and Range Region. The former stretches all across the northern section, covering about two fifths of the state. There has been much exaggeration concerning this region and its alleged inaccessibility and ruggedness. The plains and steplike escarpments here are often labeled mesas and plateaus, yet the territory is fairly easily traveled, the Grand Canyon of the Colorado River being the main exception. That, as anyone will admit, is tough to get across.

The Colorado Plateau is also broken by a few mountains, the chief ranges being the San Francisco Peaks, which are pretty rugged, and the gentler White Mountains. Humphreys Peak, near Flagstaff, is the state's highest mountain, rising 12,670 feet. There are a good many heavy forests in the mountains, but in contrast, the plateau also has bone-dry deserts with precious little vegetation. Probably the most spectacular of the dry areas is Monument Valley, in the northeast, along the Arizona-Utah border, where beautiful rock formations rise from the valley floor. This is where the famous Painted Desert and the Petrified Forest are located.

The two hundred miles of the southern border of the Colorado Plateau are dramatically marked by a series of gigantic rock walls, nearly 2,000 feet high, called the Mogollon Rim. They extend from central Arizona to the Mogollon Mountains in southwestern New Mexico.

The second major region, the Basin and Range, covers the whole southern part of the state plus a narrow strip in the west, and is characterized by mountain ranges running from northwest to southeast. The ranges are rugged and close together in the northern part of the region; farther south the mountains have more forests and broader, more fertile valleys, where the state's largest cities developed; the mountains in the extreme south and west are low and barren, with wide desert basins lying between the ranges.

The Colorado is Arizona's most important river, running 688 miles from the point it enters in the north from Utah, winds west through the Grand Canyon, and then turns south, forming almost the entire western boundary of the state. This spectacular river and its tributaries drain most of the state.

CLIMATE

Most people who have never been to Arizona probably believe that most of the state is hot and dry and hardly gets any rain. And they are right. For instance, in Phoenix the mean maximum temperature during January is 65 degrees, and during the summer the city has daily maximum readings averaging 104 degrees, with night temperatures dropping to an average 78 degrees.

Moisture can be pretty scarce in much of Arizona, half of which is semiarid, one-third arid, and the rest humid. However, there can be wide variations: The southwestern desert region receives only about two to five inches of moisture a year, while the high mountain areas may get as much as thirty inches annually.

But don't be misled by the temperature and precipitation figures—many people love the Arizona climate, and many will swear to its healthful and health-giving qualities. And it is a fact that the more arid regions of the state attract thousands of winter visitors and a good many new residents each year.

In the mountainous northeastern regions the mercury seldom rises above 90 degrees during summer, and winter readings can drop below zero. As a matter of fact, the lowest temperature ever recorded in Arizona was minus 37 degrees, in 1963 in the town of Maverick. (The record high was 127 degrees, recorded at Parker in 1905.)

THE ARIZONANS

Although many of the last sad conflicts between frontiersmen and Indians took place in Arizona, few of that state's tribes experienced the decimation and forced relocation that occurred in states like Florida and Georgia, where such tribes as the Cherokee and Seminole died in large numbers during extended warfare and removal to Oklahoma territory. Kit Carson led a campaign that defeated Arizona's Navaho tribe in 1863, but the Apaches continued to fight on fiercely until 1886. Their famous chief Geronimo finally surrendered on September 4 of that year.

Primarily for those reasons Arizona today has more Indians than any other state—nearly 100,000, grouped into fourteen tribes on nineteen reservations. The famous Navaho tribe accounts for over half the Indian population; the remaining 40,000 to 50,000 are divided among the Apaches and Hopi—who, like the Navahos, are well organized and maintain vigorous development of their land and people—and the less well known Papago and Pima tribes.

About 450,000 Arizonans are of Mexican descent and call themselves Mexicans. Social and residential segregation, in varying degrees, is still a problem for some of these people—there are, for instance, plenty of Spanish-speaking-only areas, called *barrios*. However, many thousands of Mexicans are dispersed throughout the state's urban areas and are influential in their communities' business, politics, and social life.

The 1970 census counted 1,770,900 people in Arizona, attendant with a prediction that by 1980 the population would be around 2.4 million. Those of white European ancestry, referred to as Anglos in Arizona, dominate the population numerically, and although they have a variety of European backgrounds very few are foreign-born. As a matter of fact, including all the various groups—Anglos, Mexicans, Indians, blacks, and Chinese-Americans—about 95 of every 100 Arizonans were born in the United States.

HISTORY

As early as several thousand years ago there were Indians living in what is now Arizona, the first discernible settlements having been made by the Anasazi—the ancestors of the present-day Pueblos—the Mogollon, and the mysterious Hohokam, the people who built a fairly complicated system of irrigation canals for their farms and who, after several centuries of prosperity, quietly disappeared.

After the ancient tribes had gone, Navahos and Apaches moved into Arizona, along with the Hopi and Zuñi Indians, and had the place pretty much to themselves until Spanish explorers came in the early 1500s, lured by tales of the fabulous treasures of the legendary Seven Cities of Cibola. One of the first was Francisco Vásquez de Coronado, who never found the Seven Cities of gold, most likely because they never existed.

The next wave of Spaniards, who came in the following century, had better motives. Many were priests, sent to establish missions. Father Eusebio Kino began his work in 1692, founding twenty-four missions and traveling thousands of miles. But along with the priests came more Spanish soldiers, which made the Indians hostile. Their attempts to drive out the Spaniards failed, and by 1752 the first white settlement and fort was established at Tubac. Tucson was settled later, in 1776, on the site of an Indian village.

The Spanish kept control of the region until 1821, when Mexico won independence from Spain, and Arizona became part of that new country. But not for long. The United States and Mexico were at war from 1846 until 1848, when they settled their differences with the Treaty of Guadalupe Hidalgo, giving the United States New Mexico territory, which included Arizona as far south as the Gila River. The treaty angered a lot of Easterners who thought the United States was given worthless desert. Despite such opposition, the Gadsden Purchase added the rest of Arizona to the United States in 1853.

The Civil War was a turning point in Arizona's political history. Many of the settlers there were from the South, and when the Confederacy was formed they wanted to join it, even going so far as to elect a delegate to the Confederate Congress. The Confederates thought they saw a chance for a quick victory and sent troops west in 1862 with the intention of occupying New Mexico and Arizona. But in Arizona, Union forces defeated them. The next year, in a fit of political folly, the Southerners created the Confederate Territory of Arizona, a completely meaningless act since they couldn't even get into Arizona.

But the effect of these events was to prompt the federal government into a long-delayed action—creating Arizona Territory, which it did on December 27, 1863.

The new territory was not a peaceful place, for the Indians kept everyone in a continual state of fear with their raids. The famous frontier scout Kit Carson tried to put a stop to them with a concerted campaign. He defeated the Navahos in 1863, but the fierce Apaches continued to fight, under the leadership of such famous chiefs as Cochise, Geronimo, and Mangus Coloradas. Geronimo didn't surrender until 1886. On September 4 of that year he gave himself up to Brigadier General Nelson Miles of the United States Army, after coming out of hiding in a canyon of New Mexico's Sierra Madres.

But Indian wars couldn't stop progress. Discovery of gold and silver brought miners streaming into the territory, and in the 1870s and

1880s rich copper finds brought more prospectors. Farmers came too and began large irrigated developments, and by the 1870s cattle and sheep ranching was big business. The Southern Pacific Railroad came to Arizona from California in 1877 and that also encouraged settlement.

By the 1890s many groups were agitating for statehood, but Congress kept sidelining the issue. In 1910 Arizona was permitted to draw up a constitution and apply for statehood, but President Taft vetoed the measure because the proposed constitution allowed removal of judges by recall. When the clause was finally stricken from the document, Arizona became a state on February 14, 1912.

George W. P. Hunt, Arizona's first governor, may have been its greatest, serving seven terms and supporting development of dams and irrigation systems, and working for laws favorable to ranching and mining. The first big dam was the Roosevelt, completed in 1911. The following twenty-five years of dam building and irrigations projects served to create a burgeoning and prospering population. The warm, dry climate lured health seekers and tourists, and the federal government aided by preserving and developing many scenic and historic places.

Mining production increased through the 1920s and 1930s as rich new veins of copper were discovered; agricultural production also increased as more land was irrigated, making Arizona a haven for farm workers from many parts of the nation who had been uprooted by the Great Depression.

The industrial and military needs of World War II caused enormous growth in Arizona. The state's major resources of cattle, copper, and cotton were in great demand, and its clear weather was perfect for air training bases. The wartime boom doubled the size of Phoenix and Tucson.

After the war the state grew even faster, increasing in population about 50 per cent in the 1940s and about 74 per cent in the 1950s, spurred by economic progress in manufacturing.

In the midst of this prosperity, Arizona's Indians were having a tough time. In 1948 they finally got the right to vote. However, things have gotten better for them, especially the Navahos, whose wealth was increased by the discovery of coal, oil, and uranium deposits on their land. The tribe also enhances its income with a lumber mill, some motels, and recreation areas.

Today, Arizona is facing serious problems, mostly as a result of its huge population growth. Water resources are being strained nearly to the limit. The situation was eased in 1963 when the Supreme Court decreed to Arizona the use of 2.8 million acre-feet of water a year from the Colorado River. And in 1968 Congress authorized the ten-year Central Arizona Project, a plan to bring the waters of the Colorado River to Phoenix and Tucson.

INDUSTRY

Over the past three decades Arizona has had a rather dramatic increase in manufacturing, to the point that manufactured products currently account for about a third of the state's income from all goods produced. Growth was especially rapid during the 1950s and 1960s, when the state's manufacturing income rose at a faster rate than that of any other state.

World War II was the turning point for Arizona industry, and the rise in industrial employment since then has given the state one of the most vigorous economies in the country. Today, it boasts more than 1,000 manufacturing plants, 800 of them located in the cities of Tucson and Phoenix.

The biggest employers are the electronics and electrical machinery industries, with aircraft and ordnance (weapons) second. Food processing ranks as the third-largest industry, in terms of the number of workers. Coinciding with an increasing output of minerals is the continued growth of metal smelting, while clothing, lumber, metal products, printed matter, and stone, clay, and glass products are manufactured by other plants.

During the 1960s many smaller cities built manufacturing plants, including a sugar refinery in Chandler, a pulp and paper mill near Snowflake, an electrical appliance factory in Prescott, and a plant in Parker to make cotton yarn.

Tourism also must be considered a top industry in Arizona, almost a natural result of the state's beneficent climate and spectacular scenery, plus historic, scientific, and recreational areas that have been carefully protected and developed by the state government.

The natural features that benefit tourism also benefit the manufacturing industries, for the climate attracts not only visitors but also large numbers of permanent residents each year, creating a huge, multitalented labor pool.

Mining is also a vastly important part of Arizona's industry, generating around $475 million worth of income annually. Copper is the leading mineral and is the state's most significant contribution to the national economy, amounting to over half the country's total output and about one eighth the world supply. Some by-products of copper ore are gold, molybdenum, and silver. Other mineral products are asbestos, gypsum, lead, natural gas, petroleum, stone, uranium, and zinc.

AGRICULTURE

Although only 2 per cent of Arizona's land is used for growing crops, the state realizes an annual income of over $525 million from all goods produced. This is a prime example of efficient use of land. Cotton and lettuce are the two leaders, with cotton accounting for more than half the state's crop value.

Because of its mild winters Arizona provides a good many winter vegetables and fruits for northern regions of the United States, the most important, besides lettuce, being melons, potatoes, oranges and other citrus fruit, barley, grapes, greenhouse plants, hay, and sorghum grains.

About a million head of cattle in Arizona, plus around 500,000 sheep, use more than 80 per cent of the state's land area for their grazing. Arizona is famous for vast ranches and pasture lands, and the beef from its cattle provides about 80 per cent of the state's livestock income.

Besides the crops and livestock there are other important farm products, including milk, eggs, wool, hogs, turkeys, and honey.

There is irrigated land in all of Arizona's fourteen counties, with three of them—Maricopa, Pinal, and Yuma—having the most productive irrigated regions. But the state may face a water shortage crisis resulting from urban areas expanding into surface-water irrigation districts, plus the ever-increasing cost of pumping from declining water tables. The problem can best be illustrated by this fact: Farms and ranches account for over 90 per cent of the water used annually for all purposes.

NATURAL RESOURCES

Water is Arizona's most constant concern, and because the water is actually diminishing, it must be considered the state's most valuable resource. Far too little rain falls for the state's agricultural demands, so water must be transported to crop lands from streams and reservoirs, or pumped up from wells. Farms and urban areas get only about a third of their water from streams and storage reservoirs and the rest must come from underground. But the demand on those subterranean resources has been so great that the water is being used faster than it can be replaced naturally. Since 1945 there has been a steady drop in the water table, in some places as much as two hundred feet.

To offset the declining water resources and to assure careful conservation, Arizona entered into an agreement with the states of California and Nevada for sharing of the waters of the mighty Colorado River. In 1963 the United States Supreme Court divided by law the waters of the Colorado among the three states.

But there is more beneath Arizona's surface than water. The state has vast deposits of copper, enabling it to provide half the United States supply. There are also large deposits of gold, silver, lead, barite, tungsten, and zinc.

Arizona has a scarcity of good earth, though, for only about an eighth of its soils are suitable for growing crops. For instance, in some areas of the southwestern region there are fine red soils, but beneath them is a layer of lime rock called *caliche* that is so hard that power tools sometimes must be used to dig holes.

There are many forests, covering a quarter of the state, but only about a sixth of those areas grow trees that are commercially valuable, about 3,180,000 acres' worth. However, Arizona's mountains do contain one of the country's largest stands of ponderosa pines. Other valuable trees are the blue spruce, Douglas fir, and white fir.

The cactus plant has nearly become symbolic of Arizona. In the desert areas are sharp-spined cholla cactus, creosote bushes, pricklypear cactus, and organ-pipe cactus. The saguaro, common in the southern regions, is the largest cactus in the country, and its blossom has become the state flower. Other unusual plants include the Joshua tree, the night-blooming cereus, and the yucca plant.

Animal life is abundant, including black bear, elk, mountain sheep, pronghorn antelope, badger, beaver, fox, javelina (a kind of wild pig), raccoon, skunk, squirrel, and weasel. Members of the cat family flourish in the forested regions, including mountain lion, bobcat, margay, and ocelot.

There are thirty-seven species of lizards crawling around Arizona, including the famous poisonous Gila monster. Rattlesnakes are found all over the state, and in the deserts there are coral snakes, scorpions, and tarantulas.

CITIES

Arizona's fastest-growing city is its capital, **Phoenix,** with a population of over 600,000, grown from 106,000 in 1950 and only 11,000 in 1910. Spreading over a wide flat valley, richly irrigated by a complex system of canals and reservoirs on the Salt and Verde rivers, the city is a booming commercial center, with dozens of fast-growing industries, and is an increasingly popular winter resort.

Fortunately for the citizens of Phoenix and for Arizona's much-vaunted clean air, the rapidly expanding factories in the city are mostly the kind with no smokestacks, such as those producing electronic components, aircraft parts, and air-conditioning units. The air is not as clear as it used to be, for that would be impossible with so much growth, but it is still clear enough for everyone to enjoy the fine city parks, the beautifully manicured residential districts, the dozens of hotels and motels, plus the attractive ultramodern office buildings downtown.

Phoenix is Arizona's economic, political, and cultural nerve center, and the miracle of irrigation made it what it is today, for all the city's growth can be attributed to the reclamation projects that began with Roosevelt Dam on the Salt River in 1911. Agriculture was the city's first significant economic endeavor and it is vital today, although industry and tourism have since passed it in importance. Irrigated fields still surround the city, growing some of the most profitable crops of citrus fruits, cotton, dates, alfalfa, and vegetables anywhere in the country.

Modern Phoenix reflects a combination of its past, an attractive blending of its Indian, Spanish, and Old West heritage. It was first settled by the prehistoric Hohokam Indians, who made the place livable with irrigation ditches. But they disappeared long ago and no one has ever determined why they abandoned the area.

So Phoenix was hardly even a place on the map when a man named John Smith came there in 1865 and set up a fodder depot to supply Camp McDowell nearby. Tall grass growing all around the Hohokam's ancient canals provided ample harvest for forage. Those same canals attracted more settlers several years later, who enlarged them and began using them to form a farming community. In the 1870s the first cotton fields were planted, which became the basis for an agricultural industry that was to support the city for decades. The settlers named the town Phoenix after the mythical bird said to have been reborn from the ashes of its nest every five hundred years. They felt it appropriate because the settlement had risen from the remains of the Hohokam civilization.

In the 1870s and 1880s there were extensive mining, ranching, and farming enterprises around Phoenix, contributing to its growth. A stagecoach route was opened to the town, and then in 1887 the first railroad came to Phoenix. All that activity and fast growth caused Phoenix to become a wild and nearly lawless town. By the turn of the century a rather severe law-and-order process had been instituted and Phoenix was being tamed.

But its tough, frontier character hung on well into the twentieth century. On January 12, 1912, exactly one month before Arizona became a state, an outlaw gang had its final showdown with marshals on the streets of Phoenix. The outlaws were captured after a wild, running gun battle.

Visitors to Phoenix will find the city beautiful and culturally rewarding. Nowhere is the beauty more vivid than in Encanto Park, a veritable "Central Park" of palm-shaded lagoons and gardens. *Encanto Queen,* an old-fashioned stern-wheeler, takes passengers on a twenty-minute cruise several times daily. Other diversions include tennis courts and two golf courses, picnicking grounds, and facilities for swimming, badminton, shuffleboard, and dancing.

On the city's eastern side is Papago Park, where hiking and riding trails wind through desert terrain. It also contains an eighteen-hole golf course, the municipal stadium, a state fish hatchery, and seven small lakes. Within Papago Park are the Phoenix Zoo and the Desert Botanical Garden. The zoo has an impressive collection of animals, including the only breeding herd in captivity of Arabian oryx, which was saved from extinction. The Desert Garden is the only public garden that has only desert plants, and contains a huge array of cacti and other succulents.

South Mountain Park, eight miles south of the city, is huge, covering nearly 15,000 acres of wilderness and semiwilderness terrain. There are forty miles of bridle and hiking trails, and improved picnic sites.

Phoenix has a fine selection of museums. The most outstanding is the Heard Museum, which has exhibits of anthropology and primitive art, focusing on American Indians of the Southwest. It also has the largest collection of Hopi and Zuñi kachina dolls. The Civic Center contains the Phoenix Library, the Phoenix Theater Center, and the Phoenix Art Museum, which has a large collection of paintings and sculptures.

Although **Scottsdale,** with its population of around 70,000, is third in population of Arizona's cities, it actually is considered a suburb of Phoenix, maintaining nonetheless its own identity. It is so closely tied to the larger city that many of the resorts listed as those of Phoenix are actually in Scottsdale, where the city lines meet around Camelback Mountain. Scottsdale's most charming attraction is its oldest downtown section of Old West buildings. It's a sports-minded city, too, with forty-five tennis courts and fifteen golf courses.

Mesa, with over 60,000 residents, is also a Phoenix suburb, founded by Mormon settlers in 1878, who used the irrigation canals left by the ancient Hohokam tribe to set up agricultural industries. Mesa's Mormon Temple is one of its most beautiful attractions.

Tucson, Arizona's second-largest city, is one of the oldest communities in the United States. Today it is the chief urban center of the southern Arizona desert. It began as a thriving Indian settlement which grew up around a Spanish mission founded in the 1700s; later it became a royal Spanish presidio, a trading post, and a fort. Only after it was discovered that its fine climate could help in curing respiratory ailments did Tucson grow into a city of any size.

During World War II it became an important base for military training, and since then has developed as a winter resort center as well as the base for air force activities and aircraft manufacture. Today, this city, which retains so much of the flavor of the colonial and frontier days of the previous centuries, is growing at the rate of about a thousand persons a month. Its population now is over 260,000. Most of the valley south of Tucson is irrigated, supporting prosperous ranches and dozens of luxurious guest ranches.

The University of Arizona is in Tucson, and the campus has a number of buildings of special interest to visitors. One of the most fascinating is the Arizona State Museum, containing one of the major collections of prehistoric to contemporary Southwest Indian art and artifacts. Other attractions are the University Art Gallery; the Geological Museum; the Library, which has a large Western collection; and the College of Engineering, which has a nuclear reactor.

Fourteen miles west of the city in Tucson Mountain Park is the Arizona-Sonora Desert Museum, which is the best introduction a visitor can have to the kind of life to be seen in the desert regions. It is a living museum of fauna and flora, containing everything from desert insects and birds to black bears, jaguars, and mountain lions.

The Mission San Xavier del Bac is nine miles southwest of the city on the Papago Indian Reservation. This twin-towered, historic mission is called the "White Dove of the Desert." Although the original was destroyed by Apache warriors, the present church is still one of the oldest churches in the nation in use.

Yuma, population around 29,000, in southwestern Arizona on the Colorado River, is one of the hottest, driest, and sunniest cities in the country. It began as a mission center and later developed as a trading post and fort, at a point where trails crossed the river into California. In recent years it has been a control point for water diverted from the Colorado, and the center of a richly productive irrigated district. It is also a popular stop for travelers on the important U.S. 80, and has many accommodations.

Flagstaff, with a population of over 26,000, is the largest city in northern Arizona. It is a popular stopping place for tourists because of its rugged, western atmosphere. There are large Navaho and Hopi Indian reservations near the city; the Indians, and cowboys from the surrounding cattle ranches, are common sights on the streets.

Flagstaff is situated at a 6,900-foot altitude near the San Francisco Peaks. Because of its altitude, the city may have snow anytime from October through May, with an average yearly snowfall of seventy-three inches.

The city is especially known for its scenic appeal—meadows and ponderosa pines are all around the city, creating a luxuriant natural beauty that is missing in the state's dry southern regions.

The main attraction at Flagstaff is the Lowell Observatory, founded in 1894 and one of the nation's most prestigious astronomy laboratories. It is situated deep in a pine forest on the outskirts of Flagstaff and houses seven separate telescopes. There are lectures and guided tours Monday through Friday.

SPORTS AND RECREATION

Having a good time in Arizona is easy because the weather generally is so fine. Pleasant summer days with cool evenings are the rule in the northern and eastern regions of the state, while southern Arizona is noted for dry, mild winters. The mountain areas offer abundant hunting and fishing, and cold-weather sports such as skiing during the winter.

There are good stocks of bass, crappie, catfish, and trout in most all the lakes and streams, but the very finest trout fishing is in the remote rivers in the Grand Canyon and in mountain lakes.

Wintertime in Arizona affords some exciting skiing opportunities, especially at places like the Arizona Snow Bowl near Flagstaff, which has twenty miles of ski trails. Some other lovely spots are Mount Lemon, an hour from Tucson, and the Sunrise Ski Area, near Springerville, owned and operated by the White Mountain Apache Tribe.

For those who like to sit and watch other people exercise there are major league baseball exhibition games in the Cactus League from March to April, plus the Cleveland Indians training in Tucson, and the San Francisco Giants doing likewise in Casa Grande. Rodeos are held all year round, with the biggest at Phoenix, Tucson, Prescott, Payson, Yuma, Mesa, Scottsdale, and Wickenburg. There are summer horse races at Prescott, and dog racing at Tucson, Apache Junction, Amado, and Black Canyon.

One of the most popular forms of recreation in Arizona is vacationing on either a farm or a guest ranch. Tucson and Wickenburg are the main centers, with other dude ranches scattered around places like Patagonia and Douglas. Dudes are advised to buy their riding duds there, where they are authentic.

For hunters, hikers, and campers Arizona's national forests offer beauty and abundant game. The Apache-Sitgreaves National Forest covers 2,623,000 acres along the south rim of the Colorado Plateau in the east-central part of the state. There are camping and picnicking sites, plus scenic drives through ponderosa pine, spruce, fir, and aspen forests.

Other forests are: Coconino National Forest, 1,834,000 acres of forests and deep canyons, the most outstanding being Oak Creek Canyon and the fabulous Mogollon Rim; Coronado National Forest, 1,800,000 acres scattered over twelve different areas, ranging from desert to wooded mountains; Kaibab National Forest, divided into three separate sections covering 1,738,000 acres in north-central Arizona; Prescott National Forest, 1,250,000 acres of mostly two mountain ranges in central Arizona; Tonto National Forest, 2,960,000 acres, beautiful but hard to get to because of inadequate roads and water in the wilderness mountain areas.

POINTS OF INTEREST

Going to Arizona without seeing the Grand Canyon would be about like attending a feast without eating. It is one of the most awesome and spectacularly beautiful creations of Mother Nature on this globe. Although only 105 of the 217 miles of this gargantuan gorge are within the Grand Canyon National Park, they are the best miles, with widths varying from four to eighteen miles from the South to North Rims, and with depths of up to 5,700 feet from North Rim points.

The Grand Canyon is so deep that it has all the climatic changes one would encounter traveling from Canada to Mexico, and it has six of the Northern Hemisphere's seven botanical life zones. It took the Colorado River millions of years to carve out the canyon, exposing a panorama of geologic time like nowhere else on earth. Each of the multicolored strata of rock distinctly marks a period of the earth's history; some of the strata took over 170 million years to be formed, and each layer was built upon another that took about as long for its creation.

A trip down the Bright Angel Trail, on foot or muleback, will even reveal marine fossil outcroppings where parts of the canyon once formed the bed of an ancient sea. Hiking this trail is recommended only for those in top physical condition and with good hiking experience—going down is not too bad, but wait till you try to get back up! Muleback trips are popular, but there are limitations—no one under twelve years old and no one over two hundred pounds.

Most visitors see the canyon from South Rim because it is open all year, more developed, and easier to get to. The South Rim Drives are around thirty-five miles long. At many points along these drives are splendid viewing points, where one can get complete, panoramic views of the canyon depths.

The North Rim is only fourteen miles away straight across the canyon, but unless one wants to hike or ride a mule on a two-day trip to the bottom, across the river, and up the other side, the only way to get there is a circuitous two-hundred-mile drive. Heavy snows usually prevent a visit to North Rim from October to April.

There are many trails, lookout points, visitor centers, museums, sight-seeing trips on buses, nature walks, horseback trips, and other activities available in Grand Canyon National Park. Some of the best are: Yavapai Museum, at Yavapai Point, features high-powered binoculars affording expansive views of outstanding features in the canyon, and exhibits of Grand Canyon history; the Tusayan Ruins and Museum, about four miles east of Moran Point, featuring the ruins of an eight-hundred-year-old Indian village, plus a museum with displays of artifacts taken from the ruins: the Visitor Center and the park headquarters, with exhibits of the natural history of Grand Canyon, Navaho and Hopi jewelry and other crafts, historic river-running boats, plus books, pamphlets, and maps for sale.

The Painted Desert, extending northeast of the Grand Canyon, is extremely dry and has practically no flora, but its beauty is famous because of the multicolored layers of sand on its surface.

The Petrified Forest National Park has what may be the world's largest collection of petrified wood, logs, and parts of ancient trees infused with semiprecious stones.

The Navaho National Monument, part of the Navaho Indian Reservation, contains a group of prehistoric cliff dwellings.

Many of the state's other national monuments afford visitors a close look at the remains of ancient cultures, historical sites, or native vegetation: Canyon de Chelly National Monument has thousand-foot walls that for three hundred years provided a sanctuary for the Navahos against their enemies; Casa Grande Ruins National Monument, in southern Arizona, contains the ruins of strange structures built by the mysterious Hohokam Indians, who developed a series of canals in this region as early as 300 B.C.; Chiricahua National Monument, in southeastern Arizona, contains lava beds that have been carved into unique forms by natural forces over the centuries; Montezuma Castle National Monument, in the central part of the state, preserves a huge cliff-dweller apartment house over five hundred years old, stituated high on a vertical cliff; Saguaro National Monument, near Tucson in southern Arizona, preserves the huge, towering saguaro cactus, which can live hundreds of years; Tumacacori National Monument, in southeastern Arizona, preserves the Mission San José de Tumacacori, built by Franciscans about 1800; Wupatki National Monument, in northern Arizona, has more than eight hundred ruins of ancient Indian villages, among them Wupatki (Hopi for "tall house"), which dates from the twelfth century had more than a hundred rooms built on three levels.

After wandering about a few arid regions, a visitor may want to get a look at some water, and Hoover Dam has about as much as anyone could ask for. The dam, at 726 feet, is one of the world's highest, and the water it backs up on the Colorado River in northwestern Arizona is one of the largest artificial lakes (Lake Mead) in the Western Hemisphere, extending over a hundred miles up the Colorado. Lake Mead National Recreation Area has become enormously popular as a fishing and resort area.

So much has been written and filmed about Tombstone, Arizona, "The Town Too Tough to Die," that the events of its past have reached legendary proportions. It was a rough place in the 1870s and 1880s, and it was often violent, but much that has been written about this silver and gold mining town was exaggeration, and sometimes pure fiction. The lore was created in only about eight years, during the town's peak production period, before its mining operations were doomed by water seeping into the underground shafts. Water pumps were installed, but they failed to prevent disaster. Still, by 1886, when people started giving up and moving out in large numbers, the mines already had produced millions of dollars in precious ore.

The town's days of wildness and violence were climaxed during the time when Wyatt Earp and his brothers were the more or less legal overseers. Their gun battle with the Clantons at the O.K. Corral was one of the West's most famous shoot-outs.

Sight-seeing in Tombstone is easy because most of the relics of the bad old days are conveniently grouped within a few blocks: The O.K. Corral is still there, where the Earp brothers and Doc Holiday gunned down the Clantons (there are fiber glass figures of the participants); the Crystal Palace Saloon looks like it did then, complete with a long bar equipped with mustache towels; the office of the Tombstone *Epitaph,* in publication since 1880; the Bird Cage Theatre, the scene of bawdy entertainment in the days of Wyatt

Earp; Boothill Graveyard, containing the graves of men who did not survive gun battles in town; Wells Fargo Museum, containing historical pieces relating to Tombstone's wild days, including wax figures of famous people; the Tombstone Courthouse State Historic Monument and Museum, built in 1882, which also has displays of the town's early days; and St. Paul's Episcopal Church, the state's oldest Protestant church, which is still in use. There are also tours of an old silver mine shaft.

Another Arizona tourist attraction is located at Lake Havasu City, on the western edge of the state. In 1968, when England announced that the old London Bridge was obsolete and would have to be replaced with a new one, some resourceful Arizonans decided it would be a shame to destroy the grand old bridge. So they bought it from the British Government, shipped it to this desert region block by block—all 130 tons of granite—and reassembled it in its original form. It now spans a man-made river and is fast becoming the most popular tourist site in the state other than the Grand Canyon. Its popularity has spawned a hotel and motel building boom nearby.

SPECIAL EVENTS

Arizonans love to have something going on all the time, it seems. For instance, in Phoenix, there are almost too many special events, five hundred or so every winter season, from October through April. Some of the highlights of this vigorous schedule are the Thunderbird Tennis Open in October, the Arizona State Fair in November, and the Fiesta Bowl, with top college football teams, in December. The city starts off the year with the Arizona National Livestock Show in January; the Dons Club Annual Travelcade Show, the Arizona Yacht Club Invitational Regatta, and the Phoenix Open Golf Tournament are also in January. February features the Annual Cactus Show.

Major league baseball teams come to Phoenix in March for their spring exhibitions. Also in March is the Rodeo of Rodeos, which gathers the best riders and ropers from the United States and Canada. The St. John's Indian Festival, the Gem and Mineral Shows, and the Dons Club Superstition Mountain-Lost Dutchman Gold Mine Trek round out the month.

In April there are the Firebird Festival of the Arts and the Valley of the Sun Square Dance Festival.

Now those are just a few of the happenings in Phoenix. Meanwhile, the folks in Tucson aren't just sitting around counting cacti. The city's La Fiesta de los Vaqueros takes up all of February, a wild typical western celebration, complete with rodeo. Just to help everybody get warmed up for that, during January Tucson hosts the Annual Southern Arizona Square and Round Dance Festival and the Dean Martin Open Golf Tournament.

The town of Scottsdale, which is near Phoenix, has several lively events, including an All-Arabian Horse Show and the Parada del Sol, in February, with parades and rodeos among other things. The town also has a PGA Championship golf tournament in mid-November.

Elsewhere around the state, there is the colorful annual Indian Powwow in Flagstaff from July 4 to 6, and Navaho Tribal Fairs in the town of Window Rock in late August through early September, featuring Indian art, a carnival, and traditional rites. Thanksgiving weekend features the Outboard Championship Races at Lake Havasu.

During May there are bullfights in Nogales and a regatta on the Colorado River at Parker. And in June you can see teen-age cowboys compete in the Annual Junior Rodeo in the towns of Globe and Sedona. Prescott has a real treat in July, the Annual Frontier Days, the oldest rodeo in the country, featuring two shows daily.

Tombstone puts on a fine show in October with its Helldorado Celebration, in which historical incidents are re-enacted on the city streets. The town of Sells holds the Papago Tribal Fair and Rodeo in November.

At Wickenburg in February during the Annual Gold Rush Days, you can pan for gold and keep what you find. At Yuma, that same month, is the Annual Silver Spur Rodeo, with Brahma bull riding and calf roping, among many events. Also in February, at Sacaton, is the Mul-Cha-Tha, the annual Pima tribe festival with ceremonial, crafts, and barbecue.

N.C.

CHRONOLOGY

1540   Francisco Vásquez de Coronado led expedition into Arizona region.

1692   Eusebio Kino began missionary work and travels.

1776   Tucson was founded.

1821   Arizona became part of Mexico.

1848   At end of Mexican War, territory including Arizona ceded to United States.

1853   Arizona enlarged by Gadsden Purchase.

1861–72   Almost constant warring between Apaches and white settlers.

1863   Arizona Territory organized by U. S. Congress.

1886   Apache chief Geronimo surrendered.

1911   Roosevelt Dam completed, first big dam providing irrigation water.

1912   Arizona became forty-eighth state on February 14.

1936   Boulder (now Hoover) Dam completed.

1948   Indians in Arizona get right to vote.

1963   Arizona given rights to large amounts of Colorado River water by Supreme Court.

1965   Arizona Judge Lorna Lockwood became first woman chief justice of a state supreme court.

1967   Arizona legislature revised state taxation system, reducing local property taxes and providing more money for local school districts.

One of the state's worst blizzards struck in December. Thousands were stranded in small communities and towns as seven feet of snow—one of the heaviest snowfalls on record in the state—fell in northern Arizona. Air force planes and helicopters dropped food and supplies. Worst affected were the Navahos. Nine people died; thousands of cattle and sheep were killed.

1968   London Bridge purchased from British Government. Opened to public as tourist attraction in October 1971.

Congress authorized Central Arizona Project—a plan to bring the waters of the Colorado River to Phoenix and Tucson.

Former senator and presidential candidate Barry Goldwater regained a place in the Senate by defeating ninety-one-year-old Carl Hayden, who had been in Congress since 1912.

1973   An all-out drive to remove Governor Jack Williams from office by means of the recall device of the state constitution failed. The drive was led by United Farm Workers under the leadership of César Chávez, who opposed Williams because he had signed a controversial farm labor bill.

1976   U.S.S. *Arizona* (sunk at Pearl Harbor) anchor sited and dedicated in Phoenix.

1978   According to a study made by the United States Geological Survey, groundwater levels in a 120-square-mile area southeast of Phoenix sank more than seven feet since 1952. As a result, narrow cracks appeared in the earth's surface.

1979   A stretch of Interstate 19 in southern Arizona became the longest highway distance in the nation in which distance calculations were posted in kilometers rather than miles. The interstate highway south of Tucson is 67 miles long and a mile is equal to 1.61 kilometers.

New Mexico

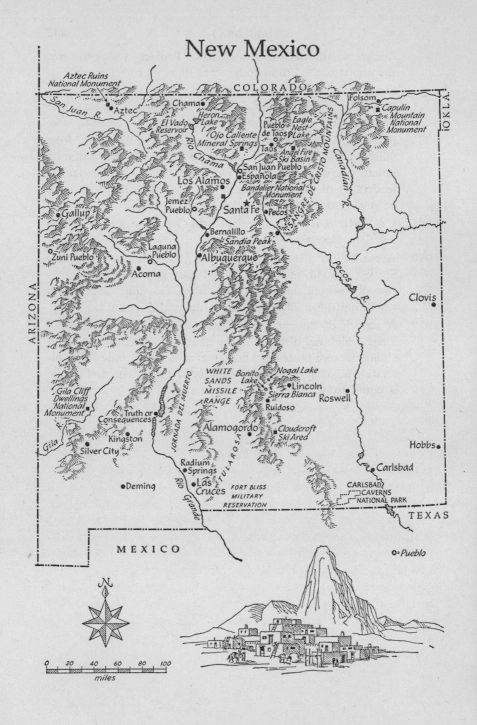

COLORADO

Aztec Ruins
National Monument

San Juan R.

Aztec

Chama

Heron
Lake

El Vado
Reservoir

Ojo Caliente
Mineral Springs

Rio Chama

Pueblo
de Taos

Eagle
Nest
Lake

Taos

Angel Fire
Ski Basin

San Juan Pueblo

Los Alamos

Española

Bandelier National
Monument

Jemez
Pueblo

Santa Fe

Pecos

Gallup

Laguna
Pueblo

Bernalillo

Sandia Peak

Zuni Pueblo

Albuquerque

Acoma

Folsom

Capulin
Mountain
National
Monument

OKLA.

SANGRE DE CRISTO MOUNTAINS

Canadian R.

Pecos R.

Clovis

ARIZONA

Gila Cliff
Dwellings
National
Monument

Gila R.

Kingston

Silver City

Deming

Truth or
Consequences

JORNADA DEL MUERTO

Rio Grande

Radium
Springs

Las
Cruces

TULAROSA

WHITE
SANDS
MISSILE
RANGE

Bonito
Lake

Nogal Lake

Lincoln

Sierra Blanca

Ruidoso

Alamogordo

Cloudcroft
Ski Area

FORT BLISS
MILITARY
RESERVATION

Roswell

Hobbs

Carlsbad

CARLSBAD
CAVERNS
NATIONAL PARK

TEXAS

MEXICO

o = Pueblo

N

0 20 40 60 80 100
miles

NEW MEXICO

In 1942 the United States Government secretly built an entire town high up in the mountains of north-central New Mexico. The town was called Los Alamos, and the population was almost exclusively scientists and technicians. It was there that the first atomic bomb was constructed, in secret; it was there that the bomb was tested, in secret, on a desert in southern New Mexico, near the town of Alamogordo, on July 16, 1945.

Now, the fact that anyone or anything, including the United States Government, could accomplish that much in almost total privacy without the curious finding out about it seems impossible. But there are vast regions in New Mexico that are very sparsely populated.

Just consider this, for instance: If the 1,041,000 population of this fifth-largest state was equably spread over its 121,666 square miles, there would be a density of only eight people per square mile (the national average is sixty). But there is not an even spread. Seventy per cent of the population lives in urban areas, one third in Albuquerque and surrounding Bernalillo alone. That leaves a lot of elbow room for people in places like Catron County, where there is one person for every three square miles.

And what is all that wide-open space like? New Mexico is not called the Land of Enchantment for nothing. Its scenic beauty is almost unsurpassed, and its diversity may be a surprise to many: great mountain ranges and wild forests covering millions of square miles, rugged canyons and rocky deserts. And throughout it all is one of the largest population of Indians in the nation, most of whom have preserved their traditional way of life.

THE LAND

There's a definite schizophrenia to New Mexico's landscape: It has some of the flattest land found anywhere, and some of the most barren, places devoid of streams where even tough cacti are hard put to survive; but it also has some of this country's most rugged mountains, and areas of thick pine forests, abundant meadows, and streams fairly crowded with fish.

The state can be divided into four distinct regions. The eastern part is an extension of the Great Plains, part of the huge Interior Plain that sweeps from Canada to Mexico. This region covers roughly the eastern third of New Mexico and is characterized by deep canyons carved by streams as the plateau slopes away from the Rocky Mountains.

Extending from Colorado into the north-central part of the state are the Rockies, reaching almost to Santa Fe. The Rio Grande, flowing from Colorado, slices through these mountain ranges, whose highest point is Wheeler Peak, 13,161 feet. The many valleys between the ranges form some of the state's most important agricultural and livestock areas.

The Basin and Range Region extends south and west from the Rockies to the Arizona and Mexican borders, covering about another third of the state and including scattered mountain ranges. The Rio Grande also cuts through this region. Between the mountains are broad desert basins, the largest of which are the Jornado del Muerto (Journey of the Dead) and the Tularosa.

The northwest part of New Mexico is a region of wide valleys and plains, canyons, sharp cliffs, and rugged, flat-topped hills called *mesas*. This area is called the Colorado Plateau. The Continental Divide winds through it; streams west of the Divide flow into the Pacific, and streams east of it flow to the Gulf of Mexico.

There are four major rivers other than the Rio Grande—the Pecos, Canadian, San Juan, and Gila. The fertile valley of the Rio Grande has since prehistoric times been a prime agricultural region, and the Pecos, like the Rio Grande, was a popular route for early explorers.

CLIMATE

New Mexico's dry, warm climate is seldom interrupted by a drenching, for the average annual rainfall is about 15 inches. The northern mountainous regions get anywhere from 20 to 40 inches a year (the higher up, the more rain), while the south and central regions get only 8 to 10 inches. Although snow falls throughout the state, the south receives only about 2 inches, whereas the higher mountains may get as much as 300 inches.

The mean annual temperature is about 53 degrees, but there are some rather awesome extremes, all the way from 29 degrees below to 110 degrees plus. The state's absolute lowest thermometer mark was minus 50, in 1951, and the highest was 116, recorded in 1918 and 1934. Average July temperatures are about 74 degrees, but even in midsummer, because of the thin, dry air, when the sun goes down the temperature drops sharply, creating wide day-night variations on the same day.

THE NEW MEXICANS

Three major groups of people settled the area that is now New Mexico—first the Indians, then the Spaniards, and finally English-speaking Americans. Today, most of the state's residents are descended from those groups, and there are few blacks or Chinese.

Because the Spaniards intermarried with the Indians, their descendants are called Spanish-Americans or Hispanos, and not Mexican-Americans, as they are in other southwestern states, such as Arizona. Hispanos made up the largest proportion of the New Mexican population until the 1940s, but by 1970 they were only 25 per cent of the population, a result primarily of a large Anglo influx after World War II.

The number of Indians, however, has continued to increase, from 34,510 in 1940 to around 73,000 by 1975. The largest tribe is the Navaho, which has a huge reservation in the northwest corner of the state which extends over into Arizona. There are also more than 20,000 Pueblo Indians scattered around on nineteen different land grant areas; the Zuñi, Utes, Jicarilla, and Mescalero Apaches also live on reservations.

Most of the Indians in the tribes mentioned above still live like their ancestors, as sheepherders and producers of beautiful handcrafts. On the surface that would seem fine and romantic, but the fact is, the Indians have had to endure years of low income, poor health, bad housing, and substandard education. Consequently there has been, in recent years, an ever-increasing number of Indians deserting the reservations for the cities. Coinciding with that exodus has been the growth of militant Indian organizations demanding better treatment for their people.

HISTORY

New Mexico's Indian history goes way back—probably at least 20,000 years. One of the earliest cultures has been detected by stone spearheads found at Folsom in northeastern New Mexico, indicating that Indians hunted there around 10,000 years ago. Anthropologists call this culture Folsom man. Other ancient cultures were the Mogollon and the Anasazi, from whom the modern Pueblo tribe is descended.

Sometime around A.D. 1500 the Navaho and Apache tribes moved into the New Mexico regions from the north, followed some years later by the Utes and Comanches. Their more or less peaceful existence was interrupted soon after when Spanish explorers began entering the territory. The most significant explorations were by Francisco Vásquez de Coronado, who came in 1540 looking for the fabled Seven Cities of Cibola, as he had in Arizona and with the same discouraging results.

European civilization got its first toehold in New Mexico in 1598 when Juan de Oñate established a colony at the Pueblo of San Juan de los Caballeros, near the Chama River. That colony served as his provincial capital when Oñate became governor, but his successor, Pedro de Peralta, moved the capital to Santa Fe in 1610. It is still the capital of New Mexico, making it the oldest seat of government in the United States.

The colony was fairly poverty stricken and kept going mostly because of the missionaries, who started schools to teach Christianity to the Indians. But coexistence had many problems. The Spanish church and civil authorities quarreled among themselves, and the Spaniards quarreled with the Indians.

The Indians had good reason for discontent. The Spaniards worked them like slaves and prevented them from worshiping their traditional gods. Revolt was inevitable, and it came in 1680, when the Pueblos killed more than four hundred Spaniards and drove the rest to El Paso del Norte (now El Paso, Texas). But the Spanish recaptured the province in 1692 and after four years of fighting inflicted final defeat on the Pueblos.

The colonists maintained control of this lonely outpost of the Spanish Empire until 1821, when Mexico won independence from Spain and made New Mexico part of its territory. It was also a significant year for another reason—the American trader William Becknell opened the Santa Fe Trail to bring goods there from Missouri. This was the beginning of Santa Fe's importance as a frontier trading and travel center.

The Mexicans controlled the region for twenty-five years, until the outbreak of war between the United States and Mexico in 1846, when forces under General Stephen W. Kearny wrested away New Mexico from Mexican troops with little resistance. Two years later the Treaty of Guadalupe Hidalgo ended the war and gave the United States possession of New Mexico.

In 1850, when Congress officially organized New Mexico as a territory, with James C. Calhoun as governor, the area also included what is now Arizona and parts of present-day Colorado, Nevada, and Utah. It was enlarged by the Gadsden Purchase in 1853. But not until 1863 did New Mexico get its present boundaries, when Colorado and Arizona were organized as territories.

The Civil War brought trouble when Confederate troops captured much of New Mexico, including Albuquerque and Santa Fe. But Union forces recaptured it in March 1862. After that there were two years of battles with the Mescalero Apache and Navaho tribes, who were finally forced to live on reservations. Kit Carson, the famous frontier scout, led the New Mexicans during the Indian campaigns.

One of the bloodiest chapters of New Mexico's late nineteenth-century history was the famous Lincoln County War, in the 1870s, when cattlemen and other groups were fighting for political control. It was during this time that Billy the Kid and other such desperadoes took part in the fighting. The gunslinging ended when newly appointed territorial governor Lew Wallace declared martial law and used troops to back it up.

A cattle and mining boom furthered New Mexico's prosperity in the late 1800s, after railroads linked the territory to the rest of the nation. During this time, bands of Indians who refused to give in to the white man spread terror with constant raids. One of the last to surrender was Geronimo, in 1886.

When New Mexico became a state on January 6, 1912, it had 330,000 residents and promise for a bright future. Things generally went well until the early 1920s when a long drought brought financial crisis to farmers and ranchers, starting a chain reaction of lowered stock prices, bank closings, and financial ruin for many people. But the state's economy was rescued by the discovery of oil and of huge potash deposits at Carlsbad. The famous caverns near Carlsbad also helped out by increasing tourism.

During World War II the federal government built the town of Los Alamos in New Mexico's mountains. The first atomic bomb was constructed there and tested three years later on the White Sands proving ground near Alamogordo in southern New Mexico. The date was July 16, 1945. The government continued to pour atomic research money into the state after the war. Atomic power development and rocket experiments, plus discovery of uranium in the northwestern part of the state in 1950, caused the economy and the population to grow.

But during the 1960s New Mexico had to attract new nongovernment industries after the federal government closed several military bases and reduced its number of Albuquerque employees. The economy was aided by the continued growth of the coal and molybdenum mining industries.

Today, New Mexico is flourishing. It is still a leading center of space and atomic research, and its tourist industry continues to grow. As a matter of fact, from the mid-1960s to 1970, state income from tourism almost doubled.

Getting enough water for farms and cities has always been, and still is, one of the state's major problems. The completion of the San Juan–Chama project, begun in 1964, is expected to ease much of the water problem by bringing water to the state through three tunnels from rivers in the Rocky Mountains.

INDUSTRY

Although New Mexico's manufacturing industries have had a fairly steady increase since World War II, their output still only accounts for around 7 per cent of the value of all goods produced in the state. Food processing leads the field, but lumber production is also important, with a rate of around 328 million board feet annually. Other leading products are stone, clay, and glass, printed materials, and electrical equipment.

However, one significant New Mexican industry is world-famous, and that is atomic research, carried on chiefly at the Los Alamos Scientific Laboratory, with testing areas at Sandia Military Base in Albuquerque and White Sands Missile Range near Alamogordo. The atomic research activities have also created spin-off industries such as ordnance (weapons), electronics, and precision instruments.

Where New Mexico really shines is in mining, by far and away the top income producer, with mineral products valued at more than 1 billion dollars a year. The discovery of gold and silver started it all in the nineteenth century, but those two resources peaked out in 1915 and have been in decline ever since.

Nowadays, the leaders in mineral production are petroleum, about 120 million barrels' worth a year, making up about two fifths of the state's mineral output; natural gas, the second most valuable product; uranium production, in which New Mexico leads the country with two fifths of the national output; and potash mining, which provides 85 per cent of the nation's supply.

Copper mining is important in New Mexico, and coal mining is enjoying a strong revival following a decline resulting from the increased use of other fuels. Improved technology helped greatly to expand coal mining during the 1960s.

AGRICULTURE

There are more than twice as many cattle and sheep in New Mexico as there are people, which should indicate just how important ranching is there. The approximately 2.25 million above-mentioned animals take up around 45 million acres for grazing, in areas where the scarcity of rainfall or the meanness of the land prevents crop farming.

Cattle raising is by far the more important of the two, beef sales accounting for more than half the market receipts from agricultural products. It wasn't always that way. Sheep were the dominant livestock until the early twentieth century when Anglos brought cattle raising from Texas.

There is a good deal of crop farming, too, 1,117,000 acres' worth, with cotton the leading cash crop, followed by hay, wheat, and sorghum grains. Dry farming is still used in the eastern half of the state, where the wheat and sorghum are grown, but that method always involves risks because of irregular rainfall. However, New Mexican farmers are irrigating their dry farming areas as fast as possible, for the construction of new dams and deeper wells is providing more water. Half of the total crop land has already been irrigated, and those regions that are provided more water produce the greatest share of the state's income from crops.

Other important produce are lettuce, onions, and dairy products. The irrigated river valleys, especially that of the Rio Grande, are good for growing fruits and vegetables. One of the nation's largest pecan groves is in Dona Ana County, containing nearly 200,000 trees that produce about 7.5 million pounds of pecans annually.

NATURAL RESOURCES

Half of New Mexico's soil may be stony and shallow, and water certainly may not be overly abundant, but the state makes up for all that with its wealth of energy-giving minerals, such as coal, natural gas, petroleum, and uranium, which is the main source of atomic energy. It also has the country's largest reserves of a vital fertilizer material, called potash, and the state is a leader in copper reserves.

New Mexico also has significant deposits of helium gas, natural gas liquids, perlite, salt, sand and gravel, stone, and zinc, followed by some minerals in lesser abundance such as clays, gemstones, gold, gypsum, iron, lead, manganese, mica, pumice, and silver.

The scarcity of water, of course, has to be dealt with, for nothing can function without it. One of the most important steps New Mexico has taken is to join with other Western states in sharing the use of water in various streams. For example, the state of Colorado used the water of the Rio Grande heavily, but it is obligated to allow a certain specified amount to flow into New Mexico. Underground water and artesian wells are also included in New Mexico's water resources. Besides those there are seven major storage projects that regulate the flow of the Canadian, Pecos, Rio Grande, and San Juan and some of their tributaries.

In contrast to the vast areas of substandard soils are eight mountain areas with plenty of commercially valuable timberlands. About 18 million acres, around one quarter of the state, are covered by forests. The most common trees are the aspen, cottonwood, Douglas fir, juniper, piñon (nut pine), ponderosa pine, scrub oak, spruce, and white fir.

The yucca is New Mexico's state flower and grows in most areas of the state. In earlier times the plant's dried stems were used by the Indians to make fires. The deserts provide some of the most unusual and some of the most beautiful plant life, such as cactus, creosote bush, mesquite, white and purple sage, grama grass, and soapweed. In the mountains there are wild plants like the forget-me-nots, saxifrages, sedges, and alpine larkspur.

New Mexico's wildlife includes some of the most majestic beasts in the country, such as black bears, mountain lions, and pronghorn antelopes. Other creatures are plentiful, too, for example white-tailed and mule deer, badgers, beavers, bobcats, chipmunks, foxes, jack rabbits, minks, otters, and prairie dogs. The state also has an abundance of game birds, among which are ducks, grouse, pheasants, quail, and wild turkeys. And the fishing is good, too, for black bass, catfish, crappies, perch, and trout.

Some other wildlife—not too popular—are rattlesnakes and coral snakes, tarantulas and black widows.

CITIES

Albuquerque, with nearly a third of a million people living in it, is New Mexico's largest city. The Old Town of Albuquerque was founded 250 years ago, and from that original point the city has sprawled out onto the riverside mesas and all the way to the foothills of Sandia Mountain. Such growth is not so remarkable until it is pointed out that as late as 1940 Albuquerque was still a small town.

So most of Albuquerque is what could be called a brand-new city.

The Old Town part is still there, though, but it has been engulfed by the spreading metropolis. The original section is one of the oldest towns in the Southwest, starting with a Spanish settlement on the banks of the Rio Grande in 1706. It gradually grew into a prosperous small town, devoted almost entirely to farming. Today, the Old Town is preserved and maintained almost as it appeared a hundred years ago, and draws thousands of visitors each year.

Albuquerque began to grow rapidly toward the end of World War II and in succeeding years, when it became a base for activities of the Atomic Energy Commission, which in turn attracted dozens of new industries devoted to electronics and related interests.

The University of New Mexico, with a student body of 20,000, is nationally famous for its distinctive Pueblo Indian architecture, and it was the university that popularized the revival of this style for new buildings in the city.

Old Town, with its shops and galleries, arts and crafts produced by resident artists, and its fine restaurants, is one of the prime tourist attractions, but the most spectacular treat for visitors is the Sandia Peak Aerial Tram, America's highest-riding elevator ride, to the peak of Sandia Mountain. At the top there's a bar and restaurant and a view that will never be forgotten.

Santa Fe lies at the southern end of the Rocky Mountains and is one of the highest cities in the country in elevation, at nearly 7,000 feet. Its ancient Palace of the Governors, still standing on the plaza, was built in 1609–10 for the Spanish governor of Spain's territory of New Mexico, making it the oldest capital city in the nation, first under the Spanish, then under the Mexicans, and since 1846 under the United States.

For many years Santa Fe was the commercial center of the Southwest, for the great trade routes of earlier years centered there—the Chihuahua Trail of Mexico, the Gila Trail, the Old Spanish Trail to California, and the Santa Fe Trail itself, crossing the plains and mountains from Kansas.

But the city is no longer important commercially, and the major routes bypass it. Before the inception of Amtrak, it was the only capital in the United States that could not be reached by passenger train, but now, accessible by train and highway and equipped with good accommodations, its population of 41,000 welcomes many thousands of visitors each year.

What the visitors are treated to is a city of great charm, with many historical monuments and museums. Much of the residential and commercial architecture is adobe-style, fronting on winding, narrow streets. The picturesque quality of the streets is accentuated by blanketed Indians who stroll the lanes or squat in open-air markets with their wares of turquoise jewelry, leather, and pottery spread before them.

No visitor should miss the Palace of the Governors. It is a massive adobe building with six-foot-thick walls, the oldest public building in the country. It was in this palace that Spanish colonists were besieged and defeated by Pueblo Indian rebels in 1680; and it was also here that Territorial Governor Lew Wallace wrote his novel *Ben-Hur,* with the shades in his windows drawn, according to legend, because Billy the Kid had vowed to assassinate him.

The Mission of San Miguel of Santa Fe, near the plaza where the Palace of the Governors is situated, was founded in 1610 and is one of the oldest churches in the country. It contains religious relics and the oldest bell in the United States.

Santa Fe's Museum of New Mexico has about six separate units in various parts of the town. The principal units, other than the Palace of the Governors, are: the Fine Arts Museum, which features regional artists; Hall of the Modern Indian, which has such Indian art as sand paintings, kiva paintings, and medicine-men dolls; the Museum of International Folk Art, which has folk art from fifty countries; and the Laboratory of Anthropology, which has displays of Indian silverwork of the Southwest.

Las Cruces, with a population of close to 40,000, is the state's third-largest city. It is the trade center of a highly irrigated agricultural area where the most important crops are cotton, alfalfa, pecans, and vegetables. There is also a good deal of dairy farming in the region. The city was founded in 1848 and is the home of New Mexico State University. Near the city are the White Sands Missile Range and Fort Bliss Military Reservation.

SPORTS AND RECREATION

There are a number of hot springs in New Mexico that have been popular rejuvenating spas for a good many years. Indians supposedly have been using them for centuries, and some of the early European explorers and American pioneers are said to have taken more than an occasional dip in the warm waters.

One of the best is the Ojo Caliente Mineral Springs, north of Santa Fe, which claims to have the only arsenical waters in the world other than those at Baden-Baden, Germany. There is also a well-known hot springs area at the town of Truth or Consequences; another called Radium Springs, north of Las Cruces; and the Ponce de Leon springs near Taos.

After a plunge into some hot springs a visitor may want to try the challenge of snow-covered ski slopes. Despite its undeserved all-desert image, New Mexico has lots of mountain areas that are prime skiing country. Some of the best are: Angel Fire Ski Basin, east of Taos, which features cross-country skiing; Cloudcroft Ski Area, east of Alamogordo, with 11 slopes, plus 75 miles of snowmobile trails; Sierra Blanca, at Ruidoso in southern New Mexico; Taos Ski Valley, with 54 slopes and trails, plus well-equipped lodges; the Red River Ski Area, which has cross-country tours and snowmobiling; Sandia Peak Ski Area, northeast of Albuquerque; the Santa Fe Ski Basin, northeast of Santa Fe; and Siapu, near Taos, which has five ski runs.

One of the top snowmobiling resorts is at Chama, in the extreme northern part of the state. It has more than 300 miles of trails for snowmobilers.

Hunters will find abundant and widely varied game over large areas of New Mexico. Approximately 40 million acres are included in hunting territory. Some of the favorite game are elk, antelope, deer, black bear, wild turkey, and grouse. There are also bighorn sheep, and cougars. There are particular seasons for various species, and special licenses for such species as antelope, cougar, bear, elk, and bighorn sheep. Species not so closely regulated are coyotes, rabbits, squirrels, quail, doves, pheasants, prairie chickens, geese, and ducks.

Some of the choicest hunting regions are around Ruidoso, Cloudcroft, the Santa Fe National Forest, which covers more than 1,526,489 acres, and Carson National Forest, covering 1,393,720 acres. The other national forests are: Cibola, covering 1,850,000 acres in central and western New Mexico; Gila National Forest, spread over 3.3 million acres; Lincoln National Forest, approximately 1.1 million acres.

For those who want to be close to the good earth again there are vacations at farms and guest ranches, a form of recreation that is growing in popularity throughout the Southwest. Some of the best are: Spanish Stirrup Guest Ranch, southeast of Deming in south-western New Mexico, popular because of its authenticity; Tres Lagunas Guest Ranch, north of Pecos, situated high up in the Sangre de Cristo Mountains of northern New Mexico; and the Bishop's Lodge, one of the state's oldest resorts, which covers 1,000 acres north of Santa Fe, and offers sports activities like tennis, and entertainment, besides the usual horseback riding and camping trips.

Fishing is good throughout most of the state, and seasons for most fish generally extend year-round. Trout is the prize most anglers go for. The best fishing is done in the streams, but there are also good catches in some of the reservoirs and lakes. Some of the top fishing waters are: Nogal Lake, Bonito Lake, Eagle Creek, El Vado Reservoir, Heron Lake, Eagle Nest Lake, and Storrie and McAlister lakes. Besides trout, bass, catfish, crappie, and perch are abundant in these waters.

POINTS OF INTEREST

The most famous attraction in New Mexico is a hole in the ground, one of the world's largest. The massive rooms of Carlsbad Caverns must be seen to be believed, and the best way to do the seeing is by taking the standard four-hour, three-mile guided hike from the outside entrance all the way through. For less vigorous visitors there are shorter tours, or an elevator that goes 750 feet down into one of the cavern rooms to a dining area.

The caverns are part of the seventy-three-square-mile Carlsbad Caverns National Park, in the southeast corner of the state, situated in the foothills of the Guadalupe Mountains. Geologists estimate the formation process of Carlsbad Caverns took millions of years, the result of slow water action gradually eating away the solid limestone. The natural sculptures and rock formations that have been formed by this water action are renowned for their beauty.

There are twenty-three miles of caverns and passages altogether, and visitors take one or both of the excursions to two principal cave areas, 750 and 850 feet below. The main rooms on these tours are the King's Palace, Queen's Chamber, and Big Room, which is 300 feet high and a half-mile wide. There are huge columns in Big Room, and gigantic limestone domes.

From way down in the ground a visitor can also go way up, to

Acoma, the "Sky City," located west of Albuquerque in west-central New Mexico. This town, which sits atop a rock formation over 350 feet high, has been continuously occupied by the Acoma Indians since the fifteenth century.

Visitors are welcome in Acoma, and they can get there one of two ways: a vehicle road provides easy access to the village, but the more adventurous may want to climb up the footpath, the one the Acomas and their ancestors have been using for centuries.

One of the best-preserved pueblo ruins in the Southwest is found at the Aztec Ruins National Monument, just north of the town of Aztec. The monument contains one of the largest of the prehistoric towns built by the Pueblo Indians.

In the canyon and mesa country of northern New Mexico, on the Pajarito Plateau, is the 29,660-acre Bandelier National Monument. Within this monument, in the cliff of Frijoles Canyon, are man-made cave rooms, unique in this country.

The Capulin Mountain National Monument is a 775-acre region in the northeast corner of the state. The main attraction there is an extinct volcano. Visitors can travel around the rim of the crater, or descend to the bottom.

Gallup, New Mexico, has a large population of Navahos in and around it, who use the picturesque town as the hub of their trading enterprises. Consequently, Gallup is referred to in New Mexico as the Indian Capital of the World. Large numbers of Zuñi Indians also come to the town to do business from their nearby reservation. The Zuñis are particularly known for the exquisite jewelry they produce.

No one who visits New Mexico should fail to see the ancient village of Taos, founded in 1615, and for many decades the home of a fairly renowned bohemian colony of writers and artists.

Coexisting with Taos' bohemia is a fascinating Indian culture. Navahos wearing blankets mingle with ranch hands in the dusty streets lined with adobe houses. The general atmosphere is a good deal more rustic than that of Santa Fe, which is also known for its adobe architecture, and its art colony. Back in the nineteenth century, the renowned scout and explorer Kit Carson made his home there, and the house where he lived with his Spanish wife and six children is a museum today.

There is plenty to see and enjoy in Taos. The Harwood Foundation Art Museum has a large collection of eastern and American Indian art, plus works by well-known Taos artists. The Mission of St.

Francis of Assisi is a lovely old Spanish church, built in the eighteenth century, featuring twin bell towers. The Stables Art Gallery
and Museum traces the cultural history of Indians, Spanish, and
Anglo-Americans and also contains works by top contemporary local
artists.

Three miles north of Taos is the Pueblo de Taos, the highest one
in the Southwest, still inhabited by about 1,500 Indians. Some of the
adobe homes in this village are five stories high. At various times
there are native ceremonial dances in the pueblo, such as Corn
Dances. Visitors should inquire about any special events.

In southwestern New Mexico, about fifty miles north of Silver
City, is the Gila Cliff Dwellings National Monument, which contains
six natural caves with thirty-five to forty rooms. The cave rooms were
used by prehistoric Indians up until about A.D. 1100. A ranger is on
duty, but there is also a self-guiding tour through the dwellings.

SPECIAL EVENTS

Considering the fact that New Mexico has a huge Indian population,
it is no surprise that Indian events dominate the seasonal attractions.
There are Indian fairs and ceremonies, especially traditional dances,
in towns all over the state throughout the year. There are deer
dances, turtle and buffalo dances, eagle and elk dances, feather and
butterfly dances, corn dances, and harvest dances. To name them all
would involve a practically endless list, so only some of the more
popular or significant ones are named here:

The annual return of the Council of the Gods to Zuñi Pueblo in
early December, an exciting and unforgettable twenty-four-hour Sha-
lako ceremony (the Shalakos are messenger birds, personified by
Zuñis wearing great bird-form masks ten feet tall); Feather and Butterfly Dances during February, in the Taos Pueblo; a Deer Dance in
February in the Santa Clara and San Juan Pueblos; a Harvest Dance
in Laguna Pueblo in March; Spring Corn Dances in Laguna, Santa
Ana, and Acoma; the Inter-Tribal Powwow dances in Albuquerque,
in June; a Buffalo Dance in Santa Clara in June; the Puye Cliffs Ceremonial in July; the Mescalero Apache Gahan Ceremonial in July;
the Jemez Pueblo medieval drama *Los Matachines,* in December;
and the Inter-Tribal Ceremonial at Gallup in August.

Among the non-Indian events, one of the most exciting is the International Balloon Fiesta and World Hot Air Balloon Championships in Albuquerque in early October. The State Fair and Rodeo are held there during September.

The town of Truth or Consequences hosts a number of adventuresome activities during the year: canoe races on the Rio Grande in April; annual fiesta, rodeo, fiddler's contest, jeep races in May; State Trapshooting Championships in June; and the New Mexico PGA Golf Tournament in August.

Also in August is the Fiesta de Santa Fe, one of the oldest festivals in the United States (started in 1712). It runs for three days, opening with the burning of Old Man Gloom. During each Tuesday of July there are Santa Fe Opera, House and Garden Tours.

The Town of Lincoln holds a three-day celebration commemorating the Lincoln County War during the first week of August. It includes a portrayal of Billy the Kid, who took part in the war, stagecoach races, and a fiddlers' contest.

The Fiesta de Oñate guarantees three days of fun and good times in Española during the second weekend in July, and the Taos Fiesta is held in late July.

Artistic events include the Southwest Indian Art Show, in Albuquerque in May; the New Mexico Arts and Crafts Fair, in Albuquerque in late June; the Santa Fe Opera, House and Garden Tours in July, and August; the Symphony Orchestra of Albuquerque, whose season opens in January; the Black Range Artists' Exhibit, in Kingston in August; and the Rio Grande Arts and Crafts Show, in Albuquerque, in November.

N.C.

CHRONOLOGY

1540–42   New Mexico region explored by Francisco Vásquez de Coronado.

1598   Juan de Oñate founded first permanent Spanish colony at San Juan.

1610   Provincial Governor Pedro de Peralta moved capital to Santa Fe.

1680   Pueblo Indians revolted against Spanish, killing hundreds, driving the rest from New Mexico.

1692   Spanish recaptured New Mexico from Pueblos.

1706   Albuquerque founded.

1821   New Mexico became part of Mexico.
William Becknell established the Santa Fe Trail.

1846   U.S. forces took possession of New Mexico.

1848   Treaty of Guadalupe Hidalgo, ending the Mexican War, gave New Mexico to the United States.

1850   Territory of New Mexico created by U. S. Congress.

1853   New Mexico Territory enlarged by Gadsden Purchase.

1862   Union forces recaptured New Mexico from Confederates, who had taken it some months earlier.

1864   Mescalero Apaches and Navahos defeated by forces under Kit Carson.

1876   Beginning of five-year Lincoln County War.

1886   Apache chief Geronimo surrendered.

1912   New Mexico became forty-seventh state on January 6.

1922   Oil discovered in southeastern and northwestern regions of state.

1930   Carlsbad Caverns became a national park.

1945   First atomic bomb tested at White Sands near Alamogordo.

1950   Uranium found in northwestern New Mexico.

1964   San Juan–Chama project begun, designed to bring water through Rocky Mountains by tunnels to Albuquerque area.

1967   Project Gasbuggy, the first commercial use of thermonuclear energy, was begun on a site in the northwestern part of the state. Its purpose was to assess the possibility of using thermonuclear energy to aid in the recovery of natural gas.

1970 The University of New Mexico in Albuquerque was closed down during a strike by students and faculty protesting national and local affairs. The National Guard was called in. Several students and Albuquerque newsmen were injured.

1974 Senator Jerry Apodaca, a Democrat, was elected to succeed retiring Governor Bruce King, thereby becoming the first Spanish-surnamed person to win the governorship since 1918.

1976 Indian Pueblo Cultural Center opened in Albuquerque.

1979 A new law reinstated the state's death penalty (replacing a law found unconstitutional in 1976) in which a lethal injection becomes the cause of death.

OKLAHOMA

ARCHAEOLOGISTS made a most remarkable discovery of three rune-stones along Oklahoma's eastern border a few years ago. What the find seemed to indicate was that Vikings, who reached the American continent a thousand years ago, ventured much deeper inland than anyone had believed. The theory is that the Vikings may have reached the Gulf of Mexico and then wandered up into Oklahoma via the Mississippi, Arkansas, and Poteau rivers.

No one is certain exactly when the first Indians came to Oklahoma, but it has been the "home of the red man" for hundreds of years. Even the name of the state signifies that fact, being derived from two Choctaw words, *okla,* meaning "people," and *humma,* meaning "red."

When European explorers first began penetrating into what is now Oklahoma, looking for "lost cities of gold," they found many indigenous tribes already there. Over the years more Indians came, but the largest Indian migrations were in the early 1800s when the American government, in one of its least glorious enterprises, forced tribes of the southeastern United States to settle there.

Today, there are more Indians in Oklahoma, representing more different tribes, than in any other state in the country. But the days of Indians enduring a subsistent existence on crowded reservations are gone, for Indians have been almost completely integrated into Oklahoma's mainstream. Indians are successful businessmen, captains of industry, directors of oil companies. A good many prospered during the oil booms, when petroleum reserves were discovered beneath their lands.

Oklahomans still like to wear cowboy boots and hats, and saddle up for rodeos, but they're keeping up with the twentieth century. For instance, the Phillips Petroleum company, headquartered in Bartlesville, is operating eight nuclear reactors for the Atomic Energy

Commission—which means Oklahoma will most likely play a vital role in helping to solve the ever-growing energy crisis.

The state also has military bases vital to the nation's defense. Tinker Air Force Base at Midwest City is the world's largest air matériel center; the Strategic Air Command is at Clinton-Sherman Air Force Base; a major naval ammunition depot is at McAlester; and Fort Sill, at Lawton, has for many years been the Army's principal artillery school.

In terms of education, during the early 1970s Oklahoma sent a considerably greater proportion of its high school graduates to college than the national average. Also, the University of Oklahoma had by that time become second only to Harvard in the number of Rhodes scholars among its graduates.

THE LAND

Three of America's large topographical regions extend into or across Oklahoma: the Interior Highlands in the east; the Coastal Plain in the south, extending through Texas to the Gulf of Mexico; and the Interior Plain, including the Central Lowland and the Great Plains, which covers the remainder.

Within those large areas are ten subregions. There are three mountain areas: the Ouachita in the southeast, and the Arbuckle and Wichita in the south. There is a fourth region in the northeast called the Ozark Plateau, which is almost mountainous. It is the western fringe of the Ozark Mountains, which lie mostly in Missouri and Arkansas. In Oklahoma this fringe is a chain of low sandstone hills and beautiful rivers that make it a major recreation and tourist attraction.

The Sandstone Hills region is a wide band stretching through the east-central part of the state between the Red River and the Kansas border; it is poor in agriculture and timber but important for oil, gas, and coal deposits. The sparsely populated Gypsum Hills region of western Oklahoma has hills that rise between 150 and 200 feet, capped by layers of gypsum fifteen to twenty feet thick.

The four remaining areas are flat to rolling. The Red River Region is a gently rolling prairie in the extreme southern part of the state; the Red Beds Plains, extending from Kansas to Texas in a wide sweep through the middle of Oklahoma, is a gently rolling plain with soft red sandstone and shale lying under the soil; the Prairie Plains, in the

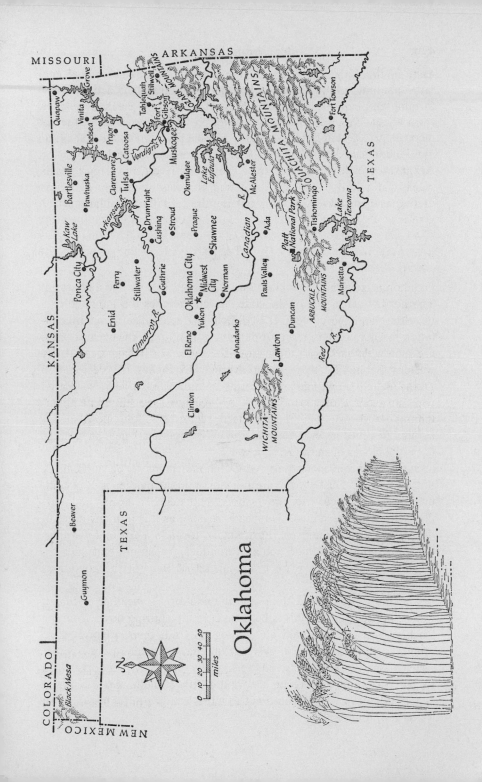

east, south of the Ozark Plateau, has most of the state's coal and large amounts of oil deposits, but its most important activities are farming and cattle ranching; the High Plains, in the Panhandle, rises from about 21,000 feet above sea level on the eastern edge of the region to 4,978 feet at Black Mesa, the highest point in Oklahoma.

Oklahoma is drained by two great river systems, the Red and the Arkansas, which carry water from the state's rivers and streams eastward to the Gulf of Mexico. The state also has more than two hundred man-made lakes and about one hundred small natural lakes.

CLIMATE

Oklahoma, generally speaking, has a climate that is dry and warm. The northwestern part of the state, which includes the Panhandle, is the driest and the coolest. It is difficult to generalize about precipitation in Oklahoma in terms of definite over-all patterns because there are such wide variations throughout the state. For instance, in the dry western Panhandle there is an average 15 inches of precipitation (rain, melted snow, and other forms of moisture) a year, compared with an average of around 50 inches yearly in the hilly and mountainous southeast. The northwestern region gets the most snow—about 25 inches a year—whereas the entire southeast gets an average of only 2 inches of snow.

Summertime in many parts of Oklahoma tends to be particularly hot and dusty. Dust storms are not uncommon; neither is it uncommon for the mercury to crawl above 100 degrees during midafternoon. In addition, summer is tornado season, as it is in many areas of the Midwest and Southwest. Fortunately, tornado alerts and warnings are more frequent than actual tornadoes, meaning that meteorological prognosticators are aware ahead of time of the conditions that spawn tornadoes.

The most predictable thing about Oklahoma's weather is that it will be unpredictable. This is because cold air pouring down from the Rockies and warm, humid air coming up from the Gulf of Mexico usually collide somewhere over Oklahoma, launching vast weather systems that sweep eastward across the country. Humorist Will Rogers, Oklahoma's favorite son, had a little something to say about Oklahoma weather: "If you don't like the weather in Oklahoma, just wait a few minutes."

THE OKLAHOMANS

Oklahoma has had a large population of Indians for much of its modern history, primarily a result of the great tribal migrations from the southeastern United States beginning in 1819, migrations that were forced by the United States Government. This resulted in eastern Oklahoma becoming known as Indian Territory.

The five principal tribes involved in the migration were the Cherokee, Chickasaw, Choctaw, Creek, and Seminole. Because they had for more than one hundred years lived in close contact with white men, adopting many white habits and customs, they became known as the Five Civilized Tribes.

One custom that the Indians picked up was slavery. Most of the blacks in Oklahoma are descendants of slaves that belonged to the Five Civilized Tribes. After the Civil War the blacks stayed in the territory on freedman land allotments under terms of the treaties of 1866. Today, the blacks outnumber the full-blooded Indians in Oklahoma, the 1970 census determining that 7 per cent of the population was black and 4.1 per cent was composed of other races, mostly American Indians. However, the Indian population is increasing. During the 1960s Oklahoma's Indians, most of whom live in the former Indian Territory in the eastern part of the state, increased in greater numbers than other races. Also, census figures do not take into account the thousands of Oklahomans who have varying mixtures of Indian bloodlines.

Most of the blacks live in the eastern and southern regions of the state or in urban centers. There are several towns with entirely black populations.

But Oklahoma also has a cosmopolitan mixture of many other racial and ethnic strains in its peoples. From early colonial times, names and bloodlines were left by the French explorers, usually in conjunction with the Indian families into which they had married. The great land rushes of 1889 to 1906 brought large numbers of Germans, as well as homesteaders from China, Japan, Mexico, England, France, and Canada. Wheat farming in northwest Oklahoma attracted German Mennonites and Czechs. A coal mining boom of the 1870s and 1880s brought to Oklahoma's Choctaw nation an influx of Italians, Slavs, Greeks, Welsh, Poles, and Russians, and descendants of these miners still live in a section known as Little Dixie in southern Oklahoma.

HISTORY

The period between the years 1820 and 1842 was a tragic time for the Indians of the southeastern United States. The members of the five major tribes of that region—the Cherokee, Chickasaw, Choctaw, Creek, and Seminole—were forced to leave their native lands and travel the best way they could to the territory of eastern Oklahoma. Many died along the way, and the Indians named it the Trail of Tears. They had been forced westward by the American government, which wanted to remove them from the path of burgeoning white settlement in the Southeast.

The Indians were given all rights to the land in the territory of Oklahoma, and each of the five tribes formed a nation. Under a guarantee by the U. S. Government to protect them, the Indian nations established their own legislatures, courts, and laws, and built schools, churches, farms, and ranches. Most of the settlements were in the eastern section, and since they were protected by treaty from white settlement, most of the westward pioneer movement passed them by.

But the protection didn't last long, because the Indians in Oklahoma got in trouble with the federal government as a result of the Civil War. The people of these Five Civilized Tribes, as they were called, were Southern in their background and institutions (which included slavery), and when the Civil War began, there was pressure from the Southern states for them to join the Confederacy. Despite widespread sentiment to stay out of the "white man's war," leaders of the Five Tribes signed treaties annexing Indian Territory to the Confederate States of America.

Because they had supported the South, the U. S. Congress forced the Five Tribes to give up the western part of their land, some of which was given or sold to other Indian tribes. After that, the land bordering Indian Territory soon filled with settlers. When there was no more free or cheap land available, the whites began coveting the fertile Indian lands in Oklahoma.

By the 1880s organizations of men called Boomers were clamoring for the government to open the Indian lands for settlement. Finally, the government yielded, buying more than 3 million acres from the Creeks and Seminoles, and then declaring 1.9 million acres of the purchase, in central Oklahoma, open for settlement at noon, April 22, 1889.

Congress established the Territory of Oklahoma in May 1890, adding the Panhandle region in the same act. Three years later, on September 16, 1893, the greatest land rush occurred when the government opened the Cherokee Outlet, in north-central Oklahoma, and the Tonkawa and Pawnee reservations. About 50,000 people got into the 6.5-million-acre area and staked their claims during the first day.

After 1890, official maps showed Oklahoma divided into Oklahoma Territory and Indian Territory, the latter region owned by the Five Civilized Tribes, plus a small area owned and settled by other tribes. It was a situation that made white settlers living outside Indian Territory envious for more land when they looked at a map.

In 1893 the Dawes Commission was created by Congress to bargain for the land and to dissolve the Indian nations. The commission divided the remaining land among members of the tribes and then helped them incorporate and prepare for citizenship. By 1905 the commission felt the region was ready to become a state, which it did, though not until two years later, on November 16, 1907.

Even before it became a state, Oklahoma had become a center of oil production, starting with the first small well near Chelsea in 1889, and the first important well at Bartlesville in 1897. Tulsa became an oil center after the Red Fork–Tulsa oil field was opened in 1901.

Meanwhile, however, the farmers were having trouble. They were not getting decent prices for their products, and many of them found they did not have enough land to make a profit. That situation changed dramatically after the United States entered World War I in 1917, creating a huge demand for the state's farm and fuel products.

During the 1920s the old problems returned, farm prices dropped again, and there was economic distress. In this atmosphere secret radical organizations like the Ku Klux Klan gained strength. During the period from 1921 to 1926 the Klan won a large membership in all parts of the state and controlled or elected a good many city and country officials. Its power was eventually curbed by the efforts of such hard-nosed politicians as Martin E. Trapp, who served as governor from 1923 to 1927.

However, the economic picture was improving during those years, due to important oil and gas discoveries, particularly the huge Oklahoma City field that opened in 1928. Within ten years it had more than 1,500 producing wells.

The Great Depression of the 1930s brought terrible hardships to Oklahoma—farm prices plummeted, banks failed, and there was a series of severe droughts and unusually hot summers. High winds stripped away thousands of acres of fertile topsoil, creating tremendous dust storms, turning the plains area into the "Dust Bowl." The state experienced a large population loss as farmers, miners, and oil workers left by the thousands.

World War II brought prosperity again, however, with increased demand for Oklahoma's fuels and foods. Soil conservation programs, meanwhile, had helped to restore much of the land damaged by the ravages of the hard times during the 1930s. During the war tremendous quantities of the state's oil, beef, and wheat went to support the Allied armies in Europe. Also during this time, Robert S. Kerr became governor, serving from 1943 to 1947, urging important reforms in education and state finances.

Kerr was followed by Roy J. Turner, who supported road building and the removal of educational institutions from politics, and he was succeeded by Johnston Murray and then Raymond D. Gary, both of whom promoted industrial development.

Today, Oklahoma is forging ahead politically and economically, most dramatically in politics, with the election to governor in 1962 of Henry Bellmon, the first Republican ever elected to that office in Oklahoma, succeeded by another Republican in 1966, Dewey Bartlett. Meanwhile, a revised tax structure and energetic advertising of the state's abundant supplies of fuel, water, and electric power have been forwarded as means of attracting new industry.

INDUSTRY

Generally speaking, Oklahoma still has a long way to go in manufacturing. In a way, it still functions more like a colony of the industrial North and East, which needs its petroleum fuels, its foods and raw materials. There have been efforts to diversify, but in 1970 only 13 per cent of the state's workers were employed in manufacturing, which is about half the national average.

The manufacturing that the state does have is based mostly on agricultural and mineral products: Agriculture provides raw materials for meat packing, canning, flour milling, feed manufacturing, and textile plants, while mineral resources supply raw materials and fuels for refining, smelting, glassmaking, and petrochemical industries.

The greatest number of Oklahomans are employed in wholesale and retail trade, followed by government agencies, service industries, transportation and public utilities, finance, insurance and real estate, construction and mining. An indicator of the employment situation is the low union membership. In 1968 nearly 30 per cent of all nonagricultural workers in America were unionized, but in Oklahoma only about 17 per cent were members of unions.

Oil refining is concentrated in the north-central and south-central sections of the state, with Tulsa and Ponca City as the leading refining centers. The towns of Enid, Duncan, and Cushing also have large oil refineries. Natural gas is processed in about seventy different plants.

Tulsa and Oklahoma City lead the state in the manufacture of machinery, and they have developed electronics and space equipment industries. The two cities are also important in the construction of transportation equipment, especially aircraft and trailers. Nine glass plants around the state use a good portion of the glass sands and limestone resources, and there are large cement plants in Ada, Pryor, and Tulsa.

Oklahoma City is the state's most important food-processing center; there are also vegetable canneries in Muskogee and Stilwell. The towns of Enid, Shawnee, El Reno, and Yukon are leading centers in grain milling.

One truly remarkable project that will most likely have prime significance for Oklahoma's developing industry has been the massive dredging of the Arkansas and Verdigris rivers. Called the McClellan-Kerr Arkansas River Navigation System, it has, by a series of seventeen locks, turned the two rivers into a commercial route that rivals the St. Lawrence Seaway in shipping potential. The project was the largest ever undertaken by the U. S. Army Corps of Engineers, and enables ocean vessels from the Mississippi River to come as far as the port of Catoosa, near Tulsa, making it the westernmost inland port in the United States.

AGRICULTURE

Beef cattle are the largest source of agricultural income in Oklahoma. There are about 4.5 million head of cattle in the state, comprised chiefly of Herefords, Aberdeen Angus, and Shorthorns. The most important cattle-growing areas are in the south-central region and in an area known as the Blue Stem Bowl in Osage County.

Oklahoma has been great cattle country for a long time, even before the first opening of land to white settlement in April 1889, for the Indians were, and still are, adept at cattle ranching.

In crop farming, wheat is the most important, and Oklahoma is the third most important wheat-producing state in the nation. Up until the 1930s cotton was the leading crop, and it is still important, along with hay, peanuts, corn, sorghum, soybeans, barley, oats, pecans, and peaches.

Soil erosion, the result of wasteful farming methods on wide grasslands that were not suited to crop farming, began to show up even before Oklahoma became a state in 1907. When the great drought of the 1930s hit the heavily eroded farming regions of northwestern and western Oklahoma, the whole area became blighted. What was left was dust. The same thing had been happening in neighboring farming districts in other states, and the region became known as the Dust Bowl.

Added to these misfortunes was the Great Depression. Oklahoma farmers by the thousands were wiped out and began migrating West, to California mostly, desperately looking upon that state as a land of hope. These migrating farmers, the "Okies," were the subject of John Steinbeck's famous novel, *The Grapes of Wrath*.

Since that period, improved technology and soil conservation methods have restored agriculture to its prosperous, vital position in the state's economy. In 1937 a state soil commission was created to educate farmers in contour cultivation and terracing of farm lands, and planting of cover crops to keep the soil from washing away. By the 1960s the soil commission had brought over 95 per cent of the state within soil conservation districts. These districts are under the organization and control of local farmers and ranchers.

Also vital to agricultural well-being has been the state's water resources program, combining flood control, irrigation, and municipal water supply. Reclamation work to reduce flood damage along rivers and streams has been particularly important. By the 1960s, about 560,000 acres, principally in western Oklahoma, had been irrigated.

According to agricultural statistics of the late 1960s, there were about 90,000 farms and ranches in Oklahoma, half of which were owned by their operators.

NATURAL RESOURCES

Petroleum is Oklahoma's most valuable mineral resource, responsible for bringing at least $1 billion of income annually into the state. That figure includes the natural gas, liquefied petroleum gas, and natural gasoline that accompany oil production.

Oklahoma ranks fourth in the country in oil production and is second in the number of producing oil wells, which amount to more than 81,000. Those regions that have wells, and produce oil, extend over most of the state's counties, with a concentration in the north-central to the southwestern sections. There is also a large natural gas field in the western part of the Panhandle.

Besides all those fuel minerals, Oklahoma also has large amounts of metallic and nonmetallic minerals, such as zinc, dolomite, granite, lead, salt, sand and gravel, limestone and sandstone, clays, glass sand, volcanic ash, sulphur, gypsum, asphalt, and ground silica.

But the state outdoes everybody in one resource—helium, which is found in the Panhandle. This particular region, with limited fields extending into the Texas Panhandle and the southern Kansas border, is the only place in the United States, and possibly in the world, where helium is found in sufficient quantities for commercially profitable extraction.

Oklahoma also has a fairly healthy lumber industry, with about 5.3 million acres of commercially exploitable timber divided almost equally between softwoods and hardwoods.

CITIES

Oklahoma City, the capital of Oklahoma, was founded in 1889, quite suddenly. The United States Government had purchased 3 million acres in the central part of the state from the Creek and Seminole tribes. It then declared that 1.9 million acres of that territory would be open for settlement starting at noon on April 22, 1889.

By noon of the appointed day there were thousands of potential homesteaders on horseback, in covered wagons, in buckboards and surreys, and on foot, held back at the border by army troops, waiting for the signaling shot to be fired. When the gun went off, a wild, frantic race began—it is now known as the first Great Land Rush—to claim the best farms and townsites. Some of the settlers, however, had slipped in early, before the gun, to get the best land. These people were labeled Sooners, and today Oklahoma is still nicknamed the Sooner State. By that night Oklahoma territory had some 50,000 new residents; about 10,000 had settled in the same area, which became known as Oklahoma City.

From that day to this, Oklahoma City has kept on growing and prospering. Today this city of over 366,000 residents is an important manufacturing and industrial center, with around 600 manufacturing plants. The city's top employer, however, is Tinker Air Force Base, with civilian employees numbering about 21,000.

The city's industries include electronics, aircraft, oil products, food processing, iron and steel, furniture, electrical equipment, printing and publishing firms, and tire manufacturers. It has the state's largest meat-packing and stockyard plants, and is one of the eight top livestock markets in the United States. It is also a cotton-processing and grain-milling center.

But the most impressive aspect of Oklahoma City is the oil, for the city is situated in the middle of an enormous oil field. Thousands of oil derricks can be seen within the city limits and surrounding areas. There are even wells on the lawn of the state capitol. As a matter of fact, the building sits atop a large deposit, and one of the wells is "whipstocked"—drilled at an angle—in order to get the oil underneath the building.

Immediately south of Oklahoma City is the town of **Norman,** most of which is the University of Oklahoma, covering 3,000 acres and housed in 532 buildings. One of the most popular on-campus attractions is the superb Stovall Museum, which has Indian art, displays of prehistoric beasts and contemporary wildlife of the Oklahoma region, and artifacts of the Greeks and Romans. Other campus cultural centers are the Art Museum, which has an extensive collection of Oriental, European, and American art; and the W. B. Bizzell Memorial Library, specializing in volumes of Oklahoma history.

Tulsa, nestled in the beautiful, rolling hills section of northeastern Oklahoma, is a lovely city. As a matter of fact, in a recent national rating of cities (physical beauty, environment, facilities, per capita income, lack of pollution, cultural achievements were some of the categories) Tulsa earned the number one spot as the most all-around desirable place to live.

Tulsa is also the center of oil activity in the state. However, there are few vestiges left of its early history as a rough-and-tumble boomtown. Today, a visitor can cruise the hilly residential areas and marvel at the veritable castles and chateaux built by the princes of the oil empire.

For many years Tulsa was known as the Oil Capital of the World, mainly because so many of the nation's oil companies headquartered there. But that title has slipped away to Houston, Texas, following the relocation of many of the oil firms' central offices. But, by way of making up for the loss, Tulsa has since become an important port city, the result of a mighty effort to dredge and deepen the Arkansas River. Also, the aerospace and aviation industries are becoming primary employers in the city.

Tulsa University, originally an Indian educational institution founded in the 1890s and known as Kendall College, draws students from all over the world to its famous petroleum engineering school. The new Oral Roberts University is remarkable for its ultra-modern architecture and its 200-foot-high glass and steel Prayer Tower.

Despite the loss of its oil capital title, the International Petroleum Exposition still comes to Tulsa every five years, luring businessmen and petroleum entrepreneurs from all over the globe.

SPORTS AND RECREATION

Oklahoma has 1,750 square miles of lakes, ponds, and rivers, which amply provide residents and visitors with outdoor diversions. There are also a good many reservoirs which, like most of the natural water areas, have state or privately operated developments near them offering boating, swimming, fishing, camping, and picnicking.

There are lovely mountain regions, too, in the south and southeastern sections of the state—the Wichita, the Arbuckle, and the Ouachita mountains, all of which have fine recreational areas. Platt National Park, founded in 1906, is in the Arbuckle Mountains area and is well known for its mineral springs. The park is located within the holdings of the Choctaw Nation; most of the area was purchased from the Indians in 1902. Although Platt is the smallest national park, it has the second highest number of visitors, a statistic that attests to its charms. The excellent facilities are partly responsible for the popularity—they include camp sites with water, lights, and picnic tables.

Oklahoma also has twenty-eight state parks and twenty-three state recreation areas, open all year and free to everyone. There are complete camping facilities in most areas and seven state-owned resort lodges. There are housekeeping cabins and duplexes in quite a few park areas.

One of the most popular areas is Lake Texoma State Park. It has 93,000 acres of lakes and 2,600 acres of park land, a resort lodge and cottages, camping and picnic areas, trailer park, rental boats and motors, guide service, enclosed fishing dock, beach, ski tow service, ski dock, trap shooting, airstrip, café, grocery store, coin laundry, golf course, and excursion boat.

Oklahoma is truly a state for hunters and fishermen. One of the prime areas is the state's "green country," which covers approximately twenty-one counties around and near the city of Tulsa, which is located in the northeast. The top wild game of that region includes deer, rabbit, squirrel, wild turkey, ducks, and especially quail. Oklahoma has a reputation for being one of the finest quail-hunting states in the country.

Fishermen have no complaints about what they can reel in from the lakes, streams, rivers, and reservoirs. Most all the water areas abound in trout, crappie, bass, catfish, and perch.

POINTS OF INTEREST

Tulsa has many ways of entertaining and edifying its visitors. Among the most outstanding are the Gilcrease Institute of American History and Art and the Philbrook Art Center, both legacies of prominent Tulsa oilmen. The Philbrook Art Center has a great many artifacts which trace the prehistoric era of eastern Oklahoma. Included are exhibits of pottery, baskets, pipes, beads, and other ornaments from Oklahoma's mound culture. An outstanding collection of American Indian paintings and Italian Renaissance art is also displayed in the museum, which was the residential mansion of the late Waite Phillips.

The Gilcrease Institute is especially outstanding for its art of the Old West. The most popular displays are the sculptures and paintings of Frederic Remington and Charles M. Russell. There are also extensive collections of ancient and contemporary Indian art.

Tulsa is also proud of Mohawk Park, which has miles of horseback riding trails, picnicking grounds with large permanent shelters of stone and wood, a 36-hole golf course, water areas for fishing and boating, and a zoo, which has a small buffalo herd. Mohawk is one of the largest city-owned parks in the country.

Tulsa has an active cultural life, too, with a symphony orchestra of distinguished reputation in that area, and the Tulsa Little Theater, which has been staging fine performances for fifty years. Movie and stage star Tony Randall got his start in the Little Theater.

Northeast of Tulsa is Claremore, which has the Will Rogers Memorial, commemorating the life and works of this humorist, writer, movie star, cowboy, and generally much-loved gentleman. His tomb is in a small garden in front of the memorial. Directly across from the memorial is the Mason Hotel, which has the J. M. Davis Gun Collection, one of the world's largest, containing more than 20,000 pieces mounted throughout the hotel.

Anyone interested in Western history should visit the National Cowboy Hall of Fame and Western Heritage Center in Oklahoma City, created as a tribute by representatives of seventeen Western states. There are galleries of Western art and a library of books and documents on frontier development. Displays include antique vehicles and clothing, life-size dioramas depicting an Indian camp, a roundup chuck wagon camp, and frontier cavalry. The Rodeo Hall of Fame is also located in Oklahoma City.

Animal lovers will enjoy Oklahoma City's Lincoln Park Zoo, which has the world's largest collection of hoofed animals, plus a few animals not normally found in zoos, such as mountain gorillas.

South of Bartlesville is the Woolaroc Ranch and Museum, covering 3,400 acres of ruggedly beautiful timberland where wild and domestic animals, such as buffalo, longhorn cattle, and deer, roam free. Woolaroc was the ranch of the late oilman Frank Phillips, who had a deep love for the Oklahoma countryside. The name he gave to the ranch signifies that love, combining parts of the words "woods," "lakes," "rocks." The museum emphasizes the local art of the Southwest. Its more than 60,000 items of anthropology, archaeology, and natural history also include artifacts from around the world.

The town of Tahlequah, once the capital of the Cherokee Nation, is the home of a popular tourist attraction, the Tsa-La-Gi Cherokee

Indian Village, a historically authentic restoration of an Indian village in the 1700s.

Indian City, U.S.A., at Anadarko, is also an Indian village restoration, guaranteed for authenticity by the University of Oklahoma, whose staff supervised its construction.

SPECIAL EVENTS

Rodeos are about the most popular entertainment attraction in Oklahoma. There are events almost daily throughout the summer, and the Sooner State hosts some of the major rodeo events in the world.

Oklahoma City has the National Finals Rodeo each December, and Tulsa has the International Finals Rodeo in February. The country's largest "behind prison walls" rodeo is held each Labor Day weekend in the State Penitentiary in McAlester. Other annual rodeos are the Will Rogers Rodeo each June in Claremore; the Ben Johnson Memorial Steer Roping in June in Pawhuska; the All-Black Rodeo in August in Drumright; the Will Rogers Memorial Rodeo in August in Vinita; and the 101 Ranch Rodeo in mid-September in Ponca City.

Because there are so many different Indian tribes in Oklahoma, colorful powwows and other tribal ceremonies and events take place throughout the year. One of the most important takes place in August at Anadarko—the American Indian Exposition includes tribal dancing, native games and feats of skill, war dances, and parades. Also in August there is the Tulsa Powwow, the Ponca Powwow at Ponca City, and the Seneca-Cayuga Indian Green Corn Feast at Grove. During June there is the Osage Indian Camp at Pawhuska, which includes tribal dancing, and an Indian celebration in Clinton. July features a powwow in Okmulgee, one at Pawnee for the Pawnee tribe, a Sac and Fox Powwow at Stroud, a Quapaw tribal powwow at Quapaw, and a Chickasaw Festival at Tishomingo.

State fairs are popular in Oklahoma. In September, Oklahoma City hosts the Oklahoma State Fair, and in October the second-largest city sponsors the Tulsa State Fair. Besides scientific, technical, and cultural exhibits, the fairs feature midways, rides, and carnival attractions.

Some of the special festivals around the state include a Czech Festival in October in the town of Yukon, and another in May in the town of Prague, called the Kolache Festival; a World Championship

Watermelon Seed Spitting Contest at Pauls Valley in July; and a Strawberry Festival in May at Stilwell.

One of the country's truly unique events takes place in Oklahoma each April—the World Cow Chip Throwing Contest, commemorating the cattle dung used as fuel that facilitated the survival of so many homesteaders and ranchers during the state's frontier days. The contest is part of the Cimarron Territory Celebration in the Panhandle city of Beaver.

There are also other historical celebrations, such as the Cherokee Strip Celebration in Perry in September; the No Man's Land Pioneer Days in Guymon in early May; and the Love County Frontier Days in Marietta in June.

N.C.

CHRONOLOGY

1682   Robert Cavelier, Sieur de La Salle, claimed Oklahoma as part of French Louisiana.

1762   France gave Louisiana, including Oklahoma region, to Spain.

1803   United States bought Oklahoma region, except for Panhandle, as part of Louisiana Purchase.

1824   Fort Gibson and Fort Towson established as the region's first military outposts.

1820–42   The Five Civilized Tribes—the Cherokee, Chickasaw, Choctaw, Creek, and Seminole—were moved to Oklahoma from southeastern United States.

1870–72   The Missouri-Kansas-Texas railroad was built across Oklahoma.

1889   Oklahoma opened to white settlement, and its first producing oil well was brought in, near Chelsea.

1890   Territory of Oklahoma established by U. S. Congress.

1907   Oklahoma became the forty-sixth state on November 16.

1910   Oklahoma City became the capital, which was moved from Guthrie.

1920   Osage County oil fields began production.

1928   Oklahoma City oil field opened.

1953   Tulsa–Oklahoma City toll road opened.

1965   Lake Eufaula completed, creating Oklahoma's largest lake.

1970s   Completion of the McClellan-Kerr Arkansas River Navigation System, which links Tulsa to the Gulf of Mexico.

1971   Mrs. Patience Latting became the first woman mayor of Oklahoma City, the state's largest city.

1973   One of the nation's costliest prison riots occurred at Oklahoma State Prison at McAlester, resulting in the deaths of several prisoners, injuries to prisoners, officials, and guards, and causing $20 million damage.

1974   The state elected its youngest governor ever—David Boren, thirty-three, a Rhodes scholar and political science professor at Oklahoma Baptist University. His nomination was considered an upset victory in the Democratic primary.

1976   A $100,000 Oklahoma City heritage plaza was planned for downtown's Civic Center Park.

1978   Oklahoma City proved to be one of a handful of U.S. cities with a detailed evacuation plan in case of foreign attack, according to civil defense authorities.

1979   The first teachers' strike ever to take place within the state occurred in late August when teachers in Oklahoma City refused to report for work, seeking a pay increase.

Texas

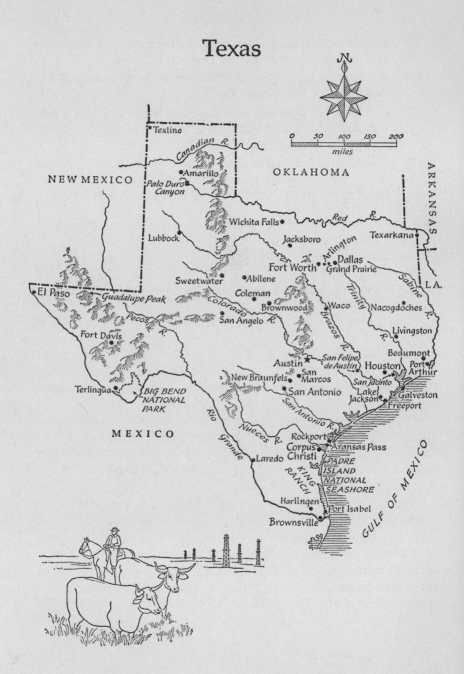

TEXAS

THERE IS a line in the state anthem "Texas, Our Texas" that used to be "largest and grandest." Nowadays, when the anthem is sung, that line is "boldest and grandest." The word "largest" was grudgingly changed when Alaska entered the Union. Little things like that hurt in a state as prideful—deservedly prideful, albeit—as Texas.

But in case the mention of the change in lyrics has elicited smiles over the possible discomfort of the Texas Chamber of Commerce, just remember one thing—Texas didn't do any actual shrinking. It's still big. There were 262,840 square miles of land and 4,500 square miles of water there before the anthem was changed, and the figures were still the same afterward. From the town of Texline in the northwest to Brownsville in the southeast corner is a distance of 939 miles; from west to east—El Paso to Texarkana—is 813 miles. And there are some 11,197,000 people living within that expanse.

Mighty big and awesome, but mighty friendly, too. As a matter of fact, that's the state motto, "Friendship," taken, presumably, from the state's very name, which is derived from "Tejas," the name of a confederacy of local Indian tribes. It is generally accepted that the word means "friendly."

The way Texas looks, too, would no doubt surprise some folks harboring prejudicial images of the state. It does not, for instance, all look like that famous scene in the 1950s movie *Giant*—one big old ranch house surrounded by endless expanses of completely undistinguished pasture, with no trees, no hills, nothing. Nothing but cattle, of course. Instead, the Texas landscape is beautifully diverse: mountains, prairies, forests, thousands of lakes, rivers, subtropical beaches.

THE LAND

The image of Texas as being all wide, arid plains filled with cattle and cowboys is simply not so. The state comprises a series of gigantic steps, from the fertile and densely populated Coastal Plains in the southeast to the high plains and mountains in the west and northwest.

There are four principal topographical regions. The West Gulf Coastal Plains is a fertile lowland that lies along the Gulf Coast, ranging from 150 to 350 miles wide, and in elevation from sea level to about 300 feet above sea level. The southernmost part of the Coastal Plains consists of the fertile valley of the lower Rio Grande, one of the longest and most historic rivers in the United States. For 1,241 miles it forms the boundary between the United States and Mexico.

The North-Central Plains have under them large deposits of oil. On the surface there are deep, rich soils producing prime farm land. This area lies west of the forest belt of the Coastal Plains.

The Panhandle makes up the major portion of the Great Plains, which stretches westward from the North-Central Plains into New Mexico, rising from about 700 feet above sea level to more than 4,000 feet in the west.

The westernmost part of Texas is the Basin and Range Region (also called the Trans-Pecos Region), which includes high, partly dry plains crossed by extensions of the Rocky Mountains. The state's highest mountains are in this region, including 8,751-foot Guadalupe Peak, the highest point in Texas.

The general coastline of Texas is 367 miles, but the many bays, offshore islands, and river mouths extend the tidal shore line to 3,359 miles. The coast is partly protected from ocean storms and tidal waves by a series of narrow sand bars. By removing the silt left by the many streams emptying into the Gulf, engineers have made possible thirteen deep-water ports and fifteen ports for barges and small ships along the Texas coast.

Texas also has thousands of lakes that have been enlarged by man. Most of the lakes were created as part of the state's program for generating hydroelectric power, irrigating farm lands, and storing water.

CLIMATE

Texas is so large that it is impossible to generalize about the weather on a state-wide basis. The climate range is from subtropical in the lower Rio Grande Valley, the warmest part of the state, to moderately temperate in the northwest.

The lower Rio Grande area stays warm most of the year—January averages 60 degrees, for instance—and summertime is a scorcher, with average July readings of 85 degrees. That is in significant contrast to the coldest section of the state, in the northwest Panhandle, where the average January temperatures are around 35 degrees and average July readings are 79 degrees.

The Gulf of Mexico region is warm and damp, where winds from the Gulf reduce the summer heat and winter cold. Central Texas has about the most agreeable weather; there, the climate is usually mild and delightful, making it a popular year-round resort area. The northeastern section is usually damp and cool; in the northwest the winters are long and cold. In the western region the climate is cool but dry.

As a matter of fact, Texas gets drier from east to west. East Texas has an average 46 inches of precipitation (rain, snow, sleet, and every other form of moisture) a year, while parts of western Texas get only 12 inches a year. A good example would be Port Arthur, in the southeast, which gets about 45 more inches of rain a year than El Paso, in the far west.

Wind is a fairly constant factor in Texas. Strong winds often blow throughout the Great Plains, and during droughts these winds carry away the soil. Occasionally, during the winter, winds, sleet, and heavy rain from the north sweep across the state. Snow seldom falls in the south-central and central regions, but the High Plains have an average of more than 24 inches of snow a year.

THE TEXANS

When Spanish adventurers and explorers in the sixteenth century first penetrated the vastness of what is now Texas, there were more than twenty tribes of native Indians living and thriving there; in the following centuries other tribes came, like the Comanche and Kiowa, who had been driven from their lands to the north, and the Choctaw, Chickasaw, and Alabama-Coushatta, who had been pushed westward across the Mississippi by expanding American settlement.

But the Indians got in the way of white settlers, who considered all of them a threat, despite the peace efforts of certain tribes. There were many military campaigns against the various tribes, seldom distinguishing between friend and foe. By 1867 the federal government came down hard on the Indians, forcing leaders of the Comanche, Kiowa, and Apache tribes to sign a treaty restricting them to 3 million acres in what is now eastern Oklahoma, then called Indian Territory. Some Indians broke out now and then, pulling off some damaging raids, but finally, in the 1870s, they were subdued and permanently restricted.

Today, according to a recent census, there are only about 18,000 Indians living in Texas, but that figure fails to account for the rather large heritage left in the state by the Indians, for there are many families with Indian blood. Most of the Indians today are unobtrusive city dwellers, but there are two tribes still maintaining their unity—the Alabama-Coushatta tribe, which occupies the only reservation in the state, in east Texas; and about 300 Tiwa living at a site now enveloped by the town of El Paso.

A significantly large part of the Texas population is composed of chicanos, although discussing this group involves some difficulties of definition. The dictionary defines chicano as an American of Mexican descent, but in Texas subtle differences exist between such terms as Mexican-American and chicano, although popular usage has tended to fuse them. The federal census combines them all into a single group through the criterion of Spanish surnames. That sort of measurement fails to account for all the centuries of intermingling of Mexican with Indian and European bloodlines, including families whose surnames have lost all Mexican-American flavor. The fact is, around 20 per cent of Texans are of Mexican-American descent. A number of communities along the American side of Texas' southwestern border are almost totally Mexican-American.

Chicanos have gained a progressively better way of life since World War II, but in Texas they are still at the bottom of all ethnic groups in terms of education, income, and political power; to overcome these deficiencies has become the overriding goal of the chicanos.

Layers of rock formed over 225 million years ago
and Canyon's Inner Gorge.

PLATE 74 Montezuma Castle National Monum
cliff dwelling built by Pueblo Indians in the 120

PLATE 7
in the Gr

PLATE 76 Horseback riding over desert trails in the Valley of the Sun, near Phoenix.

PLATE 77 Monument Valley in Arizona, where red sandstone walls tower over the canyon floor.

PLATE 78 Prehistoric cliff dwellings in Bandelier National Monument near Santa Fe.

PLATE 79 San Xavier del Bac mission near Tucson.

PLATE 80 The terraced, multi-storied communal dwellings of Taos Pueblo in New Mexico.

PLATE 81 The impressive formation of the "Giant Dome" in Carlsbad Caverns.

PLATE 82 San Miguel Mission, the oldest mission church in the United States, is in Santa Fe.

PLATE 83 Will Rogers Memorial in Claremont, Oklahoma, birthplace of the beloved humorist.

PLATE 84 Venus' Needle, a towering monolith, in northwestern New Mexico.

PLATE 86 Cattle ranch in West Texas.

defeated the Mexicans in a surprise attack at San Jacinto, during which Santa Anna was captured.

In October 1836 the Republic of Texas was officially established, with Sam Houston as president and Stephen Austin as secretary of state. But the republic was to last only ten years—a very difficult ten years. The financial situation was very bad and no foreign country would give the new republic loans. There was constant harassment—raids from Mexico and from the Indians. It was during this period that the famous Texas Rangers were formed, armed riders whose duties were to travel long distances quickly to repel or punish raiding forces.

The Texans finally gave up and signed an annexation treaty in 1845 with the United States, and Texas became the twenty-eighth state on December 29, 1845. The annexation agreement included a provision permitting Texas to retain title to public lands, a situation unique among the states of this country.

In 1861 Texas seceded and joined the Confederacy, despite the fact that Governor Houston adamantly opposed secession and refused to take an oath of allegiance to the Confederate States. He was removed from office for his stubbornness. No major battles of the war were fought in Texas, but the citizens did have to defend themselves from Indian attacks, Mexican encroachment, and federal gunboats and troops. Federal forces gained control of much of the Gulf Coast, but they didn't get any farther inland.

After Texas re-entered the Union in 1870, there were rapid developments in population and economy. Aided by immigration from the North, the South, and Europe, farming spread throughout the central areas; the cattle industry began to flourish on the plains; railroad building and increased shipping forged new links with the rest of the world; manufacturing grew, and by 1900 the population was more than 3 million.

In the following decades there were few interruptions—except for the Great Depression—of progress and prosperity. In 1901 the Spindletop oil field was discovered, which gave birth to Texas' fabulous petroleum industry: great refineries and other manufacturing plants were built; coastal harbors were deepened to help ship oil and other products. Between 1900 and 1920 railroad mileage was increased and the state built a road system; between 1900 and 1910, the total value of manufactured goods more than doubled. Between 1900 and

1920 the number of cities and towns also doubled, because more Texans were becoming workers in city-oriented industries.

In 1953 there was federal legislation of great significance to Texas. Three years before, in 1950, the U. S. Supreme Court ruled that Texas had lost ownership of its oil-rich tidelands (submerged offshore lands) when it entered the Union in 1845. Great reservoirs of oil had been discovered beneath the shallow tidewaters, and the court's decision meant that the oil belonged to the federal government. After a bitter dispute in Congress, President Dwight D. Eisenhower signed a bill in 1953 that restored the tidelands to Texas.

Today, Texas is in a period of rapid industrial growth, spurred in large measure by the construction and continued development of the Lyndon B. Johnson Space Center near Houston. The center covers 1,600 acres, has thousands of employees, and has been responsible for the growth of related industries.

The most tragic incident in modern Texas history was the assassination of President John F. Kennedy in Dallas on November 22, 1963. Texas Governor John B. Connally was wounded during the shooting. On that same day, Lyndon B. Johnson, Kennedy's Vice President and a native of Texas, became the first southern President since the Civil War. Lee Harvey Oswald, accused of shooting the President, was shot to death two days later by Jack Ruby, a Dallas nightclub owner.

INDUSTRY

With so much oil lying beneath its surface in practically every part of the state, it was only natural that petroleum and petroleum-related products came to dominate the industry of Texas.

The chemical industry is the most important industry in Texas, accounting for about one fourth of the state's manufacturing income, surpassing even petroleum refining. However, it is a petroleum-related industry, for most of the products are based on oil and natural gas. The most important are ammonia, caustic soda, chlorinated solvents, glycols, hydrochloric acid, polyethylene, and synthetic rubber. The centers of chemical production are located mostly in the Gulf Coast cities.

Texas is first among the states in petroleum refining, with more than one hundred refineries throughout the state, the largest located along the Gulf Coast in Baytown, Beaumont, Houston, Port Arthur, and other port cities. Oil is also brought to these coastal refineries by pipelines from all over Texas and other states as well.

Since World War II the manufacture of transportation equipment has greatly increased in Texas, most of the growth concentrated in aircraft and aerospace production. However, boat and mobile home construction have also been expanding.

Food processing had become very important to the Texas economy by the late 1960s, employing at least 86,000 workers. The meat-packing industry is based in Fort Worth, which has the largest stockyards south of St. Louis. Other important industries involve the cleaning and polishing of rice; sugar refineries; manufacturing of cottonseed, peanut, sugar-dextrose, and vegetable oil products; canning and preserving fruits and vegetables; and milling flour.

Texas forestry products are also significant. There are more than 1,000 wood-using plants in the state, most of them in the northeast, where mills and factories manufacture furniture and fixtures, lumber, poles, posts, pulp, veneer and plywood, and wooden containers. Texas also has a healthy fishing industry, for it is a leader in shrimp production, with an average yearly catch of about 70 million pounds.

America's space explorations have been responsible for substantially enlarging the industrial complex of Houston and the upper Texas Gulf Coast. In the early 1960s the National Aeronautics and Space Administration built the $125-million Manned Spacecraft Center (renamed the Lyndon B. Johnson Space Center after the former President's death in 1973), about twenty miles southeast of Houston at Clear Lake City. The center directs the nation's spacecraft program, but more important to Texas economically was the rapid development of an industry new to the region—electronics—to work in coordination with the Space Center.

AGRICULTURE

Texas produces more beef cattle than any other state. Because the winters in the state's cattle-growing regions are usually mild, the cattle can graze outdoors all year around, enabling Texas farmers to raise cattle more cheaply than northern farmers. The vast cattle empires of the nineteenth century have tended to shift to the coastal areas during this century, the reverse of the path of cotton. Such empires now produce about 10 million head of beef cattle a year, providing around $900 million.

Texas also raises the most sheep in this country, producing the most wool—about 37 million pounds a year. In fact, 60 per cent of the world's mohair and 95 per cent of the United States total comes from the Angora goats of Texas.

Long before the Civil War, farmers found that the fertile land of east Texas was just right for cotton growing, and in the years after the war, cotton became the state's major crop. But as mechanized farming developed, cotton growing shifted to the High Plains country in West Texas, where irrigation and fertilizer maintained the bountiful production. Today, cotton is still Texas' most valuable crop, and more of it grows there than in any other state.

Primarily because of its size, Texas has always been an agricultural leader, and in recent years it has consistently ranked third or fourth among the states in total value of farm crops. It is a leading producer of grain sorghums, rice, wheat, grapefruit, pecans, peanuts, and watermelons. And it also ranks high in the production of chickens, eggs, turkeys, vegetables, and honey.

NATURAL RESOURCES

Drillers first discovered oil in Texas near Nacogdoches in 1867. During the ensuing years it was determined that impressive quantities of "black gold" were tucked away beneath east Texas fields.

But it wasn't until 1901 that large-scale oil production began, with the opening of the Spindletop field near Beaumont. Later, large fields were opened in the Panhandle, the Pecos Valley, and central, east, and north Texas—all over, practically. The greatest discovery was in 1930, when drillers brought in the famous East Texas oil field, which became the largest in the world, with more than 19,000 producing oil wells.

Today, Texas leads all the other states in the value of mineral production, primarily because of its oil. Texas wells account for about a third of the U.S. oil production, and nearly a tenth of the world's supply. Along with the oil came natural gas, which occurs in all the state's oil-producing regions, making it Texas' second most valuable mineral. There are also large deposits of sulphur and salt: Texas supplies half the nation's sulphur and is second in salt production.

Texas also has great coal deposits, about 8 billion tons' worth, the largest extending through north-central Texas; beds of lignite cover about 60,000 square miles, from Laredo to Texarkana; in the western mountains and the central hills regions are deposits of copper and gold, and silver is in the Basin and Range Region; there is a broad belt of limestone extending from the Red River to the Rio Grande, and across north-central Texas; and gypsum deposits lie in the North-Central Plains and the Basin and Range Region.

Soils, or the lack of them, are vital in determining an area's history and well-being, and Texas has been liberally blessed with five hundred different soil types, enabling farmers to grow a great variety of crops. Forests cover more than 26 million acres, nearly 15 per cent of the state. There are more than 120 kinds of trees, but the most commercially valuable are the pines and hardwoods, like gums and oaks, which grow on about 12.5 million acres.

Wildlife is plentiful in the eastern forests and the western plains, and landowners in these areas earn millions of dollars a year selling hunting leases to sportsmen. The principal game are deer, pronghorn, and wild turkeys. Texas is also a bird watcher's paradise, inhabited at one time of the year or another by nearly two thirds of all North American species north of Mexico. The lowlands of the Texas coast are especially noteworthy for the great variety and abundance of birds, especially in the town of Rockport, near Corpus Christi, the center of the Aransas National Wildlife Refuge. It is there that the famous whooping crane is making what may be its last stand.

CITIES

Probably the most remarkable aspect of modern Texas is its cities, for they are the most dynamic and fastest-growing in the country.

Houston, for instance, with a population of some 1,959,000, is already the largest city in the Southwest. Its citizens seem obsessed with the future, and with massiveness, good examples being the Astrodomain and the Lyndon B. Johnson Space Center. The original part of the $100 million Astrodomain is the Astrodome, designed to house a variety of sporting events (such as Houston's pro football team, the Oilers, and its baseball team, the Astros) in all sorts of weather, heated and air-conditioned, capable of holding 45,000 to 66,000 spectators, depending on the event. Next door to the Astrodome is

Astrohall, one of the world's largest exhibition centers and home of the Houston Livestock Show and Rodeo and of Ringling Bros. and Barnum & Bailey Circus.

Although the Space Center is south of Houston, in Clear Lake City, the complex is considered part of the city. The center is of prime significance to America's space program, for it was the headquarters of the *Mercury, Gemini,* and *Apollo* flights and is now the training center for NASA's Space Lab and Space Shuttle programs.

Houston is now called the Oil Capital of the World, replacing Tulsa, Oklahoma, the former long-time title holder, by virtue of the fact that a majority of the nation's oil companies have their headquarters in Houston. Also, it is, and has long been, a center of oil refining.

But along with all its dynamism and economic accomplishments, Houston is also a fiercely cultural city. It is enriched by facilities for symphony, opera, and jazz concerts, ballet, musical comedy, and theater. Its Museum of Fine Arts contains American, European, and Far Eastern art objects; and its medical facilities—including 17 institutions, hospitals, and research centers making up the Texas Medical Center—rate among the finest in the world.

The city's educational institutions include the University of Houston, founded in 1934 and now among the largest in the state system; Rice University, founded in 1912, and one of the nation's great privately endowed institutions; and Texas Southern University.

Dallas—"Big D"—is Texas' second-largest city, with a population of around 850,000, referring to the city itself, or about 1.6 million, if considered as Metropolitan Dallas, which includes the six counties of Dallas, Collin, Denton, Rockwall, Kaufman, and Ellis.

Another way of looking at Dallas is as part of the Dallas–Fort Worth complex that is rapidly nearing the day when it will become one huge megalopolis. There are two towns in between the cities— Arlington and Grand Prairie—which will be swallowed up in the process.

It is generally recognized that Dallas is the New York of the Southwest, a leader in sophistication and culture. Its culture consciousness began in the 1850s when over two hundred French artists, writers, musicians, and scientists settled there hoping to found a utopian colony. The colony failed but the venture gave Dallas its cultural nucleus.

The Dallas Symphony is a major orchestra, and the Frank Lloyd

Wright-designed Theater Center is well known for its productions; the Metropolitan Opera Company of New York makes an annual tour to Dallas; Dallas Summer Musicals are held at State Fair Music Hall; the Dallas Civic Opera offers a full season; ballet may be seen during the year at the State Fair Music Hall.

Dallas' Fair Park is a tremendous $36-million facility with ten permanent exposition buildings, an ice skating rink, and an amusement park. Among the features of Fair Park are the Cotton Bowl, the Dallas Aquarium, the Dallas Garden Center, the Dallas Health and Science Museum, the Museum of Fine Arts, and the Museum of Natural History.

Dallas is an important business and industrial center, with more than 200 insurance companies (more insurance firms are headquartered there than in any other American city), fifty hospitals and clinics, thirty-eight trucking lines, a great many wholesale operations, and the fourth-largest number of million-dollar businesses. It is the Southwest's largest banking center, and ranks as one of the nation's top three fashion centers.

One of the most impressive commercial centers of the city is the Market Hall, which has 188,000 square feet of exhibit space in three connected halls, all designed for easy, efficient buying. The Dallas Convention Center has a main exhibit hall that can seat 28,000 people, and an arena with seating for more than 10,000. It has a total of more than 600,000 square feet of exhibit space.

The world's second-largest airport is the Dallas-Fort Worth Regional Airport, a facility intended to be the world's largest (the one in Toronto has more acres).

Dallas is significant in education also, with the famed Southern Methodist University, the University of Texas Southwestern Medical School, the Baylor University College of Dentistry, and the Southwest Center for Advanced Studies.

Dallas has built three distinct memorials to assassinated President John F. Kennedy: one is a polished granite marker at the corner of Houston and Main streets, to mark the spot where he was shot; another is a cenotaph and memorial park at Main and Record streets; the third is the John F. Kennedy Museum in Dealey Plaza.

Although **Fort Worth** is one of the state's fastest growing cities, and is a major industrial center, it still retains much of its rugged, western flavor. It has oil and aircraft industries, grain industries, and it is one of the nation's leading food production and packaging centers. But this city of over 400,000 people has not gotten too far away from its frontier past, for it is still headquarters for the cattle industry. Just as it has been since shortly after the Civil War, it continues to be one of the leading shipping points and supply depots for cattlemen and for other agricultural enterprises.

The city began as a military camp in the late 1840s, established to protect settlers from the Indians, and was named for General William J. Worth, a hero of the Mexican War. In the 1850s it became a major stop on the old Chisholm Trail, which eventually led to its becoming a gathering place for herds of cattle being driven to Kansas railheads.

Today, the cowboy atmosphere is tempered by an expanding cultural awareness: Fort Worth has its own symphony orchestra, opera, and ballet, summer and winter theater seasons, and many art galleries and museums. One of its proudest possessions is the new Tarrant County Convention Center, covering fourteen downtown city blocks.

The Amon Carter Museum of Western Art, across the street from the Fort Worth Art Center and the Will Rogers Auditorium and Coliseum, lures art connoisseurs from all over the nation. The museum houses an outstanding collection of some of the most famous cowboy and Indian paintings and bronzes of Frederic Remington and Charles Russell.

The newest addition to the arts is the Kimbell Art Museum, exhibiting an international collection of European, Oriental, Near East, and pre-Columbian art. The city also has some fine higher-education institutions: Texas Christian University, Texas Wesleyan College, and the Southwestern Baptist Theological Seminary.

Austin, the state's capital, has experienced truly incredible growth during recent decades. Between 1950 and 1960 the population leaped from 132,000 to 187,000; and from 1960 to 1970 it soared to 252,000. Most likely, this increase has resulted from the rising importance of state administrative and governmental functions.

The city, founded in 1839 and named for Stephen F. Austin, the "father of Texas," is situated in Texas' Hill Country, and the many species of wildflowers that grow on the gently rolling hills that surround Austin present a lovely vista for travelers.

There are two establishments worthy of attention in Austin. One is the massive state capitol, built of the famous Texas pink granite, modeled after the U. S. Capitol. It dominates forty-six acres of landscaped grounds and flowering gardens. The other is the University of

Texas, founded in 1833, the largest university in the state, with about 40,000 students. The buildings are of a striking Mediterranean-style architecture. The Lyndon Baines Johnson Library is also one of the outstanding attractions. The archives have documents of the Johnson Administration and the presidency in general. There are also slides, motion pictures, closed circuit TV, and mobile exhibits.

San Antonio, third-largest city in Texas with a population of over 650,000, is a busy city with military-industrial enterprises, but it has not lost its Old Spanish atmosphere. Since its founding as a mission center in the early 1700s the city has been under six flags—Spain, France, Mexico, the Republic of Texas, the Confederate States of America, and the United States.

The influence of all those nations is still apparent in the architecture and general flavor of this lovely city. It has a modern skyline with tall office buildings that blend with remnants of the past, such as La Villita, a restoration of San Antonio as it was in the time of Jim Bowie and Davy Crockett. They and 185 others died in the Alamo in 1836, defending against a Mexican army. The Alamo is the city's foremost shrine and one of the nation's most famous historical landmarks. Another outstanding vestige of San Antonio's past is the eighteenth-century Spanish Governor's Palace, which is near La Villita.

Situated on the Mexican border, **El Paso's** international atmosphere is evident in a thousand ways. The cultural influences of the Indians, Mexicans, Spaniards, and American pioneers have all been preserved in this wide-open, sprawling city of 330,000. In El Paso is Ysleta, the oldest community in Texas, which was established by refugees from the bloody revolt of Indians against the Spanish along the upper Rio Grande in 1681, in what is now New Mexico.

Ysleta's ancient flavor has been preserved, for today whitewashed adobe stands in stark contrast to modern structures hundreds of years newer. The Tiwa tribe, which has many direct descendants of the Indians who fled the 1681 Pueblo revolt, still makes its home in Ysleta.

Old Fort Bliss was established in El Paso in 1848 as a defense post against the Indians. Today, it is a major rocket research and combat training center for the U. S. Army Air Defense Command.

Corpus Christi has doubled its population four times in the past forty years and now has a population of over 200,000, making it the state's seventh-largest city. It is a major port, ranked ninth in America, where a cosmopolitan array of flags can be seen on ships loading and unloading cargo. It is also liberally endowed with cultural efforts in art, drama, literature, and music—its huge Memorial Coliseum hosts a big roster of events, including the All-Texas Jazz Festival. But for visitors, the city is most popular as a convention and resort center, with its beaches, bays, yacht basins, plush motels, clubs, and beautiful climate.

Amarillo, a large, modern city with a population over 127,000, is the oil and gas center of the Texas Panhandle, with pipelines from nearby fields extending to the east coast of the state. It also has one of the world's largest helium plants and one of the world's largest carbon-black plants. A source of civic pride is the 417-acre Amarillo Medical Center, composed of ten different institutions.

Galveston on Galveston Island in the Gulf of Mexico, is a city of 62,000 people, connected by causeways to the mainland. A ten-mile sea wall guards it from flooding. Because of its sunny location and its thirty-two-mile-long beach, Galveston has become a popular resort and fishing area. It is also one of the Southwest's leading ports.

Waco, in east-central Texas on the Brazon River, was founded in 1849 and has a population of nearly 100,000. Baylor University was chartered by the Republic of Texas in 1845. Its Armstrong Browning Library contains the world's largest collection of Browning works and personal memorabilia.

SPORTS AND RECREATION

There are truly fine experiences to be had just about anywhere in Texas. One of the prime areas for sportsmen are the inland waterways, the hundreds of creeks, rivers, and lakes making up 6,000 square miles of fresh water.

Freshwater fishermen from throughout the Southwest come to the region for black bass, smallmouth or Kentucky bass, bluegills, crappie, white or sand bass, channel, blue, and flathead catfish. Less abundant and more highly prized are rainbow trout, pickerel, northern pike, walleye, and striped bass.

Saltwater fishermen love the Gulf Coast, where there are 624 miles of shoreline and around 250 species of fish. The most popular are speckled trout, king and Spanish mackerel, wahoo, tuna, marlin, bonito, sailfish, pompano, flounder, grouper, jewfish, red snapper, sheepshead, redfish, and drum.

Like fishing, hunting in Texas ranks as some of the best in the country. Top game animal is the white-tailed deer, which is found almost all over the state, but most abundantly in the Hill Country of central Texas, where they occur in greater numbers than anywhere else in the United States. Mule deer and pronghorn antelope are found in dense numbers in West Texas. Other game animals include javelinas, wild boars, and squirrels.

Game birds are plentiful too, including a great variety of waterfowl which winter in Texas. There are wild turkey, several types of quail, mourning and white-winged doves, pheasants, prairie chicken, sandhill cranes, and chahalacas.

There are also some ranches where exotic game animals are stocked for hunting year round. Among the species are wild Corsican rams, Indian blackbuck antelope, African aoudad sheep, axis and sika deer.

The state's four national forests are situated in East Texas, and cover a total of 658,023 acres. Except for two small game management areas, all lands in the forests are open to the public, where visitors may see abundant wildlife, exotic flora, and controlled timbering industries. The forests—Angelina, Sabine, Davy Crockett, and Sam Houston—have hiking trails, shelters, boating and swimming areas, camping grounds, and picnicking areas.

Texas also has four state forests, which are wildlife refuges, where hunting is prohibited and where fishing is permitted only in designated areas. They are under management of the Texas Forest Service, which is part of Texas A&M University. Fairchild covers 2,896 acres, Jones covers 1,725 acres, Kirby has 600 acres, and Siecke comprises 1,722 acres.

A popular way to get to know the real Texas is to sign for a farm or dude ranch vacation. There are many ranches catering to guests in the Bandera and Hill Country northwest of San Antonio. The dude ranches savor the Old West, but are not without concession to the twentieth century, such as runways for guests who are flying in.

One of the state's most popular resort areas is the Gulf Coast. Corpus Christi, Aransas Pass, Port Isabel, and Galveston are some of the top resort towns. Off the coast from Corpus Christi is the Padre Island National Seashore, an 80-mile stretch on Padre Island, which, at 110 miles, is the nation's longest. This unspoiled island offers one of the last entirely natural seashores in the United States.

POINTS OF INTEREST

When visiting San Antonio, remember the Alamo, where 187 defenders died on March 6, 1836, after holding off the huge army of Mexican General Santa Anna for two weeks. The Alamo, located in downtown San Antonio, was built in 1744. It is open every day of the week and holidays except for December 24 and 25. Remember the Alamo Theater, opposite the mission fortress, presents films about the battle.

Six Flags Over Texas, just northeast of Arlington, is a huge recreational and entertainment park that draws several million visitors every year. History and fantasy are combined to celebrate Texas' colorful past. There are rides, Indian ceremonies, gunfights, riverboat excursions, cave explorations, and staged entertainment.

Big Bend National Park is a gigantic wilderness area covering 708,221 acres of desert, mountains, and canyons. Fossil remains of the ocean that covered this area millions of years ago can be seen on the canyon walls. Visitors can see mule deer, javelina (collared peccary), squirrels, cougar, gray fox, bobcat, coyote, pronghorn antelope, an occasional rare desert bighorn sheep, and more than 200 species of birds.

The Palo Duro Canyon Scenic Park, in the Panhandle, exposes over 200 million years of geological formations. There are fifteen miles of scenic drives, twenty miles of bridle paths, and thirty miles of hiking trails.

The W. J. McDonald Observatory, near Fort Davis, north of the Big Bend National Park, has telescopes that are among the largest in operation in the world. There is free access during the day to a viewing gallery.

The Fort Worth Museum of Science and History features both live and mounted animals, historical artifacts, and special exhibits for youth. Museum displays include a diversity of subjects, such as the history of Texas, health, astronomy, dolls, and the natural history of man. There is also a planetarium.

Lion Country Safari, just north of the Dallas-Fort Worth Turnpike, uses its 500 acres to imitate an African plain, complete with lions, elephants, rhinoceros, giraffes, zebras, antelopes, chimpanzees, cheetahs, and other animals and birds.

On April 21, 1836, Texan revolutionaries and the Mexican Army met in a fierce battle, some twenty-one miles east of the present city of Houston, a battle that ended the war and won Texas its independence. Today that battle of San Jacinto is commemorated in the 460-acre San Jacinto Battleground Park. Within the park is the San Jacinto Monument and Museum of History, a 570-foot building that contains a museum in its base which traces the region's history from ancient times.

The Alabama-Coushatta Indian Reservation, east of the town of Livingston, home of several hundred Alabama and Coushatta Indians, is the state's oldest reservation. Visitors can enjoy the Living Indian Village, where tribal members make jewelry, basketry, and leather goods.

The King Ranch, in southern Texas west of the town of Kingsville, is the largest ranch in the United States, covering about 823,000 acres. It was established in 1853 by Captain Richard King, and his descendants still control it. The original stock was only Texas Longhorns, but the ranch led in introducing purebred cattle such as Hereford, Shorthorn, and Brahman. The famous Santa Gertrudis breed, the first strain of cattle originated in the Western Hemisphere, was developed on the King Ranch. Visitors can follow a twelve-mile loop drive to observe the ranch operations.

SPECIAL EVENTS

The year begins with the end of a rousing salute to the Texas climate, the Southwestern Sun Carnival in El Paso. From December 20 to January 1, the folks in El Paso enjoy beauty contests, balls, swimming, golf, tennis, polo meets, sports car races, rodeos, and the annual Sun Bowl football game. On January 1 is the big finale, the Sun Carnival Parade.

Also on the first day of the year is the traditional Cotton Bowl football game in Dallas.

February is the time for pre-Lenten festivals, which are called Mardi Gras in the Gulf Coast towns of Freeport and Lake Jackson, and Charro Days in Brownsville, a four-day international fiesta on both sides of the border.

San Antonio stages its stock shows and rodeo at mid-month, and the historic Salt Grass Trail Ride opens the Houston Livestock Show and Rodeo during the closing week.

March is rattlesnake-catching season. There are rattlesnake round-ups for hunters and spectators at Brownwood, Coleman, Jacksboro, and Sweetwater.

The most dramatic moments of Texas history are celebrated during the third week of April. On April 21, 1836, Texas won its independence from Mexico at the battle of San Jacinto near Houston. State-wide ceremonies mark the occasion, with the feature event at the San Jacinto Battleground, including a review of the Texas Navy, composed of yachts and pleasure boats.

Also around April 21 is the Fiesta San Antonio, a Latin-accented carnival for nine days, featuring the famous Battle of Flowers Parade, a nighttime water parade on the San Antonio River through midtown, and a night parade called the Fiesta Flambeau. The festivities are centered around La Villita, a re-created Mexican village of a century ago, in the heart of San Antonio.

Pirates invade Corpus Christi in May and subject the city to a reign of fun during the last days of April and the first days of May, called the Buccaneer Days, with parades, balls, beach activities, and a music festival.

There are a good many food festivals in the fall. Some of the most outstanding are San Antonio's Texas Folklife Festival in September; the annual Republic of Texas Chilympiad, a chili cooking contest in San Marcos in September; the World Championship Chili Cook-Off at the ghost town of Terlingua in November; and the Wurstfest (sausage festival) during the last days of October and the first days of November in New Braunfels.

Autumn is also the time for country and regional fairs, the biggest of them all being the State Fair of Texas, which runs for sixteen days in Dallas in October.

In November, at Harlingen, the Confederate Air Force presents its annual flying spectacular, featuring military aircraft of World War II from the United States, Great Britain, Germany, and Japan.

N.C.

CHRONOLOGY

1519   Alonso Álvarez de Pineda of Spain mapped Texas coast.

1541   Francisco Vásquez de Coronado traveled across part of west Texas.

1542   Hernando de Soto's expedition explored part of northeast Texas.

1682   Spanish missionaries built first two missions in Texas, near present-day El Paso.

1685   Robert Cavelier, Sieur de La Salle, founded Fort St. Louis, a French settlement, on Texas coast.

1718   Spaniards established mission and fort on site of present-day San Antonio.

1821   Texas became part of new Empire of Mexico. Americans led by Stephen F. Austin settled in Texas.

1835   Texas began revolution against Mexico.

1836   Independence from Mexico declared; Mexican forces overwhelmed and defeated American defenders at Alamo; Sam Houston defeated Mexicans in Battle of San Jacinto; Texas won its independence and became Republic of Texas.

1845   Texas admitted to Union on December 29, becoming twenty-eighth state.

1861   Texas seceded from Union and joined Confederacy.

1870   Texas readmitted to Union.

1901   Oilmen discovered great Spindletop oil field.

1925   Texas became second state to have a woman governor—Mrs. Miriam A. Ferguson.

1947   Ship explosion in Texas City harbor killed about 500 persons, injured about 3,000.

1953   Congress restored Texas tidelands to the state.

1962   Construction of Manned Spacecraft Center at Houston was started.

1963   President John F. Kennedy was assassinated in Dallas on November 22, and Lyndon B. Johnson, of Texas, Kennedy's Vice President, was sworn in as the thirty-sixth President.

1964   The Manned Spacecraft Center near Houston became permanent headquarters of American astronauts.

1967   Hurricane Beulah struck Texas Gulf coast on September 20, resulting in fourteen deaths and property damages of $225 million.

1968   HemisFair '68, an international exposition, was held in San Antonio, marking the city's 250th anniversary.

1970   Hurricane Celia devastated Corpus Christi area, killing eleven people and causing $750 million damage.

1971   Lyndon Baines Johnson Library dedicated in Austin.

1974 $210 million Union Terminal area redevelopment in Dallas.

1976   Horizon '76 Program—a plan to preserve, restore, and enhance Austin's waterways.

Opening of El Paso amphitheater with Southwest history outdoor drama.

1977   National Women's Conference held in Houston.

1979   An August oil slick from Mexico's Extoc I offshore oil rig fouled huge sections of the state's coastline with the region near Brownsville especially affected.

When Republican William P. Clements, Jr., took the oath of office as governor, he became the first member of his party to fill the post in 105 years.

THE FAR WEST

Alaska

ALASKA

ALASKA officially joined the Union as its forty-ninth state on January 3, 1959. As the first new state in forty-seven years, Alaska promptly claimed a host of superlatives.

Alaska is, first of all, the largest state: nearly two and a quarter times the size of Texas. It is also the most sparsely populated, with only one third as many citizens as Rhode Island. It has the coldest temperatures, the longest coastline, and the most surface water area, and it is the site of the nation's most northerly, most westerly, and, because the Aleutian Islands extend into the Eastern Hemisphere, most easterly points in the United States.

Alaska's vast expanses embrace North America's highest mountain peak and almost all of its active volcanoes. Earthquakes in Alaska are commonplace. So are glaciers, islands, and spectacular scenery. Alaska also has the longest and shortest days and nights.

Alaska's name is derived from the term "Alyeska," used by the Indians native to the Aleutian Islands to describe their "great land." Today, Alaskans like to refer to their state as the Last Frontier, because the potential wealth of its natural resources is so tremendous and because so much of the land is unsettled and essentially unexplored.

At the present time Alaska is experiencing a more dramatic change than any of the other states. In 1959, as Alaska attained statehood, economic historian George W. Waters, of the University of Alaska, wrote: "Alaska is not something that is or has been; it is a promising potential of something that can be." Today, a great deal of that potential is being realized in a flurry of economic activity triggered by the discovery of massive oil reserves along its Gulf and Arctic coasts.

But Alaska has had booms before. Men have come and exploited its mineral wealth, its fishing waters, its magnificent stands of timber, and then returned to their homes, leaving Alyeska to its Indians,

Eskimos, and sourdoughs, who not only have made their peace with Alaska's sometimes violent climate but love it with a passion.

THE LAND

The overwhelming size of the forty-ninth state in comparison to the others is difficult to conceptualize. Its 586,412 square miles could encompass the next three largest states—Texas, California, and Montana—with room to spare. Alaska's general coastline measures 6,640 miles, but when all the coastline of the mainland and major islands is added, the result measures 33,904 miles.

Alaska is shaped like a giant trident crown tipped on its side with two streamers attached, one flowing southeasterly and one southwesterly. The southwesterly ribbon is formed by the Alaska Peninsula and the Aleutian Island chain, the southeasterly by Alaska's "Panhandle," a strip of islands and coastal glaciers and mountains separated from Canada by the Coast Range. The Panhandle is some 400 miles in length, and the Alaskan Peninsula and Aleutian Islands reach out for 1,400 miles. The bulk of the state would fit roughly into a square about 750 miles on each side.

Alaska is bounded on the east by Canada's Yukon Territory at about 141° west longitude and, from Mount St. Elias (18,008 feet) southward, by the Coast Mountains of British Columbia. The Arctic Ocean and Chukchi Sea delineate the north and northwest coastline; the west and southwest coasts look out on the Bering Sea and Bristol Bay. The south coast and the Panhandle have been carved by the waters of the Gulf of Alaska and the Pacific Ocean.

Topographically, Alaska can be divided into three main areas. The Arctic Region north of the Arctic Circle, comprising nearly one third of the state, is one. South of the Circle is a broad plateau, called by Alaskans the Interior, which is drained by a number of rivers of which the most important is the famous Yukon. The Interior is also roughly equal to about one third of Alaska's area. The third topographical region is the mountainous southern section of the state, shaped like a giant arch with one base in the Aleutian chain, the other in the Panhandle. Its apex reaches inland and northward nearly three hundred miles from the Gulf of Alaska coast.

The most prominent topographical feature of Alaska's Arctic Region is the Brooks Range, which spans the state east to west. Though its major peaks—Mount Chamberlain at 9,131 feet, Mount Michelson at 9,239 feet, and Alapah Mountain at 8,500 feet—are less than half the height of the major mountain peak of the more southerly Alaska Range, they are nevertheless imposing in their stark, saw-toothed, treeless, snow-covered beauty.

The Brooks Range separates the Arctic Slope, to the north, from the Interior at the south. The Slope, as it is referred to, is a flat, dreary plain, snow-covered for most of the year. The entire area is underlaid with permafrost—solidly frozen ground that never thaws—to depths estimated at 1,000 feet or more. Trees do not grow on the Slope. Instead, the area is covered with tundra—a low, dense, ground-hugging vegetation that withstands the long sunless winter periods of extreme cold and bitter winds to blossom into a multi-hued blanket of flowers during the brief summers.

The Central Plateau, between the Brooks Range in the north and the Alaska Range in the south, is a broad, vast expanse of rolling hills, their peaks eroded by a millennium of ice movement. The Interior is drained by the Yukon River and its tributaries. The Yukon thrusts northward from its source in Canada to the Arctic Circle, then meanders southwesterly on its 2,081-mile journey into the Bering Sea.

The main tributaries of the Yukon are the Koyukuk, which drains the southern slopes of the Brooks Range, and the Tanana, which drains the northern slopes of the Alaska Range.

There are few settlements in the Central Plateau, even along the Yukon River, which is navigable by small boats and barges as far as Canada. The primary reason is not so much the long and arduous winters but the underfooting in summer. Much of the Plateau's underlying ground turns into mushy peat bog, known as muskeg, when not frozen.

The mountainous arch in the southern section of the state consists of a number of mountain chains. From east to west, the major ranges include the Coast Range, St. Elias Mountains, Wrangell Mountains, Alaska Range, and Aleutian Range. It is within this area that practically all of Alaska's thirty-five volcanoes can be found, the vast majority of which are still active.

The highest point in North America is Mount McKinley, 20,320 feet, in the Alaska Range. Nearby is Mount Foraker, another giant at 17,400 feet.

Of the volcanoes, Mount Wrangell at 14,163 feet in altitude is the tallest and lies in the Wrangell Range. Other volcanoes of more than 10,000 feet in altitude include Torbert and Spurr, which both erupted in 1953, Mount Redoubt, which erupted in 1966, and Mount Iliamna. The balance of the state's volcanoes lie primarily in the Aleutian Islands, and few of these are in the dormant stage.

Where there are mountains, of course, there are valleys, and where Alaska is concerned, there are also glaciers. The fertile Matanuska Valley, south of the Alaska Range, near Anchorage, is the most famous of the valleys and basins within the south-central mountains. Nearly three fourths of Alaska's agricultural produce is grown in this valley. Other valleys turned into agricultural wonderlands in spite of the shortness of the growing season are the Tanana, near Fairbanks, and portions of the Kenai Peninsula, south of Anchorage, as well as isolated, smaller acreages on Kodiak Island and some of the Aleutians.

The Susitna Valley, another agricultural realm of south-central Alaska, extends north and east from Cook Inlet. Melting ice and snow pour into this and other smaller valleys, forming shallow lakes and the tributaries that feed into Cook Inlet and the Gulf of Alaska. These coastwise areas are what geologists call flood plains, with the water table only a few feet below the surface.

Alaska offers some of the world's most spectacular glaciers. There are literally thousands of them, ranging up to thirty miles in length, filling the mountain valleys. Peculiarly, perhaps, most of Alaska's glaciers are located in the south and southeast, which is the state's most benign climatic area. Nevertheless, there they are, and, fortunately for the tourist, many of the most impressive are reachable by boat or car.

Malaspina, at the head of Alaska's Panhandle, is the largest glacier. It spills into the Gulf of Alaska, an ice sheet fifty miles wide. Another spectacular glacier, reachable by boat from Cordova, is Columbia, a massive ice cliff ending in the Gulf of Alaska.

Another of Alaska's more noted glaciers, Mendenhall, is but a few miles outside Alaska's capital city, Juneau. It can be reached easily by car.

Although most of the land forms that give Alaska its vast and varied character have stabilized, it is obvious as well that the major forces of nature—earthquakes, volcanic and glacial action, and the force of great water runoffs—are changing the face of many areas much more quickly than those found in more temperate climes.

CLIMATE

Alaska's lowest recorded temperature in history was registered in the Arctic Region at Prospect Creek near the village of Barrow in January 1871. And how cold is coldest? A mere −80° F. Still, generally, the coldest temperatures in Alaska occur not in the Arctic Region but in the vast Central Plateau. The town of Fort Yukon at the confluence of the Porcupine and Yukon rivers often experiences −70° weather in winter.

Though extremes such as these are impressive and oft reported in the press, Alaska is not quite so cold as many people believe.

January averages for the Arctic Slope range from −30° to −20°. The Central Plateau is slightly warmer, with temperatures averaging −20° to 0°. South-central Alaska, including a strip of the Central Plateau looping southeasterly from the mouth of the Yukon, has January averages from 0° to 20°, moderate, even for the north-central contiguous states. In the Panhandle and on many of the more westerly Aleutian Islands January temperates range from 20° to 40°. It rarely reaches below zero in Juneau or, in fact, most of the towns and villages of southeast and south-central Alaska located directly on the Pacific or Gulf of Alaska shore line. The Japan Current is responsible for the mildness of the latter area's winters, just as it is responsible for its slightly cooler summers.

It can be very hot in Alaska in the summertime. Remember Fort Yukon? Plus-100° weather has been recorded there. In fact, the warmest area of Alaska on the average is in the upper reaches of the Central Plateau, where daily high temperatures in July will average 68° to 76°. The balance of the Plateau, to the west but excluding a strip directly bordering the Bering Sea, averages 60° to 68° during the same month. Most of south-central Alaska, including the Panhandle, falls within the same climatic range during July.

Alaska's coolest summers are experienced on the Arctic Slope, along the Bering Sea, on the outermost Aleutian Islands, and in a small stretch of the Panhandle where the mighty glaciers are. Here the average of daily high temperatures in July will range from 44° to 52°.

If Alaska has a great range and variety of climate, it has an even greater range of precipitation within its borders. At some points in the Arctic Slope country as little as 4 inches of precipitation fall each year.

Even central Alaska is quite dry. Most of the Plateau averages between 8 and 16 inches. The southwest section of the Plateau and that area of the mountainous south-central district north of Anchorage receive 16 to 32 inches of rain annually.

A narrow strip of coastal land extending from the Aleutians clear down the Panhandle receives considerable rainfall each year, with averages ranging between 32 and 100 inches. And selected areas can receive much more than that. Fact: Port Walter, on Baranof Island, has the highest average annual precipitation in the continental United States—a very wet 221 inches. But many places in southeastern Alaska receive more than 200 inches—mostly in rainfall—per year.

As famous as Alaska's reputation for coldness is its fame as the land of the midnight sun. The winter solstice brings twenty-four-hour-a-day darkness to the slope, but in summer the sun does not drop below the horizon for eighty-two days—at least in that portion of Alaska that falls north of the Arctic Circle.

A more spectacular visual experience is the occasional fanciful plays of the northern lights, or aurora borealis, across Alaskan skies. Most occur in September and October or in March and April.

THE ALASKANS

Until recent years, the giant wilderness of Alaska had changed little since its first civilizing influence in 1741. Fur trading brought the first influx of white men, who set about harvesting the wealth of fish, game, and timber.

A few small settlements were established by the Russians during the 125 years they controlled Alaska from Sitka. A few more were set up by French and English explorers from Canada. Even the Spanish ventured into Alaskan waters and established bases of exploration.

When the United States purchased Alaska in 1867 for $7.2 million (which at 2 cents an acre was one of the world's greatest bargains), the huge tract remained essentially untouched for many years. A land of spectacular beauty but ofttimes bitter climate, Alaska was populated largely by indigenous folk who lived simply, wresting their livelihoods from the uncompromising land until well into the twentieth century.

The Klondike and Alaska gold rush of 1897 and 1898 brought thousands of miners, drifters, journalists and poets, boatmen, dance hall girls, and whiskey drummers, but unlike the California gold rush of 1849, not many of the adventurers hung around after the yellow metal petered out. Still, a few stayed to tell tall tales, and some not so tall, of the horrors experienced crossing Chilkoot Pass—from Skagway to the gold fields of the Yukon Territory—in the dead of winter, of cabin fever, of claim jumping, and even of murder. It has been said that Alaska is one of the few classless societies in the civilized world, but the gold seekers who came and stayed to endure as sourdough citizens have been, as long as they lived, the most revered of Alaskan pioneers.

Other smaller waves of immigration came to Alaska with the building of the first fish canneries in the early twentieth century, but, again, many of those immigrants stayed only for a few seasons before they went "Outside," which is what the contiguous United States was called in territory days.

Influxes of "Outside" workers also occurred during the building of the Alaska Railroad—Seward to Fairbanks—in the early 1920s. Farmers came to the Matanuska Valley during the federal government's relocation program of 1935, and in the late 1930s until 1942, thousands of workers made their homes near Fairbanks working on the construction of the Alaska Highway, but except for the farmers of Matanuska, most returned when the specific work they had contracted for was completed.

During World War II, the United States Armed Forces had about 152,000 men stationed in Alaska. Though only a handful of these returned after victory, their presence and the attention given the territory by the federal government in recognizing Alaska's strategic importance in global war helped immeasurably in focusing attention on Alaska.

The Distant Early Warning system, or DEW Line, is a series of radar stations reaching from Barrow across Canada to Greenland. Designed to provide early warning of potential aerial attack, the DEW Line is supplemented by a series of microwave communications units known as White Alice.

Installed and funded by the Radio Corporation of America, Alice is manned by Eskimos trained for the project. It also functions as an interior communications system for residents of northern Alaska, carrying news and personal messages between villages.

Only about one third of the current population estimate of some 330,000 people were born in Alaska. And about half of the state's residents have lived there less than five years. Although the great land affords an average of nearly two square miles per resident, 80 per cent of the population lives in the southern coastal areas.

About one sixth of the total population is comprised of people indigenous to the area—Indians, Aleuts, and Eskimos. No other state has such a high proportion of indigenous citizens, and in no other state have their life-styles been so late in catching up to modern patterns.

The Eskimos have lived in Alaska for thousands of years, their race probably originating in the frozen wastes of Siberia. Centuries of living with extreme cold have made the Eskimo physically and psychologically well adapted to the stern environment of Alaska's Arctic plains and the freezing coastline of the Bering Sea.

Physiologists believe the Eskimo's short chunky build to be an adaptation to the cold. Certainly the severity of the environment has demanded a specialized capacity for survival. The Eskimos have learned not only to respect but to relish the bitter temperatures while wresting a living from barren terrain and cold seas.

The Aleuts are cousins to the Eskimos, physically similar but with different language and customs. They are of mixed descent, mostly from Siberia and other northern Asian areas, and many call themselves Russian. The early fur traders treated the Aleuts as slaves and massacred thousands of them for insubordination. Today, fewer than 7,000 Aleuts inhabit the Kenai and Alaska peninsulas and the Aleutian Island chain.

Among the approximately 28,000 native Indians in Alaska there are four major linguistic groups. The Haida, the Tsimshian, and the Tlingit are basically sea hunters and fishermen who live along the Gulf coast and on the islands of the Panhandle. The Athabascans, historically nomadic hunters, are native to the Central Plateau.

The Tlingit are highly skilled in crafts, are resourceful businessmen, and, among all Alaska's natives, have blended more easily into modern society. Their barter system had prepared them for a cash economy. Clever traders, as well as expert hunters and fishermen, the Tlingit accumulated wealth rapidly and thereby lived a life of conspicuous consumption with little thought for the future. In fact, the central feature of their ceremonial "Potlatches," held frequently to honor deceased nobles of their tribe, entailed giving away or destroying much of the wealth of their village.

The Tlingit fared well as middlemen between the white traders and the Athabascans and, jealously guarding their position, managed to keep the Athabascans confined to the interior and to keep the white man out for many years.

Relatively few Haida and Tsimshian remain in Alaska, although many of their tribes still live in Canada. Some of Alaska's most outstanding totem poles and slate carvings are tributes to the craftsmanship and skill of the Haida. And the Tsimshian model village at Metlakatla has a community-owned fish cannery, water system, hydroelectric plant, and commercial landing field.

The Athabascans flourished in the plateau forests as nomadic hunters for six hundred years until diseases introduced by the white man, for which they had no immunity, reduced their numbers by half. The onslaught of fortune seekers during the years of the gold rush completely disrupted their way of life. Some briefly found work in the gold fields, later in building the railroad, but when they returned home they found game scarce and fur prices low. There was little place for them in the new society, in contrast to other Indians, who were valued for their knowledge pertinent to the budding commercial fishing industry, or the Eskimos, whose ability to deal with the Arctic made them invaluable.

As recently as 1960, the plight of Alaska's natives was lamentable. In some of the most far-flung villages, life-style had changed little. Outboard motors might power the little fishing boats, rifles might have replaced the old harpoons, and gasoline might have supplanted seal oil, but for the most part, the Indians' old balance with nature had been irreparably destroyed. There was poverty, poor health, inadequate sanitation and medical service, plus a generalized inability to cope with the inroads of civilization.

Since that time, much effort by both the state and the federal governments has been directed toward easing the transition of Alaska's natives into the mainstream of the modern state. Extensive programs have been developed to improve living conditions and provide education, job training, and work opportunities.

Recently, the natives themselves have taken an aggressive stand on their own behalf. A native-owned and oriented newspaper established in 1962 has done much to foster awareness on the part of the natives of their own needs and rights.

In 1966 a federation of native organizations filed claim to more than half of Alaska on the basis of aboriginal rights. In 1971 the Alaska Native Claims Settlement Act recognized twelve regional native corporations which were granted title to some 40 million acres—much of it rich in oil and mineral potential—and royalties amounting to $962.5 million over the ensuing twenty years. Natives own shares in the corporations, which are empowered to make investments and undertake projects for the members' benefit.

The tenor of Alaska's nonnative population has been much the same since the first fur traders arrived. Few outsiders, as has been mentioned, come to stay. Alaska has been, to them, a place where a stake can be quickly accumulated and success achieved in short order.

Opportunities for riches have certainly come with the booms—fur trading, mining, railroad and highway construction, seasonal lumbering and fishing—and they will again. Construction of the Alaska pipeline, completed in 1977, employed hundreds of thousands of workers.

About one tenth of Alaska's residents are servicemen, always on the move and rarely involved in the business of their communities. Alaska also has a high percentage of federal employees. A recent survey showed that 56 per cent of the labor force was employed by either the state or the federal government. Many of these workers are on relatively short-term assignment. Another highly transient group is comprised of the technicians assigned to Alaska for periods ranging from a month to several years by the giant corporations involved in the utilization of Alaska's resources.

It is not then surprising that the average age of the state's population is twenty-three and that men outnumber women by a ratio of 132 to 100.

Alaskans love, among other things, tall stories, flying (one of every fifty-five adults holds a pilot's license), and, apparently, the writing of checks. It is a fact that Alaskans write more checks per capita than the residents of any other state. Although Alaska's cost-of-living index consistently stands much higher than elsewhere in the United States, there is an all-pervasive, easy-come, easy-go attitude toward money and material possessions and a lack of social distinctions and rigid societal mores typical of such a mobile population.

While resident in Alaska, the citizens are greatly affected by the immensity and diversity of their environment. Awed by its spectacular beauty, they are likewise cowed by its intractable winters—particularly in the less temperate climes. Cabin fever affects virtually all to some extent during the long winters with little sunlight. Frustrations abound. Automobile engines and toilets freeze, and tires go "square." Walls crack, floors heave, and pipes burst as the ground alternately freezes and thaws. Modern ingenuity is continually outshone by the vagaries of nature. Alcoholic intake increases, and accident and suicide rates hold at an alarmingly high level.

There is, of course, a small percentage of rugged individualists who make their homes in Alaska because they like it there. They are fiercely protective of Alaska "as it has always been," yet eager to see it developed to its full potential.

HISTORY

Vitus Bering, a Dane sailing in the service of Peter the Great of Russia, proved on his first voyage in 1728 that Asia and America were not a single continent by sailing through the strait that bears his name. Heavy fog, however, prevented him from sighting the continent. On his third voyage, in 1741, Bering sighted Mount St. Elias at the southeastern corner of the Alaska mainland. The group later landed at Kayak Island.

Georg Steller, a German naturalist sailing with Bering, wrote extensively of the fur seals, sea otters, blue foxes, and other wildlife encountered in the Alaskan environment, and soon thereafter the country was overrun by Russian fur traders.

Bering's discovery was immediately claimed by Russia, and the czars ruled the land for more than a century and a quarter.

Explorers and traders from England, France, and Spain also made minor inroads. In 1778 British Captain James Cook traversed the south coast and left his name on Cook Inlet, south of Anchorage.

One of the Russian fur traders, Gregory Shelikof, established the first permanent white settlement in Alaska at Kodiak Island in 1784. Fifteen years later the Russian-American Company was chartered, the only governing power Alaska was to see for the following sixty-eight years. Alexander Baranof was its first manager.

The Russian-American Company prospered under Baranof during

his eighteen-year administration, though his treatment of the Indians —he practically enslaved the Aleuts—left something to be desired. The only major massacre of this period occurred at Sitka in 1802. The Tlingit tribe sacked and burned the town, killing many settlers. The Russians rebuilt the town in 1804 and named it their capital.

The charter of the Russian-American Company called for the building of schools and churches and the fostering of agriculture. It did much to improve relations, eventually, with the Indians, who had been shamefully treated.

After Baranof was replaced in 1817, Alaska was governed by a succession of Russian naval officers who had little nose for the business of the Russian-American Company. Further, there was increased competition from Canadian and American traders cutting into company profits as well as hurrying the depletion of the animal herds.

The development of the Canadian and American West had brought the question of territorial boundaries to the fore, and in 1824 and 1825 Russia signed treaties with the United States and Canada establishing latitude 54°40′ as the southern boundary of Alaska (and Russian territory) in the New World.

In 1847 the Hudson Bay Company established the first English-speaking trade settlement in Alaska. The site was Fort Yukon.

The decade of the 1850s was a particularly trying one for Russia. The Crimean War (1853–56) had drained Russian treasuries. This, combined with dwindling numbers of fur-bearing animals in Alaska, made Russia particularly eager to sell their American territory. So in 1867 Russia found a buyer for one of the world's largest real estate deals. The United States Secretary of State, William H. Seward, championed the purchase, and the deal was consummated for $7.2 million.

The sale made little difference to those living in Alaska—Indian and white alike—but Americans at home were anything but enthusiastic. They chidingly called the great land Seward's Folly, and it was not until gold was discovered toward the end of the nineteenth century that the derision turned to respect for Seward's farsightedness.

Under United States rule, Alaska was administered first by the Army, then the Navy. In 1884 Alaska was declared a district under the Organic Act and placed under the direction of the Secretary of the Interior, but no provisions were made for local government or congressional representation.

The first important immigration into Alaska from the United States occurred with the gold rush, which started late in 1897. The rush for gold sparked recognition of Alaska's vast potential in other mineral resources and impelled scattered exploration and mining of mineral deposits. Among these, and perhaps the most important, were the Kennecott Copper mines in the Copper River area southwest of Cook Inlet. And during the first years of the twentieth century, the fishing industry flourished with the building of canneries.

The 1897 gold rush drew thousands of treasure-seeking Americans up the Inland Passage and made Skagway, the jumping-off point for the Yukon Territory gold fields, a metropolis practically overnight. Two years later another strike was made at Nome, far west on the Seward Peninsula. Three years after that more gold was discovered in central Alaska, near Fairbanks.

The influx of so many miners and camp followers during the years of gold naturally caused certain legal problems in Alaska. Since 1884, the territory had a federal judge and a code of laws adapted directly from those used in governing Oregon Territory, and they were not particularly suited to adaptation for Alaska.

The gold rush prompted Congress to act on this matter, and it passed a criminal code for the territory in 1899 and a civil code the following year. In 1906 Alaska had its first delegate to Congress. It was a nonvoting post, but the electee could speak for the people of Alaska on the floor of the House of Representatives. In 1912 Alaska was made a territory of the United States. With this status a territorial legislature was formed.

With the gold rushes over, Alaska settled down to a more leisurely pace. Furs, ores, and fish provided the living for most Alaskans who were not involved in lumbering. Farming was encouraged by the federal government, which opened up Matanuska Valley in 1935 for fugitives from the Midwestern dust bowls.

In the early years of the twentieth century, Alaska was also drawing the attention of conservationists. Through their pressures and through mining and military development, vast areas were set aside by the federal government for various purposes: national parks and monuments, sanctuaries and wildlife preserves, military reservations, water conservation districts, mineral withdrawal areas, road rights of way, and so on. The potential for Arctic Slope oil was recognized in 1923 when the Navy and Interior departments put the entire region into Petroleum Reserve.

World War II emphasized Alaska's strategic location, and that period brought about rapid and widespread development in the north land. The Alaska Highway was pushed through Canada 1,523 miles to Fairbanks. Military bases and outposts mushroomed throughout the territory. Roads, airfields, and landing bases were built. Development under the aegis of the military has continued ever since, though on a lesser scale, and in many cases concomitantly with industrial interests.

There had been many attempts to gain state status for Alaska in the years following the gold rushes, but none had been adopted. Finally, on June 30, 1958, Congress passed an Alaska statehood bill, and the following January 3, 1959, President Dwight D. Eisenhower proclaimed Alaska the forty-ninth state of the Union.

Though land-rich beyond measure, Alaska had economic problems in the first years of statehood. Things that had once been paid for by the federal government, road construction, utility services, schools, fire departments, and law enforcement, were now to be paid from the new state's treasury. Transportation service, particularly, in the mountainous but heavily populated south-central and southeastern coasts required great expenditures.

But Alaskans persevere. During the 1960s they created a state ferry system along the Inland Passage that eventually was increased sufficiently to serve Kodiak Island and Prince William Sound.

Two natural calamities beset the people of the forty-ninth state in the 1960s. The biggest earthquake ever experienced on the North American continent struck near Anchorage in March 1964. The quake took a heavy toll—130 people were killed, and property damage was recorded at $750 million.

Three years later, in August 1967, Fairbanks suffered the largest flood in its history. Five people lost their lives in that calamity, and property damage was listed at $84.5 million.

Discovery of the massive oil fields—one of the greatest discoveries of all time—in 1968 has triggered the most explosive developmental thrust in Alaska's history. Although work on the oil transport pipeline, proposed soon after the discovery, could not begin in earnest until the signing of the authorizing bill in November 1973, preparations for the removal of the oil had been intensive since 1968. Leasing of state-owned land on the Arctic Slope in 1969 enriched the state by $900 million alone. Most of this was allocated to improving roads and public facilities in readiness for the anticipated activity.

Alaskans seem to be on the verge of another boom of such magnitude it will make the gold rushes seem like penny ante poker.

Anticipated revenues to the state of $250 million a year when the oil started flowing in 1977 mean further rapid development for the state. But in the meantime, despite the planning and preparation of the previous five years, Alaska's public facilities are strained beyond reasonable limits. Boom conditions are apparent in prices, especially for housing and food. City fathers wait uncomfortably for production royalties to begin, wrestling with the problems of how far to develop before the money is forthcoming.

Alaska enthusiasts predict that the state will leap into the forefront of industrial society with the flow of oil, pointing to 100 million acres of potentially petroleum-rich lands still unexplored, plus reserves of at least thirty other minerals.

Pessimists, on the other hand, note that with the pipeline completed, employment needs to maintain operational capacity will drop to fewer than five hundred persons. This will be no more important than any of Alaska's previous booms, they say; the new folk will soon pack up their full pokes and disappear—as all the rest.

There is one major difference, however, between the "oil rush" and the one for gold so long ago. This time, a great bulk of wealth will remain in the hands of Alaskans and their government. How they put it to use will have a tremendous influence on the future of the Last Frontier.

INDUSTRY

Oil stands unquestioned today as Alaska's most important industry and its most valuable resource. The discovery of oil reserves on and around the Kenai Peninsula near Anchorage in 1957 was described as "perhaps the single most important date in all of Alaska's colorful history."

Within five years, oil and natural gas production accounted for more than three quarters of the dollar value of all mineral production in the state. In one year the value of oil and gas surpassed the value of gold mined during the best year of the gold rushes.

In 1975 oil production, mostly from the offshore fields in Cook Inlet, accounted for $360 million of the state's total $524 million mineral production.

The potential in the Prudhoe Bay fields in the Arctic Slope country is projected in tens of billions of barrels, and the estimates that Alaska will benefit some $250 million per year in royalties have been called conservative.

The Alaska pipeline carries Slope oil eight hundred miles to a port on the Gulf of Alaska. A consortium of seven major oil companies was formed to plan and finance the construction. A delay of several years before actual construction could begin was brought about by controversies over land rights and ecological concerns.

Among other mineral production, gold mining has long been prominent, and in 1975 the value of gold production was $2.6 million. Other important mineral production includes about 16 million tons of sand and gravel annually, most of which is used in the state for highway construction and some 667,000 tons of coal, also used mostly within the state to provide heat and power. Barite, copper, mercury, platinum, silver, and stone are also mined currently, and reserves of these and other minerals are incalculable. Less than 1 per cent of Alaska's total land area has been adequately explored for its mineral potential.

Harvesting of fish and timber resources constitutes Alaska's second and third most important industries. Alaska is the leading state in commercial fishing, the annual catch valued at about $144 million in 1975. Many factories for canning, freezing, salting, and smoking the catch operate in the coastal areas processing salmon, halibut, sablefish, trout, king and Dungeness crab, clams, shrimp, and other fish and sea food.

Some 28 million acres of commercial timberland have been developed out of Alaska's vast forests. Logging companies cut more than 500 million board feet a year, about three fourths of which is processed through pulp mills at Haines, Ketchikan, and Sitka. Total timber product value is over $134 million yearly—mostly spruce, cedar, hemlock, and birch.

Fur seal herds maintained at the Pribilof Islands produce pelts valued at more than $3.5 million annually. Trappers bring in other pelts valued at nearly $3 million, including sable, ermine, wolverine, otter, muskrat, beaver, mink, fox, lynx, and marten.

Tourism, including sports hunting and fishing, is becoming important to Alaska's economy. Tourism is currently listed as a $45-million annual industry, with the number of visitors per year estimated at about 125,000.

Goods manufactured in Alaska represent $200 million a year in value added by manufacture. Nearly all this is produced by Alaskan companies processing raw materials of the state.

AGRICULTURE

Relatively little of Alaska's great terrain is suitable for agriculture. Farms cover about 2 million acres, but of this less than 25,000 are planted to crops and more than two thirds of that acreage lies in the Matanuska Valley near Anchorage.

Perhaps as much as 50 million acres could be used for raising livestock and about 6 million more could be farmed, but the costs of clearing and fertilizing the land are huge. Neither are there suitable farm-to-market roads. But the one thing handicapping Alaska's development as an agricultural state is the most necessary of all. There is no great wave of immigrating farmers into the Last Frontier.

Alaska's agricultural products are now valued at about $4.2 million annually. About 75 per cent of that amount is in livestock.

The growing season, though short, offers summer sun as much as twenty hours a day, and crops mature very quickly. Most fruits and vegetables that grow in a cool climate can thrive in Alaska as far north as the Arctic Circle. Chief crops are potatoes, barley, oats, and other grains. Eskimos keep herds of reindeer for meat and hides, and other livestock ranchers raise cattle, sheep, hogs, and poultry. Greenhouse and nursery products are also major agricultural commodities.

NATURAL RESOURCES

In many respects there is little to differentiate Alaska's store of natural resources from its industrial production. Both are enmeshed, one with the other, to a greater degree than the resources and industry of any other state.

For example: The total value of goods produced in Alaska in 1971 was more than $624.7 million. Of that, 53 per cent was in mineral products and 14 per cent in fish products. Agriculture and wildlife contributed 1 per cent. The balance, 32 per cent, was contributed by manufactured products—most of which are processed natural resources such as lumber.

The greatest natural resource in Alaska is the vastness of the land itself. The soil of Alaska is mainly that called loess—fine particles of clay and sand. It is a highly productive agricultural soil but requires much fertilizer.

The mineral wealth of Alaska has been noted elsewhere. There is still gold aplenty, coal, magnetite iron ore, barite, copper, mercury, platinum, antimony, nickel, silver, tungsten, and uranium in valuable quantities. Still, it is the potential of Alaska's mineral wealth that intrigues those with a vested interest in the state. A case in point: Explorations reveal that Lost River might be one of the most important tin-producing centers in North America.

Nearly all of Alaska's timber wealth lies within the boundaries of two great national forests—Chugach and Tongass—where western hemlock and Sitka spruces are the prime money crops. There are forests in the interior of the state as well, though it is of less commercial value. Among these are birches and white spruces.

Of all the states, Alaska is the richest in animal life. Fish abound. The Pribilof Islands offer harbor to the largest fur-bearing seal herds in the world. Brown bears, the largest flesh-eating mammals in the world, live on Kodiak Island, the Kenai Peninsula, and other south-central locations. There are polar bears in the polar regions, caribou on the Central Plateau, moose near the lakes and rivers, and grizzly bears in the forests.

Other big-game animals include elk, mountain goats, and mountain sheep. Alaska is also a summer nesting place for every species of duck on the Pacific Flyway. Other game birds include grouse and ptarmigan (the willow ptarmigan is Alaska's state bird).

Among nongame species are bald eagles, wolves, coyotes, marmots, and hair seals, the latter sometimes raising havoc with fishermen's nets.

As far as natural resources go, Seward's Folly, it has been noted, not only is blessed with abundance but might very well be the most important natural resource the United States possesses.

CITIES

Only five towns in Alaska, and four military bases, listed populations
of more than 5,000 in the 1970 census, and that tally does not include some of the better known such as Nome, Seward, Valdez, Fort
Yukon, Kodiak, and Barrow. In Alaska a big town (such as these are
to Alaskans) can support a population of 3,000, 2,000, and less.

With the oil boom, accurate population counts in many towns
most affected fluctuate wildly. For example: Valdez, listed at 1,005
residents in the 1970 census, now estimates its population at 4,600.
City fathers expect Valdez to harbor 10,000 people by the end of
1976.

Anchorage, Alaska's largest city, has grown from a counted
48,081 in 1970 to an estimated 76,610 at year-end 1974. Greater
Anchorage, which includes suburban areas and air bases sprawling
around the city, estimates its current population at 165,000—approximately half the population of the state. Both Valdez and Anchorage
lie in the south-central section of mainland Alaska.

The emergence of Anchorage as the biggest, richest, and most
powerful city in Alaska is a comparatively recent development. The
town did not even exist in 1910. Its beginnings in 1914 were as a tent
town erected as a construction camp for railroad workers building an
eastern extension of the Alaska Railroad from Seward to Fairbanks.

The community of tent residents swelled to some 6,000 persons,
with two hotels, three churches, two movie theaters, and a hospital
before World War I halted progress on the railroad and the bulk of
the population quietly folded their tents and went elsewhere.

In the spring of 1940, Hitler's inroads in Norway spurred a long-
sought Alaskan air base, and construction on Elmendorf Field outside Anchorage brought the town a new breath of life. A sevenfold
increase in the following decade found the greater Anchorage area
described in 1950 as a "lusty, brawling, hard-drinking community of
32,000 energetic, vigorous people."

With continued growth, Anchorage became less distinguishable
from other small American cities. Its personality mellowed, new businesses were being established, a new oil field, only fifty miles away,
indicated a new security, and Anchorage seemed well on its way to
achieving "king city" status.

Then the earth shook. It was Good Friday 1964 when the most devastating earthquake in North American history struck down the town. Streets and buildings dropped into twenty-foot crevices. Seventy-seven homes in one suburb slid into Cook Inlet. Ninety-five per cent of Anchorage's high-rise buildings were declared unsafe. The total damage topped $750 million.

But with the aid of disaster loans from the federal government, the city was quickly rebuilt and has been since described as one of the most modern and well-laid-out cities in the world.

Today, most Alaskans agree that while Juneau remains the titular capital of the state, Anchorage serves as capital for all practical purposes. Roughly half of the state's retail sales occur there and more than half its wholesaling. Anchorage banks control more than half the state's total assets. The city housed the headquarters of construction crews building the trans-Alaska pipeline.

Anchorage is a major seaport, it is headquarters for the Alaska Railroad, and its international airport is the largest in Alaska. It is served by five foreign airlines and a dozen American carriers on busy routes to the Orient and transpolar routes to Europe. Thousands of small planes, which fly regularly "into the bush" to Alaska's scattered communities plus all the aerial activity at the nearby military bases, make Anchorage one of the busiest air traffic centers in the nation.

Visitors find familiar names on department stores and supermarkets—and noticeably higher prices on the merchandise.

The modern town of Anchorage boasts of a highly rated public education system, with campuses of both the University of Alaska and Alaska Methodist University.

Five hospitals afford modern medical facilities to residents. A half dozen major hotels and motels offer convention facilities, and a host of small ones afford comfortable accommodations. Two daily newspapers, three television stations, and seven radio stations keep residents informed and entertained.

An active cultural community supports a fine-arts museum, several smaller museums, four theater groups, a community concert organization, and a festival of music each June.

Other important towns in the south-central area include **Seward,** founded in 1903 as a starting point for the Alaska Railroad and long an important port. **Homer,** located in the lower reaches of the Kenai Peninsula, was known as Summerland to the Russians. **Kodiak,** on the island of the same name, dates back to the days of Russian exploration and is, today, an important fishing and hunting center. Cordova and Seldovia can be reached only by ferry or by plane and, hence, retain much of the flavor of the old Alaska.

Valdez, as has been mentioned, has caught the full brunt of the oil and pipeline boom. It was originally named as a port by a Spanish explorer in 1790 and became a small settlement in the days of the first gold rush. Later, when the Fairbanks rush began, Valdez became one of that interior city's supply bases. Men and supplies made the 365-mile Valdez Trail by dog team and horseback. Today, the same trail has become the much-traveled Richardson Highway. Valdez was also hard hit by the 1964 earthquake and has been modernized in the rebuilding. It is destined to become one of Alaska's most important cities as the southern terminus and shipping point for pipeline oil.

Juneau, capital of Alaska, is the largest city in the Alaskan Panhandle. It is set in a lushly green area frequently shrouded in fog and mist or heavy rain. The entire area has been sculpted by glaciers into a network of waterways surrounding dozens of islands and stubby peninsulas jutting out from the Coast Mountains. Flat land is scarce. Many of the downtown buildings of Juneau and other Panhandle cities are built on pilings driven deep into the mud flats.

Juneau lost population between 1960 and 1970. Some 6,000 persons live within the city, which is dominated by a ten-story federal office building. Another 15,000 residents make their homes in the surrounding metropolitan area. Some of the residential areas cling to the slopes of Mount Juneau. Others string for miles alongside the Gastineau Channel. In its strikingly beautiful, if somewhat impractical, site near the northern end of the Inside Passage, Juneau is connected to the balance of Alaska only by ferry or by air.

Juneau remains Alaska's capital, having successfully overcome a strong bid by Anchorage to replace it during the campaign for statehood. Strong rivalry exists between the two cities today, and most Alaskans believe Anchorage will continue to petition to become Alaska's seat of government.

Tourism is becoming an increasingly important part of Juneau's economy, and, aside from its picturesque qualities, Juneau offers a surprisingly cosmopolitan atmosphere for such a small community.

The Alaska Historical Museum houses an excellent collection of Eskimo and Indian crafts along with relics of early-day mining. The renowned Old Witch totem at the governor's mansion and nearby

Mendenhall Glacier and Glacier Bay National Monument are usually included on sight-seeing itineraries.

Ketchikan, a town of about 7,000, is the most southerly in Alaska and calls itself the world's salmon capital. **Wrangell,** third oldest community in Alaska, is important to the lumber and fishing industries. It was the site of an 1834 Russian fort.

Petersburg, an important fishing center since 1897, reminds one of old Scandinavia, with boardwalks and false fronts lining the colorful fishing fleet at anchor.

Sitka, capital of Alaska for more than a century and once known as New Archangel, is beautifully located at the edge of Mount Edgecumbe, a volcano many claim is reminiscent of Fujiyama. This second-oldest white settlement in Alaska was founded in 1799, and it was here, also, that formal ceremonies transferring ownership of the territory to the United States were held. A Japanese-owned pulp mill opened here in 1960, and Sitka's population has since grown to nearly 3,500.

A museum at the Sheldon Jackson High School and Junior College has an outstanding collection of Alaskan artifacts. The federal government maintains a school and hospital for natives, in Sitka, that is interesting to visit. A disastrous fire in 1966 destroyed much of Sitka's business district as well as historic St. Michael's Cathedral, said to have been the finest example of Russian architecture in the United States.

Haines-Port Chilkoot is the home of the Chilkat Indians, famed for their dancing, arts, and crafts. The Alaska Indian Arts Center here is dedicated to preserving the Chilkat culture.

Skagway was once a bustling outfitting town serving Yukon miners across Chilkoot Pass, and it reached 20,000 population before the gold ran out. Today, though still a sourdough town and, hence, an interesting town to visit, only about 750 Alaskans call it home.

Fairbanks, in Alaska's interior, has poignantly felt the effects of the economic activity and population boom of the pipeline. Already Alaska's second-largest city, Fairbanks counted 14,771 residents in the census of 1970. In the years since, it is estimated that the population has more than doubled. Despite massive public expenditures, service facilities are strained at present.

Fairbanks lies on the Tanana fork of the Yukon River, about 250 miles northeast of Anchorage, and is the major trading center for all communities north of the Alaska Range. It is the terminus of both the Alaska Highway and the Alaska Railroad and is connected by highway to Anchorage and other south-central cities as well as to Fort Yukon farther north. Completion of road building and bridge construction concurrent with the building of the pipeline will give Fairbanks a midpoint position on coast-to-coast auto routes from the Gulf of Alaska to the Arctic Sea.

When Barnette's Cache, a trading post for gold prospectors, was established in 1901 on the site that was to become Fairbanks, it was more by chance than by choice. Shallow waters made proceeding farther north impracticable in the eyes of E. T. Barnette. At that point in time, Barnette encountered Felix Pedro, whose confidence in the gold potential of the area persuaded Barnette to stay, and it was Pedro who made the strike the following year that, though slow in developing, proved in the succeeding decade to be the second richest in Alaska's history, topped only by the Klondike.

By 1906, the thriving community, by then renamed in honor of Vice President Charles Fairbanks, had electricity, a water system, a fire department, schools, churches, hotels, a hospital, daily newspapers, railways to major mining centers, and a telephone system that linked Fairbanks to outlying camps and other communities.

Fairbanks was less flamboyant than other mining towns, serving more as a supply center for the scattered trading posts that sold directly to the miners. The gold stampede fizzled out as prospectors discovered that the worthwhile ore lay mostly under 100 to 500 feet of bedrock. Fairbanks dwindled to about 1,000 hardy souls after that —until its revival during World War II.

Today, Fairbanks is still a gold town, but the bearing gravel is now worked by huge corporation-owned dredges. The city's main industry has been the production of construction materials, and it now thrives on pipeline demands. The Tanana Valley around the city is a good agricultural area and supplies much of Fairbanks' vegetables and dairy products.

The University of Alaska with its internationally famed Geophysical Institute, Arctic Research Laboratory, and Institute of Arctic Biology, was founded in 1922 and has affiliated community colleges at Ketchikan, Anchorage, Matanuska-Susitna, Kenai, Sitka, and Juneau-Douglas. Fort Wainwright military base nearby contributes much to the economy.

A fine museum is maintained by the university, and visitors can enjoy a Disney-type park called Alaskaland, which features re-creations of Alaskan history.

Other important towns of the interior are **Fort Yukon, Nome,** and **Kotzebue** on the west coast. The latter two towns are favored places to see Eskimo culture firsthand. Nome was once the most raucous of the gold rush towns with a population of more than 40,000, but today, although it is a busy trading center, its population is about 2,500.

Barrow is the only town of appreciable size in the Arctic area, its population nearing 3,000 with the influx of pipeline workers. Located about two hundred miles west of Prudhoe Bay, Barrow holds title as the most northerly village in the United States and, aside from its proximity to the oil fields, is an important research center for the Navy.

SPORTS AND RECREATION

Sportsmen's eyes light up at the mention of Alaska. Both hunting and fishing are superb, and few places in the world surpass Alaska as a photogenic subject or a place for observing wildlife. Skiing, hiking, camping, boating, and flying are becoming increasingly popular as recreational pursuits.

Hunting and fishing lodges and resorts are scattered throughout the state, but most are concentrated in the south-central and southeastern sections. Bush pilots fly sportsmen into wilderness areas. Hunting and fishing licenses and game tags must be obtained from the Department of Fish and Game, but bag limits are generous.

Favorite hiking and camping areas are mostly within the state's many national parks, monuments, and wildlife preserves.

Mount Alyeska near Anchorage is among the most popular of the dozen ski areas near Alaska's major cities. Alyeska boasts a two-mile double-chair lift. Aside from skiing, Alaskans enjoy all the sports of winter—snowmobiling, curling, hockey, and many others, including dog-sled racing.

The plentitude of waterways from Anchorage south makes boating more than a pastime. It is the only way, except for the airplane, that a person can travel for any distance in a private conveyance. So the docks and marinas, particularly of the Inside Passage communities, are full of watercraft of every shape and size.

Alaskans further entertain themselves with friendly competition—organized and unorganized—in baseball, basketball, football, bowling, and most other conventional competitive sports. Fishing derbies are many throughout the coastal cities. And nearly every Alaskan buys a chance to guess the exact time of the seasonal ice breakup in Nenana.

POINTS OF INTEREST

If the visitor to Alaska is not a fisherman stunned by the size and fighting spirit of the king and the silver salmon—or the plentitude of trout, char, grayling, pike, and sheefish—he has a lot of entertainment to attend and/or a lot of imposing sights to see.

The rugged beauty of Alaska itself is its own best tourist attraction, but even within this monument of beauty there are special pockets worth seeking out.

Three of the nation's largest national park areas are located in Alaska. Glacier Bay National Monument, for example, encompasses over 2.8 million acres and is the largest in the national park system, surpassing even Yellowstone. More than twenty tremendous glaciers and many smaller ones are located here. The most famous, Muir Glacier, is almost two miles wide and rises 265 feet at the mouth of the inlet where great chunks occasionally break off and float away in the bay.

Many of Alaska's thousands of spectacular glaciers can be visited easily from the major cities. These awesome giants have been formed over thousands of years, each annual snowfall adding that amount not melted during the brief warm season to the mass.

Piling up for years, the great glaciers eventually cake into ice, and their own weight impels them to inch downward toward the sea, a new ice pack continually forming behind it.

Mount McKinley National Park straddles the Alaska Range between Fairbanks and Anchorage where the majestic peak dominates the landscape. Its nearly 2 million acres also serves as a wildlife preserve. McKinley Park Hotel is open from mid-June through Labor Day and serves as headquarters for hiking, fishing, canoeing, mountain climbing, and other outdoor activities. Camp Denali, with lodge and cabin just outside the park boundary, is a wilderness camp favored by sportsmen.

Katmai National Monument dominates the Alaska Peninsula, a

huge 2.7-million-acre tract of lava ash. The remaining crevices from which steaming gases still escape give the name Valley of the Ten Thousand Smokes to the area.

Residents of the peninsula had fled during a series of earthquakes that preceded the eruption of Mount Katmai in 1912. Today, the crater contains a jade-green lake about a mile in diameter. Glaciers have already formed on the inside walls, and the valley has cooled to less than a dozen "smokes." But nearby volcanoes still rumble.

Visits to Eskimo and Indian villages to see remaining strains of their primitive life-styles and to purchase prized native arts and crafts are one of the foremost lures of Alaska.

Gigantic produce—seventy-pound cabbages, turnips the size of basketballs, strawberries big as baseballs—draws many visitors to the Matanuska Valley.

But when all is said and done, the grandness of Alaska and the magnificence of its land forms and waterways, wildlife and forests, are the greatest tourist attraction, perhaps, in the world.

SPECIAL EVENTS

Perhaps because Alaskans are few and share the same hardships of winter and wind and know the feeling of isolation better than most other United States citizens, they celebrate like the devil whenever they get the chance. Almost every city, town, hamlet, or settlement in the state has one period a year—for a day or a week, sometimes more —when they go all out for a good time.

The best known of these annual shindigs is the week-long Fur Rendezvous in Anchorage in February. Among the scheduled events is a fur auction, the world championship dog-sled races, sports car races, parades, Eskimo dancing and blanket-tossing demonstrations, balls, dinners, and art shows, and, it is said, impromptu drinking challenges in Anchorage's pubs can reach epic proportions.

The Gold Medal Basketball Championship tournament is held in Juneau, also in February, and numerous ski races from January through May are highlighted by the Alyeska Ski Festival in March. That same month, Juneau holds its annual Alaska Arts and Crafts Show, and Fairbanks, Dillingham, and Soldotna have blowouts all headlined with dog-sled races.

The annual Salmon Derby in Ketchikan in April readies the visitor for Kodiak Island's King Crab Festival in May. Also in May, Petersburg entertains itself with a Little Norway Festival; Skagway recreates the gold rush era with its Days of '98 Show. Marathon river races from Fairbanks to the Yukon and back and the Copper Basin Spring Festival are also popular May events.

The midsummer Midnight Sun Festival in Nome is highlighted by a raft race with push-off time at midnight, and in Fairbanks the summer solstice is marked by the Midnight Sun baseball game, starting at midnight without benefit of artificial lights. The Chilkat Indian dancers perform throughout the summer, and at Anchorage, June features the annual music festival, which offers a variety of concerts, recitals, and lectures.

The Fourth of July is widely celebrated with gala festivals throughout the state, the more outstanding of these, perhaps, being the Golden Days Celebration in Fairbanks and the Marathon Mountain Climbing Race in Seward. Sitka produces the All-Alaska Loggers Championship in July, which features lumbermen's competitions, parades, and carnival.

August in Alaska features the Alaska State Fair in Fairbanks, Klondike Days in Fort Yukon, the Silver Salmon Derby at Seward, and several harvest fairs. Sourdough Days, Skagway's second major celebration, occurs in September, and the big Alaska Day Festival in Sitka, commemorating the transfer of Alaska from Russia to the United States, in October, round out the carnival season.

T.B.

CHRONOLOGY

1741   Alaska was discovered by Vitus Bering, sailing for czarist Russia.

1778   Captain James Cook explored the Gulf of Alaska, naming Cook Inlet and Turnagain Arm.

1784   First settlement was established by Russian fur traders on Kodiak Island.

1799   Russian-American Company was chartered by Russia and established headquarters at New Archangel, subsequently renamed Sitka.

1825   In treaties with the United States and England, Russia recognized latitude 54°40′ as the southern boundary of Alaska.

1847   First English-speaking settlement established at Fort Yukon.

1867   United States purchased Alaska from Russia.

1870   Pribilof Islands were declared a sealing reservation.

1878   First canneries for salmon were established at Sitka and Klawock.

1879   Gold was first discovered at Mount Juneau.

1884   Alaska was declared a district with passage of the Organic Act, which provided laws and a federal court.

1897   Klondike and Alaskan gold rush brought thousands of prospectors.

1903   An international commission settled a dispute between the United States and Canada over Alaska's southeastern boundary.
Initial work began on construction of the Alaska Railroad at Seward.

1906   Alaskans elected their first delegate to the U. S. Congress. Work began on the Copper River Railroad into the Kennecott mines.

1912   Alaska became a territory under the Second Organic Act, which provided for a territorial legislature.

1914   Aviation was introduced to Alaska, which has since become more dependent on air travel than any other state.

1917 Mount McKinley National Park was established.

1922 Agricultural college, now the University of Alaska, was opened.

1923 Alaska Railroad was completed.

1935 Midwest farmers resettled in the Matanuska Valley under a federal program.

1942 Japanese forces invaded the Aleutians.

Alaska Highway was completed.

1956 Alaska's current constitution was adopted.

1957 Oil was discovered on the Kenai Peninsula and in nearby Cook Inlet.

1958 Alaska's statehood was approved by Congress in June.

1959 Alaska became a state on January 3, and the state legislature convened.

1963 Alaska State Ferry System went into operation.

Construction began on Alaska's first oil refinery at Kenai.

1964 North America's most disastrous earthquake occurred, causing more than $750 million in property damage to Anchorage and neighboring towns.

1967 Flooding caused extensive damage in Fairbanks.

1968 Huge oil reserves were tapped on the Arctic Coast.

1969 Alaska State Government received more than $900 million from sale of oil and gas leases in the Arctic Slope area.

1971 Alaska Native Claims Settlement Act awarded title to 40 million acres and royalties amounting to $962.5 million to Eskimos, Indians, and Aleuts.

1973 Federal bill was signed authorizing construction of the trans-Alaska pipeline to carry crude oil from the Arctic Coast to the Gulf of Alaska.

1974 Contracts were awarded for pipeline construction and the bridging of the Yukon River.

1977 Completion of the trans-Alaska pipeline.

1979 Thanks to successful game management, the Pacific walrus, once an endangered species, reached a population of about 200,000, a point unequaled since its mid-nineteenth-century high.

California

OREGON

Redwood
National Park

Mount
Shasta

Eureka

Shasta Dam
Lassen Volcanic National Park

SACRAMENTO VALLEY
SACRAMENTO R.

Mendocino

Nevada
City

Donner Summit
Lake Tahoe

RUSSIAN R.

Coloma

Fort Ross

Santa
Rosa
Napa

Sacramento

Volcano

Bodega Bay
Sonoma

Murphys

Yosemite National Park

Sausalito
Columbia
Historic
Park

San Francisco
Oakland

San Mateo

San Jose

Hornitos

SAN JOAQUIN R.

SIERRA

NEVADA

Kings Canyon
National
Park

Monterey Bay
San Juan
Bautista

Monterey

SAN JOAQUIN VALLEY

Mount
Whitney

PANAMINT RANGE

Death Valley
National Monument

Carmel

Owens
Lake

AMARGOSA RANGE

Big Sur

Sequoia
National Park

COAST   RANGES

San Simeon

Kern R.

Kern

MOJAVE DESERT

Colorado R.

Solvang

Valencia

San Fernando
Hollywood

Santa Barbara

Malibu

Pasadena

San Bernardino

Parker Dam

Culver City

Los Angeles

Palm Springs

Long Beach

Anaheim

Disneyland
San Juan
Capistrano

Mount San Jacinto
Indio

ARIZONA

Santa
Catalina Island

Salton
Sea

Del Mar

San Diego

MEXICO

N

PACIFIC   OCEAN

0   50   100
miles

NEVADA

CALIFORNIA

CALIFORNIA comes by its nickname—the Golden State—honestly. It was gold that drew thousands of prospectors back in 1849 and it was the golden sunshine that brought millions more over the years. California today is the most populous state and the most varied. The land itself ranges from 282 feet below sea level in Death Valley to 14,495 feet at Mount Whitney, the highest peak in the United States outside Alaska. And then there's the climate—temperatures ranging from 120 degrees in the desert to 10 degrees below zero in the mountains. The vegetation is equally varied—scrub desert mesquite to lofty redwoods and sequoias. And the land itself ranges from sandy beaches to rugged snow-capped mountains and lush fertile valleys.

Perhaps most important, Californians themselves are an equally fascinating mix. Settlers came from every state in the Union, every country of Europe, from China, Japan, Mexico, and Africa. They're a hardy, individualistic lot who went West in search of a more open way of life on the nation's last frontier.

The big appeal for many was the weather—mild the year round in most parts of the state, with ample sun for the free and easy life southern California has fostered. Add to that the glamour of Hollywood, the sophistication of San Francisco, the majesty of Yosemite, the rugged beauty of the coastline, and you can see what drew so many millions to the shores of the Pacific. There they live with a zest and flair that the rest of the country strives to imitate—an indoor-outdoor life where only sliding glass doors separate living room from garden, terrace, and, frequently, swimming pool. "California style" has become a watchword for the rest of the country—it means relaxed, informal living; sun tans and swimming pools; a healthy, open attitude toward life; and an easygoing tolerance of others.

THE LAND

California ranks third in size of the states. Its nearly 159,000 square miles are bounded on the north by Oregon, on the east by Nevada and Arizona, on the south by Mexico, and on the west by the Pacific Ocean.

California's geography is easy to grasp: There is a mountain fringe along the coast, called the Coast Ranges, and a second mountain system, the Sierra Nevada, along the east border. In between is a magnificent valley called the Sacramento Valley in the north and the San Joaquin Valley in the south. Much of the rest of the state is desert. The northern section has great forests. Along the coast are many fault lines, the reason the area is earthquake-prone.

Coastal range altitudes vary from 2,000 to 8,000 feet. In the east the Sierra Nevada is far taller and grander—one continuous mountain chain that boasts about forty peaks between 5,000 and 8,000 feet and eleven peaks over 14,000 feet. The granite pinnacles of the highest sierra opposite Owens Lake drop 10,000 feet into a valley. Equally spectacular are the snowy volcanic cone of Mount Shasta; the grandeur of Yosemite Valley; Lake Tahoe, 6,229 feet above sea level and surrounded by peaks rising to 5,000 feet; and the extinct or dormant volcanoes in Owens Valley, east of the Sierra Nevada.

The great central valley, 450 miles long and 40 miles wide, is closed to the north and to the south, surrounded by a mountain wall broken at only a single spot—the gap behind the Golden Gate at San Francisco. Two rivers, the Sacramento and the San Joaquin, drain the 18,000 square miles of this lush interior basin. Of the two valleys, the San Joaquin is the larger, comprising over three fifths of the area.

Southern California includes both fertile coastal plains and arid desert. The two vastly different areas are separated by mountain ranges from 5,000 to 7,000 feet high, and with peaks much higher, the San Jacinto being 10,831 feet. Unlike the mountainous areas of the north, however, those in the south are broken by many passes which permit railroads to cross to the Pacific Coast.

South and east of the Coast Ranges are the Open Basin and the Great Basin, about 50,000 square miles of desert. The famous Mojave Desert belongs to the Great Basin; a narrow strip along the Colorado River that separates California from Arizona belongs to the

Open Basin. A feature of the latter is the Salton Sea, a lake of about three hundred square miles, created by trapping water from the Colorado River and from numerous desert creeks and small rivers when the beds are not dry.

To the north, about forty miles east of Owens Lake, is the famous Death Valley. It was named for a party of "Forty-niners," as those who set out for the gold rush of 1849 were called, thirteen of whose members died of thirst and starvation. Death Valley is the lowest point on the continent, 282 feet below sea level, and one of the most remarkable parts of the state, rich in borax and nitrate of soda.

CLIMATE

Only 1 per cent of the world's surface and no other part of the United States has the climate of California. It is often called Mediterranean because of the short, mild, wet winters and long, dry summers of that area. Most of California has only two seasons—mild winter and dry summer. Spring and fall are either so short as not to be noticeable or don't occur at all except in the high elevations or in the north. The Pacific Coast has an even climate—cooler in summer and warmer in winter than the same latitudes in the interior of the country.

The greatest range in temperature occurs in the interior lowlands, farthest from the moderating effects of the Pacific Ocean. In the summer the extreme temperatures are more comfortable there due to the dryness of the air. Rainfall varies from an annual 110 inches in the northwestern part of the state to less than 2 inches in Death Valley. In winter there are apt to be snows in the mountains and in the north, depths ranging from a few inches a year in peninsular ranges to many feet in the Sierra Nevada. The scant rainfall makes for water shortages in certain areas.

In the lowlands of southern California, the climate is mild, with warm, almost rainless summers and agreeable winters with occasional mild storms. At the Los Angeles airport the mean temperature in January is 54 degrees and in July, the hottest month, 69 degrees. Very few nights go below freezing and few summer days go over 100 degrees. In winter, rainfall varies from 12 to 25 inches and there are sunny days in all seasons.

The inland mountain climate boasts summer temperatures similar

to interior lowlands. Mountain temperatures decrease 3.5 degrees
with every 1,000 feet of elevation. In winter when ocean breezes are
insignificant, normal temperature variations prevail and, of course,
the mountains are colder. Mount Wilson at 5,710 feet elevation registers an average 42 degrees in January and 72 degrees in August.

In the desert the picture is entirely different. Death Valley is the
hottest place in the United States. The mean January temperature is
52 degrees while a July mean is 102 degrees.

Northwestern California is mountainous, heavily forested, and the
wettest part of the state, receiving over 60 inches of precipitation annually. Near the Oregon border, rainfall often tops 100 inches per
year. However, temperatures are mild with a January average of 47
degrees and an August average of 57 degrees. There is considerable
coastal fog in the summer.

The so-called Bay Area—the counties of Alameda, Marin, San
Francisco, San Mateo, southern Napa, Sonoma, and small parts of
Solano and Santa Clara—is noted for its cool summers and mild winters. Snow is rare here and rain is found only during the six months
of winter, in any quantity. The famous fogs of San Francisco form in
the ocean air and are floated in by breezes in the afternoon, the fogs
disappearing in the morning. Day and evening temperatures only vary
a little; September is the warmest month and January is the coldest.
Temperatures range from around 50 degrees to 70 degrees. The annual rainfall is about 18 inches.

The central, coastal part of the state extends some two hundred
miles from the Bay Area to the Transverse Ranges of southern California. Here, too, the climate is mild, with coastal summers cool and
interior summers warmer. Summer fog is limited to the coast; summer sun is the rule in the interior areas. Winters are rainy, especially
on the west sides of the mountain ranges. Temperatures range around
50 degrees in January and 60–65 degrees in September.

The Sacramento Valley enjoys a warm, Mediterranean-like climate. Winters are cool and rainy with frequent fogs; summers are
sunny, hot, and dry. The northernmost parts of the San Joaquin Valley have a climate similar to that of the Sacramento Valley. Farther
south, the climate is drier in summer but offers cooler, moist winters
when fogs may blanket the whole area for days or even weeks. The
summers are often quite hot, with temperatures reaching 100 degrees.

The Sierra Nevada region is wet, with many parts receiving 50
inches of precipitation annually, three quarters of it during the win-

ter. The central part records heavy snows. In the foothills, summers
can be very warm, but days are cooler as elevations increase. In winter it can be somewhat cool to extremely cold.

THE CALIFORNIANS

California's earliest settlers were the Indians of many different
tribes. It is not surprising, then, that the first Europeans to come into
the region were the Spanish missionaries who came to convert and
colonize them, and the Spanish were the first to settle the land to any
extent. In terms of colonization, the Spanish period was roughly from
1770 to 1822. During this time the Russians established a trading
post at Fort Ross near San Francisco. The settlement was relatively
short-lived, however, and added little to the over-all ethnic composition.

When Mexico took over control of California in 1822, many Mexicans came north. The chicanos, as the Mexican-Americans are called
today, form important colonies in many large cities and in rural areas
and have preserved both their language and their customs.

As the overland routes from the eastern United States were developed, more and more Anglo-Saxon and German settlers pushed into
California. The biggest influx came as a result of the discovery of
gold in 1848, a date that coincided with the end of Mexican authority. Both of these events opened the area for massive settlement.
Gold fever brought men from all over the world, although it is estimated that three fourths of the 80,000 who came in 1849 alone
were Americans.

This was the real beginning of the melting pot California was to
become. The area became a state in 1850, an event that spurred a
new wave of immigration and settlement. The advent of the railroads
accounted for an influx of some 15,000 Chinese; later thousands of
Japanese poured into the state, most settling in the San Francisco
area.

Others who have made a deep and colorful impression on California are the Italians, many of whom came early in the twentieth century as fishermen from Naples. Today their descendants form a large
and powerful segment of San Francisco. Portuguese fishermen came,
too, gravitating toward the southern coastal cities.

More recent immigration has been from other parts of the United

States, especially farmers from the Midwest who fled states afflicted by the terrible drought of the 1930s. During 1936–37 alone, 200,000 went West, and by 1938 immigration was 10,000 a month. But the greatest population boom came between 1940 and 1970. During those years millions migrated to California and the population almost tripled, making it the most populous state in the Union. The population per square mile in 1970 was 125.7, compared with 56.2 for the country as a whole.

Racially, the population in 1960 was: 92 per cent white; 8 per cent nonwhite, with 5½ per cent black, 1 per cent Japanese, ½ per cent Chinese, and slightly less than ½ per cent Filipino. At that time the state had nearly 40,000 American Indians.

HISTORY

Until California became a state, its history was one of sporadic change rather than consistent development. It was discovered sometime before 1542 when the southern part of the Colorado River was sighted by the Spanish explorer Hernando de Alarcón. He failed to cross it into what is now California. It remained for Juan Rodríguez Cabrillo and Bartolomé Ferrelo to push north, exploring the entire coast. In 1579 Sir Francis Drake repaired ships north of what is now San Francisco and called the area New Albion. Spanish galleons running from the Philippines to the Mexican coast traveled the length of California, the most documented voyage being that of Sebastián Vizcaíno in 1602. He explored the coast thoroughly and discovered Monterey Bay. However, the Spanish largely ignored California for the next hundred or so years as of little value except as a stopping-off place for more important maritime commerce.

It remained for the Catholic Church to spearhead settlement and as early as 1697 Jesuit missionaries entered Lower California. The Church remained active even after the Jesuits were expelled and their property turned over to Franciscan monks. Then, in 1772, the Dominicans took over the few existing missions and from then until 1823 many more were set up, twenty-one of them, extending from San Diego north to Sonoma. These were about a day's travel apart, along a crude trail called El Camino Real (Royal Highway), which survives approximately as U. S. Highway 101. These missions, while doing little to upgrade the life of the Indians, were an important force in bringing civilization and commerce to California.

Fear of the Russians' growing expansion in Alaska and along the Pacific Coast finally prompted Spain to settle northern California. The Spanish needed safe refitting points there for ships plying the Manila trade. By the end of the eighteenth century there was some semblance of Spanish authority the length of the area. Three types of settlements were created: presidios (military bases), missions (religious centers), and pueblos (towns).

When revolution occurred in Mexico in 1810, California remained loyal to Spain, but by 1822 Mexico was independent of Spain and had received California's allegiance. Upper and Lower California were jointly represented in the Mexican Congress, but there was growing dissatisfaction with Mexican rule and great friction between north and south. There was also bitterness over secularization, the detachment of mission land from the control of the Catholic Church, which resulted in a series of Mexican governors being driven out. By 1845 there was talk of independence.

During this period the Russians founded Fort Ross (1812) on the coast north of the mouth of the Russian River. It was a trading post and a source of supply for sea-otter hunters. However, in 1841 after the otters had been largely exterminated, the Russians abandoned the outpost. Hunters from the United States began entering the province, adding to the already important trade with the East. Also, Yankees in ships hunted whales along the coast and developed a hide and tallow trade with the ranch owners. Just as the Spanish period was dominated by the missions, the Mexican period was dominated by cattle ranches.

By 1830 an extension of the Santa Fe Trail brought American traders overland to Los Angeles. Many of the men who came from the United States as hunters or traders married into influential California families. Perhaps the most important of these settlers was John A. Sutter, a Swiss who amassed both land and influence.

By the mid-1840s there was a consensus among the American residents that California should become a state. The United States consul in Monterey was instructed to engineer the withdrawal of California from Mexico, and at the same time pressure was building in Washington for war with Mexico.

In 1846 American settlers seized Sonoma near San Francisco and raised a flag with a grizzly bear emblem. For a few heady days California was independent. But less than a month later Commodore John D. Sloat raised the Stars and Stripes over Monterey, proclaiming California part of the United States. The whole matter was concluded by the treaty of Guadalupe Hidalgo in 1848 whereby Mexico formally ceded California. A battle then raged in Congress as to whether it should be admitted as a free or a slave state. Finally, admission as a free state was assured as part of the Compromise of 1850.

While all these issues were being debated, gold was discovered at John Sutter's mill in January 1848. In one year the lure of gold brought 80,000 people. These "Forty-niners" came by land and sea from the far corners of the world.

The next big wave of migration came after the Civil War, when thousands of Easterners went West in search of cheap land and high wages. Some 15,000 Chinese laborers were brought in to help construct the Central Pacific (later the Southern Pacific) Railroad, the first transcontinental line to link Sacramento with points east. Unhappily, the Chinese took the brunt of public discontent with the depression of the 1870s—ten years of widespread unemployment and bank failures. There were anti-Chinese riots in Los Angeles in 1871 and in San Francisco in 1877. Hostility toward Orientals continued into the twentieth century. In 1913 the state legislature passed the Alien Land Act (also called the Webb Act) designed to restrict Japanese landholdings. Even more bitterness was generated during World War II when the federal government interned Japanese living along the California coast for the duration of the war.

California experienced another land boom after the depression of the 1870s. The twentieth century brought continued economic growth and a great natural disaster—the earthquake of 1906 that virtually destroyed San Francisco and killed about 700 people. Another quake was to hit the Los Angeles area in 1971. This one killed 64 people, injured hundreds of others, and caused more than $500 million worth of damage.

A continuing problem for the state since the early years of the twentieth century has been the water supply. Colorado River floods plagued California until 1928, when Congress authorized construction of Boulder Dam, which today controls floods and helps relieve the recurring droughts in southern California and nearby states. Nevertheless, water remained in short supply until the 1960s, when work began on a system of canals, dams, and reservoirs to divert excess water in northern California to dry areas in the south.

Despite setbacks to the economy affecting both the state and the nation as a whole in recent years, California remains a powerful political and social force. Like other sections of the country, it suffered from racial problems during the 1960s. A riot in Watts, a black section of Los Angeles, took thirty-four lives in 1965 and resulted in millions of dollars in property damage. The state's college campuses were a focal point for student unrest during the 1960s—the demonstrations at the University of California at Berkeley are remembered as the first major student protest of the decade.

The state's politicians also have made names for themselves nationwide. Richard Nixon, born in Yorba Linda, served as Vice President under Dwight D. Eisenhower and became President himself in 1968. He won re-election in 1972 only to resign in 1974 as a result of the Watergate scandal.

INDUSTRY

Heavy industry in California was minimal for many years simply because the state lacked fuel resources. However, the development of the big oil fields in the 1890s changed the picture dramatically. By 1920 manufacturing had overtaken agriculture as the leading commercial enterprise. By the mid-twentieth century, the development of electric power, natural gas, oil, and water supplies along with the discovery of new sources for steel, aluminum, chemicals, and other raw materials helped boost the state's manufacturing output. Aircraft, automobile parts and accessories, and shipbuilding are major heavy industries. In fact, California's aerospace industry is the largest in the country.

Machinery and electrical equipment are also important, as is lumber production. Much of the glamour of California is associated with film-making and television. Film makers from New York City moved to the Los Angeles area because of the assurance of year-round sunlight, since most film-making took place outdoors in the early days. By the 1920s, Hollywood was the film capital of the world. During the depression of the 1930s when entertainment lightened the nation's worries, film-making boomed and accounted for an important part of the state's income. After World War II and the advent of television, the film industry changed, but the Los Angeles area adapted to it and the major studios became the producers of TV films.

The fishing industry has always been an important one here. Fleets from Eureka, Monterey, San Francisco, Los Angeles, and San Diego bring in huge catches of tuna, anchovies, barracuda, salmon, sole, mackerel—nearly a half million pounds a year.

AGRICULTURE

In the Spanish and Mexican periods the big ranchos with their immense grazing lands made cattle the basis of wealth. The production of fruits and vegetables was negligible because of the dryness of the climate. Until the available water power was harnessed in the mid- and late nineteenth century and irrigation systems were brought into play, farming was limited. However, by 1890, about a million acres of land were under irrigation. By 1960 this had increased eightfold, making California first among all states in irrigated acreage.

Along with this development came a careful study of what crops were suited to the climate and the soil leading to the importing of two seedless orange trees from Brazil, the forefathers of the millions of trees in California today. These orange groves, once limited to the southern part of the state, are now found also on the foothills of the Sierra Nevada and in the Central Valley. Lemons and walnuts are also grown in these areas, while almonds, peaches, apricots, and many other fruits are grown in the north. Prunes, raisins, and olives are other big crops.

Grapevines date back to the Franciscan fathers in 1770 who tended the so-called mission grapes. Later, almost all varieties of European grapes were introduced and today California is first in grapes and raisins and produces 90 per cent of the wine of the United States.

Although some mission wine was sold as early as 1798, it wasn't until Jean-Louis Vignes, a Frenchman from Bordeaux, arrived that wine making took on any commercial importance. He brought vines from Europe and cultivated them on four hundred acres near Los Angeles. By 1850 wine production had reached 58,000 gallons. Most of the vineyards at the time were in the Los Angeles area and in Sonoma, Santa Clara, and Solano counties.

In the 1860s more than 100,000 vines representing some three hundred varieties of grapes were imported from Europe. Since then the California vineyards have flourished. They are now distributed through five regions of the state classified according to climatic conditions and producing an impressive variety of wines—everything from reds like burgundy and beaujolais to white chablis and sauternes, rosés, and sweet and dry champagnes.

NATURAL RESOURCES

Nature has blessed California with an abundance of natural resources —lush forests of redwood, cedar, and pine, a dazzling array of wildlife, vast mineral wealth. The only thing that's not in ample supply is water. While there is plenty in the mountains, nature hasn't provided nearly enough for the arid regions in the south of the state. As a result, the state has had to harness the waters of the Colorado River to serve the Los Angeles area and the Sacramento and Trinity rivers to supply the San Joaquin Valley. Today, massive engineering feats such as the Hoover Dam, the Colorado River Aqueduct, and the Shasta Dam and Reservoir have relieved much of the chronic water shortage in the dry areas.

No one was thinking about water, however, when California experienced its big boom back in the mid-nineteenth century. The natural resource that fired men's imagination was gold—the rich lode discovered at John Sutter's mill in 1848. Gold was mined in the state for one hundred years until in 1950 the big mines were closed by government order.

But gold isn't the state's only valuable mineral. There are boron, uranium, magnesium, mercury, asbestos, and tungsten along with oil. The state ranks third in the nation in oil production. It produces about 15 per cent of all the nation's oil—upwards of 375 million barrels a year.

California is also third in lumber production. Redwood, fir, cedar, pine, and other trees logged in its mountains and valleys bring the state about $600 million every year. The California redwoods are legendary. Forests encompass eight counties in the northern part of the state. While second-growth redwoods are used for timber, the huge, old trees are preserved forever by the state and federal government in Redwood National Park. Here, visitors may stand beside the world's tallest tree—a 367-foot giant. The oldest tree in the country is in California, too. It's a 300-foot-thick giant sequoia called General Sherman, believed to be 4,600 years old. It's protected by law along with other giant sequoia in the vast pine forests that stretch the length of the Sierra Nevada and along the inner ranges from Oregon south.

The forests and mountains are populated by at least six kinds of deer, mountain lions, black bears, and a variety of small animals— everything from jack rabbits to gray squirrels and spotted skunk. Among the most picturesque of the animals is the mountain sheep, or bighorn—a creature that stands about three feet high at the shoulder, weighs two hundred pounds, and sports enormous curving horns.

There's a good bird population, too—ranging in size from the tiny Wilson snipe to the California condor, the largest flying bird in the northern hemisphere. And California has more wild geese than any other state, although only the Great Basin Canada goose is a native. The rest are migratory species that come south from Canada each winter.

As far as fish are concerned, there are more than enough to satisfy the most demanding angler: five kinds of salmon, four types of trout. Steelhead trout sometimes reach a weight of twenty pounds while king salmon up to fifty pounds have been reported.

Huge California gray whales weighing up to forty tons migrate back and forth along the coast from the Arctic to Mexican waters. Sea otters, an endangered species, can be seen around San Mateo and Santa Barbara. The California sea lion, weighing five and six hundred pounds, range all along the coast. They, too, are protected by law.

CITIES

Los Angeles is the largest city area in the country, encompassing 450 square miles, and boasting the second-largest population after New York City. Greater Los Angeles has nearly 10 million residents and covers over 4,000 square miles, divided among Los Angeles County, Orange and parts of Riverside, Ventura, and San Bernardino counties. It epitomizes the city of the automobile age, with many sections inaccessible by bus or rapid transit. Day and night, the freeways, parkways, and highways are choked with traffic, accounting for the city's famous smog.

The city dates back to 1781 when Felipe de Neve and forty migrants founded El Pueblo de Nuestra Señora la Reina de los Ángeles de Porciuncula, a long-winded appellation which can be anglicized to

Our Lady Queen of Angels of Porciuncula, fortunately further short-ened long ago to Los Angeles. By 1800 there were 315 inhabitants, and by 1820 650 souls were scattered among the small farms of the area. During the Mexican Colonial period, settlers arrived from the south, making a village of 1,200 by 1830, the largest community in California.

Compared with San Francisco, which boomed with the gold rush, Los Angeles' growth was sluggish, and when incorporated in 1850, it had only 1,600 inhabitants, mostly Indians and Mexicans. It was, however, a center for the many large ranchos created during the Mexican period. Adobe huts eventually gave way to brick and wood residences; gas lamps appeared in downtown areas, and in 1869 a short railroad line was built to Wilmington on San Pedro Bay.

By 1880 the population was over 11,000, swelled in part by the city's reputation as a beneficial haven for those afflicted with asthma, arthritis, and respiratory diseases. Another boon was the arrival of the Southern Pacific Railroad in 1876, and after the Santa Fe Rail-road reached the town in 1885, growth was swift, due in part to a rate war between the two competing railroads. By 1890, the census registered 50,000 residents.

Another boom came from 1902 to 1914, when the population rose to 300,000. During this period, petroleum production, which com-menced in 1892, increased by leaps and bounds; oil wells in back yards were a common sight. The citrus fruit industry was consoli-dated at this time, too, and the Sunkist Co-op—the California Fruit Growers' Exchange—spurred marketing on a national basis. Los An-geles had lacked a port until granite blocks were piled up across San Pedro Bay to form a breakwater. When this was completed in 1910, the city had an important deep-water seaport which added to its growing commerce. At about this time, too, the motion picture indus-try found its way to the area and Hollywood, a quiet orange grove village, became a center whose name is still synonymous with the glamour of films and film stars. By 1920 Los Angeles boasted over half a million residents.

World War II quickened the pace of life. Industrial output soared, especially of aircraft; shipyards were temporarily active; the first total steel-making plant was constructed at Fontana; and the Los Angeles International Airport was built. After the war, thousands of service-men settled and brought the population into balance as against the high percentage of elderly citizens who retired to the city. Suburban development grew at a frenzied pace until today there are some fifty incorporated cities in Los Angeles County. Housing tracts replaced farms; shopping centers and parking lots now stand where there were bean fields and chicken farms. Today Los Angeles claims over 3 million residents, with nearly 10 million in the metropolitan area.

Los Angeles is now a cosmopolitan city with impressive cultural and educational advantages. Foremost is the Civic Center in the heart of the downtown area. It includes the five buildings of the Music Center for the Performing Arts, a seven-acre complex with the Dorothy Chandler Pavilion for opera and symphony, the Ahmanson Theater for drama and musical productions, and the Mark Taper Forum for more intimate drama and musical events. The Hollywood Bowl to the north is the site of summer concerts; nearby is Griffith Park with its Greek Theater, Travel Town Museum, planetarium, and zoo.

The Los Angeles County Museum houses one of the nation's most impressive art collections with works dating from the Renaissance to the present. Surrounded by pools and fountains, it is located on Wilshire Boulevard facing the Miracle Mile, a section of fine shops and hotels. Other important art museums include the Huntington Library, Art Gallery, and Botanical Gardens in San Marino, the J. Paul Getty Museum in Malibu, and the Southwest Museum in Pasadena.

Still other attractions are the County Museum of Natural History in Exposition Park, Antelope Valley Indian Museum, Frank Lloyd Wright's Hollyhock House, Hollywood Wax Museum, Lomita Railroad Museum, Museum of Science and Industry, Seabee Museum, Trolley Museum, and Roy Rogers Museum. One of the old Hollywood studios offers a tour through the movie and TV back lot, a tram ride at Universal which is a fascinating glimpse into movie-making. The little theater movement emanating from the Pasadena Playhouse, Hollywood's Call Board Theater, the Circle Theater, and the Horseshoe Stage have been outstanding.

Institutions of higher learning are numerous and serve the expanding population. The University of Southern California, southern California's largest private university with 18,000 students; the University of California at Los Angeles, a great center of learning with 20,000 students, 2,000 faculty members, a large campus, and a full range of technical and professional schools; and the California Institute of Technology (Cal Tech) in Pasadena, a respected engineering and scientific center, are all fine centers of learning. Since 1948 six state colleges have opened in the metropolitan area while private four-year colleges include Occidental, Chapman, Loyola, Immaculate Heart, and Whittier. Los Angeles City College on the eastern fringe of the Hollywood section is the largest of the junior colleges with 20,000 students.

Because of its enormous, sprawling physical area, Los Angeles is hard to grasp as a city entity. Downtown L.A. focuses on Pershing Square, below which is a five-level underground garage. For years buildings in this central area were limited to five stories, making for an even skyline. Today this is punctuated by new, higher structures including the fifty-two-story Atlantic-Richfield Plaza and the forty-three-story Crocker-Citizen Plaza. Newest is Union Center, rising from the eastern edge of the Harbor Freeway.

In the heart of the downtown area, the thirty-two-story City Hall for years towered over the skyline. A monumental progression of public buildings leads west uphill to the new Water and Power Building, for years kept illuminated at night and visible for miles. Eastward from the Civic Center, along First Street, is "Little Tokyo," the city's Japanese area which includes a community center, Yamato Hall, and a Buddhist temple. To the northwest is Chinatown, a new creation replacing the original Chinatown, which was razed to make way for Union Station and the Civic Center.

Girdling the downtown area are a variety of residential areas and suburban complexes, ranging from depressed to wealthy, all interconnected by the freeways that are the lifeblood of the city. Hollywood, once the film capital of the world, is now a mixed residential and commercial section.

Wilshire Boulevard, a sixteen-mile thoroughfare leading from the downtown area all the way to the Pacific Ocean, includes the Miracle Mile, a midsection of fine hotels, department stores, and specialty shops. Nearby is Beverly Hills, a beautiful residential enclave, completely surrounded by Los Angeles. From there the boulevard passes through elegant Westwood Village, then turns toward another separate community, Santa Monica, where it ends in a bluff overlooking the ocean. A group of beach towns parallels the shores of Santa Monica Bay from Santa Monica to Redondo Beach. Another huge part of Los Angeles is the San Fernando Valley, two hundred square miles of it.

While not large by today's standards—**San Francisco** has 716,000 people—this magnificent city is the commercial, cultural, and social hub of northern California and draws from a population of over 4 million. Located on San Francisco Bay, one of the largest landlocked harbors in the world, and surrounded by picturesque hills, the city has a history to match its intriguing beauty.

Sixteenth-century explorers Cabrillo and Francis Drake came close but missed the entrance into the bay, very likely because it is so often shrouded in fog. So it remained for a scouting party sent by Gaspar de Portolá in 1769 to discover the area, and six years later the first Spanish vessel, the *San Carlos,* entered what explorer-soldier John C. Frémont much later named the Golden Gate. In 1776 Juan Bautista de Anza brought the first colonists from Mexico, and an adobe presidio, or garrison, was built on the hills above Fort Point. That year Mission Dolores, the sixth in the eventual chain of twenty-one, was established along the coast.

It was San Francisco's strategic position along a land-girdled deep-water port that kept up the Spaniards' interest. It thrived as a seaport, a supply base for foreign ships from all over the world—English, Yankee from the East Coast, even Russian.

By 1835 San Francisco was recognized by its rulers in Mexico City as an important trade center. The missions were being broken up and the presidio was falling into decay, so the government established a new pueblo, Yerba Buena (Good Herb), which became the forerunner of the present city. It was laid out on a cove on the lee side of what is now Telegraph Hill, a spot where there was deep water close to shore.

By the 1840s pressure was building to bring California and San Francisco along with it into the Union, and in 1846 Captain John Berrien Montgomery of the U.S.S. *Portsmouth* had raised the American flag over Yerba Buena plaza. Two years later when the village passed formally from Mexican to American control there were 900 inhabitants.

The discovery of gold that same year forever changed the character of the area. As people began to pour in by sea, Yerba Buena became the point of debarkation and supply. Soon a shanty, waterfront town grew up along the coast. The name Yerba Buena didn't seem appropriate to what would be the great port of the West and in 1847 the town became San Francisco.

The first years were boisterous and disorderly. The Barbary Coast became the center of all kinds of vice, with the roughnecks and brigands from the world over congregating there. Finally, in 1851 a vigilante committee cleaned out the thieves and troublemakers. From then on the city grew in an orderly way. Tidal flats were filled in and much land along the water was reclaimed. In 1876 the Embarcadero was laid out as a waterfront boulevard extending from the China Basin on the south to what is now Fisherman's Wharf.

Progress continued and the city grew until April 18, 1906, when a series of earth tremors, caused by the periodic flexing of the San Andreas Fault, toppled chimneys and cracked masonry walls. The tremors were not so extreme. What caused the terrible destruction was the fires that followed. By 8 A.M. there were fifty or more fires and a strong wind was blowing. The water system, crippled by the tremors, could not be brought into play. That was Wednesday. By Saturday when rain mercifully extinguished the last flames, more than 500 blocks and $500 million of property had been destroyed. A few sections survived—the top of Telegraph Hill and the area west of Van Ness Avenue where dynamiting curbed the spread of the flames. By 1910 rebuilding was well under way and by 1915, when the Panama-Pacific International Exposition opened, a bright, shining new city greeted visitors.

Since that time progress has been steady. In 1936 the Oakland Bay Bridge was opened, linking San Francisco to Berkeley and Oakland across the bay. A year later the fabulous Golden Gate Bridge, the second-longest single-span suspension bridge in the world, opened to link Sausalito and Marin County to the north. Two more bridges were built, spanning the South Bay, and later, the five and one half miles between Richmond and San Rafael on opposite sides of North Bay were linked by a two-level span. Another pair of bridges crossed the western end of the Carquinez Straits. Then in 1962 a seventh bridge was opened linking Benicia and Martinez. These bridges have largely replaced the ferries of which there were at one time forty-three, carrying 50 million passengers across the bay annually.

There is very little flat land in San Francisco, so both business and residential areas take to the hills. Residential areas include Nob Hill with its elegant apartment houses and fine hotels, pretty park, and magnificent church; Russian Hill with its few skyscraper apartments and many single-family homes and small apartment complexes; Telegraph Hill, the scene of the famous Coit Tower, an architectural adaptation of the fire hose nozzle; and Pacific Heights with its mansions and schools.

The city is tightly built and San Franciscans are usually apartment dwellers or have small homes with even smaller gardens. Near, around, and between the hills are many interesting areas: Cow Hollow, a fine residential and shopping neighborhood; North Beach, the center of the city's large Italian colony, descendants of seamen who arrived in trading ships from Genoa; and, nearby, Chinatown, certainly the most picturesque and authentic oriental settlement in the nation.

Located along Grant Avenue and its adjacent streets, Chinatown has a population of 50,000 descendants of settlers who came from Kwantung province, an area near Canton, China, to help build the railroads. By 1860 there were 38,000 in California. Today they are important property owners in San Francisco as well as proprietors of every kind of business, especially curio shops and restaurants. Cantonese customs, language, and dress still prevail, giving great color to the area.

Manufacturing is of secondary importance in the city, although publishing, printing, metal fabrication, and food handling and processing are thriving businesses. Primarily, San Francisco is a financial and managerial center with offices of more than 2,000 corporations. Montgomery Street, the Wall Street of California, is a skyscrapered canyon of brokerage houses, banks, and insurance companies. The city is also an important port, staying competitive to keep its share of the shipping business, since Oakland, Richmond, Stockton, and Redwood City also boast modern port facilities.

San Francisco is also the cultural center of the West. The city has a rich heritage and its people are enthusiastic about the arts. The symphony orchestra, ballet, and opera companies—among the best in the country—are well endowed and well attended. There is good legitimate theater with productions by the American Conservatory Theater and other groups playing Broadway shows as well as original works. Interest in the arts is kept alive by the De Young Museum with its American and European collections, period rooms, and topical exhibits. The city's oriental focus, due to kinship with China and Japan, is seen in the Asian Art Museum with the Avery Brundage Collection of oriental art, one of the finest in the world. The San Francisco Museum of Art is primarily a collection of contemporary works, while the Palace of the Legion of Honor has a collection of French painting and furniture along with current exhibits of different art genre. A high point of tourist interest is the Japanese Tea Garden near the De Young Museum in Golden Gate Park, an authentic replica of a formal Japanese tea garden with a two-story entrance gate, Buddhist and Shinto shrines, half-moon wishing bridge, and ceremonial teahouse, where the public is invited to partake of tea and cookies.

Other sights are the Steinhart Aquarium, Morrison Planetarium, the Mexican Museum, the Museum of Natural History, Fleishacker Zoo, Mission Dolores (the area's first habitation), and Candlestick Park. Churches not to be missed are the lovely Grace Cathedral on Nob Hill with copies of the famous Ghiberti doors and St. Mary's Cathedral on Geary Boulevard, perhaps the most magnificent contemporary ecclesiastical design in the country. Ghirardelli Square, a shopping center and restaurant complex developed around an old brick chocolate factory, and the Cannery, a gallery of distinctive shops in what was once a fruit and vegetable cannery, are interesting waterfront attractions near Fisherman's Wharf, a perennial tourist favorite.

As for institutions of higher learning, although those in San Francisco proper are dwarfed by the University of California in Berkeley and by Stanford University to the south, the city does have the University of California's Medical School, the University of San Francisco with nearly 7,000 students, and San Francisco State College with about 18,000 students. The San Francisco Art Institute is well regarded, as is the California Academy of Sciences, founded more than a century ago.

Pushing San Francisco for second place in terms of population is **San Diego,** with nearly 700,000 inhabitants. The county seat of San Diego County, it is the site of California's finest mission, San Diego de Alcala. Its superb harbor serves as headquarters for many Pacific Fleet activities as well as for an extensive fishing fleet. It is the country's leading tuna center. In addition, San Diego has developed an impressive industrial complex, manufacturing aircraft and parts, missiles, boats, and electronics. It is the site of atomic laboratories. Tourism is an important source of revenue, too, since the city has an excellent climate and is a well-known sports and recreational center.

Educational facilities include the University of California at San Diego, the State University, and City College. There are many attractions including Old Town, with its authentic restorations of early Spanish settlements; the Zoological Gardens, one of the largest and most complete zoos in the world; the Cabrillo National Monument; the Star of India Maritime Museum; Sea World in Mission Bay Park;

the Reuben H. Fleet Space Theater and Science Center in Balboa Park; and the San Diego Wild Animal Park. To the northeast, within easy distance of the city, is Mount Palomar Observatory.

San Jose in Santa Clara County claims to be the fastest growing major city in the United States. Its population has more than doubled every ten years since 1940 when it had a population of 68,000. Today there are 527,500 people in the city proper and 1,189,000 in the county. Founded as a pueblo in 1777, it was the state capital from 1849 to 1851. The center of a vast agricultural complex, it has vineyards, wineries, packing plants, frozen food processing factories, and canneries. It is the largest center of fruit drying in the world. Lately the city has made a determined effort to diversify and there are now companies manufacturing computers, atomic power equipment, and agricultural machinery.

Educational facilities in the city proper include San Jose State University, the oldest and largest state college in the system, San Jose Community College, and San Jose Vocational Center and Adult Education. The city takes pride in its seventy parks and fifty theaters, its symphony orchestra, eleven full golf courses, and five nine-hole courses. Alum Rock Park covers 776 acres; the Municipal Rose Garden is world-famous.

Tourist attractions include the Winchester Mystery House, the bizarre lifetime project of the daughter-in-law of the rifle manufacturer who was told early in life to atone for those killed by the Winchester rifle by constantly adding to her house. Now a museum, it includes 160 rooms, 47 fireplaces, 476 doors, 10,000 windows, and cost $5.5 million. The Mission Santa Clara de Asis, founded in 1777, was the eighth in the chain of missions. All that remains of the original church is the wooden cross which today faces the mission. The present structure built after the fire and earthquake has a ceiling painted by renowned Mexican artist Augustin Dávila and the structure is surrounded by lush gardens and olive groves. The Rosicrucian Egyptian Museum is situated in a setting reminiscent of the land of the Nile and has a collection of rare, authentic Egyptian, Assyrian, and Babylonian artifacts. The complex also includes an art gallery and planetarium. The San Jose Center for the Performing Arts was designed by the Frank Lloyd Wright Foundation to house a wide variety of entertainment—symphonies, opera, rock concerts, jazz bands, ballets, and theater. The San Jose Historical Museum depicts life and commerce in the early days of the area. The weekend San Jose Flea Market regularly attracts fifty thousand buyers and six hundred dealers and claims to be one of the largest in the United States.

Although part of its fame rests on the fact that it is, in a sense, the sister city of San Francisco, **Oakland** has an importance and distinct character of its own. The county seat of Alameda County, incorporated in 1852, it is the fifth-largest city in the state with 370,000 people. A busy port with an excellent harbor, it has other major industries besides shipping. Shipbuilding, transportation, chemicals, fabrics, glass, machinery, and food processing are also big contributors to its economy. It is the world headquarters for the far-flung Kaiser Industries, and also the center for the Bay Area Rapid Transit System, the famous new BART subway of which all Bay Area residents are so proud. Main Oakland attractions include the Oakland Museum, Jack London Square, the Sports Coliseum Complex, the Knowland State Park and Arboretum, and the Paramount Theater—a landmark of the 1920s meticulously restored to its original brilliance.

Sixth-largest city in California, **Sacramento** was incorporated in 1850 and has a population of about 270,000. It has been the capital since 1854 and is the county seat of Sacramento County. This historic city is the site of Sutter's Fort, an early outpost in the interior of the state. It was for many years the western terminus of the Pony Express. The city boasts an inland harbor for ocean-going ships and is the center of water, rail, and motor transportation for the agricultural Sacramento Valley. Industries include food processing, canning, rice mills, and the manufacture and testing of rockets for the United States space program. Large military installations are found in the area. Sacramento College on the western bank of the American River is an important institution of higher education in the state.

Main attractions in Sacramento are the State Capitol and State Library, the E. B. Crocker Art Gallery, State Indian Museum, and William Land Park. Chinatown, an unusual downtown shopping mall, and restored Old Sacramento are always of tourist interest. The capitol building dominates the center of the city, set in a park of more than forty acres, with over one thousand varieties of trees and shrubs from all over the world. Nearby is the restored Sutter house and fort, now a historic exhibit, once a complex that played a major role in the gold rush days. Sacramento is a handsome city with its site at the junction of two rivers, the American and Sacramento, and with its deep-water channel to the sea via San Francisco.

SPORTS AND RECREATION

Sports and recreation in California go hand in hand. Nature offers an abundance almost unmatched anywhere in the world. It includes 1,200 miles of scenic coastline, more than 4,000 lakes, dramatic desert areas, 30,000 miles of streams, more than 40 million acres of forests, and many magnificent mountain ranges. Californians have made the most of all these bounties for recreational purposes, and in so doing have attracted myriad tourists.

Federal and state governments own most of the recreational land, some 45 million acres. The National Forest System administers its vast preserves for hunting, fishing, winter sports, swimming, boating, camping, picnicking, hiking, and scenic touring. Natural conditions are preserved and protected as much as possible and man is allowed as a temporary visitor on foot or in his car. Reservoirs created for water storage do double duty on federal lands: Millions of visitors enjoy boating, fishing, water-skiing, and swimming at reservoir recreation centers.

The state also has seventeen national wildlife refuges to maintain wildlife populations and preserve endangered species. To help people learn about wildlife, visitor centers, nature trails, and picnic areas have been arranged for nature study. Some of these refuges permit hunting and fishing.

In addition to the federal projects, California has one of the largest state park systems in the country. Over two hundred units include over 800,000 acres of parks, reserves, campgrounds, beaches, and historic areas.

California has been called the sports capital of the world, largely because the climate and topography permit so many types of sporting activity so much of the year. There are beaches for swimming, mountains for climbing, and many modern stadiums and sports facilities.

Major golf tournaments sponsored by the Professional Golfers' Association include the Los Angeles Open, which began in 1926 and opens the golfing season in January each year; the Bing Crosby Professional-Amateur, which takes place on the Monterey Peninsula; plus tournaments in San Diego (sponsored by Andy Williams), in Palm Desert (sponsored by Bob Hope), in San Francisco, and in Napa, and the Tournament of Champions in San Diego County.

PLATE 87 The San Antonio River meanders for several miles through the heart of the city.

PLATE 88 The Alamo is San Antonio's best-known attraction.

PLATE 89 The Dallas skyline from the Turtle Creek Park area.

PLATE 90 Houston's Astrodome, the world's first plastic-domed, air-conditioned stadium.

PLATE 91 The Lyndon B. Johnson Library is one of the outstanding attractions in Austin.

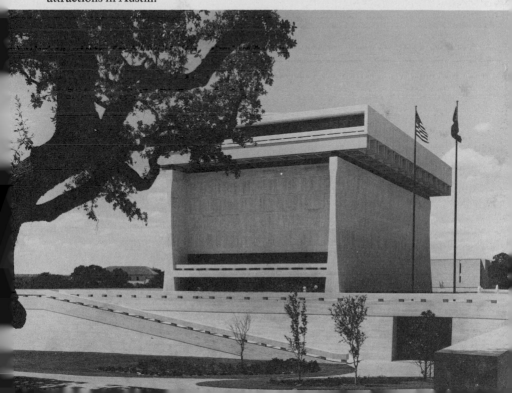

PLATE 92 Rugged mountain terrain of Mount McKinley National Park.

PLATE 93 Hikers descend into the Valley of Ten Thousand Smokes, a portion of Katmai National Monument on the Alaska Peninsula.

Plate 94 Cable cars are a familiar sight on San Francisco's steep hillsides.

Plate 95 Golden Gate Bridge, the second-longest single span bridge in the world.

PLATE 96 San Simeon, the fabulous William Randolph Hearst Castle, is a museum and historical monument in California.

PLATE 97 San Diego's
Yacht Club.

PLATE 98 Ansel Adams
captures the beauty of a
redwood grove in northern
Mendocino County,
California.

PLATE 99 The picturesque Monterey coastline.

History, a Space Theater and Science Center, and an Aerospace Museum. Also in Balboa Park is the San Diego Zoo, over 100 acres of rugged terrain with 5,000 animals, said to be the world's largest collection. Also under zoo management is a new 1,800-acre San Diego Wild Animal Park, thirty miles from downtown, where wild animals are viewed by visitors in monorail trains.

Also in the San Diego area is Mission Bay Aquatic Park—4,600 acres along the Pacific with beach bathing, sailing, golfing, surfing, and picnicking. Sea World in Mission Bay shows marine life in a specially landscaped setting. Here are also found a Japanese Village where divers go for pearls, and shows feature a killer whale, dolphins, seals, and penguins. Near San Diego are Old Town State Historic Park, the Star of India Maritime Museum, Torrey Pines State Park, Shelter Island, and Harbor Island, all worth a visit.

While in southern California, visitors can enjoy the Undersea Gardens at Santa Catalina Island, Magic Mountain in the foothills of Valencia, Busch Gardens in Van Nuys, and Ports o'Call Village in San Pedro. In the desert at Palm Springs, the Aerial Tramway is reportedly the largest passenger carrier of its type in the world. It rises two and a half miles from the desert floor to Mount San Jacinto, over 8,000 feet above. Over three hundred tons of moving cable are supported by five steel towers, the first taller than a twenty-one-story skyscraper.

Central and northern California: Moving north, visitors can discover the many attractions of the San Francisco Bay Area. The cable cars are always intriguing and there is a Cable Car Barn with a visitors' gallery and a museum with old photographs of the picturesque trolleylike vehicles which are the nation's only landmarks on wheels. Around Union Square, the city's prime shopping area, tourists can enjoy the surprising talents of strolling musicians and mimes along with equally surprising palm trees and the delightful St. Francis Hotel with its tower-top restaurants which offer magnificent panoramic views.

Along the waterfront, Fisherman's Wharf takes one to the Mediterranean, to a seaside complex of restaurants and shops with a backdrop of fishing boats and distant mountains. Nearby is the Maritime State Historic Park with replicas of old-time ships that were built on the coast and plied the coastline years ago.

Other pleasant strolls are along Union Street with its specialty shops, antique and art stores, and picturesque cafés, and through

Jackson Square, a restored area of old brick warehouses and commercial buildings that survived the earthquake and fire of 1906. Today there are handsome showcases for antiques and the wares of furniture and fabric houses that serve the city's interior designers. Not far from Jackson Square is the new Embarcadero Center, a complex of the city's new skyscrapers clustered near the fascinating Transamerica pyramid building.

Within relatively short distances of San Francisco are many points of tourist interest. Across the Oakland Bay Bridge one can visit Jack London Square, the Paramount Theater, Mormon Temple, and Lake Merritt in Oakland, and the Berkeley campus with its handsome Zellerbach auditorium. Continuing on, the tourist can visit the famous wine country in Napa and Sonoma counties and tour many of the wineries. Still farther north, Santa Rosa's city park features Luther Burbank's historic gardens and the Church of One Tree, built in 1875 from a single redwood. Along the Pacific Coast at Mendocino are the Pygmy Forest and botanical gardens and the Carson mansion at Eureka.

To the south are picturesque Monterey and Carmel with their fascinating shops and lovely scenery, especially the spectacular Seventeen Mile Drive which connects the two cities along the coast. Continuing along the rugged, cliff-hanging coastal highway are Big Sur and below that San Simeon, the fabulous William Randolph Hearst Castle, now a museum and state historical monument, which includes 127 acres of land, the main house of one hundred rooms, three guest houses, and magnificent grounds. The structures, created around Mr. Hearst's lifetime collecting of furniture, paintings, sculpture, and other artworks gathered from the four corners of the world, can be intimately studied in a series of three guided tours which take one whole day and part of another.

For buffs of the gold rush days, Columbia State Historic Park has restored several blocks of an early town, with a blacksmith's shop, Wells Fargo office, and an old-time firehouse. In the Mother Lode area, there are the towns of Volcano, Hornitos, Murphys, and Nevada City near old mining sites.

No list of California tourist attractions would be complete without mention of the Sierra Nevada, one of the country's main recreation and tourist regions. Five national parks—Yosemite, Kings Canyon, Sequoia, Lassen Volcanic, and Redwood—are the site of magnificent mountain scenery and trees. There are also a number of recreation areas and state parks, including six near Lake Tahoe.

A most interesting tour is one of the missions along Route 101, approximately the old Camino Real. Most of these are open to the public and all give a fascinating insight into what life was like in the early Spanish and Mexican days. Some of the missions have been completely rebuilt—Santa Clara de Asis, for example; others are being restored; and a few are almost exactly as built in the eighteenth century. From San Diego in the south to Sonoma in the central part of the state, this string of missions includes San Juan Capistrano of the famous swallows, now partially restored, and San Juan Bautista, which has the church and museum as part of a restored plaza with an old hotel, livery stable, and living quarters of bygone days (it is also a delightful, peaceful little town with antique shops lining the main street).

SPECIAL EVENTS

All major cities and many smaller cities and towns have their special happenings each year. Many take place June through September, the best weather months, but there are some throughout the year. For example, every county in the state has a fair and these occur regularly. Below is a list of major events:

Pasadena Tournament of Roses, January (Rose Bowl football game)

San Francisco Sports and Boat Show, January

Gold Discovery Days in Coloma, January

Palm Desert Golf Classic, February (the Bob Hope Tournament)

San Diego Golf Tournament, February (the Andy Williams Tournament)

National Date Festival in Indio, February

Chinese New Year Celebration in San Francisco and Los Angeles, February

California Five Hundred Auto Race in Ontario, March

San Francisco Grand National Livestock Exposition, Horse Show, and Rodeo, March

Jumping Frog Jubilee in Angels Camp, Calaveras County, May
Glenville Roundup in Kern County, June
Southern California Exposition in Delmar, June
Santa Barbara Horse and Flower Show, July
California Exposition and State Fair in Sacramento, August
Bach Festival in Carmel, August
Scottish Gathering and Games in Santa Rosa, August
Monterey Jazz Festival, September
Danish Days in Solvang, Santa Barbara County, September

W.E.H.

CHRONOLOGY

1542 Juan Rodríguez Cabrillo explored the California coast.

1579 Sir Francis Drake visited New Albion.

1602 Vizcaíno's Spanish expedition discovered Monterey Bay.

1769 Father Junípero Serra and Gaspar de Portolá explored upper California.

Father Serra founded San Diego Mission and Presidio.

1770 Monterey Mission and Presidio were founded.

1774–75 Juan Bautista de Anza opened overland route to California.

1776 San Francisco Mission and Presidio were founded.

1777 San Jose, the first pueblo, was founded.

1781 Los Angeles, the second pueblo, was founded.

1812 Russian Fort Ross, near Bodega Bay, was established.

1821 Mexico gained independence from Spain.

1826 First United States citizens reached California overland led by Jedediah Smith.

1833 Secularization of the missions was begun.

1846 Bear Flag was hoisted and Republic of California proclaimed.

1848 Gold was discovered.

Mexican War ended.

California became part of United States.

1849 The gold rush began; nearly 100,000 settlers arrived.

First state constitution was adopted.

1850 California was admitted to the Union as the thirty-first state.

1861 Telegraph line was completed to California.

1869 First transcontinental railroad was completed.

1878 Constitutional Convention was called.

1880 Second state constitution was adopted.

1906 Earthquake and fire nearly destroyed San Francisco.

1915 Panama-Pacific Exposition was held in San Francisco; city rebuilding was completed.

1932 Los Angeles and Long Beach hosted the Olympic Games.

1936 Oakland Bay Bridge was opened in San Francisco.

1937 Golden Gate Bridge was opened, second longest single-span suspension bridge.

1939 Golden Gate International Exposition was held in San Francisco.

1945 United Nations was founded in San Francisco.

1951 Japanese peace was signed in San Francisco.

1964 California became the most populous state.

1971 Earthquake hit Los Angeles area.

1973 Bay Area Rapid Transit train made a first run underwater from Oakland to San Francisco.

1976 San Jose celebrated its 200th anniversary along with the nation's Bicentennial.

1978 Californians voted to approve Proposition 13 for a slash of almost 60 per cent in property-tax revenues. The referendum was a result of a voter-initiative effort.

1979 In April, with the cutoff of oil from Iran and cutbacks from Saudi Arabia, California became the first state hit by gasoline-shortage panic. The crunch triggered an odd-even rationing system, eventually imitated in many other parts of the country.

HAWAII

FOR A GROUP of islands which were isolated from all contact with the Western world until the arrival of Captain James Cook in 1778, the fiftieth state has seen the swift forces of change transform it into a crossroads of commerce and trade, a mecca for vacationers, a prosperous Pacific paradise still holding onto its natural beauty while the cost of living shakes it up more than the occasional eruption of its volcanoes.

If the essence of Hawaii were to be capsulized into one word, surely that word must be "unique." The youngest of the United States is one where, in just fifteen years, the low-profile, semisleepy city of Honolulu on Oahu has become a fast-paced city with hundreds of high-rise structures; yet, in another part of the multi-island state, there are still islanders (on Niihau) who lead lives without television, automobiles, even electricity. Hawaii is the only one of the states with only air and sea access, with a royal palace, with a population entirely composed of ethnic minorities.

Known popularly as the Aloha State, Hawaii is a place of beauty where one tends to pull out all the stops in choosing adjectives that connote visual delight. Perhaps Mark Twain put it as well as anyone when he described Hawaii as "the loveliest fleet of islands anchored in any ocean." But the price of beauty comes high. Hawaii has become one of the most expensive housing markets in the country, with the general cost of living from 10 to 30 per cent more than elsewhere in the states. There is great wealth, but extremes of poverty, too, brought on by the decline of agriculture on those sparsely populated islands where tourism is just beginning.

Some Hawaiian residents mutter that the powers-that-be are more concerned about keeping the state bird, the rare nene (Hawaiian goose), from extinction than the rights of the descendants of the original settlers. A significant number of those descendants have looked at the recent accomplishments of fellow minority-group Americans, especially blacks and American Indians, and are pressing for the acquisition of federally owned land and cash subsidies for Hawaiians and part-Hawaiians.

The state's population is an ever-changing mix and although there is some local skittishness about the social pecking order, tolerance prevails. Of course there is no such thing as complete harmony, but perhaps the nearest thing to it is the majority attitude toward visitors. Friendliness is everywhere; the so-called Aloha Spirit permeates the sweet-smelling, unpolluted air. Tourists are welcome to peek into the governor's office; receive courteous answers from patient bus drivers who guide the municipal transportation facility, TheBus (this is the actual name and spelling of it), in Honolulu's traffic lanes; smile when they recognize Hawaii's legislators Patsy Mink or Daniel Inouye.

Hawaii knows that tourism is sweeter to its economy than the finest quality of sugarcane. The state has even added an official with the title Director of Visitor Satisfaction to its bureaucracy. It wants to guarantee that its motto be more than mere words. Translated from the Hawaiian, it is: "The life of the land is perpetuated in righteousness."

THE LAND

In describing the topography of Hawaii, one is tempted to pull out all the stops in the use of superlatives. The islands are dramatically beautiful, incredibly lush, and yet offer stark contrasts of inhospitable terrain. Rugged slopes are draped in a rich verdure of tropical and semitropical trees, plants, and flowers. Waterfalls drop hundreds of feet against a background of a profusion of green and gay color and terminate in the trim, geometric neatness of sugar and pineapple fields.

Seas in all tonalities of blue rim palm and pandanus-fringed shores; talcum-powder-smooth beaches of white, coral, and black sand can be but a short distance from coasts so rocky that some can be reached only by helicopter.

There is the bleak appearance of volcano lands, barren cinder cones—both similar to the surface of the moon. Then there are incredibly rich motion-picture-type settings that have been just that.

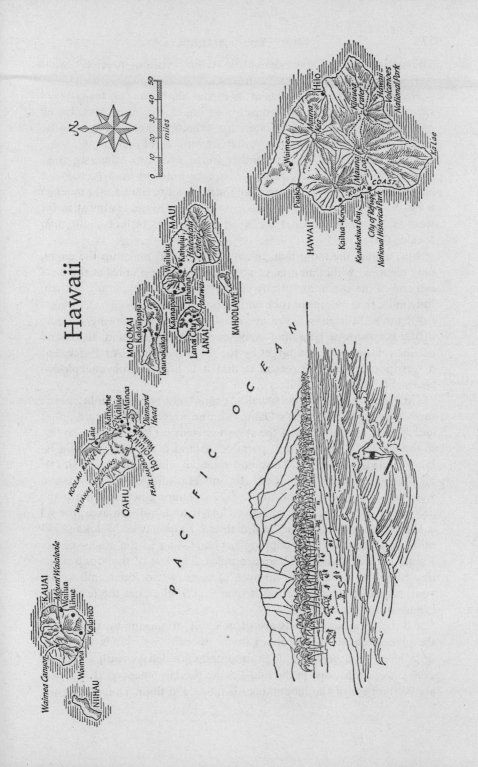

Hawaii

The natives of the state delight in telling visitors precisely what scenes from which films have been shot in specific locales.

Hawaii offers wooded areas at its higher elevations, cactus-covered ranch land, and, above all, a mind-boggling variety of orchids. In the nurseries of the island of Hawaii, for example, there are said to be more than twenty-two thousand different varieties of orchids.

The United States' fiftieth member consists of one of the longest island chains in the world. Its 6,425 square miles of land (somewhat larger than the state of Connecticut) stretch more than 1,600 miles in a vast arc across the Pacific. The most western island is almost as far west as New Zealand, and the most southern is farther south than Mexico City.

But, among the more than twenty islands that make up the chain, only eight, all within an area of about four hundred miles at the eastern end of the chain, are of any size. The rest are tiny, many of them little more than clumps of rock and reefs.

Of the eight islands, seven are inhabited. (At this writing, in spite of the pressures of Hawaiian activists to reclaim the land, the island of Kahoolawe, used as a target by the U. S. Navy and Air Force, has a zero population. The reason is that it is littered with unexploded shells and considered unsafe.)

Only one island, with Hawaii's capital city of Honolulu, has a fairly dense population. It's Oahu, with an area of 598 square miles, and more than four-fifths of the state's citizenry. (It's the third-largest in the chain.) The next most populous island is Hawaii, the "Big Island," which, with its 4,037 square miles, is almost twice the size of all the other islands combined. Beyond Hawaii, going from east to west, are Maui with a land area of 728 square miles, making it the second-largest of the islands; Lanai, 141 square miles in area; the 45 square miles that make up uninhabited Kahoolawe; Molokai, 259 miles in area; and then—skipping beyond Oahu in the chain—comes Kauai, with an area of 551 square miles. The last of the group is the tiny island of Niihau, with an area of seventy-two square miles. Beyond Kauai, stretching northwest over 1,200 miles, are the rest of the islands of the chain.

All the Hawaiian Islands are of volcanic origin, the tops of one of the highest chains of volcanoes in the world. The islands are really little more than peaks of huge mountains hidden beneath sea level, even though this ridge in the mid-Pacific rises in places to 26,000 feet above the base of the mountains on the ocean floor. Dominating the volcanic landscape are Mauna Kea (13,796 feet) and Mauna Loa (13,680 feet) on Hawaii.

On the basis of geologic age, the Hawaiian chain can be classified into three types. The oldest islands are the small ones of the northwestern arc. These submerged rocks, islets, and small uninhabited islands are the remains of very ancient volcanoes. Here the formerly high mountains have been eroded to or near sea level.

The second group consists of the seven islands, from Niihau to and including Maui, now volcanically quiescent or dormant. Many have been eroded to only a remnant of their former height. Also in this group are small, quiet, and eroded "pimple volcanoes" located on the sides or flanks of the former large volcanoes. Diamond Head, landmark of Oahu, is one of these.

The major volcanoes that form this second island group rise to various heights above sea level. While the highest point of Oahu is a shade over four thousand feet, Mount Haleakala on Maui, which has one of the largest craters in the world, is 10,025 feet high.

The third type is the young and active volcanic island of Hawaii with the "greats": Mauna Kea, Mauna Loa, and the very active crater of Kilauea, a little over four thousand feet. These have erupted in the past and continue to do so with astonishing regularity. On occasion, lava flows reach the sea and fall over the wave-cut sea cliffs in rivers of fire. It's not unusual for forests, sugarcane fields, roads, and buildings to be burned or buried. Yet Hawaii's volcanoes don't spew out the heavy cloud of ash which has proven disastrous in other of the world's volcanoes. With reasonable precautions, the volcanoes, considered in Hawaiian legend to be the home of the fire goddess, Pele, can be watched and photographed safely.

The Hawaii Volcanoes National Park, with more than 200,000 acres, has been set aside by the government to incorporate volcanic features. In the southern section of the park on Hawaii are the Mauna Loa and Kilauea craters, and in the northern part, on Maui, is the now-quiet crater of Haleakala. Overlooks for tourists are at Kilauea. Here one can view the crater with its constantly bubbling lava. The National Park Service maintains rangers in this park. Its experts and others on a university level study and record volcanic activity.

The islands are fringed by coral reefs, built in the shallows of the ocean by polyps, tiny sea animals attached to the rocks. As each generation dies, it leaves the coral limestone it has built in place. Later generations build the reefs higher. Ultimately, waves, breaking on the reefs as they roll in from the Pacific, bound the coral and in time break it into sand.

CLIMATE

The Aloha State's pleasant climate is one of its greatest natural assets. The island chain stretches across a subtropical latitude. The happy result is air that is usually comfortably balmy and temperatures with little seasonal change. Within the state, summer temperatures average 78 degrees and in winter the temperature hovers around 72 degrees. Year-round, nights bring a temperature drop of about 12 degrees. The highest official temperature recorded for Honolulu is 88 degrees; the lowest, 57 degrees. The annual average in the city is 75.1 degrees.

As for water temperatures, they are always fine for bathing, between 75 degrees and 82 degrees. (It's not chill waters but waves that cause problems. Winter is the season for high surf, and North Pacific storms have been known to generate waves twenty-five to thirty feet high.)

The Hawaiian Islands lie in the path of the northeast trade winds which blow steadily, with moderate velocity at lower altitude, but often with great force at higher levels. Sometimes, when the air is banked against a mountain wall or funneled through a pass, the force of the wind may make walking difficult. Hawaiian women invariably carry a scarf to protect their hair. When a spell of kona (leeward wind) comes along, high humidity and southwesterly breezes accompany it. In summer—usually August—kona weather is the same as very-sticky weather. In winter it can bring storms, even torrential rain.

The eastern and northeastern sides of an island are windward. They are toward the wind, which here blows from the ocean to the land. The western and southwestern sides of the islands are leeward. Here the trade winds travel across the land to the sea. On Oahu, the suburbs of Honolulu such as Kailua and Kaneohe and their neighboring eastern-side areas are spoken of as windward Oahu. The western shore of the island is leeward Oahu.

Windward coasts receive thirty to forty or more inches of rain a year at sea level; leeward coasts can get as little as eight to fifteen inches. The Koolau range, facing the eastern side of Oahu, has more than a hundred inches of rain near its windward base, and three hundred inches at places near its crest; this is fortunate for Honolulu's water supply.

Although the overall impression of the Neighbor Islands is that of green (indicating sufficient rainfall), the variations there are truly remarkable. The wettest spot on earth, according to the Hawaii Visitors Bureau, is at Mount Waialeale, in the center of the island of Kauai, where the bureau reports a mean annual rainfall of 486 inches. Yet, just a few miles away on the same island there is an area with less than twenty inches of rain a year. The driest spot recorded in the islands is Puako, on Hawaii, where a raincoat is about as much needed as a mink lap robe. The mean average rainfall is about ten inches a year. On Oahu, within the city of Honolulu, it is possible to live in a place where the annual rainfall is 125 inches, or in a place four miles away that receives eight inches. In Honolulu, by the way, residents, ever-conscious of the tourist industry, seldom mention rain. They talk about "liquid sunshine" or "pineapple juice falling from the heavens."

Tourists headed for an excursion on the Neighbor Islands are always advised to take a sweater if they anticipate a change in altitude. In just one day, a jaunt can go from an island's coast—bikini-type weather—to, say, Maui's Mount Haleakala, where a jacket is always in order. During the months of January and February, snow is found on the summits of the Big Island's Mauna Kea and Mauna Loa. There is even skiing here at times, although local conditions will never be a challenge to the Austrian Alps.

Thus, in Hawaii, you can really choose your climate. Rarely are there any surprises. In spite of the enormous range of rainfall, one can count on the overall pattern being a combination of the natural air conditioning of the trade winds and equable temperatures.

THE HAWAIIANS

When, on January 18, 1778, the sloops *Discovery* and *Resolution* under the command of the great English explorer Captain James Cook sighted the natives of Waimea on the Hawaiian island of Kauai, they were looking upon the descendants of islanders who had inhabited the mid-Pacific archipelago for hundreds of years. What is amazing is that, with all the previous crisscrossing of the Pacific, these people had not been discovered much earlier.

Although there are no written records of the history of the islands in pre-Cook years—the Hawaiians had no written language—nor knowledge of the size of their population when they were discovered by the white man (figures of anywhere from 100,000 to 300,000 natives are among the estimates), anthropologists have constructed a rough chronology of early settlement.

Nobody, of course, knows when Hawaii was first inhabited. For a long time it was thought that the original settlers set foot on the islands about A.D. 1000, but new research places the time of the first immigration closer to A.D. 700–750.

Historians believe that the Polynesians who conquered the Pacific in double canoes (probably some hundred feet long) originally came from Southeast Asia. Although Tahiti is considered one center of Polynesian development from which the exploration may have had its roots, other evidence points to the Marquesas. Be that as it may, the consensus is that the navigational skills of the pioneers were enormous, their feat of fantastic proportions.

Presumably these people who settled the islands—large, brown-skinned, and good-looking—lost contact with other lands for several centuries. From a study of their chants, songs, and sagas, and from the oral histories of the natives of other islands, it is theorized that in the eleventh century there were fresh waves of immigration and then, once more, there ceased to be new arrivals.

It is believed that in their canoes the original settlers brought food plants, including coconut, taro, bananas, breadfruit, sweet potatoes, and possibly sugarcane. Chickens, pigs, and dogs were the source of meat. Drinking water for the voyage was carried in gourds or bamboo pipes.

The first Hawaiians evidently lived in a relatively primitive state in villages near the shores of the islands. Knowing nothing of metals, they made tools of stones, shells, bone, teeth, and wood. Having no beasts of burden, they performed the heaviest labor themselves. As the population spread slowly over the islands, stone axes were used not only to fell trees but to build grass-covered huts and hollow out the mammoth canoes which were the inter-island means of transportation.

Life was highly organized, with the social order divided between the nobility (alii) and the common folk (makaainana). At the top of this pyramid was the alii nui, the leader, who, if he controlled an entire island, was given the title of King (moi). (Note the relationship to the French word for King, roi.) The alii nui, who could be a woman as well as a man, was tended both by nobles owing fealty and by priests, who also came from the noble class.

Although the alii were at the apex of the social order and spent their time in the performance of rituals in a complicated, stratified system, the priests (kahunas) were almost equally important. They were in charge of the ritual code of kapu. (Interestingly, this word is similar to tabu, the expression for a forbidden act used in other parts of Polynesia.)

No common person, for example, could let his shadow fall on the chiefs without being in danger of instant death. Women, in particular, suffered severe restrictions in this highly organized scheme. They were forbidden to dine with the men or eat certain foods (normally, the most appetizing). During some periods of religious festivals the lower classes could not venture out of doors. Indeed, there were some people who were always forbidden to emerge into the daylight!

The ancient Hawaiians followed a polytheistic form of nature worship. Although the universe was supposedly ruled by a supreme being, there were hundreds of important deities, including Kane, Ku, and Lono, the gods, respectively, of light, war, and the harvest; Kaneola, ruler of the land of departed spirits; and Pele, the fire goddess.

The gods were invisible spirits, symbolized by natural objects or human or animal images made by skilled craftsmen. There were stone temples (heiaus) all over the islands, and on almost any occasion a ceremony took place. (The remnants of one ruin where there were heiaus is at the City of Refuge at Honaunau on the island of Hawaii. For all its bloodthirstiness, the religion provided places such as this for fugitives. After a period of repentance, they were allowed by the priests to re-enter tribal life. Honaunau, dating from the twelfth century, is noteworthy for its stonework and is now a National Historic Park.)

Although there was certainly human sacrifice, usually the victim would be a captured warrior. Cannibalism was practiced, but not as widely as some have once thought, and infanticide was common, as a means of population control.

The ordinary man wore a loincloth (malo); the woman, a skirt of kapa, a cloth beaten from the inner bark of a tree. Either sex might cover the shoulders with a loose mantle or, then again, often choose to go naked. As for the chiefs, those of highest rank wore long feather cloaks as the visual symbols of prestige; lesser chiefs, shorter cloaks. Colors were red, yellow, black, and green, worked into designs in which triangles and crescents prevailed.

Although life was certainly stratified, it was not overwhelmingly grim. The Hawaiians excelled at all sorts of water activities: swimming, boating, and, as every modern-day tourist soon sees, surfing. The Hawaiians were fond of coasting down hillsides on ti leaves and had forms of boxing, wrestling, foot racing, and games akin to checkers or chess.

They gambled, got drunk on fermented brews made from awa and ti roots, sang to the accompaniment of wind instruments and drums. (Contrary to common belief, the Hawaiians did not invent the ukulele. It's an instrument of Portuguese origin.) The common man danced a form of the hula which differed somewhat from that of the sacred dance performed at religious rituals.

The early Hawaiians had casual attitudes toward sex. People were free with their bodies and the exchange of wives and husbands was quite common. Jealousy was rare, as was the concept of private ownership.

What evolved between the initial visit of Captain Cook and 1820, when the first American missionaries arrived on the islands, is outlined in the "History" section of this chapter. In the interim, the Polynesian population began to drop because these long-isolated people had no natural immunities from the white man's diseases. Within a century after the coming of Cook, the native population had been reduced to about fifty thousand.

The coming of the missionaries represented the first of many migrations which have ultimately resulted in the cosmopolitan aspect of the people of Hawaii today. Pure Hawaiians represent only about 1 per cent of today's population. About 250 of them are found on the privately owned island of Niihau where they raise livestock and are completely cut off from communication with the rest of Hawaii. No visitors are allowed, except by special permission.

The uninformed tend to think of Hawaii as a happy melting pot in which racism has not simmered. Not so. As each group arrived, it experienced racial prejudice before it was assimilated. Even today there is a racial pecking order, with pure Hawaiians recently demanding the social equality which they have seen being achieved by other American minority groups.

It was during the middle of the nineteenth century, when Hawaii was a center of whaling activity, that most of the white Anglo-Saxons (haoles) came to the islands. But it was agricultural needs that attracted other groups, coming as they did with a dwindled, disease-ravaged native population. The first groups recruited—work-oriented toward the sugar industry—were the Chinese, who came around 1852. The ethnic pattern which followed brought streams of migration in which Japanese, Koreans, and Filipinos followed. Other immigrants, most of whom came to the islands between 1878 and 1930, included Portuguese, Puerto Ricans, and in lesser amounts people from the South Seas, Germany, Russia, Italy, and Spain, among others.

After Pearl Harbor there were doubts about the loyalty of Hawaii's large Japanese population. They were totally unfounded and no anti-American action took place. When thousands of Americans of Japanese Ancestry (AJA's) volunteered to fight for the United States, they were organized into the 100th Infantry Battalion and 442nd Regimental Combat Team. They became the most decorated units in our military history.

More than half the Hawaiian population today is under twenty-five years old. As a rule of thumb in determining the contemporary ethnic pattern, Hawaii's people are about one-third Caucasian and two-thirds nonwhite. According to a survey completed in 1972, 28.4 per cent were white and 27.4 per cent Japanese. Hawaiians of Filipino descent numbered 10 per cent of the population and those of Chinese origins, 4.3 per cent. Pure Hawaiians, as mentioned earlier, are only 1 per cent of the population and Samoans, Koreans, Puerto Ricans, blacks, and other groups of unmixed ethnic origin were each less than 1 per cent of the people. Part-Hawaiians numbered 18.1 per cent of the population while peoples of mixed ancestries figured at 7.3 per cent.

On July 1, 1974, the population of our youngest state was 846,900, including 54,600 members of the armed forces and 68,300 of their dependents. Oahu is the home of 81.6 per cent of the population and households average 3.44 persons, with males and females about equally divided.

Since World War II, one out of three marriages in Hawaii has been interracial and, of course, everywhere English is the universal language. (Some Hawaiians, however, do use pidgin when communicating among themselves.)

Immigration to Hawaii still continues, with most of the newcomers young people. Retirees in 1974 accounted for only 3 per cent of new arrivals. Hawaii may be, physically, a kind of paradise, but it's not one that the citizen who lives on a pension can normally afford. The cost of living is high, with housing taking the largest financial drain. Newcomers tend to be from the western states of the mainland but those from overseas destinations are still arriving. In 1974 the largest group from a foreign land came from the Philippines. They were followed by people moving from Korea, Japan, and Taiwan, in that order.

HISTORY

The first Western tourist to discover Hawaii was the English explorer-navigator-cartographer, Captain James Cook. But he wasn't enchanted by his balmy, verdant find. The purpose of his expedition wasn't to sail to tropical enchantment; his mission was to seek a passage to the Atlantic along the northwest coast of North America. In this he failed.

When, on his third voyage to the Pacific, Cook set anchor at Kauai on January 18, 1778, he was received as a deity by the natives, who assumed he was the god Lono. The Polynesians supplied Cook with provisions and water and he and his crew sailed off once again in two middling-size sloops which, to the Hawaiians, surely appeared enormous.

Frustrated by a lack of success in ferreting a path through the ice to the north, the explorers once again turned south. On this segment of the trip, Cook sighted Maui and then, on November 30, 1778, the big island of Hawaii. He named the island chain the Sandwich Islands, in honor of the first lord of the admiralty, the Earl of Sandwich. Cook sailed around the island, charting Hawaii's coastline, and on January 17, 1779, he landed on the west shore, at Kealakekua Bay.

Cook was once again treated as a god, even given a temple in which to live. Gifts were heaped upon him. In exchange, he proferred trinkets. By the time the British visitors were ready to set sail once again, Cook's deity-like image had apparently tarnished a bit. His sloops left the islands on February 4, but storm damage forced his return in just a few days.

This time, Cook was received without adulation, and friction quickly developed between his crew and the natives. When some iron tools and a ship's boat were stolen—the latter presumably for its nails by a metal-less people—Cook led an expedition ashore. Taking a chief as hostage, he further enraged the natives by firing a charge at another member of the Hawaiian nobility.

Chaos erupted. Cook was clubbed and in minutes he and four of his crewmen were dead. Not until the sloop *Resolution* fired its cannons at the Hawaiians did they retreat, bearing with them the bodies of many of their chiefs and commoners. As for Cook's remains, it wasn't until after a week of fighting that a few grisly parts of it were recovered.

The sailors who returned leaderless to Britain told tales of the Sandwich Islands, but several years elapsed before other white voyagers arrived. At this time, each of the islands was ruled as a separate kingdom by hereditary chiefs. One such chief, Kamehameha I (The Great) (reign: 1795–1819), consolidated his power in a series of battles in which he gained control over most of the islands. By the time of his death, the Kingdom of Hawaii was established and lasted until 1893.

Although Kamehameha followed the Hawaiian religion, he ended some of its more extreme measures, notably human sacrifice. He was also an active and shrewd trader who stocked his warehouses with foreign treasures. He learned that sandalwood, which grew in the mountains, was much in demand in the Orient. Somewhat later, Hawaii's sandalwood forests were almost totally destroyed and agriculture neglected, while the Polynesians felled trees, leaving hunger to additionally sap the energy of natives already reduced in numbers by white men's illnesses to which they had no natural resistance.

After Kamehameha I's death the authority of the Hawaiian priests started to decline. His son, Kamehameha II (Liholiho) (reign: 1819–24), made sweeping reforms in the religion and broke down the old kapus. Sadly, the young King and his Queen gave personal evidence of his people's lack of immunity to what are considered common diseases in the western world. The pair both died of measles within a few days of each other while on a visit to London.

Actually, it wasn't this King but New England missionaries who forged the decisive change in Hawaiian beliefs and changed the lifestyle of the people. The Vermonter Hiram Bingham and a party of Congregational missionaries arrived in the islands in 1820 and promptly began to exert a profound influence on the people. In their effort to convert the Polynesians to Christianity, they were helped by the early acceptance of their religious tenets by their first convert, the head Queen of Kamehameha I and other members of the royal class. The first church built for Christian use, Kawaiahao Church, made of coral blocks in 1841 in Honolulu, is still in use, with Sunday morning services still conducted in both Hawaiian and English.

Rigidly New England in their morality, the Congregational missionaries helped pave the way for the efforts of what, in contrast, seemed the almost-liberal thinking of the Catholic and Mormon missionaries who followed. The Congregationalists saw many of their new native converts leave the flock for the more acceptable newer religious groups.

The missionaries gave the Hawaiians a written language, using only twelve letters: the five vowels and H, K, L, M, N, P, and W. Thus, all names of Hawaiian origin are made up of all or some of these twelve. Anyone asking for directions in Hawaii, visitor or native, finds the points of orientation are Hawaiian: mauka (toward the mountains), makai (toward the sea), ewa (toward Ewa Plantation, i.e., west), and waikiki (toward the famous beach).

The missionaries made another contribution to the culture. Shocked by the lack of clothing of the Polynesians—sometimes carrying an umbrella made a woman "dressed"—they persuaded the women to wear a long sacklike shape which has since become known as the muumuu and is worn not only by the contemporary women of the state, but by comfort-conscious females in many parts of the world. Hawaiian men were, in missionary days, encouraged to emulate the apparel of visiting ship crews which resulted in their adopting forms of western dress.

Two groups of haoles (white foreigners), the missionaries and the whalers, arrived in Hawaii about the same time. Starting in about 1820 and continuing until after the end of the Civil War on the mainland, Hawaii became a winter base for a fleet of more than four hundred whaling vessels, mostly from New England. Whale oil was the fuel then used for lamps, but whaling declined once petroleum was discovered in Pennsylvania.

When they aligned themselves with the monarchy, the Protestant missionaries gained great political, as well as religious, success. Some, in fact, became advisers to a second son of Kamehameha I, Kauikeaouli (reign: 1825–54), who took the name of Kamehameha III.

During his long years as monarch, the King promulgated a series of decrees which gave his people stronger individual rights and a government which, in but a bit more than a quarter of a century, saw the pendulum swing from a semifeudal system to a constitutional monarchy.

This was a time when the islands prospered and their independence was recognized by the great governments: France, England, and the United States. Hawaii became a tempting prize and several times French naval forces made demands of the monarch. Indeed, a British naval force actually usurped the kingdom. This strange situation lasted but a few months, but remnants of the English influence remain in Hawaii. Case in point: the Hawaiian flag—now the state flag—has a field in one corner which resembles the Union Jack, while eight red, white, and blue stripes, representing the eight main islands, suggest the U.S. flag.

In 1845 the King and legislature moved from Lahaina, the whaling center on Maui, to Honolulu. On August 31, 1850, King Kamehameha III declared officially that Honolulu was a city and the capital of the kingdom.

In the years which followed, the growing importance of sugar had its ramifications on the political as well as economic scene. Among missionaries who gave up religion for commerce were the founders of the sugar company, Castle & Cooke. The descendants of other missionaries started another sugar venture, Alexander and Baldwin. Together with three other foreign groups, C. Brewer and Company, American Factors, and Theodore H. Davies, they became known as the Big Five—the economic establishment.

The sugar planters favored annexation of Hawaii by the states, knowing that this would give them a firm market for their product. But, in one way or another, this move was opposed by a succession of monarchs who supported the policy of Hawaii for the Hawaiians.

Yet, to be pro-Hawaii didn't mean a King couldn't be pro-British as well. In addition to being nationalistic, the next two kings, Kamehameha IV (Alexander Liholiho) (reign: 1854–63) and Kamehameha V (Lot) (reign: 1863–72), who was the brother of his predecessor, often favored the British over the Americans in cultural and political matters. During the reigns of both monarchs, there was inconclusive wrangling between those who wanted to limit the powers of the sovereigns and those who wanted to strengthen the power of the throne.

With the death of Kamehameha V, the line of direct descent from the first Kamehameha ended. Although related by blood to the royal family, the next two kings were elected by the legislature. First came the pro-American Lunalilo (William Kanaina) (reign: 1873–74), then Kalakaua (David Kalakaua) (reign: 1874–91). Disorders caused by followers of Kalakaua's rival, Queen Emma—widow of Kamehameha IV—reached such a state that the government had to call on the marines, both British and American, to restore normalcy.

During Kalakaua's reign a reciprocity treaty with the United States (1876) was negotiated. It gave Hawaiian sugar preferential treatment in America, and, at the same time, American products a similar status in the islands. The treaty was extended in 1887 but at that time Hawaii was forced to assign Pearl Harbor to the United States for exclusive use as a coaling station.

King Kalakaua was a fun-loving chap who was known informally as the Merry Monarch. He had a number of stormy moments, in addition to his troubles with Queen Emma. He was personally ambitious, nationalistic, and had grandiose schemes that included creating a Polynesian empire. During his reign, Iolani Palace was built as an official residence. The King even proposed the idea of marrying a Hawaiian princess to a Japanese prince for political reasons. That idea was turned down.

Under pressure from the white planters, he signed a new constitution in 1887 which limited his power and set up a cabinet-type government, responsible to the legislature. These reforms were far from popular and led, in 1889, to an unsuccessful rebellion by those who opposed this constitution.

The struggle was still going on when, on a visit to San Francisco, the King died in his hotel. Kalakaua was succeeded by his sister Liliuokalani (Lydia Papi) (reign: 1891–93), the wife of an Englishman. She is best remembered as the creator of the beautiful song "Aloha Oe." The Queen was even more nationalistic than her brother and tried to circumvent the 1887 constitution. This led to her deposition as Queen in a "bloodless revolution."

A provisional government—its aim was annexation by the United States—was established under the leadership of Sanford B. Dole. But President Grover Cleveland didn't sympathize with either the government or the revolution and wouldn't condone annexation. The provisional government then changed Hawaii into a republic and, in 1894, Dole was proclaimed its President.

The next U. S. President, William McKinley, presented a more sympathetic ear to the annexation issue. The outbreak of the Spanish-American War in 1898 brought matters to a head—Hawaii's importance militarily in the Pacific couldn't be overlooked. And so, the annexation of Hawaii was made formal by a joint resolution of Congress. A formal transfer of sovereignty took place; in 1900 the new possession became a territory and Dole its first President.

From annexation in 1898 until World War II Hawaii surged forward. The sugar and pineapple industries developed. Hawaii became the hub of Pacific transportation. Older workers tended to leave agriculture for other pursuits but, although there were labor disputes, even violence, labor was not effectively organized until later.

During the 1920s the first efforts toward tourism were made. Although the Depression was not as marked in Hawaii as in more industrial areas, international tensions caused the United States to accelerate its military power in the islands.

With stunning suddenness, those international tensions exploded on December 7, 1941, with the bombing of Pearl Harbor by the Japanese. The American fleet was seriously damaged. Nearly four thousand casualties resulted. Eventually, Hawaii became the nerve center of the United States' Pacific operation and semimartial law, curfews, and blackouts were the way of life until the celebration of V-J day on August 14, 1945.

The idea of statehood for Hawaii had been fermenting for decades. By the war's end it was widely endorsed. Previous arguments about the distance of the islands from the mainland and the threats to national security by Hawaiians of Japanese descent were outmoded. But the late 1940s brought union-management problems with alarmist talk about an imminent Communist takeover and a serious waterfront strike which lasted six months. During the Korean conflict, priorities shifted but the statehood movement marched on. A constitutional convention which wrote Hawaii's modern constitution was held in 1950 and, finally, in 1959, statehood was achieved on August 21. The next Fourth of July, the official United States flag boasted fifty stars.

In the Vietnam years Hawaii's people had their share of casualties. The islands themselves became an area of rest and recuperation for combat troops.

At this point in history, the youngest state, with its young population, is participating in discoveries in outer and inner space and a rapid expansion of oceanographic research. Its greatest concern is to preserve its greatest asset: natural beauty.

INDUSTRY

Hawaii is one of the most prosperous of the states. In 1974, it ranked eleventh among all the states and the District of Columbia in per capita personal income: $5,882.

What places it in this happy position? Not principally industry, if one equates the word with revenues from manufacturing. Hawaii's major sources of income are federal government expenditures (particularly in the military area) and tourism. The other mainstays of the economy are sugar and pineapple, in that order. (More about sugar and pineapple are found in the section on agriculture which follows.)

The state's dependence upon the federal government is dual: as its chief economic indicator in the monetary sense and as a provider of jobs. Obviously, Hawaii's location is the key to governmental interest in the islands. It is close enough to the Far East for the military to extend protection to Pacific lands and defend its own; near enough to the mainland to be supplied with armed forces and weapons.

The U. S. Pacific Command, largest of six which embrace all forces, is headquartered there. In 1974, federal spending in Hawaii was $1.7 billion. Most of this went to defense. In the middle of 1975 the state was the home base of about 54,000 armed force members and some 90,500 of their dependents. Their presence generated over 19,000 jobs, accounting for more than 5 per cent of the non-agricultural jobs within the state. Nearly all the direct impact of federal spending is upon Oahu, where the major bases are found, including the Pearl Harbor Naval Base, the Army's Fort Shafter, Hickam Air Force Base, and Kaneohe Marine Corps Air Station. Collateral results are evident in many ways, from housing, to retailing, to the service industries.

For more than a decade, tourism has been a pivotal force in the economy. In 1922, Hawaii entertained 9,676 visitors. By 1961, the tourism figure was up to 319,807. Only fourteen years later, according to the Hawaii Visitors Bureau, Hawaii said aloha to 2,823,673 travelers, an increase of over 1 per cent from 1974 figures—and this despite the country's recession woes and an airline strike which dealt a heavy blow to tourism in December, a month when hotels were fully booked, staffed, and left waiting. Problems or not, in 1974 visitor expenditures went over the $1 billion mark.

In 1961 there were only about ten thousand hotel rooms in all of Hawaii. By 1975 available space for guests had almost quadrupled. Until just a few years ago most visitors gravitated to Waikiki, on Oahu. Now, using both air transport and a newly created inter-island hydrofoil service, a significant number travel beyond Honolulu's hotel strip to the Neighbor Islands, which aggressively (and deservedly) have promoted themselves as unspoiled destinations. While high-rise buildings mushroomed in Waikiki, major resort areas developed on Maui, Hawaii, and Kauai, where there has been a determined effort to stick to a low-profile, maintain the natural beauty, and avoid the too-zealous construction of hotels and condominium apartments that took place on Oahu. (The Waikiki proliferation is now under control, its formerly feverish pitch checked by strict zoning.) Molokai, for a long time agricultural, has just started to concentrate on tourism, but the last of the five major Hawaiian Islands, Lanai, is still pineapple country, although there are long-range plans to develop some of the non-pineapple land into low-density resorts.

As tourism has expanded from the geographical standpoint so, too, has it in ever-widening markets. In the early 1970s, visitor industry sources stretched their mainland promotions to entice tourists not only from the western part of the country, the traditional visitors to the fiftieth state, but from the midwestern and eastern states as well. They have succeeded, aided by new concepts in air charter travel.

Visitors don't just come from the other states, however. Foreign travelers make up almost 29 per cent of the temporary arrivees. For example, in 1974 the Japanese represented 14 per cent of Hawaii's visitors. What's truly staggering is that they spent an average of $123 a day in that year.

The Japanese tourist is interesting from a cultural as well as an economic point of view. A quick indoctrination in western bathing practices was instituted by Japanese tourism people for Hawaiian vacationers-to-be. The Japanese, it seems, habitually soap and shower outside of a tub and use a bathtub exclusively for relaxation in hot water. Unaccustomed to the western scheme of ablution, Japanese hotel guests were continuing their usual practices to the horror of maids running around with mops to wipe up flooded bathrooms, and hoteliers were enraged by the repair costs of peeling paint and loosened tiles. (Now hotel room literature and signs are usually in Japanese as well as English.)

Other than the processing of sugar and pineapple, Hawaii's manufacturing is diversified and, in the main, directed at the local market. The fact that this manufacturing effort is rapidly growing is rather remarkable, considering the state's mid-Pacific location, relatively small population, and sources of power.

Few things that Hawaii consumes are made entirely on the islands. Bedding, boxboard, steel pipe, and apparel, for example, are fabricated locally only after the importation of raw or semifinished materials. Manufacturing covers two oil refineries, two cement plants, a steel mill, metal fabricators, handicraft factories, and a food-processing industry which concentrates on Hawaiian specialties such as guava confections, tofu (bean curd), and poi.

Important locally is the manufacture of Hawaiian clothing: gay aloha shirts, muumuus, swimwear, and such. Although the shirts are worn at home by Hawaiian men and his-and-her print outfits of shirts and muumuus are seen on the streets camouflaging the silhouettes of tourists, about half the sportswear output is exported. In 1975, about 130 companies, mostly small, were engaged in some facet of the garment industry.

Most manufacturing takes place on Oahu because it offers both the largest labor supply and biggest local market. Labor unions are solidly entrenched in the majority of fields (except textiles) and pay scales approximate those of mainland metropolitan areas. In industries where salaries fall behind, union forces soon push for parity.

The number of available jobs has doubled in the past twenty-five years but, although manufacturing has increased both in output and value, the number of workers within this category has remained steady for the past two decades. It's in government-related civilian posts and the visitor industry that the job opportunities are found. Because of tourism, for example, some forty to fifty thousand Hawaiian residents find employment, directly and indirectly. Interestingly, the labor force includes a large number of working wives. For them, employment is not a ramification of the women's liberation movement but a reflection of the high cost of living in Hawaii.

AGRICULTURE

Although no longer the mainstay of the state's economy, agriculture is still a big money-maker, one which has sympathetic treatment from the state's government. The third-largest source of income are agricultural products: sugar and pineapple.

The saga of sugar, however, is one that has grown a bit sour with the passing of time. Until the United States and Hawaii signed a Reciprocity Treaty in 1875, sugarcane was grown only in modest amounts on the islands. Once the fact was established that sugar would be admitted to the United States duty-free, plantations increased their sugarcane acreage and new plantations were established.

Companies called "factors" grew in size and importance. Factors supplied materials and goods to the plantations and took charge of the shipment and sale of raw sugar. Eventually, Hawaii developed the most advanced sugar technology in the world. Other countries, notably Peru and Iran, turned to the state for aid in developing their own sugarcane industries.

The sugarcane industry in Hawaii is highly industrialized, maintained by large companies, and strongly dominated by trade unions. Facing ever-stiff competition, Hawaii's sugar producers must still pay ever-higher wages. Including their fringe benefits, the almost ten thousand workers in the sugar industry covered by union contracts in their work on the plantations averaged almost forty dollars a day in mid-1975. This made them the highest-paid agricultural workers in the world.

Sugarcane is grown at low elevations, most of it irrigated. Therefore, land surface must be flat or only gently sloping. Plantations are large, with fields found on nearly every island. The planting of cane is done mechanically. Some fifteen to eighteen months later, before harvest, the mature cane is burned, removing leaves and excess vegetation, but leaving an unharmed stalk.

Stalks are harvested by machines, loaded into giant cane carriers, and taken to sugar mills for crushing. Some eight thousand workers are employed in Hawaii's sugarcane factories. From these mills, most of the raw sugar is transported for shipment to refineries on the mainland.

Sugar companies are currently developing new irrigation systems, cultivation and harvesting methods. Several have consolidated. Of twenty-three sugar plantations in Hawaii in 1970, only sixteen remained in 1975. Agricultural task forces appointed by the state government have as their main job to find substitutes for the land taken out of sugarcane production.

Although compliance payments to Hawaiian companies under the U. S. Sugar Act ended in 1974, the industry is trying to have them restored, for, to some growers, they mean the difference between profit and loss.

Sugar prices gradually rose over the 1963–73 decade. In 1973 they were $181 a ton. A year later, they were atypically high: $634 per ton. Such a sugar year isn't expected to repeat itself. Perhaps a more "normal" year for quoting sugar value would be 1972. That's when what is still Hawaii's number one agricultural product brought $203 million to corporate coffers.

Tourists don't tote home sugarcane but almost every returnee to the mainland has a box of fruit tucked under his feet on the airplane. Pineapples, Hawaii's number two agricultural product, got their start in importance due to the efforts of James D. Dole, a descendant of missionaries. He made the name Dole almost a synonym for pineapple when he chose the Cayenne, a type of pineapple, as most suitable for cultivation on the islands.

Shortly after the start of this century, pineapple plantations began to proliferate in Hawaii. Pineapples, grown on high, unirrigated land, are cultivated on five of the islands, with one island, Lanai, owned by the Dole Company, devoted solely to raising the fruit.

From what was once a bit of exotica has come a fruit that is almost a pantry staple. In 1903, Hawaii shipped 1,893 cases of pineapples to the mainland. An important development in increasing exports took place in 1912. In that year a cannery employee invented what was to be to the pineapple what the cotton gin was to cotton: the Ginaca machine. This invention peels and cores the fruit as fast as it can be fed through the machine. By 1971, Hawaii was producing 42 per cent of the pineapples used in the world.

The pineapple industry is big business in the literal sense. Only a few small farmers are engaged in its production. Machines first lay paper strips at planting time. Then, another machine punches a hole in the paper and a pineapple slip is inserted. This paper, which keeps weeds from growing, in time disintegrates into fertilizer.

When pineapples are ready for picking, another machine takes over. It is driven along roads that have been left in the fields and a long boom extends over the plants. Workers pick the fruit, cut off the leaves, and toss the pineapples onto a moving belt on the boom. In a highly mechanized industry, this is about the only hand labor that remains. The fruit moves to the machine and into boxes and is then taken to canneries. The ecology-conscious take note: the dried centers of the pineapple are used to feed cattle.

Although, in 1972, Hawaii supplied 85 per cent of the pineapple consumed in juice form in the world, the industry is—no pun intended—in the midst of a serious squeeze. The reason is the high cost of labor in the state. Example: A worker who, for doing the same chores, would get 15 cents an hour in the Philippines in 1975 commanded $3.28 an hour in Hawaii.

In 1969 Hawaii had six pineapple companies. Seven years later, there were only three. Obviously, the state's pineapple business faces serious problems from the competition of new, fast-growing foreign pineapple enterprises. Hawaii's biggest companies, including the so-called Big Five which still control the pineapple industry (as well as sugar and some shipping), are being forced to diversify, branch out to the mainland, and depend on overseas acquisitions to remain profitable.

Hawaii grows some tropical fruits, however, besides pineapple, which have commercial potential. Avocados, first brought to the islands in the early nineteenth century, rank third in commercially grown fruits. Guava, the most common wild and backyard-grown fruit, is considered something of a sleeper. Increasingly, in processed forms of fruit juice, jams and jellies, it's being exported. Papayas have also become a substantial export crop, and tangerines from the Big Island have all but replaced mainland imports. Bananas, passion fruit, and oranges are also on the list of local tropical fruits.

A wide variety of vegetables and other agricultural crops grown mostly on small farms include some for which Hawaii is virtually the only U.S. source. These include macadamia nuts, coffee, and taro. And several seed companies are experimenting with hybrid seed corn on the islands, including Maui, as the islands' year-round growing season makes three crops possible instead of the single one common on the mainland.

The unique macadamia nuts, grown on about two thousand acres, most of them on the island of Hawaii, are part of an industry with a bright future. Not so coffee. Usually grown by farmers of Japanese ancestry, most of it comes from the same island's Kona district. The Arabian-type coffee, very strong, is used mainly in blending with weaker coffees. At its peak in 1957, the industry is currently in the doldrums due to the high cost of production and a scarcity of harvesting labor.

Most people fail to identify beef cattle with Hawaii, yet the Parker Ranch on the Big Island, with its half-million acres, is the world's second-largest ranch. (Tourists rarely see this part of Hawaii, as nearly all of the cattle ranches are inland and on rougher land than that used for crops. Some of the ranches extend up the slopes of the volcanoes on the island.)

Hawaiians and part-Hawaiians are the usual cowboys, with a life-style much like that of those on mainland ranches. But Hawaii doesn't produce enough beef even for its own use and depends on meat shipped in from the mainland and Australia.

Truck crop farmers grow about twenty of the major vegetables sold locally, including such ethnic favorites as Chinese cabbage, Japanese daikon (turnip), ginger root, burdock, and lotus root. Some rice is grown on these islands, where it is a starch preferred by the populace to the usual staple of the potato. There is not enough, however, to meet local needs, so Hawaii imports rice from California. As for the not-so-lowly spud, in a Honolulu supermarket it costs about five times per pound more than its counterpart in Manhattan.

Although some of Hawaii's crops, notably the more exotic vegetables, specialty items such as passion fruit (lilikoi) juice, and an abundance of flowers and foliage, especially orchids and anthuriums, are on the export list, the state is self-sufficient only in tropical vegetables. Food is one of the chief items shipped into Hawaii.

NATURAL RESOURCES

The variety of rocks we know on the mainland simply doesn't exist in Hawaii. Here there are only two major kinds: lava and coral lime-stone; yet, they are both available in sufficient quantity to support more than one local cement manufacturing plant.

Few minerals have been found in the islands' volcanic rock. In recent years, there has been the discovery of bauxite and titanium but, because of the high extrication costs, neither is exploited commercially. The islands also offer trace deposits of nickel, chromium, zirconium, vanadium, and cobalt.

It is believed that the sea beds around the islands are rich in mineral deposits, such as manganese, but the mining of such minerals is in the noncommercial stage. Outside of some peat deposits in the Waianae Mountains of Oahu, there is no trace of coal. Nor are there any oil resources. Green gems called olivines, formed by explosions of lava, are used in jewelry manufacturing, as is coral.

What is truly scarce on the islands is land, with mountains and lava flows eating up a large percentage of the available area. (In 1961 Hawaii became the first of our states to have a general land-use law enacted. A special commission establishes districts for the utilization of land for urban, rural, agricultural, and conservation uses.) Although some logging goes on on Maui and Hawaii, forestry officials don't expect Hawaii to become a state self-sufficient in timber production.

Paradoxically, each island on land-shy Hawaii has a sufficient supply of fresh water, with subterranean reservoirs used to store rain, the main water source. The water quality is deemed excellent and it is rare that chemical purifiers such as chlorine are used. Water use is efficient and Hawaii is especially proud of the engineering methods used within the state to irrigate agricultural crops.

The ocean surrounding the islands offers fascinating future opportunities. A coral jewelry industry has emerged, a result of encouragement by science, business, and government, in which a system of harvesting utilizes beds of pink, black, rose, and gold-colored coral.

Shellfish raising is a distinct possibility. Malaysian prawns are now grown commercially. Experiments with other shellfish, including lobsters and clams, is under way. The state is interested in developing Hawaii's natural ocean strengths in areas other than food fish, however. There is a study under way to determine the potential of using temperature variations in the water to produce energy. Other long-range projects investigate ways to make Hawaii a center for oceanographic research.

PRINCIPAL INHABITED ISLANDS

•

Hawaii is unique, the only one of the states comprised entirely of islands. In descending order, based on population rather than size, the major Hawaiian islands* are:

OAHU

The majority of those who call the Aloha State home live on Oahu. Based on a 1974 estimate, there are 847,000 people, some 691,000 of whom live in what is called metropolitan **Honolulu.** Small wonder that Oahu is known informally as the Gathering Place.

Oahu has mountain ranges, agriculture, construction and manufacturing, military bases, fine beaches, charming hamlets—and, above all, it has Honolulu, a far cry today from the tiny village which the first Westerners, arriving aboard British ships, saw in 1786.

Dominant features of the Honolulu shoreline are the extinct volcano Diamond Head and the far-from-extinct coral strand known as Waikiki—a half mile long, three blocks wide, and filled with hotels and tourists, surfers and sailors.

At first glance at Honolulu, one might think he is in any mainland metropolis. The freeways, high-rise buildings, traffic jams are all there. But the population is a mix of East and West, and the religious edifices range from Christian churches to Shinto temples. The older buildings are a curious blend of New England and tropical island styles, the newer ones of striking design which takes advantage of indigenous features. Case in point: the outstanding State Capitol. A rectangular structure, it has a volcano-shaped crown with the domes of the legislative chambers also like volcanic cones. Volcanic rock decorates the exterior; fluted columns encircling the building evoke palm trees, reflecting pools symbolize the ocean; native art adorns the interior. The grass-shack image of Hawaii is gone forever.

Culturally, Honolulu is cosmopolitan indeed. Among museums is the multifaceted Bishop, which is best known as custodian of an outstanding collection of Hawaiiana and Polynesian antiquities; the Honolulu Academy of Arts is a gem known for everything from

---

* Niihau is eliminated because this livestock-raising enclave, privately owned, welcomes no uninvited visitors.

Egyptian art to its Pacific galleries. Honolulu boasts: several "little theater" groups; the Honolulu Symphony which plays under the stars in the Waikiki Shell; the Royal Hawaiian Band; buildings of historical association such as Iolani Palace, only throne room under the American flag, where royalty once lived, reopened for the Bicentennial after extensive refurbishment (termites are an ongoing island problem); Mission Houses, the oldest frame buildings (1821) erected; and the Royal Mausoleum, resting place of former rulers. Punchbowl Memorial Cemetery of the Pacific is the final resting place of thousands of veterans; Pearl Harbor is etched in history.

Hawaii has a state university system spread over nine campuses and five independent four-year colleges. The main University of Hawaii campus at Manoa in Honolulu has over twenty-one thousand students and includes oceanography, Asian studies, and tropical agriculture among its specialities. Its broad spectrum of courses and fifteen-minute proximity to Waikiki Beach are drawing cards which make its summer sessions among those most popular in university offerings to mainlanders. The U. S. State Department co-sponsors the East-West Center at Manoa for cultural and technical interchange. Among well-known Honolulu secondary schools are the Punahou School, one of America's top preparatory schools, scholastically speaking, and Kamehameha School, founded in 1887 for children of Hawaiian blood.

Elsewhere on Oahu are the Mormon Temple in **Laie,** largest temple west of Utah, and the nearby Polynesian Cultural Center, a popular tourist attraction which delineates six cultures in separate villages, and superb all-island expanses of beaches, parks, and coastline.

HAWAII

Almost twice the land size of all the other islands combined, the Big Island has a population over sixty-three thousand. Also known as Volcano Island and Orchid Island, it offers spectacular contrasts from Mauna Loa, the world's largest active volcano, and Mauna Kea, highest point in the islands, to Ka Lae, the southernmost tip of the entire United States. Much of the island's splendor is confined within Hawaii Volcanoes National Park, where one can view giant tree ferns, steaming craters, unique volcanic formations, and a volcanological museum.

The most important city, chief port, and the islands' second-in-status airport (Honolulu is first) is **Hilo.** Home to over 26,000 people, it has a branch of the University of Hawaii, Lyman Memorial Museum of Hawaiian artifacts, a missionary-established church, fantastic gardens, and nurseries.

At the western side of the island, on the Kona Coast, is the village of **Kailua-Kona,** south of which Captain Cook landed (and was later killed); several sites of historic interest (including a nearby City of Refuge, further described in "The Hawaiians" section of this chapter); and, a bit farther away, the little town that is the headquarters of the not-so-little Parker Ranch, **Waimea.**

The rest of Hawaii is a fascinating amalgam of orchid fields, macadamia nut tree and Kona coffee orchards, rainbow waterfalls, and black sand beaches.

MAUI

Over forty-five thousand people live on Maui, the Valley Island. (It gets this name because of two mountain masses at east and west, linked by a narrow isthmus.) Islanders say, "Maui no ka oi," which, translated from Hawaiian, means, "Maui is best." Be that as it may, the island assuredly is a winning blend of landmarks and modern resorts. It's the second-most-touristed of the entire island chain.

Maui is dominated by Haleakala, the largest dormant volcano crater in the world. At its summit is **Science City,** multisponsored by governmental, educational, and commercial interests, a research complex of which only the University of Hawaii's Solar Observatory is accessible to visitors, by appointment.

Most arrivals are at the airport in **Kahului.** Next to the town is the provincial village, **Wailuku,** where the Maui Historical Society Museum is a good place to investigate Hawaiiana. From the town, the visitor can take off either for Haleakala or the lush Iao Valley, dominated by a needle of rock which towers twelve hundred feet into the heavens.

Probably the island's greatest "urban" place of interest is **Lahaina,** Hawaii's capital before 1845, which still has lots of old whaling-town atmosphere, the Baldwin Home Museum of missionary days, Lahainaluna School (the oldest—1831—educational institution west of the Rocky Mountains). The town delights in the largest banyan tree in all of Hawaii, many intriguing boutiques, an old prison (Hale Paahao), and is a good place to sample Maui's grease-free potato chips, which have been extolled in mainland newspapers. Four miles away is the multihotel resort development of Kaanapali which is linked to Lahaina by Hawaii's only remaining railroad.

KAUAI

Kauai, whose total population hovers around thirty thousand, is the oldest island, geologically, in the island chain and, even to the majority of Hawaiians, the most beautiful of the group. It's called the Garden Island and it's appreciated equally by movie companies, who do considerable "on-location" work here, and by vacationers. Awesome scenery includes Waimea Canyon State Park, the island's answer to the mainland's Grand Canyon; the tropical valley of Kalalau; Fern Grotto in Wailua River State Park, scene of ancient Hawaiian rites and contemporary weddings; lava slides, four botanical gardens, and many Bali Ha'i-type beaches, some accessible only by helicopter.

The island's business center is **Lihue.** Not far from the town of three thousand are the remnants of an old Russian Fort of 1817 and the historical house, Wailoli Mission Home, built in 1834.

MOLOKAI

Now called the Friendly Isle, Molokai, which has over a shade more than five thousand residents, was once called the Lonely Isle, for victims of Hansen's disease (leprosy) were segregated at Kalaupapa. The treatment center, established by the Hawaiian monarchy in 1866, was made internationally famous by the efforts of the Belgian priest, Father Damien de Veuster, who chose to isolate himself with the disease victims. Now, modern medicine has virtually eliminated the illness and guides, former patients, conduct tours of the settlement.

The tiny village of **Kaunakakai,** which became known because of the song "The Cockeyed Mayor of Kaunakakai," is the island's chief settlement. A touch of modernization to the basically agricultural isle: it has the world's largest rubber-lined reservoir, Kualaupuu Reservoir, completed in 1969.

LANAI

Lanai, the pineapple island, takes its name from the luscious fruit. Most of the two thousand folks here work at Dole's pineapple plantation and live in **Lanai City,** a peaceful, easy-going town perched on an interior plateau. Beachcombing and hunting are principal recreations. At **Kaunolu,** there are ruins of an ancient Hawaiian village. At **Palawai,** there is evidence that the Mormons tried to found a colony in 1861.

SPORTS AND RECREATION

It is said that toboggan racing is about the only sport not available on sporty Hawaii. (There's skiing, on the snowy peaks of Mauna Kea on Hawaii, in the winter.)

Water sports lead the list of what is available year-round. Surfing, the Hawaiian sport of kings, can be tried almost anywhere. Beginners rent boards to learn on the two-footers at Waikiki; pros challenge the giant waves of Oahu's north shore in winter.

Swimming beaches are on all the islands; reefs present opportunities for scuba and skin-diving enthusiasts. Outrigger canoes and catamarans have their fans, while sailing is another popular island sport. Small boat harbors are being developed for interisland cruising.

Deep-sea fishing is special. Some of the world's largest marlin have been hooked in local waters. Other prized gamefish are mahimahi (the Pacific dolphin), a'u (swordfish), ono (wahoo), aku (skip jack), and ahi (yellowfin tuna). Shore fishing is popular; there is even freshwater trout to be caught on Kauai.

Hunters are challenged by wild pigs of Hawaii and Kauai while wild goats, axis deer, trophy sheep, pheasants, and quail await hunters on all islands.

Other back-to-nature options include hiking, camping (cabins are available in some state or national park areas), four-wheel drive safaris in the country, birding, backpacking, horseback riding, and even mule train trips.

There are thirty-seven golf courses scattered through the island chain, from public courses with no greens fees to elegant private clubs. Interest in tennis has accelerated rapidly. There are even rooftop courts in Waikiki.

Hawaii has the usual spectator sports—football, baseball—and some unusual ones such as hukilaus (fishing parties) and other Polynesian-type activities. If eating is a sport, then attending a luau (native feast with roast pig the specialty) qualifies. Hula dancing has its following and Hawaii offers instruction in other local specialties from traditional quilt-making to cooking.

POINTS OF INTEREST

With tourism so interwoven in the Hawaiian economy, it's difficult to isolate attractions specifically for visitors. Case in point: Honolulu's Ala Moana Shopping Center. Would one consider a complex of more than 150 consumer-oriented establishments touristic? Yes, when it's one of the world's largest centers, a multilevel, fifty-acre complex with pools, ponds, sculpture, and entertainment like a weekly children's hula show. On all the islands, where they exist, the best touristic shopping possibilities center on the centers. Hawaii doesn't exactly abound in wares one can't get anywhere else. Best ideas: coral jewelry, local handcrafts, macadamia nuts (a bit less expensive than on the mainland), Hawaiian sportswear, and local, sweetish perfumes.

Typically touristy are lei stands, a wax museum, rickshaw riding; less so, industrial plant tours such as (in season) a visit to a pineapple cannery. Oahu, has the Kahuku Sugar Mill and the adjacent cultural-entertainment facility and many parks; Hawaii, the Volcano House, right on the rim of Kilauea Crater (for dining or overnighting); Kauai, motorboat cruising with musical entertainment, helicopter sightseeing; Maui, the sugarcane train and a whaling museum; Molokai, muleback trips to the former leper colony.

All major hotels offer Polynesian-style entertainment, much of it free, such as evening torchlight ceremonies and hula instruction. There are also dinner cruises, intimate lounge entertainment, and Radio City Music Hall-type spectaculars. Interestingly, until recently the emphasis has been on the entertainment, not the performers. Generations of tourists know but one name: Don Ho. A new group of Hawaiian showfolk aims at emphasizing personal talents.

SPECIAL EVENTS

Hawaii loves celebrations and, in addition to the usual national holidays, enjoys festivals which emphasize its diversified cultural heritage. In January (or February) the islands celebrate the Narcissus Festival, for the Chinese New Year; in late March or April comes the Cherry Blossom Festival. Lei Day is celebrated on May 1; June 11 is

Kamehameha Day, with parades and pageants. Bon Odori, a Buddhist Festival, comes in June, July, or August with the Hawaii state fair another summertime event. Aloha Week is in October. At various times of the year there are flower shows and festivals, athletic competitions and sports events. Dates of special events vary from year to year, unless already specified.

J.A.

CHRONOLOGY

A.D. 700–750   First Hawaiian settlers, probably Polynesians, arrived in the islands.

1200s   A second wave of immigration, again, probably Polynesian, to the islands.

1778   Hawaiian Islands discovered by Captain James Cook.

1789   First American ship, *Eleanore,* visited Hawaii.

1792–95   King Kamehameha I fought and conquered all the islands and became sole ruler of Hawaii (except for Niihau and Kauai).

1810   Cession of Kauai to Kamehameha I.

1819   Abolishment of kapu system (ancient restrictions) by Kamehameha II.

1820   Arrival of first New England missionaries.

1825   First coffee and sugar plantations established.

1831   First English school at Lahaina, Maui.

1840   Under Kamehameha III, Hawaii was transformed into a constitutional monarchy with its first written constitution.

1840s   The United States, Great Britain, and France recognized Hawaii's independence.

1852   Chinese immigration to Hawaii began.

1887   After renewing the Reciprocity Treaty of 1875, the United States received Pearl Harbor as a base. At the same time, Hawaiian sugar was allowed U.S. entry without paying a tariff.

1893   Overthrow of the monarchy when Queen Liliuokalani lost her throne.

1894   Republic of Hawaii established. First President: Sanford B. Dole, son of American missionary parents.

1898   Annexation of Hawaii to the United States by joint resolution of Congress.

1900   Hawaii became a territory on June 14.

1919   Eruption of both Mauna Loa and Kilauea volcanoes.

1925   Genesis of Hawaii's modern tourist industry.

1941   Sneak attack by Japanese at Pearl Harbor, December 7, plunged United States into World War II.

1950   A new constitution was signed by constitutional delegates, providing for an elected governor, senate, and house of representatives.

1959   Hawaii became the fiftieth member of the United States.

1959   to the present   Hawaii's tourism expanded to become the state's major income source. Credit given to jet air transportation.

1968   New $30 million State Capitol in Honolulu has its first legislative session.

1970   Beginning of major Japanese investment in Hawaiian land and businesses.

Beginning of movement by full and part Hawaiians to protect their ethnic identity.

1975   Inter-island hydrofoil service established on limited basis after lapse of inter-island ferry service for over two decades.

Eruption of Kilauea. At 7.2 on the Richter Scale, it was the strongest earthquake in a hundred years.

1976   3.2 million tourists visited the Hawaiian islands.

1977   New hotel on Molokai spurred the island's first major wave of tourism.

1979   After twenty years of statehood, Hawaii's unemployment rate stood at over 14 per cent. Hawaiians and part-Hawaiians were at the bottom of the economic scale in the multi-racial state.

1980   A new state agency was scheduled to be created—the Office of Hawaiian Affairs. Its aim: to deal with the unique problems of Polynesian-descended Hawaiians. Following the example of other minorities, this group has shown a resurgence of recognition of its ethnicity.

OREGON

OREGON was celebrated in name and poetry long before it was settled. In 1817 while the United States had barely begun to venture west of the Mississippi, William Cullen Bryant published his epic *Thanatopsis,* with the lines "where rolls the Oregon and hears no sound save its own dashing."

Bryant's romantic image of the Pacific shore was based largely on the reports of the Lewis and Clark expedition, which reached the mouth of the Columbia River in 1805. Other observations about the mountains, forests, rivers, and sea coast of Oregon came from fur traders and missionaries, and by the 1840s a major immigration to the Pacific Northwest was under way.

The pioneers experienced the great geographic shock that is common from viewing Oregon and its sister state, Washington. On the near side of the Cascade Range is an arid land of sagebrush, dry canyons, and lava beds. On the far side is a temperate, timbered region which, with its wildlife and rich soil, must have seemed the Promised Land. So Oregon proved to the pioneers and their descendants. The stands of Douglas fir, ponderosa pine, and cedar have provided a bountiful harvest, as has the lush Willamette Valley with its multitude of crops.

Perhaps more than any other state, Oregon has been able to maintain a balance between the use of its natural resources and their preservation. Fully a quarter of its total acreage is parkland; it has more than four thousand campsites and six thousand picnic spots; and nearly the whole of a 400-mile stretch of seacoast, among the great wonders of the world, has been saved from commercial exploitation. Small wonder, perhaps, that Oregonians have been trying, albeit gently, to stem the flow of new immigrants who want to share nature's bounty. More than anything else, Oregon fears overpopulation will upset the balance.

Economic growth is better controlled, but it is not diminished. Portland, Oregon's premier city at the juncture of the Columbia and Willamette rivers, is a major United States seaport which began shipping out timber products and wheat more than a century ago. In recent decades, it has proved equally attractive to industry ranging from aluminum smelting to electronics and frozen foods.

Portland's dependence on the Pacific is symbolic. For water is the key to Oregon's present and future, whether for fishing, shipping, and hydroelectric power or for the irrigation that has turned vast areas east of the Cascades into fertile farm land.

THE LAND

Oregon has it all: rugged coastline, sandy beaches, heavily timbered ranges, snow-capped peaks, broad river valleys, lava fields, and rolling upland plains cut by deep gorges. Perhaps nothing so typifies the scenic drama as that December day in 1843 when explorer John C. Frémont and his party ascended to an altitude of seven thousand feet amid the snows of south-central Oregon. From there they looked down three thousand feet on a lake surrounded by grass and green trees, and they descended in a matter of hours from winter to summer. Frémont named the two points Winter Rim and Summer Lake.

The present state, formerly the major portion of a vast area known as the Oregon Territory, measures some 280 miles from north to south and 380 miles from east to west. It is split down the middle, as is the state of Washington to the north, by the imposing barrier of the Cascade Mountains, a chain crowned by volcanic peaks. The greatest is the perpetually snow-clad Mount Hood, easily visible from the city of Portland. Another of the natural wonders, forming the larger part of Oregon's northern boundary, is the Columbia River, which gives Oregon somewhat the shape of a saddle. Forming part of the eastern boundary is the mighty Snake River, with a rugged gorge deeper than the Grand Canyon of the Colorado. These two rivers, added to the three hundred miles of coastline, comprise more than two thirds of Oregon's perimeter. Within the boundaries are the 96,699 square miles of one of the largest states in the United States.

The Cascades divide Oregon, as they do Washington, into two unequal parts. To the east is the broad plains-plateau section; to the west, and accounting for about one third of the total, lies the more

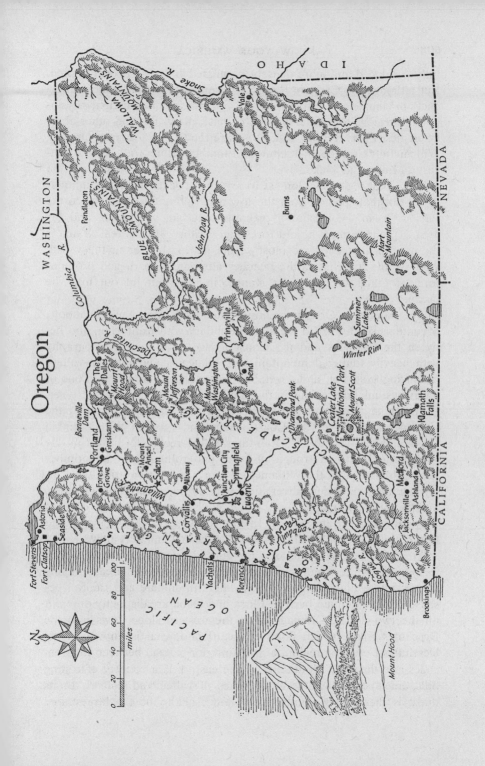

fully developed and more densely populated valley and coast section. But although the Cascade Range is responsible for the major differences in climate and topography, it is possible to discern eight physiographic regions that differ in soil, climate, plant life, and other characteristics. From west to east, these are the Coast, Southern Oregon, Willamette, Cascade, Deschutes-Columbia, Blue-Wallowa, Southeastern Lake, and Snake River.

The Coast region is a long strip less than twenty-five miles in average width that spreads from the low and rolling Coast Range to the Pacific Ocean. High rainfall prompts luxuriant vegetation, and the area is prime farm, fish, and foresting territory. But its real drama is the coastline, perhaps the most scenic marine border in the world. Along some stretches, white beaches alternate with rugged promontories—foothills of the Coast Range, in fact—that jut out into the ocean.

The Southern Oregon region, extending from the Calapooya Mountains southward to the state boundary with California, and between the Cascades and the Coast Range, is of rough topography with heavily timbered mountainsides, plateaus, and interior valleys producing fruit, nut, and vegetable harvests. In addition, it is one of the richest mineral regions in the state and has abundant waterpower. Although the climate is varied, there are no extremes. West of the Cascades and east of the Coast Range and between the Columbia River and the Calapooya Mountains is the rectangle known as the Willamette Valley, a trough of level and rolling farm and timber lands. Nourished by the Willamette River and its tributaries, the Valley maintains a widely diversified agriculture, great timber stands, and the overwhelming majority of Oregon's population in the cities of Portland, Eugene, and Salem. In fact, no Oregon city of more than thirty thousand people is located outside the Willamette Valley.

To the east of Willamette is the rugged grandeur of the Cascade region. The western slope is more precipitous, while the eastern side merges into a high plateau, which differs in climate and rainfall because of the mountain barrier. Flora and fauna are distinctly different on the two slopes. Drainage from the western slope flows into the Deschutes River, which flows eastward into what is known as the Deschutes-Columbia region, a great interior plateau between the Cascades and the Blue Mountains to the east. It is a country of rolling hills, interspersed with level stretches of valley and upland. In its midst is the great Columbia lava flow, said to be the largest and deepest in existence, etched by erosion into canyon walls fifteen hundred to two thousand feet deep.

To the northeast is the 20,000-square-mile Blue-Wallowa region, with two great mountain masses. The Blue range consists of rolling terrain, covered with park-like stands of timber; the Wallowa is rugged, precipitous country, with mountain lakes as part of the striking scenery. Southward from the Blue-Wallowa is the Southeastern Lake, including the high desert wasteland of sagebrush, dry lakes, and lava beds. The area for the most part is treeless, but portions of the Deschutes and Frémont National Forests have stands of pine. Finally there is the Snake River region, a strip along the Idaho boundary which consists of an open plateau from thirty-five hundred to four thousand feet in altitude. Semi-arid, its chief features are narrow and deeply cut river valleys, low ranges of mountains, buttes, and sagebrush plains.

CLIMATE

Oregon's climate suffers from the split personality that affects the neighboring state of Washington. In the western portions, the rains are heavier, the snows deeper, and the foliage greener as the sea winds moving in from the coast lose their moisture against the central spine of the Cascade Range. Precipitation along the coast averages about seventy-five inches a year, concentrated in the fall and winter months. Portland, one hundred miles in from the coast, has an average temperature of about 38 degrees in January and 67 degrees in the summer. Indicative of the mild, moist weather in the west is the overwhelming abundance of flowers of all kinds during the spring, summer, and fall months.

East of the Cascades, however, the climate verges on the semi-arid, with the average rainfall barely exceeding ten inches annually and summers equal in intensity to the Great Plains states. The city of The Dalles, for example, on the eastern slope of the Cascades, has had temperatures ranging from 30 degrees below zero to 115 degrees above, and as little as six inches of rain. So varied is the climate, in fact, that Portland's television news programs carry five sharply different forecasts.

THE OREGONIANS

Oregon's racial and ethnic background is essentially American. The first white inhabitants—the hunters, trappers, explorers, traders, and farmers of the early nineteenth century—were either American-born or American in their general outlook, habits, and ambitions. The state has always had a fairly homogeneous, overwhelmingly Protestant population; Roman Catholics still comprise only 11 per cent of the state, less than half the national average.

White settlers represented the second major wave of immigration to Oregon. According to anthropological evidence, men have lived in Oregon and the Pacific Northwest, especially on lake and river shores, for about ten thousand years. The original native Americans migrated from Asia to North America by an Alaskan land bridge and moved down the coast to settle along the Columbia River and in the interior basin. Pacific Northwest Indians were unique in the great number of languages used in a relatively small area. The many languages of the Oregon coast may have been derived from successive waves of migration from Asia, which brought in new customs and tongues, and the rough country, where heavily forested headlands divided one tribe or village from another.

To trade, the Indians used a common sign language. East of the Cascades in the plateau country, language divisions were few and tribal organizations were larger, with the patterns of life closer to those of the Plains Indians, especially after the introduction of the horse in the mid-eighteenth century. The coast Indians were not warlike, though occasional attacks were made on white fur traders. It was these Indians who first saw Europeans and Americans, who supplied trading ships with furs, and who took their goods in exchange.

The immigrants of a hundred years ago came from nowhere in particular, despite the claim that Oregon's conservative manners came from New England stock. In the first census taken, in 1850, Oregon had some 13,300 white residents, of whom only a few hundred came from New England, compared to far heavier representation from Missouri, Illinois, Ohio, and Kentucky. It had been just a few years earlier that the first great westward migration of settlers reached Oregon, in the wake of the Methodist missionaries who arrived in 1840.

During the 1850s, gold hunters, adventurers, and settlers drifted into Oregon from California; merchants, mechanics, laborers, and professional men arrived from New England, the eastern seaboard, and the Mississippi Basin seeking more favorable economic opportunities than could be found in their hometowns. Thus, by 1860, Oregon's population had swelled to over 52,000, and by 1900 to nearly 414,000. The number of foreign-born, which never exceeded 20 per cent of the total population, varied with the extent of railroad construction when swarms of common laborers were imported, many of them to remain.

Their arrival corresponded to Oregon's boom decades of 1890 to 1910. The population increase in the first ten years was largely due to the completion of the transcontinental railroads and construction of local lines, affording easy transportation for settlers. The second was the combined result of the World's Fair held in Portland in 1905, bringing vast crowds of visitors; the development of irrigation which opened large tracts of land for settlement; and the modern exploitation of Oregon's great lumber resources. Nevertheless, the thoroughly American character of Oregon's population has its exceptions in the state's past and present. Among these are the Basques of southeastern Oregon who came in the late nineteenth century to tend the great sheep herds; Finnish and other Scandinavian immigrants drawn to Astoria, Oregon, because of the fishing, sailing, shipbuilding, and lumbering—their occupations in the Old Country; and the German community at Aurora in Clackamas County. That settlement dates from 1856 when a band of Germans from Missouri established an experiment in communal living lasting more than twenty years. The death of their religious leader signaled the beginning of the colony's disintegration and assimilation of its members into the outside world.

The change was traumatic, but it was easier than the situation faced by another of Oregon's minorities, the Chinese. Their immigration to Oregon began in 1850 to replace the laborers who had gone off to the California goldfields. The influx increased with the years and construction of the railroads, to the point where Chinese laborers were competing with whites for a variety of jobs. Accommodation was replaced by anti-Chinese demonstrations which grew in violence from 1870. Oregon's militia was finally called out to cope—unsuccessfully—with the situation. It was only through the passing of the Chinese Exclusion Act of 1882 that race prejudice was finally appeased.

The anti-Chinese feeling itself was one of the starting points of a strong union trend which culminated in the International Workers of the World (IWW) movement of the early twentieth century before and just after World War I. For years, the genius of the IWW was "Big Bill" Haywood, a former miner who knew conditions in western mining and logging camps. In 1907 he helped organize a massive strike in that part of the state's lumber industry centered around Portland, which led to increased wages and improved working conditions.

Oregon was also an organizing crucible for Samuel Gomper's American Federation of Labor, which was fighting the Knights of Labor for national leadership in the 1890s. The AF of L outlasted the Knights, and ultimately the IWW, whose radicalism alienated many of the workers the IWW sought to recruit.

As the labor situation eased in the years between the world wars, so did population growth. Oregon did not cross the one million mark until the Depression, when like Washington and California it served as a beacon for dispossessed farmers and factory workers of the mid-western states. But the years after World War II changed all that—and not necessarily for the better, as far as native Oregonians are concerned. Oregon's natural wonders, many of them preserved from the ravages of industrial expansion, now attract nine to ten million visitors a year, and more than a few decide to stay. They accounted for a major share of Oregon's population growth of 56 per cent from 1,338,000 in 1946 to 2,091,385 in 1970. California, itself crowded, now provides a large number of emigrants who often began their journeys in the East or Midwest.

Perhaps the most celebrated statement of Oregon's wish to keep population in balance with the environment came in a talk by then-Governor Tom McCall. "Welcome to Oregon," he told a group of conventioneers meeting in Portland a few years ago. "While you're here, I want you to enjoy yourselves. Travel, visit, drink in the beauty of our great state. But for God's sake, don't move here."

HISTORY

For two centuries before the "Oregon Country" even had a fur-trading post, it was an area of legend, appearing first in the mapmakers' unknown kingdoms of Quivira and Anian. Many explorers came to

search for the fabled Northwest Passage they thought might be entered somewhere on its coast. The first white men to view the Oregon shore line came in Spanish vessels under the command of Juan Rodríguez Cabrillo, a Portuguese in the service of Spain, and his chief pilot Bartolome Ferrelo. They are believed to have sailed up from Mexico to southern Oregon in 1542–43. About the same location was reached in 1579 by Sir Francis Drake, who there abandoned his search for a northern passage to England and returned southward.

Nearly two hundred years passed before further discoveries were made by the Spanish and various English expeditions under James Cook and John Meares. It was an American sea captain and trader, Robert Gray of Boston, who actually verified the existence of the hitherto legendary "River of the West," however. Gray named the river the Columbia, after his ship, the first to anchor in its waters, in May 1792. Five months later, an English naval officer, Lieutenant William R. Broughton, explored the Columbia for nearly one hundred miles inland, sighted and named Mount Hood on October 29, and formally claimed the region for Great Britain.

Despite the name given by Gray, for a good many years after his discovery the river was commonly referred to as the Ouragon, Oregan, Origan, or Oregon. As now spelled, it first appeared in Jonathan Carver's *Travels in Interior Parts of America,* published in 1778, although it remained unfamiliar to the public at large until William Cullen Bryant referred to "Oregon" in his poem *Thanatopsis,* which appeared in 1817.

The name applied to one of the most prominent geographical features was also applied to the region as a whole. The so-called Oregon Territory, or Oregon Country, originally comprised all the land between the Rocky Mountains and the Pacific, from the somewhat vague border of the Spanish Southwest to the Russian possessions on the north, above Canada. By the Treaty of Florida in 1819, the southern boundary was fixed at the 42nd parallel; and in 1846, Great Britain and the United States agreed to the northern boundary along the 49th parallel. From the vast area of more than 300,000 square miles within these coordinates were later created the present states of Oregon, Washington, and Idaho, and considerable parts of Montana and Wyoming.

Into this uncharted wilderness came the American explorers Meriwether Lewis and William Clark, heading an expedition authorized by President Thomas Jefferson. They reached the headwaters of the

Columbia in October 1805, journeyed downriver to Cape Disappointment in November, and passed the winter in log quarters which they named Fort Clatsop, after a neighboring Indian tribe.

The accounts of their journey, which ended back in St. Louis on September 23, 1806, aroused widespread interest, particularly among those seeking to develop the fur trade. The first such post in the Columbia River region was established by John Jacob Astor's Pacific Fur Company in 1811 in Astoria, close to Fort Clatsop. It was short-lived, however. Fur-trading was scarcely under way when the War of 1812 began, and the more powerful British North West Company took advantage of the opportunity to buy out the Astor group. Astoria was returned to the United States in 1818 during a period which marked the elimination of the Spanish interests in the region and the renunciation of Russia's claims on territory south of Alaska.

The dominant commercial factor at that time was the Hudson's Bay Company, which bought out the rival North West Company in 1821. And the dominant individual was Dr. John McLoughlin, Chief Factor of Hudson's Bay, who built Fort Vancouver on the north bank of the Columbia, a few miles east of the mouth of the Willamette, and from there ruled the fur-trapping fortunes of white men and Indians alike. McLoughlin held sway for twenty years, during which time American interests began to take root. When Nathaniel Wyeth of Boston came to establish the Fort William salmon fishery on Sauvie Island in 1834, he brought with him Methodist clergymen Jason and Daniel Lee, the first missionaries to settle in the Northwest. Others followed, among them Dr. Marcus Whitman and Henry Spalding in 1836. Until the early 1840s, Hudson's Bay's word was quite literally law, and Americans in the Oregon Territory were largely ignored by successive administrations in Washington. But the missionaries' glowing reports of the Northwest did prompt interest back East, and in 1843 the first significant wagon train made the journey over the Oregon Trail.

As the American population increased, the influence of Hudson's Bay diminished. Pioneers built cabins and barns from the surrounding forests, and took food from the newly tilled ground. Their numbers grew, a provisional governor was elected in July 1845, and on August 14, 1848, Congress passed the bill admitting Oregon as a territory. That same year, the gold rush swept into California, bringing with it two thirds of the available male population in Oregon. Many did strike it rich, returning to Oregon with their new-found wealth.

Those who remained at home prospered as well, supplying the miners in California with wheat at $4 a bushel, flour at $15 a barrel, and lumber at $100 a thousand feet. Oregon took on the appearance of well-being, with log cabins giving way to substantial homes in the New England style.

The Indian wars dispelled any illusions about the comfortable East, however. The rising tide of immigration in the 1840s greatly disturbed the Indian population, estimated at twenty-seven thousand in 1845. Goaded by what they saw as invasion of their rights, a band of Cayuses attacked the Presbyterian mission near the site of Walla Walla, killed Dr. Marcus Whitman, his wife, and twelve others, and destroyed all the buildings. The settlers immediately declared war, and although the Cayuses were defeated, other incidents brought about other engagements between Indians and settlers until the defeat of the Spokane tribe in 1858.

Meanwhile Oregon's economic condition continued to prosper, as roads and bridges were constructed and more than a score of academies and two universities were established. Salem became the official capital in 1856, where legislators organized the state government following President Buchanan's signature of the bill granting statehood on February 14, 1859. Indian troubles erupted again after the Civil War and flared intermittently for more than a decade until soldiers quelled the final uprisings in 1880.

With the completion of the Union Pacific Railroad to Promontory Point, Utah, in 1869, and construction of a connecting line to Portland in the early 1880s, a new era of population growth and economic expansion began for Oregon. Homesteads were established in remote areas, turning the eastern plains and ranges into land for wheat and livestock. The *Sally Brown,* sailing from Portland to Liverpool, England, in 1868, carried the first full cargo of Oregon wheat, and Portland has since emerged as one of the world's more important wheat-shipping ports. From 1870 to 1900 the state's population grew more than fourfold to 413,526.

Oregon achieved stature with the Lewis and Clark Centennial Exposition held in Portland in 1905. There was considerable social and political progress as well: The direct primary was adopted in 1904, women's suffrage in 1912, and workmen's compensation in 1913. Perhaps the most significant development in recent decades was the construction by the federal government of Bonneville Dam and lock on the Columbia River, forty-two miles east of Portland. Begun in

1933 and completed just before World War II, this $70 million project supplies hydroelectric power to a huge area in the Columbia River region and permits navigation by ocean-going vessels far inland.

Federally built dams along the Willamette and the Columbia have done much to prevent erosion and flood damage, which used to plague Oregon. Since World War II, the land around Eugene and Springfield, once flooded every few years, is now filled with homes. In the postwar years Oregon has been as much concerned about its environment as it has about its economy. The state got off to a good start when advances in forestry enabled it to avoid the overcutting that stripped Michigan, Wisconsin, and Minnesota of their timber resources. Oregon took the initiative more recently when it proposed water pollution controls up to the standards of the Water Quality Act of 1967—one of the first states to do so. A state authority published an enforcement plan covering every stream and every city and industry on each Oregon waterway. The Willamette has been among the chief beneficiaries: the famous Chinook salmon, which abandoned the river because of the level of pollution, have returned to ancestral spawning grounds.

INDUSTRY

Oregon used to rely entirely on a resource-oriented economy, highly dependent on timber, agriculture, and fishing, but in recent decades the state has diversified. By the end of the 1960s, only 17 per cent of over 800,000 workers were employed in the lumber and farm industries, compared to 30 per cent in 1950. The growth in new industries, ranging from freeze-dried foods to electronics and sports clothes, has been responsible for the increase in Oregon's job rolls, which grew at an annual rate of 2.7 per cent in the 1960s, nearly three times that of the 1950s. At present Oregon's annual industrial output from all sectors approaches $10 billion a year. Timber is the biggest, at close to $2 billion, followed by agriculture and tourism. The past ten to fifteen years have brought a doubling of employment in metals and machinery and a 66 per cent growth in such services as finance and realty. All told, workers in Oregon received wages of $5 billion in 1970, twice that of 1960, and over three times the amount recorded in 1950.

Among the fifty states, Oregon has perhaps the most to gain through trade with Japan, which is interested in its wheat, cattle, timber, and aluminum output. Portland is the point of departure for these products, as well as the focus for the newer industries, such as one company which keeps more than six thousand workers busy assembling oscilloscopes and other electronic devices. A rash of new office buildings in Portland, worth perhaps $75 million in construction costs, will significantly change the city's skyline and greatly add to its industrial and business space. Port activity is also healthy. Improved access to the inland farm lands, via the Columbia River, has increased barge traffic, while shipping connected with the Alaskan pipeline development has had a positive impact. Industrial facilities will be improved with the construction of an automated plant in Portland which allows for the more efficient transfer of uniform-size shipments.

AGRICULTURE

Waving fields of wheat are emblematic of Oregon's major agricultural crop. East of the Cascade Range, irrigation has enabled the state's wheat farmers to harvest over one million acres of the crop annually, or 5 per cent of the twenty million acres devoted to agriculture.

The variations in topography, climate, and soils in Oregon have been the major factor in a diversity of agricultural production. A wide variety of crops are grown, many of which Oregon supplies to other states. Oregon is responsible for 23 per cent of the country's snap bean production, a third of the sweet cherries, all of the rye grass, and half of the peppermint. Growers produce 95 per cent of all United States filberts and a considerable quantity of grass—nearly 30 per cent of Merion Bluegrass, all the red fescue seed, and nearly all the bent grass and crimson clover seed. A thriving greenhouse and nursery business has also made the state the first in the United States in Christmas holly and Easter lily bulbs.

But the potential in agriculture has not been fully tapped. It is thought that if Oregon would press harder and faster to get more land under irrigation, especially in the sagebrush regions east of the Cascades, it could share in the large-scale "agribusiness" farming that has developed in California. Irrigation has already meant huge potato crops along the Idaho border and a threefold increase in some crops in the Columbia River Valley. Experts think more of the same is feasible elsewhere. Commercial fisheries are another expanding source of agricultural income, bringing in a harvest of salmon, tuna, crabs, clams, and shrimp worth well in excess of $20 million a year.

Farming has been integral to the state from the beginning. Vegetable crops were planted by early explorers and fur traders at the start of the nineteenth century, and favorable reports about the fertile valleys of Oregon brought a trickle of eastern farmers into the new and unclaimed country in the late 1830s. Thereafter immigration increased rapidly until the trickle grew to flood proportions. By 1846 wheat had become the pioneers' first and principal crop, with more than 160,000 bushels harvested. An act of the provisional government made wheat legal tender, worth $1 a bushel, and its value to the California gold-seekers was such that the export commerce provided the economic foundation for towns and seaports, wagon roads, steamship lines, and railways. For the next half century, in fact, the Willamette Valley, with its brown loams and silty clay soils, was predominately "wheat country."

Willamette Valley is also a particularly good example of Oregon's agricultural diversity. The prime population center of the state, it also grows more than a dozen major crops, including caneberries, strawberries, walnuts, sweet corn, snap beans, and all grass and legume seeds except alfalfa. Cattle and calf herds are concentrated east of the Cascades, where nearly 80 per cent of beef is raised. Umatilla County, on the northeastern edge of the state, is important in hog production, while Douglas in the southwest leads in the value of sheep and lambs. Dairy products are big in western Oregon: Together the Willamette Valley and the coastal areas account for over 70 per cent of the milk and cream sold by the state's farmers.

The number of farmers in Oregon is subject to the same trends present elsewhere in the United States. Increased capitalization, mechanization, and specialization have resulted in the reduction of individual farm output to one, two, or three major commodities; more machines, fewer workers, and greater investments have transformed the basic nature of Oregon's farm sector, bringing about a decline in rural population. Thus about 67 per cent of Oregon's population was urban in 1970, compared to 62 per cent in 1960.

At the same time, farming has become a more important—and more closely integrated—part of the Oregon economy. Sales at the farm gate registered over $600 million in 1975, while food processing

—packing, canning, freezing—added nearly $400 million more to the aggregate value. Overall the food industry ranks second only to forest products in importance to the state's economy. Projections of future agricultural output vary, but a significant increase by 1980 may be expected with normal trends.

NATURAL RESOURCES

Timber is dominant in Oregon's industrial and commercial life. Other natural resources are much less in evidence. Oregon receives a small, albeit steady, income from the mining of gold, copper, silver, and lead. The occasional prospector exists still, but more indicative of mining's limited value are the ruins of ghost towns built hurriedly and as swiftly abandoned in the eastern and southern parts of the state.

Activities connected with lumbering spread over all regions but the grasslands and the high plateaus of the southeast. So important is timber and its products that even the state's tax-supported schools derive a good portion of their income from the forests. Indeed, the importance of the Douglas fir, spruce, hemlock, and ponderosa pine is symbolized in the state shield, which the founding fathers inscribed with a forest and a ship.

It is understandable: One of the most awesome sights to the pioneers must have been the immense stands of virgin forest on the western flank of the Oregon Territory, covering the land from the Pacific to the flanks of the Cascades, with Douglas firs as high as 280 feet towering above hemlock and cedar. There was enough timber to build millions of ships or many times that number of houses. Oregon still claims to have enough lumber to rebuild every home in the fifty states.

The lumberjacks put their arms and backs to the task in earnest in the 1850s when teams of oxen began hauling logs down skidroads which are now Portland streets. The lumber industry had its beginnings then, along the shores of the Columbia River. But it wasn't until 1890, when the exhaustion of the forests of the Great Lakes region was in sight, that Oregon became prominent as a lumber state. Shortly after 1900, widespread corruption in the lumber industry was uncovered in the great Oregon Timber Fraud cases, exposing entrepreneurs who had acquired forest lands through "dummy" corporations.

A happy outcome was the setting aside later of thousands of acres of forest, forming national reserves within the state. Thus the northwestern lumberman never inflicted the damage that was done in the north-central cities. There is still much controversy over the policy of clear-cutting, whereby timber is harvested in big patches—usually fifty to a hundred acres—which make Western forest lands look like giant checkerboards from the air. Nevertheless as more and more land has been set aside for wilderness and park lands, a number of the major timber firms such as Weyerhaeuser, Crown Zellerbach, and Boise Cascade have seen the need for sophisticated reforestation on their own property. It is thought these techniques can increase the yields of lands by perhaps 50 per cent. In 1941, Weyerhaeuser initiated the United States' first tree farm near Aberdeen, Washington, and a number of others have since been established in Oregon.

Along with reforestation have come more efficient means of cutting timber. Now Oregon lumberjacks have high-powered saws to fell trees, automatic chippers that strip logs of bark and branches and cut them into convenient small pieces on the spot, and mechanical movers that can pick up as much as sixty-five tons of wood in a single motion. Often logs are brought out of remote forests by balloon to avoid road construction costs and the scarring of the landscape. The invention of plywood in Oregon in 1905 has led to the use of waste products—sawdust, bark, chips, and the like—which consume the whole tree.

All this is accomplished with significantly fewer workers. Nearly ninety thousand people were employed in the timber trades in 1950; by 1970 that figure had declined to just over sixty-seven thousand, less than a twelfth of the state's total work force. Nevertheless, Oregon continues to rank as the nation's top producer of timber, a position held since 1937 when it passed Washington. It also leads in plywood, with about 70 per cent of the United States' output to its credit.

CITIES

With a 1970 population of 382,619, **Portland** sits nestled at the northern end of the Willamette Valley at the junction of the Willamette and Columbia rivers. The city is quiet and discreet, the scenery around it green and spectacular. To the east of Portland, itself containing seven thousand acres of parkland including wilderness trails, is majestic Mount Hood, elevation 11,235 feet. On clear days, Mount Hood can take on an almost magical appearance to Portlanders. The mist which settles just below its peak appears to leave the top floating on the horizon.

The other distinctive feature is the city's position in a zone of moist, coastal climate. Here vegetation flourishes, and each June since 1909 Portland has been the site of the famous Rose Festival. Football's Rose Bowl notwithstanding, Portland is well known as the "City of Roses."

With its access to the Pacific, the city is also renowned as a port. Chinook Indians found the site a good place to tie up their canoes on trading trips between the Columbia and Willamette rivers. Later, Portland's commercial possibilities were noted when in 1840 Captain John Couch came from New England to investigate the prospects for a salmon fishery. "To this point," he told a fellow traveler, "I can bring any ship that can get into the mouth of the Great Columbia River."

So he could, and salmon fishing matured into an industry by the 1870s, joining lumber and flour as major aspects of the Oregon economy. Both were shipped out of Portland on sailing vessels that crowded the city's wharves. Rebuilding after two devastating fires in 1872 and 1873, Portland helped complete the final rail link connecting it to the eastern states in 1883, annexed the towns of East Portland and Albina in 1891, grew to a population of 207,314 during the height of the Alaskan gold rush, and celebrated the Lewis and Clark Centennial Exposition in 1905. This last drew three million visitors to the city, and many new residents.

The city itself has grown relatively little since then—its population in 1960 was almost the same as that ten years later—but the suburbs, including those across the Columbia in Clark County, Washington, have increased markedly. At present, metropolitan Portland accounts for more than 40 per cent of the state's population, and its growth has spilled over to the south and west where Clackamas and Washington counties have spawned subdivisions.

As befits its size, Portland is the business and economic center of the state. It is home to a variety of industries, reflecting the diversity of Oregon's economy: electronic component manufacturers, textile firms specializing in woolens, aluminum plants drawing on abundant hydroelectric power, chemical plants, logging equipment producers, and lumber mills. Unlike Seattle, Portland has never gone after aerospace and other military-related companies—a point much in its favor during the 1970 recession. Portland's unemployment rate was only one half that of the metropolis to the north. In fact, Oregon, and therefore Portland, ranks near the bottom of the fifty states in the percentage of its population employed in defense-related industries. The search for new industry has led Portland away from "dirty" products and, in keeping with strict air quality standards, toward "clean" businesses such as finance and electronics. Their appearance in force accounts for the extensive construction of new office buildings in downtown Portland.

The bustling Port of Portland is a major business attraction. The value of imports and exports passing through the docks and terminals lining the Willamette River broke through the $1 billion mark in 1969. In addition, the Port has been deepening the 110-mile channel connecting Portland to the Pacific; the earth turned up by the dredging has created prime industrial land which is being converted into a well-planned industrial park on the North Portland Peninsula. The city's other point of departure is its International Airport, completed in 1958. With far more airport land than Seattle, it could become the flight center of the Northwest, especially with the completion of a $110 million expansion plan that will boost passenger capacity significantly.

Portland is divided by the Willamette River which runs on a north-northwesterly course through the heart of the city. On the west side are the high-rise structures of a revitalized downtown, most of the city's seven thousand acres of parklands, and handsome residential districts. East of the river are a variety of older neighborhoods. Still farther east are suburban towns like Gresham, on the way to Mount Hood, which has a large Japanese farm community and Oregon's biggest strawberry crops, and Oregon City, the old territorial capital.

The city's reputation for caution and conservatism hasn't stood in the way of civic improvements, including the impressive Memorial Coliseum, docks and schools, and a new zoo. The $100 million Lloyd Shopping Center features flowered malls, walks, and a twenty-story office building among the retail establishments. During the 1960s, southwest Portland, a mixture of rundown homes and businesses, was torn down and rebuilt into a corporate center for such companies as Boise Cascade. Conversely the Skidmore Fountain area near the Willamette River has been renovated to preserve several Victorian commercial buildings that represent nineteenth-century Portland. Within one of the Portland Development Commission's urban renewal projects is a block square of grotto, park, and public plaza that contains a series of man-made waterfalls, cascading thirteen thousand gallons a minute into a sunken pool. Terraced steps and platforms enable the visitor to walk behind the falls.

Universities are the center of cultural life in Portland, especially Reed College, known nationally for its intellectual freedom and the number of Rhodes scholars it graduates. Portland State University, severely damaged by the Columbia River flood of 1958, has recovered to become one of the nation's fastest-growing institutions for higher learning. Its Music Department sponsors chamber concerts each summer, in addition to the Oregon Symphony Orchestra appearances at the Civic Auditorium. The Portland Civic Theater hosts a variety of productions year-round, including children's plays, while the Portland Art Museum offers a collection of Northwest Indian artifacts, African art, and collections of classical painting and sculpture. At the Oregon Museum for Science and Industry, occupying four acres overlooking the Zoological Gardens, visitors can examine the "walk-in" heart, demonstrating the functions of the human heart, and a replica of a ship's bridge which can take them on an imaginary sea voyage.

Out-of-doors Portland is a feast for the senses. On its Scenic Drive, which leads motorists to the summits of three hills affording a spectacular view of the city and its environs, are rose, rhododendron, and azalea test gardens, the Portland Zoo, and Hoyt Arboretum.

Aside from Portland, only Eugene and Salem have populations exceeding 50,000. **Eugene,** about 110 miles south of Portland, has grown the faster of the two, jumping from 20,838 inhabitants in 1940 to 76,346 in 1970. Lane County, of which it is the center, has over 213,000 residents.

Eugene has changed relatively little over the years, with a landscaped park, comfortable houses, and long lines of shade trees giving it a turn-of-the-century appearance. Early in its history—in the mid-1850s—Eugene claimed to be the popular choice for territorial capital, but there was a dispute over the majority of votes cast, and Salem was the eventual winner.

What Eugene does have is the University of Oregon, whose 14,000 students, faculty, and support personnel give a significant boost to the local economy. The city also benefits from its location at the center of great fir and cedar forests whose harvest provides employment at lumber mills and industries arising from the diversification of timber use. On the university campus are the Museum of Art, housing over three thousand objects from Russian and Far Eastern cultures, and the Natural History Museum, with its collection of fluorescent minerals, Northwest Coast Indian masks, and primitive weapons. Adjacent to the campus is the Maude I. Kerns Art Center, with an art workshop and exhibits of painting, sculpture, weaving, and glassblowing.

Salem, population 68,296 as of 1970, rests in the shadow of Portland, only forty-five miles to the north. Sharing Portland's facilities—airport, shopping centers, and the like—limits the growth of its own, but the city has found a comfortable niche for itself as state capital and as a center of the Willamette Valley's timber and fruit and vegetable canning industries.

Dominating Salem's Capitol Mall is the modern, white-marbled Capitol, facing northward and flanked by four other structures. Completed in 1939 at a cost of $2.5 million, the Capitol replaced a classic Greek statehouse that was destroyed by fire in 1935, after serving Oregon for more than half a century. Its dome, topped with a statue depicting the pioneer, offers a fine view of the Willamette Valley.

Also in Salem are the Bush Barn Art Center, which features exhibitions by Northwest artists, and Bush House Museum. The latter was the home of Asabel Bush, pioneer banker and newspaper publisher. Bush's name was given to Bush Pasture, an eighty-acre city park planted with rare trees and shrubs.

SPORTS AND RECREATION

Oregon has the range of outdoor activities that befits a state with its scenery and varied terrain. In the summer, for example, there is swimming at countless locations along the coast and inland in rivers and lakes. Seaside, south of Astoria, has long been the most popular site for the former, and Rooster Rock State Park, a half hour's drive from Portland, is first choice for the latter. But swimmers used to warmer climes should be forewarned—Oregon's natural waters generally are on the cool side year-round. One important exception is at Kah-nee-ta, a spa on the Warm Springs Indian Reservation; and there are numerous heated pools among those that dot the state. Each town of five thousand or more residents—and sometimes fewer—has one, often in a city park.

With water, water everywhere there are ample opportunities for motorboating, sailing, and water-skiing, particularly in the area along the coast between Yachats and Florence. Fishing also has its adherents: More than a half million anglers are drawn yearly to fifteen thousand miles of streams and hundreds of lakes. Along the Pacific, the principal game fish are chinook and silver salmon, steelhead and cutthroat trout, striped bass, and shad. Inland on the Columbia, Umpqua, and Rogue rivers, there are substantial runs of salmon, chinook, and silver in the spring and fall.

From fly casting to "Fore!" is as simple as a trip to one of Oregon's hundred or so golf courses, with twenty in the Portland area alone. Most courses are open to public play, and many are in use year-round in the mild western section of the state.

Oregon's mountains aren't to be denied their share of excitement, which runs the gamut from hiking, backpacking, and horseback riding in the central and eastern high country to climbing Mount Hood. The same high country also provides the best hunting in the state, where the game includes birds, deer, and pronghorn sheep. Bighorn sheep can be sought in special hunts on Hart Mountain in September, while mountain goats are tracked in the Eagle Gap Wilderness Area in late August.

Concurrent with summer activities is the winter favorite of skiing. The alpine slopes of Mount Hood and other peaks remain hospitable to skiers from November through September. Mount Hood, because it is so close to Portland, gets the largest crowds, and offers the most complete facilities, including twenty-five different runs. Twenty-passenger Sno-Cats transport skiers and sightseers alike as high up as ninety-five hundred feet.

Spectator sports play their part. At the professional level are the Portland Trailblazers of the National Basketball Association, who play home games at the Memorial Coliseum; the Portland Mavericks of baseball's Northwest League; and the Portland Buckeroos of the Western Hockey League. Top golfers in the Northwest journey to Portland for the Payless Classic in May and the Open Golf Tournament in the fall. That time of year also brings out collegiate football at Eugene, where the University of Oregon holds forth, and at Corvallis, home of Oregon State.

POINTS OF INTEREST

As much as any state, and more than most, Oregon is in the public domain. Nearly 25 per cent of Oregon's total land area has been set aside in thirteen national forests; they account for 15.4 million of 61.5 million acres.

The jewel in the state crown is Crater Lake National Park, fifty-seven miles north of Klamath Falls in the rugged southeastern region. First seen by white men in 1853, the 1,932-foot-deep lake was formed by the collapse of a prehistoric volcano, Mount Mazama, and is encircled by lava cliffs. No one has yet found an outlet for Crater Lake, which is fed by melting snows. A thirty-five-mile drive around the lake's rim offers a succession of impressive views: Wizard Island, a symmetrical cone rising 760 feet above the water's surface; Phantom Ship, a mass of lava resembling a ship under sail; Llao Rock, a lava flow to the north that fills an ancient glacial valley. Among the many mountain viewpoints are the 8,060-foot Garfield Peak and the 8,926-foot lookout station atop Mount Scott.

The mountains are the center of several other national park attractions. The Cascade range alone has six such preserves along its flanks, including Mount Hood, Willamette, Deschutes, and Fremont. In fact, the Willamette National Forest, containing 1,667,189 acres, is the most heavily timbered in the United States. Access to three of the peaks in its midst—Mount Jefferson, Mount Washington, and Diamond Peak—and the Three Sisters Wilderness Area is restricted to foot and horseback, and on some trails horses are not permitted. Much of northeastern Oregon is covered by two national forests, the Umatilla and the Wallowa-Whitman, comprising well over three million acres. Together they offer more than a hundred camp areas and recreation from swimming to skiing.

If the national parks excel in mountains, the state parks offer the best of Oregon's spectacular coastline and the Pacific. Nearly all the tideland—including sand dunes, broad beaches, deep inlets, and the sea lions that inhabit them—belongs to the residents. More than thirty state parks, encompassing the choicest scenic spots, are reserved for public use. Moreover, they are generally easy to reach; Portlanders, for example, have access to well over a dozen. Among the better known are Fort Stevens, ten miles west of Astoria; Ecola State Park, about twenty miles to the south, where Lewis and Clark came in 1806 for oil and blubber from a grounded whale; and Jessie M. Honeyman, two and a half miles south of Florence, which features great stands of rhododendrons, sand dunes, and a magnificent coastal lake. In all, Oregon's Pacific seashore stretches for four hundred miles, served by the Oregon Coast Highway.

There are man-made attractions as well, ranging from the lush flower gardens in Portland to the annual Shakespearean Festival in Ashland, and Bonneville Dam. The most westerly of all the dams on the Columbia River, Bonneville is only thirty-five miles from Portland. It offers the sight of vessels being raised and lowered through the rocks and the salmon pools, where the fish continue their upstream swim.

SPECIAL EVENTS

Tourists and residents alike have ample opportunity to celebrate Oregon's great outdoors in a variety of special events that begin with the end of winter and continue through fall.

March opens the festivities with the Original All-Northwest Barbershop Ballad Contest and Gay 90's Festival in Forest Grove. April features the Pear Festival in Medford, and then comes a series of flowery celebrations—the Rhododendron Festival at Florence in May, an Azalea Festival in Brookings on Memorial Day weekend, and the Rose Festival at Portland in June.

The arrival of summer presents the festival goer with the dilemma of choice, ranging from the round of Shakespearean plays offered at Ashland to the World's Champion Timber Carnival at Albany on the first weekend in July and the Crooked River Roundup at Prineville that same month. The highlights of August include a four-day Scandinavian Festival at Junction City and the Peter Britt Gardens Music and Arts Festival at Jacksonville.

Portland offers a series of concerts and plays called the Music by Moonlight Festival, while Astoria lives up to its historic past as a port city by hosting the Astoria Regatta on the fourth weekend in August. Salem's Oregon State Fair—running from the last week in August through Labor Day—signals the end of events for most visitors.

For those who can stay, though, there remains one of Oregon's best-known events, the Pendleton Roundup, featuring the Westward Ho parade and Happy Canyon Rodeo. It takes place in mid-September, followed by the Oktoberfest at Mount Angel and the International Livestock Exhibition at Portland.

S.G.

CHRONOLOGY

1542–43 Juan Cabrillo's pilot, Bartolome Ferello, sailed along the coast of Oregon.

1579 Francis Drake passed Oregon coast; named region of southwest Oregon and northern California "New Albion."

1765 First known use of the territory's name "Oregon" by Major Robert Rogers appeared in petition asking permission of King George III to explore territory in search of Northwest Passage; the word was spelled "Ouragon."

1778 Name "Oregon" appeared for the first time in Carver's *Travels,* which mentioned "the River Oregon, or the River of the West."

1792 Captain Robert Gray, an American, discovered and named Columbia River.

Lieutenant William Broughton, of the British Navy, reached the Cascades after traveling up the Columbia for about a hundred miles; he named Mount Hood.

1793 Sir Alexander Mackenzie completed first overland trip across Canada to Pacific coast, opening the Pacific Northwest to fur trappers.

1803 United States purchased Louisiana Territory, the land west of the Mississippi River.

1804–6 Lewis and Clark, under orders from President Jefferson, led an exploring expedition from St. Louis to mouth of Columbia River.

1811 Astoria, first permanent American foothold in Pacific Northwest, founded as trading post by John Jacob Astor's Pacific Fur Company.

1818 Fort Walla Walla was built by North West Company.

Astoria returned to the United States.

Great Britain and America agreed to occupy for ten years disputed region between Columbia River and the present north boundary of the United States.

1824 Dr. John McLoughlin, Chief Factor of the Hudson's Bay Company, arrived in Oregon.

1827 Second treaty with Great Britain extended provision for joint occupancy of Oregon Territory.

1834 Nathaniel Wyeth established a fishery on Sauvie Island at mouth of Willamette River.

The Reverend Jason Lee founded Methodist mission on French Prairie in Willamette Valley.

1836 Dr. Marcus Whitman and H. H. Spalding established missions in Walla Walla and Clearwater valleys.

1839 First American settlers, the "Peoria Party," came to Oregon from Illinois.

1843 Influx of immigrants began; first considerable wagon train west from Fort Hall.

1846 United States title to Oregon was established by treaty with Great Britain.

1848 Oregon Territory was established by Congress on August 14.

1852 Great immigration took place across plains into Oregon.

1853–59 Indian Wars under way.

1859 Oregon admitted to the Union on February 14.

1868 First full cargo of wheat was shipped direct to Europe in the ship *Sally Brown*.

1876 University of Oregon opened.

1905 Centennial celebration of Lewis and Clark expedition took place in Portland.

1933 Erection of Bonneville Dam began.

1935 Capitol in Salem destroyed by fire.

1938 First ocean-going vessel, the S.S. *Charles L. Wheeler*, passed through Bonneville Locks.

1939 Opening of the new Capitol in Salem.

1967 Oregon among first states to fully adopt Federal Water Quality Act.

1975 Completion of Tualatin Project to provide water for irrigation of 17,000 acres of Oregon's land.

1979 Exploration for natural gas accelerated. A well, for example, drilled about forty-five miles from Portland, was estimated as having a potential yield of as much as 8 million cubic feet a day.

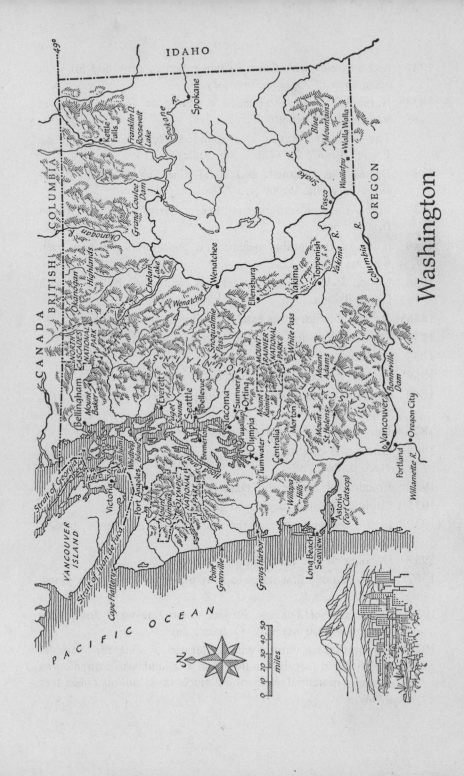

WASHINGTON

EVEN for part of a nation in the New World, Washington State is new. Barely more than a hundred years ago, the region was largely unexplored. The eastern region was a semiarid plateau of rolling hills covered with sagebrush and bunch grass, the habitat of prairie dogs, coyotes, and rattlesnakes, and the domain of numerous Indian tribes.

Through these barrens the mighty Columbia River cut its way to the Pacific Ocean. The great natural barrier—the Cascade mountain range—changed the nature of Washington radically, as it did the neighboring state of Oregon. West of the Cascades the region becomes moist and heavily timbered. In the mid-nineteenth century it was a dense forest of spruce, Douglas fir, cedar, and hemlock down to the coast, unbroken except for Indian trails and occasional prairies and lowland valleys.

The geographic settings have helped define the human characteristics of Washington as it underwent settlement. Eastern Washington shares the cautious, landlocked attitudes of the Great Plains states; western Washington, open to the sea, is more volatile, even radical in its attitudes.

Oregon and Washington are of a geographic piece, so Congress applied its own measurements in determining state boundaries. The result is that Washington is 31 per cent smaller in area, measuring 340 miles east to west and 230 miles north to south. Its borders—nearly rectangular except for a chunk in the northwestern corner given over to the Pacific—make Washington the West's smallest state in terms of area. But the state's seaport access and an abundance of natural resources have attracted their share of settlers: Washington now has half again the population of Oregon, and the numbers continue to grow.

The coming of the settlers greatly altered the face of Washington. Forests have been cut, grasslands broken and planted to wheat, and the arid range in the east turned into feeding grounds for sheep and cattle. Much has been destructive, much has not. The Grand Coulee Dam and Roosevelt Lake backed up behind it are marvelous sights in themselves, and they have provided the irrigation waters that have turned deserts into productive gardens, orchards, and farm tracts.

Even the densely populated Puget Sound area, with the city of Seattle and the giant industrial complex of Boeing, is close by the state's most mysterious and remote area, the Olympic Peninsula. To native Betty McDonald, who wrote *The Egg and I,* it is "the most rugged, most westerly, greatest, deepest, largest, wildest, gamiest, richest, most fertile, loneliest, and most desolate" land anywhere.

THE LAND

Within Washington's 68,192 square miles—1,483 of which are inland water—are seven distinct physiographic areas representing nearly every topographic variation known in the coterminous United States. They are the Olympic Mountains, Willapa Hills, Puget Sound Basin, Cascade Mountains, Okanogan Highlands, Columbia Basin, and Blue Mountains.

The Olympic Mountains, part of the coastal range, lie to the west, between Puget Sound, Juan de Fuca Strait, and the Pacific. It presents a labyrinth of peaks—three of them towering over 7,000 feet— and rugged ridges separating valleys, lakes, and fast-running rivers. South of the Olympics are the Willapa Hills, a region of sedimentary and igneous rocks with elevations rarely exceeding 3,000 feet. The Puget Sound Basin lies between the Olympic and Cascade mountains as a broad trough. It extends from Juan de Fuca Strait, connecting Puget Sound with the Pacific, halfway to the Columbia River, which carves through central Washington before swinging west to Seaview and the ocean.

The basin's flanks of sedimentary rocks and lava flows rise to join the mountains. It drains into Puget Sound, a body of water 80 miles long and up to 900 feet deep flanked by forested bluffs and containing some three hundred islands. Of these, the most noteworthy are the inhabitable islands of the San Juan group and Whidbey Island, the second largest in the continental United States.

Extending across the state from north to south at its approximate middle, paralleling the Columbia River, is the Cascade range. Shaped somewhat like an hourglass, it is 100 miles wide at the Canadian and Oregon boundaries and 50 miles at its middle, with numerous peaks of 6,000 to 8,000 feet and Mount Rainier at 14,410 feet. A great volcanic cone, Rainier is a startling backdrop to Seattle and the leading tourist attraction of the Northwest. On its slopes are twenty-six live glaciers, wildflower fields in the summer, a wide variety of wildlife including mountain goats and elk, and great stands of timber. There is also the threat of future volcanic activity which could melt the 4 cubic tons of snow and ice on Rainier's slopes and cause massive, catastrophic mud slides. Geologic evidence indicates that some five thousand years ago a wave of mud descended from Rainier to inundate 125 square miles of Puget Sound lowlands.

North of the Big Bend of the Columbia River and north of the Spokane River are the Okanogan Highlands, which merge into the Cascades on the west and the Rockies on the east. Rounded, broad low hills, these are largely open and parklike, unlike the heavily wooded Cascades. The Columbia Basin is south of the Okanogan from the Oregon boundary to the Idaho line, containing 1.5 million acres of sage and scabland. The area of the Big Bend is scarred by great, ancient, long-dry river courses, or coulees, some of which still hold chains of strongly alkaline lakes. The Columbia Basin is probably Washington's least attractive region. Only in its southeastern section, in the area of the Blue Mountains, an uplift of some 7,000 feet, is there enough rainfall and thick fertile soil to support a diversified agriculture.

CLIMATE

Geography plays a key role in the climate of Washington. Located on the Pacific, the state's winter weather is dominated by warm moist ocean air masses moving eastward across the state. This moisture-laden air passes over several mountain ranges, losing more moisture each time it rises over a peak. Because of this, the state has a very wide range of rainfall—from 200 inches a year in the forests west of the Olympics to 15–35 inches a year on the eastern slopes. Still farther eastward, the vast area behind the Cascade range, which runs north-south through the center of the state, receives only 5–15 inches a year.

What results are the three basic climates in Washington. West of the Cascades, winters are mild and rainy with only very infrequent snow. In the Cascades and Olympics themselves, there is heavy snowfall, as much as 400 inches in Snoqualmie Pass. East of the Cascades, winters are moderately cold and dry with snow in moderation. During the summer, even though cool marine air still moves across the state, temperatures are not low enough to bring on heavy rainfalls. So the west side enjoys cool, dry weather and the east, hot and dry. Seattle, in the west, has a mean average temperature of 38 degrees in January and 64 degrees in July; Spokane, in the west, goes from a low of 25 degrees to a high of 74 degrees.

This weather pattern has helped make western Washington heavily forested, allowing less room for farming, while the eastern part of the state has vast regions with sparse natural vegetation.

THE WASHINGTONIANS

Washington and the lure of the Far West have drawn people since the mid-nineteenth century. Attracted by timber, free lands, minerals, railroad construction, fishing, big dams, and atomic energy, successive waves of settlers have come first to the territory and then to the state: Southerners uprooted by the Civil War; immigrants from Europe and the Orient; discouraged farmers from the Dust Bowl farm lands of the Great Depression; engineers and professionals seeking postwar opportunities.

The first permanent American settlement took root in 1845 when the provisional government of Oregon, dominated by England's Hudson's Bay Company, turned away a train of eighty overland wagons because they bore one Negro, freeborn George Bush. The party made its way to a site near what is now Olympia. In 1851 the settlers north of the Columbia River, separating Washington and Oregon, started to campaign for separate territorial status, a request the United States Congress granted two years later.

But before the imported Americans, there were the native Americans. The Northwest Indians of Washington—the Nisquallys, Puyallups, and Yakimas, among others—were divided into two major groups, one comprising those bands east of the Cascade range and the other those to the west of it. The sharp cultural differences that developed between them rose in large measure from the mountain barrier. Contributing also to the formation of distinctive cultural pat-

PLATE 100 Panoramic view of Oahu's yacht harbor, resort hotels, Waikiki Beach, and extinct volcano Diamond Head.

PLATE 101 Sleeping Beauty's Castle is the entrance to Fantasyland in Disneyland.

PLATE 102   A tranquil white sand beach on the island of Kauai.

PLATE 103   The crater of Haleakala, the largest dormant volcano in the world, on Maui.

PLATE 104 Giant fern forest in Hawaii Volcanoes National Park.

PLATE 105 Many-shaded, colorful domes and ridges abound in the Painted Hills area of Oregon's John Day Fossil Beds National Monument.

PLATE 106 Majestic Mount Hood dominates the horizon north of Portland.

PLATE 107 Bonneville Dam is constructed in two sections over the Columbia River and stands between Oregon and Washington.

PLATE 108 Oregon's beautifully blue Crater Lake is set in the crater of the extinct volcano Mount Mazama.

PLATE 109 This Indian chief is symbolic of six different Indian tribes who participate in Pendleton, Oregon's annual Round-Up.

PLATE 110 Washington's Olympic National Park, dedicated in 1946.

PLATE 111 The snow-crested peak of Mount Rainier rises 14,410 feet above sea level.

PLATE 112 Delicious apples grown in Washington's central valley.

PLATE 113 Apple blossom time in the Wenatchee Valley in central Washington.

terns was the sharp contrast in the physical character and climatic conditions of the two areas, rain forest on the Pacific Coast, grasslands and semiarid plateaus in the interior.

The same natural barriers and the Indians themselves hampered the white settlers. Nevertheless, the decades just before and well after the Civil War brought explosive growth. Thousands of Midwesterners mixed with New Englanders who came to homestead and found the new cities of Seattle, Tacoma, Spokane, Walla Walla, and Olympia. The population grew from 1,201 in 1850 to 350,000 in 1889, the year Washington gained statehood. Lumber defined the economy, and lumbering was dominated by Swedes and Norwegians, many of them from the timber-stripped regions of Wisconsin and Minnesota.

The first railroads reached Washington in the 1860s, bringing with them thousands of Chinese laborers who settled in the cities and on the farms after that construction boom ended. They accounted for only a tiny fraction of the immigrant whole: fully 97 per cent of the foreign-born, who made up 15 per cent of the total population, were English-speaking, German, or Scandinavian by the 1890s. All were caught up in the furor of the Alaskan gold rush of 1897, which helped swell Washington's population past 1 million by 1910.

The Scandinavian element remained strong and with it an affinity for the Populist-farmer-labor politics of the upper Midwest. Washington remains today one of the most Protestant of the fifty states—only 14 per cent of the people are Catholic or Jewish.

Washington's population has also made it among the most active in the labor movement. From the beginning, workers were mainly migrants, laboring in gangs in the woods, mines, and fields, often living in camps and bunkhouses that any day might be knocked down and transported elsewhere. This lack of security coupled with a rugged, no-nonsense environment fed the fires of radical unionism around the turn of the twentieth century.

The Knights of Labor established itself in Washington before statehood, advocating such progressive measures as industrial compensation laws and graduated income taxes—and restrictions on Chinese laborers. With depressed working conditions, the Knights of Labor agitated against their employment, and played an important part in the anti-Chinese riots of 1885. From this and other union movements, many Washington workers and their sympathizers entered the Socialist party and then between 1905 and 1910 became the spearhead of the new Industrial Workers of the World.

Better known as the "Wobblies," the IWW ran into violent opposition in its organizing efforts and often retaliated in kind. Shipyard workers in Seattle in 1919 triggered a general strike that paralyzed the city for several days and aroused fears of a genuine revolution on American soil.

Later, after a pitched battle between the Wobblies and American Legionnaires in Centralia, the IWW declined in strength. But the idea of union radicalism, almost unthinkable in the United States before, had been planted. It rose again during the Great Depression, given fresh impetus by the Dust Bowl farmers who occupied shantytowns on the edge of the cities, taking farm jobs where they could and helping to build the Grand Coulee Dam.

The prosperity following World War II dampened the enthusiasm for political extremism. It has not stemmed the migration of Americans looking for employment and the allure of the Pacific Northwest. Washington's population now stands at more than 3.5 million, more than half of whom live in the Central Puget Sound region encompassing Tacoma, Seattle, Bellevue, and Everett. From 1960 to 1970 the region grew some 28 per cent as newcomers sought to take advantage of the expansion of aerospace, forest product, and transportation industries. Washington likely will grow apace throughout the 1970s and 1980s, guaranteeing the state a population of continuing diversity.

HISTORY

The story of Washington long predates the arrival of American pioneers anxious to settle a new land. In fact, for two centuries before the mid-nineteenth-century influx, European naval powers sought the fabled Northwest Passage, a navigable waterway across the upper half of North America, in the waters off the coast of Washington.

Imperial Spain was foremost in the quest. In 1542 Bartolemé Ferrelo, commanding a Spanish expedition sent northward along the coast of what is now California to look for the passage's western opening, sighted the coast of southern Oregon. Then, in 1578, Francis Drake, representing Spain's greatest rival, England, reached the northwest coast and named the land New Albion; this was followed by another expedition whose pilot, Juan de Fuca, claimed entrance in 1592 of a broad inlet between the 47th and 48th degrees of north latitude. Little has been verified about his voyage, but his name has been given to the strait between the Olympic peninsula and Vancouver Island.

A century and a half later the struggle for control over the Northwest was still between England and Spain, with the Russians in Alaska as interested observers. Spain strengthened her claims when Bruno Heceta and Juan de Bodega y Quadra landed near Point Grenville in 1775. It is possible that Heceta saw the Columbia River without recognizing it as the "River of the West" so long sought.

With the explorations of Captain James Cook, English interest became more determined, and by 1788 two British traders—Meares and Douglas—joined in the rush for furs that had replaced the search for the Northwest Passage. Meares and Douglas established themselves at Nootka, laying claim to a tract of land supposedly bought from an Indian chief. Later that year an American flag appeared in northwest waters with the arrival of two vessels, the *Washington* and the *Columbia,* financed by a Boston syndicate interested in the fur trade.

When a Spanish naval force, seeking to reinforce Spain's rule, appeared at Nootka in 1789, the stage was set for a major confrontation. The Americans were unmolested, but the Spanish seized several English ships and were reinforced by a second expedition in 1790. Rather than go to war, England sent Captain George Vancouver to mediate. Vancouver met American Captain Robert Gray, who was there to find the Northwest Passage, at the entrance to the Strait of Juan de Fuca.

Their meeting is now commemorated each April 29 as Discovery Day, with good reason: After their parting, Gray turned south, found the great harbor that bears his name and then the mouth of the Columbia, which he named in honor of his ship, *Columbia Rediviva.* Gray's accomplishment gave the United States a firm claim to the whole of the territory including Oregon and Washington. Vancouver continued his exploration of Puget Sound, giving their present names to many of the region's prominent geographical features; he then sailed north through the Strait of Georgia and Queen Charlotte Strait, circumnavigating Vancouver Island. Almost as an afterthought, Spain and England mutually agreed to abandon Nootka Sound, and Spain agreed to make restitution for the property seized, eliminating itself as a contender for territory.

England and the United States then began a long contest for ownership of what became known as the Oregon Territory, an area bounded on the east by the Rockies, the south by California, and the west by the Pacific. The growing fur trade provided the competitive spark. Aiding the British were the explorations of such men as the Canadian Alexander Mackenzie and David Thompson for England's North West Company. On the American side was the Lewis and Clark expedition, which followed the Columbia to its mouth and established Fort Clatsop in 1805. In 1810 John Jacob Astor of New York organized the Pacific Fur Company in Astoria, but sold out to the British at the outbreak of the War of 1812. Thereafter the North West Company and its successor, the Hudson's Bay Company, controlled the economy and development of the region.

An uneasy coexistence continued for several decades, as American fur traders and then missionaries began to appear. By 1844 American settlers were as numerous as the British French-Canadians in the Willamette Valley, and others were on the way. On May 2, 1843, they established the Provisional Government of Oregon out of dissatisfaction with the Hudson's Bay Company's rule. A year later, the Oregon question loomed so large in national politics that the slogan "Fifty-four-forty or fight!" helped sweep James Polk to the presidency. Britain, engrossed in European troubles, decided to compromise. The Oregon question was settled on June 15, 1846, by a treaty fixing the line at the 49th parallel, with England retaining Vancouver Island.

The Oregon Territory came into being on August 13, 1848; Abraham Lincoln was offered the governorship but declined. The hazards and inconveniences of travel to Oregon City, where the territorial legislature met, and the tendency to slight the needs of the northern settlers inspired a movement for division into two parts. On March 2, 1853, President Millard Fillmore signed the bill creating Washington Territory, which included northern Idaho and western Montana. It eventually lost those sections to separate states but gained the San Juan Islands administered by England, the result of the so-called Pig War in 1859 that in fact was settled amicably.

It did not start out that way, even though the point at issue was by all accounts insignificant. England and the United States both claimed the San Juan Islands, and both attempted to collect taxes and customs. The constant state of tension felt on either side came to a head in 1859 when a pig belonging to Charles J. Griffen, an Englishman, raided a vegetable garden belonging to Lyman A. Cutler, an American. Cutler shot the pig and threatened similar action against British authorities who might move against him. Troops of both nations were sent to the islands to protect the rights of their people. Commanding the American force was Captain George Pickett, who led the famous charge at Gettysburg during the Civil War. In time the quarrel simmered down to an exchange of parties and banquets between the two garrisons. Emperor William I of Germany, selected to arbitrate the dispute, awarded the San Juan Islands to the United States in 1872. The boundary between the United States and British Columbia was fixed in Haro Strait.

There were other conflicts, less easily resolved. During the winter of 1854–55, many Indian tribes of the Northwest organized to drive the whites out of the territory. A series of conferences did result in a treaty, but the Indians, angered by the methods used in obtaining their signatures, massacred settlers in western Washington. War followed, led by the so-called "Horse" tribes, east of the Cascade Mountains, and after losses to the Indians, the territorial government closed part of Washington to settlement in 1856. After the Indians were finally subdued in 1858, the treaties were revised to give them larger and better reservations.

In spite of considerable Indian trouble, the territory's population increased as an economy based on mining, lumbering, stock raising, and shipping developed. But not until completion of the Northern Pacific Railroad in 1883 unleashed a flood of settlers were Washington's calls for statehood heard. It entered the Union on November 11, 1889, and a week later Elisha P. Ferry, former territorial governor, took the oath of office as the new state's first chief executive.

Washington's population as a state was over 357,000, nearly a fourfold increase since 1880. The rapid growth was due to the coming of the railroad. Then in 1893, the Great Northern was completed, giving Washington its second transcontinental railway system and giving the young industries of lumbering, fishing, mining, and shipbuilding ready access to the populous markets of the Eastern and Middle Western states.

Economic conditions were greatly improved by the discovery of gold in Alaska in 1897. Seattle became the port of embarkation for the thousands of prospectors who rushed to the Yukon and the Klondike; it was their outfitting station, their source of supplies, and, often, their port of re-entry. The result was a boom for the whole state.

The decade from 1890–1900 witnessed major reclamation of the semiarid lands of eastern Washington. "Apple fever," which dominated the Wenatchee Valley, helped convert thousands of acres to orchards, still bearing fruit. The federal government spurred development when it authorized irrigation projects in the Yakima and Okanogan valleys in 1902.

By the turn of the century, Washington began to foster an active labor movement which led to the creation in 1905 of a state Bureau of Labor. Progressive legislation, well in advance of most of the rest of the United States, marked that period as well. Washington's legislature enacted the direct primary law in 1907; woman suffrage in 1909; and the initiative, referendum, and recall laws in 1911. Also in that year, prodded by the unions, the state started to enforce an eight-hour-day law for women workers, a pure food and drug act, and mandatory industrial insurance.

The population in 1910 exceeded 1,140,000, paralleling the expansion of the rich farming districts of eastern Washington and such cities as Spokane, Pasco, Ellensburg, and Yakima. The entry of the United States into World War I spurred further growth. Indeed, the shipyards of Puget Sound, the lumber industry, the wheat belt of eastern Washington prospered as never before—and not again until World War II. For a number of years in between, Washington suffered from the full effects of the Depression. Federal projects, such as the construction of the Grand Coulee Dam, begun in 1933 and completed in 1941, were vital in providing labor, as well as the basis for future growth. But it was the Second World War that had the major reviving effect upon the state. Business prospered again, and many of those in uniform or recruited as civilian workers stayed on.

In recent years technology has changed the character of industry. Aerospace manufacture, as represented by Boeing, and the allied electronic arts have replaced lumber and agriculture as the dominant forces—although they are no less subject to the whims of the economy. The shift has been to industrial development. But with the growing awareness of environmental values, there has also been a concern for preserving Washington's natural beauty that captivated generations of explorers.

INDUSTRY

Washington's shift from an industrial base of wheat, timber, and mining to a manufacturing economy has been rapid. Before World War

II, about 75 per cent of employment was in agriculture and forest products; now aerospace and other businesses account for nearly 70 per cent of all jobs. The production of transportation equipment, particularly aircraft, is the basis of the state's economy, followed in importance by chemicals, atomic energy, primary and fabricated steel, and machinery. Manufacturing contributes more than $3 billion a year to Washington, with aerospace accounting for $1 billion in peak years. The cheap power from the hydroelectric dams along the Columbia River is responsible for a $400-million-a-year aluminum reduction industry, developed from plants first built in World War II.

Shipbuilding also provides employment for more than ten thousand workers, a number which has grown in recent years because of the Alaskan oil pipeline. The state's shipbuilders have worked on a variety of construction projects including fishing boats, oil rigs, and barges, as well as engaging in an assortment of repair activities. With the superior deepwater facilities of its extensive harbor complex —and the fact that it offers the shortest shipping route between the continental United States and the Far East—Washington's foreign trade has increased sixfold to nearly $6 billion in the past ten years. The state handles a major portion of cargo headed for inland markets from Japan. The key is the 2,500-square-mile Puget Sound, which is wide enough to allow ships to navigate at full speed and runs 70 to 200 feet deep as close as 500 feet from shore.

It's no accident, then, that the Port of Seattle has boomed of late, passing its archrival, Portland, in total tonnage. The port authority also runs the Seattle-Tacoma Airport, which has been expanded to accommodate rising passenger loads, including heavy traffic to Alaska and the Orient. Port activity provides some seventeen thousand jobs and hundreds of millions of dollars in payrolls, and it could grow larger with the shipments of building materials and service supplies to the oil field and pipeline construction sites on Alaska's North Slope. Yet another positive influence on Seattle's—and Washington's—economy is the beginning of construction on the Trident submarine base at nearby Bangor Naval Station. Hundreds of contracts will be awarded and up to three thousand people employed to build $600 million worth of waterfront, administrative, and housing facilities for ten nuclear-powered submarines and five thousand people.

In all, the central Puget Sound region, encompassing Seattle, accounts for nearly two thirds of Washington's total personal income. Forest products and farming continue to be important sources of employment. For example, the wood and paper industry provides a yearly average of roughly twenty thousand jobs, worth hundreds of millions of dollars. The largest employer group in the region is the transportation equipment sector, dominated by the aerospace industry. Aerospace, which translates to the Boeing Co., has been subject to the ups and downs of the economy, declining sharply during the 1970–71 recession but on the rebound since. Rebounding with it have been allied industries such as electronics, electrical machinery, and metal fabrications, which are component parts of aerospace manufacture.

Industry in various forms is spread throughout the rest of the state, but its impact, compared to forest products and agriculture, is considerably diminished. A major exception is found in the Two Rivers region in southeastern Washington, bordering on Oregon. With the establishment there of the Hanford nuclear energy power project in 1943, the area witnessed the sudden emergence of a permanent solid industrial base. Gradually this base was transformed from a group of plutonium-producing reactors to a nationally recognized complex for scientific research and development of nuclear technology, and the production of atomic-related materials. The so-called Hanford Project, located in an isolated arid region along the Columbia River, now houses such facilities as the commercial nuclear fuel processing plant operated by Exxon Nuclear and a full-fuel cycle for the U.S. government programs.

AGRICULTURE

Washington is not just apples. The state actually has a highly diversified agricultural output, with apples ranking around sixth in value. In 1974 Washington also ranked among the leading states in the harvest of pears, asparagus, wheat, cranberries, and grapes. Within the state in 1974, wheat ranked first, dairying second, beef production third, and potatoes fourth. Overall, farming and food processing are a multi-billion-dollar segment of the state's economy; a small but growing portion of the whole is commercial fisheries, whose catch now amounts to about 135 million pounds a year, worth over $160 million annually after processing.

One of the more intriguing forms of farming, in fact, is "aquaculture," raising such "crops" as salmon in large pens floating in Puget Sound. The technique, a variation on the long-established hatcheries,

which produce salmon fingerlings released to return eventually upstream and be caught, was first tried in 1970. It is expected to supply
136 million pounds of salmon by 1985.

Nature and geography have given Washington an unusually plentiful water supply, about 275 million acre-feet during the average year.
But the water is not everywhere, either geographically or seasonally.
Thus the state's agriculture depends greatly on man's efforts at irrigation, such as the over seventy-five dams and reservoirs that have been
built to date. About 10 per cent of the 16.5 million acres under cultivation is irrigated, and another 10 million acres could be as food
demand increases.

By far the largest project involves over 1 million acres in the Columbia Basin, bringing water to the arid lands of Grant, Adams, and
Franklin counties. The keystone is the mammoth Grand Coulee
Dam, which will eventually cost $1.5 billion when construction of the
third powerhouse is completed in 1990. Behind the Grand Coulee is
Roosevelt Lake, holding 9.6 million acre-feet of water for 2,200
miles of irrigation canals. Most of the land in the Mid-Columbia was
formerly sagebrush-covered, fit only for cattle or dry-land wheat
farming. After irrigation, crops with much higher value per acre, such
as potatoes, sugar beets, and fruits, have been cultivated. Yields rise
substantially as well. Wheat harvests, for example, are half again
higher in the Columbia Basin than in the rest of the state.

Nuclear power, discussed in an earlier section, may have more to
do with future irrigation projects than one might imagine. These
power plants produce huge amounts of heat that must be removed
continuously, and water—large volumes of it—is the economical con-
ductor. The resulting warm water is ideal for irrigation because it
protects crops from early frost and thus significantly extends the
growing season; it also opens up the possibilities for raising several
crops a year and introduces foodstuffs normally grown in warmer
climes. The combination of dry land and water is available along the
Columbia River, at the location of several nuclear plants planned for
the Hanford Project.

NATURAL RESOURCES

Paul Bunyan's real home is Washington, which ranks as the major
lumber-producing state in the United States. Though distinctly
different in composition, the forests on both the east and west sides of

the Cascades are mostly softwoods. Eastward lies the white and ponderosa pines, cottonwood and aspen, hugging the Pacific are Douglas fir, cedar, hemlock, soft maple, alder, and spruce.

Lumbering began in earnest almost with the arrival of the first white settlers in the late eighteenth century. A hundred years later, when the north-central states had been largely deforested, Michigan and Wisconsin lumbermen bought enormous tracts of timber from the railroads. They brought in hundreds of thousands of laborers and organized a forest products industry that still ranks as a major economic force in Washington. Where the forests stand—especially on the Pacific coast—they are the source of from 30 per cent to 65 per cent of total employment in the South Puget Sound region.

There is more to Washington than timber. With the Columbia River creating a third of the total hydroelectric capacity of the country, it has the nation's largest base of water power—the only source of replenishable energy currently available. The dams built to store and utilize this resource can generate over 17 million kilowatts, equal to about fifteen nuclear power plants, and additional construction now under way will nearly double Washington's hydroelectric capacity. Other forms of energy are available: over 6 billion tons of recoverable coal, uranium deposits, and quantities of natural gas.

While Washington has never had a major mining industry comparable with that of other Western states, its cumulative production of some three dozen minerals, ranging from platinum and cobalt to gold and asbestos, is now worth over $3.5 billion.

CITIES

Seattle vies with San Francisco for first place in dramatic settings, the kind that draws stares from airline travelers presented with the spectacle of oceans and mountains in a single, sweeping view. It is especially true when the rain clouds coming in over the Olympic Mountains are swept away, and the sun reveals the water surrounding this isthmus city of over 530,000 people and a metropolitan population of about 1,422,000. Puget Sound is on the west, Lake Washington on the east. In the distance are the mountains, among them Mount Rainier to the south and Mount Baker to the north. And then there are the precipitous hills of the city itself, drawing for visitors the final physical parallel with San Francisco.

Unlike San Francisco, though, Seattle was settled comparatively late. Seagoing explorers patrolling the northwest coast left no permanent imprint, and it wasn't until the mid-1800s that overland settlers reached the area. In 1851 several families at Alki Point gave the name of a local Indian chieftain to their rough colony—Sealth. The settlement relocated to a spot near present-day Pioneer Square, in what is now downtown Seattle, about the time local entrepreneurs began to appreciate the potential of the expanse of virgin timber that engulfed them.

So Seattle became the setting for Washington's first industry, Henry Yesler's sawmill, which cut timber for export and gave birth to the expression "Skid Road" for the path used to roll logs. It came to mean a run-down district inhabited by poor, transient workers as Seattle expanded away from its original center, and the phrase survived as "skid row" to describe similar areas of other American cities.

Seattle didn't pay much heed, however. It was more concerned with building and, after a disastrous fire in 1889, rebuilding. The Klondike gold rush of 1897, for which Seattle served as the jumping-off point, provided the impetus for rapid growth that carried the city well into the twentieth century. The transcontinental railroad, extended to Seattle in 1893, and a bustling port made it the hub of trade with the Orient and points east. Seattle has remained that, from the men and matériel of World War II to the pipeline supplies for the present Alaskan oil boom.

The city has retained much of its natural good looks, and even managed to add a few man-made attractions like the 607-foot Space Needle, built for the World's Fair of 1962, and the subterranean tour of the Seattle waterfront that existed in 1880. The fire in 1889 destroyed much of Seattle, especially the downtown area. When the city fathers made plans to rebuild, they decided that the new streets should be raised ten feet above the old level. The original waterfront became the foundation of reconstruction, yet still remains accessible to guided excursions of the underground.

Among Seattle's unusual sights are Lake Washington, with its varied shore line of marinas, parks, and homes, and the smaller Lake Union, where some six thousand to seven thousand people live permanently on houseboats. Lake Washington, one of several in metropolitan Seattle, was the object of a vigorous cleanup campaign in the 1950s and 1960s that cost more than $140 million in water treatment facilities; later another citizens' movement stopped helter-skelter commercial development on the Lake Union shore line, got a 12-acre city park built along its banks, and improved the quality of its water as well.

Seattle has had a penchant for recapturing the past as well as preserving the present. Pioneer Square, the site of that first sawmill, has also been refurbished in an effort—largely successful—to keep in touch with Seattle's rich past. The old Skid Road has become a fashionable dining and shopping area, dotted with art galleries and tastefully restored buildings. Nearby is the Pike Place Market, set in a downtown location of wooden stores and rooming houses, which never lost its original character: Farmers, fish dealers, fruit sellers, and butchers sell their goods as they did at the turn of the century, protected in a 7-acre tract by a city law passed in 1971 that requires any development to be restorationist in character.

More up-to-date is the Seattle Center, the $90 million legacy of the 1962 World's Fair, which went a long way toward bringing the city out of its provincial shell. The Center includes the Space Needle, a 3,100-seat Opera House (home of the Seattle Symphony), the 750-seat Repertory Theater, a Modern Art Pavilion, and a Science Center which is housed in the building the U.S. government had built for itself as exhibit space. Another vestige of the fair, Seattle's monorail, takes visitors from the Center to downtown in less than two minutes. It was considered the forerunner of a major mass transit system, designed along the lines of San Francisco's Bay Area Rapid Transit, but the construction of such a system was defeated at the polls in 1968 and 1970.

The same effort, however, did succeed in expanding Seattle's already impressive array of parks. There are now forty-five, including bits of forest, salt-water and lake beaches, among them the 95-acre Woodland Park Zoological Gardens, which contains 1,400 animals. Two of the more impressive are the Japanese Tea Garden in the University of Washington Arboretum and the 267-acre Arboretum itself, which has shrubs and plants from all countries. The University of Washington has its main campus, with over 34,000 students, in Seattle, making it the largest university in the Pacific Northwest. It houses the Thomas Burke Memorial State Museum, devoted to Northwest Indian artifacts, and the Henry Art Gallery, featuring European and American paintings. Another half-dozen or so museums are scattered throughout the city, including the Seattle Art Museum with its famed collection of oriental art and one of the two Tiepolo ceilings in America.

Seattle, in fact, as one ballplayer noted when the city refused to put up the necessary money to keep its American League baseball team, "seems to care more for its art museums than its ball park." Not that the city is without its spectator sports. Completion of a domed stadium will make Seattle eligible for major-league baseball and football, and the city is already represented by the Supersonics in the National Basketball Association and the Totems in the Western Hockey League.

Spokane, with a 1970 population of 170,516, is the second-largest city in the state and the largest inland metropolitan area in the region west of Minneapolis–St. Paul and north of Salt Lake City. It serves as the economic center of the vast Inland Empire, a loosely defined area encompassing all of eastern Washington, the northern Idaho panhandle, and the mountainous reaches of western Montana.

Spokane has none of Seattle's dramatic setting. There are mountains and forests within reach, but the overriding topographical feature is the so-called Channeled Scablands, an evenly surfaced plateau of thin, stony glaciated soil, interspersed with numerous lakes. Spokane lacks Seattle's urban graces also, with two railroad lines slicing through the middle of the city. The railroads, of course, helped build Spokane to its current size. Spurred by their appearance and mining activities to the north and east, its population accelerated sharply during the period of 1870–90, making Spokane a regional trade center before the turn of the century. Growth leveled off until World War II, when rapid industrial expansion resumed. Since the mid-1950s, however, the rate of growth has eased sharply.

Unlike Seattle, Spokane's more diversified agricultural-mining-manufacturing economy continued to prosper during the 1970–71 recession. Indeed the city's importance as a transportation juncture has been reaffirmed by Burlington Northern Railroad's decision to undertake a series of extensive construction projects in and near Spokane, including a $30 million freight classification yard.

Spokane helped make a vital contribution to the northwestern economy through its Expo '74, which provided employment for several thousand workers. Among the benefits is the transformation of the Expo site into a 3,800-acre Riverfront Park along the Spokane River. It contains the United States Pavilion, with its environmental exhibit center; the Opera House and Convention Center, formerly the

Washington State Pavilion; and an outdoor amphitheater that seats 1,200 people. Riverfront Park is in welcome contrast to the tangle of railroad tracks and warehouses that comprised the area before Expo '74.

Spokane does have its share of amenities, among them more than sixty parks and gardens, including the famous Duncan Gardens and Japanese Tea House in Manito Park. There are several museums—Cheney Cowles Memorial on plateau Indian art and culture, and Spokane Valley Pioneer, for example—and several institutions for higher learning. Metropolitan Spokane is home to Eastern Washington State College, Gonzaga University (Bing Crosby's alma mater), Whitworth College, and Fort Wright College of the Holy Names.

Tacoma is the third-largest city in Washington, with a population of around 155,000. It is almost due south of Seattle, near the southernmost tip of Puget Sound, and shares much of the same physical characteristics and panorama.

Like Seattle and Everett, a smaller city at the north end of Puget Sound, Tacoma is a major deepwater harbor, significant in the early development of the region. It is linked to the neighboring communities by ferries and bridges and to the world beyond by the Seattle-Tacoma International Airport, midway between the two cities. The present Tacoma Narrows Bridge had a famous predecessor called Galloping Gertie because it swayed so much—collapsing finally in 1940. Its 5,450-foot replacement is one of the longest suspension spans in the country.

More than Seattle, Tacoma is an industrial town, with wood-processing plants and a great copper smelter accounting for employment, income—and environmental problems. In recent years, the city has attempted to diversify its economy, attracting businesses in fishing, concrete, food processing, clothing, chemicals, and candy, many of which want to take advantage of its excellent deepwater docking facilities.

Tacoma has been busy improving its downtown business district, converting four blocks into the Broadway Plaza pedestrian mall. When the Local Improvement District project is completed, sixty downtown blocks will have new lighting, sidewalks, trees, shrubs, and benches. The new Port of Tacoma grain elevator and the West Coast Orient Lumber Mill represent efforts to further expand agricultural and lumber markets outside the city.

Another aspect of Tacoma is its forty-four parks, including Point

Defiance at the northernmost end of the city with its 600 acres of flower gardens, virgin forest, zoo, and deep-sea aquarium. The park can be reached on the Kla-how-ya Trail, which also takes walkers to the Wrights Park botanical observatory, the State Historical Society Museum, and the 105-foot totem pole, carved from a single cedar tree.

Some 30 miles southwest of Tacoma is the Washington State capital of **Olympia,** with a population of 23,000. The city has played a role in Washington's development as a center for shipping and for lumber, but Olympia is primarily a governmental center—among the most attractive anywhere. Its natural setting and such man-made delights as the beautifully landscaped capitol grounds, planted with Japanese cherry trees, have helped defeat attempts to move the seat of power elsewhere in the state.

Olympia's planners certainly were confident the capital would last: The Legislative Building, which is the central building of the governmental group, has a 287-foot dome, fourth highest of its kind in the world and resembling the Capitol dome in Washington, D.C. Among the other points of interest are the State Capitol Museum, concentrating on history, natural history, and art; Washington State Museum of Pharmacy; and the Judge Daniel R. Bigelow Home, constructed in 1854, five years before Olympia's incorporation, and containing the original furnishings. A second settler's home has a more contemporary tie—it's the Crosby House built in 1860 by the grandparents of singer Bing Crosby.

SPORTS AND RECREATION

With its ready access to mountains and the ocean, Washington is a mecca for the outdoorsman, in summer and winter. There are more than fifty state parks, six national parks and recreation areas, and a half-dozen national forests, which encompass about 9 million acres; nearly all of them offer some combination of camping, boating, hiking, fishing, and winter sports. Mountain climbing is probably the best in the Mount Rainier, North Cascades, and Olympic National parks.

Hikers in the Olympic National Park, for example, will find over 600 miles of trails traversing stands of spruce, fir, and hemlock as well as ridge tops and mountain passes. Fishing, for trout especially, can often be enjoyed in the upper reaches of the mountain parks. Deer, elk, and bear are also plentiful, in addition to a number of game birds such as pheasants, ducks, geese, and quail. Hunting season for one game or another is open all year somewhere in the state, although fall and winter are the busiest.

These attractions extend beyond the mountains, of course, especially in a state with eight thousand lakes stocked with a variety of fish. At the mouths of rivers that run to the Pacific, the game fish of note is the steelhead, a large seagoing trout, which is sought in winter. Farther out, off Grays Harbor and at the outer end of the Strait of Juan de Fuca, salmon fishing is at its peak in the summer. It isn't necessary to venture that far afield for a taste of the ocean. Seattle has fresh-water activities on Lake Washington and salt-water activities on Puget Sound, with locks and a canal connecting the two.

Seattle, which calls itself the "small boat capital of the world," has mooring space for thousands of craft and rents anything from canoes to ocean-going yachts and cruisers. Golf is popular in Seattle, as it is in the rest of the state, which boasts over 150 courses. Washington is also well represented in such family activities as archery, bicycle riding, bowling, and tennis; Seattle alone maintains nearly one hundred courts for the last-mentioned.

There is perhaps less to choose from in winter, but what does exist is plentiful—skiing. With the amount of snowfall Washington generally receives, the slopes are open for business from mid-November to mid-May, and some areas occasionally stretch the season to include summer training. Facilities for downhill and, increasingly, cross-country skiing abound, including several such as Alpental, Crystal Mountain, and White Pass Village within two hours' drive of Seattle.

For lookers rather than doers, Washington offers plenty to watch in university football, basketball, and track and field, horse racing, and professional sports. Seattle, which has the Supersonics in pro basketball, is trying to land an American League baseball team. It had one for a year, lost it to Milwaukee, but expects to acquire another.

POINTS OF INTEREST

The major cities—Seattle, Tacoma, Spokane, Olympia—have their attractions, of course. But no man-made structure is going to match the awesome beauty of the towering mountains and lush forests of the

Pacific coast. One does give it a good try: the Grand Coulee Dam and Franklin D. Roosevelt Lake. This immense, elongated blue jewel stretches 151 miles through eastern scrublands to the Canadian boundary. The lake was formed originally to boost electrical power production when the Columbia River dropped during the winter, but now it is nearly as prominent as a recreational attraction, replete with campgrounds and beaches. The Grand Coulee itself is an engineering marvel best described by its dimensions: 550 feet high, 500 feet wide at its base, and 4,173 feet long, producing well over its rated capacity of 2,295,000 kilowatts. The irrigation waters released by the dam have reclaimed nearly 500,000 acres of Columbia Basin lands and another 500,000 acres can be reached.

The Yakima Valley, southwest of Grand Coulee, is an impressive result of irrigation. Often called the "Fruit Bowl of the Nation," Yakima has a mile and a half of warehouses and processing and packing plants that handle cherries, peaches, pears, apples, and other small fruit by the thousands of bushels. The apple crop alone is valued at more than $50 million a year—all of it from what had been sagebrush desert.

But it is the natural wonders that predominate, most of them now part of national parks and forests. Among the more prominent is one of the newer sites, the North Cascades National Park in north-central Washington. It was established in 1968 and its 1,053 square miles contain jagged peaks, glaciated canyons, over three hundred active glaciers, and numerous mountain lakes and streams. Its centerpiece is 55-mile-long Lake Chelan, which originates in the glacial peaks of the Cascades. Another inland attraction is the Gifford Pinchot National Forest, which straddles the Cascade range from central Washington to the Columbia River. On opposite edges of 1,251,051 acres of densely wooded mountains are the peaks of Mount Adams (12,326 feet) and Mount St. Helens (9,677 feet). The vast fields of wild huckleberries surrounding Mount Adams draw hordes of pickers each autumn.

It is toward the coast that Washington's scenery becomes truly spectacular: Mount Rainier National Park, named for the 14,410-foot ice-clad volcano with six primary glaciers originating at the summit; the 1,760,000-acre Mount Baker Snoqualmie National Forest, on the western slopes of the Cascades, which contains some of the most primitive regions in the state; and the Olympic peninsula. The Olympic National Park is the wilderness core of the peninsula, between Hood Canal on the east and the Pacific on the west. Within its 896,600 acres are rain forests, wildlife, glaciers, and some 50 miles of unspoiled scenic ocean coastline. The Olympic range, including the 7,965-foot Mount Olympus, is composed of rugged cliffs and crags, clothed with trees, many of them more than 200 feet high and more than 10 feet in diameter.

Offshore is the San Juan Island Historical Park, which commemorates the struggle for possession of 172 bits of land by American and British settlers.

SPECIAL EVENTS

Flower festivals, fairs and rodeos, and international activities dominate the year's special events calendar in Washington.

In April, the Puyallup Valley Daffodil Festival is held concurrently in Puyallup, Tacoma, Sumner, and Orting. That same month the Washington State Apple Blossom Festival takes place in Wenatchee. Two horse shows, the Apple Blossom Horse Show in Wenatchee and the Washington State Open Horse Show in Yakima, are held in May.

Well-known to visitors in Washington is Seafair, a ten-day-long event in Seattle in late July and early August, featuring parades and hydroplane races on Lake Washington. Also during the summer are the Washington State Square Dance Festival in Tacoma in June; the Logger's Jubilee in Morton and the Salmon Derby Days in Port Angeles, both in August; and the Western Washington Fair in Puyallup in September.

Among the rodeos are the Diamond Spurs Rodeo in Spokane in March; the Little Britches Rodeo in Bremerton in June; the Toppenish Pow Wow and Rodeo in Toppenish, also in June; and the Long Beach Rodeo in Long Beach in August. On Labor Day weekend Walla Walla holds Frontier Days and Ellensburg sponsors the Ellensburg Rodeo, one of the major rodeos in the state, including dances, Indian exhibits, a horse show, and parades.

International events, reflecting Washington's diverse population, include the week-long Scandinavian Festival in Tacoma in October, and the Christmas Around the World celebration in Seattle in December.

S.G.

CHRONOLOGY

1578   Francis Drake sailed to the Pacific Northwest coast, naming
       the region New Albion (New England).

1592   Juan de Fuca is believed to have found a strait between Van-
       couver Island and the mainland.

1775   Bruno Heceta and Juan de Bodega y Quadra landed on
       Washington coast (near the present Point Grenville) and
       took possession for Spain.

1778   Captain James Cook, on his last voyage, named Cape Flat-
       tery, missed discovery of the strait nearby, and made a survey
       from the 44th to the 70th parallel.

1789   Estevan Martínez, a Spaniard, confiscated British ships at
       Nootka Sound.

1792   Captain Robert Gray discovered and named Bulfinch
       (Grays) Harbor; he discovered and named the Columbia
       River, anchoring on the north side to trade for furs.

       Captain George Vancouver, while negotiating with Bodega y
       Quadra a settlement between England and Spain, explored
       Admiralty Inlet and Puget Sound; and at a point near
       Everett, took possession for George III of England, renaming
       New Albion New Georgia. Lieutenant Broughton, under
       Vancouver's orders, ascended the Columbia River to Point
       Vancouver.

1803   United States purchased Louisiana Territory, increasing inter-
       est in the Oregon country.

1805–6   Lewis and Clark reached the mouth of the Columbia River
       and returned to St. Louis, giving the United States further
       claim to the Oregon country.

1810   North West Fur Company established Spokane House (9
       miles northwest of present Spokane), the first white settle-
       ment within the limits of the present state.

1811   Astoria, in present Oregon, was founded by John Jacob As-
       tor's Pacific Fur Company.

       David Thompson reached the mouth of the Columbia River
       after exploring from Kettle Falls to the mouth of the Snake

River, and claimed all land north of the Snake River for England.

1812   Fort Spokane was established by the Pacific Fur Company, near Spokane House, to compete with the North West Company.

1813   The North West Company, taking advantage of the War of 1812, purchased all of the property of the Pacific Fur Company in the valley of the Columbia.

1818   Joint occupancy of Oregon country by Americans and British was established.

1836   Marcus Whitman and H. H. Spalding, missionaries, arrived with their wives, the first American women in the Oregon country. Whitman established a mission at Waiilatpu near Fort Walla Walla.

1838–41   A number of religious missions were established in Spokane and elsewhere on the coast.

1843   Influx of immigrants assumed large proportions.

Oregon Provisional Government formed at Champoeg.

1844   Boundary slogan, "Fifty-four-forty or fight," was prominent in the presidential campaign.

1845   Michael T. Simmons and his party, the first American settlers in the Puget Sound region, reached Tumwater.

1846   United States-Canadian boundary was fixed at the 49th parallel.

Hudson's Bay Company planned to move headquarters to a site at Victoria on Vancouver Island.

Settlement began on the site of Olympia.

1848   Oregon Territory, including all of present Washington, was created.

1851   Schooner *Exact* brought members of Denny pioneer party to Alki Point (now in Seattle).

1852   First settlers come to Bellingham Bay. Nicholas DeLin settled on Commencement Bay, at the site of Tacoma.

First Washington newspaper, the *Columbian,* was printed in Olympia, strongly advocating the new territory.

1853   Washington Territory was created; the white population numbered 3,965. Olympia was named the temporary capital.

1855–58 Indian war was waged both east and west of the Cascades.

Eastern Washington was opened to settlement.

1859 The Fraser River gold rush began.

San Juan Islands boundary controversy between England and the United States became acute.

1863 Territory of Idaho was created from Washington Territory, establishing the present eastern boundary of the state.

1864 Completion of the first transcontinental telegraph lines.

1872 The San Juan dispute was settled.

1881 The transcontinental line of the Northern Pacific was completed to Spokane Falls.

1889 The enabling act was passed by Congress and signed on February 22. The constitution convention assembled in Olympia on July 4, and the constitution was adopted October 1. President Harrison proclaimed Washington a state November 11.

1919 Labor unrest led to armed clash, fatal to several, at Centralia between marchers in Armistice Day parade and members of International Workers of the World.

1938 President Roosevelt signed the bill to create Olympic National Park January 29.

1941 Grand Coulee Dam, on the Columbia, was completed.

1962 Seattle World's Fair opened; its legacy included the Space Needle and the Seattle Center, now the cultural and recreational heart of the city.

1974 Spokane held Expo '74, which also left behind a number of significant public buildings, as well as an extensive waterfront park along the Spokane River.

1975 Columbia Basin Project at Grand Coulee Dam scheduled to begin power generation.

1976 The Kingdome, a new domed stadium in Seattle, opened.

1979 In a study by the Department of Housing and Urban Development, Seattle was cited as a prime example of an urban area in which the middle classes were being displaced by such factors as central-city revivals and a shortage of new dwelling units.

Photographic Credits

VOLUME II

WE GRATEFULLY acknowledge the cooperation and assistance of the following photographic sources for this volume:

Alaska Department of Commerce & Economic Development   Plate 93

American Airlines   Plates 94, 96, 97, 99, 101

Ansel Adams   Plate 98

Arizona Office of Tourism   Plates 74, 77, 79

Chicago Convention and Tourism Bureau   Plates 2, 3

Cincinnati Convention and Visitors Bureau   Plate 28

Cleveland Convention and Visitors Bureau   Plate 25

Colorado Division of Commerce and Development   Plates 48, 50, 52, 53, 54, 55

Denver Convention & Visitors Bureau   Plate 51

Hawaii Visitors Bureau   Plates 100, 102, 103

Homestake Mining Company   Plate 49

Idaho Department of Commerce and Development   Plates 56, 57, 58

Illinois Division of Tourism   Plate 1

Indiana Department of Commerce   Plates 4, 5, 6, 7

Iowa Development Commission   Plate 8

Kansas Department of Economic Development   Plates 31, 32, 33, 34

Michigan Tourist Council   Plates 9, 10, 11, 12, 13

Minnesota Department of Economic Development   Plates 14, 15, 16, 17, 18

Missouri Division of Tourism   Plates 19, 20, 21, 22

Montana Travel Promotion   Plates 59, 60, 61, 62

National Park Service   Plate 104

National Park Service/Photo by George A. Grant   Plates 65, 110

National Park Service/Photo by John Hansen   Plate 73

National Park Service/Photo by M. Woodbridge Williams   Plates 75, 92

Nebraska Game and Parks Commission   Plates 35, 37, 38, 39

Nevada Department of Economic Development   Plate 64

658 PHOTOGRAPHIC CREDITS

INDEX

Aberdeen, Wash., 620
Abilene, Kans., 219, 223, 229–30, 237, 238, 242
Absaroka Mountains, 403, 419
Acoma, N.Mex., 462, 463
Acoma Indians, 462
Ada, Okla., 475
Adair County, Iowa, 76
Adams, Jane, 9
Adams, Mount (Wash.), 651
Adams County, Iowa, 63
Adams County, Wash., 643
Adler Planetarium (Chicago), 22
Admiralty Inlet, 653
Adrian, Mich., 172
Aerial Fire Depot (Missoula, Mont.), 358
Agassiz, Lake (N.D.), 266
Agassiz Refuge (Minn.), 120
Agate Falls (Mich.), 84
Agate Fossil Beds (Nebr.), 258
Agriculture Hall of Fame (Bonner Springs, Kans.), 236
Ahmanson Theater (Los Angeles), 554
Air Defense Command, 501
Air Force (See also specific installations): Academy, 321, 322, 326; Accounting and Finance Center, 319; Museum (Dayton), 181
Akeley, Minn., 129
Akron, Ohio, 165, 169, 173, 174, 176, 179, 183, 188, 189
Alabama-Coushatta Indian Reservation (Livingston, Tex.), 505
Alabama Indians, 490, 505
Alameda County, Calif., 544, 561
Alamo, the, 492, 504, 507
Ala Moana Shopping Center (Honolulu), 601
Alamogordo, N.Mex., 454, 460, 465
Alapah Mountain, 513
Alarcón, Hernando de, 546
Alaska, 510–39, 641; University of, 530, 533, 539

Alaska, Gulf of, 512, 514, 515, 526, 538, 539
Alaska Highway, 517, 524, 533, 539
Alaska Historical Museum, 531
Alaska Indian Arts Center, 532
Alaskaland, 534
Alaska Methodist University, 530
Alaska Native Claims Settlement Act, 520, 539
Alaska Peninsula, 512, 518, 535
Alaska Railroad, 517, 529, 530, 533, 538, 539
Alaska Range, 513, 532, 535
Alaska State Ferry System, 539
Alaska Territory, 523, 538
Albany, Oreg., 627
Albert Lea, Minn., 118
Albert Lea Lake, 126
Albina, Oreg., 621
Albion, Ill., 8
Albuquerque, N.Mex., 449, 453 ff., 457–58, 460, 462 ff.
Alder Gulch (Mont.), 360
Aldrich, Bess Streeter, 248
Aleutian Islands, 511, 512, 514 ff., 518, 539
Aleutian Range, 513
Aleuts, 518, 522, 539
Alexander and Baldwin, 585
Alexandria, Minn., 107, 127, 128
Algonquian Indians, 10, 61, 111, 196. See also specific tribes
Alien Land Act, 548
Alki Point (Seattle), 645, 654
Allegheny Plateau, 166
Allen County, Ind., 44
Alliance, Ohio, 169
Allouez, Claude Jean, 197
Alluvial Plain (Missouri), 136
"Aloha Oe," 586
Alpena, Mich., 92, 100
Alpental (ski area—Wash.), 650
Alpine Scenic Loop (Utah), 395
Alta, Utah, 386, 398
Alton, Ill., 3, 12, 27

Alum Rock Park (San Jose), 560
Alyeska, Mount, 534
Amado, Ariz., 440
Amahl and the Night Visitors, 398
Amana, Iowa, 65, 73
Amana Heim (Homestead, Iowa), 73
Amana Refrigerator Company, 65, 73
Amana Society (Colonies), 60, 63, 73, 77
Amarillo, Tex., 502; Medical Center, 502
American Conservatory Theater (San Francisco), 558
American Factors, 585
American Falls, Idaho, 342
American Federation of Labor, 144, 612
American Fork Canyon, 395
American Fur Company, 102, 272, 350
"American Gothic" (Wood), 75
American Indian Movement, 294
American Legion, 636
American Merino sheep, 175
American Metal Climax, 317
American Motors, 192, 207
American Quartette (Dvořák), 74
American Revolution (Revolutionary War): Illinois and, 11; Indiana and, 40; Michigan and, 86, 88; Wisconsin and, 197
American River, 561
Amish, the: and Iowa, 60, 75; and Ohio, 165, 169, 188
Amtrak, 458
Anaconda, Mont., 361
Anaconda Company, 352, 356, 357; Aluminum Company, 364; Copper Company, 351
Anadarko, Okla., 482
Anaheim, Calif., 563
Anasazi Indians, 430, 452
Anchorage, Alaska, 514, 521, 524, 525, 527, 529–30, 531, 533, 534, 536, 539
Ancient, Fort (Ohio), 184–85
Anderson (house—Lexington, Mo.), 159
Anderson, Ind., 39, 43
Anderson, Sherwood, 170
Andrew County, Mo., 143
Angel Fire Ski Basin (N.Mex.), 460
Angelina National Forest, 503
Angel Mounds State Memorial, 47
Angels Camp, Calif., 568
Anheuser-Busch Brewery, 147
Anian, 612
Ann Arbor, Mich., 87, 92, 98, 104–5
Annunciation Greek Orthodox Church (Milwaukee), 204
Antelope Valley Indian Museum (Los Angeles), 554
Anza, Juan Bautista de, 556, 569
Apache Indians, 490; in Arizona, 429 ff., 439, 440, 446; in New Mexico, 452, 453, 463, 465

Apache Junction, Ariz., 440
Apache-Sitgreaves National Forest, 440
Apodaca, Jerry, 466
Apollo flight, 498
Apostle Islands National Lakeshore, 209–10
Aransas Pass, Tex., 503
Arapahoe Basin (ski area—Colo.), 322
Arapahoe County Fairgrounds, 323
Arapaho Indians, 311, 406, 420, 422
Arbor Lodge (Nebraska City), 261
Arbuckle Mountains, 468, 479
Arcadia, Calif., 564
Arcadia, Mo., 150
Arches National Park, 396–97
Arctic Circle, 512, 513, 516, 518, 527
Arctic Coast (Alaska), 511, 539. See also specific locations
Arctic Ocean, 512
Arctic Region (Alaska), 512–13, 515
Arctic Slope, 513, 515, 516, 523, 524, 526, 539
Argonia, Kans., 222, 242
Argonne Cancer Research Hospital, 14
Argonne National Laboratory, 14
Arikara Indians, 269 ff., 289, 291–92
Arizona, 381, 426–27, 453; University of, 439
Arizona, U.S.S., 447
Arizona Snow Bowl, 440
Arizona-Sonora Desert Museum, 439
Arizona State Museum, 439
Arizona Territory, 431, 446, 453
Arkansas National Wildlife Refuge, 497
Arkansas River, 220, 225, 234, 241, 325, 467, 470, 475, 479. See also Fryingpan—Arkansas project
Arkansas Valley, 317, 326
Arlington, Tex., 498, 504
Armco Steel, 186
Armstrong, Louis, 9
Armstrong, Ohio, 187
Armstrong (Neil) Air and Space Museum, 187
Armstrong Company, 60
Army, U. S. (See also specific battles, installations, wars): Engineers, Corps of, 475
Arrowhead Country (Minn.), 125
Arrow Rock State Park, 159
Art Museum. See specific towns
Arvilla, N.D., 278
Ash Hollow (Nebr.), 259
Ashland, Kans., 239
Ashland, Oreg., 626, 627
Ashland, Wis., 215
Ashley, James, 402
Ashley, William H., 409
Asian Art Museum (San Francisco), 558
Asians, 610. See also specific nationalities

Aspen, Colo., 321, 323
Assiniboin Indians, 269, 271, 349
Astaire, Fred, 248
Astor, John Jacob, 102, 115, 614, 628, 638, 653
Astoria, Oreg., 611, 614, 624, 627, 628, 653
Astrodomain (Houston), 497
Astrodome (Houston), 497
Astrohall (Houston), 498
Atchison, Kans., 223, 231
Atchison County, Mo., 143
Atchison, Topeka and the Santa Fe Railroad, 226
Athabascan Indians, 518, 519
Atkins (Mary) Museum of Fine Arts, 154
Atlantic-Richfield Plaza (Los Angeles), 555
Atomic Energy Commission, 14, 32, 173, 334, 344, 372, 381, 458, 468
Atsina Indians, 349
Auditorium (Chicago), 22
Augsburg College, 123
Auraria, Colo., 313, 314
Aurora, Oreg., 611
Au Sable River, 100
Austin, Minn., 118
Austin, Moses, 146, 492
Austin, Stephen F., 146, 162, 492, 493, 500, 507
Austin, Tex., 500–1, 508
Austrians, 169
Auto-Aviation Museum (Cleveland), 178
Avila College, 155
Aztec, N.Mex., 462
Aztec Ruins National Monument, 462

Bach, Johann Sebastian, 188
Badger Pass (Calif.), 563
Badlands: North Dakota, 265–66, 268, 275, 279, 280; South Dakota, 286, 302
Bad River, 194, 291, 297
Bad River Reservation (Wis.), 196
Badin, Stephen, 46
Baha'i Temple (Wilmette, Ill.), 22
Baird, Bil, 248
Baird Carillon (Ann Arbor), 98
Baker, Jim, 407
Baker Furniture Company, 99
Baker, Mount (Wash.), 644; Snoqualmie National Forest, 651
Balboa Park (San Diego), 560, 564–65
Baldwin Home Museum (Lahaina, Hawaii), 598
Baldwin-Wallace College, 188
Ballet West, 398
Bancroft, Nebr., 261
Bandelier National Monument, 462
Bandera (Tex.), 503
Bangor Naval Station, 641

Bank of North Dakota, 273
Bank of South Dakota, 304
Bannack, Mont., 350
Bannock Indians, 331, 333, 342–43, 344, 406, 422
Baptists, 290
Baraboo, Wis., 212–13
Baraboo Range, 192
Baraboo River, 213
Baraga County, Mich., 84
Baranof, Alexander, 521–22
Baranof Island, 516
Barbary Coast (San Francisco), 556
Barbed Wire Museum (LaCrosse, Kans.), 238
Barberton, Ohio, 176
Barnette, E. T., 533
Barnette's Cache (Alaska), 533
Barrow, Alaska, 515, 517, 534
Barta, Joseph, 210
Bartlesville, Okla., 467, 473, 481
Bartlett, Mount (Colo.), 317
Barton, David, 142
Basin and Range Region: Arizona, 428; Idaho, 328, 336, 337; Nevada, 365, 384, 450; Texas, 488, 497
Basket Makers, 311, 325
Basques, 331, 342, 368, 611
Batavia, Ill., 14, 32
Battelle Planetarium (Columbus, Ohio), 180
Battle Creek, Mich., 92
Baumeler, Joseph, 186
Bay Area (Calif.), 544, 561, 563, 565; Rapid Transit System, 561, 570
Bay City, Mich., 86, 87
Bayfield, Wis., 210
Bayfield Peninsula (Wis.), 196, 210
Bayh, Birch, 54
Bayhorse, Idaho, 341
Baylor University, 499, 502
Bay Ridge golf course (Wis.), 209
Baytown, Tex., 495
"Beale Street Blues," 153
Beall Woods Natural Preserve, 20
Beanblossom, Ind., 52
Beardstown, Ill., 27
Bearmouth Ghost Town (Mont.), 360
Bear's Paw Battlefield, 361
Beatrice, Nebr., 250, 264
Beatty, Nev., 378, 380
Beaumont, Tex., 495, 496
Beaver, Okla., 483
Beaver Creek (Kans.), 223
Beaver Island (Mich.), 84, 87, 102–3
Becker, Carl, 240
Becknell, William, 140, 151, 162, 226, 241, 453, 465
Beechcraft (aircraft), 219, 231
Behlen (Nebr.) Manufacturing, 252

Belgians: and Indians, 37; and Texas, 491
Bell, Ham, 230
Belle Fourche, S.D., 294, 303
Belle Fourche River, 404
Belle Isle (Mich.), 84, 96
Belleville, Ill., 30
Bellevue, Nebr., 264
Bellevue, Ohio, 186
Bellevue, Wash., 636
Bellingham Bay, 654
Bellmon, Henry, 474
Belmont, Wis., 198
Beloit, Wis., 214
Bemidji, Minn., 132
Ben-Hur, 459
Benicia, Calif., 557
Benton, Fort (Mont.), 350, 361
Benton, Thomas Hart, 135, 156, 158–59
Benton County, Iowa, 63
Bent's Fort, Colo., 313
Berea, Ohio, 188
Bering, Vitus, 521, 538
Bering Sea, 512, 513, 515, 518
Berkeley, Calif., 557; University of California at, 549, 559, 566
Berlin-Ichthyosaur Paleontologic State Monument, 379
Bernalillo, N.Mex., 449
Berthold Reservation, Fort (N.D.), 270
Bertrand (steamboat), 76
Bethany College, 239
Bettendorf, Iowa, 65, 70, 76
Beverly Hills, Calif., 555
Bierce, Ambrose, 170
Bierstadt, Albert, 416
Big Arkansas River, 235
Big Bend Dam (S.D.), 295
Big Bend National Park, 504
Big Blue River, 250
Bigelow (Judge Daniel R.) Home, 649
Big Foot, 293
Big Hole (Mont.), 351; National Battlefield, 361
Big Horn Basin (Wyo.), 408
Big Horn Canyon (Wyo.), 419; National Recreation Area, 419
Big Horn Lake (Wyo.), 419
Big Horn Mountains, 402, 406, 415, 419
Big Horn National Forest, 415
Big Horn River, 404, 419
Big Mountain (Mont.), 358
Big Piney, Wyo., 420
Big Sioux River, 288
Big Sky of Montana, 358, 359; Historical Museum, 361
Big Stone City, S.D., 300
Big Sur, 566
Big Thompson River. *See* Colorado–Big Thompson project

Billings, Mont., 355, 360, 362, 363
Billy the Kid, 453, 459, 464
Bily, Frank and Joseph, 74
Bily Clocks, 74
Bingham, George Caleb, 153, 156, 159
Bingham, Hiram, 583
Bingham Canyon Copper Mine, 392–93
Binion's Horseshoe (Las Vegas), 374
Bird Cage Theatre (Tombstone), 443–44
Bishop Hill, Ill., 8, 28
Bishop's Lodge (N.Mex.), 461
Bismarck, N.D., 269, 272, 277–78, 281; Junior College, 278
Bison Gallery (Fargo, N.D.), 276
Bitterroot Mountains, 332
Bizzell (W.B.) Memorial Library, 478
Black Canyon (Ariz.), 440
Blackfoot, Idaho, 341, 343
Blackfoot Indians, 349, 350, 363, 406
Black Hawk (chief), 9, 28, 59, 62, 69, 158
Black Hawk Purchase, 79
Black Hawk State Park, 29
Black Hawk Trail, 28
Black Hawk War, 12, 31, 196, 198, 215
Black Hills: North Dakota, 277; South Dakota, 285 ff., 291, 292, 294, 295–96, 298 ff., 300–2, 304, 351
Black Jack, Battle of, 241
Black Kettle, 350
Black Mesa (Okla.), 470
Black River, 194
Blacks (Negroes): and Arizona, 430; and California, 546; and Colorado, 314, 315; and Hawaii, 581; and Idaho, 331, 332; and Illinois, 3, 14; and Indiana, 37, 41, 42, 46, 53, 54; and Iowa, 61; and Kansas, 222, 224, 242; and Michigan, 87, 90; and Minnesota, 113; and Missouri, 139, 141; and Montana, 349; and Nevada, 369; and New Mexico, 450; and Ohio, 169, 173, 179, 189; and Oklahoma, 471; and Texas, 491; and Utah, 387; and Wisconsin, 196
Black's Beach (Calif.), 563
Bliss, Old Fort (Tex.), 501
Bliss (Fort–N.Mex.) Military Reservation, 459
Bloody Run (Iowa), 72
Bloomfield Hills, Mich., 81, 103
Blooming Prairie, Minn., 118
Bloomington, Ill., 24
Bloomington, Ind., 48
Blossom Music Center (Ohio), 179, 182
Blue, Vida, 72
Blue Grass Region, 166
Blue Hole (Castalia, Ohio), 186
Blue Mounds (Wis.), 212
Blue Mountains, 608, 609, 632, 633
Blue Stem Bowl (Okla.), 476

Bluff, Utah, 396
Board of Trade (Chicago), 15
Bodega Bay (Calif.), 569
Bodega y Quadra, Juan de, 637, 653
Boeing Company, 231, 632, 640, 642
Bohemians: and Kansas, 221; and Ne-
  braska, 248
Bois Blanc Island, 84
Boise, Idaho, 330, 333, 337–38, 341 ff.,
  344; Gallery of Art, 338; State Univer-
  sity, 338
Boise Cascade (company), 620, 622
Boise River, 337
Boise Valley, 331, 337*
Bonanza (TV show), 378–79
Bonanza, Idaho, 341
Bonanzaville (N.D.), 282
Bond Falls (Mich.), 84
Bon Homme, S.D., 289
Bonito Lake (N.Mex.), 461
Bonner Springs, Kans., 236
Bonneville, Benjamin-Louis, 385, 409
Bonneville, Fort (Wyo.), 409
Bonneville, Lake, 393
Bonneville Dam, 615–16, 627, 629, 655
Bonneville Locks, 629
Bonneville Salt Flats, 386, 398
Bonney, William H. *See* Billy the Kid
Boomers, 472
Boone, Daniel, 136, 142, 159–60, 162
Boone, Daniel Morgan (son), 142, 154
Boone, Nathan, 142, 159–60
Boone (Squire) Caverns, 51
Boone County, Nebr., 248
Booth (family), 103
Boot Hill. *See* specific towns
Borah, William E., 334, 344
Borah Peak, 328
Boren, David, 484–85
Borglum, Gutzon, 300, 304
Borgund Stavkirke, 298–99
Bosin, Blackbear, 235
Botanical Center (Des Moines), 80
Bottineau (N.D.) Winter Park, 278
Boulder, Colo., 315, 321, 325, 326
Boulder, Mont., 361
Boulder City, Nev., 379
Boulder Dam. *See* Hoover Dam
Boulder Junction, Wis., 214
Boulder Mountains, 341
Boundary Peak (Nev.), 366
Boundary Waters Canoe Area, 125
Bourgmont, Étienne Venyard, Sieur de,
  241
Bowen, Otis R., 54
Bowie, Jim, 492, 501
Bowling Green University, 183
Boyer River, 58
Boys Town (Nebr.), 256, 264
Bozeman, John M., 357

Bozeman, Mont., 357, 362, 363
Bozeman Trail, 410
Bradley, Omar, 135, 145, 159, 162
Bradley University, 24
Brainerd, Minn., 129
Brancusi, Constantin, 255
Brando, Marlon, 248, 256
Brazon River, 502
Breckenridge ski area (Colo.), 322
Bremerton, Wash., 652
Brewer (C.) and Company, 585
Bridger, Fort (Wyo.), 410
Bridger, Jim, 136, 313, 388, 399, 407
Bridger Bowl (Mont.), 358
Brigham City, Utah, 398
Bright Angel Trail (Grand Canyon), 441
Bristol Bay, 512
British, the. *See* English, the
British Columbia, 639
Britt, Iowa, 77
Britt (Peter) Gardens, 627
Broadmoor (courses—Colorado
  Springs), 321, 323
Broadway Theatre League (Lincoln,
  Nebr.), 255
Broken Boot Gold Mine, 301
Broken Bow, Nebr., 262
Bronxon, Mich., 104
Brookings, Oreg., 627
Brookings, S.D., 303
Brooks, Gwendolyn, 9
Brooks Range, 513
Broughton, William R., 613, 628, 653
Brown, John, 76, 227, 241
Brown County, Ind., 52
Brown County, Minn., 113
Brown County, Wis., 202
Browning, Mont., 363
Browning (Armstrong) Library, 502
Browning (John M.) Museum, 395
Brownlee Dam, 344
Brownsville, Tex., 487, 505
Brownville, Nebr., 259, 260, 262–63
Brown vs. *Board of Education*, 222, 242
Brownwood, Tex., 506
Brueghel, Pieter, 96
Brulé, Étienne, 85–86, 88, 106
Brundage (Avery) Collection, 558
Bryan, William Jennings, 9, 248, 260
Bryant, William Cullen, 605, 613
Bryce Canyon National Park, 397
Buchanan, James, 390, 615
Buchanan County, Mo., 143
Buckingham Fountain (Chicago), 20
Bucyrus, Ohio, 188
Buena Park (Los Angeles), 564
Buffalo, N.Y., 60, 63, 89, 95
Buffalo, Wyo., 411
Buffalo Bill. *See* Cody, William
Buffalo Bill Dam (Wyo.), 416

Buffalo Bill Historical Center, 416
Buffalo Horn (chief), 333, 344
Buffalo River, 127
Buick Motor Company, 98
Bulfinch Harbor. *See* Grays Harbor
Bulgarians, 87
Bull Shoals Lake (Mo.), 138
"Bunyan, Paul," 129
Burbank, Luther, 97, 566
Burke, John, 277
Burke (Thomas) Memorial State Museum, 646
Burlington, Iowa, 77
Burlington Northern Railroad, 647
Burnet, David G., 492
Burnett, Peter, 143
Burton, Ohio, 188
Burton Memorial Tower (Ann Arbor), 98
Burwell, Nebr., 262
Busch Gardens (Calif.), 565
Busch Stadium (St. Louis), 156
Bush, Asabel, 624
Bush, George, 634
Bush Barn Art Center (Salem, Oreg.), 624
Bush House Museum (Salem, Oreg.), 624
Bush Pasture (Salem, Oreg.), 624
Butler (Hugh) Lake (Nebr.), 257
Butler University, 45
Butte, Mont., 352, 356–57

Cable, Mont., 361
Cable Car Barn (San Francisco), 565
Cabrillo, Juan Rodríguez, 546, 556, 569, 613, 628
Cabrillo National Monument, 559
Cache la Poudre River, 312
Cache Valley, 395
Cadillac, Antoine de la Mothe, 88, 94, 106
Caesar's Palace (Las Vegas), 374
Cahokia, Ill., 11, 27, 31
Cahokia Indians, 10
Cahokia Mounds State Park, 27
Cairo, Ill., 7, 20
Calamity Jane, 249, 285, 290, 301, 360, 407
Calapooya Mountains, 608
Calaveras County, Calif., 568
Caldwell, Idaho, 337, 338, 342
Caldwell, Kans., 230
Calhoun, James C., 453
California, 143, 250, 264, 370, 381, 435, 540–70, 612, 614–15, 618; Republic of, 547–48, 569; University of, 554; University of, at Berkeley, 549, 559, 566
California Academy of Sciences, 559
California Fruit Growers' Exchange, 553

California Institute of Technology, 554
California Trail, 415
Call Board Theater (Hollywood), 554
Calumet City, Ill., 15, 36, 38, 42, 46
Calumet-Sag Channel, 16
Cambridge, Ohio, 187
Camelback Mountain (Ariz.), 438
Camino Real, El, 546, 567
Campbell Hill (Ohio), 166
Campus Martius State Memorial Museum, 186
Canada and Canadians, 40, 269–70, 272, 282, 321, 654 (*See also* specific areas); and Alaska, 522, 538 (*See also* specific border areas); and Kansas, 222; and Minnesota, 112; and Oklahoma, 471
Canadian River, 450, 457
Candlestick Park (San Francisco), 559
Cannery (San Francisco), 559
Canton, Ohio, 169, 174, 186–87
Canyon de Chelly National Monument, 442
Canyon of Las Animas Perdidas, 323
Cape Canaveral (Kennedy) (Fla.), 147
Cape Disappointment, 614
Cape Flattery, 653
Cape Girardeau, Mo., 160
Capitol Reef National Park, 397
Capone, Al, 10
Capulin Mountain National Moument, 462
Carbonate Hill (Leadville, Colo.), 326
Carbondale, Ill., 15, 24
Carillon Park (Dayton), 181
Carl Gustaf, King, 222
Carlin Mine (Nev.), 372
Carlsbad, N.Mex., 454
Carlsbad Caverns, 454, 461; National Park, 461, 465
Carlton County, Minn., 116, 134
Carmel, Calif., 566, 568
Carmichael, Hoagy, 33
Carquinez Straits, 557
Carson (mansion—Eureka, Calif.), 566
Carson, Fort (Colo.), 321
Carson, Johnny, 248
Carson, Kit, 136, 313, 376, 381, 407, 429, 431, 453, 462
Carson City, Nev., 366, 371, 375–76, 380
Carson House (Brownville, Nebr.), 260
Carson National Forest, 460
Carson Sink (Nev.), 366
Carson Valley (Nev.), 375
Carter (Amon) Museum of Western Art, 500
Carthage, Mo., 150
Carver, George Washington, 135, 159
Carver, Jonathan, 114, 613, 628
Carver (George Washington) National Monument, 159

Carver's Cave (Minn.), 114
Casa Grande, Ariz., 440; Ruins National Monument, 442
Cascade Falls (Minn.), 170
Cascade Range (Mountains), 605, 606, 608, 609, 617 ff., 626, 628, 631 ff., 639, 644, 651, 655
Cascade River, 110
Case (Francis) Lake (S.D.), 288, 299
Case Western Reserve University, 179
Casper, Wyo., 402, 405, 413, 414–15, 420
Casper Mountain (Wyo.), 415
Cass, Lewis, 88
Cassel, Peter, 112
Castalia, Ohio, 186
Castle & Cooke, 585
Castle Ghost Town (Mont.), 360
Castle Rock (Kans.), 239
Caterpillar Tractor Company, 24
Cather, Willa, 245, 248, 261
Catholics (See also specific nationalities): and California, 546, 547; and Hawaii, 584; and Idaho, 332; and Indiana, 37; and Nevada, 369; and Oregon, 610; and South Dakota, 290; and Utah, 387; and Washington, 635; and Wyoming, 422
Catoosa, Okla., 425
Catron County, N.Mex., 449
Cave-in-Rock (Ill.), 28
Cave of the Mounds (Wis.), 211–12
Cavett, Dick, 248
Cayuga Indians, 482
Cayuse Indians, 615
Cedar Point, Ohio, 184
Cedar Rapids, Iowa, 60, 61, 65, 69, 73; Art Association, 69
Cedar River, 58, 69
Centennial Coliseum (Reno), 375
Center of Science and Industry (Columbus, Ohio), 180
Central Arizona Project, 433, 447
Central City, Colo., 313, 323
Centralia, Wash., 636, 655
Central Lowland, 266, 468
Central Pacific Railroad, 390, 398, 548
Central Plain, 192–94
Central Plateau (Alaska), 513, 515, 516, 518, 528
Central Utah Project, 399
Central Valley (Calif.), 550
Century of Progress Exposition, 32
Century II (Wichita), 234
Cessna (aircraft company), 219, 231
CF&I Steel Corporation, 315, 321
Chadron State Park (Nebr.), 257
Chaffee (Roger B.) Planetarium, 99
Chalet of the Golden Fleece (New Glarus, Wis.), 212
Chama River, 452, 454, 465

Chamberlain, Mount, 513
Chamberlain, S.D., 303
Champaign, Ill., 14, 24
Champlain, Samuel de, 88
Champoeg, Oreg., 654
Chandler, Ariz., 433
Chandler (Dorothy) Pavilion, 554
Channeled Scablands, 647
Chanute, Octave, 24
Chanute, Kans., 238
Chanute Technical Training Display Center, 24
Chapel in the Hills (S.D.), 299
Chapman College, 555
Chardon, Ohio, 188
Chariton County, Mo., 151
Charles L. Wheeler, S.S., 629
Charless, Joseph, 142
Charleston, Ill., 15, 27
Charlevoix, Mich., 87, 102
Charlotte, Mich., 104
Chartres, Fort de (Mo.), 139
Chartres (Fort de—Ill.) State Park, 27, 30
Chávez, César, 447
Chelan, Lake (Wash.), 651
Chelsea, Okla., 473, 484
Cherokee Indians, 471, 472, 481–82, 484
Cherokee Outlet (Okla.), 473
Cherry Creek (Colo.), 312, 316
Cherry Hills Country Club (Denver), 321
Chevrolet factory, 98, 106
Cheyenne, Wyo., 319, 325, 402, 405, 407, 408, 414, 420, 422, 423
Cheyenne Indians, 251, 269, 271, 292, 311, 349 ff., 355, 361, 364, 406
Cheyenne Northern Railway, 411
Cheyenne River, 286, 288, 289, 291–92, 404
Chicago, Ill., 3, 6, 8, 9, 11–12 ff., 18, 20–23, 25, 27, 29, 31, 32, 89, 199, 408; Art Institute, 21, 23; Historical Society, 23; Lyric Opera, 23; Public Library, 21; Sanitary and Ship Canal, 31; Symphony, 3, 23; University of, 14, 21, 22, 23, 24
Chicago Creek (S.D.), 313, 325
Chicago River, 10, 11, 21, 31
Chicanos, 170, 490, 545
Chickasaw Indians, 471, 472, 482, 484, 490
Chihuahua Trail, 458
Children's Museum (Detroit), 96
Chilkat Indians, 532, 537
Chilkoot Pass, 517, 532
Chillicothe, Ohio, 171, 172
Chimney Rock (Nebr.), 257, 259
China Basin (San Francisco), 557

Chinese (and Chinatowns): and Arizona, 430; and California, 545, 546, 548, 555, 558, 561, 567; and Hawaii, 581, 601, 603; and Michigan, 95; and Missouri, 140; and New Mexico, 450; and Oklahoma, 471; and Oregon, 611–12; and Utah, 387; and Washington, 635
Chinese Exclusion Act, 611
Chinook, Mont., 361
Chinook Indians, 621
Chippewa Indians, 85, 192, 195, 196, 209, 210, 265, 269 ff., 349; and Minnesota, 107, 111, 115, 128, 133
Chippewa River, 194
Chiricahua National Monument, 442
Chisholm, Minn., 128
Chisholm Trail, 219, 229, 500
Choctaw Indians, 467, 471, 472, 479, 484, 490
Chouart, Médart. See Groseilliers, Médart Chouart, Sieur de
Chouteau, Auguste, 141, 152, 153, 162
Chrysler Corporation, 81, 91
Chugach National Forest, 528
Chukchi Sea, 512
Churchill, Sir Winston, 163
Church of One Tree. See One Tree, Church of (and similar references)
Cibola National Forest, 460
Cimarron River, 220
Cincinnati, Ohio, 165, 167, 168, 172 ff., 179–80, 183, 188, 189; Ballet, 180; Reds, 183; Symphony, 180; University of, 180
Circle Theater (Hollywood), 554
Circleville, Ohio, 188
Circus Circus (Las Vegas), 374
Circus World Museum (Baraboo, Wis.), 212–13
City of Refuge (Hawaii), 579, 598
City Park (Denver), 320, 323
Civic Center. See specific city
Civilian Conservation Corps, 334
Civil War: Arizona and, 431; California and, 548; Illinois and, 12–13; Indiana and, 41–42; Iowa and, 63–64; Kansas and, 228, 242; Michigan and, 89; Minnesota and, 115; Missouri and, 144; New Mexico and, 453, 465; Ohio and, 172, 189; Oklahoma and, 472; Texas and, 493; Utah and, 390; Wisconsin and, 198
Clackamas County, Oreg., 611, 621
Clanton family, 443
Clare, Mich., 104
Claremore, Okla., 481, 482
Clark, Dick, 65, 80
Clark, George Rogers, 11, 28, 31
Clark, Georgia Neese, 222
Clark, Mo., 159

Clark, William, 142, 159, 226. See also Lewis and Clark
Clark, William A. (copper king), 351–52, 357
Clark College (Dubuque), 69
Clark County, Ind., 44
Clark County, Kans., 239
Clark County, Wash., 621
Clark National Forest (Mo.), 157
Clarksville, Mo., 150
Clatsop, Fort (Oreg.), 614, 638
Clatsop Indians, 614
Clayton County, Iowa, 61
Clear Lake City, Tex., 495, 498
Clearwater River, 328–30, 332
Clearwater Valley, 629
Cleaveland, Moses, 177
Clemens, Orion, 376
Clemens, Samuel. See Twain, Mark
Cleveland, Grover, 586
Cleveland, Ohio, 165, 167, 169, 172 ff., 177–79, 183, 189, 190; Barons, 183; Browns, 183; Cavaliers, 183; Crusaders, 183; Health Museum, 178–79; Indians, 183, 440; Playhouse, 177, 179; Symphony, 177, 179, 182; Zoo, 178
Clinton, Iowa, 65, 75–76, 77
Clinton, Mo., 138
Clinton, Okla., 482
Clinton Inn (Greenfield Village), 97
Clinton-Sherman Air Force Base, 468
Cloquet, Minn., 118
Cloudcraft Ski Area (N.Mex.), 460
Cloud Peak (Wyo.), 403
Coastal Plain. See specific states
Coast Range (Oreg.), 608
Coast Ranges, 512, 513, 531, 542. See also specific ranges
Cobo Hall (Detroit), 95
Cochise, 431
Coconino National Forest, 441
Cody, William ("Buffalo Bill"), 75, 229, 259, 407, 416
Cody, Wyo., 416, 420
Cody Park (North Platte, Nebr.), 262
Coeur d'Alene, Idaho, 334, 339, 344
Coeur d'Alene, Lake, 339
Coeur d'Alene Indians, 331, 332
Coffeyville, Kans., 220
Coleman (camping equipment), 234
Coleman, Tex., 506
Colfax County, Nebr., 248
Collegeville, Ind., 37
Collin County, Tex., 498
Collins, Casper, 415
Colman, Norman J., 149
Coloma, Calif., 567
Colorado, 250, 308–26, 453, 456–57; University of, 320, 321, 325

Colorado–Big Thompson project, 316–17, 326
Colorado College, 325
Colorado Plateau, 386, 428, 440, 450
Colorado River, 379, 381, 396, 398, 404, 428–29, 433, 435, 439, 441, 443, 446, 447, 542–43, 546, 548, 551 (*See also* Colorado–Big Thompson project); Aqueduct, 551
Colorado Springs, Colo., 310, 314, 320–21 ff., 326
Colorado State Fairgrounds, 321
Colorado State Hospital, 321
Colorado State University, 321
Colorado Territory, 314, 325, 453
Colorado Women's College, 320
Colter, John, 350, 406, 422
Colt Tower (San Francisco), 557
Columbia (ship), 637
Columbia, Mo., 138, 149, 155 ff., 161, 163
Columbia Basin, 632, 633, 643, 651; Project, 655
Columbia Exposition (Chicago), 408
Columbia Falls, Mont., 364
Columbia Glacier, 514
Columbia Heights, Minn., 118
Columbian (newspaper), 654
Columbiana County, Ohio, 189
Columbia Plateau, 328, 336, 366
Columbia Rediviva (ship), 637
Columbia River, 346, 404, 605, 606, 608–9, 610, 613 ff., 623, 625, 627, 628, 631, 633, 634, 637, 638, 641 ff., 651, 653, 655
Columbia State Historic Park, 566
Columbia Valley, 618, 654
Columbus, Christopher, 180
Columbus, Ohio, 165, 169, 172, 174, 180–81, 183; Seals, 183
Comanche County, Kans., 238–39
Comanche Indians, 311, 452, 490
Commencement Bay, 654
Community Playhouse (Lincoln, Nebr.), 255
Como Bluffs (Wyo.), 404
Como Park Zoo (St. Paul, Minn.), 122
Comstock Lode (Nev.), 370, 371, 378, 381
Concordia Senior College, 47
Concordia Theological Seminary, 153
Conejos River, 325
Congregationalists, 583–84
Congress of Industrial Organizations (CIO), 14
Connally, John B., 494
Connecticut, 171
Connecticut Land Company, 177
Contemporary Art, Museum of (Chicago), 21

Continental Divide, 310, 315, 317, 320, 346, 403, 404, 450
Convention Center (Cleveland), 177
Cook, James, 538, 571, 577, 580, 582–83, 598, 603, 613, 637, 653
Cooke, Jay, 124
Cooke City, Mont., 362
Cooke County, Minn., 128
Cook Inlet, 514, 521, 523, 525, 530, 538, 539
Coors (brewery), 315
Copperheads, 172
Copper King Mansion, 357
Copper Mountain (Colo.), 322
Copper River, 523
Copper River Railroad, 538
Cordova, Alaska, 514, 531
Cornishmen, 86
Corn Palace (Mitchell, S.D.), 302
Corn Stock Theater (Peoria, Ill.), 24
Coronado, Francisco Vásquez de, 225, 241, 264, 430, 446, 452, 465, 507
Corot, Jean Baptiste Camille, 180
Corpus Christi, Tex., 497, 501–2, 503, 506
Corvallis, Oreg., 625
Corydon, Ind., 42, 45
Costeau, Jacques, 564
Cotton Bowl (Dallas), 499, 505
Couch, John, 621
Couderay, Wis., 196
Council Bluffs, Iowa, 66, 70–71, 76
Courbet, Gustave, 68
Courthouse Rock (Nebr.), 259
Coushatta Indians, 490, 505
Couzins, Phoebe, 158
Cow Hollow (Calif.), 558
Cowles (Cheney) Memorial Museum, 648
Cox, George B., 172
Crabtree Corners (Jackson, Wyo.), 417
Cranbrook Foundation (Mich.), 103
Crane, Hart, 170
Crater Lake (Oreg.), 626; National Park, 626
Craters of the Moon National Monument, 341
Crawford County, Ind., 36
Crawford (Frederick C.) Museum, 178
Crazy Horse (chief), 251, 264, 285, 292, 301, 351
Crazy Horse Campground (Jacksonville, Ill.), 3
Cree Indians, 349
Creek Indians, 471 ff., 477, 484
Crerar (John) Library (Chicago), 23
Cresco, Iowa, 78
Crested Butte ski area (Colo.), 322
Crève Coeur, Fort (Ill.), 10
Crimean War, 522

Cripple Creek, Colo., 313, 320
Crocker (E. B.) Art Gallery, 561
Crocker-Citizen Plaza (Los Angeles), 555
Crockett, Davy, 492, 501
Crockett (Davy) National Forest, 503
Crook, George, 351, 406
Crooksville, Ohio, 188
Crosby, Bing, 648, 649
Crosby House (Olympia), 649
Crow Indian Reservation (Mont.), 355, 361
Crow Indians, 349, 350, 355, 406, 422
Crown Zellerbach, 620
Crow Wing River, 110
Cuba. See Spanish-American War
Cultural Arts Center (Las Vegas), 382
Cumberland foothills, 48
Cumbres & Toltec Railroad, 323
Curtis, Charles, 224, 242
Cushing, Okla., 475
Custer, George Armstrong, 238, 281, 285, 292, 303, 304, 350, 351, 355, 361, 363, 364, 406, 416
Custer, Idaho, 341
Custer Battlefield National Monument, 355, 361, 363
Custer State Park (S.D.), 296, 300
Cutler, Lyman A., 638–39
Crystal Mountain (Wash.), 650
Crystal Palace Saloon (Tombstone), 443
Cuyahoga Falls, Ohio, 182
Cuyahoga River, 166, 178
Cuyuna Range (Minn.), 113, 116, 119, 133
Czechs: and Illinois, 3, 9; and Iowa, 60, 63, 74–75; and Kansas, 222; and Nebraska, 248, 262; and Oklahoma, 471, 482; and South Dakota, 290, 303; and Texas, 491; and Wisconsin, 206

Dairymen's Association (Wis.), 201, 215
Dakota Indians, 195, 289
Dakotas, the, 269–70 ff. See also Dakota Territory; North Dakota; South Dakota
Dakota Territory, 272, 284, 289, 293, 304. See also Dakotas, the
Dakota Zoo (Bismarck), 278
Daley, Richard J., 32
Dali, Salvador, 178
Dali Museum, 178
Dallas, Tex., 491, 494, 498–99, 505, 506, 508; Aquarium, 499; Civic Opera, 499; Convention Center, 499; –Fort Worth Regional Airport, 499; Garden Center, 499; Health and Science Museum, 499; Symphony, 498
Dallas County, Tex., 498
Daly, Marcus, 351–52

Danbury, Wis., 195
Danes: and California, 568; and Iowa, 63; and Michigan, 104; and Minnesota, 112, 115; and South Dakota, 290, 303; and Texas, 491; and Wisconsin, 206, 213
Danville, Ill., 17, 19
Daughters of the American Revolution (DAR), 27
Daumier, Honoré, 68
Davenport, George, 70
Davenport, Iowa, 24, 28, 63, 70
Davies, Theodore H., 585
Dávila, Augustin, 560
Davis, Jefferson, 12, 198
Davis (J. M.) Gun Collection, 481
Davis (Julia) Park (Boise), 338
Dawes Commission, 473
Dawson, Minn., 118
Dayton, Ohio, 165, 169, 172 ff., 181, 189; University of, 183
Deadwood, S.D., 285, 290, 297, 301, 303
Deadwood Dick, 285
Deadwood Gulch, 301
Dearborn, Fort (Ill.), 11, 31
Dearborn, Mich., 81, 87, 89, 90, 96–97, 104, 106
"Death's Door," 209
Death Valley, 541, 543, 544; National Monument, 378
Debs, Eugene, 14
Decatur, Ill., 17
Decatur County, Iowa, 60
Decatur County, Kans., 229, 242
Decorah, Iowa, 59, 77
Deere, John, 15–16, 28, 65
Deere (John) Company, 65, 69
Deer Flat National Wildlife Refuge, 338
Deerlodge National Forest, 357
Deer Mountain (S.D.), 299–300
Defense Depot Ogden (Utah), 395
Defiance, Mo., 159–60
De Kalb, Ill., 15
DeLamar, Idaho, 341
Delaware Indians, 38, 168, 170, 402
DeLin, Nicholas, 654
Dells, the (See also Wisconsin Dells): Illinois, 25
Delmar, Calif., 568
Deming, N.Mex., 461
Denali, Camp (Alaska), 535
Denny pioneer party, 654
Denton County, Tex., 498
Denver, Colo., 310, 312, 314 ff., 318–20, 321, 323, 325, 326; Art Museum, 319; Broncos, 321; City and County Building, 318; Community College, 320; Museum of Natural History, 320, 323; Nuggets, 321; Public Library, 319; University of, 320

Denver and Pacific Railroad, 325
Denver & Rio Grande Railroad, 319–20, 323
Denver-Julesburg Basin, 317
Descanso Gardens (La Canada, Calif.), 564
"Descent of the Holy Spirit," 49
Deschutes National Forest, 609, 626
Deschutes River, 608
Deseret, State of, 389, 399
Desert Botanical Garden (Phoenix), 437–38
Desert Inn (Las Vegas), 374
De Smet, Pierre Jean, 410, 422
Des Moines, Iowa, 59, 61, 65, 66, 67–69, 72, 77, 80; Art Center, 68; Capitols, 72
Des Moines River, 56–58, 69–70
De Soto, Hernando, 507
De Soto National Wildlife Refuge, 76
Des Plaines River, 10
Detroit, Mich., 81, 82, 87 ff., 94–97, 100, 103, 106; City-County Building, 95; Symphony Orchestra, 95; University of, 100; Zoo, 96
Detroit River, 84, 94, 95, 96
Devils Lake, N.D., 274, 278
Devils Lake (N.D. lake), 266, 270, 281
Devils Tower (Wyo.), 404; National Monument, 402, 423
Dewey, George, 145
Dewey, Idaho, 341
DEW Line, 517
Dexter, Kans., 233
De Young Museum (San Francisco), 558
Diamond, Mo., 159
Diamond Head, 575, 596
Diamond Peak (Oreg.), 626
Dickens, Charles, 8
Dickinson, N.D., 274, 283
Dickson Mounds (Ill.), 28
Dillingham, Alaska, 536
Dinosaur National Monument (Utah), 397
Dinosaur Park (S.D.), 298
Discovery (sloop), 577
Discovery Basin (Mont.), 358
Disney, Walt, 563
Disneyland, 563–64
Dissected Till Plains, 56, 286
Distant Early Warning System, 517
Dixon, Ill., 20
Doane, Gustavus, 409
Dobberstein, Paul, 75
Dodge, Grenville M., 71
Dodge, Henry, 142
Dodge City, Kans., 219, 225, 230, 237–38, 241
Dole, James D., 592

Dole, Robert, 224, 243
Dole, Sanford B., 586, 587, 603
Dole Company, 592, 599
Dolores, Mission (Calif.), 556, 559
Domínguez, Francisco Atanasio, 325, 388
Dona Ana County, N.Mex., 456
Donnelly, Phil, 146
Donner Summit, 563
Door County, Wis., 209
Dos Passos, John, 9
Doty, James Duane, 204
Douglas (British trader), 637
Douglas, Alaska, 533
Douglas, Ariz., 440
Douglas, Oreg., 618
Douglas, Stephen A., 9, 12–13, 27, 31, 70
Drake, Sir Francis, 546, 556, 569, 613, 628, 653
Drayton, N.D., 274
Dreiser, Theodore, 33, 47
Dresser, Paul, 33, 47
Drummond, Mont., 360, 362
Drumright, Okla., 482
Dubrovnik Festival Orchestra, 256
Dubuque, Iowa, 62, 69–70; University of, 69
Dubuque, Julien, 62, 69, 79
Dubuque County, Iowa, 69
Dull Knife, 406
Duluth, Daniel Greysolon, Sieur, 111, 114, 133
Duluth, Minn., 116, 118, 123–24, 132
Duncan, Okla., 475
Duncan Gardens (Spokane), 648
Dunes, the (Las Vegas), 374
Dunn County, Wis., 202
Du Quoin, Ill., 29
Durango, Colo., 323
Durant, W. C., 91
Dust Bowl, 232, 242, 474, 476
Dutch, the (and Holland): and Iowa, 55, 59–60, 63, 76–77; and Michigan, 86, 103, 104; and South Dakota, 290
Du Tisne, Claude, 225, 241
Duveen Collection (Madison, Wis.), 205
Dvořák, Anton, 74
Dyche Museum (Lawrence, Kans.), 236–37

Eagle, Wis., 216
Eagle Creek (N.Mex.), 461
Eagle Gap Wilderness Area, 625
Eagle Nest Lake (N.Mex.), 461
Eagle River, Wis., 214
Earhart, Amelia, 222
Earp, Wyatt, 9, 55, 60, 75, 230, 234, 443
Earp brothers, 443
East Amana, Iowa, 73
East Chicago, Ind., 37, 42, 46
Eastern Interior Basin, 19

Eastern Washington State College, 648
East Lansing, Mich., 97
Eastman Kodak, 186, 315
East Nishnabotna River, 58
East Portland, Oreg., 621
East St. Louis, Ill., 6, 16–17, 27
East Texas (oil field), 496
East-West Center (Hawaii), 597
Eau Claire, Wis., 210
Eberhart, Mignon, 248
Ecola State Park (Oreg.), 626
Edgecumbe, Mount, 532
Edison, Thomas A., 96–97, 170, 187
Edwardsville, Ill., 24
Eel River, 36
Effie Afton (steamboat), 70
Effigy Mounds National Monument, 74
Egg Harbor, Wis., 209
Eisenhower, Dwight D., 223, 248, 494, 524, 549
Eisenhower Center (Abilene), 223, 238
Eisenhower Tunnel, 320, 326
Elbert, Mount (Colo.), 309
El Caney, Mexico, 145
Eldon, Iowa, 75
El Dorado, Kans., 233
Eleanore (ship), 603
Elkhart, Ind., 42–43
Elkhorn, Mont., 361
Elkhorn Ranch (N.D.), 280
Elko, Nev., 380
Elko County, Nev., 373
Ellensburg, Wash., 640, 652
Ellis County, Tex., 498
Ellison Bay, Wis., 209
Ellsworth, Kans., 230
Elmendorf Field (Alaska), 529
El Paso, Tex., 453, 487, 489, 490, 501, 505, 507, 508
El Paso del Norte, 453
El Reno, Okla., 475
El Vado Reservoir (N.Mex.), 461
Ely, Minn., 128
Ely, Nev., 371, 379, 380
Elyria, Ohio, 174
Embarcadero (San Francisco), 557, 566
Emma, Queen, 586
Emmet, Robert, 76
Emmetsburg, Iowa, 76
Emporia *Gazette*, 224
Enabling Act, 143
Encanto Park (Phoenix), 437
Encanto Queen (stern-wheeler), 437
Engineers, Army Corps of, 475
English, the (and England; the British) (*See also* specific wars): and Alaska, 521; and California, 556; and Colorado, 313; and Hawaii, 582–83, 585, 596, 603; and Idaho, 331; and Illinois, 8, 11, 31; and Indiana, 38, 40–41, 53;
and Kansas, 226; and Michigan, 81–82, 86, 88, 94, 95, 106; and Minnesota, 112, 114–15, 133; and Missouri, 140, 152, 154, 162; and Montana, 350; and Nebraska, 248; and Nevada, 369; and Ohio, 168, 171, 189; and Oklahoma, 471; and Oregon, 613, 614, 628, 629; and Washington, 634, 636, 637–39, 653–54, 655; and Wisconsin, 196, 197, 205–6, 207, 215; and Wyoming, 408, 409
Enid, Okla., 475
Enlarged Homestead Act, 352
Ephraim, Wis., 209, 213
Episcopalians, 290
Erie, Lake, 81, 82, 84, 165 ff., 170 ff., 175, 178, 181, 183–84, 185, 188, 189, 207
Erie and Kalamazoo Railroad, 172
Erie Canal, 12, 81, 82, 86, 89, 95, 106, 206
Erie Indians, 170
Erieview project (Cleveland), 177
Escalante, Silvestre Vélez de, 325, 388
Escanaba River, 84
Eskimos, 512, 517, 518, 527, 534, 536, 539
Esterville, Iowa, 78
Eufaula, Lake (Okla.), 484
Eugene, Oreg., 608, 616, 623–24, 625
Eureka, Calif., 550, 566
Eureka County, Nev., 372
Evans, Ron, 225, 243
Evanston, Ill., 22, 23
Evanston, Wyo., 420
Evansville, Ind., 39, 43, 47
Everett, Wash., 636, 648, 653
Ewa Plantation (Hawaii), 584
Exact (schooner), 654
Expo '74 (Spokane), 655, 674
Exposition Park (Los Angeles), 554
Exxon Nuclear, 642

Fairbanks, Alaska, 514, 517, 523, 524, 529, 531, 532–34, 536, 537, 539
Fairchild State Forest (Tex.), 503
Fair Lane (house–Dearborn), 97
Fair Park (Dallas), 499
Fairview (Lincoln, Nebr.), 259–60
Fall, Albert, 413
Fallen Timbers, Battle of, 40, 46, 171, 185, 189
Fallon, Nev., 380
Fargo, N.D., 271, 273, 276, 282, 283; Gallery, 276; –Moorhead Civic Opera, 276; –Moorhead Community Theater, 276; –Moorhead Symphony, 276
Fargo, William George, 276
Faribault, Jean Baptiste, 130
Farm Bureau Federation, 64

Farmer Labor Party, 116
Farmers' Union, 64
Farrell, James T., 9
Far West, 509–655
Fayette, N.Y., 383
Federal Center (Denver), 319
Ferguson, Miriam A., 507
Fermi, Enrico, 14
Fern Grotto (Hawaii), 599
Ferrelo, Bartolome, 546, 613, 628
Ferry, Elisha P., 639
Fetterman Massacre, 410, 419
Field, Eugene, 158
Field Museum of Natural History (Chicago), 22
Field's, Marshall, 21
Filipinos (and Philippines), 546, 581, 582, 593
Fillmore, Millard, 638
Fine Arts Museum. See specific city
Finns: and Michigan, 86, 101; and Minnesota, 112, 113, 115; and Oregon, 611; and South Dakota, 290; and Wisconsin, 196; and Wyoming, 407
Firestone Company, 66, 182
Fisher Body Division, 98, 106
Fisherman's Wharf (San Francisco), 557, 559, 565
Fisher Theatre (Detroit), 100
Fitzgerald, F. Scott, 122
Fitzsimons Army Medical Center, 319
Five Channels Dam (Mich.), 100
Five Civilized Tribes, 471, 472, 484
Flagstaff, Ariz., 428, 439–40, 445
Flaming Gorge Dam (Utah), 399
Flaming Gorge Lake (Utah), 396
Flaming Gorge Recreation Area, 419
Flamingo (Las Vegas), 374
Flanagan, Edward J., 256, 264
Flandreau, S.D., 289
Flathead Indians, 349, 350, 406
Flathead Lake (Mont.), 359–60
Fleet (Reuben H.) Space Theater, 560
Fleishacker Zoo (San Francisco), 559
Flint, Mich., 82, 87, 90, 91, 98–99, 106; Community Junior College, 99
Flint Hills (Kans.), 238
Florence, Oreg., 625 ff.
Florida, 141; Treaty of, 613
Florida, Mo., 159, 162
Floyd, Charles, 62, 71
Floyd River, 58
Fodor, Eugene, 256
Folsom, N.Mex., 452
Folsom man, 452
Fonda, Henry, 248, 256
Fond du Lac County, Wis., 202
Fontainebleau, Treaty of, 79
Fontana, Calif., 553
Foraker, Mount, 513

Ford, Gerald R., 92, 99, 224
Ford, Henry, 82, 89, 91, 95 ff., 106
Ford (Henry and Edsel) Auditorium, 95
Ford Motor Company, 81, 82, 89, 91, 96, 106
Ford (Henry) Museum, 96, 97
Foreign Film Society (Lincoln, Nebr.), 255
Forest Grove, Oreg., 627
Forest Park (St. Louis), 153, 157
Forest Service, U. S., 358
Forsberg House (Fargo, N.D.), 276
Fort Benton, Mont., 361, 363
Fort Calhoun, Nebr., 257
Fort Davis, Tex., 504
Fort Hall, Idaho, 342. See also Hall, Fort
Fort Madison, Iowa, 77. See also Madison, Fort (Iowa)
Fort Peck, Mont., 363; Dam and Reservoir, 362, 364
Fort Pierre, S.D. See Tecumseh, Fort (S.D.)
Fort Ransom (ski area—N.D.), 278
Forts. See by name
Fort Scott, Kans., 224
Fort Wayne, Ind., 39, 43, 46–47, 52
Fort Worth, Tex., 495, 498, 499–500; Art Center, 500; Museum of Science and History, 504
Fort Wright College of the Holy Names, 648
Fort Yukon, Alaska, 515, 522, 533, 534, 537, 538
Fossil Butte National Monument, 404–5
Foster, Stephen, 97
Fox Indians, 28, 31, 59 ff., 69, 70, 77, 79, 197, 209, 215, 482
Fox River, 8, 194, 195, 197, 206, 215
France. See French, the
Franciscans, 443, 546, 550. See also specific persons
Francis Case, Lake. See Case (Francis) Lake
Frankenmuth, Mich., 86, 104
Franklin, Mo., 140
Franklin County, Wash., 643
Fraser River, 655
Frazier, Lynn J., 273
Fredericktown, Mo., 150
Freeman, Daniel, 250
Freeman, S.D., 303
Freeport, Ill., 27
Freeport, Tex., 505
Frémont, John C., 140, 381, 388, 409, 422, 556, 606
Fremont, Mich., 92
Fremont Lake (Wyo.), 404, 421
Frémont National Forest, 609, 626
Fremont Peak (Wyo.), 422

French, the (France) (*See also* French and Indian War): and Alaska, 521; and Colorado, 321; and Hawaii, 585, 603; and Idaho, 331; and Illinois, 4, 10–11, 12, 27–28, 30, 31; and Indiana, 38, 39–40, 53; and Iowa, 59, 61–62, 63, 79; and Kansas, 225–26; and Michigan, 81, 85–86, 87–88, 94–95, 101, 106; and Minnesota, 107, 111, 112, 114, 121, 127, 133; and Missouri, 139, 140–41, 148, 152, 153, 160, 162; and Montana, 349; and Nebraska, 248, 249, 264; and North Dakota, 269, 271, 272, 284; and Ohio, 168, 170–71; and Oklahoma, 471, 483; and South Dakota, 289, 291, 302, 304; and Texas, 491, 492, 498, 507; and Wisconsin, 195, 197, 203, 205, 209, 210, 215; and Wyoming, 409
French and Indian War: Illinois and, 11, 31; Indiana and, 40, 53; Michigan and, 88, 106; Minnesota and, 114; Ohio and, 168, 189; Wisconsin and, 215
French Courthouse (Cahokia, Ill.), 27
French Creek (Iowa), 72
French Creek, S.D., 295
French Lick, Ind., 50
French Prairie (Oreg.), 629
Friends University, 234
Frijoles Canyon, 462
Frontenac, Count Louis de, 85
Frontier, the (Las Vegas), 374
Frost, Robert, 97
Fryer Hill (Leadville, Colo.), 326
Fryingpan-Arkansas project, 317, 326
Fuca, Juan de, 636–37, 653
Fuca Strait. *See* Juan de Fuca Strait
Fulton, Frank, 145
Fulton, Mo., 163
Fur Rendezvous, 422

Gabbs, Nev., 379
Gable, Clark, 170
Gadsden Purchase, 431, 446, 453, 465
Gage Park (Topeka), 235
Gainsborough, Thomas, 180
Galena, Ill., 19, 29, 30
Galesburg, Ill., 27
Gallatin National Forest (Mont.), 357
Gallatin Valley (Mont.), 357
Gallipolis, Ohio, 167
"Galloping Gertie" (bridge), 648
Gallup, N.Mex., 462, 463
Galveston, Tex., 502, 503
Galveston Island, 502
Gannett (mountain—Wyo.), 403
Gann Valley, S.D., 288
Garden City, Kans., 222
Garden of the Gods (Ill.), 25
Garfield, James A., 170, 187

Garfield Peak (Oreg.), 626
Garrett Biblical Institute, 23
Garrison Dam (N.D.), 273, 279, 284
Garst Museum (Greenville, Ohio), 187
Gary, Ind., 37, 39, 42, 46, 50, 53, 54
Gastineau Channel, 531
Gateway Arch (St. Louis), 158, 163
Gavins Point Dam (S.D.), 295
Gavin's Point National Aquarium, 298
Gaylord, Kans., 223
Gemini spacecraft, 8, 187, 498
General Mills, 122
General Motors, 81, 91, 98; Technical Center, 95
"General Sherman" (sequoia), 551–52
General Tire and Rubber, 182
Genoa, Nev., 370, 381
Geodetic Center, 238
Geographical Center, 238
George M. Verity (riverboat), 75
George III, 628, 653
Georgia, Strait of, 637
Gering, Nebr., 262
Germans: and California, 545; and Colorado, 313; and Hawaii, 581; and Illinois, 3, 8, 9; and Indiana, 38, 49; and Iowa, 56, 59, 60, 63, 65, 70, 73, 77; and Kansas, 221–22; and Michigan, 86, 87, 95, 104; and Minnesota, 112–13, 115, 131; and Missouri, 140, 152, 153, 161; and Montana, 349; and North Dakota, 265, 269; and Ohio, 168, 169, 179, 180; and Oklahoma, 471; and Oregon, 611; and South Dakota, 290, 293 (*See also* specific towns); and Texas, 491; and Washington, 635; and Wisconsin, 191, 192, 195, 196, 202, 203, 206, 207; and Wyoming, 407, 421
German Village (Columbus, Ohio), 180
Geronimo, 429, 431, 446, 454, 465
Getty (J. Paul) Museum, 554, 564
Ghent, Treaty of, 142
"Ghost Dance," 292–93
Giant (film), 487
Giant City State Park, 25
Gibson, Fort (Okla.), 484
Gila Cliff Dwellings National Monument, 463
Gila National Forest, 460
Gila River, 431, 450
Gila Trail, 458
Gilcrease Institute (Tulsa), 480–81
Gillette, Wyo., 408, 420
Gills Rock, Wis., 209
Gilt Edge, Mont., 361
Ginaca machine, 592
Girl Scouts, 402
Glacier Bay National Monument, 532, 535

Glacier National Park, 353, 358, 359, 364
Glasgow, Mont., 362
Glen Canyon Dam (Utah), 399
Glendive, Mont., 362
Glen Haven, Mich., 103
Glenn, John, 187
Glen Ullin, N.D., 274
Glenville, Calif., 568
Globe, Ariz., 445
Gogebic Range, 93, 192
Gold Creek (Mont.), 350, 364
Golden, Colo., 315
Golden Gate (Calif.), 542, 556
Golden Gate Bridge, 557, 570
Golden Gate Club (Las Vegas); 374
Golden Gate International Exposition, 570
Golden Gate Park (San Francisco), 558
Golden Nugget (Las Vegas), 374
Golden Spike Historical Site, 398
Goldwater, Barry, 447
Gompers, Samuel, 612
Gonzaga University, 648
Goodman, Benny, 9
Goodman Theater (Chicago), 21
Goodrich, Benjamin, 182, 189
Goodrich, B. F. (company), 182
Goodyear Tire and Rubber, 182, 186, 235
Gordon, Nebr., 261
Gordon Park (Cleveland), 178
Gosiute Indians, 369, 387
Gothenberg, Nebr., 259
Governor's Old Mansion (Helena, Mont.), 356
Gowdy, Curt, 408
Gowdy State Park, 408
Goya, Francisco de, 68, 180
Grace Cathedral (San Francisco), 559
Grand Canyon, 428, 440, 441–42; National Park, 441–42
Grand Coulee Dam, 632, 636, 640, 643, 651, 655
Granddad Bluff (Wis.), 207
Grand Detour, Ill., 16, 28
Grand Forks, N.D., 271, 273, 276–77, 278; Air Force Base, 276–77
Grand Huron River, 166
Grand Island, Nebr., 260–61
Grand Portage, Mich., 101
Grand Portage, Minn., 128; Indian Reservation, 128
Grand Prairie, Tex., 498
Grand Rapids, Mich., 82, 87, 91 ff., 99
Grand River: Michigan, 84; South Dakota, 288
Grand Teton Range, 403
Grand Teton National Park, 402, 403, 405, 416, 418, 423

Grange, the, 63, 79
Grangeville, Idaho, 342
Grant, Ulysses S., 29, 135, 158, 170, 187, 314
Grant County, Wash., 643
Grant County, Wis., 202
Grant Park (Chicago), 20
Grapes of Wrath, The, 476
Grasshopper Creek (Mont.), 350
Grasshopper Glacier, 362
Gratiot County, Mich., 94
Gray, Robert, 613, 628, 637, 653
Grays Harbor, 650, 653
Great Artists Concerts (Omaha), 256
Great Basin (See also Basin and Range Region): California, 542; Nevada, 366, 381
Great Bear (ski area—S.D.), 300
Great Britain. See English, the
Great Cathedral (St. Louis), 152
Great Central Plain. See Great Plains
Great Dust Bowl. See Dust Bowl
Great Falls, Mont., 349
Great Lakes, 16, 36, 81, 82, 84, 85, 88, 93, 99 ff., 177. See also specific lakes
"Great Lakes" (Iowa), 71–72
Great Lakes Plains, 34, 84, 166, 192
Great Northern Railroad, 272, 278, 639
Great North Woods (Wis.), 211
Great Plains, 249, 266, 268, 274, 286, 346, 349, 403, 450, 468, 488, 489
Great Salt Lake, 383, 384, 388, 389, 393, 394, 399
Great Salt Lake Basin, 383
Great Salt Lake Desert, 384–86
Greco, El, 182
Greeks: and Illinois, 9; and Michigan, 95, 104; and Ohio, 169; and Oklahoma, 472; and Texas, 491; and Wyoming, 407
Greek Theater (Los Angeles), 564
Greeley, Colo., 317
Greeley County, Nebr., 248
Green Bay, Wis., 197, 205–6, 209; Packer Hall of Fame, 206; Packers, 206, 208
Green Bay (body of water), 195, 209, 215
Green County, Wisconsin, 212, 213
Greenfield Village, Mich., 96–97, 104
Green River (river), 396, 398, 404, 409, 420
Green River, Utah, 396
Green River, Wyo., 409
Greensburg, Ind., 37
Greenville, Mich., 104
Greenville, Ohio, 187
Gregori, Luigi, 46
Gregory, John, 313, 325
Grenville, Point (Wash.), 637, 653

Gresham, Oreg., 622
Greving, Louis, 75
Grey, Zane, 170
Greybull, Wyo., 402, 417–18
Greysolon, Daniel. *See* Duluth, Daniel
     Greysolon, Sieur
Griffen, Charles J., 638
Griffith Park (Los Angeles), 554, 564
Grigware, Edward T., 416
Grindstone Lake (Wis.), 196
Groseilliers, Médart Chouart, Sieur de,
     111, 114, 133, 197
Grosse Isle (Mich.), 84
Grosse Pointe, Mich., 97
Gros Ventre Mountains, 403, 405
Gros Ventre River, 405
Grotto of Lourdes (Notre Dame Univer-
     sity), 46
Grotto of the Redemption (West Bend,
     Iowa), 75
Grove City, Ohio, 183
Guadalupe Hidalgo, Treaty of, 325, 381,
     431, 453, 465, 548
Guadalupe Mountains, 461
Guadalupe Peak, 488
Guernsey, Wyo., 410
Gulf Coast. *See* specific states
Gunsmoke, 237
Gunther, John, 9, 402
Guthrie, Okla., 484
Guthrie (Tyrone) Theater (Minneap-
     olis), 123
Guymon, Okla., 483
Gypsum Hills (Okla.), 468

Hackensack, Minn., 129
Haida Indians, 518, 519
Haines, Alaska, 526, 532
Haleakala (volcano), 575, 577, 598
Hale Paahao (Hawaii), 598
Hall, Fort (Idaho), 332, 344, 629
Hall County, Nebr., 248
Hallmark Cards, 147
Ham House (Dubuque), 70
Hamilton, Nev., 378
Hamline University, 123
Hammond, Ind., 39, 42, 46
Hamtramck, Mich., 81, 95
Hancher (Virgil M.) Auditorium, 70
Hancock, Camp (N.D.), 278; Museum,
     278
Hancock (John) Center (Chicago), 20
Handel, George Frederick, 239, 398
Handy, W. C., 153
Hanford Project, 642, 643
Hanna, Marcus A., 172
Hanna, Wyo., 407, 408
Hannibal, Mo., 159
Hannibal and St. Joseph Lines, 144
Hanover, Kans., 238

Hansen Planetarium (Salt Lake City),
     394
Harbor Island (Calif.), 565
Hardin, Mont., 363
Harding, Warren G., 170, 187
Harlem, Mich., 86
Harlingen, Tex., 506
Harmonie, Ind., 41, 49, 53
Harney Peak, 288
Haro Strait, 639
Harper's magazine, 264
Harrison, Benjamin, 45–46, 170, 187
Harrison, William Henry, 40–41, 53, 170,
     172, 187, 655
Harte, Bret, 378
Hart Mountain (Oreg.), 625
Hartsuff, Fort (Nebr.), 259
Harwood Foundation Art Museum
     (Taos), 462
Haskell Institute (Lawrence, Kans.), 237
Hatcher, Richard D., 54
Havasu, Lake (Ariz.), 445
Hawaii, 571–604; Republic of, 603; Ter-
     ritory of, 587; University of, 597, 598
Hawaii (island), 574, 577, 589, 594, 595,
     597, 600, 601
Hawaii Volcanoes National Park, 575,
     597
Hawthorne, Nev., 371
Hayden, Carl, 447
Hayden, F. V., 409
Hayes, Elwood, 42, 53
Hayes, Rutherford B., 170, 187
Hay Fever Club, 123
Haymarket Square Riot, 13, 31
Hayward, Wis., 210, 214
Haywood, "Big Bill," 612
Hazel Green, Wis., 191, 215
Hazelwood (Green Bay), 206
Heard Museum (Phoenix), 438
Hearst, William Randolph, 96, 566
Heceta, Bruno, 653
Heineman Winery, 185
Heinze, F. Augustus, 351–52
Helena, Mont., 348, 350, 355–56, 357–58,
     362, 364; National Forest, 356
Hell Canyon (S.D.), 301
Hells Canyon (Idaho), 340
Hemingway, Ernest, 9, 327, 341
HemisFair '68, 508
Henderson, Nev., 371, 372
Hennepin, Louis, 111, 114, 133
Henry Art Gallery (Seattle), 646
Herculaneum, Mo., 146
Hermann, Mo., 161
Hermosa, S.D., 303
Heron Lake (N.Mex.), 461
Herrin, Ill., 14
Hiawatha, Lake (Minn.), 130
Hickam Air Force Base, 588

Hickok, James Butler ("Wild Bill"), 9, 230, 249, 285, 290, 297, 301, 407, 414
Hidatsa Indians, 265, 269 ff.
High Amana, Iowa, 73
High Falls (Minn.), 110
Highland Park, Ill., 23
High Plains: Oklahoma, 470; Texas, 489, 496
Higley, Brewster, 223
Hill, James J., 122
Hill Air Force Base (Utah), 395
Hill Country (Tex.), 500, 503
Hillsboro, Ill., 4
Hilo, Hawaii, 597–98
Hinckley, Ohio, 187
Hispanos, 451
Historical Society. See specific place
Historyland Indian Village, 210
Ho, Don, 601
Hoback, John, 407
Hoback River Canyon, 419
Hocking River, 166
Hohokam Indians, 430, 436–37, 438, 442
Holiday, Doc, 443
Holiday Mountain (Iowa), 78
Holland. See Dutch, the
Holland, Mich., 86, 103, 104
Hollenberg Station, Kans., 238
Holliday, Cyrus K., 235
Hollyhock House (Los Angeles), 554
Hollywood, Calif., 541, 549, 553 ff.; Bowl, 554; Wax Museum, 554
Holmes County, Ohio, 169, 188
Holt County, Mo., 143
Holy Family, Church of the (Cahokia, Ill.), 27
"Home on the Range," 233
Homer, Alaska, 530
Homestake Mine (Lode), 292, 295, 301–2, 304
Homestead, Iowa, 73
Homestead Act, 228, 242, 250
Homestead National Monument (Nebr.), 260
Honaunau, Hawaii, 579
Honeyman (Jessie M.) State Park, 626
Honolulu, Hawaii, 571, 572, 574, 576, 577, 584, 585, 594, 596–97, 601, 604; Academy of Arts, 596–97; Symphony, 597
Hood, Mount, 606, 613, 621, 625, 628; National Park, 626
Hood Canal, 652
Hoopeston, Ill., 30
Hoosier National Forest, 48
Hoover, Herbert, 55, 60, 73–74, 224
Hoover, Mrs. Herbert, 74
Hoover Dam, 371, 379, 381, 443, 446, 548, 551

Hoover Memorial (Presidential) Library, 60, 73
Hope, Bob, 562, 567
Hopewell Man. See Mound Builders
Hopi Indians, 430, 439, 443
Hopper, Edward, 255
Horeb, Mount (Wis.), 211, 212
Hornitos, Calif., 566
Horseshoe Stage (Hollywood), 554
Horse Thief Canyon (Kans.), 239
"Horse" tribes, 639
Hot Springs State Park (Wyo.), 419
Houghton, Mich., 101
Houghton County, Mich., 93
Houghton Lake, 82
House on the Rock (Wis.), 212
Houston, Sam, 492–93, 507
Houston, Tex., 491, 494, 495, 497–98, 505 ff.; Astros, 497; Livestock Show and Rodeo, 498; Oilers, 497; University of, 498
Houston (Sam) National Forest, 503
Howard, Benjamin, 142
Howard, Fort (Green Bay), 206; Hospital Museum, 206
Howe, Oscar, 298
Howells, William Dean, 170
Hoyt Arboretum (Portland, Oreg.), 623
Hudson, Ohio, 174
Hudson's Bay Company, 552, 614, 628, 634, 638, 654
Hughes, Harold, 65
Hughes, Howard, 372
Hughes, Langston, 224
Hughes Fine Arts Center (Grand Forks, N.D.), 277
Hugo, Victor, 233
Hugoton Field (Kans.), 233
Humboldt County, Nev., 373
Humboldt National Forest, 377
Humboldt River, 381
Humoresque (Dvořák), 74
Humphrey, Hubert H., 134
Humphreys Peak (Ariz.), 428
Hungarians: and Illinois, 9; and Indiana, 37, 46; and Michigan, 87, 95, 104; and Ohio, 169
Hunt, W. P., 432
Hunter, Catfish, 72
Huntington Botanical Gardens (San Marino), 564
Huntington Library and Art Gallery (San Marino), 554, 564
Huntley, Chet, 359
Huntley Lodge (Mont.), 359
Huron, S.D., 294
Huron, Lake, 81, 82, 84, 101
Huron Cemetery (Kansas City), 236
Huron Indians, 85, 195, 197, 236
Hurricane Beulah, 508

Hurricane Celia, 508
Hutchinson, Kans., 234, 238, 239
Hutterites, 290
Hywet (Stan) Hall, 182

Iao Valley, 598
IBM, 124, 315
Icarians, 9
Icelandics: and North Dakota, 269; and Wisconsin, 196
Idaho, 327–44, 613, 638; College of, 338
Idaho City, Idaho, 337
Idaho Falls, Idaho, 334, 335, 339, 342, 344
Idaho Historical Museum (Boise), 338
Idaho Springs, Colo., 313, 325
Idaho State University, 338
Idaho Territory, 333, 344, 655
Ideal Basic cement, 315
IDS Tower (Minneapolis), 123
Iliamna, Mount, 514
Illiniwek Indians, 10, 25. See also Illinois Indians
Illinois, 2–32; University of, 14–15
Illinois and Michigan Canal, 31
Illinois Central Railroad, 69
Illinois Indians, 10, 59, 61–62, 195
Illinois Institute of Technology, 22
Illinois Ozarks, 3, 5, 25
Illinois River, 5, 10, 16, 27, 28, 31
Illinois State Museum (Springfield), 27
Illinois State University, 24
Illinois Territory, 5, 11, 198
Illinois Valley, 25
Illinois Waterway, 16, 31
Illinois Wesleyan University, 24
Immaculate Heart College, 555
Independence, Mo., 155, 159, 383
Independence Rock (Wyo.), 410
Indiana, 11, 33–54
Indiana Dunes National Lakeshore, 34, 50, 53
Indianapolis, Ind., 38, 39, 44–46, 47–48, 52, 53; Speedway, 46, 47–48, 51
Indiana Territory, 11, 31, 198
Indiana University, 45, 48
Indian City, U.S.A., 482
Indianola, Iowa, 77–78
Indian Pueblo Cultural Center (Albuquerque), 466
Indians, 224, 242 (See also specific tribes): and Alaska, 511, 518, 522, 536, 539; and Arizona, 429–31, 432, 436–37 ff., 442–43, 445, 446; and California, 545 ff., 553; and Colorado, 311–12, 325; and Idaho, 331–32, 333, 342–43; and Illinois, 4, 10 ff., 27, 28; and Indiana, 38, 39–41, 47; and Iowa, 59 ff. (See also Mound Builders; specific tribes); and Kansas, 224,

225–26, 229, 235, 238, 242; and Michigan, 85, 86, 88, 93, 102, 105; and Minnesota, 107, 108, 111 ff., 128 ff.; and Missouri, 139, 148; and Montana, 345, 349, 350–51, 353, 355, 361; and Nebraska, 245, 251, 262; and Nevada, 369, 381, 382; and New Mexico, 449, 451–52 ff.; and North Dakota, 265, 269 ff., 280–81, 283; and Ohio, 168 ff., 184–85, 189; and Oklahoma, 467, 471, 472–73, 482; and Oregon, 610, 615, 629; and South Dakota, 285, 286, 289 ff., 300, 302; and Texas, 487, 489–90, 491, 493, 501; and Utah, 384, 387, 389; and Washington, 634–35, 639, 655; and Wisconsin, 192, 195 ff., 203, 205, 209–10, 215; and Wyoming, 402, 406, 409, 410, 420, 422
Indian Springs (Idaho), 341–42
Indian Springs Shopping Center (Kansas), 236
Indian Territory, 471, 472, 490
Indio, Calif., 567
Industrial Advocate, The, 144
Industrial Workers of the World (Wobblies), 14, 612, 635–36, 655
Inge, William, 224
Inkpa-du-ta (ski area—S.D.), 300
Inland Passage (Alaska), 523, 524
Inouye, Daniel, 572
Inside U.S.A., 402
Inspirationists, 60
Institute for Regional Studies, 276
Institute of Art (Detroit), 96
Interior, S.D., 303
Interior Highlands, 468
Interior Plain, 468
Interlochen, Mich., 103
Internal Revenue Service, 394–95
International Peace Garden (N.D.), 282, 283
International Peace Memorial (Ohio), 185
International Petroleum Exposition, 479
Interstate 70, 320
Interstate 80, 255
"In the Evening by the Moonlight," 33
Iola, Wis., 214
Iolani Palace (Hawaii), 586, 597
Iowa, 55–80, 198; University of, 70, 72
Iowa City, Iowa, 70
Iowa County, Wis., 202
Iowa Indians, 59, 61
Iowa Oaks, 72
Iowa River, 58, 60, 72
Iowa Territory, 63, 79
Iran, 591
Irish (See also Scots-Irish): and Idaho, 331; and Illinois, 38; and Iowa, 56, 63, 76; and Michigan, 86, 87, 95, 102–3;

and Minnesota, 112, 115; and Missouri, 140; and Nebraska, 248; and Ohio, 169; and Texas, 491; and Wisconsin, 195, 206, 207
Irma Hotel (Cody, Wyo.), 416
Iron River, Mich., 104
Iron County, Wis., 195, 202
Iron Hill (Leadville, Colo.), 325–26
Ishpeming, Mich., 93
Isle Royale (Mich.), 84, 101–2; National Park, 101
Italians (Italy): and California, 545, 558; and Hawaii, 581; and Illinois, 3, 9; and Indiana, 37, 46; and Michigan, 86, 87, 101, 104; and Missouri, 140, 152; and Ohio, 169; and Oklahoma, 472; and Wyoming, 407
Itasca, Lake, 108, 110, 128

Jacksboro, Tex., 506
Jackson, Andrew, 142, 181
Jackson, Davey, 417
Jackson, George A., 313, 325
Jackson, Mich., 87, 89, 106
Jackson, William H., 408
Jackson, Wyo., 416–17, 418
Jackson (Sheldon) High School and Junior College, 532
Jackson Hole (Wyo.), 404, 409, 417, 418, 421
Jackson Lake (Wyo.), 404, 418; Lodge, 421
Jackson Park (Chicago), 21
Jackson Square (San Francisco), 566
Jacksonville, Ill., 3
Jacksonville, Oreg., 627
Jail Rock (Nebr.), 259
James, Frank, 131
James, Jesse, 76, 129, 131, 136, 160, 163, 228, 249
James River, 268, 286, 288
Jamestown, N.D., 280
Janson, Eric, 28
Japan(ese): and Alaska, 532, 539; and California, 545, 546, 548, 555, 565, 570; and Hawaii, 581, 582, 587, 589–90, 594, 604; and Idaho, 331, 332; and Oklahoma, 471; and Oregon, 617, 622; and Utah, 387; and Washington, 641
Japan Current, 515
Japanese Tea Garden: San Francisco, 558–59; Seattle, 646; Spokane, 648
Jefferson, Mount (Oreg.), 626
Jefferson, Thomas, 62, 141, 143, 226, 249, 269, 314, 613, 628; and Land Ordinance of 1785, 5; Mount Rushmore face, 285, 300
Jefferson Barracks Park (St. Louis), 158

Jefferson City, Mo., 150, 156, 158–59, 162
Jefferson Territory, 314
Jemez Pueblo, 463
Jester (Lewis A.) Park (Des Moines), 69
Jesuits, 88, 140–41, 162, 546. See also specific persons
Jesus Christ of the Latter-day Saints, Church (See also Mormons): Cody, Wyo., 416
Jetmore, Kans., 239
Jewel Box (St. Louis), 153
Jewel Cave (Black Hills), 301
Jews, 37, 635
Jicarilla Indians, 452
Johns-Manville, 316
Johnson, Andrew, 314
Johnson, Lyndon B., 507
Johnson, Philip, 49, 225
Johnson, Tom L., 173
Johnson County, Iowa, 63
Johnson County (Wyo.) Cattle War, 411, 422
Johnson (Lyndon Baines) Library (Austin, Tex.), 501, 508
Johnson (Osa and Martin) Safari, 238
Johnson (Lyndon B.) Space Center (Manned Spacecraft Center), 494, 495, 497, 498, 507, 508
Jolliet, Louis, 10, 31, 61–62, 79, 88, 140, 162, 170
"Jolly Green Giant," 119
Jones, Samuel, 173
Jonesboro, Ill., 27
Jones State Forest (Tex,), 503
Joplin, Mo., 150
Jordan, Alex, 212
Jornado del Muerto, 450
Joseph, Chief, 333, 344, 351, 361, 364
Joseph (Chief) Battleground Monument, 361
Joslyn Memorial Art Museum (Omaha), 256, 261
Juan de Fuca Strait, 632, 637, 650
Junction City, Oreg., 627
Juneau, Alaska, 514, 530, 531–32, 533, 536
Juneau, Mount, 531, 538

Kaanapali, Hawaii, 599
Kadoka, S.D., 303
Kah-nee-ta (spa—Oreg.), 624
Kahoolawe, 574
Kahuku Sugar Mill, 601
Kahului, Hawaii, 598
Kaibab National Forest, 441
Kailua, Hawaii, 576, 596, 598
Kaiser Industries, 561
Ka Lae (Hawaii), 597

Kalakaua, 586
Kalalau (Hawaii), 599
Kalamazoo, Mich., 87, 90, 92, 99; Nature Center, 99
Kalamazoo River, 84
Kalaupapa, Hawaii, 599
Kalispel Indians, 349
Kalispell, Fort (Mont.), 361, 362
Kamehameha I, 583, 584, 603
Kamehameha II, 583
Kamehameha III, 584–85, 603
Kamehameha IV, 585, 586
Kamehameha V, 585, 586
Kamehameha School (Honolulu), 597
Kane (god), 579
Kaneohe, Hawaii, 576; Marine Corps Air Station, 588
Kankakee River, 36, 40
Kanopolis, Kans., 234
Kansa Indians, 225–26
Kansas, 218–43; University of, 225, 236–37
Kansas City, Kans., 228, 231, 232, 235–36, 243
Kansas City, Mo., 136, 138, 140, 143, 145 ff., 154–55 ff., 163, 236, 237, 243; Art Institute, 155; Chiefs, 156, 237; Country Club Plaza, 155; Kings, 157; Philharmonic Orchestra, 155; Public Library, 155; Royals, 156, 237
Kansas-Nebraska Act (Kansas Bill), 227, 241, 250, 264
Kansas Newman College, 234–35
Kansas Pacific Railroad, 229, 325
Kansas River (and basin), 154, 220, 235
Kansas State University, 237
Kansas Territory, 227–28
Karamu House (Cleveland), 179
Kaskaskia, Ill., 11, 12, 31, 139
Kaskaskia Indians, 10
Kaskaskia (Fort) State Park, 27
Katmai, Mount, 536; National Monument, 535–36
Kauai, 574, 577, 582, 589, 599 ff., 603
Kaufman County, Tex., 498
Kauikeaouli. See Kamehameha III
Kaunakakai, Hawaii, 599
Kaunolu, Hawaii, 600
Kawaiahao Church (Honolulu), 584
Kaw Indians, 226
Kayak Island, 521
K C Ranch (Wyo.), 411
Kealakekua Bay, 582
Kearney, Fort (Nebr.), 259
Kearney, Mo., 160, 161
Kearny, Fort Phil (Wyo.), 410
Kearny, Stephen W., 453
Keeper of the Plains, 235
Kegonsa, Lake (Wis.), 204
Keith County, Nebr., 248

Kelleys Island (Ohio), 185–86
Kellogg, Idaho, 333
Kelly, Daniel, 223
Kelly, Wyo., 405
Kelsey Museum of Archeology (Ann Arbor), 98
Kemmerer, Wyo., 412, 423
Kemper, James, 179
Kemper Log House, 179
Kenai, Alaska, 533, 539
Kenai Peninsula, 514, 518, 525, 528, 530, 539
Kendall, Mont., 361
Kendrick, John B., 415
Kennard, Thomas P., 259
Kennard House (Lincoln, Nebr.), 259
Kennecott Copper, 523, 538
Kennedy, John F., 494, 499, 507
Kennedy (John F.) Museum (Dallas), 499
Kenosha, Wis., 192, 206, 207, 208
Kensack, Lucy Diana, 129
Kensington (runestone), 107, 113, 127
Kent State University, 173, 190
Keokuk, Iowa, 55, 65, 75
Keokuk Dam, 79
Kern County, Calif., 568
Kerns (Maude I.) Art Center, 624
Kerr, Robert S., 474
Ketchikan, Alaska, 526, 532, 533, 536
Ketchum, Idaho, 327, 341
Kettle Falls, 653
Keweenaw Bay (Mich.), 88
Keweenaw County, Mich., 93
Keweenaw Peninsula, 93
Keystone (ski area—Colo.), 322
Kickapoo Indians, 38, 195
Kickapoo State Park, 19
Kicking Bear, 293
Kilauea Crater, 575, 601, 603, 604
Kimball County, Nebr., 246
Kimbell Art Museum (Fort Worth), 500
Kincaid Act, 264
King, Bruce, 466
King, Charles B., 91
King, Richard, 505
Kingdome (Seattle), 655
King Ranch (Tex.), 505
Kings, Neltje, 415
Kings Canyon National Park, 566
Kingston, N.Mex., 464
Kingsville, Tex., 505
Kinnickinnic River, 202
Kino, Eusebio, 431, 446
Kinzie, John, 11–12
Kiowa Indians, 311, 406, 490
Kirby State Forest (Tex.), 503
Kla-how-ya Trail (Tacoma), 649
Klamath Falls, Oreg., 626
Klawock, Alaska, 538

Kleiber, Hans, 408
Klondike, 517, 538, 639, 684
Kneip, Richard F., 305
Knights of Labor, 612, 635
Knott's Berry Farm (Los Angeles), 564
Knowland State Park (Oakland), 561
Knox County, Ill., 3
Kodiak, Alaska, 530–31
Kodiak Island, 514, 521, 524, 528, 530, 537, 538
Kokomo, Ind., 42, 53
Kona Coast (Hawaii), 594, 598
Koolau Range, 577
Korea(ns), 581, 582, 587
Kosciusko County, Ind., 34
Kotzebue, Alaska, 534
Koyukuk River, 513
Krannert Art Museum (Ill.), 24
Ku (god), 579
Kualaupuu Reservoir, 599
Kucinich, Dennis, 190
Ku Klux Klan, 41, 473
Kutenai Indians, 331, 349

La Canada, Calif., 564
Lac Court Oreilles (Wis.), 196; Reservation, 196, 210
Lac du Flambeau Reservation (Wis.), 196, 210
Laclède, Pierre, 141, 152, 162
Laclede, Mo., 159
La Couteau ski area (S.D.), 300
La Crosse, Kans., 238
La Crosse, Wis., 207, 208, 214
La Crosse River, 194
Lafayette, Ind., 41
Lafayette, Marquis de, 145
Lafayette County, Wis., 202
La Follette, Philip, 199, 215
La Follette, Robert M., 191, 199, 215
La Follette, Robert M., Jr., 199
La Framboise, Joseph, 289, 304
Laguna, N.Mex., 463
Laguna Beach, Calif., 563
Laguna Pueblo, 463
Lahaina, Hawaii, 585, 598–99, 603
Lahainaluna School (Hawaii), 598
Lahontan Lake (Nev.), 377
Laie, Hawaii, 597
La Jolla, Calif., 563
Lake County, Minn., 110
Lake Havasu. See Havasu, Lake (and similar references to lakes)
Lake Havasu City, Ariz., 444
Lake Jackson, Tex., 505
Lake of the Ozarks, 136, 138
Lake of the Woods, 110
Lakes. See specific names
Lake Superior and Mississippi Railroad, 124

Lakeview Park (Nampa, Idaho), 338
Lamar, Mo., 159
Lambeau Stadium (Green Bay), 206
Lamoni, Iowa, 60
Lanai, 574, 589, 592, 599–600
Lanai City, Hawaii, 599–600
Lancaster, Ohio, 169
Lander, Wyo., 405, 406
Land O'Lakes, Wis., 211
Landon, Alfred Mossman, 223–24, 242
Land Ordinance of 1785, 5
Land (William) Park, 561
Lane County, Oreg., 623
Lanker, Brian, 224–25
Lansing, Mich., 82, 87, 90, 91, 97–98
La Pointe, Fort (Wis.), 209–10
La Porte, Ind., 43
Lapwai, Idaho, 344
Laramie, Fort (Wyo.), 410; National Historic Site, 410, 419
Laramie, Wyo., 402, 408, 415, 420, 422
Laramie and Cheyenne Plains, 404
Laramie Treaty. See Red Cloud
Laredo, Tex., 497
Larned, Fort (Kans.), 238
Larson (Arne B.) Collection, 298
La Salle, Robert Cavelier, Sieur de, 10, 11, 28, 39–40, 42, 62, 79, 88, 140, 170, 189, 249, 271, 284, 291, 304, 484; death, 491; and Texas, 491, 507
Las Cruces, N.Mex., 459, 460
Lassen Volcanic Park, 566
"Last Chance Gulch," 356
Last Supper, The, 210
Las Vegas, Nev., 368, 369, 371, 374–75, 376, 379–80, 382
Latin Americans. See specific groups
Latting, Patience, 484
Laubin Indian Dancers, 421
Laughing Whitefish Falls, 84
Lava Hot Springs (Idaho), 342
La Vérendrye. See Vérendrye
Lawrence, Kans., 222, 224, 227, 228, 236–37, 241, 242
Lawrence County, Ind., 44
Lawton, Okla., 468
Lead, S.D., 292, 295, 300, 301–3
Leadville, Colo., 313, 317, 325–26
Leaping Rock (Minn.), 130
Lear aircraft, 219, 231
Leavenworth, Henry, 115
Leavenworth, Fort (Kans.), 236
Leavenworth, Kans., 236
Lebanon, Kans., 238
Lebanon, Ohio, 184, 188
Le Claire, Antoine, 70
Le Claire, Iowa, 75
Lecompton, Kans., 222
Lee, Daniel, 614
Lee, Jason, 614, 629

Lee, Peggy, 277
Leech Lake Dam (Minn.), 111
Lehman Caves National Monument, 379
Lemhi, Idaho, 341
Lemhi Indians, 331
Lemon, Mount (Ariz.), 440
Lemont, Ill., 14
Lewis, Meriwether, 226. *See also* Lewis and Clark
Lewis, Sinclair, 69, 127
Lewis and Clark, 62, 71, 79, 139, 162, 226, 241, 249, 269, 284, 332, 344, 349, 350, 364, 406, 407, 605, 613–14, 626, 628, 638, 653; and Sakajawea, 277, 279
Lewis and Clark Centennial Exposition, 615, 621, 629
Lewis and Clark Lake (S.D.), 288, 299
Lewis and Clark National Forest, 358
Lewis Research Center, 173
Lewiston, Idaho, 330, 332, 333, 339, 340, 343, 344
Lewistown, Mont., 360–61, 362
Lexington, Mo., 159
Lexington, Nebr., 262
Liberal, Kans., 233, 239
Liberty Copper Pit (Nev.), 379
Liberty Memorial (Kansas City), 158
Life magazine, 224
Lihue, Hawaii, 599
Liliuokalani, Queen, 586, 603
Lincoln (family), 47, 48–49
Lincoln, Abraham, 3, 9, 10, 12–13, 23, 26–27, 31, 48–49, 198, 250, 314; and Davenport bridge affair, 70; and Kansas statehood, 228; Mount Rushmore face, 300; and Oregon Territory, 638; Saint-Gaudens statue, 22
Lincoln, Ill., 26, 30
Lincoln, Mary Todd, 27
Lincoln, Nancy Hanks (mother), 48
Lincoln, Nebr., 255–56, 258, 259–60, 261
Lincoln, N.Mex., 464
Lincoln Boyhood National Memorial, 48–49
Lincoln College, 26
Lincoln County War, 453, 464, 465
Lincoln Friends of Chamber Music, 255
Lincoln Heritage Trail, 49
Lincoln Library (Fort Wayne), 47
Lincoln Log Cabin State Park, 27
Lincoln National Forest, 460
Lincoln National Life Insurance Company, 47
Lincoln Park (Chicago), 22
Lincoln Park Zoo (Oklahoma City), 481
Lincoln (Fort) State Park (N.D.), 281
Lincoln Symphony, 255
Lincoln Tomb, 27
Lincoln Trail Homestead State Park, 27

Linda Hall Library (Kansas City), 155
Lindbergh, Charles A., Jr., 129, 134, 153, 163
Lindsay, Nebr., 252
Lindsay, Vachel, 9
Lindsay Manufacturing Company, 252
Lindsborg, Kans., 222, 239
Linn, Lewis F., 143
Linn County, Iowa, 63
Linn County, Kans., 228
Lion Country Safari, 504, 564
Lions Club, 239
Lipchitz, Jacques, 49
Lisa (Manuel) Warehouse, 158
Lisbon, Ohio, 188
Lithuanians, 113
Little Arkansas River, 235
Little Basin (Kans.), 239
Little Bighorn River, 351, 355, 364
Little Dixie (Okla.), 472
Little Egypt, Ill., 3
Little Falls, Minn., 129, 134
Little Miami River, 166, 171
Little Paint Creek (Iowa), 72
Little Pigeon Creek, Ind., 48
Little Sioux River, 58
Littleton, Colo., 323
Living History Farms (Des Moines), 80
Living Indian Village (Tex.), 505
Living Sea (Long Beach, Calif.), 564
Livingston, Mont., 363
Livingston, Robert, 141
Livingston, Tex., 505
Llao Rock (Oreg.), 626
Lockwood, Lorna, 446
Locust Grove, Ohio, 184
Logan, Utah, 395
Lolo National Forest, 358
Lombard, Ill., 29
Lomita Railroad Museum, 554
London, Ohio, 188
London Bridge, 444, 446
London (Jack) Square (Oakland), 561, 566
Lone Mountain Guest Ranch (Mont.), 359
Long, Stephen H., 139–40, 226, 246
Long Beach, Calif., 564, 570
Long Beach, Wash., 652
Longfellow, Henry Wadsworth, 123, 179
Longway (Robert T.) Planetarium, 99
Lono (god), 579, 582
Lorain, Ohio, 174
Loretto Heights College, 320
Los Alamos, N.Mex., 449, 454; Scientific Laboratory, 455
Los Angeles, Calif., 543, 547 ff., 552–55, 562 ff., 567, 569, 570; City College, 555; International Airport, 553; State and City Arboretum, 564

Los Angeles County, Calif., 552, 554;
Art Museum, 564; Museum, 554
Lost River (Alaska), 528
Lotus Glass, 186
Louis IX, 141
Louis XIV, 249
Louisiana, 31, 484, 491
Louisiana, Mo., 159
Louisiana Purchase, 59, 62, 79, 114, 133,
139, 141, 162, 226, 227, 249, 269, 271,
272, 284, 291, 304, 349, 364, 422, 484,
491–92, 628, 653. See also Louisiana
Territory
Louisiana Territory, 62, 226, 241, 312,
325. See also Louisiana Purchase
Lovejoy, Elijah P., 12
Loveland Pass (Colo.), 320
Lovell, Wyo., 419
Lowden State Park, 28
Lowell Observatory, 439–40
Lower Tahquamenon Falls, 84
Lowry Air Force Base, 319
Loyola College, 555
Loyola University, 22
Lucas, Robert, 63
Ludington, Mich., 92
Lunalilo, 586
Lutheran Church, 38, 290. See also Ger-
mans
Lyman Memorial Museum (Hilo, Ha-
waii), 598
Lyons, Kans., 234

McAfee, Mildred H., 146
McAlester, Okla., 468, 482, 484
Macalester College, 123
McAlister Lake (N.Mex.), 461
McCall, Jack, 297–98, 301
McCall, Tom, 612
McCargo Cove, Mich., 102
McCarthy, Joseph R., 199, 215
McClellan-Kerr Arkansas River Naviga-
tion System, 475, 484
McConaughy, Lake (Nebr.), 257
McConnell Air Force Base, 235
McCook, Nebr., 260, 262
McCormick, Cyrus, 15
McCormick Place (Chicago), 22
McCoy, Joseph G., 229, 242
McDonald, Betty, 632
McDonald (W.J.) Observatory, 504
McDonnell-Douglas Aircraft Corpora-
tion, 146
McDonnel Planetarium (St. Louis), 153
McDowell, Camp (Ariz.), 437
McGovern, George, 294, 305
McGuffy, William Holmes, 97
McIntosh, S.D., 288
Mackay, Idaho, 328
Mackenzie, Sir Alexander, 628, 638

Mackinac, Fort (Michilimackinac), 88,
102, 106
Mackinac Island, 84, 102, 104
Mackinac Straits, 82, 84, 88; Bridge, 104,
106
Mackinaw City, Mich., 104
McKinley, Mount, 513, 535; National
Park, 535, 539
McKinley, William, 170, 172, 187, 587
McKinley Park Hotel (Alaska), 535
McLean County, Ill., 24
MacLeish, Archibald, 9
McLoughlin, John, 614, 628
MacMorris, Daniel, 158
McNair, Alexander, 142
McNeal, T. A., 230
Macomb, Ill., 15
Madeline Island (Wis.), 209
Madison, Fort (Iowa), 62, 79
Madison, S.D., 294
Madison, Wis., 191, 199, 204–5, 211
Madison County, Iowa, 73, 76
Madison County, Nebr., 248
Madonna of the Trail Monument, 27
Magic Mountain (Calif.), 565
Mahoning River, 166
Maiden, Mont., 361
Majestic (showboat), 180–81
Malad City, Idaho, 342
Malaspina Glacier, 514
Malibu, Calif., 554, 564
Maloney, Lake (Nebr.), 257
Malmstrom Air Force Base, 357
Maltese Cross Ranch (N.D.), 279–80
Mammoth Lakes (Calif.), 563
Mandan, N.D., 274
Mandan Indians, 265, 269 ff., 281
Mangas Coloradas, 431
Manhattan, Kans., 237
Manistee, Mich., 104
Manistee County, Mich., 94
Manistee River, 84
Manistique River, 84
Manitoba, Canada, 282
Manito Park (Spokane), 648
Manitou Island (Mich.), 84
Manitowish, Wis., 211
Manitowish Waters, Wis., 211
Manitowoc, Wis., 200
Manitowoc County, Wis., 202
Mankato, Minn., 118
Manned Spacecraft Center. See Johnson
(Lyndon B.) Space Center
Manoa (Hawaii), 597
Manon, 256
Mansfield, Ohio, 183
Manual Training School (St. Louis), 154
Manville, Wyo., 406
Maquoketa River, 58
Marengo Cave (Ind.), 36, 50–51

Maricopa County, Ariz., 434
Marietta, Ohio, 168, 171, 186, 189
Marietta, Okla., 483
Marin County, Calif., 544, 557
Marine Corps Air Station (Kaneohe), 588
Marineland of the Pacific, 564
Marine Life Museum (Rapid City, S.D.), 298
Mariner's Church (Detroit), 96
Marion County, Iowa, 59–60
Maris, Roger, 277
Maritime State Historical Park (San Francisco), 565
Market Hall (Dallas), 499
Marquette, Jacques, 10, 31, 61–62, 79, 86, 88, 106, 136, 140, 162, 203
Marquette, Mich., 87, 92, 101
Marquette Range, 93
Marquette (Fort) State Park. See Père Marquette (Fort) State Park
Marquette University, 204
Marshall, James Wilson, 143
Marshall Mountain (Mont.), 358
Martin, Morgan L., 206
Martínez, Estevan, 653
Martinez, Calif., 557
Martin-Marietta Company, 315–16
Martinsville, Ind., 51
Mary College (N.D.), 278
Mason Hotel (Claremore, Okla.), 481
Massachusetts, 171
Massac (Fort) State Park, 28
Massillon, Ohio, 169
Masters, Edgar Lee, 26
Masterson, Bat, 230
Matachines, Los, 463
Matanuska Valley, 514, 517, 523, 527, 536, 539
Matthiessen State Park, 24, 25
Maui, 574, 575, 577, 582, 585, 589, 593, 595, 598–99, 601, 603; Historical Society, 598
Maumee, Ohio, 185
Maumee Bay, 167
Maumee River, 36, 166, 171
Maumee Valley, 166, 173, 189
Mauna Kea, 575, 577, 597, 600
Mauna Loa, 575, 577, 597, 603
Maverick, Ariz., 429
Maverick Mountain (Mont.), 358
Maxwell State Game Preserve, 219
Mayo, Charles H., 125
Mayo, Charles W., 125
Mayo, William, 116, 125, 133
Mayo Clinic, 116, 124, 133
Mayowood (Minneapolis), 124–25
Maytag (company), 65
Maytag, F. L., 65
Mazama, Mount, 626

Mead, Lake, 377, 379, 443; National Recreation Area, 379, 443
Meades Ranch (Kans.), 238
Meares, John, 613, 637
Medary, S.D., 289
Medford, Oreg., 627
Medicine Bow, Wyo., 402, 408
Medicine Creek (Nebr.), 257
Medicine Lake (S.D.), 288
Medicine Lodge, Kans., 223
Medicine Lodge Creek (Wyo.), 406
"Medicine Wheel" (Wyo.), 406
Medina County, Ohio, 176
Medora, N.D., 279–80; Doll House, 280
Meeker, Jonathan, 241
Meeteetse, Wyo., 402
Memorial Coliseum: Corpus Christi, 502; Portland, Oreg., 622, 625
Memorial Stadium (Lincoln, Nebr.), 258
Ménard, René, 86, 88, 197, 215
Mendenhall Glacier, 514, 532
Mendocino, Calif., 566
Mendota, Lake (Wis.), 204, 205
Mendota, Minn., 130, 131
Menlo Park, N.J., 96–97
Menninger Foundation (Topeka), 235
Mennonites, 8, 165, 169, 232, 242, 290, 471
Menominee County, Wis., 196
Menominee Indians, 195
Menominee Range, 93
Menominee River, 84, 194, 202
Menotti, Gian-Carlo, 398
Mercer, Asa, 655
Mercer County, N.D., 275
"Mercer girls," 655
Merchandise Mart (Chicago), 20
Mercury flight, 498
Meredith, Burgess, 170
Mermet Lake, 25
Merritt, Lake (Oakland), 566
Mesa, Ariz., 438, 440
Mesabi Range (Minn.), 113, 116, 119, 120, 128, 133
Mesa Verde, 325; National Park, 311, 322
Mescalero Apaches, 452, 453, 463, 465
Mesquakie Indians, 60, 77
Messiah (Handel), 239, 398
Methodists, 290, 610, 614, 629. See also specific places
Metlakatla, Alaska, 519
Metropolitan Opera Company, 499
Metropolitan State College, 320
Metz, Christian, 60
Mexican Hat, Utah, 396
Mexican Museum (San Francisco), 559
Mexico (and Mexicans) (See also Guadalupe Hidalgo, Treaty of): and Arizona, 430, 431, 446; and California,

545, 547–48, 550, 553, 556, 567, 569; and Colorado, 313, 325; and Indiana, 37; and Kansas, 222; and Missouri, 162; and Nevada, 369, 370; and New Mexico, 453, 458, 465; and Oklahoma, 471; and Texas, 490 ff., 504 ff.; and Utah, 389, 399; and Wyoming, 408, 409
Mexico, Gulf of, 16, 467, 484, 488, 489. *See also* specific states
Mexico, Mo., 147, 159
Mexico City, 556
MGM Grand (Las Vegas), 374
Miami (fort and city—Indiana), 38, 40
Miami, Fort (Ohio), 171
Miami and Erie Canal, 167, 172, 189
Miami Indians, 40, 46, 59, 61, 62, 79, 85, 168, 170, 195
Miami River, 166
Miamisburg, Ohio, 173
Miami University (Ohio), 183
Miami Valley, 173, 181, 189
Michelson, Mount, 513
Michigamea Indians, 10
Michigan, 11, 81–106, 181; University of, 97, 98
Michigan, Lake, 7, 10, 11, 15, 21, 23, 25, 31, 34, 36, 38, 42, 46, 48, 50, 53, 81, 82, 84, 85, 93, 102, 103, 194, 200, 202, 203, 206, 207, 209
Michigan City, Ind., 50
Michigan School for the Deaf, 98
Michigan State University (East Lansing), 97, 98
Michigan Territory, 62, 79, 106, 198
Michilimackinac, Fort. *See* Mackinac, Fort
MicroZoo (Abilene), 238
Mid-America All-Indian Center, 235
Mid-Continent Airport (Wichita), 234
Middle Amana, Iowa, 73
Middle Bass Island (Ohio), 185
Middle Easterners, in Michigan, 95
Middle Rocky Mountains, 328
Midland, Mich., 92
Midland County, Mich., 94
Midwest, 1–216
Midwest City, Okla., 468
Midwest Research Institute, 147
Mies Van Der Rohe, Ludwig, 22
Milan, Ohio, 187, 188
Miles, Nelson, 431
Miles County, Mont., 363
Military Academy, U. S. (West Point), 333
Mille Lacs, Minn., 114
Miller, Jack, 80
Millersburg, Ohio, 188
Millersport, Ohio, 188
Milles, Carl, 103

Milligan, Ohio, 167
Milwaukee, Wis., 192, 196, 197, 200, 201, 202–4, 208, 213, 216; Brewers, 208; Bucks, 208
Milwaukee County, Wis., 208; Zoo, 204
Milwaukee River, 194, 202
Minden, Nebr., 260–61
Mine Creek (Kans.), 228, 242
Mineral Museum (Butte, Mont.), 357
Miners Falls (Mich.), 84
Mink, Patsy, 572
Minneapolis, Minn., 106, 111, 113, 118, 121–23, 125 ff., 131; School of Art and Design, 123
Minnehaha Creek, 110
Minnehaha Falls, 110, 123
Minnehaha Park: Mendota, Minn., 131; Minneapolis, 123
Minnesota, 11, 63, 79, 107–34, 198, 270, 272; University of, 123
Minnesota Institute of Arts, 123
Minnesota Knicks, 126
"Minnesota Man," 114
Minnesota North Stars, 126
Minnesota Orchestra, 123
Minnesota River, 110, 113, 120, 129, 130
Minnesota Territory, 115, 133
Minnesota Twins, 126
Minnesota Vikings, 126
Minnilusa Pioneer Museum, 298
Minot, N.D., 278, 283
Mint (hotel—Las Vegas), 374–75
Mint, U. S., 319, 323, 402, 403
Mio, Mich., 85
Miracle Mile (Los Angeles), 554, 555
Mission Bay Aquatic Park (San Diego), 559, 565
Mission Houses (Hawaii), 597
Missions. *See* specific names
Mississippi Basin. *See* Mississippi River
Mississippi Palisades State Park, 20, 24–25
Mississippi River, 4, 5, 7, 8, 10, 11, 16, 24–25, 27, 28, 31, 34, 36, 38, 55 ff., 61, 62, 69, 70, 72, 74, 75, 77, 79, 111, 122, 123, 130, 133, 136, 139, 140, 151, 158 ff., 162, 192, 194, 207, 249, 264, 271, 284, 291, 467, 475; source, 108, 110, 128
Mississippi Valley, 25, 40, 61
Missoula, Mont., 358, 362, 363
Missouri, 135–63, 227; University of, 145, 149, 150, 155, 157, 161 ff.
Missouri Botanical Garden (St. Louis), 152–53, 161
Missouri Compromise, 143, 144, 162, 227, 241
Missouri Gazette, 142, 162
Missouri Historical Society (St. Louis), 153

Missouri Indians, 59, 61
Missouri-Kansas-Texas railroad, 484
Missouri River, 56, 58, 63, 70–71, 76, 136–37, 140, 143–44, 151, 154, 159, 161, 162, 220, 225, 226, 236, 241, 246, 256, 257, 259, 263, 264, 266, 268, 271, 272, 277 ff., 284, 286, 288, 289, 291, 295, 297, 299, 304, 325, 346, 350, 357, 362, 363, 404; and paddlefish, 298; Project, 293, 295, 304
Missouri Territory, 61, 162
Missouri Valley, 269
Mitchell, Ind., 51
Mitchell, S.D., 294, 302
Moab, Utah, 391, 396, 398, 399
Moberly, Mo., 159
Mobridge, S.D., 281, 302, 303
Modoc Indians, 406
Moffatt Tunnel, 320
Mogollon Indians, 430, 452
Mogollon Mountains, 428
Mogollon Rim, 428, 441
Mohave, Lake (Nev.), 377, 379
Mohave Desert, 452
Mohave Indians, 369
Mohawk (tire company), 182
Mohawk Park (Tulsa), 481
Mohican Indians, 38
Moiese, Mont., 361
Moigwena Indians, 10
Moline, Ill., 16, 24, 28, 70
Molokai, 574, 589, 599, 601, 604
Mondale, Walter F., 134
Monk's Mound (Ill.), 27
Monona, Lake (Wis.), 204
Monroe, James, 141, 143, 226, 241
Monroe, Ohio, 175
Monroe County, Ohio, 165, 169
Montana, 250, 333, 345–64, 613, 638
Montana College of Mineral Science and Technology, 357
Montana Historical Museum (Helena), 356
Montana Snow Bowl, 358
Montana State Forest Service, 358
Montana State University, 357, 362
Montana Territory, 333, 364
Monterey, Calif., 547, 548, 550, 566, 568
Monterey Bay, 546, 569
Monterey Peninsula, 562
Montezuma Castle National Monument, 442–43
Montfort feed lots, 317
Montgomery, John Berrien, 556
Montgomery Street (San Francisco), 558
Montreal River, 194
Monument Rocks (Kans.), 239
Monument Valley (Ariz.), 428
Moorehead, Agnes, 170
Moorhead, Minn., 111, 276

Moran, Thomas, 408
Moran Point (Ariz.), 442
Moravians, 169, 185, 209
Moreau River, 288
Mores, Marquis de, 280
Morgan, John Hunt (and Morgan's Raiders), 42, 172, 189
Mormons, 8–9, 249, 369, 370, 383–84, 386–87, 388–90, 391, 393 ff., 397, 399, 438, 584, 600; and Idaho, 331, 332, 341; and Iowa, 60, 71; and Michigan, 87, 102; and Wyoming, 408, 410, 413, 416, 422
Mormon Station, Nev., 370, 381
Mormon Tabernacle (Salt Lake City), 394, 398
Mormon Temple: Laie, Hawaii, 597; Mesa, Ariz., 438; Oakland, 566; Salt Lake City, 394
Mormon Trail, 249, 255, 264, 415
Morrell (plant—Sioux Falls), 297
Morris, Esther H., 407, 422
Morrison (Ann) Memorial Park (Boise), 338
Morrison Planetarium (San Francisco), 559
Morton, J. Sterling, 261
Morton, Wash., 652
Mother Lode area (Calif.), 566
Mound Builders (See also specific towns): and Illinois, 4, 27, 28; and Indiana, 39; and Iowa, 61, 74; and Ohio, 168, 184–85
Mountain City, Nev., 371
Mountains. See specific names
Mount Angel, Oreg., 627
Mount Carroll, Ill., 7
Mount McKinley. See McKinley (and similar references)
Mount Mary College (Yankton), 297
Mount Moriah Cemetery (Deadwood, S.D.), 301
Mount Pleasant, Iowa, 77
Muir Glacier, 535
Muir (John) Trail, 563
Mullan, Idaho, 342
Mullanphy, John, 142
Mullen, Nebr., 262
Mulvane Art Center (Topeka), 235
Muncie, Ind., 39, 43
Munger, Mich., 104
Munising, Mich., 100
Munsee Indians, 38
Munsing Falls (Mich.), 84
Murdock, Roland P., 234
Murphy, Joseph, 146
Murphys, Calif., 566
Murphysboro, Ill., 30
Museums. See specific names, places

Music Center for the Performing Arts (Los Angeles), 554
Muskegon, Mich., 87, 92, 93
Muskegon County, Mich., 94
Muskegon River, 84
Muskingum Conservancy District, 184
Muskingum River, 166
Muskingum Valley, 173, 189
Muskogee, Okla., 475

Nabisco (company), 122
Nacogdoches, Tex., 496
Nadelman, Elie, 255
Nampa, Idaho, 337, 338, 342
Nance County, Nebr., 248
Napa, Calif., 562
Napa County, Calif., 544, 566
Napoleon Bonaparte, 141, 226, 241, 249, 312
Natanuska, Alaska, 533
Nation, Carry, 223, 242
National Aeronautics and Space Administration (NASA), 173, 495, 498
National Bison Range, 361
National Cash Register Company, 181, 186
National Center for Atmospheric Research, 326
National Cowboy Hall of Fame, 481
National Elk Refuge, 418–19
National Governors' Conference, 382
National Museum of Transport (St. Louis), 158
National Music Camp (Interlochen), 103
National Professional Football Hall of Fame, 186–87
National Women's Conference, 508
Natural History, Museum of. See specific cities
Nauvoo, Ill., 8–9, 30, 31, 383, 388
Navaho Indian Reservation (Ariz.), 442
Navaho Indians: Arizona, 429 ff., 439, 442, 445, 446; New Mexico, 451 ff., 462, 465; Utah, 387
Navaho National Monument, 442
Naval Ammunition Depot (Nev.), 371
Navy, U. S. See specific installations
Nebraska, 244–64; University of, 255, 258, 264, 375
Nebraska Art Association, 255
Nebraska City, Nebr., 260, 261
Nebraska Territory, 172, 250, 264
Nebraska Wesleyan University, 255
Negaunee, Mich., 93, 106
Negroes. See Blacks; Slavery
Neihardt, John G., 247, 248, 261, 263, 264
Neligh Mill (Nebr.), 260
Nelson, Gaylord, 216
Nelson, William Rockhill, 157

Nelson (William Rockhill) Gallery of Art, 154
Nemadji River, 194
Neosho River, 220
Nevada, 314, 365–82, 435, 453
Nevada City, Calif., 566
Nevada City, Mont., 360
Nevada Indian Advisory Committee, 382
Nevada State Museum (Carson City), 376
Nevada State Prison (Carson City), 376
Nevada Territory, 370, 381
Neve, Felipe de, 552
New Albion, 546, 569, 628, 636, 653
New Archangel, Alaska, 538
New Bavaria, Ohio, 169
Newberry Library (Chicago), 23
New Braunfels, Tex., 506
New Bremen, Ohio, 169
Newcom Tavern (Dayton), 181
New Concord, Ohio, 187
Newell, S.D., 303
New England Emigrant Company, 227
New Georgia, 653
New Glarus, Wis., 196, 212, 213
New Harmony, Ind., 41, 49, 53
New Heritage Center (Bismarck, N.D.), 284
New Mexico, 323, 448–66; Museum of, 459; University of, 458, 466
New Mexico State University, 459
New Mexico Territory, 431, 453, 465
New Orleans, La., 141, 142, 162
Newport Beach, Calif., 563
New Salem Village, Ill., 26
Newton, Iowa, 65
Newton, Kans., 230
New Ulm, Minn., 113, 115, 129–30, 131
New World Symphony (Dvořák), 74
New York, 171
Nez Percé Indians, 331, 333, 343, 344, 351, 361, 364, 406
Nicolet, Jean, 85–86, 88, 106, 195, 197, 215
Nicolet Mall (Minneapolis), 123
Niihau, 571, 574, 575, 580, 596 n, 603
Niobrara, Fort (Nebr.), 259; Wildlife Refuge, 257
Niobrara River, 249
Nisqually Indians, 634
Nixon, Richard, 549
Nob Hill (San Francisco), 557, 559
Nodaway County, Mo., 143
Nogales, Ariz., 445
Nogal Lake (N.Mex.), 461
Noguchi, Isamu, 255
Nome, Alaska, 523, 534, 537
Nonpartisan League, 273, 284
Nonsense, Fort (Wyo.), 409

Nootka, Wash., 637
Nootka Sound, 637, 653
Norfolk (Nebr.) Insane Asylum, 250
Norfork Lake (Mo.), 138
Normal, Ill., 15, 24
Norman, Okla., 478
Norris, George, 248, 260
Norris Home (McCook, Nebr.), 260
North American Air Defense Command (NORAD), 321, 326
North Beach, Calif., 558
North Bear Creek (Iowa), 72
North Cascades National Park, 649, 651
North-Central Plains, 488, 497
North Clear Creek (Colo.), 313, 325
North Dakota, 63, 79, 192, 250, 265–84, 293, 302; University of, 270, 277
North Dakota Mill and Elevator, 276, 284
North Dakota State University, 276
Northern Angle (Minn.), 110
Northern Forest Fire Laboratory (Missoula, Mont.), 358
Northern Pacific Railroad, 269, 272, 276, 277, 351, 355, 364, 639, 655
Northern Rocky Mountains, 328
Northfield, Minn., 129, 131
North Platte, Nebr., 259, 262
North Platte River, 404, 415
North Platte Valley, 408
North Portland Peninsula, 622
Northrop Memorial Auditorium (Minneapolis), 123
North Star, Ohio, 187
North West Company, 128, 614, 628, 638, 653, 654
Northwestern Bank & Union Trust Company (Helena, Mont.), 356
Northwestern University, 22, 23
Northwest Ordinance, 11, 12
Northwest Passage, 613, 628, 636–37
Northwest State Company (Fargo, N.D.), 276
Northwest Territory, 11, 31, 38, 40, 53, 168, 171, 179, 189, 284
Northwood Institute, 50
Norwegians (Norway), 529, 537; Iowa and, 59, 77; Minnesota and, 112, 113, 115, 121; North Dakota and, 269, 270, 277; South Dakota and, 290, 298–99 (See also specific towns); Texas and, 401; Washington and, 635; Wisconsin and, 209, 212, 213
Notre Dame, University of, 46, 48
Nutcracker, The, 398
Nye, Bill, 408

Oahe Dam (S.D.), 288, 295, 297
Oahe Reservoir (Lake), 288, 297, 299

Oahu, 571, 574 ff., 581, 588 ff., 595, 596–97, 600, 601
Oak Creek Canyon (Ariz.), 441
Oakland, Calif., 557, 558, 561, 570; Museum, 561
Oakland Bay Bridge, 557, 566, 570
Oakley, Annie, 187
Oakley, Idaho, 342
Oak Ridge Cemetery (Springfield, Ill.), 27
Oberlin, Kans., 229
Occidental College, 555
Octonto River, 194
Offut Air Force Base, 264
Ogallala, Nebr., 259
Ogden, Utah, 387, 394–95, 398
Oglala Sioux, 286, 302, 303
O'Hare Airport (Chicago), 16
Ohio, 11, 89, 164–90
Ohio and Erie Canal, 167, 172, 177, 189
Ohio Company, 171, 189
Ohio Historical Center (Columbus), 180
Ohio River, 5, 7, 8, 28, 36, 38, 47, 52, 136, 165, 168, 170, 171, 174, 179, 188, 189
Ohio State University, 183
Ohio Turnpike, 173, 189
Ohio University, 183
Ohio Valley, 171, 189
Ojibway Indians, 196
Ojo Caliente Mineral Springs (N.Mex.), 460
Okanogan Highlands, 632, 633
Okanogan Valley, 640
O.K. Corral (Tombstone), 443
O'Keeffe, Georgia, 255
Oklahoma, 229, 467–85, 490; University of, 468, 478, 482
Oklahoma City, Okla., 474, 475, 477–78, 481, 482, 484, 485
Oklahoma State Prison, 484
Oklahoma Territory, 473, 484
Okmulgee, Okla., 482
Okoboji, Lake, 71–72
Old Courthouse (St. Louis), 158
Old Faithful, 359, 418
Old Fort Benton (Mont.), 361
Old Fort Bliss (El Paso), 501
Old Globe Theater (San Diego), 564
Old Market (Omaha), 257, 264
"Old Mist'ry River" (Ohio), 186
Olds, Ransom E., 89, 91, 95, 97, 106
Old Sacramento (Calif.), 561
Old Shot Tower (Dubuque), 70
Oldsmobile (company), 89, 95, 98
Old Spanish Trail, 370, 458
Old State Capitol (Springfield, Ill.), 26
Old Town (San Diego), 559; State Historic Park, 565
Old Witch (totem—Juneau), 531

Old World Wisconsin Museum, 216
Olentangy Indian Caverns, 181
Olmsted County, Minn., 125
Olney, England, 239
Olney, Ill., 20
Olympia, Wash., 634, 635, 649, 654, 655
Olympic (peninsula), 637, 651
Olympic Games, 570
Olympic Mountains, 632 ff., 644, 652
Olympic National Park, 649, 651–52, 655
Olympus, Mount, 652
Omaha, Nebr., 251, 252, 256–57, 261, 264, 383; Nebraska State Capitol at, 261, 264; Opera, 256; Playhouse, 256; Symphony, 256
Omaha Indians, 59, 61, 245, 262
Oñate, Juan de, 263, 325, 452, 465
One Tree, Church of (Santa Rosa, Calif.), 566
Ontario, Calif., 567
"On the Banks of the Wabash . . . ," 33, 47
Ontonagon County, Mich., 93
Ontonagon River, 84
Open Basin (Calif.), 542, 543
O Pioneers!, 245
Oquirrh Range, 393–94
Orange City, Iowa, 60, 76–77
Orange County, Calif., 552, 564
Orchard, Harry, 334
Order of Patrons of Husbandry, 13
Ordinance of 1785, 40
Oregon, 605–29; University of, 623–24, 625, 629
Oregon City, Oreg., 622, 638
Oregon Coast Highway, 626
Oregon Museum for Science and Industry, 623
Oregon State University, 625
Oregon Symphony, 623
Oregon Territory (Oregon Country), 143, 250, 606, 612–14, 619, 628–29, 654. See also Washington
Oregon Timber Fraud cases, 619
Oregon Trail, 219, 228, 247, 249, 255, 259, 264, 403, 410, 415, 419, 614
Orem, Utah, 387
Organic Act, 522, 538
Oriental Institute (Chicago), 23
Orientals, 548. See also specific nationalities
Orting, Wash., 652
Osage, Fort (Mo.), 159
Osage County, Okla., 476, 484
Osage Indians, 482
Osage Plains, 136
Osawatomie, 227
Osborne County, Kans., 238
Oscoda, Mich., 100
Oswald, Lee Harvey, 494

Oto Indians, 59, 61, 245
Ottawa, Ill., 10, 19, 27
Ottawa Indians, 59, 61, 85, 171, 189, 195
Ouachita Mountains, 468, 479
Ouiatenon, Fort (Ind.), 38, 40
Over (W. H.) Dakota Museum, 298
Overland stages, 410
Overland Trail, 247, 255, 410
Owen, Robert, 41, 49, 53
Owens Lake (Calif.), 542
Owens Valley (Calif.), 542
Oxford, Kans., 239
Ozark Mountains. See Ozark Plateau
Ozark Plateau (Ozark Mountains), 136, 151, 161, 468; Illinois, 3, 5, 25

Pabst Theatre (Milwaukee), 216
Pacific Coast, 543, 635. See also specific states
Pacific Command, U. S., 588
Pacific Fur Company, 628, 638, 653, 654
Pacific Heights (San Francisco), 557
Pacific Northwest, 610, 628
Pacific Ocean, 512, 515, 543. See also specific states bordering on
Padilla, Juan de, 225, 241
Padre Island (Tex.), 503; National Seashore, 503
Pagosa Springs (Colo.), 323
Painted Desert, 428, 442
Paiute Indians, 369, 387
Pajarito Plateau, 462
Palace of the Governors (Santa Fe), 458, 459
Palace of the Legion of Honor (San Francisco), 558
Palawai, Hawaii, 600
Palestine, Ill., 30
Palm Desert, Calif., 562, 567
Palo Duro Canyon Scenic Park, 504
Palomar (Mount) Observatory, 560
Panama-Pacific International Exposition, 557, 569
Panhandle: Alaska, 512, 514 ff., 518, 531; Idaho, 327, 330, 331, 335, 342; Oklahoma, 470, 473, 477, 483, 484; Texas, 488, 489, 496, 502, 504
Paola, Kans., 233
Papago Indian Reservation (Ariz.), 439
Papago Indians, 430, 445
Papago Park (Phoenix), 437
Paramount Theater (Oakland, Calif.), 561, 566
Paris, Treaty of, 171, 189
Parke County, Ind., 51
Parke-Davis Company, 92
Parker, Ariz., 429, 433, 445
Parker Ranch (Hawaii), 594, 598
Park of the Red Rocks, 320
Parks, Gordon, 224

Parrant, "Pig's Eye," 121
Pasadena, Calif., 554, 563, 567; Playhouse, 554
Pasco, Wash., 640
Patagonia, Ariz., 440
Patterson, John, 181
Patterson, Val, 248
Pauls Valley, Okla., 483
Pawhuska, Okla., 482
Pawnee, Okla., 482
Pawnee Indians, 225, 226, 238, 241, 245, 473, 482
Pawnee Indian Village Museum (Republic, Kans.), 238
Payson, Ariz., 440
Peace Democrats, 172
Pearl Harbor (Hawaii), 581, 586, 587, 597, 603, 604; Naval Base, 588
Pecos, N.Mex., 461
Pecos River, 450, 457
Pecos Valley, 496
Pedro, Felix, 533
Pei, I. M., 68
Pele (goddess), 575, 579
Pella, Iowa, 55, 59–60, 75, 76–77
Pembina, N.D., 269, 272, 282, 284
Pembina Mountains, 266
Pend d'Oreille Indians, 331
Pendleton, Oreg., 627
Peninsula State Park (Wis.), 209
Penney, J. C., 412, 423
Pennsylvania Dutch, 169
Peoria, Ill., 8, 10, 16, 17, 24, 30
Peoria Indians, 10
"Peoria Party," 629
Peralta, Pedro de, 452, 465
Père Marquette (Fort) State Park, 27
Perkins County, Nebr., 248
Perpetual Emigrating Fund, 381
Perrot, Nicholas, 62
Perry, Okla., 483
Perry, Oliver H., 172, 185, 189
Pershing, John S., 135, 145, 159, 163
Pershing Square (Los Angeles), 555
Peru, 591
Peru, Ind., 51
Peshtigo, Wis., 199, 215
Peshtigo River, 194
Peters, Roberta, 256
Petersburg, Alaska, 532, 537
Petersburg, Ill., 26
Peterson Air Force Base, 321
Peter the Great, 521
Petoskey, Mich., 105
Petrified Forest, 428; National Park, 442
Pettigrew Museum (Sioux Falls), 297
Phantom Ship (Oreg.), 626
Phelps County, Nebr., 260
Philbrook Art Center (Tulsa), 480
Philippines. See Filipinos

Phillips, Frank, 481
Phillips, Waite, 480
Phillipsburg, Kans., 239
Phillips Petroleum Company, 467–68
Phoenix, Ariz., 429, 432, 433, 436–38, 444, 447; Art Museum, 438; Library, 438; Theater Center, 438; Zoo, 437
Piankashaw Indians, 38
Picasso, Pablo, 21, 225
Piceance Basin, 317
Pickett, George, 639
Picnic, 224
Pictograph Cave State Monument, 355
Pictured Rocks (Mich.), 100
Pierre, Fort (S.D.), 289, 297
Pierre, S.D., 296–97, 303
Pigeon River, 128
Pig War, 638–39
Pike, Zebulon, 114–15, 133, 139, 226, 241, 325
Pike Place Market (Seattle), 646
Pikes Peak (Colo.), 313, 320, 324
Pillsbury (company), 122
Pima Indians, 430, 445
Pinal County, Ariz., 434
Pinchot (Gifford) National Forest, 651
Pinckneyville, Ill., 19
Pineda, Alonso Álvarez de, 507
Pinedale, Wyo., 409, 420
Pine Ridge, Nebr., 257
Pine Ridge Reservation (S.D.), 286, 302, 303
Pioneer Club (Las Vegas), 374
Pioneer Mountains, 341
Pioneer Square (Seattle), 645, 646
Pioneer Theater (Reno), 375
Pioneer Village (Brainerd, Minn.), 129
Pipestone National Monument, 129, 131
Pissaro, Camille, 68
Placerville, Calif., 380
Plains Indian Museum (Cody, Wyo.), 416
Plains States, 217–305
Platte County, Mo., 143
Platte Purchase Act, 143
Platte River, 245, 248 ff., 312
Plum Creek (Nebr.), 262
Plummer, Henry, 350
Plummer gang, 350
Pocatello, Idaho, 332, 338
Point, Fort (Calif.), 556
Point Defiance (Tacoma), 648–49
Point Grenville. See Grenville, Point
Pokegama Dam (Minn.), 111
Poland China hogs, 175
Poles: and Illinois, 3, 9; and Indiana, 37, 46; and Michigan, 86, 87, 95, 104; and Minnesota, 113; and North Dakota, 269; and Ohio, 169; and Texas, 491; and Wisconsin, 196

Polk, James, 638
Polynesian Cultural Center (Hawaii), 597
Polynesians. See Hawaii
Pomme de Terre Lake (Mo.), 138
Ponca City, Okla., 475, 482
Ponca Indians, 245, 482
Ponce de Leon springs (N.Mex.), 460
Pontchartrain, Fort (Mich.), 88, 94, 106
Pontiac, 171, 189
Pontiac, Ill., 17
Pontiac, Mich., 81, 87, 90; Stadium, 106
Pony Express, 238, 259, 264, 399, 410, 422
Poplar Bluff, Mo., 161
Porcupine Mountains, 84
Porcupine River, 515
Portage River, 166
Port Angeles, Wash., 652
Port Arthur, Tex., 489, 495
Port Chilkoot, Alaska, 532
Port Clinton, Ohio, 185
Porter, Cole, 33
Port Huron, Mich., 89
Port Isabel, Tex., 503
Portland, Ind., 42, 44
Portland, Oreg., 606, 608, 609, 611, 612, 615, 617, 619, 620–23 ff., 629; Art Museum, 623; Buckeroos, 625; Civic Theater, 623; Mavericks, 625; State University, 623; Trailblazers, 625; Zoo, 623
Portolá, Gaspar de, 556, 569
Portsmouth, Ohio, 167, 172, 173, 189
Portsmouth, U.S.S., 556
Ports o'Call Village (Calif.), 565
Portuguese, 545, 581
Port Walter, Alaska, 516
Potawatomi Indians, 38, 59, 85, 99, 195
Poteau River, 467
Potosi, Mo., 146
Pottawatomie Creek (Massacre), 227, 241
Pottawatomi Indians. See Potawatomi Indians
Pound Hollow (Ill.), 25
Powderhorn ski area (Colo.), 322
Powder River, 289, 304, 404
Powell, Lake (Utah), 396
Prague, Okla., 482
Prairie du Rocher, Ill., 28
Prairie Hills (S.D.), 286
Prairie Plains, 468–70
Prairie Stage (Fargo, N.D.), 276
Presbyterian Church; Presbyterians, 290, 338, 615. See also specific nationalities, places
Prescott, Ariz., 433, 440, 445; National Forest, 441
Presque Isle, Wis., 211, 214

Pribilof Islands, 526, 528, 538
Price County, Wis., 194
Priest River, 342
Prince William Sound, 524
Prineville, Oreg., 627
Proclamation of 1763, 40
Proctor and Gamble, 179, 186
Project Gasbuggy, 465–66
"Promised Valley," 397
Promontory Point, Utah, 390, 399, 615
Prospect Creek (Alaska), 515
Protestants (See also specific groups): and Indiana, 37; and Iowa, 61; and Oregon, 610; and Utah, 387; and Washington, 635
Provo, Utah, 387, 395, 391
Provo Canyon, 395
Prudhoe Bay, 526
Pryor, Utah, 475
Pryor Mountain Wild Horse Range, 419
Puako, Hawaii, 577
Pueblo, Colo., 314, 315, 321, 323; Army Depot, 321
Pueblo de Taos. See Taos Pueblo (and similar references)
Pueblo Indians, 311, 322, 430; and New Mexico, 451–52, 452–53, 458, 459, 462, 463, 465
Puerto Ricans, 170, 581
Puget Sound (and Puget Sound region), 632, 633, 636, 637, 640 ff., 648, 650, 653, 654
Pullman Strike, 13–14
Punahou School (Honolulu), 597
Punchbowl Memorial Cemetery (Hawaii), 597
Purdue University, 48
Purgatory ski area (Colo.), 322
Purina (company), 253
Put-in-Bay, Ohio, 184, 185, 188
Putnam, Rufus, 186
Putnam County, Indiana, 44
Puyallup, Wash., 652
Puyallup Indians, 634
Puye Cliffs (N.Mex.), 463
Pygmy Forest (Calif.), 566
Pyramid Lake (Nev.), 377
Pyramid State Park, 19

Quaker City, Ohio, 188
Quaker Meetinghouse (West Branch, Iowa), 74
Quaker Oats Company, 65, 69
Quakers: and Illinois, 8; and Iowa, 60, 64, 73–74
Quantrill, William, 228, 242
Quapaw, Okla., 482
Quapaw Indians, 482
Quebec, 40, 88, 197, 215
Quebec Act, 40

Queen Charlotte Strait, 637
Queen Mary, S.S., 564
Quincy, Ill., 27
Quinter, Kans., 220
Quivira, 225, 241, 249, 612

Raccoon River, 67, 69
Racine, Wis., 192, 196, 206–7, 213
Racine County, Wis., 202, 208
Radio Corporation of America, 517
Radisson, Pierre Esprit, 111, 133, 197
Radium Springs (N.Mex.), 460
Rainbow Bridge National Monument, 397
Raine, William MacLeod, 230
Rainier, Mount, 633, 644; National Park, 649, 651
Rampart Range, 321
Randall, Tony, 481
Rantoul, Ill., 24
Rapid City, S.D., 294, 298–99, 303, 305
Rapp, George, 41, 49, 53
Rathbun Dam (Iowa), 71
Ravinia Festival, 23
Rawlins, Wyo., 404, 420
Reciprocity Treaty (U.S.–Hawaii), 591, 603
Recovery, Fort (Ohio), 185
Red Beds Plains, 468
Red Cedar River, 98
Red Cliff Reservation (Wis.), 196, 210
Red Cloud (chief), 289, 292, 304, 406
Red Cloud, Nebr., 261
"Red Desert" (Wyo.), 404
Redfield, S.D., 303
Red Fork–Tulsa oil field, 473
Red Lake, Minn., 110, 131
Red Lodge, Mont., 361
Red Lodge Mountain (Mont.), 358
Redondo Beach, Calif., 555, 563, 564
Redoubt, Mount, 514
Red River, 266, 276, 468, 470, 497
Red River of the North, 127
Red River Region (Okla.), 468
Red River Ski Area (N.Mex.), 460
Red River Valley, 107, 112, 113, 118, 119, 266, 271, 274, 276
Redwood City, Calif., 558
Redwood National Park, 551–52, 566
Reed College, 623
Reeder's Alley (Helena, Mont.), 356
Regis College, 320
Reinisch Rose Garden, 235
Rembrandt Van Rijn, 123, 180, 182
Remember the Alamo Theater (San Antonio), 504
Remington, Frederic, 416, 481, 500
Renault, Philippe, 139, 152, 162
Rendezvous Peak (Wyo.), 418

Reno, Nev., 368, 371, 375, 376, 379;
—Stead Airport, 379
Renville County, Minn., 129
Reo Division, 98
Reptile Gardens (Rapid City, S.D.), 298
Republic, Kans., 238
Republican Party (*See also* specific states): founding of, 106
Resolution (sloop), 577, 583
Revolutionary War. *See* American Revolution
Rhinelander, Wis., 211, 214
Rhodes scholars, 468
Rhododendron (steamboat), 77
Rhyolite, Nev., 378
Ribault, Jean, 152
Ribicoff, Abraham, 14
Rib Mountain (Wis.), 192
Rice University, 498
Richardson Highway, 531
Richmond, Calif., 557, 558
Rifle River, 100
Riley, James Whitcomb, 33, 46
Rinehart, Mary Roberts, 408
Ringling Brothers (and Barnum & Bailey Circus), 212–13, 498
Rio Grande, 450, 457, 458, 464, 488, 491, 492, 497, 501
Rio Grande Valley, 456, 489
Ripon, Wis., 198, 215
Rivera, Diego, 96
Riverfront Park (Spokane), 647–48
River Q (paddlewheeler), 100
Riverside County, Calif., 552
Riviera (Las Vegas), 374
Roberts (Oral) University, 479
Robidoux, Antoine, 155–56
Robie House (Chicago), 22
Robinson, Fort (Nebr.), 251, 259, 264
Robinson Museum (Pierre, S.D.), 297
Rochester, Minn., 116, 124–25, 133
Rockefeller, John D., 178
Rockefeller Park (Cleveland), 178
Rockford, Ill., 23–24
Rock Harbor, Mich., 101, 102
Rockhurst College, 155
Rockies, Museum of the (Mont.), 357
Rock Island, Ill., 24, 28, 29, 70
Rockport, Tex., 497
Rock Post Museum (LaCrosse, Kans.), 238
Rock River, 5, 28, 58
Rock Springs, Wyo., 407, 408–9
Rockville, Ind., 51
Rockwall County, Tex., 498
Rocky Flats (Denver), 319
Rocky Mountain Arsenal, 319
Rocky Mountain National Park, 322, 326

Rocky Mountains, 310 ff., 316 ff., 326, 328, 330, 346, 348, 358, 384, 403 ff., 450, 454, 458, 465, 488, 613, 633
Rocky Mountain States, 307–423
Rodeo Hall of Fame, 481
Rodin, Auguste, 68
Rogers, Robert, 628
Rogers, Will, 470, 481
Rogers (Will) Auditorium (Dallas), 500
Rogers County, Mich., 94
Rogers (Will) Memorial, 481
Rogers (Roy) Museum (Los Angeles), 554
Rogue River, 625
Roi, Francis, 206
Rolla, Mo., 150, 155
Rolla View, N.D., 278
Roman Catholics. *See* Catholics
Roofless Church (New Harmony, Ind.), 49
Roosevelt, Franklin D., 223, 224, 655
Roosevelt, Theodore, 265, 279; Mount Rushmore face, 285, 300
Roosevelt Dam (Ariz.), 432, 436, 446
Roosevelt (Franklin D.) Lake (Washington), 632, 651
Roosevelt (Theodore) Memorial Park (Medora), 280
Roosevelt University, 22
Rooster Rock State Park, 624
Rosebud, Battle of the, 351
Roseville, Ohio, 188
Rosicrucian Egyptian Museum (San Jose), 560
Ross, Fort (Calif.), 545, 547, 569
Ross, Nellie Tayloe, 402, 423
Rotary International, 23
Roughing It (Twain), 376
Round Island, Mich., 84
Royal Hawaiian Band, 597
Royal Mausoleum (Hawaii), 597
Royal Oak, Mich., 81, 87
Rubens, Peter Paul, 182
Ruby, Jack, 494
Ruedi Dam (Colo.), 326
Rugby, N.D., 282
Ruidoso, N.Mex., 460
Rum River, 110
Runyon, Damon, 224
Rural Electrification Administration, 260
Rushmore, Mount, 285, 300, 304, 305
Russell, Charles M., 356, 357, 416, 481, 500
Russell, Fort D. A. (Cheyenne), 414
Russell (C. M.) Art Gallery (Helena, Mont.), 356
Russell (Charles M.) Museum (Great Falls, Mont.), 357
Russian-American Company, 521–22, 538
Russian Fort (Hawaii), 599

Russian Hill (San Francisco), 557
Russian River, 547
Russians: and Alaska, 516, 518, 521–22, 530, 532, 538; and California, 545, 547, 556, 569; and Colorado, 313; and Hawaii, 581; and Illinois, 9; and Kansas, 220, 232, 242; and Michigan, 87, 95; and North Dakota, 265, 269; and Ohio, 169; and Oklahoma, 472; and South Dakota, 290, 293; and Wyoming, 407
Ruth, Nev., 371
Rutledge, Ann, 26
Rye Patch Lake (Nev.), 377
Ryun, Jim, 225, 243

Saarinen, Eero, 22, 47, 95, 103, 158, 204
Saarinen, Eliel, 68, 103
Sabine National Forest, 503
Sabine River, 492
Sacajawea. *See* Sakajawea
Sacaton, Ariz., 445
Sac Indians, 28, 31, 59 ff., 70, 77, 79, 195, 198, 215, 482
Sacramento, Calif., 548, 561, 563, 568; College, 561
Sacramento County, Calif., 561
Sacramento River, 542, 551, 561
Sacramento Valley, 542, 544, 561
Sacred Heart Church (Notre Dame University), 46
Saginaw, Mich., 86, 87, 89
Saguaro National Monument, 443
Sahara, the (Las Vegas), 374
St. Anthony, Fort (Minn.), 115
St. Anthony's Falls (Minn.), 111, 122, 133
St. Charles, Mo., 162
St. Clair, Lake, 84, 97
St. Clair County, Mich., 94
St. Clair River, 84
St. Croix River, 110, 194
Ste. Genevieve, Mo., 149, 152, 160, 162
Ste. Genevieve County, Mo., 150
St. Elias, Mount, 512, 518
St. Elias Mountains, 513
St. Francis, Kans., 225
St. Francis, Sisters of, 116, 124
St. Francis Hotel (San Francisco), 565
St. Francis of Assisi, Mission of (Taos), 462–63
St. Francis Yacht Club (San Francisco), 563
Saint-Gaudens, Augustus, 22
St. Helens, Mount (Wash.), 651
St. Ignace, Mich., 102, 104
St. Jacob's Well (Kans.), 239
St. James, Mo., 150
St. Joan of Arc Chapel (Milwaukee), 204

St. Joe River (Idaho), 340
St. Joseph, Mo., 155–56, 161, 163
St. Joseph River, 36, 40, 84
St. Lawrence River, 34, 36
St. Lawrence Seaway, 16, 178
St. Louis, Mo., 136, 138 ff., 144 ff., 152–54, 156 ff., 161 ff., 614; Cardinals, 156; Choral Society, 153; Mercantile Library, 153; Municipal Opera Theatre, 153–54; Philharmonic Society, 153; Symphony, 153; University, 153, 154
St. Louis, Fort: Illinois, 10–11, 28; Texas, 491
"St. Louis Blues," 153
St. Louis County, Minn., 116, 134
St. Louis River, 110
St. Maries, Idaho, 342
St. Mary Church (Columbus, Ohio), 180
St. Mary's Cathedral (San Francisco), 559
St. Mary's Hospital (Rochester, Minn.), 116, 124
St. Marys River, 101
St. Michael's Cathedral (Sitka), 532
St. Paul, Minn., 107, 111, 113, 114, 118, 121–22, 123, 125 ff., 130; Cathedral, 122
St. Paul's Episcopal Church (Tombstone, Ariz.), 444
St. Peter and Paul, Church of (West Bend, Iowa), 75
Sakajawea, 277, 279, 407
Sakajawea, Lake (N.D.), 270, 279
Salem, Oreg., 608, 615, 623, 624, 627, 629
Salina, Kans., 238
Sally Brown (ship), 615, 629
Salmon, Idaho, 343
Salmon River, 328, 340
Salt Creek (Wyo.), 408, 413
Salter, Susanna Madora, 222, 242
Salt Lake City, Utah, 320, 386, 387, 389, 391, 392–93, 393–94, 397–98, 399; Art Center, 394; Oratorio Society, 398
Salton Sea, 543
Salt Palace (Salt Lake City), 394
Salt River, 436
Samoans, 581
Samsonite (luggage), 315
San Andreas Fault, 557
San Antonio, Tex., 491, 492, 501, 503 ff., 507, 508
San Bernardino, Calif., 552
San Carlos (ship), 556
Sandburg, Carl, 3, 4, 9, 10, 15, 16, 23
Sand Hills (Nebr.), 246, 261, 262
Sandia Military Base, 455
Sandia Mountain (N.Mex.), 457, 458
Sandia Peak Aerial Tram, 458

San Diego, Calif., 546, 550, 559–60, 562 ff., 567, 569; City College, 559; State University, 559; Wild Animal Park, 560, 565; Zoo, 565
San Diego County, Calif., 559, 562
San Diego de Alcala, 559
Sandoz, Jules, 248
Sandoz, Mari, 248, 261
Sandpoint, Idaho, 343
Sands, the (Las Vegas), 374
Sandstone Hills (Okla.), 468
Sandusky, Ohio, 167
Sandusky Bay, 183
Sandusky River, 166
Sandwich, John Montagu, Earl of, 582
Sandwich Islands, 582–83
San Felipe de Austin, Tex., 492
San Fernando Valley, 555
San Francisco, Calif., 541, 542, 544, 545, 547, 548, 550, 555–59, 562, 563, 565–66, 567, 569, 570; Art Institute, 559; Giants, 440; Museum of Art, 558; State College, 559; University of, 559
San Francisco Bay, 556
San Francisco County, Calif., 544
San Francisco Peaks, 428, 439
Sangamon County, Ill., 26
Sangamon River, 27
Sangamon State University, 24
Sangre de Cristo Range (Mountains), 325, 461
San Jacinto Mountains, 542, 565
San Jacinto River, 493, 505 ff.; Battleground Park, 505, 506; Monument and Museum of History, 505
San Joaquin River, 542
San Joaquin Valley, 542, 544, 551
San Jose, Calif., 560–61, 569, 570; Center for the Performing Arts, 560; Community College, 560; Flea Market, 560–61; Historical Museum, 560; State University, 560; Vocational Center, 560
San José de Tomacacori, Mission, 443
San Juan Basin, 311
San Juan Bautista (Calif.), 567
San Juan Capistrano (Calif.), 567
San Juan-Chama project, 454, 465
San Juan de los Caballeros, Pueblo of, 452–53, 465
San Juan Island Historical Park, 652
San Juan Islands, 632, 638–39, 655
San Juan Pueblo, 463
San Juan River, 396, 450, 454, 457, 465
San Luis Valley, 317, 325
San Marcos, Tex., 506
San Marino, Calif., 554
San Mateo, Calif., 552
San Mateo County, Calif., 544
San Miguel, Mission of (Santa Fe), 459

San Pedro, Calif., 564, 565
San Pedro Bay, 553
San Rafael, Calif., 557
San Simeon (Calif.), 566
Santa Ana, N.Mex., 463
Santa Anna, Antonio López de, 492, 493, 504
Santa Barbara, Calif., 552, 568
Santa Barbara County, Calif., 568
Santa Catalina Island, 565
Santa Clara, N.Mex., 463
Santa Clara County, Calif., 544, 550, 560
Santa Clara de Asis, Mission, 560, 567
Santa Clara Pueblo, 463
Santa Claus, Ind., 51
Santa Fe, N.Mex., 450, 452, 453, 458–59 ff., 464, 465; National Forest, 460; Ski Basin, 460
Santa Fe Railroad, 229 ff., 235, 553
Santa Fe Trail, 219, 226, 227, 238, 241, 453, 458, 465, 547
Santa Monica, Calif., 555, 563
Santa Monica Bay, 555
Santa Rosa, Calif., 566, 568
Santee Sioux, 249
San Xavier del Bac, Mission, 439
Saratoga, Wyo., 420
Sauk Centre, Minn., 127
Sauk County, Wis., 202
Sauk Indians. See Sac Indians
Sauk River, 110
Sault Ste. Marie, Mich., 86, 88, 89, 100, 101, 104, 106
Sausalito, Calif., 557, 563
Sauvie Island, 614, 629
Savage, Minn., 118
Sawtooth National Forest, 341
Saylorville Lake, 80
Scandinavian Cultural Center (Grand Forks, N.D.), 277
Scandinavians (See also specific nationalities): and Idaho, 331; and Illinois, 3, 8; and Iowa, 56, 59; and Kansas, 221; and Minnesota, 122; and Montana, 349; and Nebraska, 248; and North Dakota, 265, 277; and Oregon, 611, 627; and South Dakota, 293; and Washington, 635, 652; and Wisconsin, 196
Schlitz (Jos.) Brewing Company, 208
Schoenbrunn Village, Ohio, 185
Schoolcraft, Henry Rowe, 143
Science and Industry, Museum of. See specific cities
Science City, Hawaii, 598
Scioto River, 166, 171
Scioto Valley, 173, 189
Scots (Scottish) (See also Scots-Irish): and California, 568; and Idaho, 331; and Iowa, 63; and Missouri, 152

Scots-Irish: and North Dakota, 272, 284; and Ohio, 169
Scott, Dred, 144, 163
Scott, Mount (Oreg.), 626
Scott, Winfield, 70
Scotts Bluff (Nebr.), 259; National Monument, 259
Scottsdale, Ariz., 438, 440, 445
Scout's Rest Ranch (Nebr.), 259
Scribner, Nebr., 260
Seabee Museum (Los Angeles), 554
Seabury Western Theological Seminary, 23
Seagull Monument (Salt Lake City), 389, 394
Sealth, 645
Sears Tower (Chicago), 20
Seaside, Oreg., 624
Seaton, Fred, 248
Seattle, Wash., 632 ff., 639, 641, 644–47, 650, 652, 654, 655; Art Museum, 646–47; Center, 646, 655; Supersonics, 647, 651; Symphony, 646; –Tacoma International Airport, 641, 648; Totems, 647
Seaview, Wash., 632
Sea World (San Francisco), 559, 565
Sebewaing, Mich., 104
Sedalia, Mo., 160
Sedgwick County Zoo, 234
Sedona, Ariz., 445
Seiberling, Frank A., 182
Seldovia, Alaska, 531
Sells, Ariz., 445
Seminole Indians, 162, 471 ff., 477, 484
Semple, Robert, 143
Seneca Caverns (Bellevue, Ohio), 186
Seneca Indians, 482
Sentinel Butte (N.D.), 283
Sequoia National Park, 566
Serpent Mound (Ohio), 184
Serra, Junipero, 569
Sevareid, Eric, 277
Seven Cities of Cibola, 430, 450
Seventeen Mile Drive (Calif.), 566
Severance Hall (Cleveland), 179
Seward, Alaska, 517, 529, 530, 537, 538
Seward, William H., 522
Seward Peninsula, 523
Shafter, Fort (Hawaii), 588
Shannon County, Mo., 150, 151
Sharpe, Lake (S.D.), 288, 299
Shasta, Mount, 542
Shasta Dam and Reservoir, 551
Shawnee, Okla., 475
Shawnee Indians, 38, 41, 168, 170
Shawnee National Forest, 5
Shawnee Sun, 241
Shaw's Garden (St. Louis), 152–53
Sheboygan, Wis., 196, 213–14

Shedd Aquarium (Chicago), 22
Sheepeater Indians, 331
Shelby, Mont., 363
Sheldon Memorial Art Gallery (Lincoln, Nebr.), 255, 261
Sheldon Trio, 255
Shelikof, Gregory, 521
Shelter Island (Calif.), 565
Sheplers (store—Wichita), 234
Sheridan, Philip Henry, 406
Sheridan, Wyo., 405, 407, 415–16, 420; Inn, 415
Sheridan Valley (Wyo.), 408
Sherman Reservoir (Nebr.), 257
Short Bull, 293
Shoshone, Wyo., 419
Shoshone Indians, 331, 342–43, 349, 369, 387, 406, 420, 422
Shoshone Mountains, 403
Shoshone National Forest, 414
Shoshone River, 404, 416
Siapu (ski area—N.Mex.), 460
Sibley, Henry Hastings, 130
Sidney, Fort (Nebr.), 259
Sidney, Iowa, 77
Sidney, Mont., 363
Siecke State Forest (Tex.), 503
Sierra Blanca (N.Mex.), 460
Sierra Madre Mountains, 403, 431
Sierra Nevada, 365, 366, 376, 377, 381, 542 ff., 550, 552, 566
Sill, Fort (Okla.), 468
Silver Bay, Minn., 117, 134
Silver City, Idaho, 341
Silverton, Colo., 323
Simmons, Michael T., 654
Sinclair, Harry, 413
Sioux City, Iowa, 71
Sioux County, Iowa, 60, 62
Sioux County, Nebr., 246
Sioux County, N.D., 270
Sioux Empire Medical Museum, 297
Sioux Falls, S.D., 285, 289, 291, 294, 297, 300, 303
Sioux Indians: and Iowa, 59, 61; and Minnesota, 107, 111, 113 ff., 129–30, 131, 133; and Missouri, 138; and Montana, 349 ff., 355, 361, 364; and Nebraska, 249, 251; and North Dakota, 265, 269 ff., 280, 281, 283; and South Dakota, 285, 286, 289 ff., 297, 298, 300–1, 302 ff., 406, 422; and Wisconsin, 209, 210
Siskiwit Bay, Mich., 102
Sisseton, S.D., 300
Sister Bay, Wis., 209
Sitka, Alaska, 516, 522, 526, 532, 533, 537, 538
Sitting Bull, 270, 281, 285, 292, 293, 302, 351, 406

Six Flags Over Texas, 504
Skagway, Alaska, 517, 523, 532, 537
Skeleton Cave (Ill.), 28
Skidmore Fountain (Portland, Oreg.), 622
"Skid Road," 645, 646
Slant Village (N.D.), 281
Slavery (See also Underground Railroad): in Alaska, 518, 522; California and, 548; Illinois and, 11, 12, 27; Indiana and, 41; Iowa and, 60, 64; Kansas and, 222, 227, 228, 241; Missouri and, 142 ff., 158; Ohio and, 172; Oklahoma and, 471; Texas and, 491
Slavs, 472. See also specific nationalities
Sloat, John D., 548
Smith, A. L., 145
Smith, Hyrum, 8, 31, 394
Smith, Jedediah, 369, 381, 388, 569
Smith, John (Phoenix merchant), 437
Smith, Joseph, 8, 31, 383, 388, 394
Smith, Preacher, 285
Smith, Thomas James, 230
Smith Center, Kans., 223
Smoky Hill River, 220, 239
Snake River, 328, 330, 332, 334, 335, 337 ff., 344, 404, 421, 606, 653–54
Snake River Plain, 327, 330, 331, 337
Snake River Plateau (Columbia Plateau), 328, 336
Snake Valley, 330, 336, 337
Snelling, Fort (Minn.), 115, 130
Snoqualmie Pass (Wash.), 634
Snowflake, Ariz., 433
Snowy Range, 415, 419
Socialist Party, 14, 635
Soda Springs (Idaho), 342
Solano County, Calif., 544, 550
Soldier Field (Chicago), 22
Soldiers and Sailors Monument (Indianapolis), 45
Soldotna, Alaska, 536
Song of Hiawatha, The, 110, 123
"Song of Hiawatha Pageant," 131
Sonoma, Calif., 546, 547
Sonoma County, Calif., 544, 550, 566
Soo Canal, 89, 106
Sorenson, Ted, 248
Soudan Underground Mine, 128
South Amana, Iowa, 73
South Amherst, Ohio, 176
South Bass Island (Ohio), 184, 185
South Bay (Calif.), 557
South Bear Creek (Iowa), 72
South Bend, Ind., 39, 41, 43, 46
South Dakota, 63, 79, 198, 250, 272, 284, 285–305; University of, 298
South Dakota, U.S.S., 297
South Dakota School of Mines, 298
South Dakota State University, 303

Southeastern Lake (Oreg.), 609
Southern California, University of, 554
Southern Cross, Mont., 361
Southern Illinois School of Medicine, 24
Southern Methodist University, 499
Southern Pacific Railroad, 432, 548, 553
South Haven, Mich., 93, 104
South Mountain Park (Ariz.), 438
South Pass City, Wyo., 407
South St. Paul, Minn., 113, 118
Southwest, 425–508
Southwest Center for Advanced Studies, 499
Southwestern Baptist Theological Seminary, 500
Southwest Museum (Pasadena), 554
Space Needle (Seattle), 645, 646, 655
Spain. *See* Spanish, the
Spalding, Henry, 332, 344, 614, 629, 654
Spalding, Mrs. Henry, 332, 344
Spanish, the (Spain; Spaniards): and Alaska, 521, 531; and Arizona, 430–31 (*See also* specific towns); and California, 545 ff., 550, 556, 567, 569; and Colorado, 312, 313; and Hawaii, 581; and Iowa, 62, 79; and Kansas, 225, 226, 241; and Minnesota, 114, 133; and Missouri, 139, 141; and Nebraska, 249, 264; and New Mexico, 450, 452–53, 458, 465, 466; and North Dakota, 271–72; and Oklahoma, 484; and Oregon, 613, 614; and South Dakota, 291; and Texas, 489, 491, 492, 501, 507 (*See also* specific towns); and Utah, 399 (*See also* specific towns); and Washington, 636–37, 653; and Wyoming, 409
Spanish-American War, 145, 587
Spanish Governor's Palace (San Antonio), 501
Spanish Stirrup Guest Ranch (N.Mex.), 461
Sparks, Nev., 379
Sparta, Mich., 104
Spearfish, S.D., 302
Spencer County, Ind., 48
Spillville, Iowa, 74–75
Spindletop oil field, 493, 496, 507
Spirit Lake (Iowa), 71–72
Spokane, Fort (Wash.), 654
Spokane, Wash., 634, 635, 640, 647–48, 652 ff.
Spokane Falls (Wash.), 655
Spokane House (Wash.), 653, 654
Spokane Indians, 615
Spokane River, 633, 647, 655
Spokane Valley Pioneer Museum, 648
Spooner, Wis., 210
Spoon River, 3
Spoon River Anthology, 26

Springdale, Iowa, 60
Springerville, Ariz., 440
Springfield, Ill., 3, 12, 24, 26–27, 29, 30
Springfield, Mo., 149, 156, 161
Springfield, Ohio, 173
Springfield, Oreg., 616
Springfield, S.D., 303
Spring Green, Wis., 212
Spring Mountains (Nev.), 377
Spurr (volcano), 514
Squaw Valley, 563
Stables Art Gallery (Taos), 463
Standing Rock Reservation (N.D.), 270, 280, 281, 283
Stand Rock (Wis.), 211
Stanford University, 559
Stanton, Edward P., 145
Stanton, N.D., 269, 284
Stapleton International Airport, 320
Stardust (Las Vegas), 374
Starlight Theater (Kansas City), 155
Star of India Maritime Museum, 559, 565
Star Valley (Wyo.), 408, 412
Starved Rock (Ill.), 10; State Park, 28
State Capitol. *See* specific city
State Fair Music Hall (Dallas), 499
Steamboat Springs (Colo.), 323
Stearns County, Minn., 113
Steinbeck, John, 476
Steinhart Aquarium (San Francisco), 559
Steller, George, 521
Sterling, Mich., 100
Steubenville, Ohio, 169
Steunenberg, Frank, 334, 344
Stevenson, Adlai, 9
Stevens (Fort) State Park (Oreg.), 626
Stilwell, Okla., 475, 483
Stockton, Calif., 558
Stockton Lake (Mo.), 138
Stoddard, Amos, 141, 162
Stokes, Carl B., 173
Storrie Lake (N.Mex.), 461
Story, Wyo., 410
Stovall Museum (Norman, Okla.), 478
Stowe, Harriet Beecher, 179
Strang, James Jesse, 102
Strategic Air Command, 251, 264, 414, 468
Strawberry Island (Wis.), 196
Strawberry River Reservoir, 399
Stroud, Okla., 482
Studebaker brothers (Clement and Henry), 41, 42
Stuhr Museum (Grand Island, Nebr.), 260–61
Stuntz, George, 123
Sturgeon Bay, Wis., 200
Sturgeon River, 84

Sturgis, S.D., 303
Sublette, William, 407
Sugar Act, 592
Sugar Creek (Ind.), 51
Sugarcreek, Ohio, 188
Sugar Loaf Dam (Colo.), 326
Sullivan, Louis, 9, 22
Summer Lake (Oreg.), 606
Sumner, Wash., 652
Sundance, Wyo., 402
Sunflower, Mount (Kans.), 220
Sunkist Co-op, 553
Sunrise Ski Area (Ariz.), 440
Sun Valley, Idaho, 334, 339–40, 341, 344
Superior, Lake, 81, 82, 84, 100 ff., 123, 133, 194 ff., 200, 203, 209–10
Superior National Forest, 125–26, 128
Superior Upland, 84, 194
Superior, Wis., 200
Susitna, Alaska, 533
Susitna Valley, 514
Susquehanna House (Greenfield Village), 97
Sutter, John Augustus, 143, 547, 548, 551, 561
Sutter's Fort (Calif.), 561. See also Sutter, John Augustus
Swain, Grandma, 415
Swan, Alexander, 419
Swan Lake (Mo.), 151–52
Swanson Reservoir (Nebr.), 257
Swanson's (meat packers), 252
Swedes: and Illinois, 8, 28; and Iowa, 63; and Kansas, 222; and Michigan, 86, 95, 101; and Minnesota, 112, 115, 121, 131; and North Dakota, 277; and South Dakota, 290; and Texas, 491; and Washington, 635; and Wisconsin, 196, 209
Sweetwater, Tex., 505
Sweetwater River, 404
Swift's (meat packers), 252
Swiss: and Illinois, 8; and Minnesota, 115; and Nebraska, 248; and Ohio, 168, 169; and Wisconsin, 196, 212, 213
Swiss Historical Village (Wis.), 212
Swope, Thomas H., 157
Swope Park (Kansas City), 155, 157
Syracuse, Ind., 48

Table Rock Lake (Mo.), 138
Tabor, Iowa, 76
Tabor, S.D., 303
Tacoma, Wash., 635, 636, 648–49, 652, 654
Tacoma Narrows Bridge, 648
Taft, Mr. and Mrs. Charles P., 180
Taft, William Howard, 170, 187, 432
Taft Museum (Cincinnati), 180
Tahiti, 578

Tahlequah, Okla., 481
Tahoe, Lake (Nev.), 366, 376 ff., 380, 382, 542, 563, 567
Tahquamenon River, 84
Taiwan(ese), 582
Taliesin (Spring Green, Wis.), 212
Tama (settlement), Iowa, 60, 77
Tamaroa Indians, 10
Tanana River, 513, 532
Tanana Valley, 514, 533
Tank, Nils Otto, 206
Tank Cottage (Green Bay), 206
Taos, N.Mex., 460, 462–63, 464; Ski Valley, 460
Taper (Mark) Forum, 554
Tarrant County Convention Center, 500
Taum Sauk Mountain, 136
Taylor, Zachary, 198
Teapot Dome Scandal, 413, 423
Teater, Archie ("Teton"), 408
Tecumseh, 41, 53
Tecumseh, Fort (S.D.), 292, 304
Tejas, 487
Telegraph Hill (San Francisco), 556, 557
Tennessee Valley Authority, 260
Ten Sleep, Wyo., 402, 406
T. E. Ranch (Wyo.), 416
Terlingua, Tex., 506
Terminal Tower (Cleveland), 177
Terrace Hill (Des Moines), 68
Terre Haute, Ind., 39, 47
Territorial Enterprise, 378
Territorial Enterprise Building (Virginia City), 378
Terry Peak (S.D.), 299
Teton Country Prairie Schooner, 421
Teton Mountains, 408, 417, 419
Teton River, 335, 344
Teton Village, Wyo., 418, 420–21
Texarkana, 487, 497
Texas, 486–508; Republic of, 409, 493, 507 (See also San Jacinto River); University of, 499–500
Texas A&M University, 503
Texas Christian University, 500
Texas City, Tex., 507
Texas Medical Center (Houston), 498
Texas Rangers, 493
Texas Southern University, 498
Texas Trail, 411
Texas Wesleyan College, 500
Texline, Tex., 487
Texoma (Lake) State Park, 480
Thanatopsis, 605, 613
TheBus (Honolulu), 572
The Dalles, Oreg., 609
Thermopolis, Wyo., 403, 419, 420
Thief Lake Refuge, 125
This Side of Paradise, 122
Thompson, David, 350, 638, 653–54

Thompson, James R., 32
Thordardson Collection, 205
Three Lakes, Wis., 211, 214
Three Sisters Wilderness Area, 626
Thunder Basin National Grassland, 414
Thunderbird (Las Vegas), 374
Thurber, James, 170
Thurman, Ohio, 167
Tilghman, Bill, 230
Timber of the Ages Petrified Forest, 298
Timms Hill (Wis.), 194
Timpanogos, Mount, 395
Tinker Air Force Base, 468, 478
Tioga, N.D., 273, 274, 284
Tippecanoe River (Battle of), 36, 41, 53
Tishomingo, Okla., 482
Tisne, Claude du. See Du Tisne, Claude
Titan missiles, 304, 315
Tiwa Indians, 490, 501
Tlingit Indians, 518–19, 522
Toadstool Park (Nebr.), 246, 257, 258
Toiyabe National Forest, 377
Toledo, Ohio, 89, 165, 169, 171 ff.,
    181–82, 183, 189; Blades, 183; Mud
    Hens, 183; Zoo, 182
Tom, Mount, 50
Tomahawk, Wis., 210–11
Tombstone, Ariz., 443–44, 445; Court-
    house State Historic Monument, 444
Tombstone Epitaph, 443
Tongass National Forest, 528
Tonkawa Indians, 473
Tonti, Henri de, 10
Tonto National Forest, 441
Topeka, Kans., 221, 224, 231, 232, 235,
    239, 241 ff.; State Hospital, 235
Topeka Capital-Journal, 225
Toppenish, Wash., 652
Torbert (volcano), 514
Torrey Pines State Park, 565
Totten, Fort (Nebr.), 270, 281–82
Tower-Soudan State Park, 128
Towson, Fort (Okla.), 484
Trail of Tears, 472
Trail Ridge Highway, 322
Trails End (Sheridan, Wyo.), 415
Trans-Pecos Region (Basin and Range
    Region), 488, 497
Transverse Ranges (Calif.), 544
Trans World Airlines, 147
Trapp, Martin E., 473
Travels in Interior Parts of America,
    613, 628
Travel Town (Los Angeles), 564
Traverse City, Mich., 92, 100, 104
Traviata, La, 256
Tres Lagunas Guest Ranch (N.Mex.),
    461
Tressl's Frontier Town (Blackfoot,
    Idaho), 341

Tribune Tower (Chicago), 21
Trident (submarine base—Seattle), 641
Trinity River, 551
Tripp, William, 297
Trolley Museum (Los Angeles), 554
Tropicana (Las Vegas), 374
Truman, Harry S, 135, 155, 159, 163
Truman (Harry S) Library, 155, 159
Truman (Harry S) Sports Complex, 157
Truth or Consequences, N.Mex., 460,
    464
Tsa-La-Gi Cherokee Indian Village,
    481–82
Tsimshian Indians, 518, 519
Tualatin Project, 629
Tubac, Ariz., 431
Tucson, Ariz., 431 ff., 438–39, 440, 443,
    445, 447
Tucson Mountain Park, 439
Tularosa Valley, 450
Tulsa, Okla., 473, 475, 478–79, 480–81,
    482, 484; Little Theater, 481; Univer-
    sity, 479
Tumacacori National Monument, 443
Tumwater, Wash., 654
Turnagain Arm, 538
Turner, Joseph, 180
Turtle Mountain Indians, 270
Turtle Mountain Reservation (N.D.),
    270
Turtle Mountains (N.D.), 266, 282
Tusayan Ruins and Museum (Ariz.), 442
Tuscarawas County, Ohio, 169, 175
Twain, Mark, 55, 75, 135, 159, 162, 376,
    378, 471
Twain (Mark) Museum (Nev.), 378
Twain (Mark) National Forest, 157
Twain (Mark) State Park, 159
Twin Cities (Minn.), 117, 134. See also
    Minneapolis, Minn.; St. Paul, Minn.
Twin Falls, Idaho, 338
Twinsburg, Ohio, 174
Two Rivers (Wash.), 642

Uihlein Stadium (Milwaukee), 208
Uinta Basin, 389
Uinta Mountains, 384
Ukrainians, 87, 95
Umatilla County, Oreg., 618
Umatilla National Forest, 626
Umpqua River, 625
Uncle Tom's Cabin, 179
Underground Railroad, 60, 64, 222
Undersea Gardens (Calif.), 565
Union, Fort (N.D.), 272
Union, Lake (Wash.), 645, 646
Union Center (Los Angeles), 555
Union County, Ill., 20
Union Pacific Depot (Cheyenne), 414

Union Pacific Railroad, 71, 229, 248, 256, 264, 319, 325, 390, 398, 403, 407, 408, 410, 414, 422, 615
Union Square (San Francisco), 565
Union Station (Los Angeles), 555
Union Stock Yards (Chicago), 13, 15
Union Terminal (Dallas), 508
United Automobile Workers, 90, 98, 106
United Farm Workers, 447
United Nations, 570
United States Pavilion (Spokane), 647
Universal Studios, 554
Upper Tahquamenon Falls, 84
Upton, Bob, 25
Urbana, Ill., 14, 24
U. S. Forest Products Laboratory, 205
U. S. Steel Company, 42, 53
Utah, 383–99, 453; University of, 394, 398
Utah Lake, 395
Utah Museum of Fine Arts, 394
Utah State University, 395
Utah Symphony, 398
Utah Territory, 389, 399
Utah Valley, 395
Ute Indians, 311, 384, 387, 389, 406, 452

Vail, Colo., 321
Valdez, Alaska, 531
Valencia, Calif., 565
Valentine, Nebr., 257
Vallandigham, Clement L., 172
Valle, Jean Baptiste, 152
Valley City, N.D., 283
"Valley of the Elves" (Wis.), 212
Valley of the Ten Thousand Smokes, 536
Vancouver, Fort (Oreg.), 614
Vancouver, George, 637, 653
Vancouver, Point, 653
Vancouver Island, 637, 638, 653, 654
Vandalia, Ill., 12, 27
Vandiver, Willard Duncan, 135
Van Gogh, Vincent, 123
Van Nuys, Calif., 565
Van Wert, Ohio, 175
Ventura County, Calif., 552
Verde River, 436
Verdigris River, 220, 475
Vérendrye, François and Louis-Joseph de la, 291, 296, 304
Vérendrye, Pierre Gaultier de Varennes, Sieur de la, 269, 271, 284
Vermilion, Ohio, 184
Vermilion Range (Minn.), 116, 119, 133
Vermilion River, 24, 25, 166
Vermillion, S.D., 285, 289, 298
Versailles, Ind., 51
Veterans Administration Hospital (Topeka), 235
Veterans Auditorium (Des Moines), 68

Veterans Hospital (Leavenworth, Kans.), 236
Veuster, Damien de, 599
Viborg, S.D., 303
Victor, Colo., 313
Victoria, B.C., 654
Victoria, Queen, 21
Victory Hotel (Put-in-Bay, Ohio), 184
Vieau, Jacques, 203, 206
Vietnam, 587
Vigilantes (Wyo.), 411
Vignes, Jean-Louis, 550
Viking Lander project, 316
Vikings, 107, 113, 127–28, 467
Vilas Park Zoo (Madison), 205
Villita, La (San Antonio), 501, 506
Vincennes, Fort (Ind.), 38, 40, 53
Vincennes, Ind., 40
Vinita, Okla., 482
Virginia, 11, 171, 189
Virginia (steamboat), 133
Virginia City, Mont., 350, 360
Virginia City, Nev., 370, 378, 381
Virginia Military District, 171
Virginian, The, 408
Virgin Narrows (Utah), 396
Virgin River, 396
Vizcaíno, Sebastián, 546, 569
Volcano, Calif., 566
Volcano House (Hawaii), 601
Von Tilzer, Harry, 33
Voyageur National Forest, 129
Vriesland, Mich., 86

Wabash River, 20, 30, 34, 36
Waco, Tex., 502
Wagner, S.D., 303
Wagon Box (Wyo.), 410, 419
Wagons West, 421
Wahoo, Nebr., 248
Waialeale, Mount, 577
Waianae Mountains, 595
Waiilatpu, Wash., 654
Waikiki (Waikiki Beach, Hawaii), 589, 596, 597, 600
Waikiki Shell (Hawaii), 597
Wailoli Mission Home (Hawaii), 599
Wailua River State Park, 599
Wailuku, Hawaii, 598
Waimea, Hawaii, 577, 598
Waimea Canyon State Park, 599
Wainwright, Fort (Alaska), 533
Walker, Joseph, 369–70, 381
Walker, Minn., 131
Walker Art Center (Minneapolis), 123
Walker Lake (Nev.), 377
Wallace, Lew, 454, 459
Wallace County, Kans., 220
Walla Walla, Fort (Wash.), 628, 654
Walla Walla, Wash., 615, 635, 652

Walla Walla Valley, 629
Wallowa Mountains, 609
Wallowa-Whitman National Forest, 626
Walnut Woods Park (Des Moines), 69
Wapakoneta, Ohio, 187
Wapiti (canyon drive), 419
Wappapello Lake (Mo.), 138
Wapsipinicon River, 58
War Eagle, 71
Warm Springs Indian Reservation, 624
War of 1812, 11, 88, 115, 142, 146, 172, 189, 638
Warp (Harold) Pioneer Village, 260–61
Warren, Mich., 87
Warren (Fort) Air Force Base, 414, 423
Warsaw, Mo., 138
Wartburg Seminary, 69
Wasatch Front, 384
Wasatch Range, 384, 393, 395
Waseca County, Minn., 129
Washakie, Chief, 406, 420
Washburn, Henry, 409
Washburn University, 235
Washington (ship), 637
Washington, 605, 613, 630–55; University of, 646
Washington, Fort (Ohio), 179
Washington, George, 285, 300
Washington, Idaho, 336
Washington, Lake (Wash.), 644, 645–46, 650, 652
Washington, Mount (Oreg.), 626
Washington Arboretum (Seattle), 646
Washington County, Iowa, 60, 75
Washington County, Mo., 150
Washington County, Oreg., 621
Washington Harbor, Mich., 101, 102
Washington Island (Wis.), 196, 209
Washington State Museum of Pharmacy, 649
Washington State Pavilion (Spokane), 648
Washington Territory, 634, 638, 654, 655
Washington University (St. Louis), 154
Washita, Battle of the, 350
Washoe County, Nev., 373
Washo Indians, 369
Water and Power Building (Los Angeles), 555
Watergate scandal, 549
Waterloo, Iowa, 61, 65, 69
Waterloo Courier, 69
Water Quality Act, 616, 629
Waters, George W., 511
Watertown, S.D., 294
Watkins Mill, Mo., 159
Watts (Los Angeles), 549
Waubesa, Lake (Wis.), 204
Waukesha County, Wis., 208
Waupaca County, Wis., 202

Wawasee, Lake, 34, 48
Wayne, Anthony ("Mad Anthony"), 40, 46, 171, 185, 189
Wayne, John, 76
Wayne County, Ind., 34
Wayne County, Mich., 94
Wayne County, Ohio, 169
Wayne National Forest (Ohio), 184
Wayne State University, 100
Wea Indians, 38
Webb Act, 548
Weber State College, 395
Webster, Noah, 97
Webster County, Nebr., 248
"Wedding Dance" (Brueghel), 96
Weiser, Idaho, 342
Welk, Lawrence, 277
Wellfleet, Nebr., 259
Wells Fargo, 566; Museum (Tombstone), 444
Welsh: and Ohio, 169; and Oklahoma, 472; and South Dakota, 290
Wenatchee, Wash., 652
Wenatchee Valley, 639
Wendover, Utah, 398
West, Kathleen, 239
West Amana, Iowa, 73
West Baden Springs Hotel, 50
West Bend, Iowa, 75
West Branch, Iowa, 60, 73
Westby, Wis., 214
West Coast Orient Lumber Mill, 648
Westendorf, Thomas, 33
Western Federation of Miners, 334
Western Heritage Center (Mont.), 355
Western Potato Service, 276
Western Reserve, 171; Historical Society, 178
Western Reserve University, 183
Western Upland, 192
West Frankfort, Ill., 19
West Gulf Coastal Plains, 488
West Lake Okoboji, 71–72
West Nishnabotna River, 58
Weston, Mo., 159
West Plains, Mo., 149
West Point (N.Y.), 333
Westport, Mo., 143
Westwood Village (Los Angeles), 555
Weyerhauser firm, 620
Wheeler Peak, 450
Whidbey Island, 632
White, Alice, 517–18
White, T. Steward, 99
White, William Allen, 224
White Bird Canyon, 333, 344
White Motor Company, 98
White Mountain Apache Tribe, 440
White Mountains: Arizona, 428; Nevada, 366

White Pass Village (Wash.), 650
White Pine County, Nev., 373
White Pines Forest, 20
White River, 286, 288
White Sands Missile Range (N.Mex.), 454, 455, 459, 465
White Sulphur Springs, Mont., 360
Whitewater River, 36
Whiting, Ind., 42, 46, 53
Whitman, Marcus, 614, 615, 629, 654
Whitney, Gertrude Vanderbilt, 416
Whitney, Mount (Calif.), 541, 563
Whitney Gallery of Western Art (Cody, Wyo.), 416
Whitney Lake (Nebr.), 257
Whittier College, 555
Whitworth College, 648
Wichita, Kans., 219, 230 ff., 234–35, 238; Aeros, 237; Art Association, 234; Art Museum, 234; State University, 235
Wichita Indians, 225
Wichita Mountains, 468, 479
Wickenburg, Ariz., 440, 445
Wilber, Nebr., 262, 263
Wildcat Hills, 246, 257; Recreation Area, 258–59
Wildwood House (Nebraska City), 260
Willamette National Forest, 626
Willamette River, 606, 608, 614, 616, 620 ff., 629
Willamette Valley, 605, 608, 620, 624, 629, 638
Willapa Hills, 632
Willard, Arthur L., 145
William, Fort (Oreg.), 614
William I, Emperor, 639
Williams, Andy, 562, 567
Williams, G. Mennen, 96
Williams, Jack, 447
Williams, Walter, 161
Williston, N.D., 274
Williston Basin, 275, 364
Wilmette, Ill., 22
Wilmington, Calif., 553
Wilmington, Ohio, 167
Wilshire Boulevard (Los Angeles), 555
Wilson, Kans., 222
Wilson, Mount (Calif.), 544
Winchester Mystery House, 560
Wind Cave (S.D.), 301; National Park, 301
Windlass Hill (Nebr.), 259
Window Rock, Ariz., 445
Wind River (canyon drive), 419
Wind River Mountains, 403, 404, 419
Wind River Reservation, 402, 406, 407
Windsor, Colo., 315
Wingra, Lake (Wis.), 205
Winnebago Indians, 59, 195, 197, 207, 262

Winnemucca, Nev., 380
Winnewissa Falls (Minn.), 130
Winona, Minn., 118, 130
Winter Park (Denver), 320
Winter Rim (Oreg.), 606
Winterset, Iowa, 76
Winton, Minn., 128
Wisconsin, 11, 191, 216; University of, 205
Wisconsin Dells, 194, 195, 211
Wisconsin River, 194, 197, 211, 212, 215
Wisconsin Territory, 62–63, 79, 198, 215
Wister, Owen, 408
Wizard Island (Oreg.), 626
Wobblies. See Industrial Workers of the World
Wolf Point, Mont., 362
Wolfskill, William, 369–70
"Woman Mound" (Iowa), 61
Woman's Christian Temperance Union, 23
Wood, Grant, 69, 75
Woodcarving, Museum of (Spooner, Wis.), 210
Woodland Park Zoological Gardens (Seattle), 646
Woolaroc Ranch and Museum (Okla.), 481
Workingmen's Union, 144
Worland, Wyo., 421
World Museum of Mining, 357
World's Columbian Exposition (Chicago), 22, 31, 408
World's Fair: Portland (1905), 611; Seattle (1962), 645, 646, 655
World War I: Alaska and, 529; Idaho and, 334; Indiana and, 45; Iowa and, 64; Kansas and, 231; Minnesota and, 116; Missouri and, 145; Montana and, 352; Nevada and, 371; Ohio and, 169, 173; Oklahoma and, 473; Washington and, 640
World War II: Alaska and, 517, 524, 529, 533, 539; Arizona and, 432, 433, 438; California and, 548, 553; Colorado and, 318; Hawaii and, 581, 587, 604; Idaho and, 332, 334; Illinois and, 9; Indiana and, 45; Iowa and, 64–65; Michigan and, 116–17; Minnesota and, 90; Missouri and, 145–46, 155, 163; Montana and, 352; Nebraska and, 252; Nevada and, 371; New Mexico and, 454, 458; North Dakota and, 273; Ohio and, 173; Oklahoma and, 474; South Dakota and, 293, 297; Utah and, 390, 391; Washington and, 640–41, 644, 647
World War Memorial Plaza, 45
Worth, William, 500
Wounded Knee, S.D., 294, 305

Wounded Knee Creek, 291, 293, 302
Wovoka, 292
Wrangell, Alaska, 532
Wrangell, Mount, 514
Wrangell Mountains (Range), 513, 514
Wright, Frank Lloyd, 9, 22, 204, 212, 498–99, 554, 560
Wright, Orville and Wilbur, 97, 120, 181
Wright-Patterson Air Force Base, 181
Wrights Park (Tacoma), 649
Wrigley Building (Chicago), 21
Wupatki, Ariz., 443; National Monument, 443
Wyandot Indians, 168, 170, 181, 235, 236
Wyandotte, Kans., 228, 235–36, 241
Wyandotte, Mich., 92, 104
Wyandotte Cave (Ind.), 36, 50
Wyandotte Constitution. See Wyandotte, Kans.
Wyeth, Nathaniel, 332, 614, 629
Wyoming, 250, 333, 400–23, 613; University of, 415, 422
Wyoming Central Railway, 411
Wyoming Hereford Ranch, 419
Wyoming Territory, 333, 402, 422
Wyoming Valley, 212

Xavier University, 183

Yachats, Oreg., 625
Yakima, Wash., 640
Yakima Indians, 634
Yakima Valley, 639, 651
Yankton, S.D., 272, 285, 289, 297–98; College, 297
Yankton County Territorial Museum, 297
Yates, Fort (N.D.), 281, 302
Yavapai Museum (Grand Canyon), 442
Yavapai Point (Ariz.), 442
Yellowstone (steamboat), 272, 292, 304

Yellowstone Canyon and Falls, 418
Yellowstone County Museum (Mont.), 355
Yellowstone Lake, 404, 418
Yellowstone National Park, 305, 340, 359, 402 ff., 408, 409–10, 412, 416, 418, 422, 423
Yellowstone River, 346, 355, 363, 404
Yellowstone Valley, 348
Yellowtail Dam, 419
Yerba Buena, Calif., 556
Yesler, Henry, 645
Yorba Linda, Calif., 549
Yosemite National Park, 566
Yosemite Valley, 541, 542, 563
Young, Brigham, 9, 383, 388 ff., 395, 399, 408, 422
Young Drift Plains, 56, 266, 274, 286
Younger, Cole, 228
Youngstown, Ohio, 169, 174
Young (Brigham) University, 395
Ysleta (El Paso, Tex.), 501
Yucca Flat, Nev., 381
Yugoslavians, 9
Yukon, Okla., 475, 482
Yukon River, 512, 513, 515, 532, 539
Yukon Territory, 512, 513, 517, 523, 532, 537, 639
Yuma, Ariz., 439, 440, 445
Yuma County, Ariz., 434

Zanesville, Ohio, 171–72
Zanuck, Darryl F., 248
Zeeland, Mich., 86
Ziolkowski, Korczak, 301
Zion Canyon (Utah), 396; National Park, 396
Zoar Village, Ohio, 186
Zoos. See specific locations
Zuñi Indians, 430, 452, 462, 463
Zuñi Pueblo, 463

723